# CHARLESTON ALMANAC

## VOLUME I

*From Founding Through the Revolution*

## ALSO BY MARK R. JONES
### & East Atlantic Publishing

CHARLESTON FIRSTS
(2015)

DOIN' THE CHARLESTON:
Black Roots of American Popular Music
& the Jenkins Orphanage Legacy
(2013)

KINGDOM BY THE SEA:
Edgar Allan Poe's Charleston Tales
(2013)

## OTHER BOOKS

PALMETTO PREDATORS:
Monsters Among Us
(2007)

SOUTH CAROLINA KILLERS:
Crimes Of Passion
(2007)

WICKED CHARLESTON, VOL. II:
Prostitutes, Politics & Prostitution
(2006)

WICKED CHARLESTON:
The Dark Side of the Holy City
(2005)

# CHARLESTON ALMANAC

## VOLUME I

*From Founding Through the Revolution*

**MARK R. JONES**

East Atlantic
E.A.P.
Publishing

Copyright © 2017 Mark R. Jones

All Rights Reserved. In accordance with the U.S. Copyright Act of 1976, the scanning, uploading, recording and electronic sharing of any part of this book with the permission of the publisher is unlawful piracy and theft of the author's intellectual property, except by a reviewer who may quote brief passages in a review to be printed in a magazine, newspaper, or on the Web – without permission in writing from the publisher. Please contact East Atlantic Publishing: 1323 Jackwood Court, Charleston, SC, 29407.

markjonesbooks@outlook.com

Although the author and publisher have made every effort to ensure the accuracy and completeness of information contained in this book, we assume no responsibility for errors, inaccuracies, omissions or any inconsistency herein.

First Edition

First Printing 2017

ISBN: 978-0692642146

Cover & book design by Mark R. Jones

Front and back cover photos courtesy of the New York Public Library

Printed in the United States of America

# TABLE OF CONTENTS

**PREFACE** ................................................................................. 7

**PART ONE**
Pre-History of Charleston & the Roots of American Colonialism
1562-1669 ............................................................................... 9

**PART TWO**
The Proprietary City, 1670-1719 ..................................... 30

**PART THREE**
The Royal City, 1720-1770 ............................................. 124

**PART FOUR**
The Revolutionary City, 1771-1799 ............................... 267

**BIBLIOGRAPHY** ................................................................. 479

**INDEX** ................................................................................. 488

**ABOUT THE AUTHOR** ........................................................ 520

**As always,**

**for Kari Jones & Rebel Sinclair**
**wife & girlfriend**
**who happily happen to be the same woman!**

Thanks to the Beta-Brigade, who spent their time and effort reading this manuscript and pointing out the thousands of errors and inconsistencies. Some of you went above and beyond the call. Any errors left are completely mine.

Ernest Everett Blevins, Jim Brain (the *only* Brain in Charleston!) Steve Beard, Malcolm Hale, Al Hall, Bryce Mason, Jason Menz, Jill Hunter Powell, Michael Whitehurst, and Nick Smith.

# PREFACE

*"A people without the knowledge of their past history, origin, and culture is like a tree without roots." -- Marcus Garvey*

Most histories of early America have traditionally focused on Virginia and New England, relegating the history of Carolina to sidebars, or afterthoughts. However, as will be seen in the following pages, Carolina's role in forging the identity of the United States of America was second to none.

As a leading economic power, Carolina was always at the forefront of culture, military, and trade among the original colonies. Always independent and often obstinate, Carolina was the first colony to rebel against her English proprietors, took a firm hand in stamping out the golden age of piracy and endured more battles during the Revolutionary War than any of her sister colonies. Charleston's reputation as the one of the fiercest opponents of the encroaching British taxation policy, main agitator of secession, and staunchest defender of that "peculiar institution" did not develop in a vacuum. It grew out of the roots of the original colonists' desire for freedom, their passion for profits, and their embrace of opulence.

Charleston was also city of contrasts, which fully embraced its own hypocrisy. Within fifty years of its founding, Charleston had evolved into a disturbing mix of arrogance and fear, piety and hedonism, luxury and cruelty.

My goal in this project was to present an accurate and methodical timeline of events, as well as explore the undercurrents of those events and give the reader an understanding of how one event was built upon a previous one. Due to the sheer size of the project, with a goal of making the finished project affordable for most readers, I decided to break the Almanac into three volumes. Volume 1, which you hold in your hands, covers the founding of Carolina to the end of the 18$^{th}$ century. Volume 2 will cover the 19$^{th}$ century and Volume 3 will cover the years 1900 to the present.

Of course, I was unable, or incapable, of putting everything I wanted to about Charleston in this project, so there will be some readers that will disagree with what was left out, or what was put in. To those I say …

Enjoy!

*Mark R. Jones*

December 7, 2016

"The most effective way to destroy people is to deny and obliterate their own understanding of their history."

*- George Orwell*

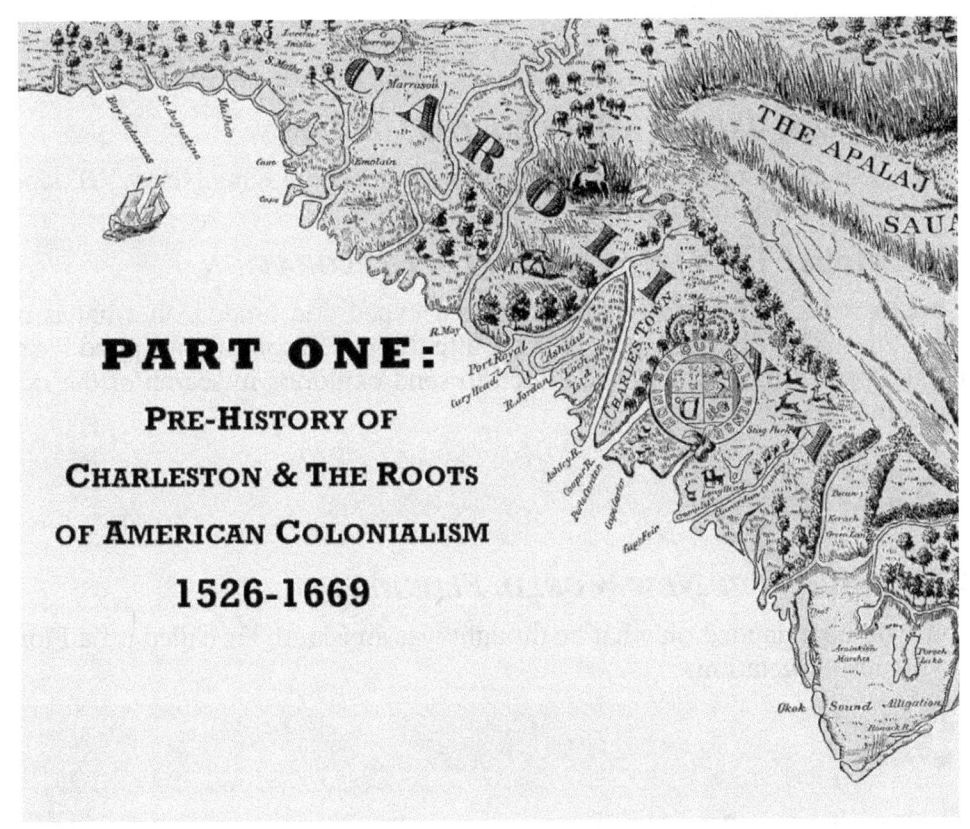

# PART ONE:

## PRE-HISTORY OF CHARLESTON & THE ROOTS OF AMERICAN COLONIALISM

### 1526-1669

"That we ... do grant full and absolute power ... for the good and happy government of the said whole province ... to ordain, make and enact, and publish any laws and constitutions whatsoever ... according to their best discretion, by and with the advice assent ... of the freeman of the said province."

- *Second Charter of Carolina, June 30, 1665*

# 1497

### 1497, June 24. *THE NEW WORLD. EXPLORATION.*

An English expedition led by Henry Cabot, financed by King Henry VII, landed on current-day Newfoundland.

### 1497, October 12. *THE NEW WORLD. EXPLORATION.*

Christopher Columbus's Spanish-financed expedition landed on what is now The Bahamas. This discovery attracted the attention of Europe and inspired France, Portugal, Spain, England, and the Dutch to send explorers in search of the riches available in the New World.

# 1513

### 1513, April 3. *THE NEW WORLD. FLORIDA.*

Ponce de Leon landed on what he thought was an island. He called it La Florida due to the lush vegetation.

# 1526

### 1526, September 29. *FIRST CAROLINA EXPLORATION. SLAVERY.*

Lucas Vasquez de Ayllón, a wealthy sugar planter of Santo Domingo sailed into what is now Wynah Bay, Georgetown South Carolina. A settlement was established in that area of about 500 men, women and children. Ayllón also brought with him African slaves. to help build the colony.

However, the slaves rebelled, fled inland and presumably settled with Native Americans. Ayllón died and the colony was abandoned.

# 1562

### 1562, May 1. *CHARLESFORT.*

Jean Ribault and a group of French Huguenots established a settlement called Charlesfortnear present day Parris Island in the Beaufort, South Carolina area.

Ribault named the region Carolus in honor of Charles IX of France and named the sound Port Royal.

Ribault left twenty-eight men to build the settlement and returned to France to arrange supplies for the new colony. However, he was arrested in England after becoming involved in the period of unrest known as the French Wars of Religion, which prevented his return.

After Ribault left, much of the settlers' stores were destroyed by a fire. A Captain Pierra, a dictatorial leader was killed by his men. Without supplies or leadership, and beset by hostility from the native population, they decided to return to France. They built their own boat and set sail, without compass, across the Atlantic. An account describes the vessel "about forty feet and some twenty tons with two masts." One man, Guillaume Rouffi, stayed behind with Native American friends.

During the long voyage in an open boat, they were reduced to cannibalism before the survivors were finally rescued by an English ship. Shortly after the colonists' departure, a Spanish force from Cuba destroyed the French fort. The site was declared a National Historic Landmark in 2001.

# 1565

### 1565, September 8. *ESTABLISHMENT OF ST. AUGUSTINE.*

Spain established a permanent settlement in Florida, named St. Augustine.

# 1566

### 1566. *FORT SAN MARCOS.*

The Spanish establish a second settlement near the abandoned Charlesfort site, which they call Fort San Marcos.

# 1585

### 1585, June 26. *LOST COLONY OF ROANOKE.*

With a charter from Queen Elizabeth, Sir Walter Raleigh's last attempt at an English settlement in the New World was at Roanoke in present day North Carolina. It was abandoned within a year and subsequent explorers found little remnants of the settlement, leading to the nickname "the Lost Colony."

# 1587

### 1587. *PORT SAN MARCO ABANDONED.*

Spain abandoned Port San Marco moving its garrison to St. Augustine.

# 1598

### 1598. RELIGION. EDICT OF NANTES.

In an effort to promote civil unity, Henry IV of France issued the Edict of Nantes, granting the Calvinist Protestants, known as Huguenots substantial rights of free worship in the very Catholic country. When the Edict was revoked in 1685, it sparked a major increase of French immigrants to the Carolina colony.

# 1605

### 1605, April 13. CAROLINA EXPLORATION.

Captain Francisco Ecija explored the area of the Kiawah River and Charleston harbor. He concluded the area was a good location to launch an operation into the interior to search for gold and other precious metals.

# 1607

### 1607, May 24. JAMESTOWN ESTABLISHED.

First permanent English settlement in the Americas was established at Jamestown, Virginia - 105 colonists, led by Christopher Newport.

# 1620

### 1620, December 21. PLYMOUTH COLONY ESTABLISHED.

The Plymouth Colony was established in Massachusetts by Puritans.

# 1625

### 1625, March. ENGLAND. CHARLES I CROWNED.

King Charles I was crowned King of England. A deeply religious man, Charles believed in the "divine rights of Kings" – that he was appointed by God to be ruler and therefore should govern by his conscious.

In addition, his marriage to the devout Catholic, Henrietta Maria, fifteen-year-old daughter of France's King Henry IV inflamed the Puritan English nobility. His reign was troubled by intense disagreements over finances and religion which ultimately led to the English Civil Wars of the 1640s.

Pilgrims at Plymouth Rock. *Courtesy of the Library of Congress*

# 1626

### 1626, May 24. *MANHATTAN PURCHASED.*

Peter Minuit, director of New Netherland purchased the island of Manhattan, and construction of New Amsterdam began.

# 1627

### 1627. *ENGLAND. THE ELEVEN YEAR TYRANNY.*

This was the beginning of what was called "the Eleven Year Tyranny" of Charles I. After the assassination of the king's friend, George Villiers, 1st Duke of Buckingham, Parliamentary criticism of his Royal rule increased. Charles realized that, if he avoided war, he could rule without Parliamentary interference. Members of Parliament arrived at Westminster to find that the doors had been locked with large chains and padlocks. They remained locked for eleven years, creating a volatile power struggle between Charles and the nobility.

### 1627, February 17. *BARBADOS SETTLED.*

Barbados was settled by Englishman Henry Powell with eighty settlers and ten slaves who were kidnapped lower class English or Irish youth. The island was established as a proprietary colony, funded by Sir William Courten, a London merchant who owned the title to Barbados. The first colonists were technically tenants since most of their profits were paid directly to Courten.

# 1629

### 1629, October 30. *CAROLINA LAND GRANT ISSUED.*

Charles I granted the American territory between the thirty-one and thirty-six degrees north latitude to Sir Robert Heath. This land included everything from Florida to the present Cape Fear River. The charter was never used. In fact, A.S. Salley wrote in *The Origin of Carolina*:

> Neither Sir Robert nor his heirs did anything toward developing Carolina, and we seldom find it referred to in any written or printed documents of that day.

The grant read:

> Charles by the Grace of God of England &c. our 1$^{st}$ patents &c. made to Sir Robert Heath Knight our Atturney Generall bearing date at Westminster 30 October in the 5$^{th}$ year of our reigne &c. tract from the Ocean on the east & soe west as far as the Continent extends & all islands "within the degrees of 31 & 36 of the Northern latitude" & c. and erect the said Region & Isles into a Province & name the same Carolina.

# 1630

### 1630, May 29. *BOSTON FOUNDED.*

Puritans founded Boston and ten other settlements in the Massachusetts Bay Colony.

### 1630, September 7. *BIRTH.*

Charles II was born at St. James's Palace in London.

# 1632

### 1632, June 20. *MARYLAND CHARTERED.*

Charles I granted the original charter for Maryland, a proprietary colony of about twelve million acres to Cæcilius Calvert, 2nd Baron Baltimore.

# 1636

### 1636, Spring. *Providence Colony.*

Roger Williams, a theologian and independent preacher, founded the Providence Colony at Rhode Island. Williams had been exiled from the Massachusetts Bay Colony due his religious views.

# 1640

### 1640. *Barbados. Slavery.*

Sugar production began in Barbados, transforming the economically struggling colony. Worldwide demand for sugar, rum and molasses increased the value of land on the tiny island. The smaller planters were bought out by larger planters and African slavelabor replaced white indentured servants. This created a small, all-powerful elite society composed of wealthy white English planters – an aristocracy transplanted from Europe.

# 1642

### 1642, August 22. *English Civil War.*

King Charles I raised his standard in Nottingham, indicating his war intention. The battle was between supporters of the king, called Royalists, and the supporters of the rights and privileges of Parliament. The first skirmish took place at the Battle of Southam the start of a nine-year struggle.

# 1643

### 1643. *Bermuda.*

Captain William Sayle became governor of Bermuda.

# 1645

### 1645, July 14. *English Civil War.*

Oliver Cromwell became Major General of the Parliamentary Army.

## 1648

**1648, August.** *CHARLES I ARRESTED.*

After six years of war, King Charles I was arrested for treason and imprisoned. Oliver Cromwell continued his campaign against the king's supporters.

## 1649

**1649, January 20-25.** *TRIAL OF CHARLES I.*

The trial of Charles I on charges of treason was conducted at Westminster Hall in London. When the king was asked to plead, he refused, stating his objection. "I would know by what power I am called hither, by what lawful authority?" He claimed that no court had jurisdiction over a monarch, that his own authority to rule had been given to him by God and by the traditional laws of England, and that the power wielded by those trying him was only that of force of arms.

**1649, January 26.** *CHARLES I FOUND GUILTY.*

Charles I was found guilty of treason and condemned to death.

**1649, January 30.** *EXECUTION OF CHARLES I.*

King Charles I "tyrant, traitor, murderer and public enemy," was executed at the Banqueting House of the Palace of Whitehall.

**1649, February 7.** *MONARCHY ABOLISHED.*

Parliament voted to abolish the English monarchy.

**1649, August.** *CROMWELL CONQUERS IRELAND.*

Oliver Cromwell commanded the English army which conquered Ireland.

## 1650

**1650, October 3.** *BARBADOS.*

Parliament passed an act which prohibited trade between England and Barbados. During the English Civil War Barbados became an asylum for Royalists seeking to avoid the conflict. After the execution of Charles I, Parliament sought to punish Barbados for remaining loyal to the King by restricting their trade. This eventually created an economic crisis on the small island.

Twenty years later, the Carolina colony became the "promised land" for many Barbadian merchants and planters.

# 1651

### 1651, October 9. ENGLAND. NAVIGATION ACTS.

The Navigation Acts were passed and signed into law by Oliver Cromwell - another law aimed to punish the West Indian islands. The goal was to stop direct colonial trade with the Netherlands, France, and other European countries.

# 1653

### 1653, October 16. CHARLES II GOES INTO EXILE.

Charles II and James, sons of the Charles I fled England to escape Cromwell's army. Landing in Normandy, France they would live in exile for nine years.

# 1658

### 1658, September 3. CROMWELL DEATH.

Oliver Cromwell died, and the office of Protectorate of the Commonwealth fell to his son, Richard, who was a weak and ineffective leader. Support for the return of Royal rule became more popular. A powerful group of Loyalists doubled their efforts in restoring the monarchy.

# 1660

### 1660, May 14. CHARLES II PROCLAIMED KING.

With the military support of General George Monck, governor of Scotland and Duke of Albemarle, Charles II was proclaimed king of England.

### 1660, April 25. RESTORATION.

Parliament met and voted to restore Charles II.

### 1660, May 29. CHARLES ARRIVES IN LONDON. SEEDS OF CAROLINA.

Charles II arrived in London. He granted amnesty to most of Cromwell's former supporters, including Baron Anthony Ashley Cooper. Fifty people, however, were excluded from the King's amnesty; nine were hanged, drawn and quartered, and the rest were given life imprisonment.

Charles II extended baronages to thirteen gentlemen of Barbados who had financially supported him during his exile including Sir John Colleton and Sir John

Yeamans. The king also appointed Colleton to the Council of Foreign Plantations along with:

- Sir William Berkeley, Governor of Virginia
- Sir Anthony Ashley Cooper
- Edward Hyde, Earl of Clarendon
- Sir George Carteret, treasurer of the Navy

Like Colleton, Sir Anthony Ashley Cooper owned property in Barbados, and like many others, his plantation failed. Due to factors such as epidemics and hurricanes, as well as strong competition in sugar production from Jamaica, several wealthy sugar plantation owners were able to absorb dozens of other, smaller estates which could not compete financially. Within a few years, most of the land on the island was controlled by a few powerful Englishmen.

Most historians agree it was Colleton and Cooper who formulated the plans for establishing a new English colony and asked Charles II to grant them the territory.

# 1661

## 1661, January 30. *Twice-Dead Body of Cromwell.*

On the 12th anniversary of his father's execution, Charles II ordered the body of Oliver Cromwell removed from Westminster Abbey. The corpse was given a posthumous execution by beheading and the "twice-dead" body was hanged in chains at Tyburn. The decapitated head was displayed on a pole outside Westminster Hall until 1685.

## 1661, May 11. *Cooper Appointed Chancellor of the Exchequer.*

Baron Anthony Ashley Cooper was appointed Chancellor of the Exchequer (equivalent of Secretary of the Treasury in the United States) by King Charles II.

# 1663

## 1663, March 23. *Carolina Colony. Lords Proprietors.*

Charles II granted the territory called Carolana to the "true and absolute Lords and Proprietors." The eight men were:

- **John Berkeley, Baron Berkeley of Stratton** - Berkeley fought on the Royalist side during the Rebellion, general of the Royal forces in Devon. He also became a Proprietor for the Colony of New Jersey.
- **Sir William Berkeley** - During the Rebellion, William served as Governor of Virginia and was a consistent supporter of Royal rule. Member of the Council of Foreign Plantations.

- **Sir George Carteret** - Served as Lt. Governor of Jersey, the largest of the Channel Islands, fifteen miles off the French coast, which became a refuge for Royalists during the Rebellion. Carteret ran an active privateering campaign against Parliament, who branded him a pirate. After the execution of Charles I, Carteret had Charles II declared King in Jersey, even though the action forced him into exile for nine years. He also became a Proprietor of New Jersey and member of the Council of Foreign Plantations.
- **Sir John Colleton, 1st Baronet** – Served in the infantry during the Rebellion and made heavy financial contributions to the Royal cause. After Charles's execution, Colleton fled to Barbados where he acquired an extensive estate and became a member of Council of Foreign Plantations.
- **William Craven, Earl of Craven** – Contributed substantial financing for the Royal cause during the Rebellion. Known for his "bawdy language," Craven was one of the few noblemen who did not flee London during the Great Plague of 1665. He remained in the city to help keep order and donated property for mass grave sites.
- **Anthony Ashley Cooper, Baron Ashley of Wimborne St. Giles** – A political opportunist who started the Rebellion as a Loyalist, then became a supporter of Cromwell after the War, but then devoted much of his energy for the Restoration of Charles II for which he was well rewarded, becoming one of the most politically powerful men in England. He was a member of the Council of Foreign Plantations.
- **Edward Hyde, Earl of Clarendon** – Maternal grandfather of two monarchs, Queen Mary II and Queen Anne, Hyde was one of Charles' closest advisors during the nine-year exile and a member of Council of Foreign Plantations. His daughter, Anne, married Charles's younger brother, James, Duke of York. Later in life he authored the acclaimed "History of the Rebellion."
- **George Monck, Duke of Albemarle** - A brilliant military leader for Charles during the Rebellion, Monck was arrested and spent two years in the Tower of London. Accepting a commission as Major General he fought with Cromwell in Ireland and Scotland. After being elected to Parliament in 1660, Monck campaigned for the Restoration of Charles II. He was rewarded as Knight of the Most Noble Order of the Garter, the most prestigious honor in England.

Each Proprietor contributed £75 sterling to establish a fund for financing a colony in Carolina. They also agreed, if necessary, to contribute an additional £500 sterling each. The Proprietors, of course, hoped that no more money would be required. There was a strong consensus that the colony could be established by luring experienced settlers from established Caribbean colonies like Barbados and Bermuda, by offering large land grants in lieu of providing financing.

### 1663, May. CAROLINA COLONY. LORDS PROPRIETORS.

Lord Proprietors met to devise their plans. They established a joint stock company to finance the Carolina colony (each Proprietor contributing equal funds) and issued liberal terms to encourage colonists. According to Peter Wood in *Black Majority* their "motives were frankly commercial" and "realized that Barbados could provide seasoned settlers from a short distance at a minimal cost."

According to the dissertation, "Servants Into Planters" by Aaron M. Shatzman:

> The very first meeting the Proprietors concluded with a decision to advertise the colony and to invite settlers from New England, Barbados and later, from Bermuda.

### 1663, June 10. CAROLINA COLONY. PLANS FOR SETTLEMENT.

Sir John Colleton informed the Lords Proprietors that due to the cramped conditions on the small island, many citizens were interested in moving to Carolina. However, due to the conditions of the 1629 Heath Charter, any settlement would be illegal. It was a problem that needed to be worked out.

Nonetheless, Peter Colleton, John's son, gathered 200 "Barbadian Adventurers", who contributed 1000 pounds of sugar to finance the settlement. In return, they were to receive 500 acres of land in Carolina. They engaged Captain William Hilton to explore the Carolina coast to search for suitable sites.

### 1663, August 10. CAROLINA COLONY. HILTON EXPLORES.

Capt. William Hilton sailed from Barbados to find a location in Carolina for settlement. He sailed into Port Royal Sound on the *Adventure* and claimed the island that protected the mouth of the harbor in his name – Hilton Head.

He was greeted by the Edistoh (Edisto) Indians who showed him the ruins of the French fort on Parris Island. Hilton wrote that he found "good Soyl [soil], covered with black mold, in some places a foot, in some places half a foot." He also reported that:

> The Country abounds with Grapes, large Figs, and Peaches; the Woods with Deer, Conies, Turkeys, Quails, Curlues ... Herons; and as the Indians say, in Winter, with Swans, Geese, Cranes, Duck and Mallard ... on and on the Sands: Oysters in abundance, with great store of Muscles ... The Rivers stored plentifully with Fish that we saw play and leap.

He also wrote of encounters with hostile natives who "acknowledged his presence by shooting arrows at him."

### 1663, August 12. CAROLINA COLONY.

A letter to the Proprietors from "Gentlemen of Barbados discussed their interest in settling in the "Province of Carolina." The letter was signed by "Tho. Modyford" and "P. Colleton."

### 1663, August 14. *HEATH CHARTER NULLIFIED.*

Charles II ordered the Heath Charter null and void due to its failure. This cleared the way for the Barbadian Adventurers to go forward with their plans.

### 1663, August 30. *CAROLINA COLONY.*

The Proprietors responded to the "Gentlemen of Barbados:

> We find by a letter from you ... that several people of Barbados have inclinations to settle and plant in some part of the Province of Carolina whom we desire by all ways and means to encourage ...

# 1664

### 1664. *CAROLINA COLONY. BARBADIAN PROPOSALS.*

The Barbadian Adventurers proposed that "for each one hundred acres ... they would have one Person white or black, young or old, transported at their Charge."

### 1664, September 8. *NEW YORK.*

New Amsterdam was conquered by the English and renamed New York, for its new Proprietor, James, Duke of York, brother of King Charles II.

# 1665

### 1665, January 7. *CAROLINA COLONY. LORDS PROPRIETORS.*

The *Concessions and Agreements* between the Lords Proprietors and William Yeamans (son of Sir John) was finalized. This document provided the guidelines for governing and distributing land in Carolina. Sir John Yeamans was named Governor of the Province of Carolina.

### 1665, June 30. *CAROLINA COLONY. LORDS PROPRIETORS.*

A second charter was drafted to the Lords Proprietors of Carolina to settle several legal issues in the original 1629 Heath grant.

The new charter claimed all land from 29° south to 39° 30' north (St. Augustine to Virginia) extending to the Pacific Ocean. It empowered the Proprietors to establish forts, towns, churches, maintain armies, and make law consistent with the laws of England "with the advice, assent, and approbation of the Freemen of said province." In return, the Proprietors were to pay the King twenty marks annually, plus one-fourth of the yield of gold and precious metals.

### 1665, October. *CAROLINA COLONY. EXPLORATIONS.*

Under the commission of Sir John Yeamans, a company of "adventurers for Carolina" was organized in Barbados. Each member was to be entitled to 500 acres in Carolina for every 1000 pounds of sugar contributed. Yeamans sailed to Carolina with three vessels.

### 1665, November. CAROLINA COLONY. EXPLORATIONS.

Yeaman's expedition was battered by a storm off the Cape Fear River. One of the vessels was wrecked with all provisions lost. Yeamans returned to Barbados. A number of colonists elected to stay in Cape Fear.

They were, however, beset upon by one misfortune after another. Supply vessels were delayed or destroyed by storms. Captain Stanyarne, master of a supply vessel "went mad and leapt overboard."

## King Charles II

**BORN:** May 29, 1630.
**DIED:** February 6, 1685
**REIGN:** May 29, 1660 – February 6, 1685
**1650 – 1660:** After his father's execution, Charles fled to France and lived in exile in the Netherlands.
**1660:** The Restoration of the English throne was accomplished through the efforts of George Monck Ist Duke of Albermarle and Anthony Ashley Cooper.

Due to his proclivities of drinking and womanizing, Charles was nicknamed "the Merry Monarch." He fathered more than a dozen children with his seven mistresses, but had no legitimate heir.
**1663:** Granted a patent for the province of Carolina
**1664:** Dutch settlement New Amsterdam was surrendered to English troops, and renamed New York, for the King's brother, James, Duke of York.
**1665:** Great plague of London killed more than 7,000 people.
**1666:** Great fire of London destroyed more than 13,000 buildings, eighty per cent of the city.
**1679:** Passed the Writ of Habeas Corpus.
**1681:** Ashley Cooper challenged the king on the question of succession. Cooper was charged with treason and thrown in the Tower of London.
**1685:** Charles II died, and with no legitimate heir, he was succeeded by his brother, the Catholic James II, Duke of York. This created a power struggle in England between the Anglicans and the Catholics.

# 1666

### 1666, June 22. *Carolina Colony. Sandford Explores.*

Capt. Robert Sandford of Cape Fear explored the Carolina coast for Sir John Yeamans. Lt. Joseph Woory, Yeaman's nephew, was part of the expedition. He wrote in his journal:

> We ran up with our ship about five miles from the river's mouth. On both sides the river is a great store of oyster banks and good creeks that run to the main ... about an hour after we came to an anchor two Indians came aboard us who told us we were in the River Grandee [North Edisto River] and that the country was called Edisto.

### 1666, June 23. *Carolina Colony. Sandford Explores.*

Capt. Robert Sandford landed on either present-day Kiawah or Seabrook Island and officially took formal possession of Carolina for England and the Proprietors. Joseph Woory wrote in his journal:

> We went a mile eastward from our ship and landed on a dry marsh where we found an Indian path which we kept, and it led us through many fields of corn ready to gather, also other corn, peas and beans. We also found many peach trees with fruit thereon near ripe. Marched three miles into the country upon an island and did not see an inch of bad land but all choice and good timber trees growing thereon, as oak, walnut, chestnut, maple, ash, elder and many other good trees.

### 1666, July 8. *Woodward Stays with Edisto.*

Dr. Henry Woodward, 20-year old ship's surgeon under Sanford, agreed to stay behind and live with the Edisto Indians in order to study their culture and language and lay the diplomatic groundwork for the future English settlers. The nephew of the tribal Cassique (chief) was taken aboard to further the relationship between the natives and the English.

### 1666, July 10. *Carolina Colony. Explorations.*

Sandford entered what is now Charleston harbor and sailed up river, which he named Ashley, for Lord Proprietor Anthony Ashley Cooper.

### 1666, July 14. *Carolina Colony. Explorations.*

Upon his return to Cape Fear, Capt. Sandford documented his commendation of the "Carolina coast as a place ideally suited for settlement." The document was attested by the officers of his crew:

Henry Brayne George Cary
Richard Abrahall Samuel Harvey
Thomas Giles Joseph Woory

### 1666, September 4. ENGLAND. BIRTH.

William Rhett was born in London. Thirty-two years later he would move to Carolina and become one of it's most prominent citizens.

### 1666, September 6. GREAT FIRE OF LONDON.

London was consumed by a great fire, which burned four days, destroying more than 13,000 buildings, about 80% of the city.

### 1666, October. LORDS PROPRIETORS. JOHN LOCKE.

Ashley Cooper went to Oxford, seeking treatment for a liver ailment and met John Locke. Locke had already graduated but was studying medicine. Ashley was impressed with Locke's brilliance and hired the young man as his personal secretary/physician and brought him to Exeter House in London.

Locke soon came to hold the positions of secretary to the Council for Trade and Plantations and secretary to the Lords Proprietors.

# 1667

### 1667, January. CAROLINA COLONY. ABANDONMENT OF CAPE FEAR.

The Cape Fear colony of "several hundreds" was abandoned. The main reason cited was the barrenness of the soil and "ill suckses [success]." Most of the colonists left for Virginia or returned to Barbados.

John Locke.
*Courtesy of the Library of Congress*

# 1668

### 1668. CAROLINA COLONY. WOODWARD CAPTURED BY SPANISH.

Henry Woodward was living with the Port Royal area Indians when the Spanish learned of his presence. The Spanish attacked and Woodward was taken to St. Augustine to be held for ransom. Robert Searle, a privateer, attacked the city several months later and during the battle, Woodward was freed. He signed on with Searle as ship's surgeon to the Leeward Islands. There he boarded a ship bound for London. However, as the ship left Barbados it was destroyed by a hurricane and Woodward managed to make it to the island of Nevis, where he waited for another ship to take him home.

# 1669

### 1669, January. COOPER'S PLAN FOR SETTLEMENT.

Ashley Cooper assumed the leadership role for the Proprietors, most of whom had little interest in the Carolina colony. Disappointed by the failure of the Barbadian efforts to colonize Carolina, Cooper was determined to make the next attempt successful.

Cooper had managed hold office under the administrations of Charles I, Parliament, Cromwell and Charles II, a rare and almost impossible feat, which illustrated his masterful political acumen. He convinced each proprietor to contribute £500 to finance his attempt, and "pledge to provide up to £200 a year for the next four years. The money was to be used for the purchase of "Shipps Armes, Ammunition, Tooles, provisions ... for the settlement of Port Royall within the Province of Carolina. At a cost of £3,000, Cooper purchased a fleet of three vessels, two frigates and a sloop – *Carolina, Port Royal* and *Albemarle*.

Cooper abandoned the Cape Fear region and determined that the new settlement would be further south, notably the Port Royal area at Hilton Head. He also began to recruit colonists from England, to supplement the expected settlers from Barbados. Within three months, more than 100 people had committed to the settlement.

### 1669, July 21. FUNDAMENTAL CONSTITUTIONS.

*The Fundamental Constitutions of Carolina* written by Anthony Ashley Cooper and John Locke, was adopted by the Proprietors. Even though the Fundamental Constitutions never became the official law of Carolina a number of its provisions were implemented and accepted by the colonists. It was an extraordinary attempt to form an aristocratic government from a colony of adventurers, and also designed to attract settlers by offering religious tolerance, liberal land grants and property rights as well as "titles of honor."

The Constitutions contained similar language of Locke's famous 1689 *A Letter Concerning Toleration,* and granted the Carolina Colony religious freedom and a liberty of conscience to all settlers, expressly mentioning "Jews, heathens, and dissenters." It would have a profound influence on Charleston society, leading to the immigration of the French Huguenots and Sephardic Jews from Portugal. Some of the religious provisions were:

- Church of England established as the tax-supported church in the colony.
- Religious freedom for anyone who believed in God.
- Seven individuals could form a "church or profession" that would be officially recognized. "No person whatsoever shall disturb, molest or persecute another for his speculative opinions in religion, or his way of worship."
- Roman Catholicism was not tolerated.

The Fundamental Constitutions also set up a County Palatine, an official who could exercise powers normally reserved to the crown Palatine and established a system of government by the landed gentry. To vote a man must own 50 acres of property and to hold a seat in the elected legislature, he must own 500 acres. The nobility consisted of:

- Landgraves (borrowed from German courts): Must possess 48,000 acres
- Caciques (the title of Indian chiefs in America): must possess 24,000 acres.

The Proprietors promised 150 acres of land to all "free settlers over the age of sixteen" and an additional "100 acres for every able-bodied servant" in their employee. "Master" Stephen Bull had nine servants and received 1050 acres. Servants could include family members (children, cousins, nieces …) and "indentured servants" who signed a work contract for a specific period of time in exchange for their passage to the colony. If an individual acquired 3000 acres, the estate could be declared a manor and the owner would have all the rights of a lord of the manor established by English law.

The Constitutions established "that all subjects who should be transported into the province, and the children born there, should be denizens and lieges of the Kingdom of England." It also set out specific and strict laws for slavery, which became one of the most important issues facing the colony during the next 200 years. "Every freeman of Carolina shall have absolute power and authority over his negro slaves."

The Proprietors also approved a "Grand Modell" for the planned colony, based on the grid pattern designed for the rebuilding of London after the Great Fire.

## 1669, July 26. CAROLINA COLONY. POLITICS.

The Proprietors issue a blank governor's commission to Sir John Yeamans, offering him leadership of the Carolina colony. If he declined, he was empowered to name his own substitute.

## 1669, July 27. CAROLINA EXPEDITION.

Mr. Joseph West, described as "a moderate, just, pious and valiant person," was appointed Commander-in-chief of the Carolina expedition until its arrival at Barbados. He was to deliver the commission to Yeamans. His instructions from the Proprietors included:

> M' West, Yo' are with all possible speed to saile with ye fleete under yo' command for Kinsaile, in Ireland, Where yo' are to endeavor to get twenty or twenty-five Servts ... & as soone as yo' have gotten them on board yo' are to saile directly to Berbados [Barbados.]

He was also instructed to obtain seeds, plants and provisions in Ireland and "to carry the seeds and roots in a tubb of earth so they may not dye before you arrive att Port Royall."

## 1669, August 3. CAROLINA EXPEDITION.

The list of seaman aboard the *Carolina* included:

| | |
|---|---|
| Henry Brayne | Thomas Sumers |
| John Comings (mate) | Henry Jones |
| Richard Dyas (gunner) | James Shepard |
| Richard Cole (carpenter) | John Williamson |
| Peter Salter (trumpeter) | John Rippertt |
| Arthur Roper (boatswain) | Alexander John |
| John More | Henry Ffaaro |
| Thomas Joy | Hails Porter |
| Georg Gray | William Orr |

## 1669, September 17. CAROLINA EXPEDITION. VOYAGE.

The expedition left Ireland for the trans-Atlantic crossing.

## 1669, September 20. INDENTURED SERVITUDE CONTRACT.

Millicent How, a spinster, became indentured to Captain Joseph West. In the 17th century, "servant" was often used to describe a formal contractual relationship between an individual and a "master." The master's responsibility was to maintain the servant for the duration of the contract, providing shelter, food and clothing. In return, the servant worked for the master for a specified period of time, traditionally two to seven years.

## 1669, November 2. CAROLINA EXPEDITON. ARRIVAL IN BARBADOS.

The ships made port in Barbados a day before a hurricane hit the island. The sloop *Albemarle* was destroyed and the other two ships were so severely damaged that repairs took more than a month. Food was so short that Sir John Colleton took "more than 20 servants" to his plantation.

Sir John Yeamans accepted the commission as Governor of Carolina.

## 1669, November 8. *Carolina Expedition.*

In a letter to the Proprietors Joseph West commented, "This is to Infome yo' of our being at Barbados where we shall stay until the 23th … then hoping to quit this island for our desired Port."

## 1669, December 9. *Carolina Expedition.*

Sir John Yeamans joined the expedition on board the *Port Royal.* A new sloop, *Three Brothers,* borrowed from the Colleton family, replaced the *Albemarle* and the three ships set out for Carolina. During the voyage they were buffeted by more storms and separated from each other.

The *Carolina* was blown west by the storm and limped to Bermuda. Passenger Affra Harleston wrote that "the stern of the ship broke in."

The storms pushed the *Three Brothers* north toward Virginia; it was presumed lost. In reality, the sloop made its way to the Nansemond River in Virginia where it was repaired and resupplied with the assistance of the Puritan settlement there.

The *Port Royal* was damaged and limped into the island of Nevis. There they discovered Dr. Henry Woodward, who immediately volunteered to accompany the expedition and give them the benefit of his experience. Yeamans immediately accepted Woodward's proposal.

They set for Carolina and yet *another* storm wrecked the *Port Royal* and left them stranded near Abaco in the Bahamas. The crew and passengers managed to patch together a small boat from the salvaged timbers where they sailed to Bermuda. They were surprised to find the crippled *Carolina* in port, being repaired.

## PASSENGER LIST OF THE *CAROLINA*
### Captain Joseph West. 1st Mate: John Coming
Masters (head of household) in CAPITAL LETTERS
Servants and free men listed beneath

CAPT. FLORENCE SULLIVAN
  Ralph Marshall
  James Montgomery
  Richard Alexander
  Stephen Wheelwright
  Thomas Kings
  Elizabeth Dimmocke
  Elizabeth Matthews
STEPHEN BULL
  Robert Done
  Burnaby Bull
  Thomas Ingram
  Jonathon Barker
  John Larmouth
  Dudley Widzier
EDWARD HOLLIS &
JOSEPH DALTON
  George Prideox
  Thomas Younge
  Henry Price
  William Chambers
  John Dawson
  William Roades
  Affra Harleston
  June Lawson
  Susanna Kinder
THOMAS SMITH
& PAUL SMITH
  Aice Rice
  Jo. Hudlesworth
  Jo. Burroughs
  Hugh Wigleston
  Elizabeth Smith
  Andrew Boorne
  Francis Noone

HAMBLETON
  Thomas Gourden
  William Lumsden
  Jo. Frizen
  Stephen Flinte
  Edward Young
  Jo. Thomas
  Samuell Morris
  Thomas Southell
  Agnie Payne
  Jo. Reed
NICH. CARTHWRIGHT
  Thomas Gubbs
  Jo. Loyde
  Martin Bedson
  Stephen Price
  William Jenkins
MORRIS MATHEWS
  Abra Phillips
  Reghnold Barefoot
  Mathew Hewitt
  Elizabeth Currie
WILLIAM BOWMAN
  Abraham Smith
  Millicent Howe
JO. RIVERS
  Thomas Poole
  Robert Williams
  Henry Burgen
  Matthew Smallwood

DR. WILL SCRIVNER
  Margaret Tudor
THOMAS MIDDLETON, &
ELIZABETH
  Richard Wright
  Thomas Wormes
WILLIAM OWENS
  John Humphreys
  Christopher Swade
  John Borely
SAMUEL WEST
  Andrew Searle
  Will West
JOSEPH BAILEY
  John Carmichaell
PASSENGERS THAT HAVE NO
SERVANTS
  Mr. Thomas Rideall
  Mr. Will Haughton
  Mr. Will Harris
  Mr. Thomas Humfreys
  Elizabeth Humfreys
  Marie Clerke
  Samuel Darkenwell
  Nathanyell Darkenwell
  Mrs. Sarah Erpe
  Elizabeth Erpe
  Martha Powell
  Mrs. Mary Erpe
  Thomas Motteshead

# PART TWO:
## THE PROPRIETARY CITY 1670-1719

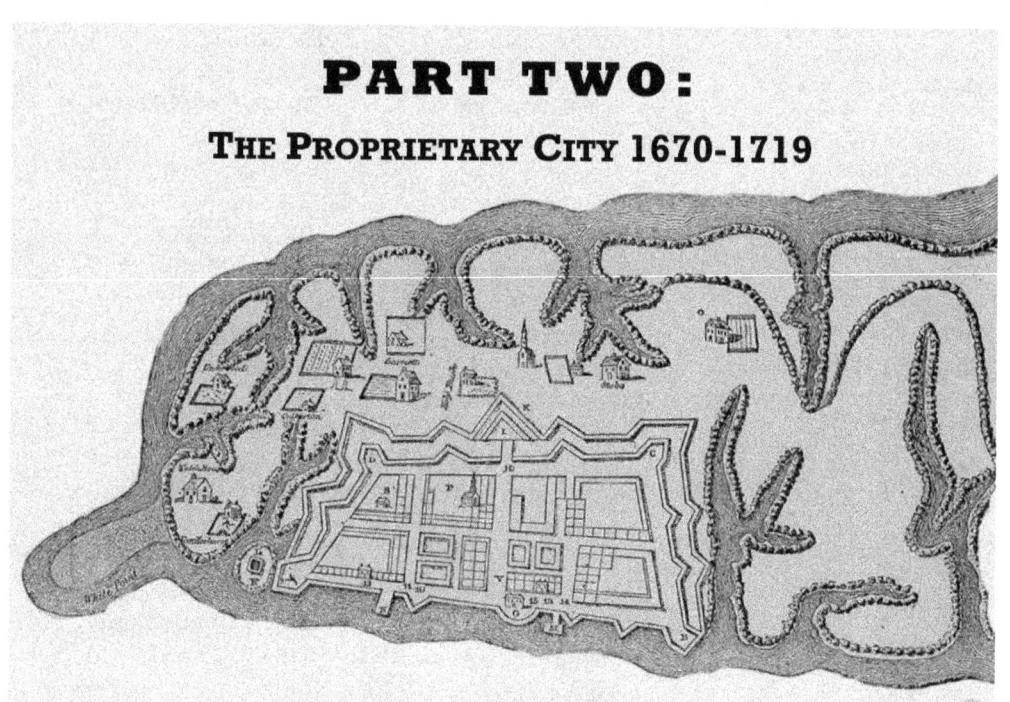

"The Proprietory-Monarchs are ... like a Landlord to his Tenant, they have their Eyes upon the Rent; their Concern, if any, is not of Affection, but of Interest ... for their Ears have been ... shut to the Complaints of their Oppress'd People."

Daniel Defoe, *Party-Tyranny, or An Occasional Bill in Miniature, As Now Practiced in Carolina* 1705

# 1670

### 1670, February 26. *CAROLINA EXPEDITION. FIRST SETTLERS.*

The expedition took on several new passengers in Bermuda. Sir John Yeamans decided to return to Barbados. In his place he named 79-year old William Sayle as the newly appointed Governor of Carolina. They left Bermuda with a plan to settle at Port Royal (current location of Hilton Head, SC.)

### 1670, March. *FUNDAMENTAL CONSTITUTIONS.*

After initial complaints from several of the settlers, the Proprietors drew up a second, revised version of the Fundamental Constitutions which was never ratified.

### 1670, March 15-16. *CAROLINA EXPEDITION. FIRST SETTLERS.*

The expedition arrived at Bull's Island, (just north of present day Charleston), 100 miles north of Port Royal. They were greeted onshore by the Cassique of the Kiawah Tribe speaking bad Spanish, "Bony Conraro Angles!" (Good English comrades!)

The Cassique was the young man, nephew of the Cassique at Port Royal, who had traveled with Captain Sanford. *(See page 23.)* He informed Sayle that a tribe called Westoes had destroyed everything from St. Helena (Port Royal) north to the Kiawha River (Ashley River).

According to Nicholas Carteret:

> We gave them [Indians] brass rings and tobacco at which they seemed well pleased ... and as we drew to the shore a good number of Indians appeared clad with dear [sic] skins having with them bows and arrows.

The Cassique tried to convince Sayle they should settle in the Bull's Island/Kiawha (Ashley) River area. Sayle, however, was determined to go south. The young Indian agreed to join the expedition and guide them to Port Royal. He was a firm friend of the English and during the journey he continued to encourage them away from Port Royal, which was closer to Spanish Florida. Most native tribes of the Carolina coast had been attacked and enslaved by the Spanish for over one hundred years. The Cassique believed the English would be better neighbors and partners. He also was concerned about the fierce Westoes tribe that controlled the area around the Savannah River. Not only were they prone to war, they were also cannibals.

## 1670, March 21. CAROLINA EXPEDITION. FIRST ELECTION.

During their short stay at Port Royal, Governor Sayle summoned the passengers and they elected five men "to be of the council" – Paul Smith, Robert Donne, Ralph Marshall, Samuel West and Joseph Dalton. This was the first election in South Carolina. The council voted to return to the Kiawha area to settle. The Kiawah were a small tribe, approximately 160 members. The population of all the coastal tribes in South Carolina was less than 2,000 when the English arrived.

William Owen, described as one who was "always itching to be in authority" questioned the legality of the election. He was described as "an egotistical Anglican." The colonists voted for a second time, with the same result. So this was the first election in Carolina as well as the first *contested* election.

## 1670, April. CAROLINA EXPEDITION. ARRIVAL IN CAROLINA.

"Early in April" (the only date recorded) the *Carolina* sailed into what is now Charleston harbor, navigated past a spit of land covered with shells at low tide, which they called "Oyster Point and sailed up the Kiawha (Ashley) River. Three miles inland they landed on the west bank of the first creek they came to and named it Albemarle Point in honor of George Monck, Duke of Albemarle, one of the Lords Proprietors.

Albemarle Point is the present-day site of Charles Town Landing, a state park. It became the third English colony in North America (Virginia, 1607 and Massachusetts, 1620).

They chose a nine-acre site on what is now called Town Creek, three miles inland around the curve of the Ashley River, making the settlement invisible to vessels sailing into the harbor. Security from the Spanish was always a major consideration. The cargo of the *Carolina* included:

- 15 tons of beer
- 30 gallons of brandy
- 59 bushels of flour
- 12 suits of armor
- 100 beds and pillows
- 1200 grubbing hoes
- 100,000 four penny nails
- 756 fishing hooks

The passengers include: Twenty-nine "Masters" (men of property) and "free" persons; sixty-three indentured white servants; and 1 black slave.

## 1670, May. CAROLINA EXPEDITION. "THREE BROTHERS" ARRIVES.

Six weeks later the *Three Brothers* arrived. The sloop left Virginia after repairs, overshot the Port Royal site and sailed into the Spanish settlement of Guale, (near present day St. Catherine's Island, Georgia). They were attacked, losing twelve passengers. The sloop turned north and was met by a group of friendly Kiawah Indians who informed them of the English settlement at Albemarle Point. So the expedition was now reunited.

The 1620 voyage of the *Mayflower* voyage was a mere two months. During the nine-month voyage of the Carolina expedition five ships were used, dozens of lives lost and only one of the original vessels that sailed out of the Thames River at Gravesend had survived.

The Carolina colonists were extremely wary of the Spanish presence at St. Augustine 200 miles south. They immediately began the construction of entrenchments and instituted a twenty-four-hour watch. Such was to become the reality of the Carolina colony for the next fifty years.

The extreme heat was another constant enemy. Captain Joseph West wrote about "pestiferous gnats called Moschetoes" and complained about the low moral standard of most of the settlers.

### 1670, May 27. FORTIFICATIONS. TO VIRGINIA AND BERMUDA.

The *Carolina* now commanded by Captain Henry Braine sailed to Virginia for supplies, most importantly, an eight- month supply of corn, peas and meal. *The Three Brothers* sailed to Bermuda for more settlers and supplies. Several crude wooden dwellings were built at Albemarle Point, as well as an earthwork fort and a pallisade with seven mounted guns.

### 1670, June. CAROLINA COLONY. SLAVERY.

The *Three Brothers* returned with three enslaved Africans on board named John, Sr., Elizabeth and John, Jr.

### 1670, June 25. RELIGION.

Governor Sayle wrote a letter to Ashley Cooper appealing for a clergyman.

### 1670, June 27. FOOD SHORTAGE.

Joseph West wrote to Lord Ashley that they only had seven weeks of provisions left. Henry Woodward was dispatched to solicit help from neighboring Indians.

### 1670, July 4. ADDICTED TO RUM.

Captain Joseph West complained that several of the settlers were "so addicted to Rum, that they will do little but whilst the bottle is at their nose." He also noted that there were "grand abuses that prophanely violate the Sabbath."

### 1670, August. ABORTIVE SPANISH ATTACK.

The Spanish considered the Carolina colony an intrusion of their land. Three Spanish frigates lay off the coast of the harbor, awaiting the return of the *Carolina*. Their plan was to starve the English colonists into submission.

### 1670, August 22. SUPPLIES ARRIVE. SLAVERY.

The *Carolina* returned from Virginia with eight months of supplies, including a slave described as "one lusty negro man." On the voyage from Virginia *Carolina* managed to slip past the Spanish force with only "token resistance." A fortuitous heavy storm approached and battered the area, making the Spanish retreat.

### 1670, September 9. TO BARBADOS. RELIGION

*Carolina* sailed to Barbados for passengers and supplies. Another letter asking for a clergyman was written and signed by Florence O'Sullivan, Stephen Bull, Joseph

West, William Scrivener, Ralph Marshall, Paul Smith, Samuel West, Joseph Dalton and Governor Sayle.

O'Sullivan also wrote a letter to Ashley Cooper.

> ... the country proves good beyond expectation, abounding in all things, as good oak, ash, deer, turkeys, partridges, rabbits, turtle and fish; and the land produces anything that is put into it – corn, cotton, tobacco ... with many pleasant rivers ... pray send us a minister qualified according to the Church of England and an able councellor [lawyer] to end controversies amongst us and put us in the right way of the managem't...

Joseph West wrote to Ashley Cooper with a warning:

> Our Governor ... is very aged, and hath much lost himself in his government ... I doubt he will not be so advantageous to a new colony as we did expect.

Joseph Dalton, Secretary of the Colony, wrote to Lord Ashley, "The Collony is ... safely settled and ... there only remains the preservation of it."

## 1670, September 15. CAROLINA COLONY.

John Locke wrote some observations about the Carolina colony.

> *Charlestowne* – Defended with a creek on the one side and a salt march overflowe at high tides on the other the neck that joynes it to the main land not exceeding 50 years palisaded and easily defensible.
>
> *Inlet* – Difficult to strangers but 3 fathom water.
>
> *Indians* - Of Edisto Ashapo and Combohe to the South, our friends. Of Wando Ituan Sewee and Sehey to the north came to our assistance and were zealous and resolute in it.

## 1670, November 1. NAMED CHARLES TOWN.

Ashley Cooper wrote to Captain West and Governor Sayle ordering that the settlement, Albemarle Point, be renamed "Charles Town."

## 1670, November 15. FIRST EXPORTS.

Sir John Yeamans wrote Ashley Cooper from Barbados: "Sending 12 cedar planks as the first fruits of that glorious province (Carolina.)

Yeamans was well-known to the Proprietors due to his success as a business man and landowner in Barbados. Yeamans already looked down upon the new English colonists as unexperienced. He was determined to use the new venture as a means of elevating his statue and wealth in the New World.

## 1670, December. ARRIVALS.

Ninety-six settlers arrived from New York on two ships, *Phoenix* and *Blessing*, lured by the promise of free land from the Proprietors.

# 1671

### 1671. *Charles Town. First Winter.*

The colony survived its first winter although they had expected to find the climate more tropical than it was. Many of the exotic crops – oranges, limes, lemons, figs, pomegranates – were destroyed by "an inch of ice" that first winter. But more traditional crops – corn, peas, tobacco – fared well.

### 1671. *England. Recruitment of Settlers.*

The Lords Proprietors launched a campaign to "attract settlers" to Carolina, by sending pamphlets across Europe. They promised "land at modest cost … freedom of religion."

### 1671. *Charles Town. Oyster Point.*

Governor Sayle decided that the peninsula, called Oyster Point between the Ashley and Cooper Rivers "was a much better permanent site for a town" than Albemarle Point. Sayle ordered 600 acres set aside for the purpose of building a town there. The elderly governor was having serious health issues at this time, and depended on the talents and energy of Captain Joseph West in running the colony.

The colony was reported to be "weak from lack of food." The council determined that come spring they would:

> … plant what plantations we can this year, it being the hope of a new settlement in the first place to provide for the belly and make some experiment in what the land will produce.

### 1671. *White Servitude.*

White servants made up the majority of the colony's population, subject to strict discipline to enforce labor and order until the end of their term of servitude. Most servants spent their time planting and harvesting the crops.

### 1671, February 8. *Arrivals.*

Forty-six settlers arrived from Barbados on the *John and Thomas*, named for the two men who outfitted the vessel, John Strode and Thomas Colleton, both of Barbados.

### 1671, February 16. *Arrivals.*

*Carolina* returned from Barbados with sixty-four settlers.

### 1671, March 4. *Death. West Appointed Governor.*

Governor Sayle, who had been ill for many months, died. In his will, he nominated Joseph West as his successor "until the Proprietors will be known."

West was entrusted with making sure the colony was profitable. To the Proprietors, Carolina was foremost a business investment. Each Proprietor expected a return on his money. During the first year, West constructed forts, public buildings, roads and fences. He also cultivated trade with the Native Indians. One of West's first jobs was the building of two houses in which to keep supplies, one for arms, the second for general stores – seeds, grains, other foodstuffs, tools, etc... A weekly allotment for each man was:

- 3 pounds of dried beef
- 4 ½ pounds of either dried peas or oatmeal or 3 ½ pounds of bread.

He wrote that thirty acres had been cleared, houses and palisades built to hold against a thousand Indians.

## 1671, March 22. *POPULATION.*

William Owen reported that the Colony numbered "about 200."

## 1671, July 1. *ARRIVALS.*

Sir John Yeamans arrived from Barbados with 50 settlers and more supplies. The lure of Carolina was simple. On Barbados there was only about 100,000 acres of arable land. A large plantation consisted of 200 acres. More than half the landowners possessed less than 10 acres. Just by arriving in Carolina a Barbadian land owner received fifteen times the amount of land he owned on the island.

According to the stipulations of Fundamental Constitutions, Yeamans expected to be named Governor upon his arrival, as he was the only Landgrave present in Carolina. The Constitutions provided that the eldest of the Lords Proprietor who should be present in Carolina should be Governor; if no Proprietor was present then the eldest of the landgraves should assume the position.

Even though the Constitutions had yet to be approved by the Grand Council, it was being used as the governmental blueprint for the colony. Yeamans' push to become governor created a power struggle and divided the colonists into two groups – the group from Barbados (aligned with Yeamans) and the group from Europe (aligned with West). Yeaman's property was about 30 miles up the Cooper River, in the Goose Creek area, which became a bastion for the Barbadians.

West wrote that Yeamans was "disgusted that the people did not incline to salute him Governor."

The Barbadians (Yeamans, Colleton, etc ...) looked down on the English immigrants. The English were novices, still adjusting to the shock of colonial life, and stood no chance against this assault by the Barbadians in controlling the government and commerce.

After, all, the Barbadians had years of experience in the New World. With their plantations and trading companies, they helped establish the most successful colonial society in the New World. They were independent, experienced, ambitious and often unscrupulous in their quest for riches. They also brought with them a fully established society and lifestyle.

The Barbadians had a well-defined slave code, which was adopted for Carolina. They were devoted to the Anglican Church and lived with:

> a combination of old-world elegance and frontier boisterousness. Ostentatious in their dress, dwellings and furnishings, they liked

hunting, guns, dogs, military titles like 'Captain' and 'Colonel', a big mid-day meal and light supper. They enjoyed long hours at their favorite taverns over bowls of cold rum punch or brandy.

They cast a long shadow and influenced much of the life in Charles Town, establishing the blueprint for what was to become romanticized as "the Old South." They also had little interest in the Proprietors' notions of a perfect government. Within the year, the Barbadians would control the Council and the Assembly.

## 1671, August 25. ELECTION.

The first election was held in Charles Town, choosing twenty men as a Parliament (Assembly) and Sir John Yeamans as speaker. Over half the councilmen were Barbadians. Five men were then selected to represent the people as the Grand Council - Mr. Thomas Gray, Mr. Maurice Mathews, Lt. Henry Hughes, Mr. Christopher Portman and Mr. Ralph Marshall. Yeamans took every opportunity to question the legality of West's appointment as governor.

John Coming, mate of the *Carolina*, wrote that "the Barbadians endeavor to rule all." Yeamans complained that "West is proud and peevish." Others called Yeamans "disaffected and too selfish." The colony was firmly divided into factions.

## 1671, August 28. LITIGATION.

First recorded case of litigation in the Carolina colony was heard by Governor West and the Grand Council – an argument over timber rights of an area - John Norton and Originall Jackson against Mr. Maurice Mathews, Mr. Thomas Gray and Mr. William Owen.

## 1671, September. COMMERCE. LACK OF FOOD.

Due to a scarcity of provisions for the coming winter, Governor West ordered that all supplies in store should be:

> ...frugally distributed to the needy; that all occupations, except for carpenters and smiths, should be suspended for the planting and gathering of a crop of provisions; that in the future no one should be entitled to assistance from the public stores who had not two acres well planted with corn or peas for every person in his family; and that slothful and loitering persons should be put under the charge of the industrious planters for the purpose of working for their maintenance and the benefit of the community.

## 1671, September 1. COMMERCE. CATTLE IMPORTED.

Sir John Yeamans imported 100 cattle from Virginia.

## 1671, September 1. POLITICS.

"We have always had some differences in this colony," Governor Joseph West wrote in a letter to Ashley Cooper a droll, understated response to the power struggle for the governorship, instigated by Sir John Yeamans.

### 1671, September 18. *Yeamans Commissioned Governor.*

Ashley Cooper wrote to Sir John Yeamans informing him of his commission as Governor and that he relied upon Yeamans to be "firm and industrious in settling the government." It would be six months until the commission arrived.

### 1671, September 27. *Indian Uprising.*

Governor West and the Grand Council declared war against the Kussoes Tribe, living up the Combahee River. The Kussoes declared themselves allied with the Spanish and began raiding English properties. Within seven days, the English had defeated the Kussoes, killing some, and enslaving many, selling them to the West Indies.

### 1671, October 24. *Survey of Oyster Point Ordered.*

The Grand Council appointed a group of citizens to "examine the banks of the Ashley and the Wando, or Cooper River, and to make a return of what places might be most convenient to situate towns upon." It was an order to begin the surveying of Oyster Point.

### 1671, November. *Arrivals.*

Ninety-six New Yorkers arrived on two ships, the *Phoenix* and the *Blessing*, lured by the promise of land.

### 1671, December 20. *Runaway Servant. Punishment.*

Dennis Mahone, who had arrived in Carolina as a servant for Richard Cole in 1670, was brought before the Council because he was "guilty of running away ... and departing this Collony to obtain the protection of the Crowne of Spaine."

He was ordered to be "strip naked to his Waste [sic] & receive thirty-nine lashes upon his naked Back."

### 1671, December 9. *Politics. Commerce.*

The Grand Council ordered Capt. Florence O' Sullivan to "admeasure and lay out ... tenn acres of land" for Susan Kinder.

### 1671, December 15. *Commerce.*

Lord Ashley wrote to John Coming:

> I ... am well satisfied with your behavior, ability and the service you have done us ... the good Character we receive of you from other hands. I take notice in particular of the care you have taken to instruct others in the Navigation of Ashley River ...

### 1671, December 16. *Slavery.*

The Proprietors forbid the enslavement of Indians. They also set out limitations for servitude – no more than seven years, and once expired, the servants were given allotments of land, tools and clothes. They also decreed that no one may retail any drink without license.

### 1671, December 23. POLITICS. COMMERCE.

Alarmed by desertions, the Grand Council ordered all shipmasters to post bond that they will not carry off any Carolina settlers.

## 1672

### 1672. ARRIVALS. CULTURE.

The majority of settlers during the first year had been English. However, that quickly changed. By 1672 more than half of the new arrivals came from Barbados and other islands of the West Indies – St. Kitts, Nevis, Anguilla, Montserrat, Antigua and Barbuda. During the next twenty years, over sixty per cent of white immigrants came from this region. Once arrived in Carolina they were generically referred to as "Barbadians," regardless of their island of origin.

They were either servants, merchants or younger sons of island-planting families seeking their own fortunes. They were of English descent, but considered themselves West Indian -tougher, and more motivated than their English counterparts. Looked upon as "rogues," these West Indian settlers were more prepared and very well-suited for the rough life in Carolina.

### 1672, January. MARRIAGE.

Sometime during the month, John Coming married Affra Harleston.

### 1672, January 13. COMMERCE. RICE.

Richard Kingdom shipped a barrel of rice to Charles Town from London on the ship *William & Ralph*, captained by William Jeffereys.

### 1672, January 20. POPULATION.

Secretary Dalton wrote that the number of colonists transported to Carolina by this date was 337 men, seventy-one women and sixty-two children – 470. Sixty-four had died, leaving a population of 406.

### 1672, February. OYSTER POINT.

Lieutenant Henry Hughs, John Coming and his wife, Affra Harleston Coming appeared for the Grand Council to voluntarily surrender half of their lands on Oyster Point for the new townsite. Hughs's land was retained, while the Coming's land was released back to them.

### 1672, April 19. YEAMANS PROCLAIMED GOVERNOR.

Sir John Yeamans was proclaimed Governor at Charles Town. In the commission letter the Proprietors praised Joseph West's service, but noted "the nature of our government ... required that a Landgrove (titled landowner) should be preferred to any Commoner."

## 1672, April 20. OYSTER POINT.

Ashley Cooper gave notice that the settlement should permanently move from Albemarle Point to Oyster Point. The Albemarle settlement did not adhere to the "Grand Modell" specified by the Proprietors. The peninsula, formed by the confluence of the Ashley and Cooper Rivers, also created a natural harbor, perfect for a commercial port. Lord Ashley ordered that the new town be:

> layd out into regular streets ... six score squares of 300 feet each ... the great street should not be less than 100 or six score feet broad; the lesser streets none less than sixty; alleys eight or ten feet.

Each owner of a lot was required to "build a house of two stories in height and at least 30 feet by 16 feet." One could make the case that this plan of wide, regular streets, laid out in "broad and straight lines" was influenced by Sir Christopher Wren's checkerboard plan for rebuilding London after the 1666 fire.

## 1672, April 23. ANTHONY COOPER TITLED.

King Charles II bestowed upon Anthony Ashley Cooper the titles, Earl of Shaftesbury and Baron Cooper of Paulet.

## 1672, May. FORTIFICATIONS.

A fort was completed at Albemarle Point. Even though plans were well underway to moving the colony to Oyster Point, security against the Spanish was still a major consideration.

## 1672, June. WEST APPOINTED NEW POSITION.

Former governor Joseph West was appointed Superintendent of the Plantation and Stores of the Proprietors.

## 1672, June 20. POLITICS.

Lord Ashley Cooper wrote to Sir John Yeaman:

> The Distinction of the Governor from the rest of our deputies is a thing rather of order than of overruling power, and he hath no more freedom thereby than any one of the council to swerve from these rules.

## 1672, July 20. OYSTER POINT.

The surveyor general, John Culpepper of Barbados, was ordered to "admeasure and layout for a town on the Oyster Point."

Most of the land on Oyster Point had been given as a grant to Henry Hughes and John Coming, first mate of the *Carolina* in 1670. Both men voluntarily surrendered half of their lands "to be employed in and toward the outlaying of a town and commons."

This made the original plan for Charles Town extending no farther west than present Meeting Street, no farther north than Broad Street and no farther south than Water Street.

> ## ANTHONY ASHLEY COOPER
>
> **BORN:** June 22, 1621, Wimborn, Minster
> **DIED:** January, 21, 1683, Amsterdam
>
> A founder of the Whig party in England, Cooper was first elected to Parliament in 1639. A devoted Anglican and fiercely anti-Catholic, during the English Civil Wars he initially fought at a Royalist, then switched to the Parliamentary side.
>
> **1660.** Cooper was one of twelve members of Parliament who traveled to the Dutch Republic and invited the exiled Charles II back to London. After the Restoration, Cooper served Charles II as Chancellor of the Exchequer and later, Lord Chancellor, becoming one of the most powerful men in England.
>
> **1669:** As one of the Lords Proprietors of the Carolina Colony, Cooper helped draft the *Fundamental Constitutions* with his secretary, John Locke.
>
> **1672:** Cooper became 1st Earl of Shaftesbury.
>
> **1681:** He was arrested for treason, due to his passionately negative views about the king's Catholic brother, James, Duke of York. James was next in line for the throne, and Cooper was violently opposed to the return of English Catholicism.
>
> **1683**: Died in exile.

## 1672, November 17. *COOPER APPOINTED LORD CHANCELLOR.*

Lord Ashley Cooper was appointed Lord Chancellor by Charles II, making him one of the most powerful men in England. Ashley, however, was becoming concerned about the King's lack of a legitimate heir. Ashley harbored a fear that if Charles died without heir, the throne would pass to the King's Catholic brother, James, Duke of York. Being a devoted Anglican, Ashley found that possibility frightening.

## 1672, November 27. *COMMENTS ABOUT YEAMANS.*

Ashley Cooper wrote about Sir John Yeamans, "If to convert all things to his private profit be the marke of able parts Sir John is without a doubt a very judicious man."

# 1673

### 1673. *Politics. Growing Pains.*

During 1673 the tensions among the colonists (Barbadian vs. English) increased, but both sides became united in their opposition against the Proprietors who increasingly quarreled about every expenditure and lack of profits. Many of the colonists found their distant masters aloof and uncaring. They were also chafing at the unpracticality of living within the confines of the Fundamental Constitutions. While a laudable plan on paper, the Constitutions were impractical for the creation of a colony and government in the wilderness. Romantic and philosophical notions of grand baronies and a genteel society born in the drawing room must bend to practical reality.

Sir John Yeamans.
*Courtesy of the Library of Congress*

### 1673. *Commerce.*

The fear of starvation had passed. The colony could produce enough corn, peas and wheat to feed the population. In addition, the surrounding waters supplied an abundance of fish and oysters and the woods were filled with game – deer, rabbits and fowl. Governor Yeamans, however, was extensively engaged in exporting these provisions for profit, leading to complaints among the colonists to the Proprietors. They clamored for the restoration of Joseph West as governor.

### 1673, January 8. *Cooper Warns About Catholics.*

Lord Ashley Cooper gave a speech in the House of Lords warning that the 16,000 Catholics living in London were on the verge of rebellion, which caused the Lords to pass an act expelling all Catholics from within 10 miles of London. Cooper introduced a measure that would require every peer, including the king's Catholic brother, James, Duke of York, to take the Oath of Allegiance renouncing the pope and recognizing the royal supremacy in the Church of England. Charles II was so angered by Ashley's actions he removed him from the Privy Council.

### 1673, May 18. *Politics. West Appointed Governor.*

Lord Ashley, having received numerous letters of complaint about Sir John Yeamans, sent Joseph West a patent making him a Landgrave and giving him the commission as Governor of Carolina.

### 1673, August 3. *Death of Yeamans.*

Sir John Yeamans died in Carolina.

# 1674

### 1674. *Commerce.*

The Proprietors refused to send out any livestock, making the colony "destitute of cows, hogs or sheep."

### 1674. *Arrivals.*

A "considerable number" of Dutchmen, arrived from New York. They complained of the severe winters and high taxes levied by the Duke of York. They settled on land near the Stono River.

### 1674, March 19. *Commerce.*

George Bedon, cooper, claimed the primary right of 240 acres of land returned by John Yeamans.

### 1674, May 6. *Proprietors Renew Commitment.*

The original agreement of the Proprietors to finance the Carolina Colony had run its course. Each Proprietor agreed to provide £100 for the next seven years.

### 1674, May 22. *Proprietor's Instructions.*

The proprietors instructed Joseph West:

> let Dr. Henry Woodward ... have out of the stores what he desires to the value of 9£ there being so much due to him of the 100£ formerly promised to him.

### 1674, May 23. *Establishment of the Proprietor's Plantation.*

The Proprietors gave instructions to Governor West and the Council that the:

> trusty & well beloved Andrew Percivall, Governor of the plantation to be settled on both sides of the Edisto or Ashipow [Ashepoo] River ... [be] afforded all Countenance, help & assistance to our plantation ...

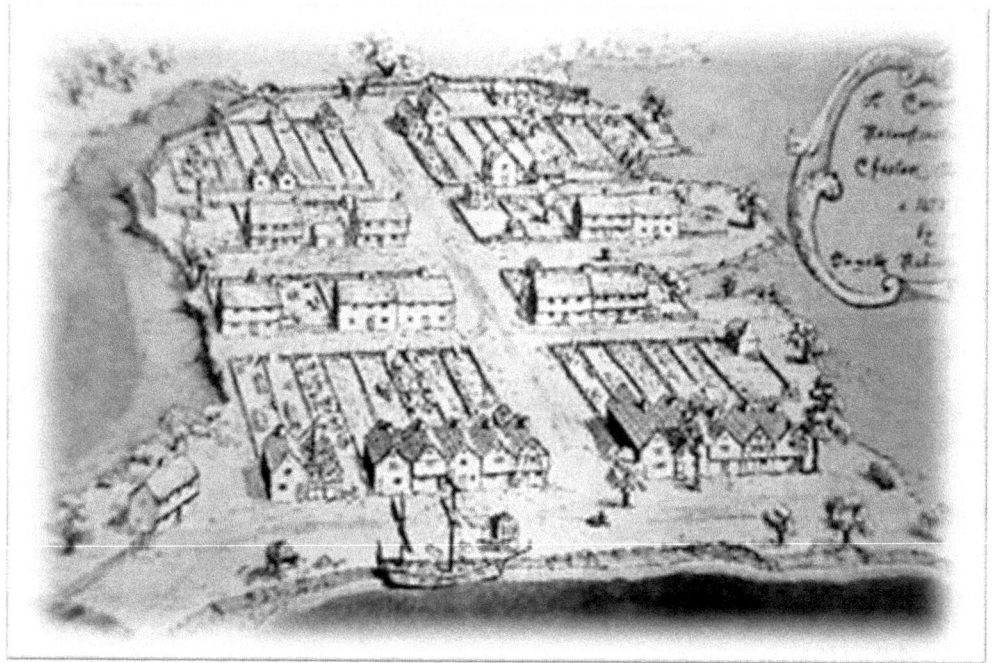

Streets of early Charles Town at Oyster Point. *Courtesy of the Library of Congress.*

## 1674, August 28. DEATH.

John Berkeley, Lord of Stratton, one of the original Proprietors, died.

## 1674. October. INDIAN AFFAIRS. SLAVERY.

After a brief skirmish with the Westo Indians south of Charles Town, Dr. Henry Woodward negotiated a treaty of alliance with the Westos, opening trade in "deerskins, furs and young (Indian) slaves."

## 1674, December 17. OYSTER POINT.

The Grand Council voted that Charles Town should move to Oyster Point.

## 1674, December 19. DEATH.

One of the original Proprietors, Edward Hyde Earl of Clarendon, died at Rouen, France.

# 1675

## 1675. COMMERCE.

John Boon purchased one-fourth interest in the *Dove of London* ship for 5,000 pounds of sugar.

## 1675, April 26. *FORTIFICATIONS.*

The Council decided that:

> in order to the better defence of this Province it is advised & resolved that the people ... be divided into three Companies ... Resolved that forty pounds of Powder be delivered to the Master of Ordinance for the Scaleing [sic] of the Great Gunns mounted at Charles Town ...

## 1675. June 10. *POPULATION.*

Carolina consisted of between 500 and 600 colonists.

# 1677

## 1677, April 10. *COMMERCE. POLITICS.*

The Proprietors required that any Indian traders more than 100 miles from Charles Town be licensed.

# 1678

## 1678. *ARRIVALS.*

A former London merchant, Arthur Middleton, arrived in Carolina with his brother, Edward. They were issued a land grant of 1,780 acres on Yeaman's (Goose) Creek, later named Otranto and Crowfield. A second grant of 1,600 acres created The Oaks Plantation. All three are prominent neighborhoods in the Goose Creek area today.

## 1678. *ARRIVALS. MEDICINE.*

Dr. William Clarke professed to be a "chirugeon" [surgeon], and became the first practitioner of medicine in Charles Town.

## 1678. *COMMERCE.*

Charles Town exported beef, pork and lumber to Barbados in return for 10,000 pounds of sugar. At this time, the Carolina colonists relied heavily on trade with Barbados.

## 1678, July 2. *PORT STATISTICS.*

Joseph West noted that he received from Stephen Clay, master of the ketch *Industrey*:

- 1 Pipe (125 gallons) of Madeira
- 32 barrels of Muscovado sugar
- 2 anchors – 570 lbs.
- 11 bundles of rod iron
- 13 bars of flat iron

- 12 barrels and 3 hogs-head of Rum (appx 1000 gallons)
- 7 barrels of Lime juice
- 9 sail
- 1 barrel of cotton seeds
- 7 Negroes by name Aboy, Cassado, Cottobo, Veter, Sarah, Moheille & Rose

### 1678, October 8. COMMERCE. REAL ESTATE.

Captain Florence O'Sullivan claimed two town lots on Oyster Point.

# 1679

### 1679. ENGLAND. HABEAS CORPUS ACT.

The *Habeas Corpus Act* was passed by Parliament, introduced by Lord Anthony Ashley Cooper. The Act's purpose was to define and strengthen the ancient prerogative writ of *habeas corpus*, a procedural device to force the courts to examine the lawfulness of a prisoner's detention. The act effectively protected an individual's personal liberty more than any other country in the history of the world. It became one of the cornerstones of the United States Constitution.

Charles II heartily supported the Act and Cooper considered it one of his greatest accomplishments.

### 1679. ARRIVALS.

Charles Drayton and his wife Ann arrived from Barbados and established Magnolia Plantation on the Ashley River. The Drayton family still own the plantation 300+ years later.

### 1679. LOCKE TRAVELS THROUGH FRANCE.

John Locke traveled through France and witnessed the harassment of the Huguenots across the country. He wrote a manuscript detailing their agricultural prowess of growing and tending silkworms, grapes, fruits and olives. Lord hley Cooper encouraged the Proprietors to recruit French settlers for Carolina.

### 1679, January 13. ENGLAND. DEATH.

Sir George Carteret, an original Proprietor, died, and was succeeded by his grandson, Earl of Granville.

### 1679, March. CAROLINA COLONY. POLITICS.

By this time, the Proprietors had invested "17 or eighteen thousand pounds" and assured the king that they had "brought the place to a prosperous condition." However, many of the settlers were not paying their debts to the Proprietors.

### 1679, September 18. COMMERCE. REAL ESTATE.

Richard Medlin, mason, sold 200 acres to Robert Brookes for £20 sterling on the south side of the mouth of the Ashley River.

### 1679, December 17. *OYSTER POINT. CHARLES TOWN.*

Governor West and the Grand Council wrote the Proprietors:

> We are informed that this Oyster Point is not only a more convenient place to build a town on than that formerly pitched ... we let you know that Oyster Point is the place we do appoint for the port town of which you are to take notice and call it Charles Town.

## 1680

### 1680. *POPULATION.*

There were more than 1200 people living in Carolina.

### 1680. *RELIGION. ST. PHILIP'S CHURCH ESTABLISHED.*

Sometime during the year, St. Philip's Church was built at the corner of Meeting and Broad Streets, establishing the Anglican Church in Carolina. The first structure was "built of black cypress on a brick foundation ... surrounded by a white palisade."

### 1680. *POLITICS. NEW PROPRIETOR.*

Seth Sothell purchased the Earl of Clarendon's (Edward Hyde) share in Carolina making him one of the Proprietors. He left England for Carolina but was captured by Algerian pirates and imprisoned for three years.

### 1680. January 13. *RELIGION.*

Four acres of land were granted to Anglican minister, Rev. Atkin Williamson by Originall Jackson who wrote he was:

> excited with a pious zeal for the propagation of the true religion which we profess ... the divine service according to the form and liturgy now established to be duly and solemnly performed by Atkin Williamson.

### 1680, March 9. *SLAVERY.*

John Lynch received of Samuel Smartt of St. Michaels, Barbados, twenty-five Negroes for £274.

### 1680. May. *OYSTER POINT.*

By spring, the Grand Council noted that more than thirty houses had been erected at Oyster Point. It was initially called "New Charles Town" by some colonists, to distinguish it from the settlement at Albemarle Point that was being abandoned.

### 1680, April 30. RELIGION. ARRIVALS. FRENCH HUGUENOTS.

The *Richmond* arrived at Charles Town carrying a group of forty-five French Huguenots. Their voyage was subsidized by King Charles II for the purpose of introducing people "skilled in ye manufacture of silks, oyles, wines." Among the new settlers were farmers, wheelwrights, grape growers, weavers saddlers, smiths, coopers, sailmakers, goldsmiths, brick makers and one doctor." The silkworms did not survive the journey.

One of the Huguenots, the mother of Gabriel Manigault, wrote of her Carolina early experience:

> After our arrival in Carolina we suffered every kind of evil. In about eighteen months our elder brother ... died of a fever. Since leaving France we had experienced every kind of affliction – disease-pestilence-famine-poverty-hard labor. I have been for six months together without tasting bread, working the ground like a slave.

Another unnamed Huguenot, wrote:

> The natives of the country are from time immemorial aboriginal Indians of a deep chestnut color, their hair black and straight, tied various ways, sometimes oiled and painted, stuck through with feathers for ornament or gallantry ... they are excellent hunters, their weapons the bow and arrow, made of reed pointed with sharp stones, or fish bones.

### 1680, May 17. PROPRIETORS. OYSTER POINT.

Instructions from the Proprietors to the Governor of Carolina:

> Oyster Point is the place that we do appoint for the Port Town, which you are to call Charles Town and to take care that all ships that come into Ashley or Cooper Rivers do there load and unload ...

### 1680, November. COMMERCE. CROPS.

Samuel Wilson, secretary of the Proprietors, noted that sixteen sailing vessels, upwards of 200 tons, were at anchor in Charles Town. He also noted that:

> Wheat, rye, barley oats and peas thrive exceedingly; and the ground yields in greater abundance than in England; ... chief produce was Indian corn ... Tar of the resinous juice of the pine was made in great quantities; several tons were transported yearly to Barbados Jamaica and the Caribee Islands.

# 1681

### 1681. RELIGION.

The first dissenting congregation in Carolina was formed by Presbyterians from Scotland and Ireland and Congregationalists from England and New England.

## 1681. *COMMERCE*

There were thousands of imported livestock in the colony, with some individuals owning more than 800 head. Every planter had an "Indian hunter" who supplied their families with game, up to "nine deer in a day." Captain Mathews claimed that "one hunting Indian had yearly killed and brought to his plantation more than 100, sometimes 200, head of deer."

Most of the colonists were thriving as traders, not planters. They exported skins and furs to England. To Jamaica and Barbados they exported pitch, tar and timber, which they exchanged for sugar, rum, molasses and ginger and other supplies.

## 1681. *RELIGION.*

Sometime during the year, the Huguenot Church was organized.

## 1681. *ARCHDALE BECOMES PROPRIETOR.*

A London Quaker, John Archdale, purchased a Proprietor's share of Carolina to be held in trust for his son, Thomas. The share, Lot 107 in Charles Town, today is bounded by Meeting, Broad, King and Queen Streets. Currently, Archdale Street runs directly through the center of Lot 107.

Archdale had married a widow, Ann Cary, in 1673 and raised her son, Thomas Cary, who later became a governor of North Carolina. Cary, North Carolina is named after him.

## 1681, March 4. *PENNSYLVANIA CHARTERED.*

William Penn was granted a charter to establish Province of Pennsylvania.

## 1681, July 2. *COOPER ARRESTED.*

Lord Ashley Cooper was arrested for treason and placed in the Tower of London. The charge stemmed from Ashley's staunch opposition to Charles' Catholic brother, James, Duke of York, succeeding to the throne.

## 1681. November 24. *ENGLAND. COOPER'S TRIAL FOR TREASON.*

Ashley Cooper's trial for treason was held. The government's case was particularly weak – most of the witnesses brought forth against Shaftesbury were witnesses whom the government admitted had already perjured themselves, and the documentary evidence was inconclusive.

This, combined with the fact that the jury was handpicked by the Whig Sheriff of London, meant the government had little chance of securing a conviction.

The case against Shaftesbury was ultimately dropped and the announcement prompted great celebrations in London, with crowds yelling "No Popish Successor, No York, A Monmouth" and "God bless the Earl of Shaftesbury!"

# 1682

### 1682. POPULATION.

From 1680-82 the population of Carolina doubled to over 2,200. The majority of the new immigrants were Dissenters (not Anglican), facilitated by Thomas Colleton, Daniel Axtell, Benjamin Blake, and Joseph Morton, all from Barbados Within the first three months of the year, more than 500 people arrived in Charles Town.

### 1682. COMMERCE. EXPORTS.

Naval stores became a major export. Turpentine, tar, rosin, and pitch, used in the processing of wood for shipbuilding. The Proprietors published a pamphlet that noted:

> Tarr, made of the Resinous Juice of pine, they make in great quantities yearly, transporting many tun [tons] to Barbados, Jamaica and the Caribee Islands.

---

**DID YOU KNOW**

**SERVANTS.**

The use of the word "servant" was an imprecise term in colonial Carolina. It denoted several different classes and statuses.

The most common use signified a person who entered into a contractual relationship with another person, agreeing to perform the defined tasks set out by the "master." The master would provide adequate shelter, food and clothing for the servant for the entire of the contract. These formal "indentures" commonly lasted from two to seven years.

The term was also used to described members of the household of the master, including junior family members.

---

### 1682. AGRICULTURE. CROPS.

Thomas Ashe wrote about crops and plants in the area:

> The peach tree in incredible numbers grows wild. Of the fruit expressed, the planters compose a pleasant refreshing liquor; the remainder of the fruit serves the hog and cattle for provision. A manufactory of silk well encouraged might soon be accomplished. The olive tree thrives there very well ... if the olive be well improved, there may be expected from thence perhaps as good oil as any the world yields ... Tobacco grows very well; and they have an excellent sort.

## 1682, January 10. *Third Fundamental Constitutions.*

A third version of the Fundamental Constitutions was drawn up. Never ratified.

## 1682, May 10. *Politics.*

Governor West signed an act for "suppressing idleness, drunkenness, and profanity."

## 1682, May 10. *Carolina Divided into Counties.*

The Proprietors announced that:

> upon the request of several eminent persons who had a mind to become settlers in the province to review the Fundamental Constitutions and to make some additions and alterations ...

Most of the changes they made were to make the colony more attractive for Dissenters. They also ordered that the province be divided into four counties that should extend thirty-five miles inland from the coast.

- Albemarle County – Between the Roanoke River (North Carolina) north to the Virginia border
- Berkeley County – Embracing Charles Town, from Sewee on the north to Stono Creek on the south
- Craven County – north of Sewee
- Colleton County – south of Stono Creek

## 1682, May 12. *Commerce.*

Dr. Henry Woodward sold to Andrew Percivall: 10 cows and 10 calves for £72 sterling.

## 1682, May 17. *Charles Town.*

A new colonist wrote:

> Of 62 that came out of England we lost three, two of them were seamen, one dyed of the scurvey, the other fell overboard, the third was a woman in child bed, her child died shortly after her. As for the Countrey, I can say but little of it as yet ... The Town which two years since had by 3 or 4 houses, hath now about a hundred houses in it, all of which are wholly built of wood, tho here excellent Brick is made, but little of it.

## 1682, May 18. *Politics. Slavery.*

Joseph Morton of Barbados replaced Joseph West as Governor. According to the Proprietors the change was due to West's involvement in Indian slave trading, which they found immoral. In reality, it was most likely a move to encourage more immigration from Barbados and other islands.

### 1682, June. *Carolina Colony Promoted.*

A promotional pamphlet about Carolina by Samuel Wilson read:

> The tools that men who goe there ought to take with them are these viz – An Ax, A Bill and Broad Hoe, a grubbing Hoe for every man, and a Cross cut Saw to every four men, a whip Saw and a set of wedgesd and fraus and Betle Rings to every family, and some reeping hooks and Sythes, as likewise Nails of all sorts, Hooks Hinges, Bolts, and Locks for their houses.

> The Merchandise that sell best in Carolina, are Linnen and Wollens and all stuffs to make clothes of; with Threat, Sewing Silk, Buttons, Ribbons, Hats, Stockings, Shoes &c.

> The Passage of a Man or Woman to Carolina is Five pound; Ships are going thither all times of the year. Some of the Lords Proprietors or myself will be every Tuesday eleven of the clock at the Carolina Coffee House in Birching Lane near the Royal Exchange to inform all People what ships are going, or any other thing whatever.

The pamphlet was translated into French for Huguenot readership in England.

### 1682, August 17. *Fourth Fundamental Constitutions.*

Under the leadership of the Earl of Craven and a new partner, John Archdale, the Lords Proprietors issued a fourth version of the Fundamental Constitutions. It was never ratified.

### 1682, October 27. *Philadelphia Founded.*

City of Philadelphia was founded.

### 1682, November 20. *Cooper Flees England.*

Ashley Cooper left England for Holland, in fear of being arrested for urging the assassination of James, the Duke of York, the king's Catholic brother.

# 1683

### 1683. *Piracy.*

The French pirate, Sieur de Grammont, after raiding several settlements in Spanish Florida, sailed into Charles Town and was treated as a hero. Any blow administered to the Spanish was met with rousing cheers by the English, and the stolen gold and other goods brought into town was a welcome boost to the economy.

### 1683, January 21. *Cooper Dies.*

Lord Anthony Ashley Cooper died in Amsterdam.

### 1683, March 21. COMMERCE. REAL ESTATE.

Arthur Middleton received 800 acres from the Proprietors.

# 1684

### 1684. RELIGION.

Rev. Atkin Williamson was dismissed for "baptizing a baby bear while drunk."

### 1684. PIRACY.

Sir Thomas Lynch, Governor of Jamaica, complained to the Board of Trade and Plantations in England of the great damage inflicted upon his Majesty by the harboring and encouraging of pirates in Carolina.

Pirates from the Caribbean had been using the Carolina coast for years. With its numerous inlets, harbors and islands, it afforded them a safe haven when pursued by enemies, to refit and repair their vessels, and (according to legend) bury their plundered treasures.

Charles II had initially encouraged privateers, and had actually knighted one of the most infamous pirates of the New World, Henry Morgan. As long as Morgan was preying on the Spanish, the King was happy to accept his share of the plunder. Morgan was made Deputy Governor of Jamaica in 1674, but was removed from power by Governor Lynch in 1682.

### 1684. ARRIVALS.

Miles Brewton arrived from Barbados. He became a goldsmith and militia officer.

### 1684, April. POLITICS.

Governor Morton was replaced by Sir Richard Kyrle of Ireland, who died within six months of arriving in Carolina. Robert Quarry, the Secretary of the Province, was chosen to replace Kyrle as governor.

### 1684, September 1. PIRACY.

An armed vessel sailed into the Ashley River. The crew pretended to have been trading with the Spanish, but Governor Quarry realized they were pirates. He reported to the Proprietors that he had prohibited the unloading or selling of the goods. In reality, however, Quarry had allowed the plundered goods to be sold.

### 1684, September 10. POLITICS.

Joseph West was commissioned as Governor, replacing Quarry, who was investigated for his role in facilitating piracy. Quarry was allowed to keep his role as Secretary.

### 1684, October 2. ARRIVALS. FOUNDING OF STUART'S TOWN.

Ten families of Scottish Presbyterians arrived, accompanied by Lord Cardross. By agreement with the Proprietors they founded Stuart's Town, on the site of the old French settlement near Port Royal.

# 1685

### 1685. RICE.

Sometime during the year, a New England trading vessel arrived in Charles Town for repairs bearing seed rice as a gift.

### 1685. RELIGION. ARRIVALS.

During the preceding three years, more than 500 Presbyterians and Baptists had arrived in Carolina. They had responding to Proprietor Archdale's vigorous campaign to attract new colonists. They settled south of Charles Town on the Edisto River.

---

**CHARLESTON FIRST**

**1685: THE FIRST RICE CROP WAS CULTIVATED IN AMERICA.**

A storm-battered ship sailed into Charles Town harbor for repairs. To repay the city's kindness, the ship's captain, John Thurber, made a gift of "golden seed rice" (named for its color) to Dr. Henry Woodward.

The low-lying marshlands bordered by fresh tidal rivers waters proved ideal for rice production. By 1700 more than 300 tons of "Carolina gold" was shipped annually to England. Charles Town planters were producing more rice that there were ships to transport it.

Rice was the main cause for the explosion of the West African slave trade to the Carolina coast.

---

### 1685, February 6. CHARLES II DIES.

King Charles II died without a legitimate heir. His Catholic brother, James, Duke of York, ascended to the throne as James II. The king let it be known that, after years of royal leniency toward privateers, he was determined to force Caribbean buccaneers to recognize royal authority. James II also was considering dissolving all Proprietary charters and converting them to a Royal charter.

### 1685, March 2. POLITICS. INDIAN TRADE.

The Lords Proprietors dismissed Maurice Matthews as Surveyor General of Carolina due to his involvement in the Indian slave trade. Stephen Bull, newly arrived to Carolina, was named his successor.

### 1685, March 5. MUSCHAMP ARRIVES.

George Muschamp, arrived as the Customs Collector, the first direct representative of royal authority in Carolina.

### 1685, March 13. *NAVAL OFFICER NAMED.*

Robert Quarry, Secretary of the Province, was named Naval Officer and required to keep lists of vessels arriving and departing Charles Town.

### 1685, April 11. *HARBOR PILOT.*

The Assembly passed "an act for settling a pilot" for the harbor.

### 1685, September. *ARRIVALS. RELIGION.*

The *Margaret* arrived in Charles Town with more than fifty Huguenots.

### 1685, September. *MORTON CHOSEN GOVERNOR.*

Joseph West resigned as governor and the Council chose Morton as governor for a second term.

### 1685, October 14. *COMMERCE.*

Christopher Kelly of Jamaica paid William Garrway £12 sterling for outfitting the ship *Unity* for a voyage to Barbados.

### 1685, October 22. *EDICT OF NANTES REVOKED.*

The Edict of Nantes was revoked by Louis XIV of France. Officially called the Edict of Fountainebleau, it removed royal protection against protestants. The king ordered the destruction of all Protestant churches and schools. Within a decade almost a million Huguenots left France, more than 1500 arriving in Charles Town. More than 70% of Huguenots who came to America settled in Carolina.

### 1685. November 23. *POLITICS. PIRACY.*

The Assembly held in Charles Town consisted of eight deputies of the Proprietors and twenty commoners. With pressure coming from James II, they passed an act for "restraining and punishing privateers," and an act for better security against hostile invasions. They also established a revenue officer under his Majesty to enforce the customs and navigation laws. George Muschamp was the first Collector of the King's Revenue.

The Barbadians were against the Collector enforcing the Navigation Act. In particular, they were against the provision that stated:

> the master and three-fourths of the mariners of every vessel importing goods into England or into any of its dependencies should also be English subjects.

They argued that the Carolina charter, issued *after* the Navigation Act, superseded the law in the province. They considered it a direct assault on their profits and claimed that the Council "totally disclaimed the authority of the British Parliament in which they were *not* represented." It was an early foreshadowing of the same argument that led to the American Revolution ninety years later.

In the end, the Barbadians ignored the law and traded as they pleased.

# 1686

### 1686. POPULATION.

During this year the population majority in Carolina shifted to the Dissenters, most recently arrived in Carolina and apprehensive about the coming persecution they imagined during the reign of the Catholic, James II.

### 1686, February 15. POLITICS.

The Proprietors recommended Governor Quarry be "dismissed from the Secretaryship for harboring pirates."

### 1686, February 26. COMMERCE.

Arnold Bruneau, Esq., Paul Bruneau, Esq. and Josias Marviland, Esq. formed a partnership for the construction of a mill (wind or water) to saw timber.

### 1686, March. ARRIVALS. JEAN BOYD.

Jean Boyd, a well-educated Huguenot merchant, arrived in Charles Towne and penned a lengthy letter to his sister back in London. He described various aspects of life and culture, and sketched a map of the town.

> Here we are at last landed in this much longed-for country. In truth, I had imagined that I would find the town of Charlestown built differently and much larger than it is ... The temperature of the air is here the same as in the southern provinces of France. The English, in truth, who are not accustomed to hearing large claps of thunder in England exclaim in surprise at those in Carolina but they would never scare a French person.

> The head of the rivers & principally the creeks are full of crocodiles so monstrous that we saw some that were 22 feet long. They do not hurt anyone and people fear them so little that several people who were bathing went swimming after them.

> When one sells something here one must specify if it will be paid for in silver; otherwise they will pay you in silver of the country, which means in corn or animals & there is a great difference, least 25% for cattle to silver. Sometimes when silver is plentiful, that is to say when the buccaneers have come, livestock is worth a lot.

> Aside from game one sees many wild beasts but a little higher up in the country, like wolves, wildcats, leopards, tigers, bears, foxes, raccoons, badgers, otters, beavers & a type of black and white cat which for its only defense (urinates) on people who pursue it, but its urine is so foul that it is capable of making one feel sick. The stench does not go away for two or three months even though one washes.

## 1686. June 10. COMMERCE.

Sam Dodson, master of the ship *Katherine* lodged an official protest with Governor Robert Quarry. According to the document written by Quarry, Dodson:

> proved by oaths of himself and others that appeared having dispatched all his business and cleared and taken out his dispatches for his return to London; Hon. Landgrave [and former governor] Joseph Morton not ignorant but maliciously intending to hinder the voyage prohibited the pilot William Watson to convey the ship and did send William Popell, Provost Marshall, with several armed men on board the vessel who broke open the hatches and afterward on 10 June did cut the hoops of several casks and carry away and damage goods and merchandise of several merchants ensuing much damage ... and passengers who may suffer for the detaining of the ship.

### CHARLESTON FIRST

**1686: FIRST ENGLISH WALLED CITY IN NORTH AMERICA.**

Due to the proximity of the Spanish at St. Augustine the English in Carolina were concerns about their safety. They wasted little time constructing walls and bastions.

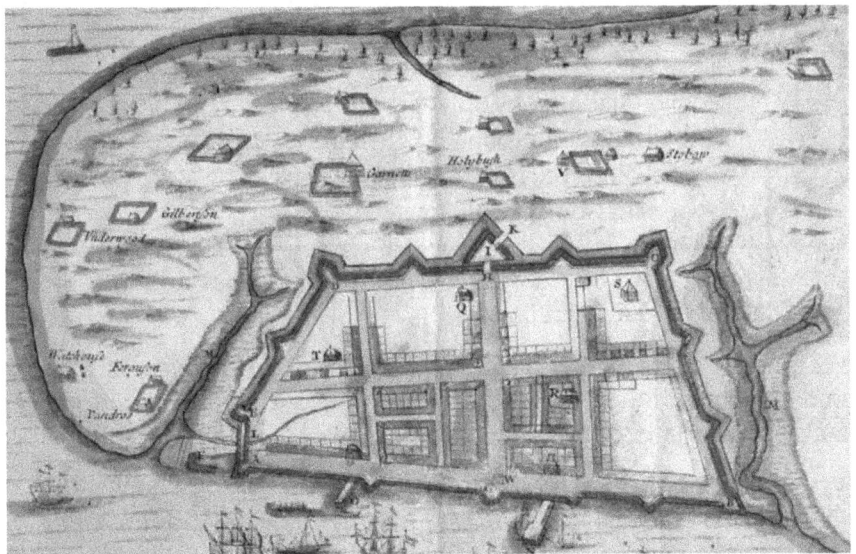

The 1711 Edward Crisp map of the walled city of Charles Town.
*Courtesy of the Library of Congress.*

## 1686, August 17. DESTRUCTION OF STUART'S TOWN.

Lord Cardross of Stuart's Town had cultivated poor relations with the authorities in Charles Town. He had also maintained an aggressive policy against the Spanish in Florida. Florida's governor Hita Salazar sent three Spanish galleons with a force of more than 150 men, who quickly destroyed Stuart's Town.

The Spanish fleet sailed up the coast near Edisto Island, and sacked the property of Governor Morton and Mr. Grimball, Secretary of the Province, damage totaling £3000 sterling. They killed the governor's brother-in-law, Mr. Bowell.

An appeal was immediately dispatched to the Proprietors for assistance, but the men of Carolina did not wait for a response. They raised £500 sterling and proceeded to outfit two vessels. Four hundred men volunteered and made preparations to sail to St. Augustine.

Edward Randolph, in his "letter to the Board of Trade described the events:

> One hundred Spaniards, with Negroes and Indians landed at Edisto, (50 miles to the southward of Charles Town), and broke open the house of Mr. Joseph Morton, then Governor of the Province. About the same time they robbed Mr. Grimball's House … they also fell upon a settlement of Scotchmen at Port Royal where there was not above 23 men in health to oppose them. The Spaniards burnt down their houses, destroyed and carried away all that they had …

## DID YOU KNOW?

**THAT CHARLESTON IS OLDER THAN:**

- Philadelphia, Pennsylvania by 12 years (1682)
- Norfolk, Virginia by 12 years (1682)
- Biloxi, Mississippi by 29 years (1699)
- Mobile, Alabama by 32 years (1702)
- New Orleans, Louisiana by 48 years (1718)
- San Antonio, Texas by 48 years (1718)
- Savannah, Georgia by 63 years (1733)

## 1686, September. *ARRIVALS.*

James Colleton of Barbados, brother of a Proprietor, arrived in Charles Town and ordered the expedition to disband. He threatened to hang anyone who persisted in the attack. He was later commended by the Proprietors.

> We are glad that you have stopped the expedition against St. Augustine. If it had proceeded, Mr. Morton, Colonel Godfrey, and others might have answered it with their lives.

## 1686, November. *POLITICS.*

James Colleton was commissioned Governor by the Proprietors. For the most part, the Proprietors had been disappointed in the governors they had appointed. Sayle had been a good man, but was weak and elderly. Yeamans was too ambitious and selfish, refusing to put the colony's interest above his own person gains; West was prudent, but lacked the will and intelligence to stand against the Barbadians. Morton and Quarry had proven undependable.

But in Colleton, they believed finally they had a man who was intelligent, forceful, through the influence of his brother, would look out for their interests.

# 1687

### 1687. *RELIGION. CHURCH OF THE TIDES.*

Reverend Elias Prileau arrived as the first pastor of the "French Church of Charles Towne." Many of the French immigrants lived up river so they would come down the Cooper and Ashley Rivers with the morning tide and moor their boats on Bay Street.

The French fell into the habit of having their services "with the tide," meaning there was no definite time for service, it was left to the vagaries of low and high tide each week. The morning service was timed with low tide and the afternoon service timed with high tide, leading to the nickname "the church of the tides."

### 1687, February 14. *POLITICS.*

Governor Colleton quickly picked up a reputation for tyranny. He wrote to the Proprietors stating that the Grand Council, "utterly denied the Fundamental Constitutions." He then disbanded the Council and proceeded to follow the Constitutions as strictly as possible.

He also imposed a large fine on a minister for a sermon he found displeasing and declared martial law due to the opposition of his heavy-handed administration.

### 1687, April. *VESSEL SEIZED.*

Mr. Muschamp, Collector, seized a vessel for violating the Navigation Act, claiming that four-fifths of the crew were Scotchmen.

### 1687, April 9. *PORT REGULATIONS.*

New port regulations were imposed. Masters of vessels had to report their arrival before unloading cargo, and must give twenty-one day notice of their departure.

### 1687, May 5. *RELIGION.*

A lot was conveyed by Ralph and Mary Izard to James Nichols "for the use of the community of the French church in Charles Town." The lot was located at the corner of Dock and Church Streets, currently the site of the 1845 Huguenot Church.

### 1687, July 23. *CROPS USED AS COMMODITY.*

The Assembly passed an act that designated certain local products to be used as Commodity - money for legal payment of public and private debts. The products included: tobacco, corn, peas, pork, beef and tar.

### 1687, August 21. *PIRACY*.

A small fleet of ships, commanded by Rear-Admiral Sir John Narborough, was dispatched "for suppressing pirates in the West Indies. It was England's first serious attempt at restraining the ever-growing threat from buccaneers. Pirates coming into any of the ports of the province [English controlled] were "to be seized and imprisoned, and their ships' good and plunder were to be taken and kept in custody until his Majesty's Royal pleasure should be known."

One observer remarked "only the poor Pyrats were hanged; rich ones appear'd publicly and were not molested in the least."

# 1688

### 1688, December 10. *THE GLORIOUS REVOLUTION*.

King James II, under siege due to his Catholicism, fled to France, escaping the armies of his daughter Mary and her husband, William of Orange – both Protestant.

### 1688. December 28. *THE GLORIOUS REVOLUTION*.

William and Mary took power as dual monarchs.

# 1689

### 1689. *ARRIVALS*.

Sir Nathaniel Johnson arrived in Charles Town. He was a strong supporter of the royal Stuart family, and served as Governor of the Leeward Islands, residing in Nevis. He refused to take the oath supporting William & Mary and was removed from his post. He moved to the Goose Creek area, invested in silk, and became one of the first successful rice planters.

### 1689, February 13. *DECLARATION OF RIGHTS*.

The Declaration of Rights was drawn up. William and Mary ascended to the throne.

### 1689, May 12. *ENGLAND. KING WILLIAM'S WAR*.

King William III of England joined other European powers to resist French territorial expansion. The war in the colonies is confined to the New England area, and had little effect on Carolina.

# 1690

### 1690. *ARRIVALS*.

After three years of being held captive by pirates, Seth Sothell arrived in Albermarle County. As a Proprietor he claimed the governorship of the area. His administration was so rapacious and self-serving that the Albermarle Parliament banished him. He arrived in Charles Town and was welcomed by the people who saw him as a good alternative to inept and heavy-handed administration of Governor Colleton.

Benjamin M'Arion, a French Huguenot, arrived in Carolina with "his wife and five servants. He received 350 acres about fifteen miles north of Charleston, on Goose Creek in St. James Parish." One of his sons would be Francis Marion.

## 1690. *POPULATION.*

The population of Carolina was estimated to be 3,500 to 4,000.

Governor Sothell entering Charles Town. *Courtesy of the New York Public Library.*

## 1690, May. *POLITICS.*

Using his power as Proprietor, Sothell called a Charles Town Parliament which voted to banish Governor Colleton. Citing the Fundamental Constitutions which stated "it is provided that the eldest proprietor that shall be in Carolina shall be governor," Sothell claimed the office.

## 1690. *RELIGION. SLAVERY.*

Sothell's banishment from Albermarle must have tempered his governing style because his administration in Charles Town was marked by substantial positive events, including:

- Established just treatment of disliked foreigners (Huguenots)
- Forbade supplying Indians with liquor and firearms.
- Required licenses for all liquor retailers.
- Provided for an organized militia and town watch.
- Provided a store of gunpowder.
- Granted a patent for a rice-husking machine.
- Enacted a slave code, heavily based on the Barbadian. It included a provision for punishment of anyone who killed a slave.

## 1690, December 22. *FORTIFICATIONS*

The Assembly established a watch on Sullivan's Island to:

> Give notice by signes hereafter appointed to bee given of enemy ship or ships, vessel or vessels that shall or may approach neare Ashley River.

# 1691

## 1691, February 7. *SLAVERY.*

The first Carolina law relating to slavery was passed. It restricted the movement of Negroes in an effort to prevent "run-aways."

## 1691, May 1. *POLITICS. CRIME.*

The Assembly appointed gaugers and packers to inspect beef and pork to eliminate fraud in the exportation of commodities.

## 1691, September 26. *RICE USED TO PAY TAXES.*

The Assembly ratified the proposal that allowed Carolinians to pay their taxes in rice, as well as other goods. By order of the Proprietors a tax was levied on all animal skins and furs exported from Carolina to help defray the cost of government.

## 1691. *RICE PENDULUM ENGINE PATENTED.*

Peter Guerard, a Huguenot and goldsmith, was granted a two-year patent on a:

> Pendulum Engine, which doth much better, and in less time and labour, huske rice than any other heretofore hath been used within the Province.

### 1691, November 8. *POLITICS. PIRACY.*

Sir Nathaniel Johnson led the "Goose Creek men" in opposition against Governor Sothell, forcing him to step down, due to his involvement in the pirate trade.

The Proprietors changed the local parliament into a bicameral system, composed of Council, appointed by the Proprietors, and Commons House elected by the freeholders, which also was given the power to initiate laws.

## 1692

### 1692. *MEDICINE.*

Dr. John Thomas, performed the first recorded autopsy in Charles Town.

### 1692, March 24. *PROTEST AGAINST THE WIND AND SEA.*

Anthony Taylor, master of the ship *Triple Crown,* officially entered his protest against the seas, extremity of winds and harbor pilot, William Bradley.

### 1692, April 9. *POLITICS.*

Philip Ludwell was commissioned as Carolina governor. Ludwell had been the secretary to Sir William Berkeley, governor of Virginia. He was faced with three separate factions of power in Carolina: the Proprietors, the Barbadian faction led by James Moore, and the dissenting newcomers led by Paul Grimball.

### 1692, May. *POLITICS. ELECTION.*

During the election for the Commons House of Assembly five of the six delegates from Craven County were Huguenots. Governor Ludwell received a petition from angry citizens asking him to prevent the Huguenots from taking their seats, asking, "Shall the Frenchmen, who cannot speak our language, make our laws?"

After several weeks of tense arguments, the Huguenots were allowed to take their seats.

### 1692, June 21. *POLITICS. RELIGION.*

The Grand Council issued an order for:

- "The better observance of the Lord's Day by prohibiting the haunting of punch houses during the time of divine service" and
- "that the French ministers and officers of their church be advised that they begin their divine service at 9 o'clock in the morning and about 2 in the afternoon of which they are to take due notice and pay obedience thereunto."

The second order was directed at the Huguenots - "the church of the tides."

### 1692, August 29. *Piracy. Arrival of the Royal Jamaica.*

A privateer with forty men, the *Royal Jamaica,* arrived in Charles Town carrying "treasures of Spanish gold and silver." They were allowed "to enter into recognizance for their peaceable and good behavior for one year with securities, till the Governor should hear whether the Proprietor would grant them general indemnity."

There is no record of the *Royal Jamaica* being seized, or its crew and passengers being arrested. A list of the passengers included some of the most prominent names in South Carolina history: Thomas Pinckney, Robert Fenwick, and Daniel Horry.

### 1692, September 19. *Marriage.*

Thomas Pinckney married Grace Bedon, daughter of George Bedon, one of the original colonists. Pinckney acquired several lots in town and a 480-acre plantation called Fetteressa.

### 1692, October. *Politics.*

Commons House of Assembly passed several important acts.

- Empowered magistrates and justices to execute the *habeas corpus* act of Charles II.
- Any person worth £10 was qualified to vote, disregarding the Fundamental Constitutions.

# 1693

### 1693, April 10. *Religion.*

The Huguenots had complained to the Proprietors of threats made upon their estates. The Proprietors replied:

> The French have complained to us that they are threatened to have their estates taken from their children after their death because they are aliens. Now many have bought the land they enjoy of us ... God forbid that we should take advantage ...

> They also complain that are required to begin their Divine Worshipp at the same time that the English doe, which is inconvenient to them in regard that severall of their congregations living out of Towne are forced to come and go by water; & for the convenience of such they begin their Divine Worshipp earlier or later as the tide serves, in which we would have them not molested.

### 1693, April 12. *Religion. Politics.*

The Proprietors wrote to Governor Ludwell to "employ no Jacobite [one who supported the return of the English monarchy to the Catholic James II]; beware of the Goose Creek men. They also authorized the Governor to "appoint some fitting person Attorney General for the prosecution of crimes."

### 1693, May. POLITICS. GOVERNOR REMOVED.

The Proprietors lost confidence in Gov. Ludwell and recalled his commission.

### 1693, November 30. SMITH COMMISSIONED GOVERNOR.

Landgrave Thomas Smith, one of the richest men in Carolina, was commissioned to be Governor.

### 1693. POLITICS. SOUTH CAROLINA.

First official use by the Proprietors of the name "South Carolina" as opposed to just "Carolina. It delineated the difference of the northern county, Albemarle, from the southern counties.

# 1694

### 1694. ARRIVALS.

Sometime during the year, William Rhett arrived in Charles Town with his wife, Sarah Ann Cooke Rhett and their child.

### 1694. FORTIFICATIONS.

The Commons House passed an act appropriating money for the construction of a brick wall along Charles Town's eastern edge (the eastern side of the present East Bay Street) "to prevent the sea's further encroachment."

### 1694, August 13. ATTORNEY GENERAL APPOINTED.

Ferdinando Gorges, of the Inner Temple, was appointed Attorney General of the province of Carolina. However, Gorges decided the office was not sufficient enough to entice him to leave England. It would be three more years until Nicholas Trott was appointed to the post.

### 1694, October. GOVERNOR RESIGNS.

Thomas Smith resigned as Governor, citing his despair in "allaying the discontents and contentions" among the citizens and "that it was impossible to settle the country except a Proprietor himself was sent over with full power to heal grievances."

### 1694, November. POLITICS. GOVERNOR APPOINTED.

Joseph Blake, son of Landgrave Benjamin Blake was chosen by the Council to act in Smith's stead until a new Governor was commissioned by the Proprietors.

# 1695

### 1695. *Religion.*

Sometime in 1695, there was the first mention of a Jew living in Charles Town. Governor Archdale, during the interrogation of four Spanish-speaking Indians, used a "Jew for an Interpreter." No record of the Jew's name exists.

### 1695, June 20. *Religion.*

Governor Blake gave £1000 sterling to the Independent Church.

### 1695, August 17. *Arrivals. Archdale Becomes Governor.*

John Archdale, a Quaker from London, who owned a Proprietary share in Charles Town, arrived as Governor of Carolina, sent at the behest of the Proprietors. He retained Joseph Blake as Deputy Governor. He wrote to the Proprietors that:

> When I arriv'd I found all matters in great confusion and every faction apply'd themselves to me in hopes of relief; I appeased them with kind and gentle words and so soon as possible call'd an assembly.

Archdale moderated restrictions against the Indians and was acknowledged for his more humane settlement of conflicts. He also reinforced the liquor act - prohibiting the sale, except by license, of any "beer, cider, wine, brandy, rum, punch or any strong drink whatsoever under the quantity of one gallon."

He also passed an act stating that "laws passed by the Commons House of Assembly ... could not be repealed by London without the consent of the assembly."

### 1695, December 20. *Founding of Dorchester.*

A group of Massachusetts Puritans, led by minister Joseph Lord, sailed into Charles Town. William Harmon, a Carolina landowner, had invited the Puritans to organize a Congregationalist church. They settled near the head of the Ashley River, which they called Dorchester.

John Archdale.
*Courtesy of New York Public Library.*

## BUILDINGS OF CHARLESTON
### The Pink House, 17 Chalmers Street

In 1695, John Breton constructed a tavern of Bermuda stone on Beresford Alley (currently Chalmers Street). The building is still standing in the 21st century, commonly called the "Pink House."

The Pink House, Chalmers Street, c. 1695. *Courtesy of the Library of Congress.*

# 1696

### 1696. *SLAVERY. POLITICS.*

A new, tougher fugitive slave law was enacted that provided a severe public whipping of up to forty lashes for a first offense. Persistent runaways were branded, whipped and mutilated and could be executed if they resisted capture.

### 1696. *RELIGION.*

Rev. Samuel Marshall arrived in Charles Town to officiate the English Church. He was "a sober, worthy, able and learned divine who left considerable benefice and honorable way of living in England to come out to Carolina."

### 1696. *POLITICS. COMMERCE.*

The Navigation Acts of 1696 required that all vessels be registered. Ten vessels were registered in Charles Town, the largest being 50 tons; the smallest, 25 tons.

### 1696, March. *FORTIFICATIONS.*

The Assembly passed a second act appropriating money for the construction of a brick wall along Charles Town's eastern edge. It became known as the "wharf wall," or the "curtain line upon the Bay." The Assembly also considered plans for building a brick "fort" at the east end of Broad Street.

### 1696, March 6. *COMMERCE. POLITICS.*

The Assembly added rice to the list of commodities which could be used as currency in Carolina.

### 1696, March 10. *POLITICS. RELIGION.*

Henry Peronneau, a Huguenot, was one of sixty-three petitioners who were granted "the rights and privileges of citizenship."

### 1696, April 10. *PARLIAMENT. NAVIGATION ACT.*

Parliament strengthened the Acts of Trade and Navigation. All officers of colonial governments must post bond to uphold the laws. Colonial customs officials were given the same power as those in England to board and search vessels.

### 1696, May 15. *PARLIAMENT.*

The Board of Trade was created. It would oversee almost every phrase of Carolina colonial life until 1776.

### 1696. December. *FORTIFICATIONS.*

The Assembly ratified an act to appropriate money for the construction of a "fortress Battery or fortification . . . at ye Point of Sand to ye Northward of ye Creek commonly called Collins his Creek." This structure, located slightly north of the eastern end of modern Water Street, was named Granville's Bastion in honor of John Granville, First Earl of Bath.

### 1696. December. *DEATH.*

Grace Bedon Pinckney, wife of Thomas Pinckney died.

### 1696. December. *POLITICS. ARCHDALE LEAVES.*

Having calmed the political turmoil, and dealt with several legal and financial issues, John Archdale appointed Joseph Blake governor and returned to England.

### 1696. December. *RELIGION. ARRIVALS.*

William Scriven, an Anabaptist minister from Maine, arrived in Charles Town. He had been imprisoned in Maine for denouncing infant baptism as an ordinance of the devil.

Granville Bastion marker. *Photo by author*

# 1697

### 1697. *SLAVERY.*

Three runaway slaves were captured and returned to Charles Town. They were publically whipped and emasculated.

### 1697. January 19. MARRIAGE.

Thomas Pinckney married Mary Cotesworth Betson. Over the next five years she gave birth to three sons, Thomas, Charles and William.

### 1697, March 8. POLITICS.

Rev. Samuel Marshall was appointed Register of Births.

### 1697, March 10. POLITICS. RELIGION.

Governor Blake signed an Act which gave "all aliens ... of what nation soever the civil rights of native-born Englishmen" and "liberty of conscience to all Christians except Paptists."

### 1697, May. EPIDEMIC.

Charles Town's first major small pox outbreak kills more than 200 people.

### 1697, May 26. RELIGION.

For the first time in Charles Town records, names of individual Jews appear on the role register for full citizenship:

- Simon Valentine, a merchant from New York
- Jacob Mendis, from the Caribbean
- Abraham Avilia, from the Caribbean

# 1698

### 1698. ARRIVALS. RELIGION.

Rev. John Cotton, Jr. arrived in Charles Town as minister of the White Meeting House, after serving thirty years in the original Pilgrim Church at Plymouth, Massachusetts. He was the uncle of the famous minister Cotton Mather.

### 1698. RELIGION.

The General Assembly passed an act giving Rev. Samuel Marshall a salary of "£150 per annum, a Negro man and woman, plus four cows and calves, all to be paid out of the public treasury."

### 1698. PARLIAMENT. SLAVERY.

Parliament removed the monopoly of the Royal African Company, opening up slave trade to other companies and individuals.

### 1698, February 5. ARRIVALS.

Nicholas Trott was appointed Attorney General of Carolina. Trott had served the same post in Bermuda. He was the Carolina official who was trained at the Inns of Court – a professional association for barristers. His uncle, Sir Nicholas Trott, had been governor of the Bahamas and was accused of harboring pirates for personal profit. Edmund Bohun was appointed Chief Justice.

### 1698, February 5. *EARTHQUAKE.*

An earthquake shook the area.

### 1698, February 24. *DISASTER. FIRE.*

A fire destroyed about one-third of Charles Town, burning the "dwellings, stores and outhouses of at least fifty families ... the value of £30,000 sterling."

### 1698, March 12. *EPIDEMIC.*

The governor wrote that "We have had the small pox amongst us nine or ten months which hath been very infectious and mortal. We have lost by the distemper 200 or 300 persons."

Mrs. Affra Coming wrote to her sister that the epidemic "killed 200 or 300 persons ... unburied, lying upon the ground for the vultures to devour."

### 1698, April 11. *POLITICS. COMMERCE*

The Proprietors conveyed Lord Berkeley's share of the grant to Joseph Blake.

### 1698, October 8. *SLAVERY. COMMERCE.*

The Assembly passed "An Act for the Encouragement of the Importation of White Servants." Fearful of the growing number of blacks being imported as slaves, the South Carolina Assembly passed a law granting £13 to anyone who would bring a white male servant into the province as "... the great number of negroes which of late have been imported into this Colony may endanger the safety thereof." For every six adult African male slave owned, a planter was required to purchase one indentured white servant, if available.

The Act also set out terms of indenture service: those over sixteen years old should serve at least four years, those under sixteen, no less than seven years.

### 1698, October 8. *PUBLIC SAFETY.*

The Assembly forbade vessels from entering the harbor until it was ascertained if there were diseases aboard.

### 1698, December. *POLITICS. COMMERCE.*

Affra Harleston Coming, widow of John Coming, made a deed in which she gave to "Rev. Samuel Marshall, minster of the Gospel in Charles Town, and to his successors ... seventeen acres of land adjoining the town as a glebe."

Currently, the property is named Glebe Street and forms part of the campus of the College of Charleston.

# 1699

### 1699. RELIGION.

William Elliott, a member of the Anabaptist Church, donated a lot on Church Street for the construction of a house of worship. The First Baptist Church of Charleston stands on the property to this day.

### 1699. COMMERCE.

The exports of rice exceeded 2,000 barrels for the year. An average barrel contained 350 pounds of cleaned rice. With the addition of expanded trade in deerskins and fur, Carolina was reaching level of prosperity never attained.

### 1699. POLITICS.

The Proprietors, under pressure by the Board of Trade, appointed Joseph Morton as Advocate General of Admiralty for Carolina.

### 1699, March 6. EPIDEMIC.

Mrs. Affra Harleston Coming, wrote to her sister in England:

> I am sorry that I should be the messenger of so sad tidings as to desire you not to come to me till you can hear better times here than is now ... it is the small pox which has been mortal to all sorts of inhabitants and especially the Indians who it is said to have swept away a whole neighboring nation, all but 5 or 6 who ran away and left their dead unburied ...

### 1699, March 14. POPULATION.

Peter Girad wrote that there were 195 French Protestants in Charles Town.

### 1699, March 16. PIRACY.

Collector of Customs, Edward Randolph, arrived and announced that the royal government was tightening its grip on all the colonies and was considering voiding all Proprietary charters. Randolph also made it clear that the royal Admiralty Courts believed the Proprietors allowed:

> illicit trade ... and sought to establish a sort of independence of the King ... traded with the Ditch, welcomed pirates as free spenders and have no regard to the acts of trade.

Randolph also discovered that Governor Blake was "a notorious offender against the act." He also accused Blake and his brother-in-law, Judge Joseph Morton, Jr. of:

fraudulently condemning vessels as contraband and then colluding to purchase, at auction, ships and cargoes at bargain prices ... took bribes to ignore smuggling and traded with pirates and the Spanish in Florida.

Affra Harleston marker on Glebe Street.
*Photo by author.*

In Memory of AFFRA HARLESTON COMING, who epitomizes the settling of this state. Com-ing by herself from England in 1670 as a bond-ed servant and serving a two-year indenture to pay for her passage, she after-wards married John Coming, first mate of the ship *Carolina*. While her husband was often at sea, Affra, despite danger from disease and often hostile Indians, cleared lands, planted crops and man-aged a remote plantation.

In 1698, after Captain Coming's death, Affra deeded seventeen acres of her Charleston lands to the rector of St. Philip's Episcopal Church and his sucessors "in consideration of the love and duty I have, and I owe to the Church, to promote and encourage ... good, charitable and pious ... work."

She died not long afterwards. The Glebe, sur-rounded by St. Philips, Coming, George and Beaufain Streets, is a living reminder of the vision and character of Carolina's first settlers.

*Erected by the Society of First Families of South Carolina, 1670-1700.* (1986)

## 1699. July 21. *Rice.*

In a letter from William Thornburgh, one of the Lords Proprietors to William Popple, Secretary of His Majesty's Commissioners for Trade and Plantations:

> I have herewith sent you a sample of our Carolina rice that the Rt. Hon. the Lords Commissrs. of Trade & Plantations may 'see what a staple the Province of Carolina may be capable of furnishing Europe withall. The Grocers do assure me its better than any Foreign Rice by at least 8s. The hundred weight, & wee can have it brought home for less than 4s. pr. tonn. web. is not dear.

### 1699, August 1. COMMERCE.

A lot on the Grand Modell "distinguished by the letter B," was granted by Governor Joseph Blake to Captain Edmund Bellinger "with the priviledge [sic] of hawking, hunting, fishing, and fowling" in return for:

> erecting and keeping in Repair a sufficient pair of Steirs or Comon [sic] Landing Place of the breadth of Eight feet and half wide with bolts, rings, and posts for comon (sic) use.

### 1699, Fall. PIRACY. EXECUTION.

A group of forty-five pirates from Cuba lay off Charles Town for several weeks, capturing a few ships and putting their crews ashore. The pirates got into a fight over the division of their spoils. Nine Englishmen were set adrift and landed at Bull's Bay and made their way to Charles Town. They told a story about being shipwrecked, but were identified as pirates by several sailors who had been earlier plundered. Seven of the pirates were executed.

### 1699, November 1. EPIDEMIC.

It was reported that since August, more than 160 people died yellow fever, including Chief Justice Edmund Bohun and English minister Rev. Samuel Marshall.

### 1699, November 16. LIBRARY ESTABLISHED. CHARLESTON FIRST.

A law passed by the Assembly established a provincial library.

## CHARLESTON FIRST

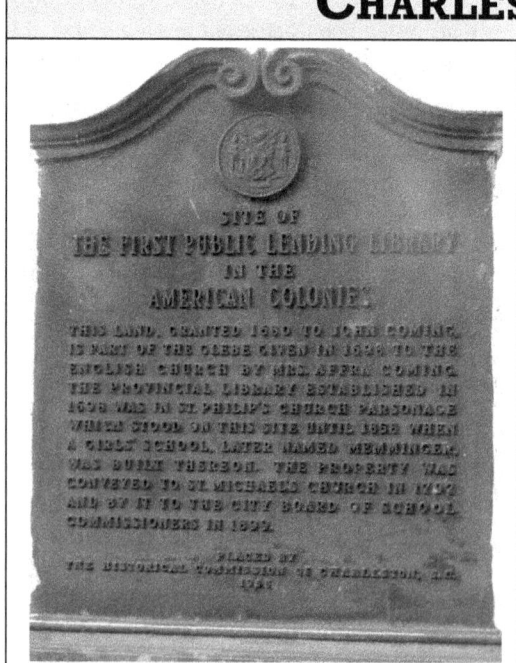

**1699. FIRST PUBLIC LIBRARY IN THE AMERICAN COLONIES.**

A law passed by the Assembly established a provincial library in Charles Town and provided for its governance. This library, located on St. Philips Street, remained in operation for fourteen years, mainly offering religious material for the citizens.

Library marker at Memminger School at the St. Philip's Street entrance.
*Photo by author*

# 1700

### 1700. *BUILDINGS OF CHARLESTON. 106 BROAD STREET.*

Sometime during the year, a wood-frame house was built on Lot no. 160 of the Grand Modell (106 Broad Street), which was granted to James DeBordeaux, a Huguenot. It later became the home of Dr. John Lining. In 1783 it housed the *Gazette of the State of South Carolina* published by Mrs. Ann Timothy. In the 21st century the building serves as a law office.

### 1700. *POPULATION.*

The population of Charles Town was 4000, which included:
- 1700 Anglicans
- 1300 Presbyterians
- 500 Huguenots
- 300 Baptists
- 100 Quakers

### 1700, January 17. *EPIDEMIC.*

Gov. James Moore wrote to the Lords Proprietors:

> A most infectious pestilential and mortal distemper ... was from Barbados or Providence brought in among us in Charles Town about the 28th or 29th of August last, and much decay of trade and mutations of your Lordships' public officers has been occasioned thereby. This distemper ... killed in Charles Town at least 160 persons.

Among the dead included:
- Mr. Ely, Receiver general
- Mr. Armory, Receiver for the public treasury
- Edward Rowlins, Deputy marshall
- Edmund Bohun, Chief Justice
- Rev. Mr. Marshall, minister

### 1700, March. *COMMERCE.*

Governor Blake wrote a letter to the Lords Commissioners of Trade and Plantations that the colony "hath made more rice ye Last Cropp then we have Ships to Transport."

### 1700, March. *POLITICS.*

Attorney General Nicholas Trott publically criticized Governor Blake and was arrested and removed from office.

## 1700, July 30. COMMERCE.

Three hundred and thirty tons of rice were exported from Charles Town to England and the West Indies. Edward Randolph, Collector of Customs wrote:

> They have now found out the true way of raising and husking Rice. There has been above 300 Tons shipped this year to England besides about 30 Tons more to the Islands."

## 1700. August 15. ARRIVALS.

John Lawson arrived in Charles Town. He was commissioned to lead an expedition from Charles Town into the interior of Carolina. He spent several months organizing the expedition.

## 1700. September 3. DISASTER. RISING SUN DESTROYED.

The *Rising Sun* arrived from Scotland, with several hundred Presbyterians, led by Rev. Archibald Stobo. Members of the White Meeting House met Rev. Stobo and invited him ashore to preach the next day. Stobo, his family, and twelve other passengers disembarked.

The next day, a fierce hurricane hit Charles Town causing extensive damage to the waterfront fortifications being constructed and destroying the *Rising Sun* and killing its crew and passengers. Stobo viewed the event as God's judgment. He wrote that "the ship's crew were so filled with wickedness that they could hold no more; they were ripe, they must be cut down with the sickle of His wrath."

Edward Hyme, a newly arrived immigrant, described the catastrophe to his wife in England:

> On Tuesday September 3 here happened a most terrible Storm of Wind or Hurricane with continual Rain; which has done great Damage to ye Country. Thousands of Trees have been torn up by ye Roots, many Houses blown down & more damnified; much Rice, Corn & c spoiled; but ye greatest Mischief fell amongst ye Shipping of which about a Dozen Sail (of all sorts) were riding at Anchor before ye Town, some of which were driven on Shoar & broke all in Pieces, some were carryed a great Way up into ye Two Rivers into Ashley River, in her way breaking down a Pair of Gallows (from which 8 Pirats at once were hanged since my coming here) some were turn'd Bottom upwards & lost.

> But ye greatest and most deplorable loss of all was that to a great Scotch Ship called ye Rising-Sun, which having lost all her Masts in a Huricane in ye Gulf of Florida was riding at Anchor with out our Bar, wth Designe to come in here & refit; but being a Ship of 800 tons & 60 guns she durst not venture in with out lightening to which Purpose One Sloop has already been on board her, but waiting for another, ye Storm rise & she foundered at Anchor, ye Captain (Gibson) & all ye souls on board (being about 100) misearbly perishing...

It was reported "their bodies strewn on the beach at James Island.

Rev. Stobo settled in Charles Town and became renowned for his oratory skills, with sermons lasting more than four hours. Church officials asked that he divide his sermons into two sessions so that members could break for dinner. Stobo refused, claiming that Charleston's spiritual reservoir needed filling. The next Sunday, Solomon Legare left the service at the two-hour mark. Rev. Stobo called out, "Aye, aye, a little petcher (pitcher) is soon full!" Legare called back, "You've said enough to fill all the cisterns in Charlestown."

## 1700, September 7. *DEATH*.

Gov. Joseph Blake died in office, which precipitated a power struggle over his successor.

## 1700, September 11. *MOORE BECOMES GOVERNOR*.

The Council elected James Moore governor of Carolina in a power coup led by the Goose Creek men, usurping the senior Landgrave Joseph Morton, Jr.

Moore originally arrived in Carolina in 1675 from Barbados, married one of Sir John Yeaman's daughters and became a member of the Goose Creek faction, opposed to the Fundamental Constitutions. He became the leading Indian trader in the colony. His father was Roger Moore (Rory O'More), one of the leaders of the 1641 Irish Rebellion against the anti-Catholic Puritan forces and evidently inherited his father's rebellious nature.

## 1700, September 11. *JOHN LAWSON ARRIVES*.

John Lawson, an English naturalist and explorer, described his first impressions of Charles Town and the colony of Carolina where he would spend eight years studying the plants, animals, and peoples of the region.

> After a Fortnight's Stay here [New York City], we put out from Sandyhook, and in 14 Days after arriv'd at Charles-Town, the Metropolis of South Carolina which is situated in 32 [degrees] 45 [minutes] North Latitude, and admits of large Ships to come over their Bar up to the Town, where is a very commodious Harbour, about 5 Miles distant from the Inlet, and stands on a Point very convenient for Trade, being seated between two pleasant and navigable Rivers. The Town has very regular and fair Streets, in which are good Buildings of Brick and Wood, and since my coming thence, has had great Additions of beautiful, large Brick-buildings, besides a strong Fort, and regular Fortifications made to defend the Town.
>
> The Inhabitants, by their wise Management and Industry, have much improv'd the Country which is in as thriving Circumstances at this Time as any Colony on the Continent of English America, and is of more Advantage to the Crown of Great Britain than any of the other more Northerly Plantations (Virginia and Maryland excepted).
>
> This Colony was at first planted by a genteel Sort of People that were well acquainted with Trade, and had either Money or Parts to make

good Use of the Advantages that offer'd, as most of them have done by raising themselves to great Estates and considerable Places of Trust and Posts of Honour, in this thriving Settlement. Since the first Planters, abundance of French and others have gone over and rais'd themselves to considerable Fortunes. They are very neat and exact in Packing and Shipping of their Commodities, which Method has got them so great a Character [reputation] Abroad that they generally come to a good Market with their Commodities; when oftentimes the Product of other Plantations are forc'd to be sold at lower Prices.

They have a considerable Trade both to Europe and the West Indies, whereby they become rich and are supply'd with all Things necessary for Trade and genteel Living, which several other Places fall short of ... Their Roads, with great Industry, are made very good and pleasant. Near the Town is built a fair Parsonage-house with necessary Offices, and the Minister has a very considerable Allowance from his Parish.

There is likewise a French Church in Town of the Reform'd Religion [French Protestants] and several Meeting-houses for dissenting Congrega-tions who all enjoy at this Day an entire Liberty of their Worship, the Constitution of this Government allowing all Parties of well-meaning Christians to enjoy a free Toleration and possess the same Privileges, so long as they appear to behave themselves peaceably and well – It being the Lords Proprietors Intent that the Inhabitants of Carolina should be as free from Oppression as any in the Universe, which doubtless they will if their own Differences amongst themselves do not occasion the contrary.

## 1700, November. *LAND GRANTS.*

Edward Hyrne wrote to his brother requesting money to purchase a plantation near Charles Town, using the illustration of another success story.

> Here is a man in this country that came over a poor Servant about 18-20 years ago, that has gotten a great Estate ... I am credibly informed he has now about 4000 head [of cattle] besides a great number of horses, hogs, etc . and that he had last year 800 calves.

## 1700, November 16. *POLITICS.*

The Assembly passed a law which doubled the rate of tax for non-residents engaged in exporting skins. Charles Town merchants complained that the law would cause the departure of vessels to be so delayed that "the Wormes shall rot their bottoms out."

## 1700, December 28. *EXPEDITION INTO THE BACKCOUNTRY.*

John Lawson left Charles Town to begin his exploration into the Carolina backcountry. He wrote:

I began my voyage from Charles-Town, being six Englishmen in company, with three Indian-men, and one woman, wife to our Indian guide … from the town to the Breach we went down in a large canoe … this breach a passage through a marsh lying northward of Sullivan's Island. At night we got to Bell's-Island, a poor spot of land.

### 1700, December 29. *BACKCOUNTRY EXPEDITION.*

From John Lawson's journal:

> The next morning we set away thro' the marshes, and about noon we reached … Dix's Island … there lived an honest Scot, who gave us the best reception his dwelling afforded, being well provided of oat-meal, and several other effects he had found on that coast; which goods belonged to that unfortunate vessel, the *Rising Sun*.

# 1701

### 1701. *POLITICS. CURFEW LAW.*

The Carolina Assembly passed a curfew law that prevented blacks from "playing the rogue at night." Town constables were to arrest any black who had "no good reason being abroad and to lock him up until morning, have him whipped severely and return him to his owner after a fine was paid."

### 1701. *FORTIFICATIONS.*

The Assembly discussed the completion of the brick Half-Moon Battery, a semi-circular fortification, at the east end of Broad Street.

### 1701. *PUBLIC WHARVES.*

The Assembly also ordered the building of two public wharves with provincial funds.

### 1701. January 3. *BACKCOUNTRY EXPEDITION.*

From John Lawson's journal:

> We entered Santee-River's mouth, where is fresh water … with hard rowing we got two leagues up the river, lying all night in a swampy piece of ground, the Weather being so cold all that time, we were almost frozen ere morning.
>
> We found some Sewee Indians firing the canes swamps, which drives out the game, then taking their particular stands, kill great quantities of both bear, deer, turkeys and what wild creatures the parts afford.

### 1701, March. *PIRACY.*

King William III of England proclaimed a pardon for pirates. Upon their surrender and taking an oath of allegiance, they would be pardoned. According to William Penn, several of Captain Kidd's pardoned crew settled in Carolina.

### 1701, June 16. *SOCIETY FOR THE PROPAGATION OF THE GOSPEL.*

King William III issued a charter establishing the "Society for the Propagation of the Gospel in Foreign Parts" as "an organisation able to send priests and schoolteachers to America to help provide the Church's ministry to the colonists."

### 1701, November. *RELIGION.*

The Dissenters charged that during the election "strangers, indentured servants, paupers, free Negroes and very many unqualified aliens [Huguenots] voted."

# 1702

### 1702. *CATHOLICS GIVEN RIGHT TO VOTE.*

The Commons House approved an act that registered Catholics could vote. They also voted to return Nicholas Trott to his position as Attorney General.

### 1702, March 8. *ENGLAND. DEATH.*

King William III died. Anne, daughter of King James II, ascended to the throne of Great Britain.

### 1702, March 8. *IRELAND. BIRTH.*

Anne Cormac was born in Kinsale, County Cork, the illegitimate daughter of lawyer William Cormac and Mary Brennan, a servant woman. Due to the scandalous birth, the couple migrated to Charles Town. Anne herself would become quite scandalous in a few years.

### 1702, May 4. *QUEEN ANNE'S WAR.*

England declared war on Spain. Known as "Queen Anne's War" in the colonies, it consumed most of her reign. The war consisted mainly of French privateering in the Atlantic and French and Indian raids on the frontier between England and France. In Charles Town rumors surface that the Spanish at St. Augustine are preparing to attack. Governor Moore encouraged a pre-emptive strike on St. Augustine.

### 1702, June 30. *BIRTH.*

Elizabeth Villin was born in Amsterdam. She would later marry Lewis Timothy and move to Charles Town in 1731.

### 1702, August. *QUEEN ANNE'S WAR. FORTIFICATIONS.*

Gov. James Moore ordered work on a seawall along the harbor to be hastened.

### 1702, December. *ST. AUGUSTINE ATTACKED.*

Gov. Moore attacked St. Augustine and the inhabitants retreated into the Castillo de San Marcos, while the English burned the city. Moore lacked sufficient artillery to batter the fortress, so when Spanish reinforcements arrived from Cuba, he abandoned the siege and returned to Charles Town, leaving a £6,000 debt on the colony due to his siege.

## 1703

### 1703. *SLAVERY.*

In order to prevent Carolina from becoming a dumping ground for troublesome slaves in the West Indies the import duty on slaves from the islands was set at a higher rate than on slaves from Africa.

### 1703. *PIRACY. ARRIVALS.*

Sometime during the year Irish lawyer, William Cormac arrived in Charles Town with his illegitimate daughter Anne and his mistress, Mary Brennan. Mary died not long after their arrival and Anne grew up a tomboy, described as "a strapping, boisterous girl of a fierce and courageous temper." She later became an infamous pirate in the Caribbean.

### 1703. *THEATER.*

Anthony Aston wrote and performed the first play in Charles Town, *The Subject of the Country*.

### 1703, February. *POLITICS. RELIGION.*

John Ash, a Dissenter, introduced a bill to regulate elections in the Assembly "granting as much freedom to the French and other aliens as could be granted." It created a tense atmosphere between the Dissenters and Anglicans.

### 1703, March. *POLITICS.*

Sir Nathaniel Johnson was appointed governor. Also there was a Commission for Nicholas Trott as Chief Justice. Trott quickly became hated by the Dissenters. He was accused of being "grossly partisan, unscrupulous in controversy and self-seeking."

### 1703, March. *FORTIFICATIONS.*

Johnson urged the Assembly to pass an act for repairing the existing fortifications and building new works to surround the town. It specified:

the severall forts, halfe moons, platforms, batterys and flankers, built on the front wall [i.e., East Bay Street], shall have gabions [*walls built on a slope to protect against erosion*] fixed upon them, and shall also be well piled, for their preservation against the sea.

The act also stipulated that the fortifications "shall be [made] by intrenchments, flankers and parapets, sally ports, a gate, drawbridge and blind necessary for the same." This plan created a ring of fortification, including four corner bastions linked by a curtain walls and punctuated by eight redans, surrounding sixty-two acres of high land.

## 1703, May 6. *Queen Anne's War.*

Due to expenses of defense and fortification, a tax was imposed upon the importation of Negroes -20 shillings a head for each negro slave from the West Indies and ten shillings per head on each Negro imported from Africa.

## 1703, May 6. *Politics. Scandal.*

Upon John Ash's death, Governor Johnson discovered some private letters of Dissenting Landgrave Smith addressed to Mr. Ash which were critical of the Goose Creek (Anglican) faction. Johnson submitted the letters to the Assembly who arrested Smith. This created several days of "rioting in which the Dissenter leaders, John Ash, Thomas Smith, Edmund Bellinger and Joseph Boone were beaten or threatened." Captain Rhett beat Landgrave Edmund Bellinger over the head with his cane.

A letter to the Proprietors described the attacks:

> John Ash – Landgrave, Thomas Smith and others were assaulted & set upon in the open street without provocation ... Smith was set upon by Lieut. Col. George Dearsly who with his drawn sword and the point held at Smith's belly swore he would kill him ... Ash walking down the Street was assaulted by a rude drunken ungovernable rabble.
>
> Ash was retired into a friend's chamber for security and the same armed multitude came to the House ... assisted by Captain Rhett & others drew him on board ... Rhett's ship ... threatening him as they dragged him along; they told him they would carry him to Jamaica ... threatened to hang him or leave him on some remote island.

No one was arrested for the riot.

## 1703, May 8. *Queen Anne's War.*

In order to pay the debt left by Gov. Moore's St. Augustine expedition, the Assembly issued £6000 bills of credit.

## 1703, June 17. *Public Library.*

Nicholas Trott informed the Assembly that Dr. Bray had sent books as an addition to the "Public Library."

# 1704

### 1704. *GOOSE CREEK FACTION TAKES POWER.*

The Goose Creek faction was now in control of the governorship and the council and they launched a:

> plan ... secretly formed for expelling from the legislature all persons not members of the Anglican Church and establishing it by law as the state religion supported at public expense.

### 1704. *FORTIFICATIONS.*

Due to the incursion of a French privateer into Charleston harbor, Gov. Nathaniel Johnson ordered the construction of a fort at Windmill Point on James Island. He also ordered the digging of trenches at Oyster Point.

### 1704, January. *ASSAULT ON SPANISH FLORIDA.*

After destroying thirteen Spanish Florida missions Col. James Moore returned to Charles Town with substantial booty, including Catholic silver plate.

### 1704, April 21. *BIRTH.*

Gabriel Manigault was born in Charlestown, son of French Huguenot Pierre Manigault and Judith Gitton. He would become the city's most successful merchant.

### 1704, May 4. *RELIGION. EXCLUSION ACT.*

A bill, called the Exclusion Act, to exclude from future Assemblies all but persons communing in the Church of England was passed by the Assembly by a vote of 12-11. The 12 "yes" votes came from Anglicans.

### 1704, May 4. *POLITICS.*

The Assembly passed legislation that prevented "Mens cohabitating with women with whom they ware not married."

### 1704, May 4. *POLITICS. CULTURE.*

The Public Treasurer paid Edward Mosley £5,15s for "transcribing the catalogue of the library books."

### 1704, October 23. *RELIGION.*

Francis Simonds, a widow, donated a plot of land for the construction of a dissenting church building, the White Meeting House, site of the current Circular Church on Meeting Street.

### 1704, November. *POLITICS. RELIGION.*

The Dissenters sent Joseph Boone to England to protest the two acts. Ultimately, Queen Anne ordered the Proprietors to declare the acts void or lose their charter.

## 1704, November 4. *ENGLISH CHURCH ESTABLISHED.*

The Assembly passed the Establishment Act making the Church of England the state religion of the Province. Minister's salaries and church construction were to be financed by an export and import tax. Local vestries were empowered to raise revenue by assessing the real and personal property of Anglicans and dissenters alike. The Act brought an immediate outcry from the dissenters.

## 1704, December. *FORTIFICATIONS.*

Governor Nathaniel Johnson reported to the Lords Proprietors in England that the earthwork entrenchments around Charles Town are "in a great measure perfected," while the works along the waterfront have been "retarded for the want of bricks." That included Lot B of Grand Modell where the Half-Moon Battery was constructed with the Court of Guard on the bottom floor and the Council Chamber above.

Sir Nathaniel Johnson.
*Library of Congress*

# 1705

## 1705. *Religion.*

The Proprietors of the Carolina Colony at this time were:

- Lord John Granville
- Lord William Craven
- Maurice Ashley
- Sir John Colleton
- Joseph Blake
- Nicholas Trott of London
- John Archdale

## 1705. *Commerce. Rice is Enumerated.*

Rice was placed on the list of enumerated goods, meaning that all rice shipped to Europe must pass through an English port before it was exported to a foreign country. This effected the profits of the planters.

## 1705, April. *Death.*

Thomas Pinckney died of yellow fever. He had been in Charles Town for fourteen years and amassed a large fortune.

# 1706

## 1706. *Religion. Arrivals.*

The Society for the Propagation of the Gospel sent its first missionaries, led by Dr. Francis La Jau, to Carolina to preach and "encourage the setting up of schools for the teaching of children."

Dr. Francis La Jau commented that he thought the idea for establishing the Church of England (St. Philip's) in Charles Town "was grounded upon true zeal for the glory of God." He soon concluded that it was for "revenge and self- interest."

## 1706. *Dissenters Allowed to Hold Office.*

An Act was passed which allowed Dissenters to hold elective office.

## 1706. *Commerce.*

George Dearsley opened a shipyard on Hobcaw, across the harbor from Charles Town, east of the Cooper River. After his death, his widow married Thomas Bolton, who continued the shipyard operation.

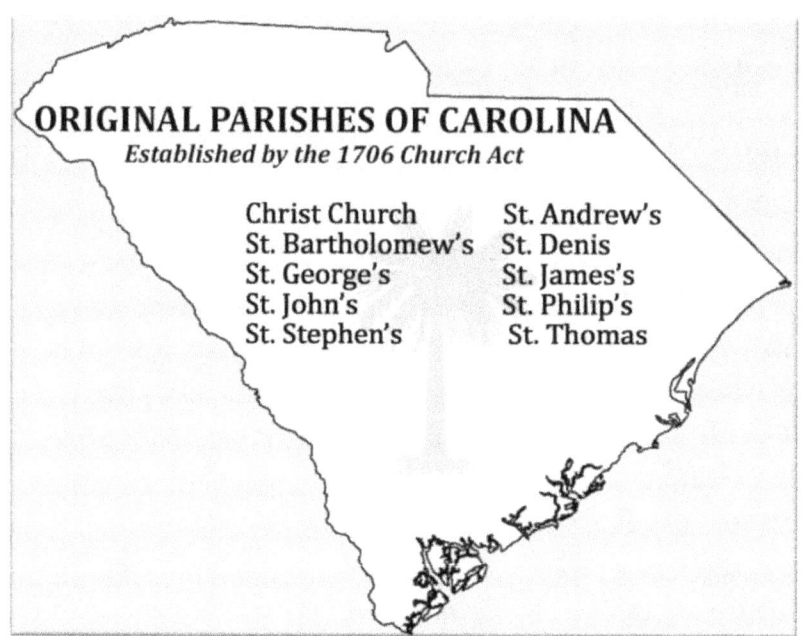

## 1706, January. COMMERCE

Parliament began to pay bounties on naval stores from the American colonies.

## 1706, March 20. POLITICS. CRIME. WITCHCRAFT.

Judge Trott convicted a woman (not named) of witchcraft. Reverend Dr. Francis Le Jau wrote:

> A notorious Maelfactor evidently guilty of Witchcraft & who had kill'd several persons by the Devils help was lately return'd by the Grand Jury. The last Sedition begun while the Judge was examining Evidence relating to the accused Witch that is still in our prisons ... that she has many powerful friends here.

Judge Trott also convicted Sarah Dickenson of murder and sentenced her to "be drawn upon a Hurdle, to the place of Execution and there shall be burned to Death.

## 1706, August 24. QUEEN ANNE'S WAR.

A Dutch privateer sloop belonging to Captain Stool from New York anchored in Charles Town. Stool reported that while in St. Augustine they learned a French ship was planning to attack Carolina. While he was making his report, five columns of smoke appeared on Sullivan's Island, the signal that a fleet was off the bar.

It was a French squadron from Martinique led by Captain De Feboure which included the frigate *Soleil* (22 guns), two 8-gun sloops, two smaller sloops and a galley. On board were more than 700 Spanish soldiers. Some of the Spanish landed on James Island and burned a plantation.

### 1706, August 27. *QUEEN ANNE'S WAR.*

The French ships crossed the Charles Town bar and anchored off Sullivan's Island awaiting winds in which to sail into the harbor.

### 1706, August 28. *QUEEN ANNE'S WAR.*

The French raised a flag of truce, and the French ships crossed the Charles Gov. Johnson sent a galley out to make inquiries. A French officer was brought to shore and kept at Granville Bastion before being escorted to the governor. As he was slow marched through the street, the Frenchman was greeted by militia stationed between buildings and on the side streets. It seemed Charles Town had more than four times the soldiers than they thought. He did not realize that he was actually seeing the same group of militia who were running from one street to the other, staying just ahead of the slow-marching prisoner.

Upon being received by Gov. Johnson the French officer demanded the city surrender within the hour. Johnson responded he "would not need a minute to reply in the negative."

### 1706, August 29. *QUEEN ANNE'S WAR.*

About 160 Spanish troops landed at Mt. Pleasant, burning and looting several plantation houses. Two vessels in Hobcaw Creek were also burned. Gov. Johnson sent out a galley with 100 men, and the Spanish recalled their ships. At the same time, forty French troops landed on James Island and burned the countryside and then retreated. That night, 300 French troops crossed Shem Creek.

### 1706, August 30. *QUEEN ANNE'S WAR.*

At daybreak, Captain Cantey and 100 militia from Charles Town attacked the French, driving them back across Shem Creek. Several French drowned and fifty-eight French prisoners were taken. One Charles Town militia was killed.

### 1706, August 31. *QUEEN ANNE'S WAR.*

Colonel William Rhett and a fleet of six small vessels drove the French / Spanish invaders from the harbor. The English fleet consisted of:

- Flagship: *Crown Galley*
- Galleys: *Mermaid* -12 guns; *Richard* -16 guns; *William*
- Sloop: *Flying Horse* – 8 guns; *Seaflower*

### 1706, September 16. *QUEEN ANNE'S WAR.*

A joint French and Spanish attack from St. Augustine against Charles Town was repulsed by Governor Nathaniel Johnson and Colonel William Rhett. Colonial forces captured a French vessel and crew.

### 1706, September 16. *EPIDEMIC.*

Yellow fever ravaged the town, killing more than one hundred.

### 1706. November 30. *Religion.*

The Council received word that Queen Anne had repealed the Establishment Act (*November 1705*). They promptly passed a new Church Act, establishing the Church of England as the official church of South Carolina, *(see page 85)* dividing the colony into ten parishes. Six of the ten parish names duplicated those in Barbados.

The Act also stipulated that the rector of St. Philip's Church was to receive £150 a year and other rectors £50 a year for three years, then £100 afterward. A registry was to be kept of marriages, births, christenings and burials of all white people within the parish.

# 1707

### 1707. *Commerce.*

During this year, seventeen ships weigh anchor in Charles Town. They left for England laden with naval stores, rice, animal skins and fur. Dozens of more vessels sail to Barbados carrying lumber, meats, cheese, butter and corn; they return with sugar, molasses and slaves.

### 1707. *Fortifications.*

The Assembly passed an act "for Repairing and Expeditious Finishing the Fortifications" in Charles Town, which had suffered breaches and other damages. Parts of the brick wall along the waterfront were apparently still incomplete.

### 1707. *Politics. Religion.*

One year after they were given the right to hold office, the Dissenter Party took control of the Assembly. Members of the party immediately began to call for the removal of Chief Justice Nicholas Trott as "an unfit man for any public office."

### 1707, April 24. *Religion.*

On Easter Sunday, Dr. Francis Le Jau conducted communion at St. Philip's. He was dismayed that only twenty-four people received the sacraments.

### 1707, May 1. *Act of Union.*

The Act of Union took effect. The Scottish Parliament and the English Parliament united to form the Parliament of Great Britain. Anne became Queen of Great Britain.

### 1707, September 15. *Politics. Religion.*

Judge Trott wrote in defense of the Church Act: "The reason why we passed the Act to exclude them [Dissenters] from being chosen was because they never did any good there nor never do any."

### 1707, September 28. *INDIAN AFFAIRS.*

The land between the Combahee and Savannah Rivers was set aside as a reservation for the Yemassee tribe. Surveys and settlements were forbidden, and white settlers within its limits were removed. It was Governor's Johnson's attempt to keep the Yemassee friendly and use them as a buffer between Charles Town and St. Augustine.

# 1708

### 1708. *FORTIFICATIONS.*

Due to the ease in which the French/Spanish fleet sailed into Charles Town in 1706, the Assembly passed an act to build a fortification at "Windmill Point on the east end of James Island.

A letter written by the Grand Council to the Queen's officers in London described the defenses:

> Charles Town the chief port in Carolina by the direction and diligence of our present governor, Sir Nathaniel Johnson is surrounded with a regular fortification, consisting of bastions, flankers and half- moon ditched and palisaded and mounted with 88 guns. Also, at the entrance of the harbor in a place called Windmill Point (within a carbine shot of which all vessels must pass by) is now building and almost finished a triangular fort and platform of capacity to mount 30 guns which when finished will be the key and bulwark of this province but wanting some large heavy guns both for the fortification and about Charles Town and the said fort and platform together with a suitable store of shot.

Windmill Point was renamed Fort Johnson, in honor of the governor. Trenches were built on Oyster Point (now the Battery). A guard was placed on Sullivan's Island, which commanded a view of the ocean, with orders to build a number of fires opposite the town equal to the number of ship that might appear on the coast.

### 1708. *COMMERCE.*

Gov. John Archdale, wrote:

> Carolina…. Produces rice the best of the known world, being a commodity for sending home, as also pitch, tar, buckskins … and it hath already such plenty of provisions, as beef, pork … that it furnishes in a great measure Barbados and Jamaica … I understand that silk is come into great improvement, some families making 40-50 pounds a year … little Negro children being serviceable in feeding the silk-worms …

### 1708, January 20. COMMERCE.

Sir John Colleton conveyed to Thomas Broughton 4.4 acres granted to Sir Peter Colleton in 1679. The property was known as "Mulberry Plantation."

### 1708, April. RELIGION. ARRIVAL OF REV. GIDEON JOHNSTON.

Reverend Gideon Johnston was appointed Bishop's Commissary in South Carolina by the Bishop of London. Johnston and his wife, Henrietta, had an arduous journey to Carolina.

After leaving England his ship stopped to re-supply at the island of Madeira off the coast of Portugal, as was customary before making the trans-Atlantic crossing to Barbados. Johnston went ashore and sampled a new drink – a golden-colored spirit named after the island, Madeira. The wine was aged for at least twenty years in casks, bottled and then allowed to mature for another thirty to seventy-five years.

Johnston enjoyed the wine so much he missed the ship's departure, even though his wife was aboard. He was forced to take another vessel to Barbados, where his wife awaited him.

When they arrived in Charles Town it was low tide and the entrance of the harbor was impassable. Impatient, Rev. Johnston struck out for shore in a small boat, but a storm blew him to the south, marooning him on a small island. Johnston wrote that he had nothing "to Eat or Drink ... but sea weeds and my own Urine."

### 1708, September 17. POPULATION. BLACK MAJORITY.

Governor Johnson wrote that the population of Carolina was 9,580 souls which included:

- 2,260 free men and women
- 120 white servant males and females
- 1,700 white free children
- 2,900 Negro men and women slaves
- 1,100 Indian men and women slaves
- 1,200 Negro children slaves
- 300 Indian children slaves

For the first time, blacks outnumbered whites in Carolina. Johnson also noted that:

> the Yamassees [native Indians situated about 80 to 100 miles south from Charles Town; they consist of about 500 men able to bear arms; they are great warriors and are continually annoying the Spanish and Indians they allies.

> From this Province are exported to several of the American islands, as Jamaica, Barbados ... and the Bahama Islands – staves, hoops and singles, beef, pork, rice tar, green wax, candles made of myrtle berries, butter, English and Indian peas ... Goods imported from the foregoing islands are – rum, sugar, molasses, cotton ... salt, and piminento.

We have also commerce with Boston, Rhode Island, Pennsylvania, New York and Virginia; to which we export Indian slaves, ... tanner leather, pitch, tar and a small quantity of rice. From thence we receive beer, cider, flour, dry codfish and marckerel ... Further, we have a trade to the Madeiras, from which we receive most of our wines ...

## 1708, September 20. *RELIGION. CULTURE.*

Reverend Gideon Johnston was not impressed at what he found in Charles Town. He wrote:

> The people here, generally speaking, are the vilest race of men upon earth. They have neither honor, nor honesty, nor religion enough to entitle them to any tolerable character, being a perfect Medley of hotch-potch made up of bankrupt pirates, decayed libertines ... who have transported themselves hither from Bermudas, Jamaica, Barbados Montserat, Antego, Nevio, New England, Pennsylvania ... Most of those that pretend to be churchmen are strongly crippled in their goings ...

## 1708, December 30. *COMMERCE.*

Since rice had become enumerated (must initially pass through an English port) in 1705, profits had suffered. It did not take Carolina merchants long to bypass this law and start smuggling rice to other countries. John Lloyd wrote to William Popple, Secretary of the Commissioners for Trade and Plantations:

> I received your Two Letters that reminded me of my Promise to the Right Honorable the Lords Commissioners of Trade & Plantations concern in 2 Ships that carried Rice to Portugal. I wrote to a Particular friend there and pray'd him to give me an account of itt ... I find he is unwilling to give any information. All that I can learn is this - That three Ships loaded at Carolina and took out clearings for Rhode Island, from whence they got certificates to Cleare their Bonds att Carolina and thence Reloaded their Ships the Masters Names are Samuel Jones Thomas Thatcher and one —— Pitts, all New England men.

> I have a Ship lately arrived from Carolina now att Portsmouth ... I presume one way to stop this Trade, would be to give power to our Consuls abroad strictly to examine all ships from Her Majystys: plantations or settlements that shall be loaded with Fish, whether part of their cargoe be nott Rice Logwood, pitch or Tarr, which are often imported in those parts. As for Rhode Island tis a place where all Roguery's are committed and great Quantitys of Goods from Portugal are Landed there, and so conveyed to severall parts.

# 1709

## 1709. RELIGION.

Rev. Gideon Johnston and his family were suffering financially. His payment from London was often delayed and he discovered £150 salary "was much too meager, for he needed £300 to £400 in Carolina money to live in a style that £100 sterling would buy in London." He also wrote that, "Were it not for the assistance my wife gives me by drawing pictures ... I shou'd not have been able to live."

Johnston called his campaign to establish the Anglican Church in Carolina "dangerous and difficult Warfare." He was verbally attacked by the Dissenting minister of different faiths. Rev. Pollock (Presbyterian) denounced the Church of England as "scandalous," and Archibald Stono called Johnston a "fierce and violent man."

---

**CHARLESTON FIRST**

**1709. AMERICA'S FIRST FEMALE PAINTER, HENRIETTA JOHNSTON.**

Starting in 1708, in order to help support her family, Henrietta Johnston painted pastel portraits of wealthy Carolina citizens such as Gov. Thomas Broughton, Col. William Rhett and Gov. Nathaniel Johnson.

According to the book, *American Colonial Portraits* by Richard Saunders and Ellen Miles, Henrietta Johnston was the earliest recorded female artist and first known pastelist working in the English colonies.

---

# 1710

## 1710, April. EDUCATION.

The Assembly passed an act to establish a "Free School ... for the instruction of Youth ... in grammar, arts and sciences and the principals of Christianity." Requirements for the teacher included being able to teach "Latin and Greek and be of the Church of England."

## 1710, April. COMMERCE.

It was estimated that twenty-two vessels traded between Charles Town and England.

## 1710, June. ELECTION SCANDAL. NEW GOVERNOR.

After the death of governor Edward Tynte, Robert Gibbes, one of the largest land owners in Carolina, was elected acting governor by the Executive Council. Gibbes received one vote more than his opponent, Thomas Broughton, by bribing a member of the Council.

### 1710, August 18. COMMERCE. POLITICS.

In a letter to Nathaniel Sayle, Receiver General, the Proprietors wrote:

> The Officers Sallaries & payments you are Directed to make by your Commission & Instructions are to be pd. out of our Quit Rents, but Moneyes which you Shall Receive for ye Purchase of Lands & wt Shall Remain of our QuitzRents after those Payments made - you are hereby Ordered to Consigne to Us and to Send them for London by ye first opportunity every Quarter of a Year in Rice or money.

### 1710, September 24. BIRTH.

William Bull, Jr. was born at Ashley Hall planation, son of William Bull, planter.

### 1710, Fall. INDIAN AFFAIRS.

In an effort to control the Indian Trade, Gov. Gibbes appointed the Commissioners of the Indian Trade of South Carolina to set guidelines for trading with the natives.

### 1710, December. COMMERCE. POLITICS. DEATH.

The Proprietors, addressing Nathaniel Sayle's successor as Receiver General, wrote:

> We being inform'd that att the time of the death of our late Receiver ... there were Effects of ours in his hands of a Considerable Value which he intended to have returned to us. According to the directions to him formerly by us Given, These are therefore to Command & require you forthwith to send Over his Accts: and Remmitt ye Ballance thereof in Rice etc: by two of the Next ships yr shall Come for England after the Receipt hereof.

# 1711

### 1711, January 17. CAROLINA COLONY. FOUNDING OF BEAUFORT.

The town of Beaufort was chartered on the Port Royal Sound, making it the second oldest town in South Carolina. It was named after Henry Somerset, the 2nd Duke of Beaufort and a Lord Proprietor from 1700-14. The Beaufort settlement made the Yemassee Indians unhappy, as it usurped a large part of their territory.

### 1711, March 11. RELIGION.

At the urging on Rev. Gideon Johnston, a law was passed for "Erecting a New Church," on the "east sde of Church-street, a few pole north of Queen Street." It was to be the new location of St. Philip's Church. The Assembly had realized that the true entrance of the city was not by road (Broad Street), but by ship, so it was determined to build the new church closer to the harbor.

### 1711, August. *Epidemic.*

The worst epidemic of yellow fever and small pox in the city's history began and would run for the next four months.

### 1711, August 3. *Indian Affairs.*

The Commissioners of the Indian Trade of South Carolina published a document titled "Instructions For the South Carolina Indian Traders."

### 1711, November 16. *Epidemic.*

Rev. Gideon Johnston commented in a letter:

> Never was there a more sickly or fatall [sic] season than this for small Pox, Pestilential ffevers, Pluerises, and fflexes have great numbers here of all Sorts, both Whites, Black and Indians ... Three Funeralls a day, and sometimes four are now very usual.

> The town looks miserably thing, and disconsolante, and there is not one house in twenty ... I speak modestly that has not Considerably suffer'd and still laborious, under this general Calamity ... But I verily think, it is a Sort of Plague, a kind of Judegement upon the Place (ffor they are a sinful People) ...

### 1711, December. *Indian Affairs.*

Colonel John Barnwell led an expedition into North Carolina to suppress an uprising of the Tuscarora tribe.

### 1711, December 25. *Epidemic.*

More than 400 slaves, and an equal number of white, had died of the small pox, a quarter of the population. Rev Johnston wrote about Christmas, "Instead of the usual Joy and festivity ... very few are seen abroad ... for fear of being Infected."

# 1712

### 1712. *Politics.*

The Assembly passed legislation stating that all English laws passed by Parliament should be enforced in South Carolina.

### 1712. *Buildings of Charleston.*

Colonel William Rhett's house was constructed at 54 Hasell Street. It is still a private residence in the present-day.

## 1712, March 12. *ARRIVALS. POLITICS.*

Charles Craven arrived in Charles Town as governor to replace the illegally elected Robert Gibbes. Craven had previously served as secretary of the Proprietors.

## 1712, June. *EPIDEMIC. POLITICS.*

The Assembly passed an act "for the more effectual Preventing the Spreading of Contagious Distempers" and appointed Gilbert Guttery the first health commissioner. He was empowered to board any ship coming into the harbor and order anyone quarantined in the "pest house" on Sullivan's Island, under penalty of fine or whipping for leaving.

**BUILDINGS OF CHARLESTON**
**William Rhett House, 54 Hasell Street**

William Rhett House, 54 Hasell Street, c.1712.
*Courtesy of the Library of Congress*

## 1712, June. *FORTIFICATIONS.*

The Assembly also passed an act to build a powder magazine "within Twenty yards of the Redoubt [redan] on the North part of Charles Town." This powder magazine still stands on the south side of modern Cumberland Street in downtown Charleston.

### 1712, June. INDIAN AFFAIRS. "TUSCARORA JACK."

Col. John Barnwell returned victorious from North Carolina against the Tuscarora tribe, and picked up the nickname "Tuscarora Jack."

### 1712, December 12. AGENT IN LONDON.

The Assembly created an office of Agent in London to solicit the interests of the province with Parliament and the Proprietors and to increase the trade of rice and naval stores. Abel Kettleby was named the first agent.

The Assembly also adopted Nicholas Trott's *Compilation of the Provincial Statues* as the official statement of law.

- The common law of England was declared in force in Carolina
- A free school was established in Charleston.

# 1713

### 1713. BUILDINGS OF CHARLESTON.

The Powder Magazine was completed for the storage of gunpowder and munitions. Today, the Magazine is operated as a museum by the National Society of The Colonial Dames of America in the State of South Carolina. It is the oldest municipal building in South Carolina.

### 1713, April 11. QUEEN ANNE'S WAR. TREATY OF UTRECHT.

The Treaty of Utrecht officially ended Queen Anne's War. The boundaries between Carolina and Florida, and Carolina and French Louisiana were left unsettled, setting the stage for further conflicts.

One of the residual effects of the War was the proliferation of pirates in the West Indies and throughout the Caribbean. After ten years of preying on Spanish and French ships with her Majesty's permission, some of these privateers were loath to give up the easy wealth and adventure.

### 1713, June 6. COMMERCE.

The leading exports of the year were:

- 73,790 deerskins
- 75 Indian slaves
- 12,677 barrels of rice
- 6,617 barrels of pitch and tar
- 661 barrels of turpentine
- 1,965 sides of leather
- 1,963 barrels of beef

### 1713, August 13. POLITICS.

Chief Justice Nicholas Trott was granted a leave of his duties in South Carolina so that he may see to his affairs in England. During his absence his salary was continued.

## 1713, September 5. *DISASTER.*

A hurricane hit Charles Town. Rev. William Livingston, pastor of the White Meeting House, survived the storm from his house on White Point. He wrote that the storm "beat off the weatherboards of the house, carried away the book that contained the church records and the furniture of the rooms on the lower floor."

Thomas Lamboll recorded:

> On September 5 came on the great hurricane which was attended with such an Inundation from the sea and to such an unknown height that a great many lives were lost; all the vessels in Charleston harbor, except one, were drove ashore. The new Look-out on Sullivan's Island of wood, built eight square and eighty feet high, blown down; all the front wall and mud parapet before Charlestowne undermined and washed away.

## 1713, December 18. *FORTIFICATIONS.*

The Assembly provided two scout vessels to patrol the Atlantic waters between the Stono River and Florida. Manned by white and Indian crews, their job was to watch for approaching enemy vessels, and track down runaway slaves and servants.

## BUILDINGS OF CHARLESTON
### Powder Magazine, 79 Cumberland Street

Two views of the Powder Magazine, Cumberland Street, 1713.
TOP: *Harper's Weekly,* 1860. *Courtesy of the Library of Congress.*
BOTTOM: Modern view. *Photo by Author, 2014.*

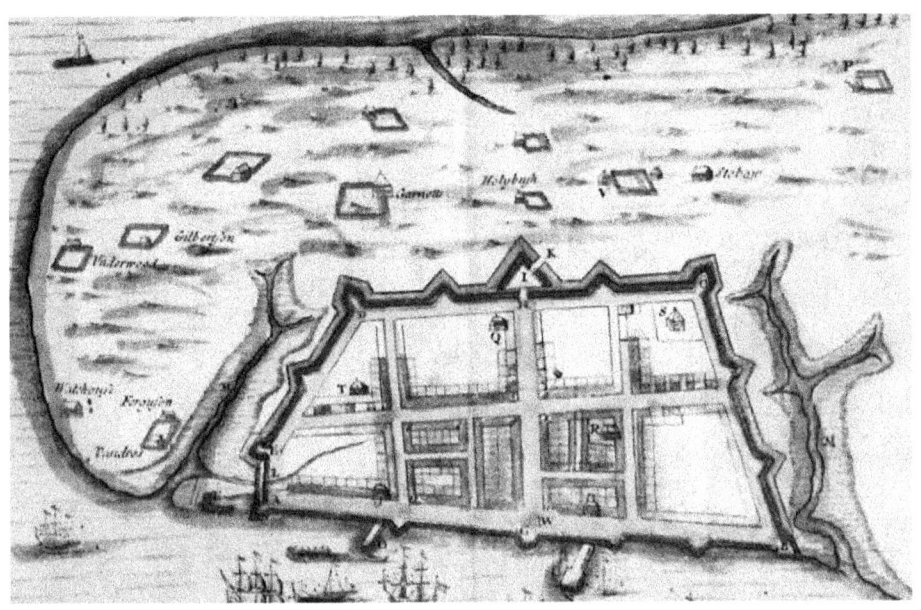

Edward Crisp map, cc. 1713. *Courtesy of the Library of Congress*

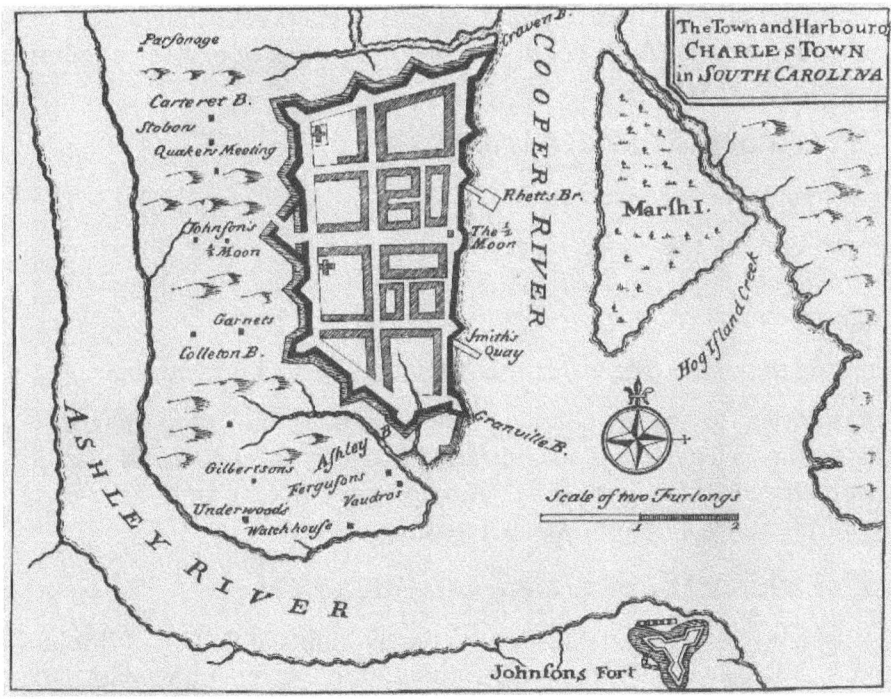

Walled city with bastions labelled. *Courtesy of the Library of Congress*

# 1714

### 1714. *SLAVERY.*

Troubled by recent acts of slave unrest, the Assembly levied heavy import duties to discourage the importation of blacks. During this year 419 black slaves were imported. During the next two years that number fell to eighty-one and sixty-seven respectively.

### 1714, August 1. *ENGLAND.*

George I became King of Great Britain.

### 1714, September 8. *POLITICS. ENGLAND.*

After several meetings with Chief Justice Nicholas Trott, the Proprietors issued an order declaring him:

> a permanent member of the Council without whose presence there should be no quorum for the transaction of business, and without whose consent practically no law should be passed.

Trott became the most powerful man in South Carolina, Attorney General and Chief Justice. Without his presence, the Council could not make decisions. Upon Trott's return to Charles Town, Governor Craven and the Assembly were obviously distressed. They wrote: "A power in one man not heard of before ... unheard of in any of the British dominions."

### 1714, December. *FORTIFICATIONS.*

The Assembly passed an act:

> for preventing the Sea's further Encroachment on the Wharfe of Charles Town, and for repairing the Bastions, Half Moon and Redoubts on the same.

According to this act, the waterfront fortifications had proved to be:

> not sufficient to secure Charles Town, especially the front thereof, against the violent storms and hurricanes, that for these two years last past hath been upon us, to the undermining and ruining great parts of the fortifications and front wall before Charles Town.

### 1714, December 18. *POLITICS. COMMERCE.*

The Assembly passed "An Act for avoiding Deceipts in Selling of Beef and Pork, Pitch and Tarr Rosin and Turpentine by appointing Packers in Several Parts of this Province." The Assembly appointed official packers at all lowcountry wharves.

# 1715

### 1715. *BLOODLESS REVOLUTION.*

At some point during the year the Assembly officially asked the London Board of Trade to void the Proprietor's charter and make South Carolina a Royal Colony.

### 1715. *COMMERCE.*

Samuel Wragg had the 150-ton vessel *Princess Carolina* built in Charles Town. Benjamin Austin supervised the construction, employing eleven shipwrights and other mechanics. She was most likely the first ship built locally designed for trans-oceanic commerce. The *Princess Carolina* proved that Carolina ship-builders were capable of building up to European standards.

### 1715, February 16. *COMMERCE. RICE.*

The Assembly granted John Thurber a gratuity of £100 out of the Public Treasury for bringing the first Madagascar rice into South Carolina. Twenty pounds were to be paid to him, and the other eighty were to be paid to Thurber's family in New England.

### 1715, April 15. *YEMASSEE WAR.*

At this point, many of the Lowcountry Indian tribes were deeply indebted to the English. Unscrupulous traders in London and Charles Town overextended credit to the Indians hoping to force them to pay in land concessions. The Yemassee were also unhappy with the town of Beaufort being settled in the middle of their territory. As the pressure to collect the debt increased, the Indian agents often resorted to cruel practices - cheating, beatings, and the raping of their women.

A Charles Town delegation was sent to negotiate with the Yemassee tribe, but they were ritually tortured and murdered. The Indians then divided themselves into two war parties. One attacked Beaufort. About 300 whites were able to take refuge on a ship in the Port Royal River while the Yemassee burned most of the town.

The other Yemassee party marched through St. Bartholomew's Parish, burning houses on the way, killing 100 people.

> Governor Craven declared martial law, lain an embargo on all vessels, impressed men and property into service for defense and appointed Robert Daniel deputy governor to administer the colony while Craven was at the front.

Terrified of being attacked, the Assembly took an unprecedented action – they armed 400 black slaves to join a force of 500 white men. The site of armed Negros marching through Charles Town frightened them as much as the possibility of Indian attack.

### 1715, May. *YEMASSEE WAR.*

Governor Craven led a force of about 240 men to the Combahee River. He engaged the Yemassee in the open terrain near the Indian town of Salkahatchie at the junction of the Combahee and Salkahatchie Rivers. Several leading Indian warriors were killed and the rest fled into nearby swamps, abandoning the battle. Casualties numbered about thirty on both sides.

News from the northern region of South Carolina indicated that about 400 Catawba warriors, joined by about 70 Cherokee, terrorized the northern parts of the colony and murdered the British traders among them.

A South Carolina force of ninety cavalry under Captain Thomas Barker went north in response, but they were massacred by the Catawba and Cherokee war party. Another Catawba and Cherokee force attacked Benjamin Schenkingh's plantation and killed about twenty people. South Carolina no longer had defenses to protect the wealthy Goose Creek district.

The Yemassee raising the "Bloody Stick" of war. *Courtesy of the Library of Congress*

## 1715, May 23. YEMASSEE WAR.

When the reality of the continuing war settled in, Governor Craven appealed for help. In a letter to Lord Townshend, Secretary of State to the new monarch, George I, Craven wrote:

> It is a great pity, my lord, so fine and flourishing a country so beneficial to the Crown by its trade and once so safe to other colonies by reason of the vast number of Indians it was in alliance with. I have no occasion, therefore, to press your Lordship to consider that if once we are driven from hence, the French from Movill (Mobile) ... will certainly get footing here if not prevented and then ... they will be able to march against any colony on the main and threaten the whole British settlements.

Governor Craven offered future rice harvests as security for arms and men. The British government supplied no soldiers but sent the following supplies:

- 1000 muskets
- 600 pistols
- 2000 grenades
- 201 barrels of powder

The Proprietors met in London and "to their great grief" were unable to afford to send any military support. The British government pressured the Proprietors to surrender their charter of a "province they would not defend." They "absolutely refused" unless the King would purchase their charter.

While South Carolina struggled against murder and wholesale destruction of their colony, three thousand miles away the politicians argued over money.

## 1715, May 25. *YEMASSEE WAR.*

Governor Eden of North Carolina called for volunteers to fight for South Carolina and sent a force of fifty men.

## 1715, June 13. *YEMASSEE WAR.*

The Cherokee war party returned north. That left the remaining Catawba force to face a rapidly-assembled militia under the command of George Chicken from Goose Creek. In the Battle of the Ponds, the Chicken militia routed the Catawba who returned to their villages and decided on peace.

## 1715, June 24. *DEATH.*

Former governor, Robert Gibbes, died.

## 1715, July. *YEMASSEE WAR.*

Catawba diplomats arrived in Virginia to inform the British of their willingness to not only make peace, but to assist South Carolina militarily.

Governor Spotswood, of Virginia, sent the H.M.S. *Valour* with 120 men, 160 small arms, ten barrels of powder and twenty-five casks of shot.

## 1715, July 19. *COMMERCE.*

The Council of Trade, in a letter to James Stanhope, Secretary of State for the Southern Department, stated:

> The Produce of this Colony, are, Naval Stores, Pitch & Tar in Good Abundance and some Masts, Rice of the best kind; & considerable Quantities of Skins, which by the Trade hereof, and the Duties On their Importation here, are very beneficial to this Kingdom, & occasion an Augmentation of his Majesty's Revenue.

### 1715, August 26. *YEMASSEE WAR. POLITICS. RICE.*

The Assembly voted to extend two gratuities, to be paid in rice for services rendered during the Yemassee War.

Captain Samuel Meade, commander of his Majesty's ship *Success* was granted six "Tuns of Rice so soon as the same can conveniently be got ready to be delivered to him." Lieutenant Alexander Coldcott was presented "one Tun of Rice ... for his services to the Publick."

## BUILDINGS OF CHARLESTON
### Dr. John Lining House, 106 Broad Street

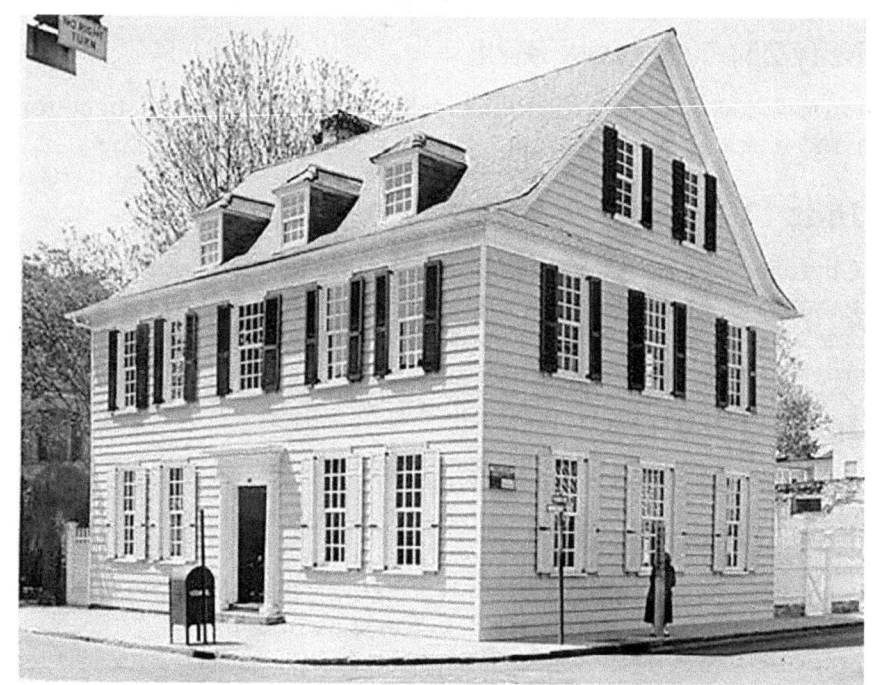

106 Broad Street, c. 1715, pictured here in the 1940s. This building holds the claim as the oldest frame structure in Charleston. A house is mentioned on this site conveyed to William Harvey. *Courtesy of the Library of Congress*

# 1716

### 1716, January. *YEMASSEE WAR.*

The Creek nation allied itself with the Yemassee. Reports of attacks from all across the Carolinas reached Charles Town. Governor Craven sent Maurice Moore with an expedition of 300 men, which included armed slaves, to the Cherokee towns along the lower Savannah, asking them to ally themselves with the English.

### 1716, January 27. *Yemassee War.*

Several weeks of negotiation bore fruit when the Cherokee tribe allied with the English. They lured Creek soldiers with a plan of hiding in the forest, lying in wait for the English. The Cherokee killed the Creek and attacked their villages. Within a few months, the Creek and the Yemassee were decimated and asked for peace.

### 1716, February 24. *Politics.*

The Proprietors yielded to the complaints of the Assembly and revoked Judge Trott's veto power but made him Judge of Admiralty. They also approved the appropriation of the Yemassee lands to be opened for white settlers.

### 1716, April 25. *Bloodless Revolution.*

Governor Craven returned to London, to plead the case of grievances against the Proprietors before the King, asking to become a Royal colony.

### 1716, April 25. *Robert Johnson Becomes Governor. Death.*

The Proprietors commissioned Robert Johnson as governor, the son of former governor Sir Nathaniel Johnson. Craven appointed Robert Daniel to serve as governor in his absence until Johnson's arrival.

Rev. Gideon Johnston accompanied Craven in a sloop out to the harbor to bid him farewell. During the return trip the sloop was swept over by a storm. Johnston drowned, and several days later his body washed up on the same bank of sand on which he had been marooned on the day he arrived in 1708.

### 1716, April 25. *Yemassee War.*

The Yemassee lands were opened to settlers.

### 1716, Fall. *Arrivals.*

A group of thirty-two Scots, political prisoners who had been sentenced to servitude in the colonies for their part in the Jacobite Rebellion against King George I, arrived in Charles Town. They were sent to the backcounty for garrison duty.

### 1716, November 27. *Piracy.*

Judge Trott held his first piracy trial. He convened a Grand Jury who returned an indictment against nine men for piracy, but a jury failed to convict them.

### 1716, December 15. *Legal. Politics*

The Elections Act of 1716 was ratified by the Assembly. It was the first to designate the parishes as election units and the church wardens as election officials.

Dutch painting of the Yemassee War. Title is: "The Gruesome Attack of the Indians on the English, in Carolina, West Indies on 19 April, 1715." *Courtesy of the Library of Congress*

# 1717

### 1717. BIRTH.

Sometime during the year, Henry Middleton was born at The Oaks Plantation in Goose Creek.

### 1717. COMMERCE.

The Collector's office reported 162 ships visited Charles Town during the year.

### 1717. PIRACY.

Captain Woodes Rogers was appointed the governor of the Bahamas, with orders to rid the island of pirates.

During Queen Ann's War, New Providence (currently Nassau, Bahamas) was over run twice by both the French and Spanish. The island became a haven of desperate men of various nationalities, most of whom had served on ships during the war. They began to cruise the Caribbean and up and down the Atlantic coast seizing vessels of all nations for cheap and easy plunder. They had hundreds of hiding places along the coast of the Carolina , the most popular being the Cape Fear River area of North Carolina and the Outer Banks.

Estimates indicate that there were more than 2,200 men operating as buccaneers between New Providence and the Outer Banks. Charles Town sat almost exactly between the two, placing the town in the midst of the golden age of Piracy.

## 1717. *YEMASSEE WAR. COMMERCE.*

During the War, trade came to a standstill in Carolina. The colony's debt to London creditors was more than £100,000. Crops outside the town had not been planted in two seasons, in fear of attack. Farm buildings and fences had been burned and livestock slaughtered or carried off. There were acute food shortages that spring and summer. One-half of cultivated land was unused, burned and abandoned. Four hundred settlers had been killed, four per cent of the white population.

### PIRACY IN CHARLES TOWN

Pirates were once encouraged in Charles Town. During the first two decades of the eighteenth century pirates preyed on the Spanish galleons carrying gold and other treasure from Florida to Spain. Charles Town tavern owners and shopkeepers embraced those free-spending agents of the sweet trade.

However, after the King's Pardon, there was a dramatic increase of attacks on British ships bound to and from Charles Town, plundering by the likes of Blackbeard, Charles Vane, Richard Worley, Calico Jack Rackham, and the "Gentleman "Pirate, Stede Bonnet.

In 1718, Charles Town would play a significant role in the demise of the Golden Age of Piracy, led by Judge Nicholas Trott, Colonel William Rhett and Governor Robert Johnson.

## 1717. *PIRACY.*

During that year, sixteen-year old, red-haired Anne Cormac started frequenting the waterfront taverns of Charles Town. She quickly picked up a reputation as a drinker and fierce brawler, quick to anger. It was reported, "That once, when a young fellow would have lain with her against her will, she beat him so that he lay ill of it a considerable time."

### 1717, March. *POLITICS. PETITION TO KING GEORGE I.*

The failure of the Proprietors to come to Carolina's aid during the Yemassee War increased the tension between the colonists and the Proprietors. The Commons House of Assembly in Charles Town, wrote a petition to King George I asking to become a Royal Colony. The petition opened with:

> We, your Majesty's most dutiful and loyal subjects, the representatives and inhabitants of the Province of South Carolina America, out of the extreme grief we are under to see our country still harassed, and our fellow subjects killed and carried away by our savage Indian enemies, with the utmost submission, are obliged again to intrude on your Majesty's more weighty affairs, and presume ... to lay before your Majesty the state of this, your afflicted Colony ...
>
> Our troubles, instead of coming to a period, daily increase upon, and we now see ourselves reduced by these, our misfortunes, to such a dismal extremity, that nothing but your Majesty's most royal and gracious (under God) protection can preserve us from ruin.

### 1717, June 24. *PIRACY.*

Stephen James de Cossey, Francis de Mont, Francis Rossoe and Emanuel Erando were charged by Judge Trott with taking the vessels *Turtle Dove, Penelope*, and *Virgin Queen* off the coast of Jamaica.

### 1717, June 30. *COMMERCE. SLAVERY.*

The Assembly once again passed an act to encourage the importation of white servants. For every ten black slaves owned, a planter was required to acquire one white servant, when available.

### 1717, July 3. *PIRACY. EXECUTION.*

The four pirates, Stephen James de Cossey, Francis de Mont, Francis Rossoe and Emanuel Erando, were hanged.

### 1717, August. *PIRACY. STEDE BONNET OFF CHARLES TOWN.*

A Barbadian pirate named Stede Bonnet lay off the Charles Town bar in a ship called *Revenge*. He plundered two vessels leaving the harbor, a New England brigantine and a sloop from Barbados. He relieved them of their cargo and kept the sloop. He returned the crews of both vessels back to Charles Town in the now empty brigantine.

### 1717, October 29. *BLOODLESS REVOLUTION.*

Governor Robert Johnson met with the Assembly for the first time. As the representative of the Proprietors he was not warmly received. The lack of assistance the Proprietors offered during the Yemassee War had soured the people's opinion. Judge Trott and Col. William Rhett, Speaker of the Assembly, were the two most powerful men in colony, more respected than the Proprietors. Johnson, however, knew that former Governor Craven was in London seeking a path to make South Carolina a Royal Colony. During his address to the Assembly Johnson said:

> I am obliged for your sakes to give you my opinion touching the disrespectful behavior that has of late been shown to the Lords Proprietors ... very unjustifiable and impolitic. If it be supposed their character is a bar to your relief, it is a mistake. His Majesty and his Parliament are too just to divest their Lordships of their properties without a valuable consideration.

## STEDE BONNET– GENTLEMAN PIRATE

Stede Bonnet was an educated man and served in the Royal Army as a major. After retirement from the military he grew wealthy as the owner of a sugar plantation in Barbados. For some unknown reason, in 1717, Bonnet purchased a ship, *Revenge*, hired a crew of seventy and sailed out of Bridgetown harbor and began to plunder ships in the Caribbean. This is the *only* recorded incident of a pirate *purchasing* a ship.

Why did Bonnet turn to piracy? One theory is that he suffered from a "disordered mind." Another theory is that he rebelled against his comfortable life and suffered what is now called a midlife crisis. Instead of sports car or a Harley, Bonnet purchased a pirate ship. The third, and most enduring theory, was that Bonnet turned to the sweet trade to escape his nagging, shrewish wife.

It didn't take Bonnet's crew long to determine that he was not much of a pirate. He suffered from seasickness, dressed in fine clothes and wore a powdered wig. He was a refined gentleman who rarely drank and spent most of his time in his cabin – reading!

The crew was talking mutiny with plans to strand Bonnet on a deserted island until the *Revenge* crossed paths with the infamous Edward Teach – "Blackbeard – off the Charles Town bar. What happened next is one of the most legendary stories in the annals of pirate history – the blockade of Charles Town, and subsequent "war against the pirates."

*Stede Bonnet's "Jolly Roger"*

### 1717, November 30. *Piracy. Bonnet meets Blackbeard.*

Stede Bonnet, the Gentleman Pirate, ran into another pirate fleet in the Leeward Islands, commanded by Edward Teach, Blackbeard. The two pirates decided to join forces. Captain Hume of HMS *Scarborough* reported on "a Pyrate ship of 36 Guns and 250 men, and a Sloop of 10 Guns and 100 men."

### 1717, December 11. *Slavery. Politics.*

The Assembly passed an act that placed a 40 duty on all Negroes imported in Carolina. The act would take effect on June 8, 1718 and expire in four years.

### 1717, December 11. *Commerce. Shipbuilding.*

The Assembly offered tariff concessions for the building and owning of ships. However, the Proprietors blocked the concessions as being unfair against British shipping.

# 1718

### 1718. *Commerce. Exports.*

The Collector's office recorded 140 ships trading in Charles Town for the year, exporting the following products:

- 9106 barrels of rice at 350 pounds each (1600 tons)
- 55,938 barrels of pitch and tar
- 43 chests of deerskins
- Other products included beef, pork, butter, lumber, leather, corn and peas.

Charles Town merchants were repaid in flour, beer, cider, fish, rum, sugar, molasses and cotton.

### 1718. *Arrivals.*

Thomas Gadsden, a sailor in the British merchant fleet, settled in Charles Town permanently.

### 1718 January 5. *Piracy. The King's Pardon.*

A proclamation from King George I was issued announcing clemency for all piratical offences, provided for those surrendered by September 5, 1718. Colonial governors and deputy governors were authorized to grant the pardon.

### 1718, January 5. *Piracy. Stede Bonnet & Blackbeard.*

Stede Bonnet and Blackbeard spotted a sloop from Jamaica, *Adventure*, making for the harbor at Turneffe Island east of Belize. She was boarded and her captain, David Herriot, after seeing the amount of riches they had gathered, was easily convinced to join the pirates.

## EDWARD TEACH - BLACKBEARD

Traditional history tells us Edward Teach, Blackbeard, was born in Bristol, England. He arrived in Jamaica as a teenager and for the next several years served his pirate apprenticeship under Captain Benjamin Hornigold, who groomed the young man as his successor.

Hornigold and Blackbeard captured a 200-ton French slave ship, *Concorde*, a substantial windfall. Hornigold accepted the king's pardon for his crimes and retired to a quiet life. As a parting gift his presented his young protégé the slave ship, which Blackbeard renamed *Queen Anne's Revenge*.

During an eighteen-month period, 1717-18, Blackbeard terrorized the Atlantic coast from Honduras to Virginia, taking at least twenty prizes – more than one ship a month. He became the most feared pirate in the West Indies. Blackbeard's blockade of Charles Town in May 1718 was one of the most daring pirate raids in history.

Blackbeard had an arrangement with North Carolina governor Charles Eden. In exchange for a share of the pirate's booty, Eden would issue the pirates a pardon. Blackbeard, and other pirates, found a willing market for their plunder in North Carolina.

Blackbeard also discovered a perfect hideout off Ocracoke Island which he called "Teach's Hole. The Hole was in the midst of the Outer Banks a bewildering labyrinth of inlets, creeks and islands which served as a perfect hideout from authorities, to bury their treasure and refit their ships in privacy.

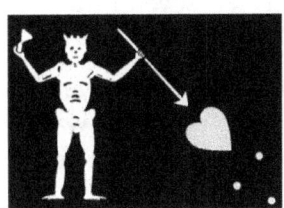

Blackbeard's "Jolly Roger"

At the time of this publication, there is an alternate theory by Kevin Dufus, who, in his book *The Last Days of Blackbeard*, claims Blackbeard was from Goose Creek, the son of Capt. James Beard.

### 1718, May 22. *BLACKBEARD BLOCKADES CHARLES TOWN.*

Blackbeard and Stede Bonnet's five ship fleet blockaded the Charles Town bar and captured the pilot boat. They quickly pillaged nine vessels, including the *Crowley*, which was headed for London. On board were several prominent citizens, including Samuel Wragg, a member of the Governor's Council and his four-year old son, William. With these hostages at his mercy, Blackbeard effectively held the city of Charles Town in his control for several days.

Blackbeard directed his ship's surgeon to compile a list of needed medicines for the fleet. He sent an armed boat commanded by a Mr. Richards into the city, along with a Mr. Marks, one of the captured citizens. Blackbeard demanded that within two days, Marks would convince Governor Johnson to meet the demand or the citizens would be hanged one by one from the bowsprit of the *Crowley*.

The deadline passed and Blackbeard sailed eight of his ships into the harbor, creating a panic among the citizens. Finally, in exchange for rations, money and medical supplies gathered from among the leading merchants, Governor Johnson was able to buy the release of the hostages. Blackbeard sailed unmolested out of the harbor with more than £1500 of gold and silver and made a beeline to his hideout on Ocracoke Island for Teach's Hole.

Stede Bonnet and David Herriot sailed to North Carolina and received a pardon from Governor Charles Eden. Bonnet then renamed the *Revenge* the *Royal James* and called himself Captain Thomas. They sailed to Delaware and plundered several vessels.

## 1718, June 5. PIRACY.

Governor Robert Johnson wrote to the Proprietors asking for help to protect their commerce:

> About fourteen days since, four sail appeared in sight of town, immediately took the pilot boat ... and in a few days took eight or nine outward-bound vessels ... Hardly a ship goes to sea but falls into the hands of the pirates.

## 1718, July 22. BLOODLESS REVOLUTION.

The Proprietors, with permission of the King, repealed the Assembly's ten per cent duty upon goods of British manufacture imported into the colony. They also repealed several other Acts passed by the Assembly, which inflamed the tension between the House and the Proprietors, including:

- The ten-year old power of the Assembly to nominate the Public Receiver was repealed.
- Act for Elections calling it "contrary to the laws and customs of Parliament and Great Britain we therefore do declare the ... Acts to be null and void ..."
- Yemassee Act for Settlement which provided 200 acres to each settler was repealed.
- Indian Trade Act was repealed since London merchants saw it as a monopoly.
- The Proprietors ordered the Governor to dissolve the Assembly.

Members of the Assembly were surprised and outraged, except for two, Nicholas Trott and William Rhett. It was discovered that Trott and Rhett had carried on a private correspondence with Mr. Shelton, the secretary of the Proprietors, encouraging the repeal of the Act for Elections, since it took control from their offices.

## 1718, August. PIRACY. STEDE BONNET.

Stede Bonnet sailed up the Cape Fear River, grounded his vessel and set the crew to overhauling and repairing the sloop.

### 1718, August. PIRACY. CHARLES VANE.

Charles Vane waited off the Carolina coast and took several ships leaving Charles Town, including the *Henry,* the *Neptune* and the *Emperor.*

In the first six months of 1718 Vane and his crew, led by first mate, Calico Jack Rackham, plundered more than two dozen ships, several off the Carolina coast. They fled north to the Outer Banks to hide. On Ocracoke Island Vane met up with Blackbeard and the two crews held the most infamous pirate party in history for two weeks, enjoying their spoils.

### 1718, September. PIRACY. RHETT OUTFITS SHIPS.

Charles Town had been thrown into terror at reports of pirate ships off the coast. Governor Johnson commissioned Colonel William Rhett to organize an expedition to protect Charles Town against Vane. Two sloops were pressed into service, the *Sea Nymph* (eight guns and seventy men) and the *Henry* (eight guns and sixty men.)

### 1718, September 15. PIRACY. RHETT SEARCHES FOR PIRATES.

Col. William Rhett's expedition left, searching for Charles Vane. Information indicated that the pirates had sailed up the Edisto River. However, the search was in vain. Rhett found no trace of the pirates and sailed north to Cape Fear to continue his patrol.

### 1718, September 27. PIRACY. RHETT ATTACKS BONNET.

In the late afternoon, Col. Rhett sailed up the Cape Fear River and spotted a suspicious ship named the *Royal James* floating at anchor. The vessel hurriedly tried to sail toward the open sea, but the *Henry* intervened and was able to maneuver the *Royal James* onto a shoal. In the process, both the *Henry* and *Sea Nymph* ran aground as well – all three ships were stuck and the tide was receding. The crews of all three vessels spent the overnight hours preparing for battle when the tide turned.

The *Henry* was within firing range of the *Royal James* and as the tide gradually came in, the ships fought fiercely for two hours, cannons booming and muskets blazing. Rhett's ships floated free first and they moved into position. The Charles Town men stormed the *Royal James* and overpowered the crew of thirty-five. On boarding the ship, Rhett discovered that Captain Thomas was none other than Stede Bonnet himself - wanted for the Blackbeard blockade four months before.

The Carolinians suffered eighteen dead and twenty-eight wounded. The pirates lost nine of their crew with two wounded.

### 1718, October 3. PIRACY. RHETT RETURNS VICTORIOUS.

Rhett triumphantly returned to Charles Town with two vessels captured by Bonnet, the *Fortune* and the *Francis*. He delivered Bonnet and his men to the Provost Marshal of Carolina, Capt. Nathaniel Partridge, who placed them in the watch-house at the Half Moon battery to await trial.

Stede Bonnet remained in the custody of Capt. Partridge at the latter's residence under armed guard. David Herriot and boatswain Ignatius Pell were also kept in Partridge's residence, as they had agreed to give evidence for the Crown.

## 1718, October 25. *Piracy. Bonnet Escapes.*

Some local merchants were nervous about Bonnet's testimony that may link them to the buccaneer's trade. Due to the lax security (and most likely a bribery of gold by merchant Richard Tookerman) at Capt. Partridge's home, Stede Bonnet and David Herriot escaped. Bonnet disguised himself as a woman to remain undetected.

Accompanied by a slave and an Indian, they stole a small boat and planned to leave the harbor under cover of night and rendezvous with Christopher Moody's ship, *Cape Fear*. However, foul winds and lack of supplies forced the four of them onto Sullivan's Island., where they cowered.

## 1718, October 31. *Piracy.*

Governor Robert Johnson wrote an account of the pirate episode to the Commissioners of trade. He expressed his apprehension that "the pirates who infest the coast in great numbers would be much irritated" at the actions of Col. Rhett. He again asked for a permanent vessel be sent for the protection of the Carolina coast.

> Almost immediately, word arrived that a pirate ship named *Cape Fear* captained by Christopher Moody, was off the bar with a vessel carrying fifty guns and 200 men. Moody was infamous for giving "no quarter" (sparing of lives). The news spread across the city like wildfire.

The Council approved Johnson's request to outfit four ships - the *Mediterranean* (twenty-four guns), the *King William* (thirty guns), the *Sea Nymph* (six guns) and, ironically, Stede Bonnet's former pirate vessel, the *Royal James*, was outfitted to hunt down pirates. The Council asked for volunteers, promising them a share of all the booty that might be taken.

Governor Johnson at once placed a £700 bounty on Bonnet's head and dispatched search teams to track him down, led by Col. Rhett.

## 1718, November. *Bloodless Revolution.*

Joseph Boone, representing the Assembly in London, had been encouraging the Board of Trade and Plantations to revoke the Proprietor's charter. The Proprietors argued that Mr. Boone represented only a small faction in the colony, not a majority of the people.

In response, Mr. Boone read an address signed by all members of the Assembly and by 568 citizens of Carolina more than half the male population. It read:

> We further take the liberty to inform your Majesty that notwithstanding all our miseries, the Lords Proprietors of the Province instead of using any endeavors for our relief and assistance are pleased to term all our endeavors to procure your Majesty's Royal protection the business of a faction or party. We most humbly assure your Majesty that 'tis so far from being anything of that nature that all the inhabitants of the Province (in general) are not only convinced that no human power but that of your Majesty can save them, but earnestly and fervently desire that this once flourishing Province may be added to those already under your happy protection.

To which the Board replied:

> Upon this occasion we cannot help repeating the advice which has frequently been given by the Board that the proper methods be taken for resuming of this and all other proprietary governments into the hands of his Majesty.

### 1718, November 4. *PIRACY. BONNET RE-CAPTURED.*

After getting reports of mysterious campfires on Sullivan's Island Rhett searched the western end and discovered Bonnet hiding. During the subsequent battle Herriot was killed and the two slaves wounded. Bonnet surrendered and was returned to Charleston, this time imprisoned in the watch-house.

That same night, Governor Johnson's fleet sailed out of the harbor to seek the pirate Christopher Moody, who had been spotted off the bar.

### 1718, November 5. *PIRACY. RICHARD WORLEY KILLED.*

That morning, off the Charles Town bar, Johnson's fleet was waylaid by a sloop, the *Eagle*, which raised the black flag and called on the ships to surrender. Johnson raised the King's standard, threw open his ports and delivered a broadside which swept the deck of the pirate ship. The Carolina crew swarmed the deck and took possession of the *Eagle*.

Johnson discovered the ship was not that of Christopher Moody, but the captain was Richard Worley, who had captured the *Eagle* in Virginia. Worley had been killed by the broadside, but his crew of twenty-four were arrested. The cargo included 106 convicts and covenant servants, thirty-six of whom were women, bound as settlers in Maryland.

### 1718, November 7. *PIRACY. EXECUTION.*

Stede Bonnet's crew was found guilty by Judge Trott. The twenty-nine men were hanged that day. Their bodies were dumped in the marsh beyond the low-water mark.

### 1718, November 8. *PIRACY. BONNET ARRAIGNED.*

Stede Bonnet was arraigned on two counts of piracy before Judge Trott.

### 1718, November 10. *PIRACY. BONNET SENTENCED.*

Judge Nicholas Trott sentenced Bonnet to death. Trott's long harangue during sentencing - quoting scripture and lecturing Bonnet on morality - probably felt like a death sentence to the pirate. Trott stated that Bonnet faced "not just physical death, but everlasting burning ... in fire and brimstone."

Bonnet was allowed an appeal, which he wrote to Governor Johnson.

### 1718, November 10. *PIRACY. EXECUTION.*

Twenty-four pirates, Richard Worley's crew, were put on trial. Five of the crew were acquitted, probably because they agreed to testify for the Crown. The other nineteen were found guilty, sentenced to death and hanged.

Colonel William Rhett (seated) and Stede Bonnet.
From *Howard Pyle's History of Pirates*

Stede Bonnet writing his appeal. Illustration from the 1902 novel, *Kate Bonnet: The Romance of a Pirate's Daughter*. *Courtesy of the Library of Congress*

## 1718, November 24. *PIRACY.*

Charles Vane ordered an attack on a frigate which turned out to be a French Navy warship. Out-gunned, Vane broke off the fight and fled. First mate Calico Jack Rackham called a vote in which the men branded Charles Vane a coward and removed him from authority, making Calico Jack the next captain.

## 1718, December 10. *PIRACY. EXECUTION. BONNET HANGED.*

Stede Bonnet, Gentleman Pirate, was hanged, supervised by Col. Rhett. He stood clutching a posey of wild flowers. He was "swung off" the cart and died "the agonizing death of strangulation."

During one month's time, the province of South Carolina executed forty-nine pirates, an unparalleled event.

Execution of Stede Bonnet.
*Author's collection*

# Stede Bonnet's Pitiful Appeal
## to Gov. Robert Johnson

Honoured Sir:

I have presumed on the Confidence of your eminent Goodness to throw myself, after this manner at your Feet, to implore you'll be graciously pleased to look upon me with the Tender Bowels of Pity and Compassion; and believe me to be the most miserable Man this Day breathing; That the tears proceeding from my most sorrowful soul may soften your heart and incline you to consider my Dismal State, wholly, I must confess, unprepared to receive so soon the Dreadful Execution you have been pleased to appoint me; and therefore beseech you to think of me an Object of your Mercy.

For God's Sake, good Sir, let the Oaths of three Christian Men weigh something with you, who are ready to depose, when you please allow them the Liberty, the Compulsion I lay under in committing those Acts for which I am doom'd to die.

I entreat you not to let me fall a Sacrifice to the Envy and ungodly Rage of some few Men, who, not being yet satisfied with Blood, feign to believe that I had the Happiness of a longer Life in this World, I should still employ it in a wicked Manner, which to remove that, and all other Doubts with your Honour, I heartily beseech you'll permit me to live, and I'll voluntarily put it ever out of my Power by separating all my Limbs from my Body, only reserving the use of my Tongue to call continually on, and pray to the Lord, my God and mourn my days in Sackcloth and Ashes to work out confident hopes of my Salvation, at that great and dreadful Day when all righteous Souls shall receive their just rewards. And to render to your Honour a further assurance of my being incapable to prejudice any of my fellow Christians, if I were so wickedly bent I humbly beg you will (as a Punishment of my Sins or my pour Soul's Sake) indent me as a menial Servant to your Honour, and this Government during my life, and send me up the fartherest inland Garrison or settlement in the County or in any other ways you'll be pleased to dispose of me.

Now the God of Peace that brought again from the Dead our Jesus Christ, that Great Shepherd of the Sheep, thro' the Blood of the everlasting Covenant make you perfect in every Good Work to do his Will, working in you, that which is well pleasing in his sight through Jesus Christ to whom be Glory for ever and ever is the hearty prayer of ...

Your Honour's Most Miserable and Afflicted Servant,

*Stede Bonnet*

# 1719

### 1719. *Marriage. Anne Cormac Marries James Bonney.*

Sometime during the year, the boisterous seventeen-year-old Anne Cormac married a sailor, James Bonny. Her father, convinced that Bonny was only after his daughter's considerable wealth, "turned her out of doors." The couple sailed for Nassau, Bahamas by the end of the year.

### 1719. *Arrivals.*

Also during the year, the Reverend Alexander Garden arrived in Charles Town as the Bishop of London's Commissary and became rector of St. Philip's Church.

Rev. Garden faced a monumental job, he was dismayed by the lack of intellectual curiosity among the Anglican elites. He noted that they were "absolutely above every occupation but eating, drinking, lolling, smoking and sleeping."

### 1719, February 27. *Politics.*

The Assembly passed an act providing funds to pay the debts incurred by Gov. Johnson and Col. Rhett their actions against the pirates.

### 1719, February 27. *Fortifications. Politics.*

The Assembly passed an act "for the more speedy putting the bastions of the Fortification of Charles Town in a posture of defence" by repairing the existing fortifications.

### 1719, March 20. *Bloodless Revolution. Politics.*

The Lords of Admiralty consented to send "a frigate as soon as possible." Governor Johnson had written a letter illustrating the Proprietor's inability to defend their territory and subsequently, their charter. .

The man-of-war *Flambourg*, under Captain Hildesly, arrived on duty in the harbor, while the *Phoenix* under Captain Pierce patrolled the coast for freebooters. Better late than never, the citizens felt.

### 1719, March 20. *Religion. Politics.*

The Assembly revised the election law, making a reapportionment of representation from thirty seats to thirty-six. The breakdown was:

- ✝ St. Philip's Parish (five members)
- ✝ Christ Church (two)
- ✝ St. Andrew's (four)
- ✝ St. John's (three)
- ✝ St George's – new parish (two)
- ✝ St. James (four)
- ✝ St. Thomas (three)
- ✝ St. Dennis (three)
- ✝ St Paul's (four)
- ✝ St. Bartholomew (three)
- ✝ St. Helena (three)

## 1719, May. *BLOODLESS REVOLUTION.*

Francis Yonge arrived in London to meet with the Proprietors. Yonge, a member of the Assembly, was sent to argue the Colony's case of grievances in person before the Lordships. He delivered a packet of letters written by Governor Johnson, Nicholas Trott and William Rhett. Yonge waited three months for a reply which never came.

## 1719, May. *PIRACY.*

Calico Jack Rackham and his men were granted the King's pardon by Bahamas Governor Woodes Rogers.

## 1719, September. *COMPLAINTS AGAINST TROTT.*

Francis Yonge returned to Charles Town never meeting with the Proprietors. Instead, after reading the letters from Governor Johnson, Nicholas Trott, and William Rhett. the Proprietors decided to accept Trott's version of events (after all, he was *their* man). They delivered a packet of letters to be returned to Carolina.

Yonge bitterly commented, "Thus, a whole province was to be governed by the caprice of one man."

## 1719, October 5. *FORTIFICATIONS.*

The first Royal Navy Station Ship, the *Flamborough,* arrived in Charles Town, commanded by Captain John Hildesley.

## 1719, November 17. *BLOODLESS REVOLUTION.*

The Land Grant office was closed by the Proprietors. New settlers were now unable to claim land, while established land owners were able to claim the best tracts, staking out 800,000 acres. The promised grants on the Yemassee lands to hundreds of settlers were ordered to be surveyed into 12,000 acre tracts for the Proprietors.

The leading citizens gathered in Charles Town to repair the fortifications of Charles Town, and formed an association to the following effect:

> That the Proprietors having pretended to repeal laws contrary to the charter and offered other hardships to the inhabitants of this country, they do resolve to choose an Assembly pursuant to the writs issued out and to support their represent-tatives with their lives, and fortunes, and to stand by such resolutions as they shall take at the next Assembly.

## 1719, December 10. *REVOLUTIONARY ASSEMBLY FORMED.*

Angry Carolinians met in Charles Town and formed a Revolutionary Assembly and elected Arthur Middleton as Speaker. The Assembly refused to recognize the Proprietors' vetoes and asked Governor Robert Johnson to:

> hold the reins of government for the King till his Majesty's pleasure be known, for the people are determined to get rid of the oppression and arbitrary dealings of the Lords Proprietors.

Governor Johnson refused the Assembly's request, supported the Proprietors and ordered the Assembly dissolved.

## 1719, December 21. *MILITIA CHALLENGES JOHNSON.*

Governor Johnson ordered a review of the militia, and upon arriving he found the militia already drawn at arms. Johnson ordered Colonel Parris "in the King's name disperse your men." Parris, in return, commanded his men to "present their muskets at him" [Johnson] and to "stand off at his peril."

## 1719, December 23. *PROPRIETORS OVERTHROWN.*

The Assembly pronounced it was convened as "a convention of the people," seeking to become a royal colony. It denounced the rule of the Lords Proprietors and officially petitioned King George I to purchase the Carolina colony from the Proprietors.

The Assembly voted unanimously for a new provisional government until his Majesty assumed control of the colony. The officers chosen were:

- James Moore, Jr., (son of former governor), Governor
- Richard Allein, Chief Justice (Trott was removed)
- Francis Yonge, Surveyor General of the Province
- William Rhett, Receiver of the Province
- Col. John Barnwell, Agent of the Province.

Col. Barnwell was ordered to England with instructions and a Declaration of Causes to present to the King which, in part, read:

> Whereas the Proprietors of this province of late assumed to themselves an arbitrary and illegal power of repealing such laws as the General Assembly of the settlement have thought fit ...and acted in many other things contrary to the laws of England and the charter to them and us freeman granted.

> Whereby we are deprived for those measures we have taken for the defence of the settlement, being the south west frontier of his Majesty's territories in America ...

> We therefore ... the Representatives and delegates of this Majesty's liege people and free born subjects of the said settlement now met in convention at Charles Town ... do hereby declare ... James Moore his Majesty's Governor of this settlement, invested with all the powers and authorities belonging and appertaining to any of his Majesty's governor in America till his Majesty's pleasure herein shall be further known.

For all practical purposes, the citizens of South Carolina had overthrown the Proprietary government, America's first Revolution. They had proven that, if need be, the citizens were willing to take matters into their own hands.

### 1719, December 30. *POLITICS. TROTT REMOVED.*

Governor Moore removed Nicholas Trott from the office of Chief Justice, and replaced him with Richard Allein.

### 1719, December 30. *POPULATION.*

During the Proprietary years, the population of Carolina grew from 200 to 16,460 (6460 whites; 10,000 Negro slaves). More than 1600 ships entered the port during the years 1707 – 1719.

## PROPRIETARY GOVERNORS OF CAROLINA
### 1670-1719

| | | |
|---|---|---|
| 1 | William Sayle | March 15, 1670 – March 4, 1671 |
| 2 | Joseph West | March 4, 1671 – April 19, 1672 |
| 3 | John Yeamans | April 19, 1672 – August 1674 |
| | Joseph West (2nd term) | August 13, 1674 – October 1682 |
| 4 | Joseph Morton | October 1682 – August 1684 |
| 5 | Richard Kyle | August 1684 |
| | Joseph West (3rd term) | August 1684 – July 1685 |
| 6 | Robert Quarry | July 1685 – October 1685 |
| | Joseph Morton (2nd term) | October 1685 – November 1686 |
| 7 | James Colleton | November 1686 – 1690 |
| 8 | Seth Sothell | 1690 – April 1692 |
| 9 | Philip Ludwell | April 11, 1692 – May 1693 |
| 10 | Thomas Smith | May 1693 – November 16, 1684 |
| 11 | Joseph Blake | November 1684 – August 17, 1695 |
| 12 | John Archdale | August 17, 1695 – October 29, 1696 |
| | Joseph Blake (2nd term) | October 29, 1696 – September 7, 1700 |
| 13 | James Moore | September 11, 1700 – March 1703 |
| 14 | Nathaniel Johnson | March 1703 – November 26, 1709 |
| 15 | Edward Tynte | November 26, 1709 – June 26, 1710 |
| 16 | Robert Gibbes | June 26, 1710 – March 19, 1712 |
| 17 | Charles Craven | March 19, 1712 – April 23, 1716 |
| 18 | Robert Daniell | April, 25, 1716 – 1717 |
| 19 | Robert Johnson | 1717 – December 21, 1719 |

# PART THREE:
## THE ROYAL CITY 1720-1770

"Carolina looks more like a Negro Country than like a Country settled by White People." – Samuel Dyssli

*AUTHOR'S NOTE: During this period the spelling of the town changed from Charles Town to Charlestown and will be reflected in the manuscript.*

# 1720

### 1720. BLOODLESS REVOLUTION.

Colonel John "Tuscarora Jack" Barnwell was sent to England to plead for the King to buy out the Proprietors.

### 1720. POPULATION.

Estimated population was 18,500. Twelve thousand were black.

### 1720. COMMERCE.

During the year "nearly 200 sail of all sorts" left Charlestown for other ports.

### 1720. SLAVERY.

The African population exploded during this period due to the demands for skilled labor for rice cultivation.

### 1720. BUILDINGS OF CHARLESTON.

Lt. Governor William Bull constructed his dwelling at 35 Meeting Street. It was also occupied by his son, William Bull II, who also later served as lt. governor. In the present-day it continues to be a private home.

### 1720. BUILDINGS OF CHARLESTON.

John Cock built the home at 71 Church Street on "Town Lott 57." The title transfer that year indicates it was acquired by merchant, Miles Brewton, Sr. and occupied by his son, Col. Robert Brewton after whom the house is still named.

It is thought to be the oldest surviving example of a "single house" in Charleston. Brewton was a wealthy merchant, wharf owner, militant officer and politician who served as the official powder receiver for Charles Town. In the present-day it continues to be a private home.

### 1720, January. BLOODLESS REVOLUTION.

Former Governor Robert Johnson set up a "government in exile" outside the city. He continued to probate wills and issue marriage licenses to Anglican clergy who supported the Proprietors. The Dissenting clergy who supported the Revolution used licenses signed by Governor Moore.

Johnson also encouraged Proprietary officials to ignore orders from Moore and the Assembly and withhold their taxes. The Assembly responded by arresting tax dodgers and firing officials who refused to obey their Acts. Twenty-eight men were ultimately arrested.

## 1720, February 20. POLITICS.

An act, the text of which has been lost, created the system of courts which lasted until the Revolution.

## 1720, May-June. SLAVERY.

"A wicked and barbarous plot" was uncovered which terrified the white population. A group of blacks outside the city were said to have plotted "to destroy all the white people in the Country and then take the town."

More than a dozen slaves were captured "and burnt ... hang'd and banished." The town watch was given more power to deal with blacks. A well-armed force of twenty-one men patrolled the streets nightly to "Quell any ... designs by Negroes."

## 1720, August 11. BLOODLESS REVOLUTION.

The Royal Privy Council commanded that:

> in consideration of the great importance of Carolina and the acute danger of its being lost at such a critical time, the government be provisionally taken into the hand of his Majesty.

Mary Read and Anne Bonny. From *a General History of the Robberies and Murders of the Most Notorious Pyrates* by General Charles Johnson.

## BUILDINGS OF CHARLESTON
### 35 MEETING STREET & 71 CHURCH STREET

William Bull, the first lieutenant governor of the Royal Colony of South Carolina built this house in 1720. It was later occupied by his son, William Bull II who also served as a lt. governor. The younger Bull was the first native South Carolinian to receive a medical degree.

William Bull House,
35 Meeting Street
*Photo by author*

Col. Robert Brewton was a merchant, powder receiver and politician, built this dwelling in 1720. It has long been cited as Charleston's oldest single house, but it may have been rebuilt after damage from the 1740 fire.

Robert Brewton House,
71 Church Street
*Courtesy of the Library of Congress*

## 1720, September 27. *POLITICS. FIRST ROYAL GOVERNOR.*

Sir Francis Nicholson was sworn in as the first Royal Governor of South Carolina. He had served as governor of Maryland, Virginia and Nova Scotia and helped found the College of William and Mary. He was a passionate supporter of the Anglican Church which made many of the Dissenters nervous. He was also instrumental in positive negotiations with the Cherokeenation but duplicitous in his dealing with the Creek nation. In a treaty he promised the English settlements would not extend west of the Savannah River.

Nicholson was notorious for his temper. He was "subject to fits of passion." In one story, an Indian said of Nicholson "The general is drunk." When informed that Nicholson did not partake of strong drink, the Indian replied, "I do not mean that he is drunk with rum, he was born drunk."

### 1720, October. *PIRACY. BONNNY CAPTURED.*

Anne Bonny, Mary Read and Jack Rackham were captured by British pirate hunter Jonathan Barnet while they were at anchor (and drunk) at Dry Harbour Bay in Jamaica.

### 1720, November 18. *PIRACY. EXECUTIONS.*

Jack Rackham and his male crew were hanged in Port Royal, Jamaica.

# 1721

### 1721. *SLAVERY.*

The Assembly passed an Act which merged the militia, the town watch and the slave patrols. The main duty of the militia became "supervision and control" of slaves.

### 1721. *POLITICS. COMMERCE.*

Act of 1721 made the courts the guardians of community morals with full power "to license all taverns, victualing houses, ale houses, punch houses and public inns." A £20 fine was levied on any tavern operating without license or:

> convicted of being disorderly, as entertaining of servants, Negroes, common drunkards, lewd and idle and disorderly persons, selling liquors on Sundays or times of Divine service.

### 1721, January 6. *BIRTH.*

Rawlins Lowndes was born in St. Kitts, son of Charles Lowndes, a sugar plantation owner, who became impoverished due to his pursuit of luxury. The family would move to Charlestown in 1730.

### 1721, April 12. *PIRACY. ANNE BONNY.*

Mary Read died in a Jamaican jail. Anne Bonny was freed after her father, William Cormac, bribed the Jamaican governor. She returned to Charlestown; she was nineteen years old.

# ANNE CORMAC BONNY
## History's Most Infamous Female Pirate

BORN: March 8, 1702, County Cork, Ireland
DIED: April 22, 1782, Charleston, South Carolina?

**1718.**

Seventeen-year old Anne Bonny arrived in Nassau with her husband, James, who became an agent for Governor Woodes Rogers turning in pirates for rewards. Disgusted by her husband's behavior Anne returned to her former life – hanging out in waterfront taverns with sailors and pirates. It was there that she met Calico Jack Rackham who recently had taken the King's pardon. They fell in love.

**1719**

Within a year, Jack Rackham returned to piracy with Anne Bonny by his side, disguised as man. She quickly earned the respect of the crew as one of the fiercest fighters on board. During battle, before she killed a man, Anne took great delight in exposing her breasts so his dying thought would be that he had been bested by a woman.

**1720**

Anne began spending a lot of time with a new crew member, Mark Read. Jack, being jealous, confronted them. Anne revealed that Mark was actually *Mary Read* who, like Anne, had been posing as a man on ships for several years. This odd trio continued to plunder ships together in Cuba and Jamaica.

**October 1720**

Rackham, Bonny and Read were captured in Jamaica off Negril Point. Rackham and the male crew members were hanged. Bonny and Read "pled their bellies" (pregnancy) and in accordance to English law, they were spared until they gave birth. Read, however, died in prison. Bonny's wealthy father, William Cormac, bribed the Jamaican governor and brought his daughter back to Charlestown.

**December 21, 1721**

Legend holds that Anne Bonny married Charlestown merchant William Burleigh and gave him ten children.

### 1721, May 22. POLITICS. FIRST ROYAL GOVERNOR ARRIVES.

General Sir Francis Nicholson arrived in Charlestown on the ship *Enterprise.*
Col. John Barnwell returned with the governor. He was commissioned as the commander of the southern forces and ordered to establish a fort on the Altamaha River, close to Florida.

### 1721, June. FORTIFICATIONS.

Rumors reached Governor Nicholson that the French were going to build an outpost between Charlestown and St. Augustine. He chose Colonel John Barnwell to construct Fort King George at the mouth of the Altamaha River (currently Brunswick, Georgia, hoping that would encourage English settlement of the region.

### 1721, September 19. POLITICS. PARISHES CREATED.

A new election law was passed, dividing the representation among parishes. It remained that was until the Revolutionary period.

### 1721, September 22. POLITICS. LEGAL.

A Court of Chancery was established.

### 1721, October. POLITICS. RHETT VERBALLY ATTACKED.

Governor Nicholson wrote to Charles de la Fay, secretary to the Lord Justices, calling Colonel Rhett "a haughty, proud, insolent fellow, and a cheating scoundrel."

### 1721, December. FORT KING GEORGE ESTABLISHED.

Close to present-day Darien, Georgia, Fort King George was the southern outpost of the British Empire in North America on the Altamaha River. A cypress blockhouse, barracks and palisaded earthen fort were constructed by Colonel John "Tuscarora Jack" Barnwell and manned by His Majesty's Independent Foot.

### 1721, December 21. PIRACY. MARRIAGE.

Anne Cormac Bonny married a successful Charlestown merchant, Joseph Burleigh. They had ten children.

# 1722

### 1722. SLAVERY.

The Negro Act passed by the Assembly stated that slave conspirators "found caching ammunition would be executed immediately" as an example. Anxiety among the white citizens over slave conspiracies was rampant, fed by reports from the West Indies and Caribbean Islands.
The duty on negroes imported from Africa was £10 per head, and £30 per head from other colonies.

## 1722. *ARRIVALS. RELIGION.*

A Moravian minister from Switzerland, Christian George arrived in Charlestown with his friend Peter Rombert The two men were followers of the gnostic mystic Jakob Böhme who, during the 1600s, wrote extensively about alchemy, astrology and religion. There were soon to create havoc in Charlestown.

## 1722. *POLITICS.*

Thomas Gadsden was appointed Collector of Customs, a post he held until his death in 1741.

## 1722, January. *POPULATION. POLITICS.*

Tax records indicate the population of Charles Town as 9,000 whites and 12,000 black slaves. It also showed that less than 6% of South Carolina was in private ownership – 1,163,817 acres. Each land owner paid a small duty (quitrent) to the British government.

Governor Nicholson wasted no time enforcing the Navigation Acts as a means to crack down on political opposition, sparking the animosity of Col. William Rhett.

## 1722, May 3. *ARRIVALS.*

Mark Catesby, the naturalist, landed in Charles Town. At the request of Sir Hans Sloane, founder of the British Museum, Catesby explored the Carolina backcountry and the Bahamas before returning to Europe.

## 1722, Summer. *PIRACY.*

The English pirate, George Lowther, appeared off the Carolina coast and attacked the merchant ship *Amy* as it left the harbor bound for England. Lowther's ship ran aground and his crew abandoned it and swam ashore.

## 1722, June 22. *POLITICS. CHARLESTON INCORPORATED.*

The city of Charlestown was incorporated by Governor Nicholson under an act titled "An Act for the Good Government of Charles Town."

The Act called for an "annual election of a Mayor on the King's birthday." The Mayor and Aldermen were to regulate "markets and fairs." William Gibbon was elected Mayor. The Act for "good government" was repealed a year later.

## 1722, December 28. *BIRTH.*

Elizabeth Lucas (known as "Eliza") was born in Antigua, West Indies at Cabbage Tree Plantation. It was customary for elite colonists to send boys back to England for their education. Her father, Lieut. Colonel George Lucas, recognized Eliza's intelligence and, against the custom of the time, sent her to boarding school in London at age eight. Her favorite subject was botany. She wrote to her father that she felt her "education, which I esteem more valuable fortune than any you could have given me, will make me happy through my future."

# 1723

## 1723. *RELIGION. POLITICS.*

Morovian minister Christian George and his friend Peter Rombert befriended the Dutartre family living in the Orange Quarter in St. Denis Parish (near present-day Huger, South Carolina. They began to teach the mystical writings of Bohme – that they were the only people on earth with knowledge of the true God.

Rombert, who married one of the widowed Dutartre daughters, began to have visions that the:

> wickedness of man is so great that, as in the day of Noah, God was determined to destroy all men from the face of it except one family, whom he would spare from which to raise a godly seed upon earth.

The Dutartre family fell completely under the spell of the George and the prophet Rombert. Rombert declared the family no longer needed to obey the laws of the colony – the laws of God trumped the laws of Man. They began stockpiling food and weapons and building a ten-foot high wall that encircled their plantation. They withdrew completely from public interactions of any kind.

## 1723, January 12. *WILLIAM RHETT DIES.*

Col. William Rhett died of apoplexy, ending the life of one of the most active and important early figures in Carolina history. He was described as:

> greedy, violent, vulgar, lawless, brave, impulsive, generous ... greedily violating law and propriety for bigger profits, insulting the noble and courteous Gov. Craven.

## 1722, February 15. *COMMERCE.*

The Assembly organized semi-annual fairs at Dorchester and St. Andrews following "the usage and customs of Fairs holden in ... England." This was an attempt to promote settlement and commerce in those two rural districts north of Charlestown.

## 1723, March 28. *RELIGION. POLITICS.*

On Easter Sunday, the congregation of St. Philip's worshipped for the first time in their new church. The structure was described as a:

> work of ... Magnitude Regularity Beauty ... not paralleled in his majesty's Dominions in America ... lofty arches and massive pillars, an octagonal tower topped by a dome and a quadrangular Lantern and weathervane soared eighty feet above the church.

The Assembly ordered that the "old church and churchyard (at the site of present-day St. Michael's) be given to the city for the "holding of their General Court and for public uses."

## Charleston Single House

The most distinctive house form associated with Charleston is the single house, so named due to its floor plan.

Traditionally a single house is a multi-story dwelling one room wide and three across including a central entrance and a stair hall. It is constructed with the narrow end to the street. The entrance is usually halfway down the length of the house which opens onto the stair hall. It typically (but not always) has a piazza along one of its longer sides, with a false privacy door opening onto the piazza.

The single house was Charleston's creative solution to the scarcity of space in the city, with the added convenience of helping to mitigate the heat and humidity.

Single house @ 69 Meeting Street
*Photo by the author.*

### 1723, May. *PIRACY.*

Edward Low captured several vessels coming out of Charles Town, cutting off the ears of one of the captains. He then left the area, but was later captured in Newport, Rhode Island and hanged.

### 1723, June 27. *ACT OF INCORPORATION REPEALED.*

By the order of the Lords Justices the "Act for the Good Government of Charles Town" was repealed.

### 1723, Fall. *RELIGION. CRIME.*

Peter Rombert, living with the Dutartre family, claimed he received a vision in which he said God commanded him to:

> Put away the woman whom thou hast for thy wife, and when I have destroyed this wicked generation I will raise up her first husband from the dead, and they shall be man and wife as before; and go thou and take as thy wife her youngest sister, who is a virgin; so shall the chosen family be restored entire and the holy seed preserved pure and undefiled.

Rombert convinced the family that he should sleep with each of the Dutartre women. If he failed to impregnate them, then each man in the family should lay with each woman to fulfill their ordained mission. Since God had commanded it, the act was not considered incest. Within several weeks, Judith Dutartre was pregnant – by

# 1724

## 1724. POPULATION.

Population of South Carolina was 46,000 - 14,000 whites, and 32,000 Negroes.

## 1724. SLAVERY.

During the year 439 African slaves were imported to Charlestown.

## 1724, February. RELIGION. CRIME.

The citizens of Charlestown learned of Judith Dutarte's pregnancy by an unidentified member of her family and:

> a warrant was issued for bringing her before the Justice to be examined, and bound over to the general sessions, in consequence of a law of the province, framed for preventing bastardy.

Captain Simmons and six men of the militia attempted to serve the warrant against the Dutartre family and Peter Rombert. Rombert told the family that:

> God commanded them to arm and defend themselves against persecution, and their substances against the robberies of ungodly men; assuring them at the same time that no weapon formed against them should prosper.

The family opened fire on the militia as it approached the compound. Simmons realized his small group had no chance of delivering the warrant and retreated back to town, where a plan was formulated to take the Dutartre's home by force.

Two days later, a militia of fifty men attacked the compound. Captain Simmons was killed and several other members were wounded. Within half an hour the militia had taken the property and:

> killed one woman within the house, and afterward forcibly entering it, took the rest prisoners, six in number and brought them to Charlestown.

The prisoners taken were:

- Peter Dutartre: father
- Peter Rombert: prophet
- Christian George: minister
- Michael Boneau
- Judith Dutartre: daughter
- David Dutartre: son
- John Dutartre: son

## 1724, February 16. *BIRTH*.

Christopher Gadsden, son of Customs Collector Thomas Gadsden, was born in Charlestown. Christopher would become one of the wealthiest and most powerful men in the city's history.

## 1724, March 6. *BIRTH*.

Henry Laurens was born in Charlestown, son of John Laurens, a French Huguenot, who owned the largest saddler business in the colonies. Young Henry became friends with Christopher Gadsden during childhood, creating an alliance between two of the most powerful men during the Revolution. Lauren's son-in-law, Dr. David Ramsay, later wrote that they were:

> Attached in their early youth to each other by the strongest ties of ardent friendship. They made a common cause to support and encourage each other in every virtuous pursuit, to shun every path of vice and folly, to leave company whenever it tended to licentiousness ... and acquired an energy of character which fitted them for acting a distinguished part in the trying scenes of a revolution ...

## 1724, June. *POLITICS*.

Gov. Nicholson wrote to the Board of Trade in London asking to be released from his position as governor.

## 1724, June. *ARRIVALS. GEORGE ANSON*.

George Anson, twenty-six-year-old captain of the H.M.S. *Scarborough* (his first important command), was sent on patrol duty at the Carolina Station. He soon became known for his social status. Mrs. Hutchinson of Charles Town wrote to her sister in London:

> Anson is not one of those handsome men ... but I think his person is what you would call agreeable ... good sense, good nature, is polite and well-bred ... is generous ... elegant without ostentation, and above all, of a most tender, humane disposition. He never dances, nor swears, nor talks nonsense. As he greatly admires a fine woman, so he is passionately fond of music. He loves his bottle ... so well, that they will not be very soon tired of their company ... that now and then his mistress may come in for a share of him.

He was to remain in Charlestown for eleven years.

St. Philip's Church, 1723. *Courtesy of the New York Public Library.*

## 1724, September. *EXECUTION*.

Peter Dutartre, Peter Rombert, Michael Boneau, and Christian George were convicted of murder. During the trial the men appeared unconcerned about their fate. Rombert claimed that if they were executed, like Jesus, they would be resurrected on the third day.

They were marched to the gallows near the public market (present-day Washington Park & City Hall) and hanged before a large crowd who jeered at them. The men responded they would see them soon. The bodies were left to dangle from the gallows for several days so the resurrection (or lack thereof) could be witnessed by the public.

They remained dead.

# 1725

## 1725. *COMMERCE*.

Margaret Kennett, possibly Charlestown's first business woman, ran a shop on the ground floor of her house on Bay Street. She described the citizens as being "Trained up in Luxury and are the Greatest Debauchers in Nature."

### 1725. *ARRIVALS.*

Robert Pringle arrived in Charlestown from Scotland. He became a successful merchant, selling dry goods and rice.

### 1725, January 20. *CULTURE.*

In a letter from Mrs. Margaret Kennett to Mrs. Thomas Brett, she described Charlestown as a city filled with houses of "Brick, Lime and Hair, and some very fine timber Houses ... glazed with Sash Windows after the English fashion."

### 1725, April 17. *COMMERCE.*

William Mellichamp was granted the rights to manufacture salt in South Carolina for fourteen years. The Act also granted a bounty of 12 pence be given him for every bushel of salt produced. Mellichamp was to certify under oath as to the number of bushels produced.

### 1725, May 7. *POLITICS. FIRST ROYAL GOVERNOR LEAVES.*

Gov. Nicholson returned to London, carrying with him Cherokee baskets that became part of the earliest collections in the British Museum. Arthur Middleton as president of the Council, assumed the administration of South Carolina.

# 1726

### 1726, February. *WEATHER.*

First recorded snowfall in Charlestown.

### 1726, March 11. *POLITICS. ENVIRONMENTAL FINES.*

The Assembly established fines for the obstruction of navigable rivers and streamed by "careless cutting of tress and for the pernicious practice of fishing by poisoning the creeks."

### 1726, March 26. *COMMERCE. ANSON BUYS LANDS.*

Capt. George Anson bought a tract of land which later would bear his name - Ansonborough. According to local legend, Anson won the entire tract in a single game of cards from Thomas Gadsden, King's Collector of Customs. In fact, Gadsden conveyed this tract to Capt. George Anson for £300 sterling. This was an unusually large sum for such a young naval officer to possess, so it is quite possible that Anson's winnings came from his prowess at cards.

### 1726, December. *POLITICS. FINANACIAL.*

The Assembly voted an addition £86,100 in bills, which agitated a group of citizens concerned about inflation.

| **Carolina Rice Exports** ||
| 1726 - 1762 ||
| 1726-27: 40,000 barrels of rice | 1755-56: 60,000 barrels |
| 1729-30: 41,957 barrels | 1757-58: 67,000 barrels |
| 1740-41: 80,000 barrels | 1760-61: 100,024 barrels |

# 1727

### 1727, January. *POLITICS.*

Thomas Smith, a leader in the Assembly organized an anti-tax association against the paper currency. Smith and other colonists were not happy about the amount of tax being charged by the colony to raise and maintain a ranger company. They believed the crown should be responsible for the protection of the colony. He declared:

> That now there was necessity for a bold stroke, and that some men (meaning Your Majesty's Council) must be put bodily in fear ... opponents were conspiring to deprive the people of their lands ... we are forced by grasping lawyers, base judges and extortionists ... to pay three or four times our debts because of the lack of law for the tender of produce.

### 1727, March. *ECONOMICS.*

An economic recession hit Carolina, due to the over-expansion of credit and excessive paper money.

### 1727, April. *POLITICS.*

Governor Middleton denounced the anti-tax meetings as "riotous assemblages to withdraw the people from obedience to the King" and he ordered the meetings ceased, or risk arrest. Thomas Smith led another protest on the street and was arrested and then released.

### 1727. May 5. *POLITICS. RIOTS*

Two hundred armed men rode into town and entered the Council Chamber to protest the excessive paper money. Governor Arthur Middleton called out the town militia only to watch most of them join the mob. When the Council refused to meet with them, Thomas Smith attempted to have himself declared President.

The crowd dispersed without any altercation.

## HENRY LAURENS
### Patriot & Merchant

**BORN:** March 6, 1724, Charlestown
**DIED:** December 8, 1792, Charleston

By the 1750s Laurens was one of the most successful merchants in the American col-onies. His shipping firm traded with all over the world from England to Jamaica, Barbados and France.

He was one of the largest slave merchants in America, handling more than 20% of the slave trade in Charlestown, the largest slave port in the colonies.

**March 1776**

South Carolina became an independent re-public and Laurens served as its Vice-President.

**January 10, 1777**

Laurens replaced John Hancock as president of the Continental Congress.

**1780**

As an envoy for the American government, Laurens was arrested off New-foundland by the British Navy and imprisoned in the Tower of London as a traitor.

**December 31, 1781**

Laurens was released from the Tower in exchange for General Lord Cornwallis. It has been estimated that Laurens lost more than £40,000 during the Revolution ($4 million).

## 1727, June 11. *POLITICS. CRIME.*

A warrant was issued for Thomas Smith. The town constable and a group of armed men surrounded his house and rushed into his chamber "greatly terrifying his wife, who was in delicate condition." He was arrested and charged with high treason. Smith was ultimately released and never put on trial.

# 1728

## 1728. *ARRIVALS.*

Dr. John Moultrie arrived in Charlestown from Scotland, establishing the Moultrie name in Carolina.

### 1728. *COMMERCE.*

John Schermmerhorn established a regular packet service between New York and Charlestown. This increased the amount of provisions from New York – flour, bread, corn, bacon and beer.

### 1728, February – March. *POLITICS. INDIAN AFFAIRS.*

Col. John Palmer led a force of 200 Carolinians on a successful attack on the Yemassee settlements near St. Augustine. This was important, as it impressed the other Indian tribes in the region of English strength.

### 1728, June. *POLITICS. SLAVERY.*

Acting governor Arthur Middleton formally complained to English authorities that the Spanish were "receiving and harbouring all our Runaway Negroes." He also accused them of supplying Indians "to Murder our White People, Rob our Plantations and carry off our slaves."

### 1728, Summer. *WEATHER. DROUGHT.*

Dr. Hewatt noted that a drought befell the area. The weather was:

> Uncommonly hot, by which the face of the earth was entirely parched, the pools of standing water dried up, and the beasts of the field reduced to the greatest distress.

### 1728, August 13. *DISASTER. HURRICANE.*

A "dreadful hurricane burst upon them in the end of August." Water overflowed the town and damaged the fortifications, houses wharves and fields. The streets were:

> Covered with boats, boards and staves, and the inhabitants were obliged to take refuge in the higher stories of their dwellings. Twenty-three ships were driven ashore ... damaged or dashed to pieces. The *Fox* and *Garland*, men-of-war stationed in Charlestown ... were the only ships that rode out the storm.

David Ramsay wrote:

> The waves roared over the town and the surrounding lowlands with disasterous consequences for fortifications, houses, wharves, shipping, and even corn fields. Twenty-three of the twenty-five ships in the harbor were either gravely damaged or dashed to pieces. As the streets filled with boats, boards, and staves, the inhabitants rushed to the relative safety of their roofs and upper stories.

### 1728, August 13. *RELIGION. SCANDAL.*

Reverend Garden had to deal with the issue of Rev. John Winteley who was dismissed from the pulpit as a "whore monger and drunkard" by the vestry of Christ Church (modern-day Mount Pleasant.)

Winteley moved to Charlestown and was seen in taverns and in the streets "much in liquor." He was also charged with making "lewd attempts" against six women.

### 1728, September – December. *EPIDEMIC.*

Yellow fever swept the area, killing "hundreds." "Multitudes" of people died, white and black. Backcountry farmers, fearful of infection, refused to bring fresh produce into town. It was noted that:

> there were scarcely to be found sufficient white persons to bury the dead, and so quick was the decomposition after death, so offensive and infectious were the corpses that even the nearest relations shrank from the duty.

# 1729

### 1729. *COMMERCE. SLAVERY.*

During this year, Charlestown imported more than 1,500 slaves and large quantities of British woolen, linens, hardware and glass. The city also exported:

- 32,384 barrels of rice
- 11,818 barrels of tar and pitch
- 1,913 barrels of turpentine
- 80,000 deerskins

### 1729. *COMMERCE.*

Solomon Legare purchased a small island contiguous to Folly Island. Today it still bears his name - Sol Legare Island.

### 1729. *FOUNDING OF GEORGETOWN.*

Elisha Screven laid out Georgetown at the head of Wynah Bay, near the mouths of the Peedee, Wacamaw, Black and Sampit Rivers.

### 1729, May 14. *BLOODLESS REVOLUTION.*

King George II bought out the Lords Proprietors, finalizing South Carolina transformation into a Royal Colony. The agreed payment was £2500 sterling ($250,000) and £5000 sterling to cover incidental expenses.

## 1729, July 12. *Naval. Piracy.*

The Spanish ship, *San Antonio*, was condemned by the Vice-Admiralty Court for non-compliance with the British Navigation Act. It was ordered that the ship be sold at auction and the proceeds be divided between the King, Acting Governor Middletonand Collector of Customs Thomas Gadsden.

## 1729, November 30. *St. Andrew's Society Organized.*

A number of gentlemen, "chiefly natives of Scotland," organized the St. Andrew's Society, the first such organization in the world. Named for the patron Saint of Scotland, its mission was to assist widows, orphans and others in need.

The hall that the Society built became part of the social life of high society Charleston. It was used for balls, banquets, concerts, and meetings of organizations like the South Carolina Jockey Club and the St. Cecilia Society.

### BUILDINGS OF CHARLESTON
### St. Andrew's Hall, 118 Broad Street

St. Andrew's Hall pictured here during the 1860 Democrat Convention. It was destroyed by the 1861 fire. *Courtesy of the Library of Congress*

# 1730

## 1730. *ARRIVALS.*

Twenty-two year-old Dr. John Lining, arrived from Lanarkshire, Scotland. He quickly became concerned with the epidemics of Charlestown which he claimed "came regularly at their stated seasons like a good Clock."

Charles Lowndes, impoverished sugar plantation owner from St. Kitts, moved to Charlestown with his family in the hope of reversing his fortunes.

Andrew Rutledge arrived from Ireland. He was trained as a lawyer at the Inns of Court in London.

Eleazar Phillips a bookseller, binder and printer arrived in Charlestown from Boston, the "first Printer to his Majesty" in Carolina.

## 1730. *POPULATION.*

The population of Carolina was approximately 30,000, with 15,000 being black.

### SOUTH CAROLINA CURRENCY
### Values 1710 - 1773

| DATE | S.C. CURRENCY | BRITISH STERLING |
|------|---------------|------------------|
| 1710 | 150 | 100 |
| 1714 | 200 | 100 |
| 1715 | 400 | 100 |
| 1717 | 575 | 100 |
| 1725 | 710 | 100 |
| 1735 | 750 | 100 |
| 1738 | 800 | 100 |
| 1749 | 725 | 100 |
| 1764 | 775 | 100 |
| 1773 | 762 | 100 |

## 1730, January 8. *BORDER OF NORTH AND SOUTH CAROLINA.*

An agreement between North and South Carolina Assemblies declared their border "to begin 30 miles southwest of the Cape Fear river, and to be run at that parallel distance the whole course of said river;" This was the beginning of an issue not officially settled until 1905.

## 1730, March 11. CAROLINA COLONY. SURVEYING.

Surveyor George Hunter began his journey northward along the Cherokee path from Charleston and eight days later he arrived at Saxe Gotha (present-day Columbia). According to Hunter's calculations it was 144 miles. Present-day mileage from Charleston to Columbia is 120 miles.

## 1730, August. SLAVERY.

Rumors of a slave insurrection spread throughout the white citizens. Black men in Charlestown were overheard talking about murdering white people and forcing young, white women for sexual partners. Dozens of suspects were arrested, tortured and those that appeared to be the instigators were executed.

## 1730, September 7. ENGLAND. COMMERCE. INDIAN AFFAIRS.

A treaty of friendship was signed in London between King George II and six Cherokee chiefs who had been had escorted to London.

## 1730, September 30. COMMERCE. NAVIGATION ACTS.

For almost thirty years, rice from Carolina could be imported *only* to Great Britain. Samuel Wragg, agent of the Provincial Assembly, persuaded Parliament to relax those restrictions. Rice could now be imported anywhere. Every white man in South Carolina believed that they had a chance of getting rich by growing rice, which created the largest rice boom in Carolina's history.

## 1730, October 20. RELIGION. FIRST CLERGY CONVENTION.

Rev. Alexander Gardner held the first convention of South Carolina clergy at Charlestown.

## 1730. November 23. BIRTH.

William Moultrie born in St. John's Berkeley Parish. He was the second son of Dr. John Moultrie and his wife, Lucretia Cooper.

## 1730, December 15. POLITICS. SECOND ROYAL GOVERNOR.

Robert Johnson who had served as the last Proprietary Governor, returned as South Carolina's the second Royal Governor of South Carolina. Also on board were the six Cherokee chiefs who had negotiated the treaty with King George II.

Johnson wasted little time in instituting his "township scheam," which established ten townships "along the outskirts of the coastal region" to be settled by "poor Protestants from Europe." The settlers would be given "King's land" and provisions.

# 1731

### 1731. *Georgetown Desginated "Port of Entry."*

King George II designated Georgetown as a "port of entry."

### 1731. *Commerce. Naval.*

During this year 107 ships left Charlestown loaded with marine stores.

### 1731. *Religion. First Scots Established.*

The Presbyterian Church was founded by twelve Scottish families who withdrew from the White Meeting House. The amicable division was over the issue of subscription to the Westminster Standards of the Church of Scotland (Presbyterian). The Scots wanted a "strict subscription" while the majority of the dissenters were "Non Subscribers."

### 1731, August 20. *Politics. Quitrent Act.*

In an attempt to establish an accurate land and rent roll, the Assembly passed the Quitrent Act. It voided all of the old Proprietary patents and ordered that, within eighteen months, these and all other land titles must be registered.

A law also established the South Carolina currency at a ratio of seven for one with sterling.

### 1731, September 1. *Commerce. Exports.*

Jean Pierre Purry wrote about South Carolina.

> The Trade of Carolina is now so considerable that of late years there has sail'd from thence Annually above 200 ships ... besides 3 ships of war ... which had above 100 Men on Board. It appears from March 1730 to March 1731 that there sail'd rom Charles Town 207 ships ... which carried ... 41,957 barrels of rice about 500 Pounds Weight per barrel ... besides a vast quantity of Indian corn, Pease, Beans, Beef, Pork and other salted Flesh ... There were between 5(00) to 600 houses in Charles Town ... most of which were very costly.

### 1731, September 10. *Arrivals. Printing.*

Benjamin Franklin sent one of his printers, Thomas Whitmarsh to Charlestown to open the *South-Carolina Gazette*.

### 1731, September 21. *Philadelphia.*

Lewis Timothy a Huguenot living in the Netherlands migrated to Philadelphia on the ship *Britannia of London* with his wife Elizabeth and four sons.

Timothy was fluent in German, French, Dutch and English. The month after arriving in Philadelphia, Timothy immediately advertised in Benjamin Franklin's *Pennsylvania Gazette* his intention to open a "Publick French School; he will also, if required, teach the said language to any young gentlemen or ladies, at their Lodgings."

Franklin, who had just sent Thomas Whitmarsh to Charlestown was in need of a new printer, and impressed with Timothy's language skills, hired him.

# 1732

### 1732, January 8. COMMERCE.

The *South Carolina Gazette* published its first edition under the editorship of Thomas Whitmarsh, under a franchise with Benjamin Franklin for "copartnership for the carrying on the business of printing in Charlestown." Franklin sent a printing press, and "400 weight of letters.'

The paper advertised it "contained the freshest Advices Foreign and Domestick."

### 1732, February 5. MEDICINE.

Mr. George Valentine, "surgeon of his Majesty's Ship the Fox," performed "tapping for the Dropsy … on Rich Evans, a Sailor of the said ship; there were ten Quarts of Water extracted and the Man is in a fair way of Recovery."

> Note: Dropsy was the medical term for modern day edema, an abnormal accumulation of fluid beneath the skin and in the cavities of the body which can cause severe pain.

### 1732, February 27. BIRTH.

Francis Marion was born in Berkeley County on his parent's plantation, Goatfield, about fourteen miles northeast of Goose Creek.

Upon his birth, Francis was described as "not larger than a New England lobster." His uncle gave Francis three slaves, "a man named June, his wife Chloe, and their son, Buddy." Buddy became Francis' childhood friend and later manservant.

### 1732, March 1. CULTURE.

The Queen's birthday was celebrated in the Council Chamber, a gathering of dignitaries, who "cheered a discharge of the great cannon in the Fort, a round of toasts and a sumptuous Entertainment."

### 1732, March 13. CULTURE. ENTERTAINMENTS.

An Assembly of Dancing and Cards, "for the Entertainment of Gentlemen and Ladies" opened at the apartment of Mr. Salter, organist.

## 1732, March 21. *BIRTH*.

William Drayton was born in Charlestown.

## 1732, Spring. *NAVAL*.

George Anson became captain of the *Squirrel* at the Carolina Station. It was a 26-gun, 377-ton ship.

## 1732, April. *PHILADELPHIA*.

Lewis Timothy unsuccessfully attempted to operate a German language newspaper, but remained employed by Benjamin Franklin.

## 1732, April. *CULTURE. ENTERTAINMENTS*.

Henry Campbell advertised a benefit concert of "vocal and instrumental musick," and "country dances for the diversion of the ladies."

## 1732, April 19. *CULTURE. FIRST ADVERTISED CONCERT*.

The notice for the first advertised concert in Charlestown appeared in the *Gazette* as a "consort [concert] of Musick at the Council Chamber, for the Benefit of Mr. Salter."

## 1732, June. *CRIME. NAVAL*.

The Vice-Admiralty Court issued a warrant against Captain Gordon of a merchant ship for a debt of £56. The marshal approached Gordon's ship at anchor and Gordon fired a shot near the marshal's boat. The marshal requested the *Squirrel's* assistance.

Captain George Anson sent a boat from the *Squirrel* and it was also fired upon. Captain Gordon was killed by musket fire from the *Squirrel's* boat.

## 1732, June 3. *CULTURE. INDIAN AFFAIRS*.

The Indian chieftains convened in Charlestown and were entertained in the Council Chamber and "introduced to some Ladies, who were in the Room adjoining."

## 1732, June 9. *ENGLAND. GEORGIA CHARTERED*.

King George II granted a charter "for establishing the colony of Georgia" in the territory west of the Savannah River.

## 1732, July. *EPIDEMIC*.

Another yellow fever outbreak crippled the town. Business came to a halt. Most of the wealthy fled to their plantations. There were so many funerals that Dr. Alexander Gardner prohibited the tolling of bells because it would have been "constant."

The death toll was more than "one hundred and thirty whites besides a great many slaves" – about 7% of the population, including Eleazar Phillips, printer.

### 1732, July 15. CULTURE.

William Brown put a notice in the *Gazette* offering instruction in "Dancing."

### 1732, October 27. ARRIVALS. SETTLEMENT OF WILLIAMSBURG.

A ship arrived from Belfast, Ireland with eighty-five passengers. This was the first contingent of "poor Protestants" to implement Governor Johnson's township plan. They journeyed north to the Black River to the new township named Williamsburg.

### 1732, November. ARRIVALS. SETTLEMENT OF PURRYSBURG.

During this month sixty-one Swiss Protestants arrived, followed by an additional ninety-one under the leadership of Jean Pierre Purry of Switzerland. They settled Purrysburg on the Savannah River.

### 1732, November 4. MEDICINE.

Dr. Varambaut, advertised that he "has a specifick Remedy for the Cure of all sorts of Fevers."

### 1732, November 30. CULTURE.

The St. Andrew's Club met for "a handsome Entertainment." It was their second anniversary celebration. In attendance was "his Excellency the Governor, Robert Wright, Esq.; Chief Justice … and about 40 members." It was announced that total subscriptions paid to the Club in two years was £700.

### 1732, December. SLAVERY.

Rumors of a slave uprising forced Governor Johnson to order out extra detachments of the militia to "ride about to keep the Negroes in due order."

### 1732, December. RELIGION. STREETS OF CHARLESTON.

By the end of the year, a new brick Independent meeting-house, sometimes called the "Brick Meeting House," was constructed on the site of the original. The new building was oblong, forty feet by sixty-two, with a tower added to the front (or west) end. It contained forty-seven pews.

Present-day Meeting Street was originally called Church Street (so-named for St. Philips Church). When St. Philips moved, the Church Street name followed to the new location and Church Street was renamed Meeting House Street.

### 1732, December. COMMERCE.

Rice was selling at 6 shillings sterling per 100 pounds.

# 1733

### 1733. *COMMERCE. TRADES.*

Samuel Holmes, possibly Charlestown's first architect, advertised that he specialized in "Brickwork and Plastering."

### 1733. *POPULATION. SLAVERY. MISCEGENATION.*

There was an estimated 22,000 Negroes living in South Carolina. Six years later that number would be doubled. Several years later, Reverend Henry Melchior Muhlenberg was surprised to discover that:

> the whites mix with the blacks ... and if a white man had a child by a black woman, nothing is done to him on account of it. One ... finds here many slaves who are only half black, the offspring of those white Sodomites who commit fornication with their black slave women.

### 1733, January 13. *ARRIVALS.*

James Oglethorpe and the first settlers for Georgia arrived on the *Anne*. The merchants of Charlestown were excited and supportive of the new Georgia colony. An English settlement between St. Augustine and Charlestown meant greater security against the Spanish.

The Assembly voted £2000 for the assistance of the Georgia effort.

### 1733, January 20. *GEORGIA COLONY.*

James Oglethorpe and Col. William Bull explored the territory around the Savannah River together, scouting for a good location for a permanent settlement. They decided on Yamacraw Bluff on the river, where Savannah sits today.

### 1733, February 12. *GEORGIA COLONY.*

General James Oglethorpe and his settlers landed at Yamacraw Bluff on the Savannah River.

### 1733, February 17. *CULTURE.*

The *Gazette* announced that:

> at the Council Chamber on Monday, the 26th, will be a Consort [concert] of vocal and instrumental music. Tickets to be had at Mr. Cook's and Mr. Sanreau's at 40s. None but English and Scotch songs.

### 1733, February 24. *COCKFIGHT.*

It was announced that "on Easter Monday, at the House of Mrs. Eldridge on the Green, there will be a Match of COCK-FIGHTING."

### 1733, March 10. *Culture. Drawing Lessons.*

Mrs. Peter Precour advertised her services in the *Gazette* for the instruction of drawing.

### 1733, April 23. *Culture. St. George Society.*

The St. George's Society was founded in honor of the patron saint of England at Mr. Thomas Batchellor's.

### 1733, May 19. *Culture. Education.*

Mr. John Miller advertised his teaching services in the *Gazette:*

> Arithmetick, Algebra, Geometry, Trigonometry, Surveying, Dialling, Navigation, Astronomy, Gauging, Fortification, *Stereographick,* and *Ortho-graphick Projection* of the *Sphere,* the Use of the *Globes*, and the *Italian Method* of Book Keeping.

### 1733, Summer. *Slavery. Execution.*

An ax-wielding slave murdered a white man and was "hung in chains at Hangman's Point opposite Charlestown in sight of all negroes passing and repassing by Water."

### 1733, June 2. *Culture. Commerce.*

An advertisement in the *Gazette* stated, "Young Ladies are to be taken to board by Mrs. Salter where they may also be taught Musick."

### 1733, Fall. *Spain. Slavery.*

The King of Spain issued a royal decree promising liberty to all slaves who desert the British colonies for St. Augustine.

### 1733, October 10. *Death.*

Thomas Whitmarsh died, which suspended the publication of the *Gazette*.

### 1733, November 16. *Philadelphia. Commerce.*

Upon learning the news of Thomas Whitmarsh's death, Lewis Timothy arranged with Benjamin Franklin to take over the publishing of the *South Carolina Gazette* weekly newspaper on a six-year franchise contract.

# 1734

### 1734, February 2. COMMERCE.

The *South Carolina Gazette* resumed publication under Lewis Timothy.

### 1734, February 2. CULTURE.

The *Gazette* advertised a horse race for a saddle and bridle, valued at £20 sterling – mile heats, four entries. Horses carried ten stone (a stone = 14 lbs) and the riders must be white. The race took place on a track in the Charlestown Neck, across from the Bowling Green Public House.

### 1734, February 2. COMMERCE. TRADES.

Samuel Holmes advertised his skills as a "Bricklayer ... draws Draughts of Houses, and measures and values all sorts of Workmanship in houses or Buildings."

### 1734, March 3. CULTURE. SHEPHEARD'S TAVERN LONG ROOM.

Charles Shepheard fitted out an upstairs room in his tavern on Broad Street for use as a public assembly room, which commonly was called the "Long Room." The first group to rent the room was the St. George's Society, which included Charles Pinckney, Speaker of the Commons House.

### 1734, April. STREETS OF CHARLESTON.

The name of Dock Street was changed to Queen Street.

### 1734, May 8. CULTURE. POETRY.

In a letter to the *Gazette*, a writer commented on an affair between an elderly gentleman and a young lady with a poem:

> In this our Town I've heard some Youngsters say
> That cold December does make Love to May
> This may be true, that warm'd by youthful charms
> He thinks of Spring, when melting in her arms
> As trees, when crown'd with blossoms white as snow
> May feel the heat, and yet no life below

### 1734, May 24. RELIGION. FIRST LUTHERAN SERVICE.

The first Lutheran Holy Communion was held by Rev. John Martin Bolzius.

### 1734, June 1. CULTURE.

A billiard table was advertised for sale at Ashley Ferry in the *Gazette*.

### 1734, June 23. RELIGION. FIRST SCOTS.

First service was held at the Scots Meeting House at 53 Meeting Street. It was a simple frame structure, southeast of the present-day First Scots Presbyterian Church building.

### 1734, July 5. RELIGION.

The vestry of St. Philip's Church signed a tax-list for £1000, authorized to use for the relief and maintenance of the poor.

### 1734, September 28. COMMERCE.

Benjamin Whitaker, member of the Commons House (and later Chief Justice) advertised in the *Gazette:*

> a corner lott in Charles-Town containing the Front on the Church-street one hundred and fourteen feet and on the Dock Street one hundred and nineteen feet. ...

> *Note: The advertisement used "Dock" street, even the name of the street had officially been changed to "Queen" earlier in the year. Locals, however, still called it "Dock Street."*

### 1734, November. POLITICS.

The Commons House of Assembly convened in the "Long Room" of Charles Shepheard's Tavern, paying £100 a year in rent.

### 1734, November 9. CULTURE.

Henry Holt, a recent arrival to Charles Town, advertised in the *Gazette* for dancing students:

> Henry Holt is ... sufficiently qualified to teach, having served his Time under Mr. Essex, Junior, the most celebrated Master in England, and danced a considerable Time at both Play Houses ...

### 1734, December 5. COMMERCE.

Benjamin Whitaker leased three-quarters of his corner lot on Queen/Church streets, to Thomas Monck. The empty quarter was donated by Whitaker to the city.

# 1735

### 1735. COMMERCE.

Statistics for the year.

- 600 homes in Charlestown
- 248 ships

- 52,349 barrels of rice exported
- 2,907 Negroes imported
- 11,333 gallons of rum imported

Sixty-eight Charleston merchants imported rum during the year, but eleven of them brought in seventy per cent of it.

## 1735. *SLAVERY.*

The most profitable commodity was African slaves to work the rice fields, construct the casks and barrels, and build and maintain the boats that transported the rice down river from plantation to port. The Carolina planters' appetite for new slaves was so strong that one merchant wrote that "Negroes are the proper bait for Catching a Carolina Planter, as certain as Beef to catch a Shark."

## 1735. *ARRIVALS. MARRIAGE.*

Dr. John Rutledge, brother of Andrew, arrived in Charlestown from Ireland.

Andrew Rutledge married Sarah Hext widow of Hugh Hext, one of the richest men in South Carolina. Hext left Sarah a plantation in Christ Church on the Wando Neck and twenty-three slaves. His other holdings were left as a legacy for his eight-year daughter, Sarah, to inherit when she turned twenty-one or upon her marriage, whichever came first. They included: two houses in Charlestown, a 550-acre plantation at Stono and a 640-acre plantation at St. Helena.

## 1735. *DEATH.*

Benjamin M'Arion died. He left eleven children, including a son named Francis. His estate, valued at £6,800 sterling, included "thirty-two slaves, forty-six cattle, sixty-four sheep, horses, hogs, pewter and chinaware …"

## 1735, January 4. *COMMERCE. TRADES.*

Peter Chassereau advertised that he "draws Plans and Elevations of all kind of Buildings whatsoever, both civil and Military" and "sets out ground for Gardens and Parks, in a grand and rural manner."

## 1735, January 24. *CULTURE. THEATER.*

The first record of a theatrical season in Charlestown began with the show *The Orphan, or the Unhappy Marriage* by Thomas Otway. It was performed in the long room of Shepheard's Tavern, which stood on the corner of Church and Broad Street. Tickets cost 40 shillings.

The announcement in the *Gazette* read:

> On Friday the 24th inst. In the Courtroom will be attempted a tragedy, called *The Orphan or The Unhappy Mariage*.[sic]. Tickets will be deliver'd out on Tuesday next at Mr. Shepherd's at 40s each.

### 1735. February. *CULTURE. THEATER.*

Construction of a theater began on the empty quarter-lot at Queen and Church Streets, donated by Charles Whitaker.

### 1735. February. *CULTURE.*

The *Gazette* advertised a "race for owners of fine horses" at the Quarter House, six miles from Charlestown. Prize was £100. The track was named the York Course, after the famous course in England. This begun an annual "race season" in February and March at various tracks in Charlestown for the next 150+ years.

### 1735, February 1. *CULTURE. THEATER.*

There was a third performance of *The Orphan* at Shepheard's Tavern. It was followed by an afterpiece, "a new Pantomimic Entertainment in Grotesque Characters, called, *The Adventures of Harlequin and Scaramouch, with the Burgomaster Trick'd*" performed by Henry Holt.

### 1735, February 18. *CHARLESTON FIRST. CULTURE.*

The first public presentation of an opera in the colonies was performed at Shepheard's Tavern. The opera was titled *Flora, or Hob In The Well*. Local musicians provided the musical accompaniment on organ and fiddle.

### 1735, March 17. *DEPARTURE. GEORGE ANSON.*

Captain George Anson left Charlestown for the last time, escorting a convoy of seven merchant ships. His career progressed to great glory, circumnavigating the world in 1740-44. He is also credited for being the officer to document that citrus fruits prevented scurvy. He later became fleet commander for the Royal Navy, made a peer and First Lord of the Admiralty.

### 1735, March 22. *CULTURE. THEATER.*

There were two performances of a comedy, John Dryden's *The Spanish Fryar, or the Double Discovery*, closing the first theater season in the American colonies. During the season there had been:

- Four performances of *the Orphan*
- A performance of the opera, *Flora*
- Two performances of *The Spanish Fryar*
- Two performances of the pantomime *The Adventures of Harlequin and Scaramouch*
- A performance of the *Dance of the Two Pierrots*.

The success of this season created a desire among the Charlestonians to establish a permanent theatrical institution.

> ## CHARLESTON FIRST
>
> **1735, FEBRUARY 18.**
> **FIRST OPERA PERFORMED IN THE AMERICAN COLONIES.**
>
> The ballad opera, *Flora, or Hob in the Well*, was performed at Shepheard's Tavern on Broad Street. Local musicians provided accompaniment and sang. The performance was so successful it convinced the city to construct the Dock Street Theatre where *Flora* again performed to great success. The play is often credited to Colley Cibber, an English actor, playwright and poet laureate. The truth, however is more involved.
>
> The comic character, Hob, the farm boy, was first created by Restoration comedian, Thomas Doggett for his five-act comedy *The Country Wake* in 1696. Hob was reborn in a condensed version called *Hob, or the Country-wake* in 1720. Nine years later John Hippisley reworked the piece as a ballad opera now re-titled after the heroine, *Flora or Hob in the Well*.

## 1735, May. *ANSONBOROUGH.*

Captain George Anson recorded the deed to his property, Ansonsborough.

## 1735, May 3. *DEATH. NEW GOVERNOR.*

Governor Robert Johnson died. Lt. Governor Thomas Broughton, Johnson's brother-in-law, assumed the office of governor.

## 1735, May 24. *CULTURE. THEATER.*

Charles Shepheard advertised in the *Gazette* for performers.

> Any Gentlemen that are disposed to encourage the exhibiting of Plays next winter, may have a sight of the proposals for a Subscription at Mr. Shepherd's in Broad Street. And any persons that are desirous of having a share in the Performance thereof, upon application to Mr. Shepherd shall receive a satisfactory answer.

## 1735, July. *ARRIVALS. SETTLEMENT OF ORANGEBURG.*

The *Gazette* announced the arrival of 450 Swiss who planned to settle a township on the North Edisto River to be called Orangeburg. Half of the immigrants were "redemptioners," indentured servants who had to "bind themselves out for two to four years in order to compensate for their Passage."

The other half had:

> Paid all for their Passages, are now going to Edisto ... The Government ... provides them with provisions for one Year, and gives them 50 Acres a head.

### 1735, August 11. RELIGION. BAPTISM.

Abraham, a Negro man owned by Mr. Samuel Jones, was baptized by Rev. Nathan Bassett of the Independent Church.

### 1735, October 14. RELIGION. WESLEY BROTHERS TO GEORGIA.

At the request of James Oglethorpe and through the offices of the Society for the Propagation of the Gospel, John Wesley and his brother Charles sailed from Kent, England on the *Simmonds* to Savannah, as minister to the new settlers.

### 1735, November 15. CULTURE. ENTERTAINMENTS

A ball was held in Shepheard's "Court-Room precisely at 5 o'clock. No Person to be admitted but by printed ticket."

### 1735, December 27. CULTURE. FRIENDLY SOCIETY.

The *Gazette* announced:

> Articles of Agreement ... We do covenant, promise, conclude and agree, That we will form ourselves (as far as by Law we may) into a Society for the mutual Insurance of our respective messuages [sic] ... and do name and call ourselves the FRIENDLY SOCIETY.

# 1736

### 1736, January 10. POLITICS.

The Commons House assembled for their session.

### 1736, January 31. CULTURE. THEATER.

The *Gazette* announced:

> On Thursday the 12th of February, will be open'd the New Theatre in Dock Street, in which will be perform'd the COMEDY call'd *The Recruiting Officer*. Tickets for the Pitt and Boxes will be delivered at Mr. Charles Shepherd's on Thursday the 5th Febr. Boxes 30s [shillings] Pit 20s and Tickets for the Gallery 15s which will be deliver'd at the Theatre the Day of Playing.

### 1736, February 3. CULTURE. CHARLESTON FIRST.

Local citizens found it nearly impossible to obtain fire insurance from English firms. This led to the establishment of America's first fire insurance company - the Friendly Society for the Mutual Insurance of Houses Against Fire, started by Charles and William Pinckney.

## CHARLESTON FIRST

**1736, FEBRUARY 3.**
**FIRST FIRE INSURANCE COMPANY IN AMERICA.**

The "Friendly Society for the Mutual Insuring of Houses Against Fire was organized in Charlestown. Four years later, the devastating 1740 fire burned over 300 buildings and bankrupted the company.

At one point Charlestown had more than a dozen fire companies that issued metal markers to policyholders to signify the property was insured against fire. In the present-day, most of the markers displayed on Charleston buildings are replications.

Fire markers on Charleston buildings. *Photos by author.*

## 1736, February 3. *CULTURE. COMMERCE.*

Lewis Timothy published Nicholas Trott's two-volume work *The Laws of the Province of South Carolina.*

## 1736, February 9. *CULTURE. HORSE RACING.*

A horse race was announced, the first prize was "a fine large Pacing Horse with Saddle and Bridle."

## 1736, February 12. *CULTURE. THEATER.*

The New Theatre on Dock Street opened with a performance of *The Recruiting Officer*. The "Doors will be open'd all the afternoon."

## CHARLESTON FIRST

**1736, FEBRUARY 12.**
**FIRST THEATER IN AMERICA.**

Sitting on the corner of Church and Dock (now Queen) Streets, the Dock Street Theatre was the first building in America constructed for theatrical performances.

The Dock Street opened with a performance of *The Recruiting Officer*, a 1706 comedic play by Irish writer George Farquhar. The second work performed was the ballad opera *Flora, or Hob in the Well*, after its successful performance the year before at Shepheard's Tavern.

Dock Street Theater. *Author's collection*

### 1736, February 16. *CULTURE. THEATER*

The tragedy, *The Orphan, or the Unhappy Marriage*, was performed at the Dock Street Theater on Queen Street.

### 1736, February 24. *CULTURE. THEATER.*

*The Recruiting Officer* was performed "By the desire of the Troop and Foot-Companies At the New Theatre [Dock Street]."

### 1736, March 1. *CULTURE*.

The Welch [Welsh] Club met to honor St. David (the patron saint of Wales) and fired several guns after Sun-set, which was "contrary to the Act of General Assembly." They were fined £10, to be paid to the Poor.

### 1736, March 2. *CULTURE. THEATER*.

*The London Merchant* opened at the Dock Street Theatre, with a rise in the cost of ticket prices - pit and box tickets were 25s.

### 1736, April. *PACHELBEL ARRIVES*.

Charles Theodore Pachelbel (baptized Karl Theodorus) arrived in Charlestown. Born in Germany in 1690, he was the son of the famous Johann Pachelbel, composer of the popular *Canon in D.*

Pachelbel initially migrated to Providence, Rhode Island to install an organ in Trinity Church in 1733. Three years later he arrived in Charlestown and stayed until his death.

### 1736, April 23. *CULTURE. CULINARY*.

An advertisement invited citizens to "the Sign of the SUGAR-LOAF ... to come and partake of the largest Plum Pudding (*gratis*) that was ever made in this country."

### 1736, May 8. *CULTURE. COMMERCE*.

The Dock Street Theater was put up for auction, "To be Sold to the best Bidder." There is evidence it was purchased by Giles Holliday, a dry-goods owner on Broad Street. Upon his death the theater was left to his widow.

### 1736, May 15. *COMMERCE. FIRST PAPER MONEY*.

Joseph Massey advertised that he was "the first that engraved and printed the Paper Currency of this Province."

### 1736, May 22. *DEATH. SUICIDE*.

Charles Lowndes committed suicide with his pistol in his jail cell.

After arriving in Charlestown with his family from St. Kitts, escaping debts due to his extravagant lifestyle, he purchased 500 acres and a house in Goose Creek and jumped into the rice business. Within two years Lowndes "owned" 1000 acres, thirty-eight slaves, everything heavily mortgaged to Charleston merchants to support his luxury. When it was discovered he could not pay his debts and was ruined, his wife left him. Lowndes refused to pay her maintenance and was arrested. In jail he was allowed a change of clothes and his pistol, as a gentleman.

On Saturday morning, May 22, he dressed and shot himself. Provost Marshall Robert Hall became the legal guardian of Lowndes's fourteen-year old son, Rawlins.

### 1736, May 28. COMMERCE. CULTURE.

An advertisement by "M. Harward" in the *Gazette* announced, "young ladies may be boarded, taught to read, embroider, and flourish, as also all sorts of Needlework."

### 1736, May 29. COMMERCE.

The Assembly offered a bound of £4 for each "hundredweight of water-rotted, well-cured, and clean dressed hemp." They also offered 50s for each hundredweight of flax and 20s for each pound of silk "fit for the foreign market."

### 1736, July 31. RELIGION. WESLEYS ARRIVE.

John and Charles Wesley arrived from Savannah where they had been serving as missionaries. Charles was returning to England due to ill health.

### 1736, August 1. WESLEY PREACHES AT ST. PHILIP'S.

John Wesley, at the request of Reverend Alexander Garden, preached the Sunday sermon at St. Philip's Church with:

> about three hundred present for Morning Service ... about fifty for the holy communion. I was glad to see several Negroes at church; one of whom told me, she was there constantly; and that her old mistress (now dead) had many times instructed her in the Christian religion.

### 1736, August 16. RELIGION.

Charles Wesley sailed back to England. John Wesley returned to Savannah to continue his ministry.

### 1736, September 6. DEATH.

Arthur Middleton, President of the Council, died.

### 1736, October 28. CULTURE. FREEMASONRY.

First Masonic Lodge in Charlestown was organized under a warrant issued by Lord Weymouth of England, Grand Master of the Ancient and Honorable Society of Free and Accepted Masons. An announcement in the *Gazette* said:

> Last night a Lodge of the Ancient and Honorable Society of Free and Accepted Masons was held, for the first time, at Mr. Charles Shepheard's, in Broad Street, when John Hammerton, Esq., Secretary and Receiver General for this Province was unanimously chosen Master, who was pleased to appoint Mr. Thomas Denne, Senior Warden, Mr. Tho. Harbin, Junior Warden, and Mr. James Gordon, Secretary.

### 1736, October 30. CULTURE.

Henry Makeroth and John Keen advertised in the *Gazette* to teach students "to blow the French Horn."

### 1736, November 11. CULTURE. THEATER.

Joseph Addison's tragedy, *Cato*, was performed at the Dock Street Theatre, kicking off the new season.

### 1736, December 11. COMMERCE. TRADES.

David Murry advertised in the *Gazette*, "Letters to be cut on Tomb stones, or Chumney pieces to be cut and laid of Marble or Free stone."

### 1736, December 30. RELIGION. BAPTISM.

Peter, an adult Negro man, was baptized by Rev. Nathan Bassett of the Independent Church.

# 1737

### 1737. CAROLINA COLONY. BOUNDARY COMMISSION.

The Boundary Commission completed the survey of the boundary between North and South Carolina.

### 1737, January 29, CULTURE. SCANDAL.

It was not unusual for husbands to place notices in the *Gazette* announcing their wayward wives, as a means of shaming them to society. However, Issac Simmons the following announcement was placed in the *Gazette* about a wife lured by the theater life:.

> This is to give notice to all people in Charles-town or elsewhere, not to credit harbor nor entertain Mary Simmons, the wife of Issac Simmons, which has made an elopement from her said husband especially to be employed in the Playhouse in Charles-Town, it being entirely against the said Mr. Simmons' request.

### 1737, February 16. MARRIAGE.

Charles Theodore Pachelbel married Hanna Poitevin in St. Philip's Church.

### 1737, March. SLAVERY. CURFEW ACT.

A Curfew Act was enacted for blacks. Any blacks who appeared on the street after sundown without a lantern and written permission from their master, could be apprehended by any white and taken to the Watch House overnight. They would be whipped in the morning and their owners could claim them after paying a fine.

## 1737, March 26. *CRIME*.

Alexander Forbes was convicted of "stealing Cloathes and other things." He was sentenced to "be whipped on the bare back at the cart's tails through the town."

## 1737, March 28. *CULTURE. AMICABLE SOCIETY*.

Members of the Amicable Society met for their "annual Feasts, in order to chuse [sic] new Stewards."

## 1737, April 2. *SLAVE POPULATION FEARS*.

The disproportionate numbers of Negro slaves versus white settlers began to concern some citizens. In a letter to the *South Carolina Gazette* a writer named "Mercator" argued about the danger of the "importation of Negroes." He argued that in the four years past there had been imported 10,447 Negroes and in the four years before only 5,153. He suggested that some method to prevent the large importation of Negroes must be speedily adopted or else there would be "the most fatal consequence to the province."

## 1737, April 14. *RELIGION. CHARLESTON FIRST*.

John Wesley returned from Savannah for a second visit to Charlestown. He noted in his diary:

> I had the pleasure of meeting with the clergy of South Carolina among whom in the afternoon there was such a conversation for several hours on 'Christ our Righteousness' as I had not heard at any visitation in England or hardly any other occasion.

During Wesley's visit he arranged with Lewis Timothy to publish the *Collection of Psalms and Hymns*, the first Anglican hymnbook published in the colonies.

## 1737, May 3. *CULTURE*.

A fair was held at the Ashley Ferry. Events included "a Race for a Saddle value 20£" and a ball was held in the evening.

## 1737, May 18. *CULTURE. THEATER SCANDAL*.

Henry Holt conducted his final ball at the New Theatre and moved to New York, with a Mrs. Simmons, the runaway wife, as a performer. *(See entry for Jan. 29, 1737)*

## 1737, May 28. *CULTURE. THEATER*.

The theater season closed with a performance of *The Recruiting Officer* for "the Entertainment of the ancient and honourable Society of Free and Accepted Masons who came to the Play-house about 7 o'clock." This was the last theater season in Charles Town for fourteen years.

## 1737, September 1. *BIRTHS*.

Rebecca Brewton, daughter of Robert Brewton, was born at her father's house, 21 Church Street.

## CHARLESTON FIRST

**1737, APRIL.**
**FIRST ANGLICAN HYMNBOOK PUBLISHED IN AMERICA**

John Wesley serving as an Anglican minister in Georgia visited Charlestown and arranged with Lewis Timothy to publish the *Collection of Psalms and Hymns*.

Author's Collection

Marker at 97 King Street.
Photo by Author

## 1737, September 1. *SOUTH CAROLINA SOCIETY ESTABLISHED.*

The South Carolina Society was established. Originally called the "Two-Bitt Club," it was organized by French Huguenot artisans and forbade the use of English in the beginning. Their goal was to support Scottish indigent and widows and orphans. The met at Jacob Woolford's Broad Street Tavern or at Poinsett's Tavern on Elliott Street, opposite Bedon's Alley.

## 1737, September 1. *CULTURE.*

The *South Carolina Gazette* wrote:

> If any gentlemen living in the Country are disposed to send their children to Charlestown, they may be boarded with George Logan, who also intends to open his School to teach to dance, next Monday being the 19th Instant. He will likewise go into the Country if he meets with Encouragement. Any white Person that plays on the Violin or a Negro may be employ'd by the said Logan living in Union [State] Street.

### 1737, November 22. *CULTURE.*

On St. Cecilia's Day (patroness of musicians) a concert of vocal and instrumental music was performed at the Dock Street Theatre. Organized by Pachelbel, this concert most likely led to the founding of the St. Cecilia Society in 1762.

### 1737, November 22. *DEATH.*

Lt. Governor Broughton died. William Bull, as President of the Council, assumed the role of Lt. Governor.

### 1737, December 3. *ARRIVALS.*

Samuel Dyssli, an immigrant from Switzerland wrote to his family and declared:

> I am over here, thank God, hale and hearty, and doing at present quite nicely. I am working with an English master. He gives me every week …. 50 shillings and … plentiful … food and drink. Carolina looks more like a Negro Country than like a country settled by white people.

### 1737, December 24. *RELIGION. WESLEY RETURNS TO ENGLAND.*

John Wesley left Charlestown for England, ending his ministry in Georgia.

---

**CHARLESTON FIRST**

1737
FIRST SCIENTIFIC WEATHER OBSERVATIONS IN AMERICA.

Dr. John Lining of Scotland arrived in Charlestown in 1730. From his house at 106 Broad Street, Lining began a systematic recording of weather in the city, painstakingly recording temperature, rainfall, barometric pres-sure, humidity and wind direction and speed. His goal was to establish the connection between weather and disease.

The observations continued until 1750.

---

# 1738

### 1738. *ARRIVALS.*

Col. George Lucas moved his family from Antigua to South Carolina, where he had inherited three plantations from his father. Tension between Spain and England was increasing and he believed his family safer in Carolina than on the tiny, exposed island in the West Indies. His daughter, Eliza, was sixteen when the family arrived in Charlestown.

### 1738. *Commerce. Drayton Hall.*

John Drayton purchased the land on which he soon built Drayton Hall.

### 1738, January 26. *Culture. Freemasonry.*

A Lodge of the ancient and honourable Society of Free and Accepted Masons, belonging to the Lodge of St. John, was organized at Mr. William Flud's at the Sign of the Harp and Crown.

### 1738, March 9. *Slave Population Fears.*

Another writer in the *Gazette* addressed his concerns about the issue of Negro population:

> I cannot avoid observing that altho'h a few Negroes annually imported into the province might be of advantage to most People, yet such a large importation of 2600 or 2800 every year is not only a loss to many, but in the end may prove the Ruin of the Province, as it most certainly does that of many industrious Planters who unwarily engage in buying more than they have occasion or able to pay for.

### 1738, March 23. *Crime. Execution.*

Sarah Chamberlain was found guilty of "the Murder of her Bastard Child." She was sentenced to death.

### 1738, April 13. *Epidemic. Slavery.*

*London Frigate,* a slave ship, arrived from Guinea infected with small pox. It spread so extensively there were not enough healthy people to take care of the ill.

### 1738, April 27-28. *Disaster. Fire.*

A fire destroyed several blocks of Charlestown.

### 1738, May 4. *Epidemic.*

The *Gazette* reported that several slaves had "the small Pox" and urged all citizens to "take all imaginable care."

### 1738, June 1. *Epidemic.*

The *Gazette* published Dr. Pitcarn's treatment for small pox to help it stop spreading. It consisted of bloodletting and the use of a syrup of white poppies. By the end of the summer 2,112 people had come down with the disease, killing more than 400. It was reported that there were not:

> sufficient number of persons in health to attend the sick, and many persons perished from neglect and want. There was scarcely a house in which there had not been one of more deaths. Inoculation was at this

time first attempted with some success and the disease soon after abated.

### 1738, July 25. COMMERCE. REAL ESTATE.

Edmund Bellinger transferred the property on Bay Street, "Distinguished by the letter B" on the Grand Modell to Ebenezar Simmons for "800 pounds of current money."

### 1738, August. RELIGION. WHITEFIELD ARRIVES.

Rev. George Whitefield, on his way to Georgia, arrived in Charlestown for the first time. Friends with the Wesley brothers, John and Charles, he was a leader of the Great Awakening movement in England and the American colonies. Ordained by the Anglican Church but was never assigned a pulpit, Whitefield began conducting services in public places - the father of the evangelical movement. He also was among the first to preach the gospel to the enslaved and campaigned to have slavery outlawed in Georgia.

At the invitation of Rev. Alexander Gardner, Whitefield preached at St. Philip's and described it as "a grand church, resembling one of the new churches in London." He also wrote that, "On my first coming the people of Charlestown seemed to be wholly devoted to pleasure."

### 1738, September. DEATH.

Giles Holliday died, leaving his widow, Elizabeth "their store, the theatre property and five hundred acres in the Peedee."

### 1738, December 25. MARRIAGE.

Dr. John Rutledge married his brother's stepdaughter, fourteen-year old Sarah Hext, acquiring the two Charleston houses and two plantations that Sarah received upon her marriage.

Although he still kept a practice on Broad Street, and served as the surgeon for the Charlestown militia, most of Dr. Rutledge's energy was devoted to becoming a planter, famous for his "grand entertainments" at which he served a "highly popular drink – Officer's Punch."

### 1738, December 30. DEATH.

Lewis Timothy, editor of the *Gazette* died of an "unhappy accident." According to the franchise agreement with Benjamin Franklin the *Gazette* contract passed to Timothy's son, Peter, who was fourteen-years old. His mother, Elizabeth, decided to carry on her late husband's work in order to keep the contract in force for her son.

### 1738, December 30. COMMERCE. HOSPITAL/WORKHOUSE.

By the end of the year the city had completed a hospital on "an acre of ... Land called the old Burying Ground, lying on the back Part of Charles Town" – along

Mazyck Street (now Logan). The hospital would also serve as a "Workhouse and House of Correction."

# 1739

### 1739. *Birth.*

Thomas Bee was born in Charlestown.

### 1739. *Commerce.*

By this time there were eight wharves along Bay Street, and more than 500 ships docked at Charles Town annually. The largest wharf was Middle Wharf, which included shops, stores and the Old Market. The other wharves were named after their owners or builders:

- Brewton's Wharf
- Lloyd's Wharf
- Pinckney's Wharf
- Motte's Wharf
- Elliott's Wharf
- Rhett's Wharf
- Crockatt's Wharf

### 1739. *Eliza Lucas Left in Charge.*

Col. George Lucas returned to Barbados to deal with the political turmoil between England and Spain. He left his eighteen-year old daughter Eliza in charge of his plantations. Eliza resided at Wappoo Plantation on the Stono River and supervised 5,000 acres of land which produced pitch, tar, salt pork and rice.

### 1739. *Exports.*

Charlestown exported 67,117 barrels of rice with an additional 4,367 barrels shipped from Georgetown and Beaufort. Rice production doubled during the 1730s.

### 1739. *Slavery. Population.*

As a direct result of the boom of rice production, so did the slave importation. More than 2,000 slaves arrived in Carolina during the year from Gambia, Calabar and Angola, and Antigua and St. Kitts from the West Indies. More than 40,000 Negroes lived in South Carolina.

### 1739, January 4. *Commerce. Charleston First.*

The first issue of the *South Carolina Gazette*, edited by Elizabeth Timothy, was published. The masthead said "Printed by Peter Timothy."

In the first issue, at the bottom of the front page Elizabeth announced that she was now publishing the newspaper, under the name of her son, making her made her the first female editor and publisher of a newspaper in America and the first female franchisee in America.

> Whereas the late Printer of this Gazette hath been deprived of his life by an unhappy accident. I take this Opportunity of informing the Public, that I shall contain the said paper as usual; and hope, by the Assistance of my Friends, to make it as entertaining and correct as may be reasonable expected. Wherefore I flatter myself, that all those Persons, who, by Subscription or otherwise, assisted my late Husband, on the prosecution of the Said Undertaking, will be kindly pleased to continue their Favours and good Offices to this poor afflicted Widow and six small children and another hourly expected.

Over the next seven years, Elizabeth Timothy increased the quality of the newspaper. She not only included local news, but news from Boston, Newport, and Philadelphia and European news from London, Paris, and Constantinople. Many times she dedicated at least a full page of her four-page newspaper to advertising.

Benjamin Franklin praised her, stating that she was a better business manager and accountant than her late husband had been. He remarked in his *Autobiography* that while her husband was "a man of learning and honest, but ignorant in matters of account," Mrs. Timothy:

> not only sent me as clear a state as she could find of the transactions past, but continued to account with the greatest regularity and exactness every quarter afterwards, and managed the business with such success, that she not only brought up reputably a family of children, but, at the expiration of the term, was able to purchase of me the printing-house, and establish her son in it.

Elizabeth Timothy also took over her husband's position as the official "public printer" for the colony of South Carolina. She printed acts, laws, and other proceedings for the Assembly of the colony of South Carolina. In addition to publishing the *South-Carolina Gazette* and government documents, she printed sermons and religious materials. She also published some twenty historical books and pamphlets between 1739 and 1745. She also was the postmaster for Charlestown, in charge of the postal deliveries of letters, packages, and newspapers.

## 1739, April 5. *Culture. Review of Troops.*

The *Gazette* announced:

> Tuesday last being the day appointed for the Review of the Troop and Regiment of St. Philips Charlestown, the two following commissions of his Majesty were published at Granville Bastion under the discharge of the cannon both there and at Broughton Battery the one constituting and appointing the Hon. William Bull Lieutenant Governor in and over the province, and the other [for] his Excellency James Oglethorpe General and Commanders of his Majesty's Forces in the provinces of South Carolina and Georgia ... In the evening his Excellency ... made a

general invitation to the ladies to an excellent supper and ball so the day concluded with much pleasure and satisfaction.

## CHARLESTON FIRST

**1739, JANUARY 4**
**FIRST FEMALE EDITOR AND PUBLISHER OF A NEWSPAPER AND FIRST FEMALE FRANCHISEE IN AMERICA.**

Elizabeth Timothy took over the publishing of the *South Carolina Gazette* after her husband's sudden death. The franchise agreement Lewis Timothy had signed with Benjamin Franklin stated that Timothy's oldest son, Peter, would continue the business upon his father's death. However, since Peter was only fourteen, his mother, Elizabeth, made the decision to keep her husband's contract intact.

For the next seven years, Elizabeth was publisher and editor of the *Gazette*.

First edition of the Elizabeth Timothy-edited *South Carolina Gazette*. *Public Domain.*

### 1739, May 19. COMMERCE. SLAVERY.

Richard Baylis advertised in the *Gazette* for "Servants or Negroes instructed in the Art of Cutting and Curing Tobacco after the same Manner as in *England.*"

### 1739, May 21. CULTURE. LECTURE.

Mr. Hugh Anderson conducted a lecture on the subject of "natural Philosophy, natural History, Agriculture and Gardening." Tickets were purchased at "Shepheard's Tavern at 15s. Currency each."

### 1739, June 9. CULTURE.

"A Prospect of Charlestown" an engraving based on a watercolor by Bishop Roberts, was printed in London.

### 1739, July. SLAVERY.

A Spanish captain, Don Piedro, sailed into Charlestown, claiming he had a communication for Governor James Oglethorpe who was in Savannah. He left Charlestown and made several landings along the coast. This aroused the suspicion that Piedro was an agent of the Spanish government trying to promote unrest and rebellion among the slaves.

### 1739, July 19. EDUCATION.

Mr. Hugh Anderson advertised that:

> On Tuesday of each Week he will attend at the Market house ... to explain and teach the Doctrine of the Globes, and Science of Geography.

### 1739, August 15. POLITICS. SLAVERY

The Security Act was passed by the Assembly in response to white fears about the majority Negro population. The Act required that all white men carry firearms to church on Sunday. Anyone not in compliance of the law by September 29 would be subjected to a fine.

### 1739, September 9. SLAVERY. STONO REBELLION.

The largest slave revolt in the British colonies prior to the Revolution took place about twenty miles from Charleston. Some forty blacks and twenty-one whites were killed. William Bull submitted his account of the Rebellion to the British authorities:

> My Lords,
> I beg leave to lay before your Lordships an account of our Affairs, first in regard to the Desertion of our Negroes. On the 9th of September last at Night a great Number of Negroes Arose in Rebellion, broke open a Store where they got arms, killed twenty one White Persons, and were marching the next morning in a Daring manner out of the Province,

killing all they met and burning several Houses as they passed along the Road. I was returning from Granville County with four Gentlemen and met these Rebels at eleven o'clock in the forenoon and fortunately deserned [sic] the approaching danger time enough to avoid it, and to give notice to the Militia who on the Occasion behaved with so much expedition and bravery, as by four a' Clock the same day to come up with them and killed and took so many as put a stop to any further mischief at that time, forty four of them have been killed and Executed; some few yet remain concealed in the Woods expecting the same fate, seem desperate . . .

It was the Opinion of His Majesty's Council with several other Gentlemen that one of the most effectual means that could be used at present to prevent such desertion of our Negroes is to encourage some Indians by a suitable reward to pursue and if possible to bring back the Deserters, and while the Indians are thus employed they would be in the way ready to intercept others that might attempt to follow and I have sent for the Chiefs of the Chickasaws living at New Windsor and the Catawbaw Indians for that purpose ...

## STONO REBELLION
### September, 10-11, 1739

During the early morning of Sunday, September 10, about twenty slaves gathered near the western branch of the Stono River twenty miles from Charlestown. They were led by an Angolan slave named Jemmy.

They marched to Hutcheon's Store and stole small arms and gunpowder. They killed the storekeepers Robert Bathurst and Mr. Gibbs, leaving their decapitated heads on the front steps.

The group moved to Mr. Godfrey's house, plundered and burned the property, killing the owner, his son and daughter. They then turned south on the road to Georgia (present-day U.S. Highway 17). Their plan was to make it to Florida and seek asylum with the Spanish.

They reached Wallace's Tavern and dawn and spared Mr. Wallace "for he was a good man and kind to his slaves." However, they killed his neighbor Mr. Lenny, his wife and child and burned the property.

They then moved on to Pon Pon Road and burned Colonel Hext's house, killing the overseer and his wife. They burned three more homes and "kill'd all the white People they found." A white man named Bullock eluded them, but they burned his house.

By now other slaves in the area had joined them. Slaves who were reluctant to join were forcibly taken with them, so as not to raise an alarm. They fastened a standard to carry and carried two drums to beat as they marched, shouting "Liberty!"

Lt. Governor William Bull was returning to Charlestown by horseback with four other men to attend the Assembly. At 11:00 A.M. Sunday morning they came directly in view with the slaves, which by then numbered more than fifty. Bull and his party turned around and "with much difficulty escaped."

By four in the afternoon Bull had raised a posse of about 100 farmers and planters at Rev. Stobo's PresbyterianChurch at Willtown on the eastern branch of the Edisto River Jemmy and his slave rebels stopped at sundown at the Edisto, in a field close to the Jacksonboro ferry.

Bull's posse attacked the rebels firing volleys into the crowd. The next morning slaves were either dead or arrested. The planters then "Cutt off their heads and set them up at every Mile Post they came to" as they rode to Charlestown.

**CASUALTIES**
41 Blacks & 20 Whites.

The revolt had long-term effects in South Carolina. It led to stricter slave codes that dictated such things as how slaves were to be treated, punished, and dressed. It forbade them from assembling with one another or being taught to read or write. The 1740 slave codes were largely unaltered until emancipation in 1865.

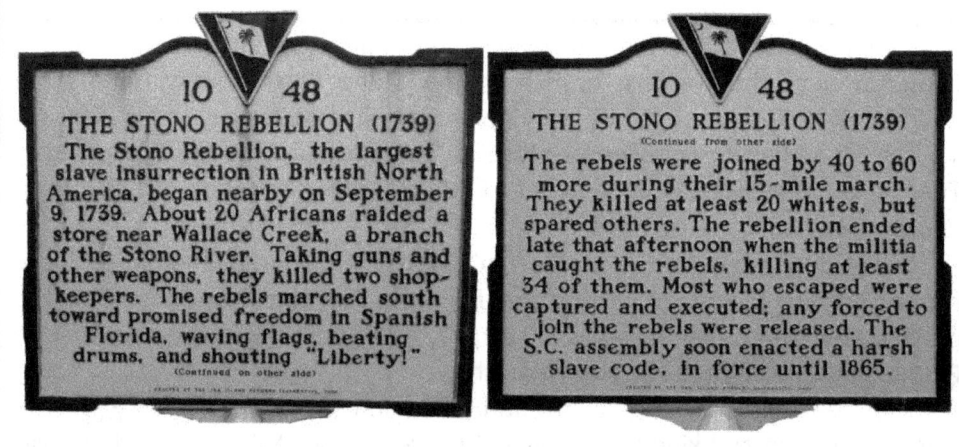

Stono Rebellion markers on U.S. Highway 17, south of Charleston. *Photos by author*

## 1739, September 17. *BIRTHS.*

John Rutledge, son of Dr. John and Sarah Rutledge was born.

## 1739, September 17. *EPIDEMIC.*

Yellow fever outbreak in Charlestown.

### 1739, October 19. ENGLAND. WAR OF JENKIN'S EAR

Great Britain declared war on Spain. The impetus was the mistreatment of English merchant sailors, in particular Robert Jenkins. He appeared before a committee in the House of Commons and reported that Spanish ships in the West Indies had boarded his vessel, plundered it and severed his ear. He presented the ear as evidence.

### 1739, October 30. MILITARY REVIEW.

The Regiment of St. Philip's Charlestown was reviewed by "his Honour the Lieutenant Governor" near Broughton's Battery in honor of "the Anniversary of His Majesty's Birthday."

### 1739, November 22. COMMERCE. POLITICS.

As hostilities between England and Spain increased, particularly in the Caribbean, Gov. Glen of Carolina granted a privateer commission to George Austin, merchant, and James Whitefield, ship shipmaster. They posed a bond of £2,000 and swore to:

> Obey all orders from the governor who empowered them to take and destroy the ships, vessels, and goods of the King of Spain and his subjects, and bring any captured prizes into English ports for adjudication in the Vice Admiralty Courts.

# 1740

### 1740. RELIGION.

The Jewish community in Charlestown received a substantial addition during the years 1740-41, when the illiberal policy of the trustees of Georgia induced both Jews and Christians to leave that colony and to flock to South Carolina.

Most Southern Jews during the colonial period were Sephardic Jews who had immigrated from London and the Netherlands, where they had settled following expulsion from Spain and Portugal in the late 15th century.

### 1740. COMMERCE. INDIGO.

Col. Lucas sent his daughter, Eliza, indigo seeds from Antigua. She expressed "greater hopes" for them, as she intended to plant them earlier than usual in the season. In her indigo-growing experiments in the new climate and soil, Eliza depended on the knowledge and skills of enslaved Africans who had grown indigo in the West Indies and West Africa.

Lucas was also on the searching for a husband for his accomplished daughter. In one of her letters, the strong-willed Eliza rebuked her father's suggestion for a husband, saying:

> As you propose Mr. L. to me, I am sorry I can't have the sentiments favorable enough of him to take time to think on the subject ... and beg leave to say to you that the riches of Peru and Chile if he had put them together could not purchase a sufficient esteem for him to make him my husband.

Eliza was charming addition to Charlestown society. She often attended entertainments at her neighbor's plantation, Belmont, owned by prominent lawyer and planter, Charles Pinckney. Pinckney often joked of Eliza's exploits in business and agriculture. However, acutely aware of her curious intellect, he gave her permission to access his large personal library.

## 1740. POPULATION.

South Carolina's population was 59,000, of which 39,000 are black. African-born slaves accounted for the largest single element of the population.

## 1740, January. WAR OF JENKIN'S EAR.

As instructed by the British government, James Oglethorpe arrived in Charlestown seeking assistance for a large-scale invasion of Florida.

## 1740, January 4. RELIGION. WHITEFIELD PREACHES.

Rev. George Whitefield returned to Charlestown for the second time, to visit his brother. By this time, Whitefield was one of the most famous public figures in colonial America, drawing massive, passionate crowds (10,000+) to his open air services and field services in New York and Philadelphia. His radial methods made traditional clergy uncomfortable.

He preached from the pulpit of Josiah Smith's Independent Meeting House and accused the people in attendance of "sin and worldliness" and being "polite and unaffected." He called upon their sins of "affected finery, gaiety of dress ... and balls and assemblies." He promised them that "God intended to visit some in Charlestown with His salvation."

## 1740, January 5. RELIGION. CULTURE.

Rev. Josiah Smith commented in the *Gazette* that Charles Town was damned due to "balls and mid-night assemblies." He also wondered how "Religion and Virtue can thrive under the shadow of a Theater." The French Huguenot Church stood opposite the Dock Street Theater on Queen and Church streets.

## 1740, January 6. RELIGION. WHITEFIELD'S JOURNAL.

Rev. George Whitefield wrote in his journal:

> Most of the town ... being eager to hear me, I preached in the afternoon in one of the dissenting meeting houses, but was grieved to find so little concern in the congregation ... I question whether the Court-End of London could exceed them in affected finery, gaity [sic] of dress and a

deportment ill becoming persons who have had such divine judgements lately sent against them.

## 1740. *RELIGION. CULTURE. WHITEFIELD'S JOURNAL.*

From George Whitefield's journal:

> I preached in the morning in the French church. The audience was so great that many stood without the door ... One of the men in town, most remarkably gay, was observed to weep.

## 1740, January 10. *COMMERCE. POLITICS. PRIVATEERING.*

The 70-ton sloop, *Sea Nymph*, owned by William Lassere, returned to Charles Town with a captured Spanish sloop, *Cruizer*. The prize and cargo netted £61,382 for Lassere.

## 1740, February. *PACHELBEL BECOMES ST. PHILIP'S ORGANIST.*

Pachelbel became the organist at St. Philip's Church.

## 1740, February 2. *EDUCATION.*

Mr. Corbett, "master of the Charleston free-school" announced he had resigned from his position.

## 1740, March. *RELIGION. WHITEFIELD CONDUCTS PUBLIC SERVICES.*

Rev. George Whitefield warned that God had been:

> Contending with the people of South Carolina... for two years with disease, the Stono Rebellion ... God has quarrel with you, for your abuse of and cruelty to the poor negroes.

While in Charlestown he conducted public services that disregarded the Book of Common Prayer, an offense against the church of which he was a licensed minister. Rev. Alexander Garden called on him to explain his offense.

## 1740, April 5. *SLAVERY.*

In response to the Stono Rebellion the Assembly passed a new Negro Act – placing high import duty on slaves, which effectively cut off new slave trading. Its stated goal was "to ensure that slaves be kept in due subjection and obedience." No slave living in town was allowed to go beyond the city limits; the sale to alcohol was prohibited as was the teaching of slaves to read and write. Only the Assembly could grant a slavefreedom. Any white person who "shall willfully cut out the tongue, put out the eye, castrate or cruelly scald" a slave, would be punished. All Negroes and mulattoes were considered slaves unless they could prove that they were born free or had been manumitted. Children of slave mothers were to be slaves. No slave could leave his master's property without a pass. If a slave resisted capture, he could legally be killed.

## 1740, April 8. *CULTURE.*

The South Carolina Society held their annual meeting.

## 1740, May 2. *CULTURE. ELIZA LUCAS.*

In a letter to a friend, Eliza Lucas wrote:

> Charles Town ... is a polite, agreeable place. The people live very Gentile and very much in the English taste ... there is two worthy Ladies in Charles town, Mrs. Pinckney and Mrs. Cleland, who are partial enough to me to be always pleased to have me with them and insist upon my making their houses my home with in town. [Note: the Pinckney house was on Union, (now State) Street.]

## 1740, May 3. *POLITICS. WAR OF JENKINS'S EAR.*

The War of Jenkin's Ear was declared in Charlestown against Spain, following England's declaration in October of the previous year. It would last for nine years.

The Assembly agreed to support Oglethorpe's invasion of Florida, naming Colonel Vander Dussen commander of 429 militiamen, 500 Indians, forty rangers and ten small boats. They also allocated full supplies for the expedition and £40,000.

## 1740, May 10. *SLAVE CODES.*

A new Slave Code was enacted by the Assembly. It provided the following:

- levied a penalty of £5 upon any person who employed a slave on the Lord's Day.
- Selling of liquor to slaves was prohibited.
- Slaves were to be provided sufficient clothing, food and shelter.
- Slaves could work no more than 15 hours a day between March 25-September 25, no more than 14 hours the other half of the year.
- Imposed a tax on newly purchased Negro slaves by height.

## 1740, July 15. *RELIGION. WHITEFIELD SUSPENDED.*

George Whitefield appeared with his counsel, Andrew Rutledge, before an ecclesiastical court at St. Philip's Church to answer for his violations of Anglican canons and rubries. He was found guilty and suspended. He appealed to the Lords Commissioners appointed by the King for hearing appeals of spiritual cause in his Majesty's Plantations in America. Whitefield was allowed to continue to practice his ministry until the appeal.

## 1740, August. *WAR OF JENKINS'S EAR.*

The English invasion of Florida was a disaster, due to Oglethorpe's hesitant and weak leadership.

## 1740, September. *WAR OF JENKINS'S EAR.*

The British government send a squadron under Commodore George Anson to attack Spain's possessions in the Pacific.

George Whitefield preaching. *Courtesy of the Library of Congress.*

## 1740, September 6. *COMMERCE. ART.*

Jeremiah Theus advertised in the *Gazette:*

> Notice is hereby given, that Jeremiah Theus Limner is remov'd into the Market Square ... where all Gentlemen and Ladies may have their pictures drawn, likewise Landskips of all sizes, Crests and Coats of Arms for coaches and Chaises.

## 1740, November 18. *DISASTER. FIRE. RELIGION.*

A fire broke out in the afternoon and consumed all the buildings from Church Street, to Broad and down to Granville Bastion. (current location of the Missroon House – Historic Charleston Foundation). With more than 300 buildings destroyed –homes, warehouses, stables - it was a major disaster, mainly because this area was along the commercial waterfront district. Losses were estimated at £200,000 ($20 million in 2014). One of the notable losses was the Dock Street Theater.

In the *Gazette* Elizabeth Timothy reported that "the wind blowing pretty fresh at northwest carried the flakes of fire so far, and by that means set houses on fire at such a distance, that it was not possible to prevent the spreading of it."

Rev. Josiah Smith responded by publishing *The Burning of Sodom*, arguing that the fire was God's response to vanity and wickedness of the city, and the Anglican Church treatment of George Whitefield. Smith wrote:

> Charles-Town is fallen, is fallen. London's plague and fire came soon after the casting out and silencing a body of ministers ... Charlestown ... should pay attention and repent ... The Pride of Sodom flourished ... Let us Enquire seriously ... whether our Streets, Lanes and Houses did not burn with Lust ... Heaps of Pollution conceal'd from Man ... which require'd Brimstone and Fire to burn up ... such abandon'd Wretches generally curse the Sun and hate the Light.

The fire bankrupted the Friendly Society for the Mutual Insurance of Houses Against Fire. William Pinckney became so impoverished, he and his wife, Ruth Brewton, were unable to care for their son Charles, who went to live with his namesake, his uncle Charles. The younger Charles began to call himself "Charles Pinckney, Junior."

## 1740, December 10. *POLITICS. CULTURE.*

The Assembly passed an Act for Rebuilding which required all buildings to be made of brick or stone and fixed the prices of building materials.

## 1740, December 13. *WAR OF JENKINS'S EAR. SHIPBUILDING.*

The Assembly announced the allocation of £2,400 to John Yermouth, shipwright. He was commissioned to build two half-galleys, a galley-style vessel without a quarterdeck. One vessel was to patrol the waters of Charlestown and look out for Spanish ships and privateers. The second ship was to perform the same duty in Beaufort.

## 1740, December 13. *CULTURE. EDUCATION.*

An announcement in the *Gazette* noted: "Mary Hext. Any Person or Persons in the County may have their Daughters boarded and taught in a true and faithful manner."

# 1741

## 1741. *CULTURE. COMMERCE.*

Middleton Place Plantation was founded. In the present-day, it is America's oldest formally landscaped gardens.

## 1741. *DEATHS.*

Thomas Gadsden, Customs Collector, died, leaving behind an estate valued at £5000 sterling to his son, Christopher.

### 1741. *CULTURE. ELIZA LUCAS.*

Eliza Lucas wrote:

> The people are in general hospitable and honest, and the better sort add to these a polite, gentile behavior. The poorer sort are the most indolent people in the world or they could never be wretched in so plentiful a country as this. The winters are very fine and pleasant, but four month in the year is extremely disagreeable, excessively hot, with much thunder and lightning and mosquitoes and sand flies in abundance.

### 1741, January 8. *RELIGION.*

In a letter published in the *South Carolina Gazette* Hugh Bryan blamed the recent fire as "part of God's wrath against the Church." He called priests "thieves and robbers who did not follow the Foot-steps of our true Shepherd, but coveted the Fleece only."

### 1741, March 12. *COMMERCE. TRADES.*

Francis Garden advertised that he "engraves in the best manner … any kind of Metal, Coats of Arms, &c."

### 1741, March 19. *CULTURE.*

The *Gazette* reported:

> … at the House of Mr. Jacob Woolford on the Bay, was established a Convention of the *Right worthy and amicable Order of UBIQUARIANS*, by some Gentlemen, Members of the GRAND CONVENTION in England, being the first coven'd in America.

### 1741, August 12. *SLAVERY. EXECUTION.*

A mulatto slave Kate, was convicted of attempting to set fire to a house on Union Street. Her execution was pardoned when she identified a conspirator named Boatswain. He was accused of setting on fire a Mr. Snowden. At his trial Boatswain said that he "looked upon every white Man he should meet as the enemy."

### 1741, August 13. *BIRTH.*

Alexander Gillon was born in Rotterdam, Holland, the son of a Scottish sea captain of French ancestry.

### 1741, August 15. *SLAVERY. EXECUTION.*

Boatswain was burned alive at the stake. The *Gazette* reported that he "died like [the] impudent Wretch he was."

# 1742

### 1742, January. *RELIGION. SLAVERY.*

Hugh Bryan began preaching to "great assemblies of Negroes" on his property in the evening. During a "religious trance" he had a vision of a successful slave insurrection that would be "the Destruction of Charles Town ... executed by Negroes with fire and sword."

Bryan was arrested for assembling blacks. However, after some days in prison, he wrote a letter to William Bull, Speaker of the Assembly:

> It is with shame intermix's with joy that I write you this. I find that I have presumed in my zeal for God's glory beyond his will, and that he has suffered me to fall into a delusion of Satan – particularly in adhering to the impressions on my mind, though not to my knowledge in my reflections and other occurrences of my journal. This delusion I did not discover till three days past when, after many days' converse with an invisible spirit, whose precepts seemed to be wise, and tending to the advancement of religion in general, and of my own spiritual welfare in particular.
>
> I found my teacher to be a liar and the father of lies, which brought me a sense of my error and has much abased my soul with bitter reflections on the dishonor I have done to God as well as the disquiet which I may have occasioned my country. Satan then appeared to me an angel of light in his spiritual conversation, but since I have discovered his wiles he has appeared a devil indeed, showing his rage.

Charges were dropped and Bryan retired to a quiet life on his plantation.

### 1742, January. *RELIGION. LUTHERANISM.*

Reverend Henry Melchoir Muhlenberg, known as the Father of American Lutherism, arrived in Charles Town.

### 1742, January 13. *WAR OF JENKIN'S EAR.*

The HMS *Pye*, under the command of Charles Hardy, arrived in Charles Town, to relieve the HMS *Phoenix*. *Pye* had been damaged during the Atlantic crossing and spent three months at the Hobcaw shipyard having her bottom cleaned and rigging refitted.

### 1742, February 13. *EDUCATION.*

An announcement in the *Gazette* noted:

William Gough continues to teach several useful Branches of Learning (in the English tongue) according to the London Method whereby Youth may be qualified for Business by Land or Sea.

Negro Camp Meeting in the South. *Library of Congress*

## 1742, March. COMMERCE. SHIPBUILDING.

Two locally constructed shallow-draft ships were launched, *Charles-Town* and *Beaufort*. Both were carried a crew of fifty men, armed with twelve swivel guns and six light guns.

## 1742, March 20. EDUCATION.

Martha Logan announced in the *Gazette*: "Any Persons desirous to board their Children … may have them taught to read and write, also plain Work, Embroidery, tent and cut Work."

## 1742, May 22. COMMERCE. CROPS.

Eliza Lucas in a letter to her brother Thomas, wrote:

> The soil near Charles Town [is] sandy … it abounds with fine navigable rivers, and great quantities of fine timber. The Soil … is very fertile, and there is very few European or American fruits or grain but what grow here. Venison and fish, Beef, veal and motton are here in much greater perfection than in the islands … peaches, nectrons and mellons … and

their Oranges exceed any I ever tasted in the West Indies of from Spain or Portugal.

### 1742, June 26. BIRTH.

Arthur Middleton, son of Henry Middleton, was born on the family plantation "The Oaks" in Goose Creek.

### 1742, July 7. WAR OF JENKIN'S EAR.

Due to the hostilities between England and Spain, the Assembly allocated £6,000 for the construction of a brick and cedar-post palisade "around Charlestown's southern and eastern waterfront." They also hired Colonel Othniel Beale to draw up the design.

### 1742, July 26. FORTIFICATIONS.

It was announced that Othniel Beale "hath received a Commission ... to carry on such Works as are further necessary to fortify Charles-Town, according to the Plans approved of in Council.

### 1742, September. BIRTH.

William Henry Drayton was born.

### 1742, September 4. SLAVERY.

The *Gazette* reported that the slave ship, *Mary Galley*, owned by local merchant Samuel Wragg, was plundered and destroyed in the Gambia River by black tribesmen who killed the crew.

### 1742, October 25. SLAVERY.

It was noted that "Matters between the whites and the blacks here are such that one fears to be seen outside the house."

### 1742, November 10. CRIME.

Peter Boez was fined £2 for "knocking down Mr. Pinckney, a Negro." Mr. Tributed was fined 10s (shillings) for "retailing Rum on Sunday."

# 1743

### 1743. CULTURE. COMMERCE. GOLF.

The first known shipment of golf equipment to arrive in the American colonies was 432 balls and ninety-six clubs shipped from Scottish port Leith to Charleston.

### 1743. COMMERCE.

Three new wharves were built by Messrs. Rober, Gibbes and Beresford. This gave Charlestown eight major wharves on the Cooper River.

## 1743, March 10. *Culture. Horse Race.*

A horse race was held "on York course, at the old Quarter-House." The prize was "a handsome and fashionable silver Punch Bowl, value *One Hundred Pounds.*"

## 1743, May 9. *Culture. Shuffleboard.*

The *Gazette* advertised:

> This is to give Notice that a SHUFFLE BOARD, ready to play at, is set up in the House of Mr. Laurans … where Gentlemen may enjoy their Bowl and Bottle with Satisfaction.

## 1743, May 30. *Culture. Entertainments.*

The *Gazette* advertised:

> To Be SHEWN, at *Five Shillings* for each Person. For the Space of a Week … at the House of Mr. *Joel Poinsett* in *Charles Town,* a WHITE Negro Girl, of Negro Parents, she is as white as any *European,* has a lively Blush in her Countenance, grey Eyes continually trembling, and Hair frisled as the Wool of a white Lamb.

## 1743, June 16. *Birth.*

Aedanus Burke was born in Galway, Ireland, and educated at a Jesuit seminary at St. Omer, France. He would arrive in America in 1769.

## 1743, June 20. *War of Jenkins's Ear.*

Commodore George Anson captured the Spanish galleon *Nuestra Señora de Covadonga*, possessing 1,313,843 pieces of eight, which he encountered off Cape Espiritu Santo. The prize money earned by the capture made him a rich man for life.

## 1743, August 31. *Disaster. Hurricane.*

Charlestown was struck by a hurricane. Every ship in the Ashley River, except two, were driven ashore by the storm.

## 1743, September 12. *Religion. Slavery. Education.*

Alexander Garden opened a free school for "educating Negro children," with more than sixty pupils.

## 1743, October 10. *Entertainments. Foot Race. Sack Race.*

A foot race was held at the *York* course at the *old Quarter-House* "for a very good handsome *French* emboider'd Waistcoat, Value 90£." Six people entered the race and ran "twice around the half Mile Course."

After the race, a "very good silver lac'd Hat" was given to the victor between "four men … each Man to be in a Sack, all but his Head."

### 1743, October 17. *War of Jenkin's Ear. Privateering.*

The privateer brigantine *Loyal William*, commanded by Capt. Mark Anderson, left Charlestown to search for Spanish prizes. She had a crew of 100, with fourteen mounted carriage guns and sixteen swivel guns.

### 1743, December 14. *Politics. Lucas Family.*

George Lucas was named Lt. Royal Governor of Antigua. He realized he would never live in Carolina again. He sent his oldest son, George, to Carolina to bring his family back to the island. His daughter, Eliza, was horrified about leaving Carolina. She had built a successful life and did not want to leave. She wrote to a friend, "We expect my brother George very shortly ... His arrival will, I sopose, [sic] determine how long we shall continue here."

### 1743, December 18. *Arrivals. New Royal Governor.*

The *Tartar* arrived in Charlestown with Governor James Glen on board.

### 1743, December 20. *War of Jenkin's Ear. Privateering.*

Captain Richard I'on of Charles Town took command of the privateer *Eagle*. He soon captured 25,000 pieces of eight from a Spanish ship.

### 1743, December 17. *Foot Race. Apple-Eating Contest.*

At the York Course at the *Old Quarter-House* a race was "Run for a handsome embroider'd Jacket ... by Foot Men, to run the half Mile Course." After the race there was a contest "for four Persons or more to eat six Apples each person, out of a Pail of Water, each Person to have his Hands tied behind his back.

# 1744

### 1744. *Commerce. Indigo Crop.*

Eliza Lucas used her 1744 indigo crop to make seed and shared it with other planters, which lead to an expansion in indigo production. She proved that colonial planters could make a profit in an extremely competitive market.

Due to her success, the volume of indigo dye exported increased dramatically from 5,000 pounds in 1745-46, to 130,000 pounds by 1748. Indigo became second only to rice as South Carolina's cash crop, and contributed greatly to the wealth of its planters. Before the Revolutionary War, indigo accounted for more than one-third of the total value of exports from the colony.

### 1744. *Commerce.*

Henry Laurens accepted a position as clerk in the London international counting-house of James Crokatt.

### 1744. *COMMERCE. SLAVERY.*

Andrew Ruck petitioned the Assembly on behalf of himself and other white boatwrights, asking for relief from slave labor in the mending and caulking of ships, which was taking business away.

### 1744, January. *DEATH.*

The wife of Charles Pinckney died after a long illness.

### 1744, February 24. *WAR OF JENKINS'S EAR. PRIVATEERING.*

A 20-ton Spanish schooner, *Cruizer*, was re-fitted and sent out as a privateer with Captain Richard I'on, who also commanded the 14-gun privateer, *Assistance*, built in Charlestown.

### 1744, March 15. *WAR OF JENKIN'S EAR. KING GEORGE'S WAR.*

France entered an alliance with Spain and declared war on Great Britain. The War of Jenkin's Ear became known as King George's War in America.

### 1744, Spring. *ENGAGEMENT. ELIZA LUCAS.*

The newly widowed Charles Pinckney had no intention in allowing the spirited Eliza Lucas to leave Carolina and return to Antigua. He proposed marriage – he was forty-five and she was twenty-two.

Eliza, who had run her family's affairs for five years, tried to allay her father's fears that she would also do the same for her husband. She wrote that she was "well assured the acting out of my proper province and invading his, would be an inexcusable breach of prudence."

### 1744, April 8. *DISASTER. NAVAL.*

The *Charles-Town* was lost when she was hit by a gale while escorting a sloop over the bar. Ten men were lost, but Commander David Cutler Braddock and the rest of the crew were saved.

### 1744, May 27. *PINCKNEY MARRIES ELIZA LUCAS.*

Eliza Lucas and Charles Pinckney were married. She took her family responsibilities seriously, vowing:

> to make a good wife to my dear Husband in all its several branches; to make all my actions Correspond with that sincere love and Duty I bear him ... I am resolved to be a good mother to my children, to pray for them, to set them good examples, to give them good advice, to be careful both of their souls and bodies, to watch over their tender minds.

### 1744, July 11. *BIRTHS.*

Pierce Butler born in born in County Carlow, Ireland. His father was Sir Richard Butler, member of Parliament and a baronet. Like so many younger sons of the British aristocracy who could not inherit their fathers' estates because of primogeniture, Butler pursued a military career. He became a major in His Majesty's 29th Regiment and during the colonial unrest was posted to Boston in 1768 to quell disturbances there.

### 1744, September 10. *CULTURE. HORSE RACING.*

Joseph Butler announced in the Gazette that he:

> Will run his Gelding CHESTNUT, from the Quarter House to *Charles Town*, with any Horse, mare, or Gelding that can be brought against him ... for 500 or 1000£.

### 1744, October 22. *EDUCATION.*

John Fouguet announced "A *French* Evening School for young Gentlemen, at 40 *sh* per month. French, English, writing, arithmetic."

### 1744, December. *KING GEORGE'S WAR. NAVAL.*

Heavily-armed Spanish vessels plagued British shipping along the Carolina coast. The French ship, *Conception,* was captured off Cuba and brought to Charlestown. Her sale brought in £80,000 sterling.

### 1744, December 3. *COMMERCE. INDIGO.*

The *Gazette* published a letter to Eliza from London which read:

> I have shown your Indigo to one of our most noted Brokers ... who tried it against some of the Best French, and in his opinion is it as Good ... when you can in some measure supply the British Demand, we are persuaded, that on proper Application to Parliament, a Duty will be laid on Foreign Growth, for I am informed we pay for Indigo to the French £200,000 per annum.

# 1745

### 1745. *COMMERCE. ANSONBOROUGH.*

Commodore George Anson ordered that his Charlestown tract, known as Bowling Green Plantation, be laid out in streets and lots. In addition to George and Anson Streets, which still bear his name, he named three streets for the most important ships he had commanded during his career. "Scarborough" and "Squirrel" had brought him to South Carolina. "Centurion" had won him fame and fortune. Scarborough and Centurion streets were later absorbed into Anson and Society streets, respectively, while Squirrel became an extension of Meeting Street.

The original suburb of Ansonborough included the area bounded by King, Calhoun, Anson streets and a line running midway between Society and Wentworth streets and parallel with those streets. Later the name came to be applied to the old suburbs of Rhettsbury, Middlesex and the Laurens Lands, to the south and east of original Ansonborough.

Some of those late 18th and early 19th century houses survive in the area now called Ansonborough, mainly in the northern part which was spared by the great fire of 1838, which swept through the southern part of the area, sparing only a few houses such as the Rhett House on Hasell Street. The destroyed buildings were replaced by handsome brick houses, most of which date from the 1840s. Many of the new houses were built with loans from the Bank of the State of South Carolina authorized by the "Act for Rebuilding the City of Charleston," passed by the General Assembly in 1838.

## 1745. January 21. *ARRIVALS.*

His Majesty's Engineer from the Bahama Islands, Capt. Peter Henry Bruce, arrived in Charles Town.

## 1745, March. *COMMERCE. CULTURE.*

Christopher Gadsden finished his apprenticeship in Philadelphia. He sailed to England to visit relatives on the British man-of-war *Aldborough.* He was appointed purser when the previous officer died on board. He remained in service to the British Navy until 1748.

## 1745, May 25. *FORTIFICATIONS.*

Work began on a new fortification north of town, digging a moat and building ramparts which cut across land and marsh between the Ashley and Cooper Rivers. The idea was to create and "island" that was easy to defend.

## 1745, May 28. *SLAVERY.*

Gov. Glen asked London for three companies of British regulars who "would give heart to our ... people [and] prove usefull in preventing or suppressing any Insurrections of our Negroes." Many citizens were growing concerned over the "great numbers of Negroes ... playing Dice and other Games."

## 1745, June 1. *COMMERCE.*

HMS *Rose* and HMS *Flamborough* sail for England as a convoy for a fleet of merchant ships from Charlestown laden with rice valued at £20,000 sterling.

## 1745, June 25. *BIRTH.*

Future Patriot physician and U.S. Treasurer, Thomas Tudor Tucker, was born to a prominent family in Port Royal, Bermuda.

After completing medical studies at the University of Edinburgh in Scotland, Tucker opened a medical practice in Charlestown. He was elected to the state assembly in 1776, where he took the Patriot side. Dr. Tucker served the Southern Department of the Continental Army as a hospital surgeon and continued in that capacity until 1783. He was elected to the Continental Congress in 1787 and 1788.

Although Tucker was an anti-Federalist who believed that the Constitution gave the central government too much power, he nonetheless held prominent positions in the new national government.

Thomas Tudor Tucker
*Public Domain*

## 1745, September 23. *BIRTH*.

Issac Hayne was born at Pon Pon Plantation.

## 1745, September 30. *WEATHER*.

Dr. John Lining noted in a letter that "in the summer the shaded air of about 2 or 3 in the afternoon is frequently between 90 and 95 degrees."

## 1745, October 7. *COMMERCE. TRADES*.

William Wright advertised that he was skilled in "Making and mending all manner of Jewelling Work ... engraving Coats of Arms on Plate, or on Copper, &c."

## 1745, December 2. *COMMERCE. INDIGO*.

Andrew Deveaux advertised, "I will teach the making of Indigo *gratis* to all that buy Seed of me."

## 1745, December 20. *CULTURE. HORSE RACING*.

There was a horse race of one mile "at Mr. Thomas Butler's Race Ground on Charles Town Neck." The prize was a "Silver Tankard of 140£."

# 1746

### 1746, January 25. *British Soldiers Arrive.*

The first of three companies of British soldiers arrived in Charlestown aboard the *Pelican*. They were to be stationed at Fort Johnson in Charlestown and Fort Frederick in Beaufort.

### 1745, February 25. *Birth.*

Charles Cotesworth Pinckney, a future signer of the U.S. Constitution, was born, eldest son of Charles and Eliza Pinckney.

### 1745, March 8. *Birth.*

Andre Michaux, the French botanist, was born in Versailles. He later arrived in Charles Town and established a 111-acre botanical garden in the area. He introduced the Camellia, tea-love and crepe myrtle to America.

### 1745, May 26. *Slavery.*

The *Gazette* announced, "Quash. RUN away ... an old Negro Man ... is a gardener."

### 1745, July 28. *Marriage.*

Christopher Gadsden married Jenny Godfrey in Charlestown. During this time, he also owned a store on Shute's Wharf. By the end of year, Gadsden had signed on as a pursor on a British man-of-war.

### 1745, October. *Commerce. Book Store.*

After Peter Timothy took over the printing business in 1746, his mother, Elizabeth Timothy, opened her own book store. It was next door to the printing office on King Street. She not only carried books, but also stationary, writing supplies such as ink, powder, and quills, as well as tallow, beer, and flour. In a *Gazette* ad, she announced the availability of books such as pocket Bibles, spellers, and primers. She also sold the books *Reflections on Courtship and Marriage, Armsrong's Poem on Health, The Westminster Confession of Faith, Watts' Psalms and Hymns,* the *Pocket Almanack* and several of Benjamin Franklin's works, including *Poor Richard's Almanack*.

### 1746, November 5. *Culture.*

The officers of the Charlestown Regiment met to commemorate the "Anniversary of our Deliverance by KING WILLIAM. The Evening was spent drinking all the Loyal Toasts ... and concluded with Bonfires and Fireworks."

### 1746, December 15. *COMMERCE. SKILLS.*

William O'Keefe advertised his skills as "Master of the Noble Science of Defence." He also mentioned that he "makes Use of his left Hand, and is to be found at French Santee."

### 1746, December 29. *COMMERCE. CULINARY.*

Peter Pekin, a "Pastry-Cook from *Paris,*" advertised that he was "willing to teach, at reasonable rates, all he several Branches of his Business."

# 1747

### 1747. *COMMERCE. INDIGO.*

Eliza Lucas Pinckney sent a substantial indigo crop to England. In all, South Carolina produced 135,000 pounds that year. England was so encouraged they offered a bounty to Carolina planters in an effort to cut out French competition. Within a few years, Carolina was exporting more than one million pounds of indigo annually.

### 1747, June. *ARRIVALS. SLAVERY.*

Henry Laurens returned from London and opened an import and export business. Through his English contacts, Laurens entered into the slave trade with Grant, Oswald & Company, who controlled Bunce Castle, the 18th century British slave castle in the Republic of Sierra Leone.

Laurens contracted to receive slaves from the "rice coast" of Serra Leone, catalogue and market the human product by conducting public auctions in Charlestown. In the 1750s, his company Austin and Laurens, was responsible for the sale of more than eight thousand Africans.

### 1747, June. *DEATH.*

Lt. Royal Gov. of Antigua, George Lucas, father of Eliza, was killed in battle.

### 1747. *COMMERCE.*

The *Gazette* announced that "Members of the LOYAL SOCIETY vulgarly called the *Laughing Club*" met at Mr. Blyth's on the Bay.

### 1747, June 13. *PUBLIC SAFETY.*

The Old Quarantine Act was revived, tightening requirements for ships that entered the harbor. A physician must board each vessel for inspection, and the ship's master was required to pay the physician £7,10s to ensure each passenger was free of smallpox, plague, infectious fever and distemper.

The approved physicians were: Thomas Dale, John Moultrie, John Martini, John Lining, David Caw and William Rind.

### 1747, October. *RELIGION. COMMERCE.*

James Peyne, a London merchant, petitioned the Commissioners for Trade and Plantations to grant him land in Carolina to settle "Foreign Protestants and others as will shew (sic) themselves attached to Your Majesty's Person and Government."

### 1747, December 22. *COMMERCE.*

Solomon DeCosta, a Jewish merchant in partnership with James Peyne, attended a meeting of the Commissioners for Trade and Plantations in London for "the settlement of several of their poor in South Carolina."

## 1748

### 1748. *WEATHER. CULTURE.*

Dr. John Lining wrote the first scientific discourse on yellow fever, *A Description of the American Yellow fever, Which Prevailed at Charlestown, in South Carolina in the Year 1748.*

### 1748. *COMMERCE.*

A total of sixty-eight ships cleared Charlestown harbor, bound for Europe during this year, with cargoes valued over £50,000 sterling. Eighty-seven smaller vessels cleared, bound to the West Indies with cargoes valued at £16,000. Thirty-seven coastal vessels sailed for the northern colonies with cargoes valued at £3,500.

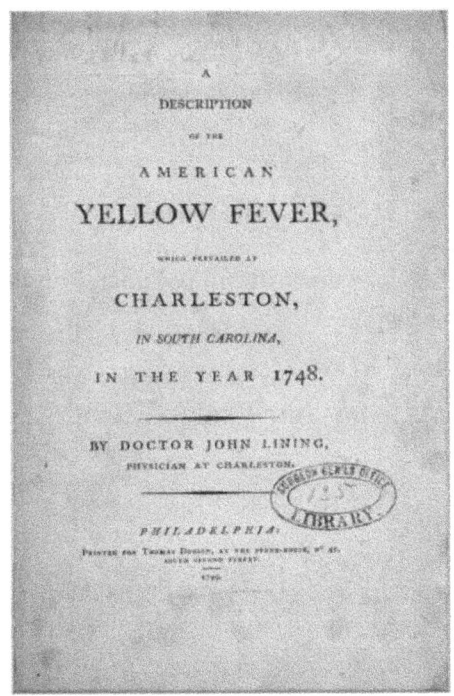

Frontpiece of Dr. John Linning's paper on yellow fever. *Courtesy of the Library of Congress*

**1748, February 17.** *Weather. Coldest Day Recorded.*

The temperature fell to ten degrees Fahrenheit, the coldest day in Charlestown in the 18th century. The cold killed most of the orange trees in the area. as will shew themselves attached to Your Majesty's Person and Government."

**1747, December 22.** *Commerce.*

Solomon DeCosta, a Jewish merchant in partnership with James Peyne, attended a meeting of the Commissioners for Trade and Plantations in London for "the settlement of several of their poor in South Carolina.

**1748, March 28.** *Culture. Business.*

William Lord announced that "I intend to open a Tavern … and keep a good Billiard Table, at my house in King-street."

**1748, Spring.** *Arrivals. Commerce.*

Christopher Gadsden returned to Charlestown. He had served for two years as purser on the British man-of-war *Aldborough*. Gadsden used his naval service to enhance his business, making money through the seizure of French ships. He opened a store on Broad Street and purchased a home on Elliot Street.

**1748, May 16.** *Arrivals. Trades.*

Patrick MacLein "Master-Bricklayer, just arrived from London" advertised that "he undertakes to finish any Kind of Building, or other Brick-Work."

**1748, June 21.** *Commerce. Interest Rate Lowered.*

The Assembly lowered the legal interest rate on debts from ten to eight per cent.

**1748, July.** *Shipbuilding*

Benjamin Darling launched the 200-ton *Mary Anne*.

**1748, July 23.** *Commerce. Culture.*

"The BOWLING-GREEN at Brampton-Bryan" was opened. It was advertised as a place "where Gentlemen that favour me with their Custom, may depend on the best Usage – Anne Shepheard."

**1748, October 8.** *King George's War Ends.*

Treaty was signed between Great Britain, Spain and France ending King George's War.

**1748, October 31.** *Culture. Electricity Demonstration.*

An advertisement in the *Gazette* proclaimed:

> THE SUBSCRIBER, Having for many Years past in his Travels thro' *Europe* … studied and made many wonderful experiments in ELECTRICITY, proposes to give Attendance at *Mr. Blythe's* Tavern … during his stay in

this Town ... to shew the surprising Effects thereof. Each person admitted to see the same, to pay 20s, who may also be *electricised* [sic] if they please, by Samuel Dömjen.

## 1748, December 28. *LIBRARY SOCIETY ORGANIZED.*

The Charlestown Library Society was organized by seventeen young gentlemen of various trades and professions who wished to avail themselves of the latest publications from Great Britain.

At first, elected librarians safeguarded the Library's materials in their homes. From 1765 until 1778, it resided in the upstairs of Gabriel Manigault's liquor warehouse. In 1792, the collection was transferred to the upper floor of the Statehouse, currently the County Courthouse at Broad and Meeting streets.

From 1835 until its 1914 move to the current King Street location, the Charleston Library Society occupied the Bank of South Carolina building at the corner of Church and Broad Streets. That building was paid for with "Brick" memberships, a permanent membership for a one-time lump sum. Several of these memberships are still in use, generations later, by Charleston families.

### FOUNDING MEMBERS OF THE CHARLESTOWN LIBRARY SOCIETY

| | |
|---|---|
| Baron, Alexander (schoolmaster) | McCauley, Alexander (wigmaker |
| Brailsford, Morton (merchant) | Middleton, Thomas (planter) |
| Brailsford, Samuel (merchant) | Neufville, John (merchant) |
| Brisbane, Robert (merchant) | Sacheverell, Thomas, Esq. (planter) |
| Burrows, William (lawyer) | Sinclair, John, librarian (merchant) |
| Cooper, John (distiller) | Stevenson, Charles (merchant) |
| Douxsiant, Paul (merchant) | Timothy, Peter (printer) |
| Grindlay, James (lawyer) | Wragg, Joseph (merchant) |
| Logan, William (merchant) | Wragg, Samuel (merchant) |

# 1749

## 1749. *RELIGION. JEWISH CONGREGATION.*

Ten heads of family, led by Joseph Tobias, formed a *minyan*, the quorum needed for the congregation they named Beth Elohim ("House of God"). Of the founding families, six were Sephardic, four Ashkenazic, including Mordecai and Levi Sheftall, both of whom were temporary residents from Savannah.

### 1749, March 6. CULTURE. SINGING SCHOOL.

Charles Theodore Pachelbel announced that he "intends to open a SINGING SCHOOL to be kept on Wednesday and Saturday throughout the Year."

### 1749, April. CULTURE. ENTERTAINMENTS.

John Gordon, who operated a tavern and Long Room, conducted a fair at his ferry on the Ashley River, which included:

> A horse race, with a saddle and furniture for the winner, a shooting match, a scramble for a soaped pig, a role of Tobacco and 3 Gross of Pipes ... and a Scharamouch-Dance ... by a Person from London, the Cat and the Barrel with the Diversion of the Goose ...

### 1749, June 1. COMMERCE. INDIGO.

Now that indigo had become the second most profitable crop produced in Carolina the Assembly required that each shipment must be certified as to the producer, place of origin and weight. Planters who mixed dirt and clay in their product would be liable to prosecution.

### 1749, June 12. KING GEORGE'S WAR.

News of the war's end reached Charlestown. A celebration lasted throughout the day and into the night with "Demonstrations of Joy ... sky-rockets ... and other illuminations." Defensive building stopped in Carolina and within a few months all fortifications fell into disrepair.

### 1749, June 19. SLAVERY. POLITICS.

The Assembly passed an addition to the Negro Act of 1740 which decreed death for any Negro who administered poison to any person.

### 1749, August 5. BIRTHS.

Thomas Lynch, Jr. was born in Georgetown. He would later sign the Declaration of Independence for South Carolina.

### 1749, August 5. CULTURE. LIBRARY SOCIETY.

Members of the Charlestown Library Society met at "Mr. Thomas Blythe's in Broad Street."

### 1749, August 18. CULTURE. SEGOON-POP CLUB.

Members of the Segoon-Pop Club met "precisely at 17 minutes after 7 o'clock" to choose a new president.

### 1749, Fall. JOHN NEWTON ARRIVES. SLAVERY.

John Newton arrived in Charlestown from Antigua as captain of the slave vessel *Brownlow*. He hired Henry Laurens as the factor selling his ship's cargo. During his several weeks in Charlestown Newton attended services at the Independent Church and met with Rev. Josiah Smith, which began his path toward converting to Christianity.

### 1749, September 3. RELIGION. FIRST JEWISH MEETING.

The first Jewish meeting in Charlestown took place. According to Jewish practice there must be a *minyan*, or ten males over the age of thirteen, for services to take place. They adopted the name Kahal Kadosh Beth Elohim– holy Congregation of the House of God. They used a small wooden house on Union Street (now State) for their worship services until 1757.

### 1749, November. CULTURE. ENTERTAINMENTS.

Mr. Stokes presented "several dramatick entertainments" in Mrs. Blythe's Court-Room. He noted that he was willing to "submit to the generosity of the Company, what Recompence he may merit."

### 1749, November 23. BIRTH.

Edward Rutledge, last child of Dr. John and Sarah Rutledge, was born.

### 1749, December 10. MARRIAGE.

William Moultrie married Damaris Elizabeth de St. Julien, from a prosperous Huguenot family in Carolina, with more and 8,800 acres to their name, and five lots in Charlestown. William obtained an estate from his brother-in-law Benjamin de St. Julien, 1,020 acres named Northhampton in Berkeley County, and settled in for a life as a planter, growing rice and indigo.

# 1750

### 1750. POLITICS. ENGLAND.

Thomas Corbet, a Charlestown attorney, moved to London and became high baliff of Westminster. Through the years, he received dozens of Charlestown's young men at his home while they were in school.

### 1750. RELIGION.

The first synagogue established at Charlestown was that of the congregation Beth Elohim founded in 1750 by Spanish and Portuguese immigrants. Several of its founders also had come from Georgia. Its first minister was Isaac DaCosta and among its earliest members were:

- Joseph & Meshod Tobias
- Moses Cohen
- Abraham DaCosta
- Moses Pimenta
- David de Olivera
- Michael Lazarus
- Abraham Nuñez Cardozo

## 1750. *Trade. Commerce.*

Governor James Glen wrote:

> The trade between South Carolina and Great Britain, one year with another, employs twenty-two sail of ships. Those ships bring from Great Britain to South Carolina all sorts of woolen cloths, stuffs and drugges, linens ... silks and muslins; nails of all sizes, hoes, hatchets, and all kinds of iron-ware; bedticks, strong beer, bottled cider, raisins, fine earthen wares, pips, paper, rugs, blankets, quilts, hats ... pewter dishes and plates ... guns, powder, bullets, flints, glass beads, cordage, woolen and cotton cards ... grind-stones, looking and drinking glasses.
>
> In return for these commodities and manufactures there are sent from South Carolina to Great Britain about seventy thousand deerskins a year; some furs, rosin, pitch, tar, raw silk, rice and ... indigo. Besides the twenty-two sail of ships which trade between South Carolina Great Britain ... there enter and annually at the Port of Charles Town, about sixty sail of ships, sloops, and brigantines, which are employed in carrying on ... trade between South Carolina and other countries.

Gov. Glen also listed the quantities of rice exported from the Province of South Carolina from 1730 to 1739 as:

- To Portugal, in all 83,379 barrels
- To Gibraltar, 958 barrels
- To Spain, 3,570 barrels
- To France, only the last two years, 9,500 barrels
- To Great Britain, Ireland and the British plantations, approximately 30,000 barrels
- To Holland, Hamburg and Bremen, including Sweden and Denmark, 372,118 barrels
- The total: 499,525 barrels

## 1750, January 1. *Culture. Education.*

Abraham Varnod and Mary Irwin announced that they:

> Will open a FRENCH SCHOOL ... and teach all sorts of plain needle work, and drawing for embroidery. They draw for Marseilles quilting and all kinds of embroidery, at a reasonable rate.

## 1750, January 15. *Culture. Smoking Club.*

The Smoking Club met "precisely at 11 o'clock in the forenoon at the House of Mrs. Wollford on the Bay, in order take into Consideration Business of great Important."

# John Newton
## From Disgrace to Amazing Grace

**BORN:** July 24, 1725

**DIED:** December 21, 1807

By the age of ten John Newton was sailing with his father, a strict sea captain. In 1744 he was impressed into service on a British man-of-war. Finding the conditions intolerable he deserted but was soon captured, flogged and demoted from midshipman to common seaman.

At his own request he was exchanged into service on a slave ship, which took him to the coast of Sierra Leone, where he became the servant of a slave trader.

*Courtesy of the Library of Congress*

He was brutally abused and forced to work along with black slaves - poorly fed, poorly clothed and unpaid – for over a year. He was rescued by another white slave captain and returned to England on the ship *Greyhound*.

During the voyage home *Greyhound* encountered a severe storm and almost sank. Newton awoke in the middle of the night and as the ship filled with water he called out to God. At that moment the cargo clogged up the hole and the ship was able to stabilize and drift to safety. Newton claimed this experience was the beginning of his conversion to Christianity.

While in Charlestown with a slave ship, Newton listened to a sermon by Rev. Josiah Smith of the Independent Church (present-day Circular Church) Newton prayed and was able to "taste the sweets of communion."

A year later, back in England, at the encouragement of John Wesley, Newton entered the Anglican ministry. As a minister Newton counseled a young politician, William Wilberforce, to remain in Parliament. For the next twenty-six years Wilberforce led the campaign to abolish slavery culminating in the passage of the Slave Trade Act of 1807. Thus, a sermon preached in Charlestown, the largest slave port in the colonies, helped lead to the abolition of the English slave trade.

In 1772 Newton wrote a religious poem which was to become the most famous Christian hymn of all time:

>*Amazing grace! How sweet the sound*
>*That saved a wretch like me.*
>*I once was lost, but now am found*
>*Was blind but now I see.*

### 1750, June 25. MARRIAGE.

Henry Laurens married Eleanor Ball, daughter of a wealthy rice planter. Laurens was on his way to becoming one of the most successful men in Charlestown. A hard worker, he rose an hour before daylight and usually worked until midnight, sleeping about four hours a day. He demanded the same work ethic in his employees.

### 1750, October 23. BIRTH.

Thomas Pinckney was born in Charleston, the second son of Charles and Eliza Pinckney.

### 1750, December 25. DEATH.

Dr. John Rutledge died, on the twelfth anniversary of his marriage to Sarah. His eldest son John was eleven, and his youngest, Edward was one-year old. His twenty-six-year-old wife was left with seven children, two houses, three plantations and 108 slaves – an estate valued at £22,000.

# 1751

### 1751, January 29. SLAVERY. CRIME. POLITICS.

The Assembly received a petition from Thomas Miles for reimbursement for his slaves, Venus and Kitt, who "were tried for Poisoning and condemned to be executed pursuant to the directions of the 'Act for the better ordering and governing of Negroes and other Slaves in this Province.'" Kitt was executed but Venus was "pardoned, and was afterwards sent off the Province."

### 1751, May 17. CULTURE. TWO-BIT SOCIETY.

The South Carolina Society was incorporated by the Assembly making it one of the most important organizations in the colony.

In 1732, a French Huguenot named Elisha Poinsett opened a tavern in Charleston. Several friends agreed to help him out his business by spending an evening or two each week in his tavern. They began to collect two bits (sixteen pence) a week for a fund to help any of their members with a need; they soon became known as the "two-bit society." When Poinsett's business no longer needed their help, they formalized their association with the idea that education would be their main charity.

### 1751, May 17. CRIME. POLITICS.

The Assembly devised a system in order to control the behavior of sailors in port, in an attempt to prevent "rowdyism, desertions and excessive debts." Ships' captains were required to provide a list of names and descriptions of sailors to the Comptroller. Tavern owners allowed to entertain sailors for "no longer than one hour nor provide them with strong drink or food costing more than ten shillings."

## 1751, June 14. *RELIGION. PARISHES DIVIDED.*

Charlestown was divided into two Anglican parishes: St. Michael's, south of Broad Street and St. Philip's, north of Broad.

## 1751, June 14. *BUILDINGS OF CHARLESTON.*

The Assembly passed an act that authorized the construction of the statehouse, and named a group of Commissioners to direct its construction "with such Materials and of such Dimensions and with such useful Offices ... [that] shall appear most conveniently and usefully to answer the Ends for which it is designed."

The Commissioners included:

- William Middleton
- Charles Pinckney
- William Bull, Jr
- James Graeme
- Andrew Rutledge
- John Dart
- Orthiniel Beale
- Benjamin Smith
- Issac Mazyck

---

### MOST SUCCESSFUL FACTORS IN CHARLESTOWN

**WHAT WAS A FACTOR?**

In the American colonies a factor acted as an agent for British firms, importing goods and selling them to retailers for a 5% commission. A factor also purchased goods locally for shipment to England.

During 1735-65 there were 337 factoring firms in Charlestown. According to the Records of the Public Treasurer, the Charlestown factors who paid the most duties on imports were:

- Gabriel Manigault: £30,330
- John Savage: £21,100
- Henry Laurens: £20,319

---

## 1751, November 25. *COMMERCE. SLAVERY.*

An advertisement for Henry Laurens' business in the *South Carolina Gazette* read:

> JUST IMPORTED in the Billander *London* Cap. Youn from Bristol and Capt. Allenby from Lancanshite, Oznabrugs, Irish shirting and sheeting, Linnen, sheat lead, bullets, shot, bottled beer and cyder, writing paper, paving stones, grind stones and millstones, Cornish tiles, white lead, tobacco plugs, iron pots, all sorts of nails, striped duffils, Tarrington rugs, linseed oil, *Gloucestire, Lancashire* and *Cheshire* cheese, butter, fine mould tallow candles, currans and raisins in small jars, earthen

ware, best sail cloth, crown glass 8 by 10 and 9 by 11, empty quart bottles and coals — also imported, a parcel of muscavado sugar in barrels and three negro men to be sold by Austin and Laurens.

# 1752

### 1752. POLITICS.

Gov. James Glen appointed Charles Pinckney Chief Justice of South Carolina.

### 1752. RELIGION. CULTURE.

Issac DaCosta was the first Jew to join a Masonic Lodge in Charlestown.

### 1752. ARRIVALS. RELIGION.

Rev. Charles Woodmason arrived in South Carolina. An itinerant clergyman, he struggled for the next ten years as a planter in the Pee Dee region before going bankrupt and moving to Charlestown.

### 1752, February 22. CORNERSTONE OF ST. MICHAEL'S.

The cornerstone of St. Michael's was laid. The *Gazette* reported that "the church will be built on the Plan of one of Mr. Gibson's Designs."

### 1752, February 28. BIRTH.

William Washington was born in Stafford County, Virginia. He was second cousin to George Washington and would later play an important role during the Revolution in South Carolina.

### 1752, April. ARRIVALS.

Dr. Alexander Garden (not to be confused with his distant kinsman, *Rev. Alexander Garden*) arrived in Charlestown, as an assistant in the medical practice of Dr. William Rose. The younger Garden also had a scientific interest in botany and medicinal plants. He began to methodically categorize local plants.

### 1752, April 27. CULTURE. FAIR.

The *Gazette* advertised:

> THE FAIR at *Ashley-River,* will begin the *first Tuesday* in May: There will be many diversions; four horses to run for a silver watch ... bear-baiting, and two women to grin for a plum pudding; some curious fireworks the like never was seen in Carolina and many other diversions too tedious to mention.

### 1752, July. POLITICS. EDUCATION.

Charles Pinckney, Jr., was admitted the South Carolina bar.

## 1752, September 1. COMMERCE.

Henry Laurens advertised the sale of 400 German indentured servants at £10 sterling from Rotterdam on board the *Upton*.

## 1752, September 13. DISASTER. HURRICANE.

A hurricane hit Charlestown, with a flood level of ten feet above the previous recorded high water mark. More than 100 died, with twice as many injuries. The *South Carolina Gazette* reported:

> All the wharves and bridges were ruined, and every house, store, & upon them, beaten down, and carried way (with all the goods, & therein), as were also many houses in the town; and abundance of roofs, chimneys, & almost all the tiled or slated houses in the town ... The town was likewise overflowed, the tide of sea having rose upwards of Ten feet above the high-water mark at spring tides ...

> All but one of the ships in the harbor were driven ashore and most of the smaller vessels soon became one with the debris. Sloops and schooners were thrown against the houses of Bay street and the wharves along East Bay street destroyed. A brigantine beat down several houses and wound up on the east side of Church street. Eight or ten small schooners, owned by Charlestonians, and three or four pilot boats were driven into the woods, corn fields and marshes of surrounding areas

David Ramsay, in his *History of South Carolina* reported:

> Colonel Pinckney, who lived in the large white house at the corner of Ellery street and French alley, abandoned it after there were several feet of water in it. He took his family from thence to ... corner of Guignard and Charles streets, in a ship's yawl. All South Bay was in ruins, many wooden houses were wrecked to pieces and washed away, and brick houses reduced to a heap of rubbish ... A brick house where Mr. Bedon lived, on Church street ... Mr. Bedon and family unfortunately remained too long in the house, for the whole family, consisting of twelve souls, perished in the water, except himself and a negro wench. The bodies of Mrs. Bedon of one of her children, and of a Dutch boy, were found in the parsonage pasture.

## 1752, October 28. POLITICS.

Gov. Glen proposed a plan for repairing and improving the city's fortifications. He claimed the defenses were "piece-meal" and suggested the hiring of a "regular Engineer." Without consulting the Assembly, Glen hired German-born engineer William De Brahm.

### 1752, November 29. *FORTIFICATIONS.*

William De Brahm presented his fortification plan to Gov. Glen and the bill for his services. The Assembly, upset they had not been consulted, refused to pay the fee. Glen paid De Brahm out of his own pocket.

### 1752, December 20. *CULTURE. TWO-BIT CLUB.*

King George II confirmed the charter of the Two-Bit Club at the Court of St. James. Soon afterward, the name was changed to the South Carolina Society and began including non-French members.

# 1753

### 1753. *BUILDINGS OF CHARLESTON.*

Construction on the State House began, at the corner of Broad and Meeting Streets.

### 1753. *COMMERCE.*

Thomas Bolton sold his shipyard at Hobcaw to James Stewart and John Rose, two immigrant shipbuilders. The shipyard covered more than 100 acres. They built the sloop *Liberty,* with a likeness of Col. William Rhett on the bow.

### 1753, January 2. *MARRIAGE.*

Charles Pinckney, Junior, married his first cousin, Francis Brewton. Both of them were grandchildren of the banker, Miles Brewton. This united two early wealthy Charleston families – the Pinckneys from the planter class, and the Brewtons from the merchant class.

### 1753, April. *POLITICS. COMMERCE.*

Former Chief Justice, Charles Pinckney, was appointed Agent for South Carolina in England. His entire family accompanied him to England: - wife Eliza, sons Charles Cotesworth and Thomas, and daughter Harriot.

The sons were educated at Westminster School and Christ Church, Oxford and France. The sons' friend, William Henry Drayton, accompanied the family and also entered school in Britain.

### 1753, June 22. *BUILDINGS OF CHARLESTON. STATE HOUSE.*

Governor James Glen convened a meeting of the Common's House of Assembly and the King's Council to observe the anniversary of King George's ascension to the throne. They gathered at the corner of Broad and Meeting Streets to lay the cornerstone of the first provincial statehouse. The entourage ended the evening at John Gordon's Tavern at the northeast corner of Broad and Church Streets for dinner.

### 1753, June 24. CULTURE.

The young Peter Manigault, while studying in England, visited Charles and Eliza Pinckney in London. He wrote to his mother about the Pinckneys:

> He already seems to have some desire to return to Carolina and I daresay he will, sooner than he at first talked of ... His wife is an excellent Woman and I venture to say she would chuse [choose] to pass her days in England; however, she is too good a Wife to ever thwart her Husband's Inclination.

### 1753, June 25. CULTURE. WAX DISPLAY.

An ad in the *Gazette* announced "Three elaborate Figures in Wax-work and other Curiosities, to be seen at Mr. *Doughty's* Long-Room, at 20*sh* each Person."

### 1753, August 7. RELIGION.

A petition was made to the Royal Governor for a parcel of land upon which to build a Lutheran church.

### 1753, November 5. CULTURE.

The members of the "ancient, venerable, and honorable Society of BROOMS" met at John Gordon's Tavern.

# 1754

### 1754. COMMERCE.

Robert Wells opened a book shop and acted as a subscription agent for English periodicals such as *London Magazine, Gentleman' Magazine* and *Monthly Review.*

### 1754. CULTURE. POLITICS.

Dr. Alexander Garden continued his studies in local flora and fauna, shipping them to John Ellis, a merchant and zoologist in London, and also to Carolus Linnaeus, a prominent Swedish botanist.

### 1754. POLITICS. ENGLAND. EDUCATION.

Twelve-year old Arthur Middleton attended the Hackney School in London and then several years at Cambridge.

### 1754. COMMERCE. COMING STREET CEMETERY.

Issac DaCosta purchased a plot of land on Coming Street to be used for his family burial site. DaCosta later conveyed this property to Beth Elohim to "be a convenient place for the Burial Ground of the Jews' Congregation in general." In present-day it is known as the Coming Street Cemetery, the oldest Jewish cemetery in the South.

## 1754. COMMERCE.

Charles Pinckney, Junior purchased a plantation from John Savage in Christ Church Parish (present-day Mt. Pleasant.) Pinckney, Jr. named it Snee Farm from the Irish word meaning "bountiful."

## 1754, February 24. CULTURE.

Peter Manigault wrote to his mother, again about Charles Pinckney:

> Coll. Pinckney is just now recovering from an Indisposition of the same kind [rheumatism] which I dare say will be a new cause for Dislike to England, as he never was attacked in that way before.

## 1754, May 28. FRENCH AND INDIAN WAR.

Called the Seven Years War in Great Britain, the war was the result of tensions between the British and French in America, with each side wanting to increase its land holdings. The French kept pushing further south from Canada, intruding into English territory.

Virginia militiamen, under the command of 22-year-old George Washington, ambushed a French patrol at the Forks of the Ohio, the Allegheny and Monongahela rivers, present day Pittsburg, Pa. His troops retreated and built Fort Necessity. For the next two years, skirmishes escalated between the French and English.

## 1754, June 11. SLAVERY. EXECUTION.

Two female slaves of Mr. Childermas Croft were burned alive for setting fire to their master's main house and several plantation outbuildings in Charleston.

## 1754, June 27. CULTURE. THEATER.

Mr. Sturgess, from London, began to perform on the slack-rope three evenings a week in the Long Room at Mr. Gordon's Tavern for 30sh. Slack-rope is similar to tightrope walking. He also performing singing and other entertainments.

## 1754, July 3. FRENCH AND INDIAN WAR.

Lt. Peter Mercier, of the Independent Company from South Carolina, was killed at Great Meadows while serving under the command of George Washington.

## 1754, August 29. SLAVERY. EXECUTION.

A South Carolina slave named Robin was gibbeted for the murder of his master in 1754. According to the *South Carolina Gazette* "till within an Hour before he expired, constantly declared his Innocence; but at last confessed." Robin declared "that he himself had perpetrated that Murder and at the same Time disclosed a Scene equally shocking," revealing a conspiracy among several slaves.

Robin and eight other slaves had planned "the Murder of two other Gentlemen in Beaufort" and then "they were to have taken a Schooner" to get to St. Augustine in Florida."

## 1754, September 28. CULTURE. THEATER.

The *Gazette* announced:

> At the New Theatre on Monday next will be presented (By a Company of Comedians from London) A TRAGEDY called *The Fair Penitent*.
>
> Tickets may be had of John Remington and at the Printers. Price: Stage Box, 50sh. Front and Side Boxes, 40sh. Pitt, 30sh. And Gallery, 20sh.

## 1754, September 28. CULTURE. THEATER.

Despite the lingering effect of George Whitefield's preaching against the loose morality of theater people, the Lewis Hallam Company of Players arrived in Charlestown for a successful theater season. The desire of the aristocracy for entertainment was stronger than their Puritanical sensibility.

The Company was run by two brothers, William and Lewis Hallam, and possessed a repertoire of twenty-four popular plays, several farces and a pantomime. Their repertoire included:

| | | |
|---|---|---|
| *The Merchant of Venice* | *Theodosius* | *The Twin Rivals* |
| *The Fair Penitent* | *Provoked Husband* | *The Lying Valet* |
| *The Beaux' Stratagem* | *Tamerians* | *Miss In Her Teens* |
| *Jane Shore* | *The Inconstant* | *The Mock Doctor* |
| *The Recruiting Officer* | *Woman's A Riddle* | *The Devil to Pay* |
| *King Richard III* | *The Suspicious Husband* | *Hob In The Well* |
| *The Careless Husband* | | *Damon and Philida* |
| *The Constant Couple* | *The Conscious Lovers* | *The Anatomist* |
| *Hamlet* | *George Barnwell* | *The Miller Deceived* |
| *Orthello* | *The Committee* | |

## 1754, October 25. CULTURE. THEATER.

The Lewis Hallam Company presented *The Orphan, or the Unhappy Marriage*.

## 1754, December. ARRIVALS.

Peter Manigault returned to Charlestown from England, where he was studying.

## 1754, December 27. CULTURE.

The Masonic election of Members was followed by a church service and then a dinner at Gordon's Tavern in the afternoon, and in the Evening, "they went to the

New Theatre, where the tragedy *The Distressed Mother* was presented ... and some Mason songs between the Acts."

# 1755

### 1755. SLAVERY.

Henry Laurens was selling "about 700 Negroes each year," more than twenty per cent of the total slave market.

### 1755. CULTURE. LIBRARY SOCIETY.

William Henderson was elected librarian of the Library Society. He moved the collections into the Free School (of which he was headmaster) on Broad Street.

### 1755, February 5. FORTIFICATIONS. FRENCH AND INDIAN WAR.

Rumors of a war between England and France reached Charles Town. The Assembly agreed to hire German-born engineer William De Brahm to build new fortifications under the direction of the Assembly-appointed Commissioners of Fortifications. They decided to concentrate on building up the southeastern seaward side of the peninsula.

### 1755, March 1. BUILDINGS OF CHARLESTON.

The new State House at Broad and Meeting streets opened. It was the largest and grandest building in South Carolina, described as a "two-story, large, commodious Brick Building ... of about 120 by 40 feet ... decorated with four ... columns."

### 1755, March 21. DEATH.

William Bull, Sr. died.

### 1755, June 2. CULTURE. MEDICINE.

The Faculty of Physic met at Gordon's Tavern, with Dr. John Moultrie elected president.

### 1755, June 19. CULTURE. JOHNSON'S DICTIONARY ARRIVES.

Samuel Johnson's dictionary, published in London in April 1755, arrived in Charles Town, imported by Robert Wells.

### 1755, July. FORTIFICATIONS.

Construction of the city's fortifications began under the supervision of De Braham. The biggest problem was the construction of a "grillage" (foundation) along the "boggy marshes" of Vanderhorst Creek (present-day Water Street). The grillage was built out of cedar posts, cypress planks and covered with layers of mud, lime and oyster shells.

### 1755, July 17. *SLAVERY. COMMERCE.*

Henry Laurens described what he most desired in a slave cargo for maximum profits:

> Two thirds at least Men from 18 to 25 years old, the other young Women from 14 to 18 the cost not to exceed Twenty five pounds Sterling per head ... There must not be a Callabar [region in Africa, present-day Nigeria] amongst them. Gold Coast and Gambias are best, next to them the Windward Coast are prefer'd to Angolas. Pray observe that our People like tall Slaves best for our business & strong withall.

### 1755, September 23. *LIGHTNING RODS INSTALLED.*

The Assembly ordered that Benjamin Franklin's new device, the lightning rod, be installed at the powder magazines in Charlestown and Fort Johnson.

### 1755, November 19. *DEATH.*

Andrew Rutledge died. The childless attorney left his estate – a house and plantation valued at £12,000 in trust for his brother's oldest children, John, Thomas, Andrew and Sarah.

John was serving a five-year apprenticeship in the Charlestown law office of James Parsons, along with another local young man, Thomas Bee.

### 1755, December 14. *SLAVERY.*

The *Gambia* arrived in Charlestown with 150 slaves.

# 1756

### 1756. *CULTURE. MACE OF LEGISTATURE PURCHASED.*

In London, South Carolina purchased, for 90 guineas, the mace which is still used the state legislature. It was crafted by Magdalen Feline, a master goldsmith, who worked in Convent Garden.

The Mace weighed about 11 pounds and it is scepter-like in appearance. Around the cylindrical head, below the crown, are four circular decorative panels that depict art work representational of craftsmanship from England, France, Ireland and Germany. Made of solid silver, with gold burnishing, it resembles the Mace of the Common Council of Norwich, England.

### 1756, January 31. *MILITIA.*

Francis Marion's name appeared on the muster roll of the St. John's Militia Company in Monck's Corner. This was the first mention of Marion in relation with military service.

Slave street auction. *Courtesy of the New York Public Library*

## 1756, February 3. *CULTURE. COCK FIGHT.*

John Gordon sponsored a cock-fight in his tavern.

## 1756, March 3. *CULTURE.*

The Artillery Association met at "the House of Mr. Elisha Poinsett."

## 1756, May 1. *FORTIFICATIONS.*

Construction of the city's fortifications were finished within ten months. De Brahm's design, a "continuous line of Ramparts, forming regular Bastions, detach'd or joined with curtains," connected Granville's Bastion with Broughton's at White Point. The new wall was four feet taller than the previous one and the *Gazette* noted that "the sea is damn'd out."

A description of the colonial waterfront from Dr. Philip Prioleau in 1803 read:

> The town was in a state of fortification ... A very strong brick wall, the curtain line extended on the east side of East Bay Street from Roper's Wharf to the Governor's bridge, at each extremity of which there was

a bastion. There wharves were few in number, the most northwardly of which is now owned by Captain John Blake. With the exception of the low stores on the wharves, the vendue store which was opposite Tradd Street, and the Old Guard House where the Exchange now stands, there was not a house on the east side of East Bay Street, nor was there any land at that time on which one could be erected.

## 1756, June 1. *ARRIVALS. NEW ROYAL GOVERNOR.*

The new governor, William Henry Lyttelton, arrived on the HMS *Winchelsea*. Crowds of citizens gathered to toast the new governor but his term would be riddled with controversies.

## 1756, July 2. *FRENCH AND INDIAN WAR.*

France and England officially declared war after two years of skirmishes in the colonies. The French had the upper hand for three years, in part due to being allied with several powerful Indian tribes.

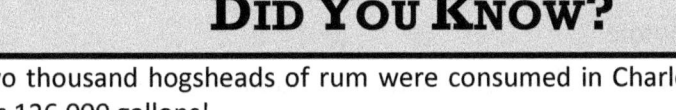

Two thousand hogsheads of rum were consumed in Charlestown in 1756 – that's 126,000 gallons!

Courtesy of the Library of Congress

## 1756, July 2. *FORTIFICATIONS.*

Gov. Lyttleton hired William De Brahm to design and build a fort in the upcountry for their Cherokee allies against the French.

### 1756, August. COLONIAL POST.

Printer Peter Timothy was appointed by Benjamin Franklin an official of colonial post. For many years he coordinated the delivery of letters throughout South Carolina arrived by sea.

### 1756, December. FRENCH AND INDIAN WAR.

Lord William Pitt became the leader of the British ministry. He adopted aggressive new policies that had a crucial effect on the latter half of the war.

# 1757

### 1757. RELIGION.

The first Lutheran church, St. John's, was organized by Rev. George Frediche. They worshiped in the French Huguenot Church until 1764.

### 1757, January 15. COMMERCE.

Henry Laurens wrote:

> Pleased to observe that we have had the good fortune thus far not to have one of the enemies' privateers come near our coast so that our trade is all safely arrived and our harbor so full of ships they may be had for any part of England at four hundred pound per ton.

### 1757, March 12. CULTURE.

The St. Andrew's Hunting Club added a new stipulation for the members ... every member was to bring a "Gun and Cartridges, to fire at a Target; and that the Time in which they are to load and fire is fixed at a Minute."

### 1757, June 5. FRENCH AND INDIAN WAR.

The First Royal Highland Battalion of over 1000 Irish officers and men arrived to supplement the 700 British troops under the command of Lt. Col. Henry Bouquet already in the city. The troops were quartered in an encampment on the northwestern edge of the city until Gov. Lyttelton ordered that the officers be given rooms in private homes.

### 1757, June 5. TROOPS QUARTERED IN CHURCH.

The enlisted men were housed in "a half-finished Church without Windows (St. Michael's) where "most of the Men were obliged to lye upon the Ground without Straw ..."

### 1757, June 20. CULTURE.

In the *Gazette,* Robert Wells, bookseller, gave:

notice to such gentleman as subscribed with him for magazines, that they may be supplied either with the *London, Gentleman's* or *Martin's* magazines, and both the *Monthly* and *Critical Reviews.*

### 1757, September. *DISASTER.*

A typhoon hit Charlestown that moved up the Ashley River with such force that eyewitness accounts (possibly exaggerated) claimed the riverbed was laid bare. The storm stranded five ships and damaged several plantations upriver.

### 1757, October 25. *BIRTH.*

Charles Pinckney, son of Charles Pinckney, Junior and Francis Brewton Pinckney, and cousin to Charles Cotesworth Pinckney, was born in Charlestown. He would later sign the U.S. Constitution as would his cousin.

### 1757, November 28. *FRENCH AND INDIAN WAR.*

The Assembly stopped paying for the rent of the British officers quartered in private homes. Outraged, Lt. Col. Bouquet ordered his officers to keep their rooms and refuse to pay their rents.

# 1758

### 1758, January 5. *EDUCATION. ENGLAND.*

John Rutledge sailed to England to study law at the Middle Temple at the Inns of Court. While in London he spent considerable time at the Carolina Coffee House on Birchen Lane, "dining, drinking and fellowship."

It was the center for Carolinians in London or Englishmen with business connections to the colony. Sixty years before, the Coffee House was the location where the Lords Proprietors met potential colonists. Many ship captains sailing to and from Carolina frequented the Coffee House so it was the best place to send and receive mail, get news from home, or book passage.

### 1758, February 28. *NEW BARRACKS BUILT.*

A "New Barracks" of pine-timber was constructed for British soldiers on what is now the site of the College of Charleston. Lt. Col. Bouquet again demanded that the Assembly pay the officers' rents in private homes. The legislature refused, claiming that the traditional right of Englishmen to be free of quartering was being violated.

### 1758, March 17. *BIRTH.*

Gabriel Manigault was born in Charlestown. He would become one of the most successful merchants in America.

### 1758, March 18. POLITICS.

A report about British quartering was presented to the Assembly. Prepared by Peter Manigault, Christopher Gadsden, Henry Laurens and Rawlins Lowndes, the report stated:

> Officers and Soldiers cannot, legally or constitutionally, be quarter'd in private Houses, without the special Consent of the Owners or Possessors of such Houses.

### 1758, April. RELIGION.

Richard Clark, rector of St. Philip's, grew a long beard and began to stroll the streets all day yelling, "Repent! Repent! The Kingdom of Heaven is at hand." Some took him seriously as a prophet, but most found him amusing, or disturbed. He soon resigned and moved back to England.

### 1758, April 3. COMMERCE.

Christopher Gadsden paid £6,000 currency for fifteen acres of high land (and twenty-nine acres of marsh) in northeastern Charlestown, which became known as Gadsdenboro.

### 1758, April 21. COMMERCE.

Charlestown cabinetmakers Thomas Elfe and Thomas Hutchinson, were paid £728.2.6 for "chairs and tables in the Council Chamber."

### 1758, May. CULTURE.

Charles and Eliza Pinckney returned to Charlestown, with their ten-year old daughter Harriot. Their sons, Charles Cotesworth and Thomas, remained in England to attend school. Charles contracted malaria soon after their return to Charlestown.

### 1758, June 28. MARRIAGE.

Rebecca Brewton married Jacob Motte.

### 1758, October 13. DEATH.

Charles Pinckney died of malaria in Charlestown. His wife, Eliza, was nearly overcome with her grief. She wrote to her sons:

> How shall I write to you! What shall I say to you! You have met with the greatest loss ... Your dear, dear father, the best and most valuable of parents, is no more! He met the king of terrors without the least terror ... and without agony, and went like a Lamb into eternity, into a blessed Eternity! where I have not the least doubt he will reap immortal joy for Ever and Ever.

## 1758, November. *French and Indian War.*

The British captured Fort Duquesne, the site of Braddock's disaster and death. Duquesne was renamed Fort Pitt, after the new English leader, and eventually became known as Pittsburgh, PA.

## 1758, November 22. *Commerce.*

The first issue of the *South Carolina Weekly Gazette*, was published by Robert Well. For the next several years, this was the only competition to Peter Timothy's *South Carolina Gazette*. Wells also operated the Great Stationary and Book Store, the largest in Charlestown, and one of the largest in America.

## 1758, December 1. *Culture.*

The *Gazette* posed:

> NOTICE IS HEREBY GIVEN, to all members of the CANDLESTICK CLUB, that they give their Attendance on the first Day of *January* next ... at the Club-room of the House of *Mr. Alexander Chisholm*, in order to elect proper officers for the coming year.

# 1759

## 1759. *South Carolina Society Purchases Land.*

The South Carolina Society purchased a block of land in Ansonborough between George & Wentworth Streets and Meeting & Anson Streets for investment purposes. The block between Meeting and Anson Streets was originally called Centurian Street but was renamed Society Street.

## 1759. *Commerce.*

Carolina exported more than 1 million pounds of indigo.

## 1759. *Real Estate.*

Francis Marion was given a portion of land on Belle Isle Plantation in St. Stephens by his brother, Gabriel. Francis became a farmer for the next fifteen years, and called his farm Hampton Hill.

## 1759, January 5. *Slavery.*

The ship *Keppel* arrived from Senegal with 50 slaves.

## 1759, April 21. *Slavery.*

A slave in Charleston:

who at the beginning of last Month most cruelly murdered several white People at the Congarees was hung in Chains ... at the dividing Path between the two Quarter-House.

## 1759, July 7. SLAVERY.

The *Gazette* reported:

> The ship *Polly,* Capt. Hamilton, and the ship *Mercury* Capt. Ingladieu, both of Bristol, were lately lost on the coast of Africa. Capt. Hamilton was destined for this port with a cargo of slaves. A sloop commanded by the brother of the above Capt. Ingladieu, slaving up the River Gambia, was attacked by a number of natives about February 27 last ... finding himself desperately wounded, and likely to be overcome when about 80 negroes had boarded his vessel, discharged a pistol into his magazine, and blew her up; himself and every soul on board perished.

## 1759, September 30. FRENCH AND INDIAN WAR.

A general muster for militia was called by Governor Lyttelton to meet the Cherokee uprising in the backcountry.

## 1759, October 16. FRENCH AND INDIAN WAR.

The *Gazette* reported. "God be praised! QUEBEC is in English hands."

## 1759, October 26. FRENCH AND INDIAN WAR.

Governor Lyttelton left Charlestown, marching for Fort Prince George (present-day Pickens County, South Carolina) with 1,500 troops (including Christopher Gads-den, William Moultrie and Francis Marion) to put down the Cherokee rebellion.

Francis Marion was a captain in his brother Gabriel's military unit. This was not a local militia, but a British Royal unit, and Marion was exposed to British army training and methods for the first time.

## 1759, November 3. BIRTH.

Martha Laurens was born, daughter of Henry and Eleanor Laurens, beginning of one of Charleston's most extraordinary lives.

Her father, Henry, was a successful merchant. Through his London contacts, Laurens entered into the slave trade with the Grant, Oswald & Company who controlled 18th century British slave castle in the Republic of Sierra Leone, West Africa known as Bunce Castle. Laurens contracted to receive slaves from Serra Leone, catalogue and marketed the human product conducting public auctions in Charles Town. His company Austin and Laurens in the 1750s, handled was responsible for the sales of more than eight thousand Africans.

Martha would reap the benefits of this privileged life.

# 1760

### 1760. POPULATION. SLAVERY.

Lt. Governor Bull estimated there were 57,253 Negroes in South Carolina, about 15,000 adult males. He also noted that with only about 6,000 white males this "must raise in our midst many melancholy reflections."

### 1760. SLAVERY.

Sullivan's Island received 3,740 slaves during the year to be quarantined before being brought into Charlestown for sale.

### 1760, January 9. FRENCH AND INDIAN WAR.

Gov. Lyttelton and the militia returned tired and hungry. They paraded down Broad Street at noon with cannons booming to welcome them.

### 1760, January 12. EPIDEMIC. MARTHA LAURENS'S FIRST DEATH.

One of the most severe small pox outbreaks in colonial America started, most likely brought to the city by returning soldiers from the Cherokee Indian expedition. More than 6,000 people contracted the disease, resulting in 380 deaths among whites and about 350 blacks.

It was also the first mass inoculation of the Charlestown population, with more than 2,000 people taking the shot within a few weeks, more than 600 in one day according to Dr. Alexander Garden.

Three-month-old Martha Ramsay was pronounced dead of smallpox. Her body was laid out in preparation for a funeral and placed next to an open window. Dr. John Moultrie arrived and pronounced her still alive, speculating she had been revived by the fresh breeze.

Eliza Pinckney wrote: "Many poor wretches ... died for want of proper nursing ... smallpox rages the city so that it almost puts a stop to all business."

### 1760, February. FRENCH AND INDIAN WAR. BACKCOUNTRY.

Cherokee Indians murdered twenty-four traders in the Carolina backcountry. Fleeing traders were chased to the settlement of Ninety-Six and seventy-five more were killed.

### 1760, February 9. ENGLAND. EDUCATION.

John Rutledge was called to the English bar and sailed home for Charlestown soon after.

### 1760, April 1. FRENCH AND INDIAN WAR.

Lt. Col. Archibald Montgomerie arrived in Charlestown with 1,200 Highlanders. They had helped take Fort Duquesne from the French and renamed it Fort

Pitt (present-day Pittsburg) after William Pitt. Three hundred and fifty South Carolina troops joined the Highlanders.

### 1760, April 23. *FRENCH AND INDIAN WAR.*

Montgomerie's army marched to join the provincial militia at the Congaree River. The provincials included the Gentlemen Volunteers, commanded by Thomas Middleton. John Moultrie, Jr., and his brother William, were part of the Volunteers. Montgomerie proceeded to burn Cherokee villages throughout the backcountry but was ultimately unsuccessful.

### 1760. July 31. *FRENCH AND INDIAN WAR. POLITICS. TAXES.*

The Assembly passed a bill to defray the cost of the war against the Cherokee.

### 1760, August 23. *COMMERCE. ART.*

Benjamin Hawes advertised in the *Gazette* that he:

> Undertakes all kinds of drawing, gilding, varnishing, painting coats of arms in water-colours; drawing on canvas for ladies work, prepares gum-colours in imitation of the Chinese.

## BUILDINGS OF CHARLESTON
### 117 Broad Street

James Laurens, brother of Henry Laurens, built his Georgian style home in 1760. Eighteen years later, the house was purchased by Edward Rutledge, signer of the Declaration of Independence, who lived here until his death in 1800.

Frederick Wagner who owned the largest grocery business in Charleston at 163 East Bay, purchased the house in 1885 and made extensive renovations. In the present-day, the house is run as a hotel called The Governor's House Inn.

James Laurens House, 117 Broad Street. *Courtesy of the New York Public Library*

# 1761

### 1761. *POLITICS.*

William Moultrie, 31-years old, was commissioned a captain in the South Carolina militia; he owned a rice/indigo plantation and about 200 slaves.

### 1761. *EXECUTION. RELIGION. BACKCOUNTRY.*

A Swiss-German named Jacob Weber was hanged for the murder of two members of his own religious sect, the Weberites. Weber killed his fellow believers in a moment of religious frenzy by burying and suffocating them under several mattresses.

### 1761, January 2. *LEGAL. JOHN RUTLEDGE'S FIRST CASE.*

John Rutledge's first legal case established his reputation in South Carolina as a leading attorney. His client, Mary Cooke sued merchant William Lennox for £7,000 for breaking repeated promises of marriage. The trial was scheduled to be heard during the November term.

### 1761, January 6. *FRENCH AND INDIAN WAR. CRESCENT INSIGNIA.*

Lt. Colonel James Grant took a force of 2,250 (British army regulars and South Carolina regiment) marched north to Fort Prince George in the upstate. .

Lieutenant-Colonel Henry Laurens served in the campaign with Colonel Thomas Middleton. Major John Moultrie, William Moultrie, Francis Marion, Isaac Huger, and Andrew Pickens all served against the Cherokee nation. All these men would later play significant roles in the American Revolution for South Carolina.

Though not professional soldiers, the Provisional Regiment at least looked the part. They wore a uniform that consisted of:

> Collarless coatees of blue with scarlet lapels, cuff and linings. Waistcoats and breeches were blue, stockings and leggings were brown, and belts and crossbelts were buff. A black light-infantry cap was fashioned by removing most of the brim of a felt hat, except the front portion, which was turned up vertically. To this false front was fastened a silver crescent believed to originated from Lt. Gov. Bull's family seal ... officers carried small swords and often wore silver gorgets suspended from their necks.

### 1761, February 2. *CULTURE. PROCLAMATION OF GEORGE III.*

The *Gazette* reported on the ceremony for the proclamation of George III as king:

> The regular troops commanded by lieutenant colonel Grant, being marched down from the barracks, and drawn up Broad Street with the

Charles Town regiment of militia, commanded by the hon. col. Beale ... and all the merchant ships in the harbor having their colours displayed; about 11 o'clock his honour the Lieutenant Governor went from his own house to the State-House, attended by several gentlemen, the regulars and the militia resting their arms all the while, and proclaimed the King in the council chamber ...

The procession then moved down Broad Street, opposite to the Guard House where the proclamation was read, repeated, and followed by three huzzahs ... and the procession went on to Granville's bastion, where the king was proclaimed for the last time; immediately after which the cannon at Granville's, Craven's and Broughton's bastions and fort Johnson were fire, followed by a general volley of small arms, and huzzaing was repeated twice more.

## 1761, February 21. *CULTURE.*

Mr. Valois, a dancing Master, organized a ball in Gordon's Long Room.

## 1761, March 3. *CULTURE. HORSE RACING.*

Horse races began with "a great deal of Diversion. There will also be Cock fighting and other Sport."

## 1761, March 21. *CULTURE.*

A theatrical entertainment was conducted by His Majesty's troops. The *Gazette* enthusiastically wrote:

> The behavior of these troops during their stay in Charles-Town has given the greatest satisfaction to the inhabitants; who on Friday and Saturday last week, were very politely complimented and agreeably entertained, by the officers of the army, with a comedy and a farce, in the council chamber.

## 1761, March 21. *CULTURE. ORANGE GARDENS.*

Mr. Wilson announced the opening of his Orange Gardens:

> where the gentlemen may depend on having the best of liquors, as well as constant attendance. The largest gardens will be laid out neat and elegant manner for Gentlemen and ladies to walk in, where may be had tea, coffee, chocolate, Salop Capilaire , etc ...

## 1761, March 28. *DESCRIPTION OF TROOPS.*

Major John Moultrie, Jr., in a letter to Eleanor Austin, called the recruits in the provincial militia:

rough and riotous fellows to manage, as ever got together; add to these some young gentlemen [the junior officers] that require a good deal of looking after ... there are some ... among us, whom though not very delicate I will call camp ladys [sic] ... who resemble noisy, riotous and troublesome cattle.

### 1761, April 6. *French and Indian War.*

Captain William Moultrie sat as a member of a regimental court-martial at the Congaree for seven men accused of desertion. Three of men were sentenced "to receive two hundred, four hundred, or eight hundred lashes on their bare backs." Three other men were sentenced to be execute by hanging. Col. Grant commuted the sentences except for one man who was hanged as an example.

### 1761, Summer-Fall. *French and Indian War.*

Lt. Col. Grant and the British forces burned fifteen Cherokee towns and destroyed all their crops, thoroughly defeating the Indians. Francis Marion was commissioned a lieutenant in the provincial infantry, serving under Capt. William Moultrie.

### 1761, June 20. *Culture.*

The *Gazette* noted: "St. Andrew's and St. Philip's Club ... spent the afternoon very merry, after killing two foxes."

### 1761, August. *Epidemic.*

A yellow fever outbreak in Charlestown caused so much alarm that Lt. Gov. Bull moved the Assembly out of town to the Ashley Ferry town.

### 1761, August 29. *French and Indian War.*

A delegation of Cherokee chiefs arrived at the British camp in the backcountry to negotiate a peace. Col. Grant furnished the chiefs with an armed escort guard to return to Charlestown to confer with Lt. Gov. William Bull. Col. Henry Laurens and Capt. William Moultrie were given command of the escort.

### 1761, September 23. *Peace With Cherokee.*

A treaty with the Cherokee was signed by Lt. Gov. William Bull at Ashley Ferry Town. The treaty provided:
- for the Cherokee to surrender all English property
- the right for the English to build forts anywhere
- the exclusion of all Frenchmen
- prompt execution of murderers of white men
- the restoration of trade between the English and the Cherokee

Francis Marion had developed a "profound distast for the cycle of vengeance that is set off when one side's atrocity is met with barbarism from the othe.r" He returned to his plantation on the Santee to grow rice and indigo and hoped he was finished with military service.

### 1761, November. *LEGAL. RUTLEDGE'S FIRST CASE.*

John Rutledge won his case for Mary Cooke, £2,500 in damages and received a large fee for his work. According to one report Rutledge's "eloquence astonished all who heard him." He quickly was retained by Lt. Col. Henry Laurens for all of his merchant firm's legal work.

Dr. David Ramsey stated about Rutledge that:

> Instead of rising by degrees to the head of his profession ... he burst forth at once the able lawyer and accomplished orator. He was employed in the most difficult cases, and retained with the largest fees.

### 1761, December 17. *DUEL.*

Col. Thomas Middleton accused Lt. Col. Grant of failing to consult him during the campaign against the Cherokee. Christopher Gadsden in the *Gazette* claimed that Grant "failed to be aggressive" toward the Indians by not allowing the men "to cut the throats of as many as they could have."

Grant challenged Middleton to a duel and "apparently could have killed him, but gave him is life."

### 1761, December 22. *ARRIVALS.*

Thomas Boone arrived as the Governor of South Carolina replacing the weak and inept William Lyttleton. He was formerly the governor of New Jersey and the nephew of Joseph Boone, former London representative of Carolina.

He was also under orders from the British government to reign in the power of the local Assembly which had become more independent during the French and Indian War.

# 1762

### 1762. *CULTURE.*

The St. Celilia Society was established to provide musical entertainment. Their annual ball, held on November 22, became the leading social event in South Carolina. Tradition holds that the Society was organized in the house at 6 Bedon's Alley.

### 1762. *RELIGION.*

Rev. Charles Woodmason moved to Charlestown, after a decade of failure as a planter in the Pee Dee region. He became a justice of the peace.

### 1762, January 12. *COMMERCE.*

The *Gazette* reported:

> the crops of rice are so great that we expect to make 150,000 barrels. I cannot express the satisfaction I feel, in reflecting on the wonderful

increase of so valuable a commodity from so small a beginning, in about, or little more than half a century.

---

## BUILDINGS OF CHARLESTON
### St. Michael's Church, 80 Meeting Street

St. Michael's Church, Charleston.
*Author's collection.*

On February 1, 1762, Rev. Robert Cooper held the first services at the newly com-pleted St. Michael's Church. Not only was the 192-foot spire the tallest in the American colonies, it also became a distinctive navigation tool. Sailors used it to distinguish "this place from the rest of the coast, where there is a sameness very dangerous to mariners."

On May 8, 1791, George Washington attended the morning service, sitting in pew #43. The graveyard is one of Charleston's most historic, with the graves of John Rutledge and Charles Cotesworth Pinckney, both signers of the U.S. Constitution, Gen. Mordecai Gist, Revolutionary War hero, and James Louis Petigru, famous Charleston lawyer.

St. Michael's is oldest surviving church building in the city.

---

## 1762, January 23. *CULTURE. RAFFLE FOR A CLOCK.*

An advertisement in the *Gazette* announced:

> To Be Raffled for, by twenty-three gentlemen at Ten Pounds a chance: THE most curious Musical CLOCK that ever was seen in this province, which plays twelve tunes on sixteen bells, and represents a concert in the arch, where every person seems to play on his separate instrument.

## 1762, March. *POLITICS.*

Gov. Boone asked the Assembly to draw up a new election act, claiming the current law "loose and general." The Assembly refused.

## 1762, April 4. CULTURE. FELLOWSHIP SOCIETY.

The artisans of Charlestown founded the Fellowship Society.

## 1762, May 29. COMMERCE. POLITICS.

The Assembly, at the urging of Governor Boone, took action to restrict clandestine and illegal trade that several Carolina merchants had with "the enemy." Boone was concerned that the shortage of proper British officials in Charlestown and other Carolina ports, as well as the suspected collusion between the merchants, Assembly and Vice-Admiralty officials, made the situation "fruitless."

## 1762, June. COMMERCE. CULTURE.

The *London Magazine* reported about Charlestown:

> It is a market town and the produce of the whole province is brought to it, for sale or exportation, its trade is far from being inconsiderable for it deals near one thousand miles into the continent ... the rich people have handsome equipages; the merchants are opulent and well bred; the people are thriving and extensive, in dress and life, so that everything conspires to make this town the politest, as it is one of the richest in America.

## 1762, June 2. COMMERCE.

Henry Laurens returned from the war against the Cherokee and purchased the 3,000-acre Mepkin Plantation in the Monck's Corner area on the Cooper River for £8,000 currency.

## 1762, August 23. CULTURE. HERMAPHRODITE SHEEP.

An advertisement in the *Gazette* announced "At *5 sh.* each, the Curious may see a very extraordinary *Hermaphrodite Sheep* at Mathias Peter's next door to the Jail."

## 1762, September 13. POLITICS. ELECTION SCANDAL

During a special election for the Assembly Christopher Gadsden was elected, but discovered the election return from St. Paul's parish was blank. The church wardens had also not taken the oath required by the Election Act.

Gov. Boone, citing the irregularities, refused to administer the oath of office to Gadsden, and called for a new Election Act to be written. This was the first time a royal governor challenged the Assembly's right to determine the validity of elections.

## 1762, September 18. CULTURE. EDUCATION.

Edmund Egan advertised he was available to teach "the use of the Small Sword."

## 1762, September 21. POLITICS. COMMERCE.

In an attempt to elevate South Carolina's reputation in overseas ports, Gov. Boone appointed Moses Lindo, a local Jew, as "Surveyor and Inspector General of indico [sic]."

## 1762, October 15. *COMMERCE. SHIPBUILDING*

Robert Cochran who had "one of the most convenient places for building or repairing vessels," announced he had sunk a wharf.

---

### BUILDINGS OF CHARLESTON
#### John Rutledge House, 116 Broad Street

John Rutledge House, 116 Broad Street.
*Courtesy of the Library of Congress*

John Rutledge built his Georgian home on Broad Street, across from James Laurens' home in 1762. President George Washington had breakfast in the home in 1791 with Rutledge's wife, Eliza-beth. The elaborate ironwork was added in 1853 by Thomas Gad-sden who employed Christopher Werner to design the ironworks.

Through the years the house has also served as the residence of Rev. John England Charleston's first Catholic bishop. During the late nineteenth century it was the home of Mayor R. Goodwin Rhett, who entertained President Taft during his 1909 visit.

In the present-day it operates as the John Rutledge House Inn.

---

## 1762, November 22. *POLITICS. ELECTION SCANDAL.*

The Assembly appointed a committee to prepare a report on the contested Gadsden election. The committee members included John Rutledge, Rawlins Lowdnes, Charles Pinckney, Junior and, in a slap to the governor, Christopher Gadsden himself.

## 1762, November 28. *POLITICS. ELECTION SCANDAL.*

The committee declared there had been no violation of the Election Act. In a brazen challenge to British authority, John Rutledge wrote on the Gadsden election issue:

> It is the undeniable fundamental and inherent right & privilege of the Commons House of Assembly of this Province Solely to examine and finally determine the Elections of their own Members.

### 1762, December 16. POLITICS. ELECTION SCANDAL.

The Assembly voted 24-6 to suspend all other business until the governor apologized for violating the rights and privilege of the House. They also sent a full account to London, asking British officials to decide the issue. They also suspended the governor's salary. From this day forward, the Assembly would become more assertive in their relationship with British officials.

### 1762, December 20. FRENCH AND INDIAN WAR. PRIVATEERING.

A Spanish privateer, *Santa Maria*, raided the Charlestown coast off, taking two local ships, *Neptune* and *General Wolfe*.

### 1762, December 24. FRENCH AND INDIAN WAR. PRIVATEERING.

The Spanish took another Carolina ship off the coast, *Mary*, which was stripped and scuttled in South Edisto.

# 1763

### 1763. COMMERCE.

Sixty-six tavern licenses were issued in Charlestown for this year.

The city's economy was booming. With a population of 8,000, almost evenly divided between black and white, it was the fourth largest populous city in colonial America behind Philadelphia, New York and Boston. The streets were teeming with royal officials, slaves, indentured servants, merchants, ministers, planters, lawyers, sailors, immigrants, beggars, orphans and prostitutes.

More than 100,000 barrels of rice were exported from Charlestown. Georgetown and Beaufort shipped an additional 5,516 barrels. More than 400,000 pounds of indigo were exported.

### 1763. SHIPBUILDING.

A square-rigged vessel of 180 tons, *Heart of Oak*, was launched from Hobcaw Point shipyard. Built by John Rose, *Heart of Oak* was the largest ship ever built in Carolina, capable of carrying one thousand barrels of rice.

### 1763. CULTURE. DESCRIPTION OF TOWN.

George Millegen-Johnston published *A Short Description of the Province of South Carolina*. Some excerpts include:

The Province is divided into four counties and nineteen parishes, Charles-town is the metropolis ... The streets are broad, straight, and uniform ...

There are about eleven hundred dwelling-houses in the town, built with wood or brick; many of them have a genteel appearance, though generally incumbered with balconies or piazzas; and are always decently, and often elegantly, furnished; the apartments are contrived for coolness, a very necessary consideration.

The town is divided into two parishes, St. Philip's and St. Michael's. St. Philip's church is one of the handsomest buildings in America ... of brick, plastered and well enlightened on the inside. The west end of the church is adorned with four Tuscan columns, supporting a double pediment ... the steeple rises octagonal, with windows on every face, till it is terminated by a dome, upon which stands a lanthorn for the bells, and from which rises a vane in the form of a cock.

St. Michael's church is built of brick; it is not yet finished.

## 1763, January 8. *Culture. Epidemic.*

Mr. Andrew Rutledge, dancing master, announced that his Ball "is put off on account of the Small-pox, til further notice be given."

## 1763, February 5. *Politics. Commerce. Election Scandal.*

In a long letter published in the *South Carolina Gazette*, Christopher Gadsden defended the Assembly's decision to cease all business until the election issue was settled. It was an early declaration of the "natural rights" philosophy which would soon sweep the American colonies during the opposition against British policies. Gadsden called their action:

> Absolutely necessary, and the only step that a *free* assembly, *freely* representing a *free people*, that have any regard for the preservation of the happy constitution handed down to them by their ancestors, their own most essential welfare, and that of their posterity, could *freely* take. 'Tis a joke to talk of individual liberty of *free* men, unless a collective body, freely chosen from amongst themselves are empowered to watch and guard it.

## 1763, February 10. *French and Indian War Ends.*

The Treaty of Paris officially ended the war in North America. France yielded Canada and all territory east of the Mississippi River to the British. France also ceded control of Louisiana to Spain, who ceded control of Florida to Great Britain.

Great Britain incurred a massive debt as a result of the war, and Parliament immediately began to look for creative ways in which to retire the debt.

## 1763, March 26. *MEDICINE. EPIDEMIC.*

Dr. William Loocock announced "An Hospital for the SMALL-POX is opened."

## 1763, April 17. *POLITICS. MARRIAGE.*

Lord William Campbell, a captain on the HMS *Nightingale* stationed in Charlestown, married a South Carolina heiress, Sarah Izard. Campbell would later serve a short term as South Carolina's last Royal governor.

## 1763, April 23. *ENGLAND. JOHN WILKES AFFAIR.*

John Wilkes, publisher of England's *The North Briton* published an article (edition # 45) critical of King George III's close friend, John Stuart, who had been appointed the Prime Minister. Wilkes considered Stuart an incompetent idiot and said so in *North Briton #45*. The King decided to prosecute Wilkes for seditious libel.

He was arrested but almost immediately released – members of Parliament were protected from arrest on the charge. His release turned Wilkes into a folk hero, as most citizens agreed with Wilkes' opinion of the Prime Minister. Parliament quickly passed a new law which did not protect its members from charges of libel.

## 1763, May 1. *MARRIAGE.*

John Rutledge married Elizabeth Grimke. There were to have ten children, eight that reached maturity.

## 1763, Summer. *POLITICS. IMMIGRATION. BACKCOUNTRY.*

With the end of the war with the Cherokee and the French threat removed, immigration to the backcountry in South Carolina turned into a stampede. Thousands of Scotch-Irish and Germans from Pennsylvania moved to acquire the cheap land offered. This dramatically increased the white population and the production of food stuffs.

## 1763, August 16. *POLITICS. EDUCATION.*

The Assembly established a committee to make plans for a public college for the young men of the province. It would be seven years before any action was taken.

## 1763, September 7. *CRIME. CULTURE.*

The *State and Public Advertiser* reported on the vandalism of the Dock Street Theater:

> Malicious and evil disposed persons ... [have] frequently broken into the theatre and cut and destroyed the scenes and furniture of the house.

## 1763, November 5. *TREATY OF AUGUSTA.*

Gov. Boone attended the signing of a treaty with the Cherokee that ceded the northern and western parts of Georgia to the English.

### 1763, November 5. CULTURE. THEATER.

David Douglass, who married the widow of Lewis Hallam, contracted to have a new theatre built for his American Company of Comedians. Douglass was described as "a shining actor, a man of sense and discretion."

### 1763, November 10. INDIAN AFFAIRS.

The Treaty of Augusta was signed by the governors of Georgia, South Carolina, North Carolina and Virginia, and the chiefs of the Cherokees, Creeks, Chickaswas, Choctaws and Catawbas. John Stuart, Superintendent of Indian Affairs, presided.

### 1763, November 12. CULTURE. THEATER.

The American Company of Comedians began a successful three-month engagement in Charlestown, performing three times a week.

### 1763, November 19. CULTURE. THEATER.

Due to the arrival of the American Company of Comedians two weeks ago, Dr. Watts complained about playhouses and midnight assemblies. He wrote, "The youth of serious religion that ventures sometimes into this infected air, finds his antidotes too weak to resist the contagion."

# 1764

### 1764, March 3. COMMERCE.

Peter Timothy announced he was suspending publication of the *Gazette* because he was unable to procure a printing assistant, his paper stock was depleted, and he had been too busy to collect bills due to him.

### 1764, April 4. COMMERCE.

The *South Carolina Weekly Gazette* was renamed *South Carolina & American General Gazette* by Robert Wells, its publisher.

### 1764, April 5. SUGAR ACT OF 1764.

King George III approved a duty on foreign molasses. This was the first of many acts to raise money in an attempt to retire the debt accruied during the French and Indian War.

### 1764, May 14. POLITICS.

Governor Boone returned to England with the ex-wife of Samuel Peronneau. Lt. Gov. William Bull was appointed acting governor, which the locals viewed as a victory, since Bull was a local man and well respected by all.

### 1764, Summer. *Religion. Bells of St. Michael's.*

The bells of St. Michael's Church arrived from the Whitechapel Bell Foundry in London. The bells were cast by Messers. Lester and Pack at the Whitechapel Bell Foundry in London – the oldest manufacturing company in Britain, circa 1570. The foundry also cast Philadelphia's Liberty Bell in 1752 and Big Ben in 1858.

### 1764, June 24. *Religion. Buildings of Charleston.*

St. John's Lutheran Church was completed on Archdale Street.

### 1764, September 22. *Religion. Bells of St. Michael's.*

The bells of St. Michael's Church tolled for the first time during the funeral of Mrs. Martha Grimke.

### 1764, October 1. *Commerce.*

The *South Carolina Gazette* resumed publication.

### 1764, October 1. *Commerce. Art.*

Thomas You advertised "A copper-plate view of St. Michael's Church *Charles-Town*, drawn by himself, and neatly engrav'd in London."

### 1764, October 15. *Timothy Asks for Debts to be Paid.*

Peter Timothy of the *Gazette* requested that all people who owed him money pay their debts as soon as possible. He pointed out that in thirty-three years he had never resorted to a summons or an attorney to collect a bill, but such measures may be forthcoming.

# 1765

### 1765. *Culture.*

John Rutledge assumed role of surrogate father toward his younger brothers, Hugh and Edward. They both clerked in his law office, and later were admitted to the Middle Temple in London.

### 1765. *Commerce. Religion.*

Rev. Charles Woodmason applied for the position of stamp collector. He did not get the job, but his application ruined his reputation in Charlestown, branding him as a "private Spy and Correspondent of the Ministry – a faithless fellow – one that is a betrayer of the Rights and Privileges of America." He returned to England to take Holy Orders in the Church of England.

### 1765. *Religion.*

A visitor to Charlestown noted "a meeting house for Jews" on Beresford Street (now Fulton) near King Street.

## 1765, January 17. COMMERCE.

Lt. Gov. William Bull reported that during the previous twelve months, 360 ships arrived from Havana, Montserrat, Lisbon, Jamaica, London, Bermuda, St. Kitts. Philadelphia, St. Augustine, and Aberdeen.

## 1765, February 2. COMMERCE.

A writer in the *Gazette* commenting on the bleak economy warned that:

> more almshouses will soon be needed, for it is no doubt that an industrious Man who does not earn more than Thirty or Forty Shillings in the Day (and few do that) cannot possibly pay House-Rent, Cloath and feed his Family.

## 1765, March 22. STAMP ACT.

In another attempt to pay the debt run up during the French and Indian War Parliament passed the Stamp Act, which required that most printed materials in the colonies be produced on "stamped paper" (an embossed revenue mark) from London. The printed materials included newspapers, legal documents, playing cards and magazines. There was quick and passionate opposition to the Stamp Act in Boston, Philadelphia and Charlestown.

South Carolina's London agent Charles Garth wrote John Rutledge informing him of the proposed Stamp Act being argued in Parliament. In Garth's opinion the Act could not be successfully opposed by the colonies.

The Stamp Act was viewed as a threat by most Charlestown's men. Just a year before they had been emboldened when they successfully managed to secure the upper hand over Governor Boone who had challenged the Assembly's right to determine the validity of elections.

## 1765, April 5. SUGAR ACT.

The Sugar Act was passed by Parliament, another means to raise revenue.

## 1765, April 13. CULTURE. ELECTRICITY DEMONSTRATION.

William Johnson delivered a series of lectures on electricity at Mr. Backhouse's Tavern. One of the lectures was called "Fire darting from a Lady's Eyes, that will kindle spirits (without a Metaphor.)."

## 1765, May 3. QUARTERING ACT.

The Quartering Act was passed by Parliament. It stated that Great Britain would house its soldiers in American barracks and public houses, inns, livery stables, ale houses and other buildings. Colonial authorities would be required to pay the cost of housing and feeding the troops.

## 1765, May 27. ARRIVALS. CULTURE. WEBSTER'S JOURNAL.

Pelatiah Webster, a Philadelphia merchant, kept a daily journal of his two-month business trip to Charles Town. His observations on this day were:

It contains about 1000 houses, with inhabitants, 5000 whites and 20,000 blacks; has 8 houses for religious worship ... The State-House is a heavy building of about 120 by 40 feet. The Council Chamber is about 40 feet square, decorated with many heavy pillars & much carving, rather superb than elegant. The assembly room is of the same dimensions, but much plainer work, 'tis convenient enough.

The streets of this city run N. & S., and E. & W., intersecting each other at right angles. They are not paved except the footways within the posts about 6 feet wide, which are paved with brick in the principal streets.

There are large fortifications here but mostly unfinished and ruinous. There is a pretty fort on James Island called Johnson's fort which commands the entrance of the harbour ...

The laborious business is here chiefly done by black slaves of which there are great multitudes. The climate is very warm; the chief produce is rice & indigo the manufacture of hemp is set afoot & likely to succeed very well. They have considerable lumber and naval stores [tar, pitch, and turpentine]. They export annually 100,000 barrels of rice & 60,000 lbs. indigo.

## 1765, May 29. *Culture. Webster's Journal.*

Pelatiah Webster observed in his journal:

Wednesday. Still sauntering about town as much as the great heats will permit. Dinner with Mr. Tho. Smith, a reputable merchant in this town & in very fine business: is an agreeable sensible kind man: passed my time with him very pleasantly several hours.

## 1765, May 30. *Slavery.*

Henry Laurens wrote to the Overseer of his plantation:

I have now to recommend to you the care of my Negroes in general, but particularly the sick ones. Let them be well attended night and day, and if one wench if not sufficient, add another to nurse them. With the well ones use gentle means mixed with easy authority first – if that does not succeed, make choice of the most-stubborn one or two and chastise them severely but properly and with mercy, that they may be convinced that the end of correction is to be amendment ...

## 1765, June 4. *Culture. Webster's Journal.*

Pelatiah Webster observed in his journal:

Tuesd. The militia all appeared under arms, about 800, & the guns at all the forts were fired, it being the King's Birthday. The artillery made a good appearance and performed their exercises and firings very well. The militia were not so well trained & exercised but made a pretty good & handsome appearance. The militia & artillery of Charlestown are said to consist of 1300 men in the whole list from 16 to 60 years old.

### 1765, June 8. *CULTURE. BUSINESS. WEBSTER'S JOURNAL.*

Pelatiah Webster observed in his journal:

> Saturday. Very hot. Met with disappointment in the sale of my flour which lies on my hands & I fear I must leave it unsold or expose it to vendue [auction] with loss of what I have procured with long pains & industry: my mind is somewhat depressed.
>
> Dined with Mr. Liston, passed the afternoon agreeably at his summer house till 5 o'clock P. M. then went up into the steeple of St. Michael's, the highest in town & which commands a fine prospect of the town, harbour, river, forts, sea, &c ...

### 1765, June 11. *CULTURE. BUSINESS. WEBSTER'S JOURNAL.*

Pelatiah Webster observed in his journal:

> Tuesday. Sold 12 BBl. flour at £4 [four English pounds] currency pr. ct. which is about first cost to Mr. Peter Boquet & the rest. Mr. Liston procured me a sale of at 90/ pr. ct. So I am over the difficulties of my sales. Dined with Mr. Liston, Capt. Bains from London & Mr. Head. Passed the evening at the Reverend Robt Smith's.

### 1765, June 14. *WEBSTER'S JOURNAL. SLAVERY.*

From Pelatiah Webster's journal:

> Friday. A hot sultry day. Went with Mr. Liston in a boat to Sullivan's Island where there were 200 or 300 Negroes performing quarantine with the small pox This island is 7 miles E. from the town, about 4 miles long, very sandy, hot, and barren, though there are some groves of trees in it. There is a pest-house here with pretty good conveniences. The most moving sight was a poor white man performing quarantine alone in a boat, at anchor ten rods from shore, with an awning & pretty poor accommodations ...

### 1765, June 18. *CULTURE. BUSINESS. WEBSTER'S JOURNAL.*

Pelatiah Webster observed in his journal:

> Tuesday: Embarked on board the brigantine *Prince of Wales*, Thomas Mason, Commander, for Philadelphia; took leave of all my Charlestown friends. At 4 P.M. made sail.

Now I have left Charlestown, an agreeable & polite place in which I was used [treated] very genteely & contracted much acquaintaince for the time I stayed here. The heats are much too severe, the water bad, the soil sandy, the timber too much evergreen; but with all these disadvantages, 'tis a flourishing place, capable of vast improvement.

## 1765, August 1. *POLITICS. LEGAL.*

William Drayton was appointed Chief Justice for the Province of East Florida.

## 1765, August 14. *STAMP ACT. DEMONSTRATIONS.*

In Boston, the stamp officer, Andrew Oliver was hanged in effigy, which was later paraded around the streets, beheaded and burned. Sheriff Greenleaf and Lt. Gov. Hutchinson were stoned when they tried to intervene.

## 1765, August 25. *ASSEMBLY OPPOSES STAMP ACT.*

John Rutledge, conveying the wishes of the South Carolina Assembly, instructed Charles Garth, their agent in London, to oppose the stamp tax, and any other tax by Parliament. Rutledge claimed it was "inconsistent with that inherent right of every British subject, not to be taxed but by his own consent, or that of his representatives."

## 1765, September 4. *STAMP ACT CONGRESS.*

Thomas Lynch, Christopher Gadsden and John Rutledge sailed for New York on the *Carolina Packet* to attend the Stamp Act Congress. At age twenty-six, Rutledge was the youngest delegate in attendance.

## 1765, October 7. *STAMP ACT CONGRESS.*

The Stamp Act Congress convened in New York City. South Carolina was the only southern colony to send representatives. For the first time, they learned of the violent protests in Boston. Christopher Gadsden gave a rousing speech which set the tone for the meeting:

> I wish the charters may not ensnare us at last, by drawing different colonies to act differently in this great cause. Whenever that is the case, all will be over with the whole. There ought to be no England men, no New Yorker, known on the continent, but all of us American.

## 1765, October 18. *STAMP ACT. DEMONSTRATIONS.*

In preparation of the Stamp Act taking effect in November, the *Planter's Adventure* arrived in carrying the hated British stamped paper,. Lt. Gov. Bull first placed the stamped paper in the warship *Speedwell*, but feared it might be attacked while docked. He secretly transferred the stamped paper to Ft. Johnson for nine days.

A forty-foot high gallows was erected at Broad and Church Streets in front of Dillon's Tavern with three effigies: that of a stamp distributor hung between a Devil on one side and a boot on the other. On the front of the gallows was a sign which read – "LIBERTY and no STAMP ACT." On the back of the gallows was another sign which read "Whoever shall dare attempt to pull down these effigies had better been born with a mill stone about his neck, and cast into the sea."

Two thousand people paraded the streets looking for the stamps. The home of the stamp officer, George Saxby, was searched and ransacked. Many in the crowd were part of Christopher Gadsden's artillery company – labor-class artisans. The mob marched to the "New Barracks" (present-day location of the College of Charleston) and burned an effigy of Saxby and buried a coffin labeled "AMERICAN LIBERTY."

## 1765, October 21. *STAMP ACT.*

Lt. Gov. William Bull denounced the mob demonstrations. He issued a £50 reward for apprehension of the "persons responsible for damages to Saxby's property."

## 1765, October 23. *STAMP ACT. DEMONSTRATIONS.*

A masked and armed mob (probably members of the Sons of Liberty) of "about 60 to 80" marched on Henry Laurens's house at midnight, suspecting that he held the stamped paper. Laurens's coolness toward the Patriot cause made him suspicious in the eyes of the public. The mob held "a brace of cutlasses across my breast" and for the next hour the house was searched. Laurens was amazed by the lack of damage to his house:

> Is it not amazing that such a number of Men many of them heated with Liquor & all armed with Cutlasses & Clubbs did not do one penny damage to my Garden not even not even to walk over a Bed & not damage to my Fence, gate or House?

## 1765, October 25. *ARRIVALS. CULTURE.*

David Douglass returned to Charlestown, hoping that his American Company of Comedians, would arrive from Barbados before the embargo. They did not, and he was forced to open the theater season with a troupe of only nine performers, six of whom were novices.

## 1765, October 25. *STAMP ACT.*

The *Carolina Packet* arrived from London. It was quickly boarded by a group of angry citizens looking for stamps, or a stamp officer.

## 1765, October 26. *STAMP ACT. DEMONSTRATIONS.*

The mob marched the streets threatening to kill the two stamp agents, George Saxby and Caleb Lloyd, unless they resign.

## 1765, October 28. *STAMP ACT.*

George Saxby and Caleb Lloyd, stamp officer and stamp distributor, who had been virtual prisoners in the fort for two days, publically promised not to perform their duties, "until Parliament had addressed colonial grievances," and to prevent "murder and the destruction of the town."

The crowd roared its approval and a celebration began, clanging of bells, and cannon fire. Saxby and Lloyd were escorted by the crowd to Dillon's Tavern.

Lt. Gov. Bull called the *Gazette* the "Conduit Pipe of northern propaganda ... poisoning the minds ... against the Stamp Act ... to directly support and engage in the most violent Opposition."

Stamp Act Protests. *Courtesy of the New York Public Library*

## 1765, October 30. *STAMP ACT.*

Attorney Richard Hutson complained that many locals were indifferent yet they praised the "laudable example of the northern provinces in endeavoring to repel the manifest encroachments on their liberty."

## 1765, October 31. *STAMP ACT.*

Peter Timothy wrote in *Gazette:*

> Tomorrow (being the First of November) ... the publication of the *South-Carolina Gazette*, will also be suspended, it being impossible to continue it without great loss to the printer, when the numerous subscribers thereto have signified *almost to a man*, that they will not take ONE stamped news-paper, if stamps could be obtained.

### 1765, October 31. *EDUCATION. MEDICAL.*

A Mr. Harrison advertised in the *Gazette*:

> Surgeon and Man-Midwife, from London, will open a Dissecting-Room next November, and will instruct any gentleman to dissect, and give them a lecture on the muscles, arteries, &c. and will go through all the operation of Surgery.

### 1765, November 1. *STAMP ACT GOES INTO EFFECT.*

The Stamp Act went to effect. Ships could not get clearances to leave Charlestown harbor and courts could not conduct any legal business without stamped paper. Lt. Governor Bull wrote that:

> the courts of common law, admiralty, and ecclesiastical jurisdiction are all silent; no grants of land are passed; all the ships remain in the harbor as under an embargo; every transaction requiring stamps is at an end.

### 1765, November 3. *STAMP ACT.*

Lt. Governor Bull claimed that the mob actions were "animated by some considerable men who stood behind the curtain," a veiled allusion to Christopher Gadsden.

### 1765, November 13. *STAMP ACT. COURT ADJOURNS.*

South Carolina Chief Justice, Charles Shinner, adjourned the court, unable to resolve the legal issue of the provincial ban on stamps.

### 1765, November 28. *STAMP ACT. STAMPS ARRIVE.*

The stamps were brought to the docks from Ft. Johnson. A crowd of about 7,000 read a pledge not to act until Parliament had acted on their petition for all of America. Merchants pledged not to use the stamped paper.

### 1765, November 29. *STAMP ACT. EFFECTS.*

The Assembly adopted a report by Christopher Gadsden which reflected the sentiments of the Stamp Act Congress, that taxes should only be enacted by the Assembly of each province. It also said:

> Sincerely as we are attached to his Majesty, we insist that we are entitled to all inherent rights and liberties of his natural born subjects within the Kingdom of Great Britain.

The *Gazette* published that day on plain paper with the headline: NO STAMPED PAPER TO BE HAD.

### 1765, December. *STAMP ACT EFFECTS.*

The harbor became clogged with ships. Lt. Gov. Bull allowed one ship to clear to carry food to the troops. Hundreds of merchants and planters demanded the same privilege for their ships, which Bull allowed. Henry Laurens wrote, "Our rice planters have gained a vast ascendant over the British owners and fairly turned the edge of the stamp tax upon them."

### 1765, December 6. *AMERICAN REVOLUTION - Foundations.*

The Sons of Liberty organized in Charlestown, directed by Gadsden. Many of "the richer folks were terrified at the spirit which themselves had conjurered up." To restore order, the "Liberty Boys ... suppressed them [the stamp mob] instantly and committed the leaders to Gaol."

### 1765, December 17. *SLAVERY.*

A possible slave revolt was suspected when slaves were heard on the streets shouting "Liberty!" Henry Laurens thought the threat was exaggerated. In his opinion he believed the slaves merely "had mimck'd their betters by crying out 'Liberty!'"

Lt. Gov. Bull ordered 100 militia out "to guard the city" and for sailors to stand nightly sentinel duty on the wharves during the holiday season. Laurens wrote that, "Patrols were riding day and night for 10 to 14 days in most bitter weather and here in town all soldiers were in arms for more than a week."

Whether the slave revolt threat was real or not, it did act as a calming influence on Gadsden and Timothy, as leaders of the mob actions. As Henry Laurens wrote, the hotheads:

> did not slacken in their opposition to the introduction of Stamps, but except for a little Private cruising along the Waterside at Nights to see if anything is moving among the Shipping they are pretty quiet & I have been assur'd that more than a few of their Brethren declare their repentance ...

### 1765, December 23. *STAMP ACT. EFFECTS.*

British Secretary of State Henry Seymour Conway informed Lt. Gov. Bull that further violence was "not suitable either for the safety or Dignity of the British Empire." He instructed Bull to call upon British General Thomas Gage to combat the violence of the mobs.

In addition to the mobs, Bull was also concerned about the 1,400 unemployed sailors who were stranded in Charlestown due to the closure of the port. The sailors spent most of their time in taverns and were increasingly disorderly.

# 1766

### 1766. *LAURENS' WEALTH.*

Henry Laurens summarized his holdings as being worth £147,900 colonial currency (£21,100 sterling) which included 8800 acres of land, 227 slaves and six ships.

## 1766, January 1. *SLAVERY.*

Due to "too great a disproportion of slaves to white inhabitants," an Act by the Assembly levied a heavy tax on all slaves brought into South Carolina. This, in effect, closed down the slave trade for a period of three years.

## 1766, January 14. *STAMP ACT. PITT CHALLENGES PARLIAMENT.*

William Pitt gave a speech in Parliament in support of the American colonies opposition to the Stamp Act:

> Gentlemen, Sir,
>
> I have been charged with giving birth to sedition in America. They have spoken their sentiments with freedom against this unhappy act, and that freedom has become their crime. America is almost in open rebellion. I rejoice that America has resisted.

## 1766, January 15. *GERMAN FRIENDLY SOCIETY.*

The German Friendly Society was organized in the home of Michael Kalteisen. The rules decreed that either German or English had to be spoken at the meetings.

## 1766, January 17. *CULTURE. THEATER.*

Although short-handed with only about half of its company in Charlestown, the American Company of Comedians presented *The Distressed Mother*.

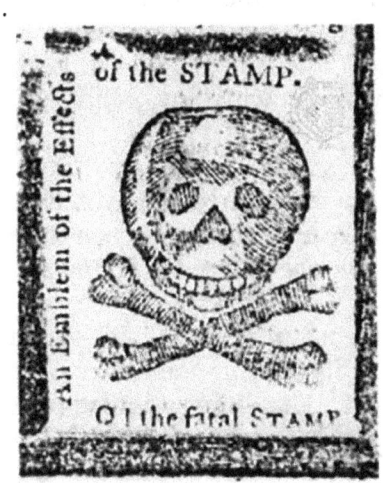

Patriot Stamp. American periodicals used this symbol instead of the proscribed British Stamp.
*Courtesy of the New York Public Library.*

## 1766, April 1. *STAMP ACT.*

South Carolina courts had shut down, due to lack of stamped paper. Lawyers presented a petition to hold court without stamped paper. They stated:

> We claim our rights under Magna Carter, the Petition of Rights, etc ...
> We cannot think ourselves bound by the Stamp Act which annihilates
> our natural as well as constitutional rights.

Chief Justice Skinner held that the court had no power to question the authority of an act of Parliament, and the fact that there was no stamped paper because of unlawful demonstrations by the people was no excuse not to follow the law.

## 1766, April 1. *CULTURE.*

At benefit concert for St. Michael's Church was held at David Douglass's theater on Queen Street.

## 1766, April 16. *SLAVERY. CONCERNS OVER POPULATION.*

Christopher Gadsden wrote to William Samuel Johnson a Connecticut lawyer, about his concerns over the large black population and the constant threat of a revolt. Gadsden said he hoped "in the case of South Carolina the enslavement of blacks would not cause the enslavement of whites."

## 1766, April 29. *CULTURE. GUITAR LESSONS.*

A Mr. Wall announced he had settled in Charlestown and was offering guitar lessons.

## 1766, May 6. *STAMP ACT REPEALED. LIBERTY TREE.*

News reached Charlestown that Parliament had repealed the Stamp Act. The city celebrated by ringing church bells and burning bonfires. Lt. Gov. Bull hosted "a very elegant entertainment" at Dillon's Tavern for the Council and Assembly. Peter Manigault, Speaker of the Assembly, wrote the news was met with "joy, jollity, and mirth."

The Assembly voted £1,000 sterling for a marble statue of William Pitt in gratitude of his exertions for the repeal of the Stamp Act. They also voted to appropriate funds for portraits of Gadsden, John Rutledge and Thomas Lynch to be displayed in the Assembly room in recognition of their service during the Stamp Act Congress.

They also learned that Parliament had passed the Declaratory Act, which stated that Parliament's authority was the same in America as in Britain - their laws were as binding on the American colonies as in England. That night, Christopher Gadsden gave a speech under the great oak tree in Mr. Mazyck's cow pasture in which he:

> harangued them at considerable length on the folly of relaxing their
> opposition and vigilance, or of indulging in the fallacious hope that
> Great Britain would relinquish their designs and pretensions.

Gadsden cautioned not to rejoice in the repeal of the Stamp Act because the Declaratory Act was a threat to the liberty of all Americans. From that night onward, the oak was called the Liberty Tree.

At the end of the meeting the men gathered hands around the tree and swore resistance to future tyranny.

## 1766, May 12. *AMERICAN REVOLUTION - Foundations.*

Henry Laurens was uneasy about the Declaratory Act writing that "all America will undergo many pangs yet before there is a hearty reconciliation."

Liberty Tree marker. Charleston, 80 Alexander Street. *Photo by author.*

## 1766, June 1. *ARRIVALS.*

The brigantine *Free-Mason* arrived in Charlestown, carrying Mary Splatt Cripps, widow of William Cripps of England, and daughter of Charlestown merchant Richard Splatt.

Master of the *Free-Mason* was Alexander Gillon. Romance had blossomed between Gillon and Mary Cripps on the voyage to Charlestown.

## 1766, June 2. *SHIPBUILDING.*

Joseph Hancock announced that he:

> Served his apprenticeship in one of his Majesty's dock yards, to one of the principal artists in England, and would be glad to carry on business for any person or persons in the art of ship building.

## 1766, June 11. *ARRIVALS. GOVERNOR MONTAGU.*

The new royal governor, twenty-five-year old Charles Genville Montagu, arrived. He presented a petition directing the Assembly to pay former Governor

Boone's salary for two and a half years. The Assembly agreed and the entire Gadsden election controversy was finally closed, leaving bitter feelings on both sides.

One of Montagu's first issues was to deal with overzealous British revenue officers who were harassing Charleston merchants, enforcing the Navigation Laws to the letter.

## 1766, July. *MARRIAGE.*

Alexander Gillon married Mary Splatt Cripps. Gillon retired from the sea and entered into the merchant trade with his father-in-law.

## 1766, September. *WOODMASON RETURNS. BACKCOUNTRY.*

Rev. Charles Woodmason returned from England ordained by the English Church. He was assigned to St. Mark's Parish on the South Carolina frontier. It was rough country. The parish had a growing population, yet had few roads and less amenities. Woodmason's circuit included twenty-six regular, periodic stops in the parish. In two years he traveled 6,000 miles. He found very little in backcountry life to his liking. The people lived in open cabins "with hardly a Blanket to cover them, or Cloathing to cover their Nakedness." Their diet consisted of "what in England is given to Hogs and Dogs," and he was forced to live likewise. He wrote:

> They are very Poor – owing their extreme Indolence for they possess the finest Country in America, and could raise by ev'ry thing. They delight in their present low, lazy, sluttish, heathenish hellish Life and seem not desirous of changing it. Both Men and Women will do any thing to come at Liquor ... rather than work for it – Hence their many Vices – their gross Licentiousness, Wantonness, Lasciviousness, Rudeness, Lewdness and Profligacy. They will commit the grossest Enormities, before my face, and laugh at all Admonition.

## 1766, December 1. *LIGHTHOUSE.*

It was announced that:

> A Beacon is forthwith to be erected upon Middle Bay Island [later Morrison Island ... and then Morris Island] near the Bar, to be built of brick, 115 feet high, with a lanthorn [lantern] on the top ... Mr. Samuel Cardy has been contracted ... for the building.

## 1766, December 7. *RELIGION. CRIME.*

Rev. Robert Smith, of St. Philip's parish, who oversaw the care of the poor complained about the "inhumane policy of housing violent prisoners with the poor and sick, who may be, and often are, pious and well-disposed persons."

## 1766, December 8. *FREEMASONRY.*

The *Gazette* noted:

The provincial GRAND ANNIVERSARY and General Communication of the Most Ancient and Honourable Society of Free and Accepted Masons in South Carolina is appointed to be holden in Charles-Town, on Saturday, the 27th of December ... The present Masters and Wardens of the seven regular constituted Lodges, under the provincial Jurisdiction ... are particularly desired to be present.

### 1766, December 10. *Exchange Building.*

William Rigby Naylor, architect, signed the plans for the construction of the Exchange Building.

### 1766, December 10. *Freemasonry.*

The "new Lodge of Freemasons," was held at Mr. Benjamin Backhouses's on the Bay. They were to meet "the second and last Monday of each month."

# 1767

### 1767. *Commerce. Gadsden's Wharf.*

Christopher Gadsden's Wharf opened on the Cooper River at the foot of present-day Calhoun Street and location of the South Carolina Aquarium. When completed, the wharf was 840 feet along the harbor, with warehouses which could hold 10,000 barrels of rice. The *South Carolina Gazette* called the wharf "a stupendous work ... which is reckoned the most extensive of the kind ever undertaken by one man in America."

### 1767. *Backcountry. Formation of the Regulators.*

In the backcountry, crime had reached a dangerous level. Robberies by wandering bandits and violent attacks on secluded households were common. John Harvey, "a roguish and troublesome man," accused of stealing a horse, was chained to a tree by a group of men, calling themselves the "Regulators." They took turns administering a total of 500 lashes on Harvey while other members of the group beat drums and played a fiddle. Due to lack of courts in the South Carolina backcountry, and their mistrust of the Charlestown leaders, these Regulators - planters, surveyors, tavern keepers, ferry operators, mill operators and merchants - decided to enforce order and justice on their own terms.

### 1767, February 16. *Culture. Electricity Demonstration.*

An advertisement in the *Gazette* announced:

> For the Entertainment of the Curious *Will be exhibited at the Library-Room, in Union-street, a course of Experiments, in that instructive and entertaining branch of Natural Philosophy called ELECTRICITY,* To be accompanied with lectures on the nature and proportion of the

Electrick Fire, by William Johnson ... *Said* Johnson *likewise proposes to exhibit* ... MAGNETISM.

### 1767, March. *POLITICS. SCANDAL.*

Daniel Moore, the new customs collector, was determined to use the position to increase his personal wealth. He increased collection fees, strictly enforced the coastal trade regulations and colluded with customs searcher, George Roupell, to "set a new standard for rapaciousness." This angered many of the local merchants, including Henry Laurens, who organized an attempt to isolate the Royal officials.

Moore was particularly interested in the coastal trade – traffic along the coast within one colony or nearby colonies. The largest coastal trade was between South Carolina and Georgia and it was vital to the economy of the inland plantation owners who used the system to ship their goods to Charlestown.

Moore insisted that the coastal trade adhere to the Revenue Act of 1764, the same as the ocean trade.

### 1767, March 23. *GOVERNOR'S BRIDGE.*

In a letter to James Grant, Henry Laurens mentioned that legislators "extended Meeting Street north to George Street and built a bridge over the creek near Craven's Bastion at the north end of the Bay." Anthony Toomer received the contract to build the bridge. Laurens also wrote that:

> We are regulating our Port and Harbour, going to build a sumptuous Exchange and Customs House ... building a new Hospital and enquiring into the State of the Poor.

### 1767, Spring. *COMMERCE. SLAVERY.*

Twenty-year old Joseph Vesey, a native of Bermuda, signed up to crew on the *Rebecca*, a "prime Bermuda Vessel" owned by South Carolina merchant Joseph Darrell. The schooner made regular trips from Bermuda to Charles Town transporting rice wine, rum and African slaves. Vesey often piloted the *Rebecca* up the rivers to make deliveries at the inland plantations. Within eight years, Vesey had become a good pilot and captain who invested his earnings in property in Charlestown.

### 1767, April 13. *CULTURE.*

The *Gazette* noted "All St. Michael's RINGERS, are desired to meet at Mr. Poinsett's on Saturday the 18th instant at seven in the evening."

### 1767, April 27. *EXCHANGE BUILDING.*

The Commons House of Assembly passed an act which granted His Majesty £60,000 to build an Exchange and Custom House. The money was to be raised by taxes on wine, rum, and flour.

### 1767, May. COMMERCE. WAMBAW SCANDAL.

Henry Laurens sent his schooner, *Wambaw*, loaded with provisions, to his Georgia plantation without clearing customs. The *Wambaw* offloaded her cargo and took on 50,000 cypress shingles as ballast to return to Charlestown.

### 1767, May 23. AMERICAN REVOLUTION – *Foundations.*

British marines from the HMS *Sardoine* were attacked by a mob as they tried to inspect the cargo of the provincial Customs schooner *Active*. British Capt. James Hawker seized the *Active*. This was the initial incident that sparked a major contest between British authorities and the Carolina merchants - all because of the Townshend Acts and the sugar tax levied against the colonies.

### 1767, May 25. NEW VAUXHALL OPENS.

Henry Poher opened the New Vauxhall, advertising a concert every Thursday accompanied with a pantomime followed by a ball. A Vauxhall was a private pleasure ground, including gardens, fountains, benches and walking paths, which at night were illuminated.

### 1767, June. COMMERCE. SHIPS SEIZED. WAMBAW SCANDAL.

The *Wambaw* returned to Charlestown. Customs Collector Moore refused to allow the ship legal clearance of the harbor. Vice-Admiralty Judge Egerton Leigh ordered the *Wambaw,* and another of Henry Laurens' vessel, the *Broughton Island Packet*, to be seized.

### 1767, June 29. AMERICAN REVOLUTION - *The Townsend Acts.*

The Townshend Acts were passed by Parliament, placing new duties on paper, paint, lead, glass, and tea that were imported into the colonies - items that were not produced in North America and that the colonists were only allowed to buy from Great Britain. The law was to become effective on November 20, 1767.

It was intended to raised £40,000 a year, earmarked for colonial defense and administration.

### 1767, July 19. CULTURE.

Nathaniel Russell helped raise £200 as well as food and clothing for a group of newly arrived Irish Protestant immigrants from Belfast. He wrote to his friend, Eliza Stiles of Newport, that the immigrants expressed "their Gratitude in very moving Term and seem astonished at the Kindness of the People."

### 1767, August. COMMERCE. WAMBAW SCANDAL.

Egerton Leigh, judge of the Vice Admiralty Court in Charleston, married Henry Laurens' niece. Leigh had once been Laurens's lawyer, and the two men were friends. He ordered the *Wambaw* be sold because Laurens admitted under oath he was planning on selling the ballast shingles for profit.

Laurens was able to purchase his own ship back for £120, but had to pay £277 in fines and court costs. These events enraged Charlestown merchants, and turned Collector Daniel Moore into the most hated man in the city. As Laurens described him as the:

> good for nothing Collector ... [who] in the space of Six Months has given more plague to the Trading people here than all the Officers of Customs put together since the memory of the oldest Merchant among us – ten to one.

## 1767, August 7. BACKCOUNTRY.

In more complaints about the dangerous conditions in the backcountry, the *South Carolina and American General Gazette* reported that:

> If we save a little for to bring to Town Wherewith to purchase Slaves – Should it be known our Houses are beset, and Robbers plunder Us, even of our Cloaths. If we buy Liquor for to Retail, or for hospitality, they will break into our dwellings and consume it ... Should be raise fat Cattle, or Prime Horses for the Market, they are constantly carried off, tho' well guarded.

## 1767, August 14. CRIME.

Gov. Montagu complained that "building a jail is a thing that is become now necessary, as the present one is so old and weak that the prisoners are frequently breaking out."

## 1767, August 17. BUILDINGS OF CHARLESTON.

The *Gazette* reported that Charlestown contained "over 900 houses and rent ranged from £80 to £800 a year."

## 1767, September 15. FORTIFICATIONS.

The Commissioners of Fortification reported they had "viewed the fortifications on White Point and find the whole in ruinous condition and some parts broke through by the sea ..."

## 1767, October 3. POLITICS. SCANDAL.

Henry Laurens confronted Daniel Moore and rebuked him over his behavior. When Moore responded with an insult Laurens grabbed him by the nose and twisted it before a crowd of people.

Laurens and other Charlestown merchants filed several lawsuits against Moore charging him with illegal extortion of fees. Moore quickly sailed to London to present his case to the Royal authorities.

## 1767, October 5. REGULATORS.

From the *Council Journal*:

His Excellency informed the Board that he had received information that a considerable number of the inhabitants between Santee and Wateree rivers had assembled, and in a riotous manner gone up and down the country, committing riots and disturbances, and that they had burnt the houses of some persons who were reported to be harborers of horse thieves, and talk of coming to Charles-Town to make complaints.

### 1767, October 9. BACKCOUNTRY. REGULATORS.

Governor Charles Montagu issued proclamation ordering those who led the Regulator movement in the backcountry to cease and desist. The Regulators were little more than brutal mob law enforcement.

### 1767, November. AMERICAN REVOLUTION - The Townsend Acts.

Word arrived that Boston had resolved not to import any taxable goods.

### 1767, November 5. BACKCOUNTRY. REGULATORS.

Rev. Charles Woodmason presented a petition to the Assembly signed by more than 4,000 backcountry settlers, which argued that the leaders of the lowcountry (Charlestown planters and merchants) treated the inhabitants of the backcountry worse than their slaves. He pointed out that the area along the coast had forty-four representatives in the Assembly, while the backcountry only had six – despite containing two-thirds of the white population of South Carolina.

The Assembly agreed to establish courts in the backcountry.

### 1767, November 5. BUILDINGS OF CHARLESTON.

Henry Middleton, John Neufville, Gabriel Manigault and John Savage "appraisers of the lands ... for an Exchange and Custom House" paid Ebenezar Simmons 5,500 pounds for his property (Lot B) on Bay Street.

### 1767, December 1. BUILDINGS OF CHARLESTON.

Construction of the Exchange in Charlestown began at the east end of Broad Street, on the site of the half-moon Battery. Builders Peter and Adam Horlbeck finished the structure in 1772 for "Forty-one Thousand Seven Hundred and Forty Pounds of lawful Current Money."

# 1768

### 1768. COMMERCE.

One hundred thirty-two tavern licenses were issued during the year. Charlestown had one tavern for every five adult males.

## BUILDINGS OF CHARLESTON
### 122 East Bay Street

TOP: Exchange Building, c. 1822. BOTTOM: Side view. *Author's Collection*

### 1768. February 1. CULTURE.

The *Gazette* announced:

> The gentlemen of the Jockey Club, we hear, are to make some regulations for the first day's sport in the future, in order that aged horses may have a chance to win.

### 1768, February 10. ARRIVALS.

The brigantine *Lord Dungamore* and *Billy* Greg brought 270 passengers from the north of Ireland to settle the backcountry.

### 1768, February 11. AMERICAN REVOLUTION - *The Townsend Acts.*

The Massachusetts House sent out a letter to the other provincial assemblies urging joint action in opposing the Townsend Acts. The British Secretary of State ordered all colonial governors to prevent their legislatures from considering the letter.

### 1768, March 4. BACKCOUNTRY.

The Assembly passed a bill for establishing courts, building jails and appointing sheriffs throughout the province.

### 1768, March 10. CULTURE. THEATER.

Bayly's Medley of Entertainments and Uncommon Performances performed at the Sign of Bacchus "on the Bay." The handbill claimed "By Dexterity of Hand, In a Manner different from all other Performs of that Art."

The handbill also claimed "Mr. Bayly continues to perform his Entertainments on Monday, Wednesday and Friday evenings, during his stay."

### 1768, March 22. CULTURE. THEATER.

In a notice published in the *South Carolina Gazette and Country Journal* Mr. Bayly reassured that "the strictest Decency and Regularity will be observed" in his theater.

### 1768, Spring. CULTURE.

The Fellowship Society of artisans sponsored a horse race and cock fight.

### 1768, April 12. PUBLIC WORKS. COLONIAL LAKE.

Colonial Lake, a Charleston landmark established by the Commons House of Assembly encompasses a city block in the midst of two neighborhoods. It was one of several public works projects initiated under Gov. Charles Greville Montagu. The original commissioners are names that still well-known in Charleston today:

| | |
|---|---|
| Henry Middleton, | William Henry Drayton |
| Isaac Mazyck, | Arthur Middleton |
| Rawlins Lowndes | William Savage |
| Edward Fenwick | |

The Colonial Commons Commission was established to oversee the lake area, specifically to:

> authorize Commissioners to cut a canal from the upper end of Broad Street into Ashley River; and to reserve the vacant marsh on each side of the said canal, for the use of a common for Charlestown.

Governor Montagu signed the Circuit Court Act, designed to solve the grievances of the backcountry men who wanted courts and jails, not the Regulators.

## 1768, April 21. *FORTIFICATIONS*.

The Commissioners of Fortifications called for bids to construct a more substantial seawall at White Point.

## 1768 May 9. *CRIME*.

The *Gazette* reported the workhouse was filled with "notorious bards, strumpers, vagrants, drunkards, and idle persons." It also complained about "too few public wells, street lamps, and public stocks, too many vagrants, taverns filthy street and bad roads, and an undermanned and underpaid town watch."

## 1768, June 8. *JOHN WILKES AFFAIR*.

Wilkes was found guilty of libel, sentenced to twenty-two months' imprisonment and fined £1,000. Wilkes was also expelled from the House of Commons. While incarcerated, he was re-elected three times with each decision overturned by Parliament. "Wilkes and Liberty!" became the rallying cry among the London middle and lower class.

Many leaders in the American colonies supported Wilkes. They saw him as a champion of the powerless against the privileged. As historian Pauline Maier wrote "In the years between 1768 and 1770 no English political figure evoked more enthusiasm in America than the radical John Wilkes.

---

### Mechanics & Artisans

Mechanics and artisans were skilled craftsmen who also ran successful businesses of retail or shipping. In Charlestown this would have included:

| | |
|---|---|
| Cabinet makers | Carpenters |
| Coopers | Gunsmiths |
| Basket makers | Silversmiths |
| Brick makers | Blacksmiths |
| Saddle & harness makers | Wheelwrights |

### 1768, July 10. *TOWNSEND ACTS. POLITICS.*

Assembly speaker, Peter Manigault, wrote to Thomas Cushing, Speaker of the Massachusetts House, that he had received the letter urging the other colonial assemblies to oppose the Townsend Acts, and that South Carolina would "join with the agents of the other provinces in obtaining a repeal of the acts of Parliament."

### 1768, September. *AMERICAN REVOLUTION - Foundations.*

The British 21st Regiment and artillery company arrived in Charlestown. The Assembly refused to pay for their quartering, stating that it was "expense incurred without our consent." Other colonies, New York and Massachusetts had also refused to pay for quartering soldiers.

### 1768, September. *POLITICS.*

With the Commons House of Assembly scheduled to meet in November, Gov. Montagu called for elections on October 4 and 5.

### 1768, September 2. *SLAVERY. FINANCING.*

Charlestown slave merchants and factors like Henry Laurens and Gabriel Manigault adopted a new method for making remittances for slave sales in twelve month installments, 3-6-9-12.

### 1768, September 3. *CULTURE. COMMERCE.*

Peter Timothy wrote to Benjamin Franklin.

> I do not suppose there is a colony on this continent in so flourishing and promising a situation as South Carolina at present. Very elegant buildings are rising in almost every street by private gentlemen.

### 1768, September 6. *COMMERCE. CROPS.*

In a letter to the Board of Trade Lt. Gov. William Bull noted that in addition to rice, South Carolina planters were also growing "tobacco, hemp, silk, wine, wheat, flax, cotton and ginger."

### 1768, October 1. *AMERICAN REVOLUTION - Foundations.*

With the elections coming in a few days, the mechanics in Charlestown nominated candidates who opposed the Quartering Act, Stamp Act, and Sugar Act. Led by Christopher Gadsden they met at the Liberty Tree "where many loyal, patriotic, and constitutional toasts were drank."

In honor of John Wilkes' *North Briton No. 45* the Liberty Tree was decorated with forty-five lights, and forty-five rockets were fired. The company marched to Dillon's Tavern where there were "45 lights ... upon the table, with 45 bowls of punch, 45 bottles of wine, and 92 glasses. They spent a few hours in a new round of toasts."

The meeting nominated five merchant-planters and one mechanic to led the Sons of Liberty:

- ✝ Christopher Gadsden
- ✝ Benjamin Dart – who, in addition to his trading business, also owned a plantation on the Ashley River. He had also served as commissioner of streets, workhouse and markets.
- ✝ Thomas Smith – who owned Broom Hall plantation in Goose Creek.
- ✝ Thomas Savage – who owned 200 acres in Berkeley County and Charlestown house.
- ✝ Thomas Smith, Sr. – a merchant since 1730
- ✝ Hopkin Price – the only mechanic chosen, had worked as a tanner and cobbler before acquiring some property in town and a plantation on the Ashley.

Henry Laurens called Gadsden's meeting a "grand barbacu [sic] given by a grand simpleton."

## 1768, October 5-6. *ELECTIONS. POLITICS.*

Charleston voters elected Gadsden, Dart and Savage. Henry Laurens, not even nominated, was elected by such a large margin that he was able to relinquish twenty of his votes to Charles Pinckney, Jr. in order to prevent the artisan Hopkin Price from winning election. Laurens stated he released his vote in order "to keep out a person who was thought unqualified to represent Charles Town."

## 1768, October 10. *BACKCOUNTRY. POLITICS.*

The people of the backcountry decided to show their unhappiness with the Charlestown politicians during the election. Many rode more than 100 miles to vote. The voters of St. Paul's parish arrived to discover the election had been held ten days *before* the announced date. They were told it was due to an error by the printer, which no one believed.

## 1768, October 18. *IMPORTATION BAN.*

When the new Assembly met, Lt. Gov. Bull read a letter from Boston inviting Charlestown merchants in joining them in refusing to import goods from Great Britain. Alarmed, Bull reported to Secretary Hillsborough that "many Charlestonians supported the political principals now prevailing in Boston."

## 1768, October 23. *IMPORTATION BAN.*

Gov. Montagu warned the Assembly to ignore any letter it received which might have "the smallest tendency to sedition, or by promoting an unwarrantable combination, to inflame the minds of the people." All twenty-six members denied they had received any such letter.

## 1768, November 16. *POLITICS. IMPORTATION BAN.*

The Assembly convened at the State House on Broad Street. The House elected Peter Manigault as speaker. They promptly endorsed the Boston letter to oppose the Townsend Acts. Gov. Montagu was furious.

### 1768, December 24. *SLAVERY. COMMERCE.*

Henry Laurens wrote:

> The planters are full of money and their rice commands money wherefore 'tis probable that the sales of slaves will be very advantageous at this market.

### 1768, December 29. *MEDICINE. MIDWIFE.*

Mrs. Grant advertised in the *Gazette* that she:

> Proposes to practice Midwifery ... having studied that art regularly, and practised it afterwards, at *Edinburgh:* Certificates of which, she can produce from the Gentlemen whose Lectures she attended, and likewise from the professors of Anatomy and Practice of Physick in that city.

## 1769

### 1769. *COMMERCE. SHIPBUILDING.*

John Rose, of the Hobcaw shipyard, retired with a fortune of £30,000 after twelve years of shipbuilding. He sold the shipyard to William Begbie and Daniel Mason.

### 1769, January. *FOREIGN SLAVERY BAN LIFTED.*

The Assembly lifted the three-year ban on foreign slave trade. Very quickly the Charlestown docks were crowded with thousands of slaves. During the first five months of the year, 5,438 Negroes were imported to South Carolina.

### 1769, January 26. *EXCHANGE BUILDING.*

The *Gazette* reported:

> Last Thursday evening arrived, in the brigantine *Jolleff* ... a large quantity of Portland stone for the new Exchange Building in this town, with Mr. John Horlbeck one of the contractors for building that edifice. This is the third importation of this kind for that work.

### 1769, February 2. *AMERICAN REVOLUTION - Foundations.*

The *Gazette* warned that unless the "revenue acts are speedily repealed the people of this province would strictly adhere to the non-importation resolutions."

### 1769, March 18. *STAMP ACT. REPEAL CELEBRATION.*

The Mechanics of Charlestown met at Mazyck's pasture to celebrate the anniversary of the repeal of the Stamp Act. After a "handsome entertainment" they walked back to town "in procession, proceded by TWENTY-SIX lights."

## 1769, March 23. SLAVERY. COMMERCE.

Christopher Gadsden advertised for "strong able-bodied COUNTRY NEGROES" to work on his wharf because they were "quiet and orderly fellows."

## 1769, March 28. AMERICAN REVOLUTION - Foundations.

In a public letter in the *South Carolina Gazette and Country Journal*, Rev. Woodmason expressed the outrage of the backcountry people of the most recent election. He publically ridiculed Christopher Gadsden as the "Scriblerus of the Libertine" and claimed he and the Sons of Liberty were hypocrites – protesting British taxation without representation yet turning around and taxing the backcountry without allowing them fair representation. Woodmason wrote:

> Lo! Such are the Men who bounce and make such Noise about Liberty! Liberty! Freedom! Freedom! Rights! Privileges! and what not ... and these very Scribblers and Assembly Orators ... keep under the lowest Subjection half the Inhabitants of this Province ... These are the Sons of Liberty!

## 1769, April. POLITICS. SCANDAL.

Egerton Leigh, Vice Admiral of the Court (and illegally the Attorney General of South Carolina) rendered a decision against a client whom Leigh had previously advised as a client.

This enraged several business men in Charlestown, including Henry Laurens, whose niece was married to Leigh. Laurens published a venomous pamphlet titled "Extracts from the Proceedings of the High Court of Vice-Admiralty in Charles-Town, South Carolina" which documented Leigh's duplicitous behavior.

## 1769, April 13. EDUCATION.

The Rev. Mr. Thomas Panting, was "appointed HEAD MASTER of the Free School."

## 1769, May 18. POLITICS. SCANDAL.

Egerton Leigh retaliated against Henry Laurens by publishing a dramatic satire in the *Gazette* titled *The Man Unmasked, or The World Undeceived.*

## 1769, June 8. SLAVERY.

The *South Carolina Gazette* published a proclamation by Governor Charles Greville Montagu:

> It has been represented to me that a large number of dead negroes who have been thrown into the river, are driven upon the marsh opposite Charles Town, and the noisome smell arising from their putrefaction may become dangerous to the health of the inhabitants of this province: In order to prevent such an inhumane and unchristian

practice, I think it fit, by the advice of his Majesty's council, to issue this my proclamation strictly forbidding this same: And I do hereby offer a reward of ONE HUNDRED POUNDS to be paid on the conviction of the offender to any person that will inform against any one person who shall be guilty of such practice.

## 1769, June 8. *AMERICAN REVOLUTION - Foundations.*

The *Gazette* announced that "several Societies of gentlemen ... in patriotic associations" agreed to dress in homespun and boycott all British goods that could be manufactured in America.

## 1769, June 22. *POLITICS.*

In the *Gazette*, Christopher Gadsden wrote:

> It seems amazing, and altogether unaccoun-table, that our mother country should take almost every means in her power, to drive her colonies to some desperate act; for what else could be the motive (besides oppressing them) of treating them with that contempt she upon all occasions affects to do?

## 1769, June 25. *COMMERCE. REAL ESTATE.*

The *Gazette* advertised a lot for sale, and a house for rent.

> TO BE SOLD by private sale,
>
> A LOT in St. Michael's Alley, opposite to Mr. John Gordon's containing 34 feet front in the alley, and 92 feet deep, on which there are two very good convenient stores, one 41 feet long, and 18 wide, two story high, with a brick cellar under it five and half feet deep. Whoever inclines to purchase said lot, may know the conditions by applying to JOHN HUME.
>
> TO BE LET, and may be entered upon immediately.
>
> A Commodious BRICK TENEMENT, in King-street, next door to Mr. Benjamin Mazyck's, lately occupied by the Reverend Mr. John Thomas; it has all necessary conveniences, four rooms neatly papered, and the whole in good order. Enquire of *Frederick Grimke*, or in his absence of *Alexander Fraizer*, Esq. in Tradd Street.

## 1769, June 28. *AMERICAN REVOLUTION - Foundations.*

An "Association" was published, pledging the non-importation of any products of Great Britain, and denounceing anyone who did not sign within a month. Many of the aristocratic leaders were upset by the surge of the mechanics in politics, usurped by men they considered their inferior. The rally cry of the "Association" became "Sign or die!"

This was the first extralegal body to formed in the colonies before the Revolution.

### 1769, June 29. *AMERICAN REVOLUTION - Foundations.*

The *Gazette* announced that the "mechanics of Charlestown are desired to meet under the Liberty Tree on Monday next at four o'clock."

### 1769, July. *CIRCUIT COURT ACT. REGULATORS.*

The demands from the Regulators forced the Assembly to pass the Circuit Court Act which gave the population of the South Carolina backcountry more equitable representation and increased the number of schools, jails and law enforcement officials. District courts were established at Beaufort, Georgetown, Cheraw, Camden, Orangeburg, and Ninety-Six.

### 1769, July 3. *AMERICAN REVOLUTION - Foundations*

Local merchants met at Dillon's Tavern and agreed to subscribe to the policy of non-importation.

### 1769, July 6. *SLAVERY.*

Peter Timothy in the *Gazette* wrote:

> From the first of January last to the first of July no less than 4,233 [Negroes] had been imported and many more were expected before the close of the year. This scarcely needs comment; every man's own mind must suggest the consequences of such enormous importation, especially at this time.

From 1756-66, more than 24,000 African slaves had been brought into Carolina, an average of 2400 each year. The doubling of the annual slaves imported during the first half of 1769 was unsettling for many citizens.

### 1769, July 6. *CULTURE.*

The *Gazette* announced:

> After the 28th Instant, a SOCIETY will be formed, which will give Premiums and other Encouragements, to those who shall raise the most SHEEP, COTTON, SILK, and FLAX, manufacture the *most* in Quantity and *best* in Quality of *coarse* and *fine* Linens, Cloths, Paper, Stockings, &c.

### 1769, July 13. *AMERICAN REVOLUTION - Foundations.*

The *Gazette* contained advertisements that called for the merchants to meet at Dillon's Tavern and the mechanics and planters at the Liberty Tree, to discuss the Townsend Duties Act. All agreed that "taxation without representation" was the main grievance.

### 1769, July 22. *Slave Ban. "Association" Formed.*

During a meeting at the Liberty Tree, both sides – thirteen merchants and thirteen mechanics and planters - accepted a unified Association. They encouraged American manufacturing and prohibited the importation of any European or East Indian goods, except a few necessary items which could not be produced in America. It was the most comprehensive protest in the American colonies.

Slave importation from Africa was banned after January 1, 1770 and all signers pledged to boycott anyone who did not sign within a month. Anyone who broke the agreement was to "be treated with the utmost contempt." The Association was to remain in effect until the Townsend Duties Act was repealed. Anyone who did not sign would have their names published in the *Gazette* as being against the Association.

### 1769, July 28. *Slavery. Execution.*

Dolly, belonging to James Sands, and Liverpoole, a slave doctor belonging to William Price, were burned at the stake on the green in front of the workhouse. Dolly was convicted of poisoning her master and his child, while Liverpoole was convicted of providing the poison.

Dick, a former slave who had been freed, was "accused as instigator of these horrid crimes." He initially escaped but was eventually retaken and given "twenty-five Lashes ... at four different Corners and the same Number last Tuesday, in all 100 each Day, and to lose his Right Ear."

### 1769, August 3. *Association. Drayton Resists.*

William Henry Drayton was a twenty-seven-year old planter who refused to join the Association. Educated in England, Drayton had expensive tastes and his fondness for gambling left him deeply in debt. He was described as "a rather frivolous young lightweight, unable to get his life in order."

When Drayton discovered there was no market for his plantation goods, he attacked the Association in the *Gazette*. The publication of his name was "an infringement of individual rights" and "only the legislature could brand a man an enemy of his country." He contemptuously called Gadsden:

> either traitor or madman who looks upon himself as a monarch ... the *ruler of the people* ... [who should be] locked in an insane asylum until the change of the moon.

### 1769, August 22. *Commerce. Trades.*

Ezra White, "Civil Architect, House-builder in general, and Carver, from London" advertised his expertise in the *South Carolina Gazette and Country Journal*. He claimed that he:

> Has finished the architecture, in the joiner way, all tabernacle frames ... and carved all the said work in the four principal rooms; and also calculated, adjusted, and draw'd at large for to work by, the Ionick

entablature, and carved the same in the front and round the eaves, of Miles Brewton Esquire's House, on White Point.

## 1769, August 28. *CULTURE. POLITICS.*

The Governor's Bridge connected the city north of Craven's Bastion by crossing Daniel Creek (present-day Market Street). The legislature fixed Boundary Street (present-day Calhoun Street) as the city's northern border.

## 1769, September 14. *ASSOCIATION.*

The *Gazette* reported that, excluding Royal officials, only thirty-one inhabitants of had refused to sign the pledge and join the Association. The names of the thirty-one were published in the paper and they quickly discovered themselves unable to sell merchandise.

Over the next several weeks Drayton and Gadsden published letters in the *Gazette*, with the attacks becoming more personal, rather than an exchange of ideas.

Christopher Gadsden
*Courtesy of the New York Public Library*

## 1769, September 21. *ASSOCIATION. DRAYTON REACTS.*

William Henry Drayton lashed out for having his name published as a non-subscriber of the Association. He argued that he would never "take orders from a mechanic" because "nature never intended that such men should be profound politicians or able statesmen." He also wondered why:

> other members of the educated elite would willingly associate with men who never were in a way to study, or to advise upon any points,

but rules how to cut up a *beast in the market* to best advantage, to *cobble* an old shoe in the neatest manner, or to build a *necessary house*.

Christopher Gadsden pointed out that Drayton was exempted from labor to make a living due to his "marriage to a rich heiress rather than from any merit of his own."

## 1769, October 4. *BACKCOUNTRY.*

In a letter to Lord Hillsborough, Lt Gov. Bull com-plained about those:

> Backcountry inhabitants who chose to live by the wandering indolence of hunting than by the more honest and domestic employment of planting ... little more than white Indians.

## 1769, October 4. *AMERICAN REVOLUTION – Foundations.*

Peter Manigault reported that only thirty-one merchants had refused to sign the Association. He also noted that many had signed the agreement "from fear of communal retaliation rather than conviction."

## 1769, October 16. *POLITICS.*

In a letter to James Habersham in London, Henry Laurens commented on the sad spectacle of the newspaper battle:

> You see in the Newspapers the sparrings between some of our Party men who like many other Men in such circumstances have each taken a side and seem to have forgot the subject upon which they began to dispute. Their contest is not now in defence of Liberty ... but about false concord and ungrammatical blunders.

## 1769, October 31. *SLAVERY.*

The *Sally* brought slaves to Charlestown. Henry Laurens wrote:

> A third poor pining creature hanged herself with a piece of small vine which shows her carcass was not very weighty ... who that views the above Picture can love the African trade?

Laurens rationalized his role as a slave trader using what was to become a tried and true Charleston excuse - tradition.

> These Negroes were first enslaved by the English ... I was born in a Country where Slavery had been established by the British Kings & Parliaments ... I found the Christian Religion & Slavery growing under the same authority ... I am not the Man who enslaved them, they are indebted to English men for that ...

## 1769, November 30. *COMMERCE. SHIPBUILDING.*

Begbie and Manson, advertised for "shipbuilding, heaving-down and repairing" at Hobcaw. They also advertised for "heaving-down, graving, repairing and mast-making" at Rose's Wharf in Charles Town. They also noted they had a good inventory of "live oak, cypress and spars."

### 1769, November 30. *SLAVERY.*

The *Gazette* announced an auction for:

> All the EFFECTS of Ezra White, deceased, consisting of two Negro Fellows, and three boys; one of the Fellows a Bricklayer' Several pieces of curious carved work, his Tools, Books.

### 1769, December 5. *POPULATION.*

Lt. Gov. William Bull reported that there were 45,000 white inhabitants and 80,000 Negroes in South Carolina. Charlestown contained 5,030 whites and 5,831 Negroes. During the year 5,438 slaves were imported and sold for £200,000 sterling.

Exports were listed to value £404,000 sterling and included:

- Hemp: 526,131 pounds
- Rice: 123,317 barrels
- Pork: 2,170 barrels
- Pitch & tar: 7,752 barrels
- Lumber: 678,350 feet
- Shingles: 1,987,000
- Bricks: 42,800
- Indigo: 309,570
- Tobacco: 214,210
- Deerskins: 183,221

He also noted that William Gibbes' wharf off South Bay Street (present-day South Battery) extended 300 feet into the Ashley River.

### 1769, December 7. *EDUCATION. NAVIGATION.*

Mr. George Hall, "mate of the Ship *Carolina Packet*", offered his services to teaching "the Lunar Method of Observation ... finding the True Latitude of a Ship, Independent of a Meridional Observation."

### 1769, December 8. *JOHN WILKES AFFAIR.*

The Assembly voted to send to £1500 sterling to help pay the debts of John Wilkes "for the support of the just and constitutional rights and liberties of the people of Great Britain and America." The Sons of Liberty who met at the Liberty Tree considered this part of "their resistance to the arbitrary rule by the same Parliament that had imposed unconstitutional taxes on America."

At the behest of Christopher Gadsden the Assembly ordered Jacob Motte, the public Treasurer, to send £10,500 provincial currency to the John Wilkes Fund in London "for assisting in the support of the just and constitutional rights of the People of Great Britain and America." Only seven members of the Assembly voted against the measure, including Speaker Peter Manigault.

This action shocked and infuriated government officials in both London and Charlestown, as it undermined official authority over the financial purse-strings of the colony.

### 1769, December 19. *COMMERCE.*

The *Peter and Ann* arrived in Charlestown carrying 100 pipes (one pipe = 127 gallons) of wine for Alexander Gillon.

### 1769, December 28. *AMERICAN REVOLUTION - Foundations.*

Peter Timothy, in the *Gazette*, stated about the Association that "such a brash step ... was a clear indication that South Carolinians were capable of independent and creative measures."

### 1769, December 31. *COMMERCE. CULTURE.*

By the end of this decade, the two wealthiest men in the American colonies were Henry Laurens and Gabriel Manigault. They enjoyed yearly incomes of approximately £3,000 a year. In comparison a successful lawyer or physician in America might make £500 sterling a year.

# 1770

### 1770, January 3. *ASSOCIATION. COMMERCE.*

The ship, *London,* sailed for England with a cargo of goods rejected by Charlestown due to the nonimportation resolutions. William Henry Drayton returned to England on the ship to express his disapproval of local actions.

### 1770, Janaury 4. *CULTURE.*

The *Gazette* announced:

> German Friendly Society. The Members of said Society, are desired to attend the Annual Meeting, on Wednesday the 12$^{th}$ day of January, 1770.

### 1770, January 24. *ASSOCIATION.*

Merchant Alexander Gillon attempted to sell the 100 pipes of wine that arrived the month before. At a meeting at the Liberty Tree, Christopher Gadsden and the Association ordered Gillon to either store the wine or reship it elsewhere. Gillon protested that he had ordered the wine in May, *before* the Association was organized, but he complied and stored the wine.

### 1770, January 30. *EDUCATION. COLLEGE.*

Governor William Bull urged the Assembly to make provisions for adequate education in South Carolina. He stated that "liberal education in the province was essential for the future of the community." A committee which included Henry Laurens and Christopher Gadsden presented a bill to the Assembly for the establishment of a college. This is often defined as the founding of the College of

Charleston, but the bill was never approved by the Assembly. The College would not officially be established until 1785.

Benjamin Smith left £500 sterling in his will, for the establishment of a college.

### 1770, February 13. *John Wilkes Affair*.

In response to the Assembly sending public money to the Wilkes Fund, South Carolina Attorney General William de Grey, advised that all three branches of government – Governor, Council and Assembly – must approve any appropriation of public funds from the treasury. He ruled that the gift to the Wilkes Fund was illegal.

### 1770, February 13. *Birth*.

Morris Brown was born in Charlestown. His parents were two of the twenty-four free blacks in Charleston, versus 5,800 enslaved blacks.

### 1770, March 1. *John Wilkes Affair*.

Word arrived in Charlestown of John Wilkes' release from prison. A group calling themselves Club Forty-Five met at Dillon's Tavern at 6:45 that evening and drank 45 loyal and patriotic Toasts" and adjourned at 12:45.

Peter Timothy wrote that "over 150 houses were illuminated, many with forty-five lights."

### 1770, March 5. *Boston Massacre*.

British soldiers fired on citizens in the street, killing five males and injured six others.

### 1770, March 8. *American Revolution - Foundations*.

In the *Gazette*, Peter Timothy reported that British merchants had lost £300,000 sterling just in the loss of slave trading, an unreasonable sacrifice in an attempt to raise £13,000 sterling.

### 1770, March 30. *Slavery. Population*.

Lt. Gov. William Bull reported to the Board of Trade that the Negro population of Carolina was 75,178. He also reported a white population of approximately 50,000, with more than 10,000 men in the militia, divided into ten regiments.

### 1770, April 5. *American Revolution - Foundations*.

The *Gazette* reported the Boston Massacre in a two-page story, bordered with thick lines. The royal insignia in the paper's masthead was blackened out by Peter Timothy, drawing the ire of many citizens for being disrespectful of the king.

### 1770, April 12. *Townsend Acts Repealed. Association*.

The Townsend Acts were repealed by Parliament. However, in an effort to avoid the appearance of weakness in the face of intense colonial protest, the tea tax was left in place.

Merchants in Albany, New York, Providence and Newport, Rhode Island abandoned their non-importation pledge a few weeks later.

### 1770, April 14. *JOHN WILKES AFFAIR.*

When King George III heard about the Wilkes Fund, he ordered his government to deny the authority of the South Carolina Assembly to appropriate funds for any such purpose, and that the Royal Council must approve any money bills. This kept the Assembly for doing any real business for the remainder of the colonial period.

### 1770, April 18. *CULTURE.*

The members of the Club Forty-Five met at "45 minutes after 6 in the Evening."

### 1770, April 19. *SLAVERY.*

An advertisement was placed in the *Gazette* for a runaway slave: : CAESAR: Absented himself from my Plantation . . . *plays well on the French horn."*

### 1770, May 2. *SLAVERY. ASSOCATION.*

The ship *Sally George* arrived from Africa with 345 slaves. Authorities refuse to allow the captain to unload his cargo due to the Association.

### 1770, May 14. *ASSOCIATION RENEWED.*

During a meeting at the Liberty Tree, which was chaired by Henry Laurens, it was decided that, due to the tea tax still in force, South Carolina would remain in support in the Association. Since Georgia had withdrawn from the boycott it was decided that any slaves purchased there would be seized.

### 1770, May 22. *DEATH.*

Henry Laurens' wife, Eleanor, died in childbirth. Laurens fought a losing battle over his sorrow for several years. He wrote:

> If I go here or there I find something or other to refresh my Sorrow and feel that some thing which constituted my Happiness is gone from me. I look round upon my Children, I lament for their Loss. I weep for my own.

He never married again.

### 1770, May 31. *JOHN WILKES AFFAIR. PITT STATUE ARRIVES.*

The statue of William Pitt ordered in 1766, arrived in Charlestown at Charles Elliott's Wharf via the ship *Carolina Packet*. The statue created great public excitement. Cannons fired, crowds cheered on the docks as it was unloaded. The bells St. Michaels would have rung "but were stopped out of regard to Issac Mazyck a very worthy member of the community, who was extremely ill near the church."

### 1770, May 31. *Association Violaters.*

Benjamin and Ann Mathews were advertised as "violators" of the Association agreement.

### 1770, June. *Death. Politics.*

The death of Public Treasurer, Jacob Motte, caused a new controversy between the Assembly and the Council, over his successor. The Assembly favored Benjamin Dart, a member of the Assembly who had voted for the Wilkes Fund. The Council proposed Henry Peronneau. Neither side would back down, so Lt. Gov. Bull appointed both men as joint Treasurers.

### 1770, June 4. *American Revolution – Foundations.*

During the celebration of King George III's birthday, Peter Timothy noted that, in comparison to the celebration over Wilkes and the Pitt statue:

> few [houses] were illuminated because the People are not Hypocrites. They will not dissemble Joy, while they feel themselves unkindly treated, and oppressed.

### 1770, June 7. *Commerce. Backcountry.*

Lt. Gov. Bull reported that 3000 wagons came to Charlestown last year from the backcountry carrying produce.

### 1770, June 18. *Association Broken by Rhode Island.*

News that Rhode Island had broken the Association led to the Sons of Liberty hanging an effigy between Dillon's Tavern and Gray's Tavern on Broad Street. The note attached read: SIMILAR TREATMENT TO ALL WHO VIOLATE THE ASSOCIATION.

The effigy was removed and placed in the Guard House. During the night, it was stolen, paraded around town and burned on the Green.

### 1770, June 27. *Non-Importation Agreement.*

At a meeting under the Liberty Tree presided over by Charles Pinckney, Jr., resolutions were adopted to castigate Georgia and Rhode Island for their violations of the non-importation agreement.

### 1770, July 5. *American Revolution - Foundations. Pitt Statue.*

The statue of William Pitt was dedicated at Meeting and Broad Streets – believed to be the first to commemorate a public figure in America - and placed upon a pedestal. A flag with "Pitt and Liberty" was raised. Members of the Club Forty-five led the crowd in three "hurrahs!" That evening Club Forty-five hosted a party at Mr. Dillon's Tavern where forty-five toasts were drunk.

## 1770, July 12. COMMERCE. ARTS.

William Adron, "who came here to erect Mr. PITT'S Statue", announced he was returning to London and would be "glad to serve any Gentleman that it may suit, by sending out Marble Chimney-Pieces, Monuments, Sideboard Tables, Tomb-Stones …"

William Pitt statue at its current location at the Charleston County Courthouse.
*Photo by author.*

## 1770, August 23. *AMERICAN REVOLUTION - Foundations.*

News arrived that Boston, New York and Philadelphia had joined Georgia and Rhode Island in breaking their agreements with the non-importation Association. Henry Laurens wrote:

> I am so disappointed in my Expectations of several Colonies North … to their late important Resolutions that I am in a humour to disbelieve the Sincerity of the majority of all Politicians …

## 1770, August 27. *CULTURE*.

A visitor upon arriving in Charlestown commented that "he had been mistakenly taken to Africa."

## 1770, December 5. *ASSOCIATION CONTROVERSY*.

Lt. Governor Bull also stated that there was "considerable division among the people" over the breaking of the Association. He wrote that "most of the merchants and some of the planters are ready to end the boycott." He also stated that:

> Mr. Christopher Gadsden is a violent enthusiast in the cause, he views every object of British moderation and measures with a suspicious and jaundiced eye ...

## 1770, December 13. *NON-IMPORTATION AGREEMENT*.

Henry Laurens and Charles Pinckney, Junior presided over a meeting at the Liberty Tree in which the continuation of the Association was discussed. Thomas Lynch:

> rode fifty miles to Charles Town and exerted all his eloquence and even the trope of Rhetorical Tears for the expiring liberties of his dear country, which the Merchants would sell like any other merchandise.

They then voted to discontinue the boycott on all items except tea, and "send a bitter letter to the northern colonies" about their conduct in breaking the Association. The non-importation crisis had a severe economic impact on the American colonies, with a dramatic drop in imports from 1768 to 1769.

- New York: £490, 673 to £75,930
- Philadelphia: £441,829 to £204,978
- New England (Boston and Rhode Island): £430,806 to £223,694
- Carolina: £306,600 to £146,273

The stage was set for Charlestown, and the rest of the American colonies, to shrug off their ties with the British motherland.

### SOUTH CAROLINA RICE EXPORTS
### 1698-1770

|  |  |
|---|---|
| 1698 | 5 tons |
| 1700 | 330 tons |
| 1726 | 5,000 tons |
| 1730 | 10,000 tons |
| 1740 | 25,000 tons |
| 1763 | 35,000 tons |
| 1764 | 40,000 tons |
| 1770 | 42,000 tons |

# SLAVE TRADE IN CHARLESTOWN

Most slave ships sailed directly from Africa to Charlestown. Some, however, stopped at one of the Leeward Islands (Puerto Rico, the Virgin Islands) before proceeding to the mainland.

*Courtesy of the New York Public Library.*

When slave ships arrived they were quarantined for a minimum of ten days on Sullivan's Island. Supplies were left on the beach. If the slaves had smallpox or other infectious diseases the quarantine period could be extended until the illness ran its course or the victim died. The clothing of the infected slaves was burned and the crew washed the ship down with vinegar and then smoked it.

The quality of the slaves was an important factor in the market value. Men should be no older than 25; women no older than 20 and without fallen breasts. Prime slaves were sold at £300 sterling.

Charleston, S.C., 1774. Cropped from "A View of Charles-Town", by Thos. Leitch. *Courtesy of the Library of Congress*

# PART FOUR
## Revolutionary City
### 1771-1799

"This town makes a most beautiful appearance as you come up to it, and in many respects a magnificent one ... in grandeur, splendor of buildings, decorations, equipages, numbers of commerce, shipping and indeed almost everything it far surpasses all I ever saw of ever expected to see in America."  – *Josiah Quincy, 1773*

# 1771

### 1771, January. MARRIAGE.

Major Pierce Butler of the British Army married Mary Middleton. She was heiress to a vast fortune, the orphaned daughter of Thomas Middleton, a South Carolina planter and slave importer. Two years later Butler resigned his commission in the British Army and settled with Mary in South Carolina.

### 1771, January 25. JOHN WILKES AFFAIR.

Lt. Gov. Bull urged the Assembly to pass a tax bill that did not include the £1,500 appropriation to the Wilkes Fund. The Assembly refused.

### 1771, Janaury 31. CULTURE. WAX EXHIBITION.

An advertisement in the *Gazette* announced:

> FIGURES IN WAX, as large as the Life, and admirably well executed; amongst them, one of that late eminent Preacher The Rev. Mr. George Whitefield. And another, of the Celebrated American Patriot, Commonly called the Pennsylvania Farmer ... entirely the Work of an ingenious Lady who exhibits them, that was born in America, and had never been out of it for Improvement.

### 1771, March 1. SLAVERY. EXECUTION.

Edmund Jones and Joseph Jordan were hanged for "aiding runaway slaves." Jones, the master of the schooner *Two Josephs*, and Jordan, a sailor, allegedly had stolen the schooner, taking with them several slaves. Several slaves who had run away on the *Two Josephs* were hanged together with Jordan and Jones.

### 1771, March 20. COMMERCE. BACKCOUNTRY.

Due to the increase of goods coming from the backcountry, an inspection system for tobacco was established at public warehouses on the principal rivers and ports.

### 1771, March 21. AMERICAN REVOLUTION - Foundations.

The *Gazette* announced:

> Monday last being the Anniversary of the Repeal of the Stamp-Act ... the same celebrated here in a suitable manner particularly by ... the Sons of St. Patrick, at Mr. Dillon's.

## 1771, March 28. *CULTURE*.

A Mr. William Partridge complained in the *Gazette* about being a member of a club he never joined.

> Whereas their [sic] appeared an Advertisement in Mr. Crouch's Gazette on the 26th Instant to call a Meeting of the JOVIAL CLUB, to which my Name was subscribed as Secretary ... my Name was subscribed thereto, without my Consent or Knowledge. William Partridge.

## 1771, April 18. *CULTURE. STREET MAGIC.*

The Grand Jury announced:

> We present John Shagnuffey, as guilty of a Nuisance, in performing, by himself and his Associates, Legerdemain Tricks [hand magic], thereby collecting a Number of idle, loose and disorderly Persons, to the Disturbance of the Peace.

## 1771, May 1. *CULTURE. EDUCATION.*

Thomas Griffith, a "Riding-Master, from London," opened a school to "teach Young Gentlemen and Ladies to ride, with the same Safety, Ease and Gentility, as is now practiced in the best Riding-Schools in London."

## 1771, May 21. *AMERICAN REVOLUTION - Foundations.*

At a meeting under the Liberty Tree, a group of citizens decided that no tea should be imported while the tax on it remained. The group included:

- Christopher Gadsden, merchant
- William Johnson blacksmith
- Joseph Veree, carpenter
- John Fullerton, carpenter
- James Brown, carpenter
- Nathaniel Libby, ship carpenter
- George Flagg, painter and glazier
- Thomas Coleman, upholsterer
- John Hall, coachmaker
- William Field, carver
- Robert Jones, sadler
- John Clavert, clerk
- H.Y. Bookless, wheelwright
- J. Barlow, sadler
- Tunis Teabout, blacksmith
- Peter Munclean, clerk
- William Trusler, butcher
- Robert Howard, carpenter
- Alex Alexander, schoolmaster
- John Loughton, coachmaker
- W. Rodgers, wheelwright
- Edward Weyman, glass grinder
- Thomas Swarle, painter
- William Laughon, tailor
- Daniel Cannon, carpenter
- Benjamin Hawes, painter

## 1771, July. *EDUCATION. COMMERCE.*

Henry Laurens left Charlestown with his three sons for Philadelphia, on his way to England to establish his children in school.

## 1771, August 16. DUEL.

In a duel that took place in the long room of a tavern, Dr. John Haley, a Charlestown Whig physician, killed Mr. Delancy, a Tory from New York and brother of Mrs. Ralph Izard. Since the duel took place without the presence of seconds, Dr. Haley was charged with murder. At his trial he was defended by Thomas Heyward, Jr. and acquitted which "was considered a great triumph by the Whigs."

## 1771, August 18. CULTURE. EDUCATION.

Henry Laurens wrote his daughter, Martha, from Philadelphia, as he was preparing to leave for England.

> My dearest Patsy, remember my precepts; be dutiful, kind and good to your Aunt ... let all your reading, your study, and your practice tend to make you a wise and virtuous woman, rather than a fine lady; the former character always comprehends the latter, but the modern fine lady ... is too often found to be deficient both in wisdom and in virtue.

## 1771, September 15. ROYAL GOVERNOR ARRIVES.

The HMS *Tartar* arrived. On board was Lord Charles Grenville Montagu, who was returning after a two-year absence for his third term as the Royal Governor. Montagu decided to take up residence at Fort Johnson as he was not pleased with the accommodations prepared for him in Charlestown.

## 1771, September 19. CULTURE. DANCING.

Pike's Dancing School opened.

## 1771, September 29. LAURENS SAILS TO ENGLAND.

Henry Laurens and his sons, John (seventeen-years old), Henry, Jr. (called Harry, eight-years old) and six-year old James, sailed for London where Harry was to attend school. Laurens left his business in the hands of his old friend Gabriel Manigault and his daughters, Martha and Mary Eleanor, in the care of his brother, James.

## 1771, October 31. BACKCOUNTRY.

After an investigation by Lt. Gov. William Bull, Gov. Montagu issued a pardon for the Regulators who had been imprisoned "for illegally though deservedly" punishing criminals.

## 1771, November 7. DUEL. TRIAL.

The trial of Dr. John Haley, accused of killing Peter De Lancey in a duel, attracted "the most crowded Audience that was ever assembled there [State House upon any Occasion." Haley was found guilty of manslaughter, mainly due to the skill of his lawyers, James Parsons, Thomas Heyward, Charles Cotesworth Pinckney and Alexander Harvey, "Natives of this Province, and lately from the Temple, who acquired no small Degree of Applause by their Pleading upon this Occasion."

### 1771, December 5. COMMERCE.

The *Gazette* reported that:

> No less than 113 waggons on the road to Town, most of them loaded with two Hogsheads of Tobacco, besides indigo, hemp, butter, tallow, bees wax and many other articles who all carry out on their Return, Rum, Sugar, salt and European goods.

### 1771, December 26. POLITICS.

Henry Laurens, in a letter to Thomas Franklin, wrote:

> I have always disliked those stupid Garnishings of No. 45, Wilkes and Liberty and drinking 45 Toasts to the Cause of true Liberty 450 Times unnecessarily.

### 1771, December 27. BIRTH.

William Johnson, Jr. was born in Charlestown. He would later serve as an associate justice of the U.S. Supreme Court.

# 1772

### 1772. EPIDEMIC.

South Carolina suffered a major measles outbreak, killing about 900 children.

### 1772, April 12. POLITICS.

Gov. Montagu had demanded that the House of Commons to surrender "the inherent right of its constituents to manage their own funds." Montagu wanted Governor and the Council to approve all expenditures. The House, under the leadership of Peter Manigault, refused to give up their right.

### 1772, May 16. NORTH/SOUTH CAROLINA BORDER SURVEY.

William Moultrie, appointed by Gov. Montagu to conduct of survey of a sixty-mile disputed section of the boundary, left his Northhampton Plantation for a three week journey to survey the border. He took with him "two slaves named Tobias and Dick, one five-gallon keg each of wine and rum, and for his bed only two blankets and a bearskin."

### 1772, June 4. SLAVERY.

The *South Carolina Gazette* ran this advertisement: "RUN AWAY: Dick, a mulatto fellow . . . *a remarkable whistler and plays on the Violin.*"

## 1772, July 3. EDUCATION. LEGAL.

Edward Rutledge was called to the English bar, along with his Charlestown friend, Thomas Pinckney.

## 1772, August 27. SLAVERY.

In the *Gazette*, a white planter wondered if "the laws of this province extend to the punishment of vices in Negroes?" Elite whites complained that their slaves:

> congregated in large numbers, frequented taverns, cursed and swore in the city streets, refused to work, dressed inappropriately, gambled and always seemed to behave in an insolent manner.

Most whites considered the city slaves more "rude, unmannerly, insolent and shameless" than country slaves.

## 1772, September 7. SLAVERY.

A visitor to Charlestown complained in the *South Carolina Gazette* that most blacks in the city refused to take off their hats to whites in the streets.

## 1772, September 24. MONTAGU MOVES ASSEMBLY TO BEAUFORT. JOHN WILKES AFFAIR.

Governor Montagu in attempt to break the stalemate in the Assembly over the Wilkes Fund appropriation, and the Assembly's ability to dispose of tax revenue without his consent, announced that in October, the Assembly would meet in Beaufort, not Charlestown.

He hoped that the distance and inconvenience might keep some of the more radical Charlestown members from attending, so some necessary legislation could be passed. He also hoped the implied threat of moving the capital from Charlestown would intimidate some of the members to moderate their views.

Montagu wrote to Secretary of State Dartmouth about his decision to move the legislature. Dartmouth replied, calling the action "ill-advised" and that it would only "increase that ill humour which has already too unfortunately prevailed."

## 1772, October 8. ASSEMBLY MEETS IN BEAUFORT.

Despite the long journey to Beaufort (seventy miles) thirty-seven members of the Assembly (more than the nineteen needed) opened the legislative session. They chose Peter Manigault as their speaker and informed Gov. Montagu they were ready for business. The surprised, and unprepared, governor refused to receive them for two days, and then ordered them back to Charlestown.

## 1772, October 22. COMMITTEE OF GRIEVANCES.

The Assembly opened in Charlestown in a foul mood. They immediately appointed a Committee of Grievances, chaired by Christopher Gadsden with prominent members including Speaker Rawlins Lowndes, John Rutledge, Thomas

Lynch and Charles Pinckney, Jr. Ultimately, the Assembly decided that the governor's actions justified a resolution to suspend all business with him.

## Buildings of Charleston
### Unitarian Church, 6 Archdale Street

Under the leadership of Rev. William Tennent, in 1772 construction on a second Independent Church began on Archdale Street. Construction was halted during the British occupation of the city, and completed in 1787.

Rev. Anthony Forster, a Unitarian minister, was the first pastor of the Second Independent Church. His successor, Dr. Samuel Gilman served from 1819 to 1858. It was chartered as the first Unitarian Church in the South in 1839.

*Courtesy of the Library of Congress*

### 1772, November. *BACKCOUNTRY.*

The courts in the backcountry opened. The circuit judges held court Camden, Orangeburg, Cheraw, Ninety-Six, Georgetown, and Beaufort.

### 1772, December 3. *CRIME. EXECUTION. SLAVERY.*

Dempsey Griffin was hanged for "stealing a Negro, the Property of Mr. Brisbane."

### 1772, December 31. *CULTURE. MAGIC.*

An advertisement in the *Gazette* announced:

> On Saturday Evening next, *And on* Monday *and* Wednesday following, the celebrated MR. SAUNDERS Will exhibit his Dexterity and Grand Deception in Mr. Strother's *Long-room behind the* Beef-Market.

# 1773

## 1773. *SLAVERY.*

During the first five months of the year 11,641 Negroes were imported to South Carolina.

## 1773. *ARRIVALS. COMMERCE.*

Francis Salvador, a Jew, arrived in Charlestown from London. He moved to the Ninety-Six area in the backcountry where he quickly established substantial land holdings.

## 1773. *COMMERCE.*

Francis Marion purchased a small, two-hundred-acre plantation on the Santee River, called Pond Bluff, about four miles east of present-day Eutawville. His plantation manager was the slave June, a birth gift from his uncle.

## 1773, January 6. *ASSEMBLY VS. MONTAGU.*

The Assembly opened its session and voted Rawlins Lowndes speaker. Gov. Montagu refused to recognize Lowndes and asked them to vote again. They again chose Lowndes and the governor dissolved the Assembly. The House accused him of "a most unprecedented oppression and an unwarranted abuse of the Royal Prerogative." They composed a letter to their agent in London to call for Montagu's removal.

Gov. Montagu also received a letter from Secretary Dartmouth denouncing the Beaufort met Assembly as "throwing new difficulties in the way of an accommodation of the former subject of dispute."

## 1773, January 10. *EDWARD RUTLEDGE RETURNS.*

Edward Rutledge returned to Charlestown on the ship *Magna Carta*, after completing his law studies in England. He was given a 640-acre plantation on St. Helena Island by his mother.

## 1773, January 12. *CHARLESTON FIRST.*

Charleston Museum was established – 1st museum in America.

The Charleston Library Society provided the core collection of natural history artifacts for the founding of the Charleston Museum (the first in America) in 1773. Residents were encouraged to donate objects for the new museum on Chalmers Street. Some of initial acquisitions included "a drawing of the head of a bird, an Indian hatchet, a Hawaiian woven helmet, and a Cassava basket from Surinam."

The museum also acquired "a Rittenhouse orrery, a Manigault telescope, a Camera obscura, a hydrostatic balance, and a pair of elegant globes."

> # CHARLESTON FIRST
>
> **1773, JANUARY 12.**
> **FIRST MUSEUM IN AMERICA.**
>
> The museum ran the following advertisement:
>
> **THE MUSEUM OF SOUTH CAROLINA**
> **IN CHALMER'S STREET, (NEAR THE CITY SQUARE)**
>
> Consisting of an extensive collection of Beasts, Birds, Reptiles, Fishes, Warlike Arms, Dresses and other CURIOSITIES – among which are:
>
> The Head of New Zealand Chief
> An Egyptian Mummy (a child)
> The Great White Bear of Greenland
> The Black and Red Wolves
>     of South Carolina
> The South African Lion
> The Duck Bill'd Platypus
>     from New Holland
> The Bones of an Ostrich as large
>     as those of a Horse
> The Boa Constrictor, or Anaconda
>     snake, 25 feet long
>
> The Grampus Whale, 20 feet long
> 800 birds, 70 beasts, 200 fishes
> 4000 specimens of minerals
> Shoes of the Chinese ladies,
>     4 inches long
> The Saw Fish, saw 4 ½ feet in
>     length
> A large collection of views of
> Public Buildings, etc. in Europe
> A Fine Electrical Machine
>
> The whole elegantly arranged in glass cases, open every day from 9 o'clock, and brilliantly illuminated every evening with occasionally a Band of Music.

## 1773, January 18. *CULTURE. HORSEMANSHIP.*

Mr. Bates, "who has finished the Tour of *Europe*" performed "Different Feats in HORSEMANSHIP, on one, Two & Three HORSES, At the Upper End of Meeting-street."

## 1773, February 22. *POLITICS.*

Peter Timothy addressed the situation between Gov. Montagu and the Assembly in the *Gazette:*

> By an unparalleled Succession of Prorogations and Dissolutions, the Inhabitants of this Province have been unrepresented in Assembly about three years – *A Correspondent asks, Whether this is a Grievance?* And *if it is*, Whether *it* is one of the *least Magnitude?*

## 1773, February 28. *Josiah Quincy's Diary. Culture.*

Josiah Quincy II, a Bostonian, arrived in Charlestown for a visit. He wrote in his diary:

> Just before sunset we passed the fort. Charlestown appeared situated between two large spacious rivers ... which here empty themselves into the sea. The number of shipping far surpassed all I had ever seen in Boston. I was told there were then not so many as common this season, tho' about 350 sail lay off the town. The town struck me very agreeably; but the New Exchange which fronted the place of my landing made a most notable appearance. On landing, Sunday Evening just before dark, the numbers of Inhabitants and appearance of the buildings far exceeded my expectation.

Quincy was a prominent Boston lawyer, who at age twenty-six, had assisted his cousin, John Adams, in the legal defense of the British officers accused in the Boston Massacre in 1770. In failing health, Quincy was advised by doctors to travel to a milder climate. He arrived in Charlestown during the social season and was astounded by "the most brilliant season in the history of the colonial American theatre." His son, Josiah Quincy III, would become a member of Congress, mayor of Boston and president of Harvard.

## 1773, February 29. *Josiah Quincy's Diary. Culture.*

Josiah Quincy, visiting from Boston, described the white residents as "the opulent and lordly planters, and poor and spiritless peasants." He also stated that:

> This town makes a most beautiful appearance as you come up to it, and in many respects a magnificent one. Although I have not been here twenty hours, I have traversed the most populous parts of it. I can only say in general that in grandeur, splendor of buildings, decorations, equipages, numbers of commerce, shipping and indeed almost everything it far surpasses all I ever saw of ever expected to see in America ... The number of shipping far surpasses all I have seen in Boston ... about three hundred and fifty sail off the town ... and the new Exchange which fronted the place of my landing, made a very handsome appearance.

## 1773, March 2. *Josiah Quincy's Diary. St. Cecilia Concert.*

Josiah Quincy attended a St. Cecilia Society Concert, which was held in the in Dock Street Theater. Quincy commented:

> The Concert-house is a large inelegant building situated down a yard at the entrance ... The Hall is (preposterously) and out of all proportion large, no orchestra for the musical performers, though a kind of loft for fiddlers ... the musick was good. The two bass-viols and French horns

were grand ... One Abercrombie, a Frenchman just arrived, played a first fiddle and solo incomparably, better than any I ever had heard ... has a salary of 500 guineas a year from the St. Cecilia Society.

Here was upward of two hundred fifty ladies, and it was called no great show .... In loftiness of headdress these ladies stoop to their daughters of the North; in richness of dress surpass them.

The gentlemen many of them dressed with richness and elegance was common with us – many with swords on.

## 1773, March 4. *JOSIAH QUINCY'S DIARY. CULINARY.*

From Josiah Quincy's journal:

Dined (with four other Gentlemen) with David Deis, Esq. (Table decent and not inelegant: provisions indifferent, but well-dressed: no apology; good wines and festivity. Salt fish brought in small bits in a dish made a corner) ... The ladies withdrew after the first round [of toasts] ... glasses were changed every time different wine was filled.

## 1773, March 5. *JOSIAH QUINCY'S DIARY. CULINARY.*

From Josiah Quincy's journal:

Dined at a very elegantly disposed and plentiful table at the house of John Mathews, Esq. in company with the Chief Justice of St. Augustine [William Drayton] and several other gentlemen. Puddings and pies brought in after hot meats taken away ... Good wines.

## 1773, March 7. *JOSIAH QUINCY'S DIARY. CULINARY. RELIGION.*

Josiah Quincy was not impressed with the church service at St. Philips. The small number in attendance shocked his Boston-Puritan ethic. In addition, he noted the minister was:

A young scarcely-bearded boy read prayers, with the most gay, indifferent and gallant air imaginable: very few men and no women stand in singing-time. Having heard a young church-parson very coxcomically advance a few days before, that no sermon ought to exceed twenty-five minutes, I had the curiosity to see by my watch ... that he shortened the space above seven and one-half minutes. It was very common in prayer as well as sermon-time to see gentlemen conversing together.

Josiah Quincy wrote in his diary of his evening at the Miles Brewton House, 27 King Street:

Dined with considerable company at Miles Brewton's, Esq. a gentleman of a very large fortune: a most superb house, said to have cost him

£8000 sterling. The grandest hall I ever beheld, Azure Blue Sateen - window curtains, rich blue paper with gilt ... most elegant pictures ... excessive grand and costly looking glasses etc.

A most elegant table, three courses. Nick nacks, jellies, preserves, sweet meats, etc. After dinner, two sorts of nuts, almonds, raisins, three sorts of olives, apples, oranges etc. By odds the richest wines I ever tasted. Exceeds Mt. Hancocks, Vassall's, Philip's and others much in flavor, softness and strength.

A young lawyer Mr. Pinckney [Charles Cotesworth] ... dined with us ... I was assured ... that neither negroes or mulattoes could have a jury; that for killing a negro ... there could be nothing but a *fine* ... that (further) to *steal* a negro was death, but to *kill him* was only fineable. Curious laws and policy! I exclaimed.

## 1773, March 9. *Josiah Quincy's Diary. Culnary.*

From Josiah Quincy's journal:

Spent all the morning in viewing the Public library, State-house, public offices, etc. being waited upon Messrs. [Thomas] Pinckney and [Edward] Rutledge, two young gentlemen lately from the Temple, where they took the degree of barrister at law. The public library is a handsome, square, spacious room, containing a large collection of very valuable books, cuts, globes, etc.

That evening Quincy dined with:

Thomas Smith, several gentlemen and ladies: decent and plenteous table of meats, the upper cloth removed a compleat course, table of puddings, pies, tarts, custards, sweetmeats, oranges, macaroons, etc. – profuse. Excellent wines.

## 1773, March 11. *Josiah Quincy's Diary. Culnary.*

That evening Josiah Quincy dined with Thomas Bee. Quincy described Bee as:

a planter of considerable opulence. A gentleman of sense, improvement, and politeness; and one of the members of the house – just upon the point of marrying Mrs. McKenzie, a young widow of about twenty with eight or nine thousand guineas independent fortune ... daughter to Mr. Thomas Smith.

## 1773, March 12. *Josiah Quincy's Diary. Culnary. Culture.*

Josiah Quincy dined with Thomas Lynch, "a plain, sensible, honest man." In his journal, Quincy wrote:

Spent the evening with the Friday-night Club, consisting of the more elder substantial gentlemen: About twenty or thirty in company.

Conversation on negroes, rice and the necessity of British Regular troops to be quartered in Charlestown.

**BUILDINGS OF CHARLESTON**
**Miles Brewton House, 27 King Street**

Miles Brewton House, 27 King Street, where Josiah Quincy was entertained.
*Courtesy of the New York Public Library*

### 1773, March 15. *GOV. MONTAGU RESIGNS.*

Governor Montagu resigned and sailed for England, the second consecutive governor forced out of South Carolina by the stubborn persistence of the Assembly.

### 1773, March 15. *COMMERCE. GADSDEN'S WHARF.*

Christopher Gadsden finally completed his wharf at the north end of town on the Cooper River (at the foot of present-day Calhoun Street). It was described as "one of the most extensive of the kind ever undertaken in America."

### 1773, March 16. *JOSIAH QUINCY'S DIARY. HORSERACING.*

Josiah Quincy wrote about race week:

> Am now going to the famous races ... well performed ... Filmnap beat Little David (who had won the last sixteen races) out and out. The first four –mile heat was performed in eight minutes and seventeen seconds. I saw a fine collection of excellent, though very high-priced

horses ... Two thousand pounds were won and lost at this race and Filmnap sold at Public Vendue for £300 sterling.

## 1773, March 17. *Josiah Quincy's Diary. Culture.*

The Friendly Brothers of St. Patrick held "a very elegant Entertainment." Josiah Quincy attended the feast. He wrote:

> While at dinner six violins, two hautboys [oboe] and bassoon with a hand-tabor beat excellently well. After dinner six French horns in concert – most surpassing musick!

## 1773, March 18. *Josiah Quincy's Diary. Culture.*

Josiah Quincy "advanced to Miles Brewton ... thirty-one pounds sterling for one pipe [126 gallons] of Best London Particular Madeira Wine."

## 1773, March 19. *Josiah Quincy's Diary. Culture.*

Josiah Quincy spent "all the morning in hearing the debates of the House, had an opportunity of hearing the best speakers in the province." He noted in his journal:

> T. Lynch, Esqr. spoke like a man of sense and a patriot – with dignity, fire and laconism. [Christopher] Gadsden Esqr. was plain, blunt, hot and incorrect – though very sensible ... The members of the House all sit with their hats on, and uncover when they rise to speak.

## 1773, March 20. *Josiah Quincy's Diary. Culture.*

Josiah Quincy departed Charlestown. He noted:

> Set out with Mr. Lynch for his plantation on Santee River on my way northward. In crossing Hobcaw ferry we were rowed by six negroes, four of whom had *nothing on* but their kind of breeches, scarce sufficient for covering.

> From what I learned from Mr. Lynch it is worth trying the experiment of planting rice in our low, marshy lands, for the purpose of feeding cows and making the most excellent flavored and yellow butter.

## 1773, March 21. *Josiah Quincy's Diary. Culture.*

Josiah Quincy spent his last day in the lowcountry. He wrote:

> Had a three hours tedious passage up Santee river: Crossed Georgetownriver or Sampit River just at dusk. Lodged in the town and now held in duress by a very high equinoxial gale from crossing Winyah Bay.

## 1773, March 24. *Culture.*

The *Gazette* reported the streets of Charlestown contained "all kind of filth," where cattle fed openly "to the great annoyance of the inhabitants."

## 1773, May 10. *Tea Act Passed.*

Parliament passed the Tea Act, which allowed only the East India Company to export tax-free tea to the American colonies.

## 1773, May 10. *Slavery. Execution.*

Seven slaves, including their leader Caesar, were apprehended and tried for raiding the plantation of John Drayton on the Ashley River, stealing "Candles, Sugar, Rum, Bacon, Soap, Wine, a Bale of Cloth, and sundry other Articles to a very great Amount." The *South Carolina and American General Gazette* reported it as "one of the most daring Gangs of Fellows that ever infested the Province."

Caesar was "brought to Ashley Ferry" where he was "tried, convicted, and executed." Four other slaves were also hanged. One turned into the main prosecution witness and therefore escaped punishment. Mingo, a slave of John Drayton, was pardoned by Lieutenant Governor William Bull. An eighth slave, Andrew, remained "yet out in the Woods" and was suspected of having joined another group of maroons at a camp called Black Swamp.

## 1773, June 4. *Education.*

Henry Laurens was unhappy with the level of education available in England for his sons. He wrote about Oxford and Cambridge saying:

> The two universities are generally, I might say universally censured. Oxford in particular is spoken of as a School of Licentiousness and Debauchery in the most aggravated heights.

## 1773, June 24. *Culture.*

Dr. Alexander Garden (the physician, not the minister) was elected to the Royal Society, nominated by Benjamin Franklin. The Society renamed the Cape jessamine the "gardenia," in his honor.

## 1773, July 20. *Education.*

David Ramsay, an Irish immigrant and graduate of Princeton, was awarded a medical degree from the College of Philadelphia.

## 1773, July 24. *Theater. Culture.*

David Douglas arrived with the purpose of building a new theatre.

## 1773, August 13. *Culture. Theater. Commerce.*

David Douglass signed a fifteen-year lease with Robert Wells, Robert Rowand and John Deas for Lot# 40 (on the western side Church Street between Tradd and Broad) to build a new theater. The lease stipulated that Douglass would pay a £100 yearly rent and within three months he was to "erect a building suitable and convenient for a public theater and for the exhibition of dramatical entertainments." There had to be a ten-foot passage on Church Street.

The lease also set out several other conditions. That when Douglass's troupe was not in town, the building could be let to other troupes or entertainers. Each season Douglass was to give a benefit performance for charity.

## 1773, August 26. *AMERICAN REVOLUTION - Foundations.*

Thomas Powell, acting editor of the *Gazette*, published the proceedings of the Council without their permission and was arrested. His lawyer, Edward Rutledge, was able to convince the justice of the peace, Rawlins Lowndes, to secure Powell's release. Rutledge declared his pleasure "in being called forth as the Defender of the Liberty of the Subject."

The case became a hot political issue which brought together several powerful men and families in defense of Powell, forming a core group of radical thinkers – the Rutledges, Middletons, Pinckneys and Draytons.

## 1773, October 25. *COMMERCE. SHIPBUILDING.*

The 200-ton *Briton* was launched at Hobcaw, bound for the London trade. The *Gazette* reported that there were "no less than twelve Carolina-built ships, constantly employed in the trade between this port and Europe."

## 1773, November. *AMERICAN REVOLUTION - Foundations.*

Charlestown learned that Parliament had passed the Tea Act, repealing all duties on tea the British East India Company shipped to America. It was designed to help the company recover from near bankruptcy.

## 1773, November 1. *CRIME. SLAVERY. EXECUTION.*

Jacob Ramos was convicted of inciting a slave to commit the robbery of Mr. William Sommerfall. The Negro slave was hanged, and Ramos was sentenced to "stand in the pillory for an hour, pay a fine of $350, and receive 39 lashes." During the time in the pillory Ramos was:

> most severel [severely] & incessantly pelted by an enraged Populace; who nevertheless were so orderly, as to not use any other Materials than rotten eggs, Apples & Onions.

## 1773, November 13. *TEA ACT.*

Peter Timothy announced in the *Gazette* that "300 chests of tea were on their way to Charlestown." He urged the citizens to "band together to take the necessary steps to prevent the landing" of the cargo.

## 1773, November 21. *CLUB FORTY-FIVE.*

Club Forty-Five, including the Rutledge brothers, John and Edward, met at the Liberty Tree where they swore to defend against the tyranny of Great Britain. The tree was decorated with forty-five lights and forty-five skyrockets were fired. Forty-men then paraded from the Liberty Tree down King Street to Broad to Dillon's Tavern. Forty-five lights were placed on the table, along with forty-five punch bowls and forty-five bottles of wine ... all of which were consumed.

### 1773, November 25. *ARRIVALS. CULTURE.*

Eight members of the Douglass Troupe arrived on the brigantine, the *Sea Nymph*.

### 1773, November 26. *CRIME. EXECUTION.*

Williamson Willis was hanged for "stealing a Negro."

### 1773, November 29. *AMERICAN REVOLUTION - Foundations.*

The *Gazette* warned that allowing the tea to land would be tacit permission of Parliament's right to tax the colonies. It warned of a plan to "raise a revenue out of your pockets, *against your consent*, and to render assemblies of your representatives *totally useless.*"

### 1773, December 1. *TEA ARRIVES.*

Two hundred and fifty-seven chests of tea arrived in Charlestown on the ship *London*. Consigned by the East India Company, the arrival of the tea set off a crisis. Handbills were passed out, calling for a mass meeting of all South Carolinians "without exception, particularly the landholders," at the great hall in the Exchange Building.

### 1773, December 1. *TEA PROTESTS.*

The meeting at the Exchange Building marked the beginning of Revolutionary government in Charleston; it was the first of the extra-legal bodies that would govern the province for the remainder of royal rule. The "principal planters and landholders" joined the artisans in demanding that merchants stop importing tea. They also demanded the tea be sent back to England and resolved not to purchase any tea being taxed for raising revenue in America.

> That the tea ought not to be landed, received or vended in this colony, nor should any be imported while the law imposing this unconstitutional tax remained ...

When the merchants agreed, it was met with "repeated thanks and loud shouts of applause." Christopher Gadsden was appointed chairman to the committee to secure signatures in support of this resolution. They also resolved to boycott the business of any non-signers. Anonymous letters arrived at the Exchange Building threatening to burn the ship *London*, and the wharf where it was docked.

### 1773, December 3. *TEA PROTESTS.*

The *South Carolina Gazette* reported:

Last Wednesday evening came in over the bar, the next morning anchored before the town, the ship *London,* Alexander Curling, master from London, with no less than two hundred and fifty-seven chests of Tea on board, which were shipped by the East India Company of London ...

## 1773, December 3. *Commerce. Charleston Firsts.*

A group of merchants met at Mrs. Swallow's Tavern and organized a Chamber of Commerce. The Chamber elected John Savage, president, Miles Brewton, vice-president, David Deas, treasurer and John Hopton, secretary.

---

### CHARLESTON FIRST

**1773, December 9**
**First Chamber of Commerce in America.**

The Charlestown Chamber of Commerce was organized at Mrs. Swallows' Tavern on Broad Street.

The formation of the Chamber was a direct result of the economic stress the British Empire suffered after the French and Indian War. The 1764 Sugar Acts and 1765 Stamp Act were passed by Parliament in an attempt to pay the debt run up during the war. In 1770 most of the "unfair" British taxes were repealed, however, the tax on tea was left in place.

Three years later, on December 1, 1773, the ship *London* arrived in Charlestown with 257 chests of tea on board. Local merchants demanded that the tea be sent back to England, and threatened to burn the ship.

It was within this volatile atmosphere that the Charlestown Chamber of Commerce was organized. Today it is called the Charleston Metro Chamber of Commerce and may be the longest continually operating business membership association in the United States.

---

## 1773, December 15. *Commerce.*

The artisans, upset about the forming of the Chamber of Commerce, met at Swallow's Tavern and discussed forming their own organization in opposition.

## 1773, December 16. *Boston Tea Party.*

A group of Massachusetts patriots, mostly merchants and mechanics protesting the monopoly on American tea importation by the East India Company, seized 342 chests of tea in a midnight raid and tossed them into the harbor.

## 1773, December 22. *Tea Protests.*

The deadline for paying the duty on the tea aboard the London passed. Lt. Gov. Bull ordered it unloaded and secured.

In the pre-dawn hours, custom officials off loaded the 257 chests of tea and stored them in the basement of the Exchange. He warned that the tea would remain locked away and any attempt to remove it would be met by force.

The next morning, many Charlestonians were embarrassed and furious when they learned that tea was unloaded. The New York Sons of Liberty called it "an evil hour for America."

## 1773, December 22. *Theater.*

The New Theater on Church Street opened with *A Word to the Wise* and *High Life Below Stairs*. The New Theater was located several blocks south from the Dock Street Theater location, on Church Street between Broad and Tradd, next door to Mr. Pike's Long Room.

## 1773, December 27. *American Revolution. - Foundations.*

Lord Dartmouth, Secretary of State for the Colonies, congratulated Lt. Gov. Bull on his handling of the tea situation, saying the events in Charlestown:

> altho not equal in criminality to the Proceedings in other Colonies, can yet be considered in no other light than that of a most unwarrantable insult to the authority of this Kingdom.

## 1773, December 27. *Last Theatrical Season Before War.*

The Douglass Company opened the last theatrical season until after the Revolution in the newly constructed theater on Church Street. The Company performed seventy-seven plays and farces.

## 1773, December 27. *American Revolution - Foundations.*

By the end of the year, Edward Rutledge was a lieutenant of the Charleston Artillery Company, a member of the Friendly Brothers of St. Patrick, and the South Carolina Society.

## 1773, December 27. *Culture. Commerce. Population.*

Surveyor for the Southern District of North America, William Gerard de Brahm, sent a report to his Majesty which said:

> The city of Charlestown is in every respect the most eminent and by far the richest city in the Southern District of North America; it contains about 1500, and most of them big houses, arrayed by straight, broad and regular streets; the principal of them is seventy-two feet wide call'd Broad Street, is decorated, besides many fine houses, with a State house near the centre of said street, constructed to contain two rooms,

one of the Governor and Council, th' other for the Representative of the people, the Secretary's office, and a Court room; opposite the state House is the Armory-house, item St. Michael's Church, whose steeple is 192 foot high, and seen by vessels at sea before they make any land; also with a new Exchange on the east end of said street upon the bay; all four buildings have been rais'd since the year 1752, an no expense spared to make them solide, convenient and elegant.

The city is inhabited by above 12,000 souls, more than half are Negroes and Mulattoes; the city is divided in two parishes, has two churches, St. Michaels and St. Philips, and six meeting-houses, vid, an Independent a Presbyterian, a French, a German and two Baptists. There is also an assembly for Quakers and another for Jews, all which are composed of several nations.

# 1774

### 1774. *JOHN WILKES AFFAIR.*

John Wilkes was elected Lord Mayor of London.

### 1774. *CULTURE. LARGEST BOOKSTORE IN AMERICA.*

Robert Wells claimed to have "the largest stock of books in America" at his bookstore.

### 1774, January. *THOMAS PINCKNEY RETURNS.*

Thomas Pinckney returned to Charlestown from England and would soon become an ardent Patriot.

### 1774, January. *DAVID RASMAY ARRIVES.*

Dr. David Ramsay arrived in Charlestown from Philadelphia, and established a successful medical practice. He was the first physician in town not to receive his medical training in Europe. Ramsay quickly used two avenues of gaining acceptance into Charlestown society: Princeton alumni and the Congregational Church.

Ramsay had two local friends, former Princeton classmates, Richard Hutson and William Tennant III, minister of the Independent Church. Huston sponsored Ramsay's membership to the Library Society, which introduced the doctor to some of South Carolina's most prominent men: Gabriel Manigault, Miles Brewton, Christopher Gadsden, and Henry Laurens.

### 1774, January 17. *AMERICAN REVOLUTION - Foundations.*

Embarrassed that the tea had landed in Charlestown, as opposed to the more radical events in Boston, the Sons of Liberty, determined to prove their patriotism, resurrected the General Committee Non-Importation Association with Christopher

Gadsden as the chairman. Their job was to coordinate and direct resistance to any further importation of tea, and to call general meetings of the people.

Currier & Ives illustration of the Boston Tea Party. *Courtesy of the Library of Congress*

## 1774, January 17. CULTURE. THEATER.

*Richard III* was performed at the New Theater on Church Street.

## 1774, February 28. CRIME. SLAVERY. EXECUTION.

The *South Carolina Gazette* reported of "a most infamous and dangerous Set of Villains, of whom the Public had entertained very little Suspicion." Two slaves were arrested as "Principals" in "several of the Burglaries and Robberies, which had been so frequent of late." After questioning the slaves, authorities also arrested "John Thomson, an Umbrella-maker and Shop-keeper, Richard Thomson, who kept a Livery Stable, and George Vargent, a Coachman."

The two slaves received a death sentence and were hanged a few days later. The three white men were sentenced to sit twice in the pillory where they were "most severely pelted," given a whipping of thirty-nine lashes each, and fine from 25 to 500 pounds.

## 1774, March 1. MARRIAGE.

Edward Rutledge married Henrietta Middleton, daughter of Henry Middleton, one of the wealthiest and most influential men in South Carolina who owned 50,000 acres and 800 slaves. This marriage solidified many alliances with other prominent South Carolina families that would play important roles in the coming Revolution.

One of Edward's sisters was the wife of Thomas Pinckney, Edward's good friend from the Middle Temple.

*Edward Rutledge.*
Courtesy of the Library of Congress

## 1774, March 16. *AMERICAN REVOLUTION - Foundations.*

At a "General Meeting," all citizens were invited to the Liberty Tree to vote on the enforcement of non-importation of taxed goods.

## 1774, March 21. *CULTURE. THEATER.*

The newly formed Light Infantry Company and Regiment of Militia paraded the streets for review and then marched to Mrs. Swallow's Tavern for "an elegant repast." Afterward, they went:

> to the Theater where the Comedy *The Recruiting Officer,* with the *Oracle*, were presented. After the Play they returned to Mrs. Swallow's to Supper, where they spent the Night in a Manner suitable to the Bay, in loyal and harmonious Joy.

## 1774, March 28. *INTOLERABLE ACTS.*

Parliament passed the Coercive Acts (called the Intolerable Acts in America), as a response to the Boston Tea party. The Acts included:

- The Boston Port Act, which closed the port of Boston until damages from the Tea party were paid.

- The Massachusetts Government Act, which restricted town meetings and turned the governor's council into an appointed body.
- The Administration of Justice Act, which made British officials immune to criminal prosecution in Massachusetts
- The Quartering Act, which required colonists to house and quarter British troops on demand, including their private homes.

### 1774, May 30. *Gadsden Writes to Adams.*

In a letter to Samuel Adams in Boston, Christopher Gadsden wrote that "members of the trading part have separated themselves from the general interest and neglected our public meetings."

### 1774, May 30. *Culture. Theater.*

The theater season concluded, and was considered the most successful in the city's history. Seventy-seven plays and afterpieces had been performed by the Douglass Troupe. Twelve Shakespearean plays were performed.

### 1774, May 31. *American Revolution - Foundations.*

Charlestown received word that Boston merchants had called upon all colonies to cut off trade with Britain, imports and exports, to force a repeal of the Tea Act. John and Edward Rutledge supported the trade embargo.

### 1774, 1. *Laurens Predicts Bloodshed.*

Henry Laurens wrote:

> I am more of opinion now, than ever, that there will be Bloodshed. God avert it. Innocent persons will fall a Sacrifice to the knavery & bad policy of wrong Heads on each Side & these will escape with the plunder.

### 1774, June 5. *Gadsden Writes to Adams.*

In a letter to Samuel Adams, Gadsden wrote that news from Boston "has raised our utmost resentment and detestation and hope will produce the desired effect of rousing us from our supiness."

### 1774, June 14. *Gadsden Assures Adams.*

Christopher Gadsden wrote to Sam Adams in Boston, assuring him that South Carolina would stand firm with Massachusetts, reminding him that South Carolina was the last to desert the non-importation agreement in 1770. He wrote:

> For my part I would rather see my own family reduced to the utmost Extremity and half cut to pieces than to submit to their damned Machinations.

### 1774, June 14. *Culture. Display.*

An advertisement in the *Gazette* announced:

TO BE SEEN *At the House of* Thomas Anderson .... The Wonderful Electrical FISHES. They are Natives of The Southernmost Part of North America, and have never been seen before that we know of ... at the small Expense of One Dollar.

| SLAVES IMPORTED 1765 – 1774 ||
|---|---|
| 1765 - 6,520 | 1772 - 4,740 |
| 1769 - 4,652 | 1773 - 7,845 |
| 1770 - 1,596 | 1774 - 4,592 |
| 1771 - 2,035 | |

### 1774, June 26. *TEA STORED IN EXCHANGE.*

More tea arrived in Charlestown and was stored in the Exchange basement. A "mob of several hundred men" chased Capt. Maitland from his ship, which was moved from the wharf in fear of it being burned.

### 1774, July 6. *FIRST CONTINENTAL CONGRESS.*

One hundred and four delegates arrived at the Exchange Building for a general meeting. Several planters, Arthur Middleton, Charles Cotesworth Pinckney and William Henry Drayton joined with the more radical artisans. Peter Timothy of the *Gazette* called it "the largest body of the most respectable inhabitants that had ever been seen together upon any public occasion here."

Charlestonians Henry Middleton, John Rutledge, Edward Rutledge, Thomas Lynch, and Christopher Gadsden were named delegates to the First Continental Congress. Dr. David Ramsay attended the meeting and wrote:

> This Convention of the people, and these resolutions, laid the foundation of all subsequent proceedings which ultimately terminated in a revolution ... The people, by virtue of their inherent right to resist illegal oppression by their rulers, delegated full powers to five men of their own choice to take care of their political interest ... the germ of representative government then planted, has grown up to the tree of liberty and happiness.

Edward Rutledge wrote to Ralph Izard boasting that he was elected by a "great majority – 397."

### 1774, July 7. *COMMITTEE OF NINETY-NINE.*

The General Meeting also appointed a Committee of Ninety-nine: fifteen merchants, fifteen artisans representing Charlestown, and sixty-nine planters to represent the backcountry. They were to act as an executive body and, with a quorum of twenty-one members, they could transact business, thus making it easy for the Charlestown members to influence the Committee.

### 1774, July 10. *RELIGION. CRITICISM OF THE COMMITTEE.*

The Rev. John Bullman of St. Michael's Church was critical of the Committee from his pulpit, lashing out at the mechanic:

> Who cannot perhaps govern his own household or pay the debts of his own contracting [yet is] qualified to dictate how the state should be governed. Every silly clown and illiterate mechanic should keep to his rank, and do his duty in his own station, without usurping undue authority over his neighbor.

### 1774, July 29. *DUELING. CULTURE.*

Dr. David Ramsay, in a letter to Benjamin Rush wrote:

> Dueling has been practiced so much here [Charlestown] that illiberal language is seldom used. Indeed I never heard on Gentleman vilify the character of another in plain terms.

### 1774, August 4. *RELIGION. CULTURE.*

Rev. William Tennant III of the Independent Church, wrote a letter to the *Gazette* titled "To the Ladies of South Carolina urging them to restrain from drinking tea, "that east-India poison" in support of the Boston Tea Party.

### 1774, August 4. *AMERICAN REVOLUTION - Foundations.*

Dr. Ramsay wrote and published a pamphlet in Charlestown and Philadelphia titled *A Sermon on Tea* which stated:

> This baleful herb is the match by which an artful wicked ministry intended to blow-up the liberties of America. They wanted to fix a precedent of taxing us at pleasure ... continuing to purchase tea is high treason ...

### 1774, August 14. *REV. BULLMAN CALLS GADSDEN "TRAITOR."*

The Sunday morning departure of Christopher Gadsden and Thomas Lynch to Philadelphia to attend the Continental Congress created a stir in Charlestown. Most of the clergy were on the side of the Revolutionaries. However, Rev. John Bullman, assistant minister at St. Michael's Church, boldly preached a sermon titled "The Christian Duty of Peaceableness." In a thinly veiled reference to the Boston Tea Party, he stated it was not the place of "a silly clown or illiterate mechanic (Sam Adams) to meddle in the affairs of princes and governors." He called Gadsden and Lynch both "traitors."

### 1774, August 16. *BULMAN DISMISSED FROM PULPIT.*

The mechanics responded to Rev. Bullman's charges, saying that he represented "civil and ecclesiastical tyranny by denying the privilege of thinking and acting to the honest and industrious mechanic."

Unfortunately for Bullman, many Charlestonians were sympathetic to the mechanics and Sam Adam's actions in Boston. The vestry voted 42-33 and dismissed him from the pulpit.

## 1774, September 5. *First Continental Congress.*

The Continental Congress opened in Philadelphia. John Adams wrote some observations about the South Carolina delegates in his diary:

- John Rutledge: "No keenness in his Eye. No depth in his Countenance. Nothing of the profound, sagaciousness, brilliant or sparkling."
- Edward Rutledge: "a perfect Bob o' Lincoln, a Swallow, a Sparrow, a Peacock, excessively vain, excessively weak."
- Christopher Gadsden: "Is violent against allowing Parliament any Power of regulating Trade, or allowing that they have any Thing to do with Us.

## 1774, September 7. *First Continental Congress.*

Silas Deane, representing Connecticut in Congress wrote, "Mr. Gadsden leaves all N. England Sons of Liberty behind, for he is for taking up his Firelock & marching direct to Boston."

## 1774, September 19. *Real Estate. Commerce.*

Robert Wells put an advertisement in the *Gazette*:

> The New Play House in Church Street, during the absence of the American Company from this province is To Be Let for the Benefit of the Charity Fund of the Union of Kilwinning Lodge; and as it is now entirely vacant, any persons desiring to rent the same for one or two years, may apply for further Particulars to – Robert Wells.

## 1774, October. *First Continental Congress.*

At the Continental Congress Patrick Henry called John Rutledge "the most eloquent orator … he shone with superior lustre."

John Adams reflected on Edward Rutledge as "Sprightly but not deep. He has the most indistinct, inarticulate Way of Speaking … good natured, tho' conceited … excessively vain."

## 1774, October 17. *Tea Protest.*

In the *Gazette:* "An ASSOCIATION OF PROTESTANT SCHOOLBOYS resolved *not to Use any* Indian Teas *after the 1$^{st}$ Day of November.*

## 1774, October 20. *First Continental Congress.*

The Continental Congress, dominated by New England Puritans, recommended that the colonists abstain from public amusements, which forced David Douglass to abandon his Charlestown investments. He sailed to Jamaica and never returned to the United States.

Congress also voted to suspend all trade with Great Britain after December 1, 1774.

### 1774, October 22. MIDDLETON ELECTED PRES. OF CONGRESS.

Henry Middleton was elected second president of the Continental Congress.

### 1774, October 31. CULTURE. EDUCATION.

Paul Albrecht Van Hagen, Jr. "proposes to teach ... Organ, Harpsichord, Piano Forte, Violin, Violoncello and Viola."

### 1774, November 3. TEA DESTROYED.

At noon, seven chests of tea aboard the *Britannia* were dumped into the Charlestown harbor. "A Committee of Observation" raised "three hearty cheers" with the dumping of each chest.

### 1774, November 6. CONTINENTAL CONGRESS RETURNS.

The South Carolina delegation returned from Congress and presented their reports to the General Committee. They had reached an agreement that would ban British imports starting on December 1, 1774.

### 1774, November 8. AMERICAN REVOLUTION - Foundations.

The General Committee called for elections for a new Provincial Congress to meet at the Exchange in Charlestown on Wednesday, January, 1775.

### 1774, December 1. BRITISH IMPORT BAN BEGINS.

The non-importation agreement went into effect.

### 1774, December 11. LAURENS RETURNS.

Henry Laurens returned to Charlestown from London, leaving his sons in Europe for their education.

### 1774, December 19. CULTURE. EDUCATION

John Abercromby advertised in the *Gazette* that he was:

> Opening a DANCING-SCHOOL ... Minuet, Minuet Dauphin, Minuet by four, Louvre, Rigadoon, English Country Dances, Paspied, Bretagne, New Cotillon, Allemande ... also teaches GUITAR.

### 1774, December 19. POLITICS. RELIGION.

During the elections Francis Salvador was elected to the First Provincial Con-gress from the Ninety-six district – the first Jew elected to office in the American colonies.

Continental Association document, suspending trade with Great Britain, Oct. 20, 1774.
*Courtesy of the Library of Congress*

A VIEW OF CHARLES-TOWN – The Capital of South Carolina engraved by Samuel Smith, 1774, from a painting by Thomas Leitch. *Courtesy of the Library of Congress.*

# 1775

### 1775, January 1. *JOHN RUTLEDGE WEALTH.*

At this time, John Rutledge owned more than 30,000 acres in his own name scattered across South Carolina. In partnership with other individuals he owned an additional 70,000 acres.

### 1775, January 2. *WRITING TEACHER. EDUCATION.*

Benjamin Waller advertised his services as a writing teacher with the following ad in the *Gazette:*

> Ladies, if your Daughters incline to write
> And in a fair Corr'spondence they delight
> At Mrs. Davis's, their Comp'ny I beseech
> It's in St. Michael's Alley where I teach.

### 1775, January 8. *COUNCIL OF SAFETY PROPOSED.*

A group of Charleston's leaders met at Ramadge's Tavern "to propose proper persons and prepare a list" of candidates for a Council of Safety.

## 1775, January 9. COUNCIL OF SAFETY.

The Provincial Assembly selected thirty individuals for the Council of Safety, whose duty was to enforce the non-importation commitment.

## 1775, January 11. FIRST PROVINCIAL CONGRESS.

Carolina's First Provincial Congress convened at the Old Exchange. Charles Pinckney, Jr. was chosen as President and Peter Timothy as Secretary. Populated with former members of the Assembly it declared itself the government of South Carolina, independent from British authority.

The General Meeting to discuss the recommendations of the Continental Congress was the most democratic assembly in South Carolina's history. It consisted of 184 delegates from every part of the colony, including the backcountry. It was feared that the backcountry delegates would steer a more radical path than the "conservative urban elite." Francis Marion was chosen as a delegate to represent St. John's Parish.

However, many of the backcountry delegates, not familiar with the Parliamentary proceedings complained at the delays and accused the Charleston delegates of "deliberately plotting to thin out backcountry ranks." Henry Laurens that the "reins are not in the hands of Town men as formerly ... according to their ideas everything might have been completed with no more words than are necessary in the bargain and sale of a cow."

Members of the First Continental Congress who had returned from Philadelphia made their formal reports.

## 1775, January 17. FIRST PROVINCIAL CONGRESS CREATES MILITIA.

The Provincial Congress formally requested that Lt. Gov. William Bull seat the Commons House of Assembly. Bull, governing in place of the absent Lord Montague, refused to recognize the Provincial Congress.

The Congress also recommended that all citizens "diligently train themselves in the use of arms and that their officers muster them for training once a fortnight." William Moultrie later wrote about that time:

> Agreeable to a recommendation of the Provincial Congress, the militia were forming themselves into volunteer companies; drums beating, fifes playing; squads of men exercising on the outskirts of town; a military spirit pervaded the whole country; and Charlestown had the appearance of a garrison town; every thing wore the face of war; though not one of had the least idea of its approach.

## 1775, January 18. BRITISH CARGO TOSSED OVERBOARD.

A ship arrived from Bristol, England carrying 3800 bushels of salt, 35 chaldrons of coal and 40,000 tiles. The entire cargo was tossed into the harbor by an excited population on the verge of open revolution. Another ship of 300 slaves was sent to the West Indies to be unloaded.

### 1775, February 9. *MARRIAGE.*

Dr. David Ramsay married Sabina Ellis, daughter of a prominent merchant.

### 1775, February 18. *JOHN LAURENS OPINES.*

John Laurens in school in London, wrote to his father Henry:

> Far be it from me when we are struggling against oppression to wish to make distinctions unfavourable to liberty, but it gives me great concern to hear that some of our lowest mechanics still bear great part in our public transactions – men who are as contemptible for their ignorance as they may be pernicious by their obstancy.

### 1775, March 14. *SMYTHE HORSE AFFAIR.*

Robert Smythe arrived from England aboard the *Proteus* with furniture and horses. The so-called "Smythe Horse Affair" tested the locals' commitment to non-importation.

Smythe, a Charlestown merchant, assumed that personal items did not violate the Association, and after debate, thirty-three members of the Committee agreed with him. However, most of the rest of the city did not.

### 1775, March 24. *SMYTHE HORSE AFFAIR.*

"Hundreds of inhabitants" assembled to denounce the decision to allow Smythe to off-load his horses and furniture. They threatened to enforce the terms of non-importation by force. Edward Rutledge, surprised by the crowd, harangued them for "questioning the authority of the committee." He was shouted down.

### 1775, March 27. *SMYTHE HORSE AFFAIR.*

By Monday Charlestown was in "universal commotion." The General Committee met at the Exchange and ordered the militia to stand by to land the horses by force. The majority of the militia refused. The jeering crowd flowed out of the hall and into the street.

Christopher Gadsden proposed that the Committee reverse its decision because "our people are highly dissatisfied with it." William Henry Drayton agreed, arguing that "the people thought an error had been committed and it was our duty to satisfy our constituents, as we [are] only servants of the public." The Committee re-voted, and reversed its decision by one vote.

### 1775, March 28. *AMERICAN REVOLUTION – Foundations.*

In a letter to Secretary Dartmouth, Lt. Gov. Bull prophetically observed:

> The men of property begin at length to see that the many-headed power of the people, who have hitherto been obediently made use of by their numbers and occasional riots, have discovered their own strength and importance, and are not so easily governed by their former leaders.

## 1775, April 14. *AMERICAN REVOLUTION – Foundations.*

Word reached Charlestown that Parliament considered Massachusetts in open rebellion and would send additional troops to subdue the colony by force.

## 1775, April 17. COMMITTEE OF FIVE FORMED.

The "Secret Committee of Five," was organized by the First Provincial Congress and included William Henry Drayton, Arthur Middleton, Charles Cotesworth Pinckney, William Gibbes, and Edward Weyman. They seized the mail that arrived from England on the *Swallow*. The official dispatches made it clear that British authorities would not hesitate to use force to keep and restore order in the colonies.

The Carolina Council notified other colonies that the British were planning on 10,000 men to suppress colonial uprising.

## 1775, April 19. THE SHOT HEARD 'ROUND THE WORLD.

The battle of Lexington and Concord took place in Boston. The British suffered seventy-three killed and 174 wounded. The Patriot "minutemen" lost 125 men. As Ralph Waldo Emerson would later describe it – "the shot heard 'round the world."

## 1775, April 21. SECRET COMMITTEE OF FIVE SEIZES GUNPOWDER.

The "Secret Committee of Five," seized the public gun powder at several magazines, including Hobcaw, on the Charleston Neck, and the arms in the State House at the corner of Broad and Meeting Streets. In all they stole 800 guns, 200 cutlasses and 1,600 pounds of powder.

The fact that South Carolina men had done this without knowledge of the massacre in Lexington two days before qualifies as one of the most radical acts leading up the Revoluion.

## 1775, May 1. *AMERICAN REVOLUTION - Foundations.*

Robert Wells of the *South Carolina and American General Gazette*, a committed Royalist, left Charlestown for England. His son, John Wells, assumed the duties of publisher and editor, and espoused the Patriot cause until 1780.

## 1775, May 1. STUART FORCED TO FLEE.

False rumors that John Stuart, British Superintendent of Indian Affairs, was plotting to incite Indians to attack backcountry settlements, forced him to abandon his house at 106 Tradd Street. He was fearful of reprisals by the Secret Committee of Five, or other Revolutionaries. He fled to live with backcountry Loyalists.

## 1775, May 3. CONTINENTAL CONGRESS.

The South Carolina delegation to the Continental Congress departed for Philadelphia.

### 1775, May 8. *REVOLUTION.*

News of the battle of Lexington and Concord reached Charlestown, creating passionate outrage among the citizens. Anti-British sentiment became rampant among the mechanics.

### 1775, May 10. *SECOND CONTINENTAL CONGRESS MEETS.*

Second Continental Congress met in Philadelphia. Representing South Carolina was Edward Rutledge, Thomas Heyward, Jr., Thomas Lynch and Arthur Middleton.

### 1775, May 26. *AMERICAN REVOLUTION. NON-IMPORTATION.*

The brigantine *Ester,* with 8,000 barrels of salt, was forced to return to England without offloading its cargo.

### 1775, June. *STUART ARRESTED AND ESCAPES.*

John Stuart, British superintendent of Indian Affairs, was arrested for "stirring up the Catawba and Cherokee tribes against provincials." He escaped and fled to Florida. His wife and daughter, were placed on house arrest in their Tradd Street home. A guard was posted to prevent her from leaving, but she still managed to escape to Florida to join her husband.

### 1775, June 1. *FIRST PROVINCIAL CONGRESS CONVENES.*

The second session of the First Provincial Congress convened in Charlestown.

### 1775, June 1. *SECRET COMMITTEE OF FIVE.*

The Secret Committee of Five ordered the tarring and feathering of James Dealy and Laughlin Martin, for rejoicing (supposedly) that Catholics, Negroes and Indians were going to be armed in an uprising against the people. The two men were carted about the streets and banished from town.

### 1775, June 3. *LOYALTY OATH.*

The Provincial Congress passed a loyalty oath, which increased the harassment of royal officials. Royal Surgeon, George Milligen, called his tormentors "that monster the mob [that] now governs Charlestown."

### 1775, June 4. *FIRST PROVINCIAL CONGRESS. COUNCIL OF SAFETY.*

The First Provincial Congress adopted the American Bill of Rights and the Articles of Confederation. On that same date, they also issued £1,000,000 in paper currency for military defense of the Province, and appointed thirteen new members to the Council of Safety, with power to command all soldiers and to use all public money in the Province. No military person could now sit on the Council of Safety.

Old State House, now the Charleston County Courthouse, pictured in 1872. Drawn and published by C. Drie. *Courtesy of the Library of Congress*

## 1775, June 6. PROVINCIAL REGIMENTS AUTHORIZED.

The Provincial Congress passed a resolution that two infantry regiments of 750 men each be organized for the defense of the coast, and a regiment of 450 mounted rangers for the defense of the backcountry. The militia were to:

> go forth and be ready to sacrifice our lives and fortunes against every foe in defense of the liberty outraged in the bloody scene on the 19th of April last near Boston.

## 1775, June 12. PROVISIONAL REGIMENTS ORGANIZED.

Christopher Gadsden was chosen as colonel of the First Provincial Regiment, while William Moultrie was chosen as colonel of the Second. Since Gadsden was in Philadelphia attending the session of the Continental Congress, Moultrie commanded both regiments at first. Francis Marion chosen as a captain in the 2nd regiment.

Moultrie ordered every officer to "provide himself with a blue cloth coatee, faced and scuffed with scarlet cloth, and line with scarlet ... also a cap and black feather." The front of the cap was to display a white or silver metal crescent, engraved with the motto "Liberty or Death.

## 1775, June 14. CONTINENTAL CONGRESS.

Edward Rutledge was appointed to a three-member committee to draft George Washington's commission and instructions as commander of the Continental Army.

## 1775, June 14. PROVISIONAL CONGRESS. COUNCIL OF SAFETY.

The Provincial Congress approved the thirteen-man Council of Safety charged with carrying out the business of the colony when Congress was in recess.

## 1775, June 17. LAST ROYAL GOVERNOR ARRIVES.

Lord William Campbell, once stationed in Charlestown as a naval officer, returned on the HMS *Scorpion* as the new Royal Governor. Married to Sarah Izard, one of South Carolina's most powerful families, Campbell expected his arrival to be greeted with typical fanfare – booming cannons and cheering crowds. However, arriving six weeks after the news of the massacre in Boston, with the rising revolutionary passions, he greeted with "sullen silence," according to Peter Timothy of the *South Carolina Gazette*.

Campbell moved into the Miles Brewton House at 27 King Street until his residence at 34 Meeting Street was ready. Lord Campbell wrote to London that he found:

> the legal administration of justice obstructed, government in a manner annihilated, the most dangerous measures adopted, and acts of the most outrageous and illegal nature committed publicly with impunity.

He quickly learned that he was little more than a figurehead, due to the power wielded by the Provisional Congress. Campbell knew of the political rift between the aristocratic lowcountry (more revolutionary) and the backcountry commoners (more loyal) in the upstate. He flooded the backcountry with pamphlets claiming that the Provisional Congress could not be trusted and had taken illegal power. He also began to secretly coordinate plans with backcountry Loyalists.

## 1775, June 17. AIRING OF GRIEVANCES TO CAMPBELL.

Charles Pinckney, Jr. led a group of citizens to call on Royal Governor William Campbell. They presented a list of grievances and explained why they formed the Provincial Congress. They claimed:

> Conscious of the Justice of our cause, and the Integrity of our Views, we readily profess our loyal Attachment to our Sovereign, his Crown and Dignity: And trusting the Event to Providence, we prefer Death to Slavery.

## 1775, June 30. REVOLUTION.

North Carolina governor, Josiah Martin, wrote to the Earl of Dartmouth that Charlestown was "the head and heart of their boasted province, and a single armed ship could conquer it."

## 1775, July. CAMPBELL MOVES TO 34 MEETING STREET.

Gov. Campbell moved from the Miles Brewton house into 34 Meeting Street, rented from Capt. John Bull.

### 1775, July 1. *British Blockade Ordered*

British Secretary of State for the Colonies, the Earl of Dartmouth, ordered a naval blockade of major American ports. It slowly crippled Charlestown's economy. Exports dropped from £579,549 in 1775 to £1,074 in 1778.

### 1775, July 6. *Continental Congress.*

The Continental Congress issued a *"Declaration of the Causes and Necessity of taking up Arms."* It stated that the Americans are "resolved to die free men rather than live as slaves." An ironic statement supported Charletown's delegation, all slave owners.

### 1775, July 10. *Revolution. Gunpowder Seized.*

A combined force from Charlestown, Beaufort and Savannah, led by Captain John Barnwell, captured an English ship, HMS *Phillipa,* carrying 16,000 pounds of gunpowder off Tybee Island, Georgia. The powder was divided between South Carolina (5,000 pounds) and Georgia (7,000). It was decided to send the remaining 4,000 pounds to the Continental Congress for use of colonial troops.

### 1775, July 17. *Regimental Enlistment.*

Col. William Moultrie reported to the Council of Safety that 470 men from Charlestown had enlisted in the Provincial Regiments. He also reported he had sent his officers to the backcountry, North Carolina, and Virginia seeking recruits.

### 1775, July 21. *Gunpowder Sent to Philadelphia.*

The 4,000 lbs. of gunpowder taken in Georgia was loaded on the schooner *Polly*, which left Charlestown for Philadelphia, commanded by Joseph Gambrell.

### 1775, July 25. *Revolution. Backcountry Campaign.*

Rev. Oliver Hart, of the First Baptist Church, and Rev. William Tennant were ardent supporters of the rebel cause and members of the "Association. They accompanied William Henry Drayton into the backcountry in an effort to explain the causes of the dispute with England, and to build support for the cause.

Due to Campbell's effective pamphlet campaign, they were met with either indifference, or adamant opposition.

### 1775, July 29. *Revolution. Council of Safety.*

The Council of Safety ordered Captain Clement Lempriere, a former British naval officer and privateer, to take the sloop *Commerce* to New Providence, Bahamas. He was given £1,000 to purchase gunpowder.

### 1775, July 29. *Council of Safety Intercepts British Mail.*

Capt. Edward Thornbrough, of the HMS *Tamar*, reported that the Council of Safety intercepted the mail from the packet *Sandwich*, but that he met the packet *Eagle* beyond the Charlestown bar and prevented the interception of *its* mail.

## 1775, August 5. *More Gunpowder Seized.*

Captain Clement Lempriere seized 12,000 pounds of powder from the British brig *Betsey* in Mantazas Bay off St. Augustine. Lempriere wrote a £1,000 draft, drawn on John Edwards of Charlestown, to Capt. Lofthouse of the *Betsey* and the rest of the 24-man crew were bribed £100. *Betsey's* guns are spiked.

## 1775, August 11. *Trial of Thomas Jeremy.*

The trial of Thomas Jeremy began. Jeremy, a free black man and harbor pilot, worth £1,000 sterling and a slave owner himself, had supposedly claimed that if British warships came, he would pilot them across the Charlestown bar himself. Using the provisions of the Negro Act of 1740, Jeremy was tried. The testimony of two slaves, Sambo and Jemmy, were particularly damning.

Sambo, also a harbor pilot, claimed that Jeremy told him a "great war to help the poor Negroes" was coming. Jemmy claimed that Jeremy had approached him "to take a few guns" to another runaway slave named Dewar. The weapons were to be "placed in Negroes hands to fight against the inhabitants of this Province ... Jeremy was to have the Chief Command of the Negroes."

Gov. Campbell declared Jeremy "innocent." He discounted the testimony of the two slaves who were "terrified at the recollection of former cruelties."

The court found Jeremy guilty of inspiring a slave insurrection and he was sentenced "to be hanged, and then burned to ashes, on Friday the 18$^{th}$.

## 1775, August 12. *Tarred-And-Feathered.*

In a report to William Henry Drayton in Philadelphia, Peter Timothy informed Drayton that George Walker, British gunner at Fort Johnson was grabbed by a mob of over 400 and gave him a "Tarring & Feathering for some insolent speech he had made" about the Patriots. They then put "him in a cart paraded through the Town ... using his very cruelly all the time."

## 1775, August 15. *Trial of Thomas Jeremy.*

Gov. Campbell felt helpless in the cause of Thomas Jeremy and was considering a pardon. He was convinced that Jeremy was innocent and believed that the swirling emotions of rebellion, fueled by the massacre at Lexington and Concord, created an atmosphere in which Jeremy was an unwitting victim.

Campbell was warned that his intervention "would raise a flame all the water in the Cooper River would not extinguish." Campbell wrote that he was told "if I grant him a pardon they would hang him at my door."

## 1775, August 17. *Trial of Thomas Jeremy.*

The slave Jemmy, retracted his testimony and declared Thomas Jeremy was innocent.

### 1775, August 18. *Execution of Thomas Jeremy.*

Thomas Jeremy was hanged at the workhouse green on Magazine Street, next to the Jail. His body was taken down and burned.

The day after Jeremy's execution Gov. Campbell wrote, "I could not save him My Lord!" Campbell also admitted that "the powers of government are wrested out of my hands. I can neither protect nor punish."

### 1775, August 22. *Revolution.*

Peter Timothy wrote that "in regard to war and peace, I can only tell you that the plebeians [Mechanics] are still for war, but the noblesse [Planters] perfectly pacific."

### 1775, August 24. *Loss of the Brewton Family.*

Miles Brewton, Charleston merchant, set sial for Philadelphia with his wife and three children. They were never seen or heard from again, listed as "lost at sea."

His sister, Rebecca Brewton Motte, inherited one of South Carolina's largest fortunes, including Mount Joseph, her brother's plantation on the Congaree River in St. Matthews Parish, and the Miles Brewton House at 27 King Street in Charlestown.

### 1775, August 31. *Provincial Congress Meets for Last Time.*

The Provincial Congress met for the last time.

### 1775, Fall. *Slavery. Council of Safety.*

The Council of Safety received information that the British fleet in Charlestown harbored runaway slaves. They warned all ship captains that, if such actiivy was proven and continued, supplies from town would be terminated.

### 1775, September 14. *Fort Johnson Seized. Council of Safety.*

During the night, under orders from the Council of Safety, Col. William Moultrie and 150 members of the Second South Carolina Regiment left Gadsden's Wharf and floated down the Cooper River to James Island. Officers of the Regiment included Captains Francis Marion, Bernard Elliott and Charles Cotesworth Pinckney. They quickly seized Ft. Johnson and its twenty-one guns, with no resistance from the British.

Moultrie ordered that the regimental flag be hoisted over the fort – a flag with a blue field and with crescent, matching the $2^{nd}$ Regiment's uniform.

### 1775, September 15. *Campbell Flees.*

Lord William Campbell dissolved the Commons House of Assembly. He also discovered that Patriot leaders had learned of his coordination with backcountry Loyalists. After the taking of Ft. Johnson Campbell feared an attack from Revolutionaries in the city. During the early morning hours he fled hos house on

Meeting Street to the HMS *Tamar*, vowing never to return "until he could uphold the king's authority." This effectively ended British rule in South Carolina.

## 1775, September 17. REGIMENTAL FLAG RAISED.

Three British warships, *Cherokee, Tamar*, and the packet *Swallow*, sailed within point blank range of Ft. Johnson. The Council of Safety dispatched an artillery unit, commanded by Capt. Thomas Heyward, to reinforce Col. Motte at Ft. Johnson.

They also hauled up he first South Carolina flag, navy blue with a silver crescent. The fact that this was done in plain view of three British warships made it particularly insulting. William Moultrie commented in his memoirs:

> It was thought necessary to have a flag for the purpose of signals ... I was desired by the Council of Safety to have one made ... I had a large blue flag made with a crescent in the dexter corner, to be in uniform with the troops. This was the first American flag which was displayed in South Carolina.

Two South Carolina Regimental Flags. One of the versions of this flag was raised over Ft. Johnson in 1775. Reports are unclear which.

## 1775, September 18. REVOLUTION. NAVAL ACTION.

Patriot troops from Ft. Moultrie attacked and seized a small vessel taking supplies from Charleston to two British ships at anchor off Sullivan's Island. The Patriots seized twenty-one casks of water, one case and two bottles of liquor, and some brown sugar.

In response to this action, the British vessels *Tamar* and *Scorpion,* blockaded Charleston harbor and five days later seized the Charleston merchant vessel *Polly*, owned by Benjamin and Isaac Huger.

Sailors who had been detained earlier during the Patriot capture of Ft. Johnson, warned that a bomb ketch would be coming to Charleston to attack Johnson, and then burn the town. This was a realistic threat since the British did burn Charlestown, Massachusetts. The Patriot government of South Carolina declared a state of emergency. Henry Laurens wrote, "We are on the eve of total suspension of all trade, stripped of gold and silver money, and have no resources. We are all mad, all wrong."

### 1775, September 26. CONTINENTAL CONGRESS. SLAVERY.

Edward Rutledge proposed that Gen. Washington "discharge all the Negroes as well as Slaves and Freemen in his Army." Rutledge was concerned about the example that armed black men would set to South Carolina's large slave population. The resolution was defeated.

### 1775, September 29. GENERAL COMMITTEE INVITES CAMPBELL.

The General Committee in Charlestown wrote a letter to Gov. Campbell, signed by Henry Laurens, asking him to return to the city, "the usual place of residence of the Governor of South Carolina" but only if "your Excellency shall take no active part against the good people of this colony."

### 1775, September 30. CAMPBELL REPLIES TO COMMITTEE.

Gov. William Campbell wrote to Henry Laurens.

> I have received a message, signed by you, from a set of people who style themselves a General Committee. The presumption of such an address from a body assembled by no legal authority, and whom I must consider as in actual and open rebellion against the Sovereign, can only be equaled by the outrages which obliged me to take refuge on board the King's ship in the harbor. It deserves no answer, nor should I have given it any, but to mark the hardiness with which you have advanced, that I could so far forget my duty to my Sovereign, and my country, as to promise I would take no active part in bringing the subverters of our glorious constitution, and the real liberties of the people, to a sense of their duty.

### 1775, October. FORT JOHNSON RE-FORTIFIED.

Over two thousand palmetto logs were floated across the harbor to fortify the tabby walls of Fort Johnson. More than 500 men composed the garrison, who camped in tents in James Island.

### 1775, October 3. COUNCIL OF SAFETY REPORT TO GADSDEN.

Thomas Ferguson, a member of the Council of Safety, wrote to Christopher Gadsden in Philadelphia:

> Our little army really wants you; Col. Moultrie is a very good man, but very indolent and easy, so that things go on very slow. We have had the Fort in possession about twenty days and he was desired to put it in good order as soon as possible, and spare no expense, but there is very little done.

### 1775, October 27. COLONIES DECLARED IN OPEN REBELLION.

King George III declared the American colonies to be in open rebellion, due to traitorous behavior. He stated:

Many of these unhappy people may still remain their loyalty, and may be too wise not to see the fatal consequence of this usurpation, and wish to resist it, yet the torrent of violence has been strong enough to compel their acquiescence, till a sufficient force shall appear to support them.

## 1775, October 29. *POLITICS.*

Daniel Cannon, "ticket seller and housewright" at the New Theatre on Church Street was ordered by the Second Council of Safety of the Revolutionary Party to cart five loads of benches from the playhouse to the State House.

## 1775, November. *SOUTH CAROLINA NAVY.*

Two pilot boats, *Eagle* and *Hibernia*, were taken into service by South Carolina. They were based up the Stono River in order to avoid the larger British ships in the harbor entrance. Their job was to patrol the coast and warn all ships to avoid Charlestown harbor. Col. Moultrie was ordered to provide nine privates and one sergeant for each vessel, who were to receive double pay.

## 1775, November. *DEFENDING DORCHESTER.*

Capt. Francis Marion took a detachment of ninety men to defend the arsenal at Dorchester. Marion publicly thanked all his officers "except Capt. Wigfall." Marion's insight was prescient. Later in the war, John Wigfall would switch sides and become a Tory, taking the field against Marion.

## 1775, November 1. *SECOND PROVINCIAL CONGRESS.*

The Second Provisional Congress was hastily called into session to deal with the threat the British war ships in Charlestown harbor. William Henry Drayton was voted President of the Congress. In anticipation of Lord Campbell sailing up the Cooper River to meet with Loyalists living in the backcountry, Drayton ordered the blocking of Hog Island Channel by the sinking of four hulks.

## 1775, November 4. *CONTINENTAL CONGRESS.*

The Continental Congress resolved that "the town of Charles Town ought to be defended against possible British attack." It also recommended that states should call for:

> a full and free representation of the People, and that the Representatives if they think it necessary, establish such a form of Government, as in their judgment will best produce the happiness of the People.

## 1775, November 7. *REVOLUTION. SLAVERY.*

John Murray, Earl of Dunmore, and governor of Virginia, issued a proclamation that promised freedom to those slaves who joined the British in the fight against the rebellious colonists. According to reports, runaway slaves flocked to Sullivan's Island in Charleston and Tybee Island in Savannah by the hundreds.

William Moultrie estimated that about five hundred slaves had found refuge on Sullivan's Island and Stephen Bull wrote to Henry Laurens that about two hundred slaves had settled on Tybee Island.

### 1775, November 7. SLAVERY.

A slave named Limus confronted his master Joshua Eden directly challenging the master's authority and power. According to Eden, Limus told him that "though he is my Property ... he will be free, that he will serve no Man, and that he will be conquered or governed by no Man." Afterwards Limus ran away.

Eden took out an ad in the *Gazette* that read:

> Limus is well known in Charles Town for his saucy and impudent tongue ... he has the audacity to tell me he will be free, that he will serve no Man.

---

## WHIGS & TORIES
### During the American Revolution

**WHIGS** were the people in rebellion against the English Crown, often called Patriots.

**TORIES** supported the English Crown, often called Loyalists or Royalists.

---

### 1775, November 11-12. BATTLE OF HOG ISLAND CHANNEL.

South Carolina's first Revolutionary War naval skirmish took place. William Henry Drayton, president of the Provisional Congress, was on board the newly-commissioned South Carolina schooner *Defence*, supervising the sinking of the hulks in the channel. Captain Edward Thornbrough ordered six shots fired from the *HMS Tamar* and *HMS Cherokee*. Drayton replied with his nine-pounders.

Over the next several hours the British fired 130 ineffective shots, which rallied public opinion to the side of the Revolutionaries. Lord William Campbell was aboard the *Cherokee* during the battle.

Even though this battle was of little military significance, the fact that it took place in full view of most of the citizens of Charlestown, was instrumental in animating their passions. From this day forward, there was no doubt in the minds of the people for independence.

### 1775, November 19-21. REVOLUTION. BACKCOUNTRY.

Major Andrew Williamson's Patriot militia was attacked by Tories at Ninety-Six during a three-day siege of the stockade around the Court House.

### 1775, November 24. DEATH.

Col. William Moultrie's wife, Damaris Elizabeth, died.

## 1775, November 28. *AMERICAN NAVY ESTABLISHED.*

The American Navy was established by Congress. Christopher Gadsden was one of seven members of the Marine Committee responsible for outfitting the Navy.

## 1775, December. *ARRIVALS.*

Aedanus Burke arrived in Charlestown. Since 1769 he had lived in Virginia where "the common law takes up most of my time." Dr. David Ramsay described Burke as:

> An Irish gentleman, who, with the gallantry characteristic to his nation, came ... at the commencement of the revolution as a volunteer to fight for American liberty.

## 1775, December 1. *AMERICAN REVOLUTION.*

Governor William Campbell wrote that:

> every rebellious measure which has been adopted in the part of the continent originated in Charlestown ... the fountainhead from whence all violence flows; stop that, and the rebellion in this part of the continent will I trust be at an end.

## 1775, December 5. *GADSDEN FLAG.*

The commander-in-chief of the Navy, Commodore Esek Hopkins, received a yel-low rattlesnake flag from Christopher Gadsden to serve as the distinctive personal standard of his flagship. It was displayed at the mainmast.

Gadsden Flag. *Public Domain.*

### 1775, December 8. *SLAVERY.*

Captain John Tollemache, commander of the HMS *Scorpion,* angrily testified that the blacks on his ship "came as freemen, and demanding protection; that he could have had near five hundred, who had offered."

### 1775, December 10. *REVOLUTION. SLAVERY.*

Henry Laurens wrote to the captain of the British ship *Tamar* that the Council had:

> daily complaints from the inhabitants of the sea-coast, of robberies and depredations committed on them by white and black armed men, from on board some of the ships under your command.

According to Laurens, those slaves who had found refuge on Sullivan's Island were especially involved in these robberies. He claimed that William Campbell had gone great lengths in "harboring & protecting Negroes on Sullivan's Island from whence those Villains made their nightly Sallies and committed robberies & depredations."

### 1775, December 15. *NAVAL OPERATIONS.*

Two small boats attempting to reach the HMS *Cherokee* were stopped by the Provincial guards at Gadsden's Wharf. The boats were carrying domestic servants for Lord William Campbell.

### 1775, December 18. *REVOLUTION. SLAVERY.*

*The South Carolina General Gazette* reported that:

> the Company of Foot Rangers...made a descent on that Island [Sullivan's] burnt the House in which the Banditti were often lodged brought off four Negroes killed three or four & also took White prisoners four Men three Women & three Children destroyed many things which had been useful to those wretches.

### 1775, December 20. *REVOLUTION. HADDRELL'S POINT.*

A detachment of 200 men under Major Charles Cotesworth Pinckney erected a battery of 18-pounders at Haddrell's Point in Mt. Pleasant. Col. William Moultrie ordered Pinckney to fire on the three British warships, *Tamar, Scorpion* and *Cherokee* which forced them to leave the harbor.

Moultrie commented on the construction:

> Everyone fell to work, and by day-light we were ourselves well covered, and in a few hours more, laid our platforms, and some guns mounted, and shortly after, opened our embrasures.

### 1775, December 21. *AMERICAN PORTS CLOSED.*

King George III issued a royal proclamation closing the American colonies to all commerce and trade, to take effect in March of 1776. The King also decreed that after the first of the year, "all vessels captured by British ships leaving American ports would be deemed lawful prizes."

## 1775, December 21. *CONTINENTAL CONGRESS.*

Continental Congress was informed that France may offer support in the war against Britain.

Haddrell's Point, Mt. Pleasant. *Courtesy of the New York Public Library.*

# 1776

## 1776, January 5. *REVOLUTION. NAVAL.*

Capt. Joseph Vesey, a privateer of an "armed pilot boat," *Hawke*, captured a British brigantine off the Carolina coast and dragged the prize up the Stono River. He was then ordered to sail to Philadelphia to pick up Christopher Gadsden and the rest of the South Carolina delegates to the Continental Congress.

## 1776, January 6. *REVOLUTION. NAVAL.*

Most of the British fleet off Charlestown sailed for Cape Fear, North Carolina carrying the last royal governor with them. Henry Laurens wrote to his son, John that "the little ships of war which were lying ... are all now going out to sea ... I believe in search of provisions."

## 1776, January 6. *COUNCIL OF SAFETY. SULLIVAN'S ISLAND.*

A committee from the Council of Safety visited the southern tip of Sullivan's Island and recommended the site be fortified. They ordered Lt. Col. Owen Roberts of the Provincial Regiment to construct a temporary fortification until a more permanent structure could be built.

### 1776, January 9. REVOLUTION. "COMMON SENSE" PUBLISHED.

Thomas Paine's *Common Sense* was published in Philadelphia. The fifty-page pamphlet was highly critical of King George III and provided strong arguments for American independence. Paine wrote, "We have it in our power to begin the world anew ... America shall make a stand, not for herself alone, but for the world."

### 1776, January 10. FORTIFICATIONS. SULLIVAN'S ISLAND.

A number of slaves and artisans were ordered to Sullivan's Island to begin construction of a fort. The Council of Safety contracted with Cornelius Dewees to supply palmetto logs "not less than ten inches diameter in the middle, one third to be eighteen feet long, the other two-thirds twenty feet long."

### 1776, January 11. REVOLUTION. FORT JOHNSON.

The HMS *Syren* and HMS *Raven* sent a force of British marines onshore at James Island. They were fired upon by Fort Johnson and driven back to their ships.

### 1776, January 17. REVOLUTION. FORTIFICATIONS.

Thomas Lynch wrote to George Washington, informing him that Sullivan's Island was being fortified and cannon being mounted on the waterfront batteries.

### 1776, January 19. REVOLUTION. COMMERCE.

The *South Carolina and American General Gazette* noted that "the markets have been of late very scantily provided and everything sold at an extravagant price." Merchant Josiah Smith, Jr. complained:

> Charlestown is now a melancholy place to behold, houses shut up, wharves and stores all empty, trade not carried on, places of worship almost deserted, scarce a woman to be seen in the streets, men continually on military duty, and no other music but drum and fife daily sounding. In short, business of no kind in a public way to be done, but that of fortifying the harbor and fitting out of vessels for defense. Our trust I hope is ultimately on the Great Ruler of the Universe.

### 1776, January 20. REVOLUTION. SULLIVAN'S ISLAND.

Workmen had mounted five guns at Ft. Sullivan.

### 1776, January 20. CONTINENTAL CONGRESS.

Edward Rutledge proposed to create a War Office.

### 1776, January 26. REVOLUTION. FORTIFICATIONS.

The Council of Safety ordered Col. William Moultrie to develop new signals to be used for the lighthouse at Morris Island, at Ft. Sullivan and Ft. Johnson to warn of the approach of British naval vessels.

## 1776, February 9. GADSDEN FLAG PRESENTED.

The South Carolina delegation returned from the Continental Congress. During the return trip from Philadelphia aboard the *Hawke*, the British man-o-war *Syren* bore down on the small pilot boat.

Capt. Joseph Vesey sailed hard for the shore and beached the *Hawke* on the North Carolina coast. The delegates and crew scrambled to safety in a nearby swamp and made their way overland to Charlestown, leaving the *Hawke* as a prize for the British.

Once in Charlestown John Rutledge warned that a British attack in the South was probable. Christopher Gadsden presented his "Don't Tread on Me" flag to the Provincial Congress. As recorded in the South Carolina congressional journals the proclamation read:

> Col. Gadsden presented to the Congress an elegant standard, such as is to be used by the commander in chief of the American Navy; being a yellow field, with a lively representation of a rattlesnake in the middle in the attitude of going to strike and these words underneath, "Don't tread on me."

Gadsden also a presented copy of Paine's *Common Sense*, which helped inflame local political sensibilities.

## 1776, February 13. REVOLUTION. GADSDEN TAKES COMMAND.

Christopher Gadsden assumed command of the provincial troops defending Charlestown harbor and made his headquarters at Ft. Johnson.

## 1776, February 27. REVOLUTION. FORTIFICATIONS.

Henry Laurens wrote that:

> The houses of Charles Town which had been emptied of their owners and their furniture are now made use of as barracks for the country rifle-men and other militia.

## 1776, February 27. SOUTHERN WAR DEPARTMENT.

The Continental Congress, convinced that the British strategy was to divide the colonies north and south, created the Middle and Southern military departments. General Charles Lee was appointed to command the South, which consisted of Virginia, the two Carolinas and Georgia.

## 1776, March 3. FORTIFICATIONS. SULLIVAN'S ISLAND.

Christopher Gadsden gave Col. William Moultrie command of Fort Sullivan. Moultrie and the Second South Carolina Regiment arrived on the island to complete the construction of a "large fort," considered to be the key to the geographically shielded harbor.

A large vessel sailing into Charlestown had to cross the Bar, a series of submerged sand banks lying about 8 miles southeast of the city. A half-dozen channels penetrated the bar, but only the southern pair could be navigated by deep-draft ships. A broad anchorage called Five Fathom Hole lay between the bar and Morris Island. A thousand yards north of that shoal loomed the newly constructed Fort Sullivan.

Moultrie's work gangs cut thousands of spongy palmetto logs and rafted them over from other islands. The fort's design was described as "an immense pen 500 feet long and 16 feet wide, filled with sand to stop the shot." The workers constructed gun platforms out of 2-inch planks and nailed them together with spikes.

Fort Sullivan was intended was to make an invasion as costly as possible, or, to prevent an invader from landing at all. Since such a fixed defensive position could not reasonably be expected to annihilate the enemy, the fort would have to be backed up by inland troops and a well-armed city.

## 1776, March 21. *Second Provincial Congress.*

The Second Provincial Congress of South Carolina began to debate about the form of government that was to be established in the state. During the debate an express rider from Savannah arrived with a copy of December 21, 1775 Parliamentary Act that declared the colonies in open rebellion.

This silenced the opposition for establishing an independent government. Very quickly, they decided to organize a General Assembly and a Legislative Council of 13 members (to replace the King's Privy Council) and called for the election of a President and Vice-President.

## 1776, March 23. *Continental Congress. Provincial Congress.*

The South Carolina Provincial Congress authorized its congressional delegates to agree to anything believed "necessary, for the defence, security, interest or welfare of this colony in particular, and of America in general." This was taken by the delegation in Philadelphia as an endorsement for independence.

## 1776, March 23. *Commerce.*

William Ancrum ordered his overseers to do the best they could on the plantation with their existing tools for "there is not a hoe nor a bar of iron to be got. If times do not become better soon ... we shall be greatly distressed for many articles."

## 1776, March 26. *Republic of South Carolina.*

Four months before the Declaration of Independence was signed, South Carolina adopted a state constitution, drafted by the Provincial Congress and the Republic of South Carolina was born. Charles Cotesworth Pinckney was chosen to chair the Constitutional Committee.

John Rutledge was elected president, Henry Laurens vice-president, and William Henry Drayton, Chief Justice. The Assembly elected thirteen members to a Legislative Council, which acted as the upper house. It also elected a six-member Privy Council to act as an advisory panel to the president.

The 1776 Constitution was considered a temporary measure until "an accommodation of the unhappy differences between Great Britain and America can be obtained." It gave the president "absolute veto power" over the acts of the legislature. Due to his power, Rutledge picked up the nickname "Dictator."

The Second Provincial Congress adjourned that morning and reconvened that afternoon as the General Assembly, electing William Henry Drayton as the Chairman of the General Assembly. As Henry Laurens described it, "Congress metamorphosed in the twinkling of an eye into a General Assembly."

Of course, the new Constitution kept government control firmly in the hands of the Lowcountry gentry, who held 126 of the 202 seats. The backcountry was sixty per cent of the population but held only thirty-eight per cent of the seats. Since only forty-nine members created a quorum, Charlestown's members easily dominated the assembly. William Tennett, minister of the Congregational Church, complained that "so many circumstances concur to give the capital and adjacent parishes in representation that there is danger that the government of this state in time will degenerate into an oligarchy."

For the second time in its history, South Carolina had forced a change in its government – in 1719 they had overthrown the Proprietors and now they had replaced British rule with a local government.

### 1776, March 26. *Campbell Plots with Clinton.*

Lord William Campbell wrote to General Henry Clinton claiming that, if the British navy seized Charlestown, then the backcountry residents of Georgia and Carolina would submit to Royal authority "driven by economic necessity. They almost entirely depend on their necessary supplies on the market of Charlestown."

### 1776, March 28. *New State Constitution Read.*

A detachment of Charlestown militia and a detachment of the provincial artillery "were drawn up in Broad Street from the State House to the Exchange, where the new South Carolina Constitution was read."

### 1776, April. *Revolution. Battle of Sullivan's Island.*

The Assembly required all ministers and lay officials of each church to support the Patriot cause. Pres. Rutledge signed an act that prescribed the death penalty and confiscation of property for anyone who aided the British. Rutledge also appointed 46-year-old Col. William Moultrie, former militiaman and Indian fighter, in charge of preparing the city's military defense.

### 1776, April. *Revolution. Armstrong Arrives.*

Brig. General John Armstrong arrived in Charlestown from Pennsylvania. He had been appointmented the second officer in command the Continental forces in South Carolina, under General Charles Lee. Since Lee had not yet arrived, Armstrong served as President Rutledge's military advisor.

**1776, April.** *REVOLUTION. RELIGION.*

Dissenting Baptist ministers, Oliver Hart and Richard Furman, invited ministers of all denominations to meet at the Baptist Church at the High Hills of Santee to draft a petition calling for disestablishment of the English Church.

**1776, April 2.** *STATE SEAL DESIGNED.*

A state seal of South Carolina was authorized to be designed by Arthur Middleton and William Henry Drayton.

**1776, April 11.** *ADMIRALTY COURT CREATED.*

South Carolina created her own vice admiralty court.

**1776, April 26.** *REVOLUTION. NAVAL.*

Col. Moultrie, under orders from Pres. Rutledge, sent a scouting party commanded by Capt. Peter Horry north up the coast to the Sampit River to observe two British men-of-war anchored offshore of Raccoon Key. They were to determine whether this was the vanguard of a larger British fleet.

William Henry Drayton.
*Courtesy of the Library of Congress*

**1776, May 3.** *BRITISH REINFORCEMENTS ARRIVE IN CAROLINA.*

After a grueling three-month voyage, a British naval squadron arrived at Cape Fear from Cork, Ireland. Commanded by Sir Peter Parker, the squadron carried Maj. General Charles Cornwallis, seven British army regiments, and two companies of Royal Artillery.

## 1776, May 17. ADAMS COMMENTS ON S.C. CONSTITUTION.

John Adams, in Philadelphia, wrote to his wife, Abigail, discussing Charlestown's politics:

> Two young gentlemen from South Carolina now in this city, who were in Charles Town when their new Constitution was promulgated, and when their new Governor and Council and Assembly walked out in procession ... told me that they were beheld by the people with transports and tears of joy. The people gazed at them with a kind of rapture.

## 1776, May 22. REVOLUTION. NAVAL.

Returning to Charlestown with captured prizes the South Carolina vessels, *Comet* and *Defense*, were met by two British ships, the 28-gun *Sphinx* and the schooner *Pensacola Packet*. One of the prizes, *St. James*, loaded with rum and sugar, was set on fire by the British. The *Defense* was run aground.

## 1776, May 31. REVOLUTION. LEE'S ARRIVAL.

A Patriot express rider brought word to President John Rutledge that British vessels were seen near Dewees Island, twenty miles away. This was Sir Peter Parker's fleet from Cape Fear.

However, the timely arrival of General Charles Lee boosted the morale of the city. He was considered the best flag officer in the colonial army, and had been considered as commander of the Continental Army, which was given to George Washington. Charles Lee was also known as an acerbic, rather unpleasant man who preferred the company of his hunting dogs to people.

His 6,500 troops in Charlestown consisted of:

- 500 Continental troops from Virginia
- 1,400 from North Carolina
- 1,950 South Carolina regulars
- 700 Charlestown militia
- 1,972 backcountry militia

## 1776, June 1. REVOLUTION. BRITISH FLEET ARRIVES.

Lord William Campbell had been urging a major expedition against South Carolina to crush the rebellion in the South. The British fleet, commanded by Peter Parker and Sir Henry Clinton, appeared and "displayed about fifty sail before the town, on the outside of the bar."

Col. Moultrie described its effect on Charlestown:

> The sight of these vessels alarmed us very much, all was hurry and confusion, the president with his council busy in sending expresses to every part of the country, to hasten down the militia; men running about the town looking for horses, carriages and boats to send their

families into the country; and as they were going out through the town gates to go into the country, they met the militia from the country marching into town ...

## 1776, June 2. *REVOLUTION. PREPARATION OF CHARLESTOWN.*

Gen. Lee placed Brig. General Robert Howe in charge of the troops in Charlestown. Families were sent to the country, upriver out of harm's way. The city's printing presses and public records were sent to "places of safety." This suspended the publishing of any of the gazettes until August.

## 1776, June 4. *REVOLUTION. FORT JOHNSON.*

Thomas Pinckney, stationed at Ft. Johnson on James Island, reported that "our men are healthy and very cheerful, so that I flatter myself if they venture in we shall be able to give a very good account of them."

Charles Lee. Head of Southern War Department. *Courtesy of the New York Public Library*

### 1776, June 4. *REVOLUTION. BATTLE OF SULLIVAN'S ISLAND.*

General Lee reviewed the defenses on Sullivan's Island called them "poorly constructed" and considered Fort Sullivan a "slaughter pen."

As much as Lee was disappointed in the preparations he inspected, he worked diligently "from sunrise to sunset" supervising the construction of the city's defenses. He also gave speeches in an attempt to elevate the local's fear of the British military superiority. He told a crowd in Charlestown that he had once served under Clinton and found he was a "dam'd fool."

### 1776, June 8. *REVOLUTION. BATTLE OF SULLIVAN'S ISLAND.*

Most of the British fleet crossed the bar and anchored in Five Fathom Hole. Sir Henry Clinton delivered a proclamation to the patriots "to entreat and exhort them, as they tender their own happiness and that of their posterity, to return to their duty to our common sovereign." Pres. John Rutledge rejected this plea.

### 1776, June 8. *CONTINENTAL CONGRESS.*

In a letter to John Jay, Edward Rutledge explained that he supported the idea of independence, but for tactical reasons he was opposed to a declaration of independence which would only give Britain "Notice of our Intentions before we had taken any Steps to execute them." He also noted that he was going to propose to delay "for 3 Weeks or a Month" the vote on the resolution for independence.

### 1776, June 9. *REVOLUTION. BATTLE OF SULLIVAN'S ISLAND.*

Learning of the construction of Ft. Sullivan, and the fact that the back (land) side of the fort was not completed, Clinton and 500 soldiers landed on Long Island (present-day Isle of Palms) just north of Sullivan's Island. Over the following days, Clinton increased his force on Long Island. His plan was to cross The Breach, an inlet between Long Island and Sullivan's, and attack the fort from its unfinished rear while Parker's ships assaulted it from the sea.

The *Polly* ran aground near Stono Creek and the Patriots scuttled and abandoned her. The HMS *Bristol* sent eight boats under the command of Lt. Molloy to investigate and attempt to refloat the *Polly*, but she had five feet of water in her hold. So, they set her on fire, and she then:

> blew up with a great Explosion... It would have been much greater but she had five feet of water in her hold, which had damaged a great deal of the Powder.

Richard Hutson wrote to his friend, Issac Hayne, that "the fort will be tendered to them at the mouth of the cannon. We are preparing for the most vigorous resistance in our power."

### 1776, June 11. *REVOLUTION. BATTLE OF SULLIVAN'S ISLAND.*

A floating bridge, comprised of a catwalk of ropes and planks fastened to empty hogsheads anchored to the bottom, was constructed across the cove to Haddrell's Point. However, the bridge was never considered practical.

Gen. Lee was so sure that the fort on Sullivan's Island would be quickly overrun by the British that he became obsessed with having some retreat for the troops. Col. Moultrie, however, had no anxiety. He wrote:

> I never was uneasy on not having a retreat because I never imagined that the enemy could force me to the necessity; I always considered myself as able to defend to the post against the enemy.

Recognizing however, that the uncompleted fort was vulnerable on its right (western) flank, Col. Moultrie suggested placing an "armed schooner," the *Defense*, near the bridge, "out of the way of damage from large ships ... and effectively secure our retreat."

### 1776, June 12-14. *BATTLE OF SULLIVAN'S ISLAND.*

Gen. Clinton took two days to survey the islands surrounding Charlestown. He ruled out landing a force on Sullivan's Island in heavy surf. He discovered that Long Island (present day Isle of Palms), to the north was unoccupied. He was also told that the inlet, the Breach, between Long Island and Sullivan's Island was only eighteen inches deep at low tide.

### 1776, June 13. *REVOLUTION. NAVAL.*

The 12-gun South Carolina sloop *Vixen*, under Captain Downham Newton, captured the British sloop *Polly*, and returned to Charlestown with her prize.

### 1776, June 13. *FORTIFICATION OF CHARLESTOWN.*

Construction crews in Charlestown raised traverses across the major streets. Lead was removed from the windows of churches and houses to make musket balls. Several buildings along the wharves were dismantled to provide fields of fire along the earthworks on East Bay Street. Charles Cotesworth Pinckney wrote to his mother:

> You would scarcely know the environs of the town again, so many lines, bastions, redans and military mince-pies have been made all around it, that the appearance of it is quite metamorphosed. All the houses on the wharves are pulled down, so that the town looks form the water much handsomer than it ever did.

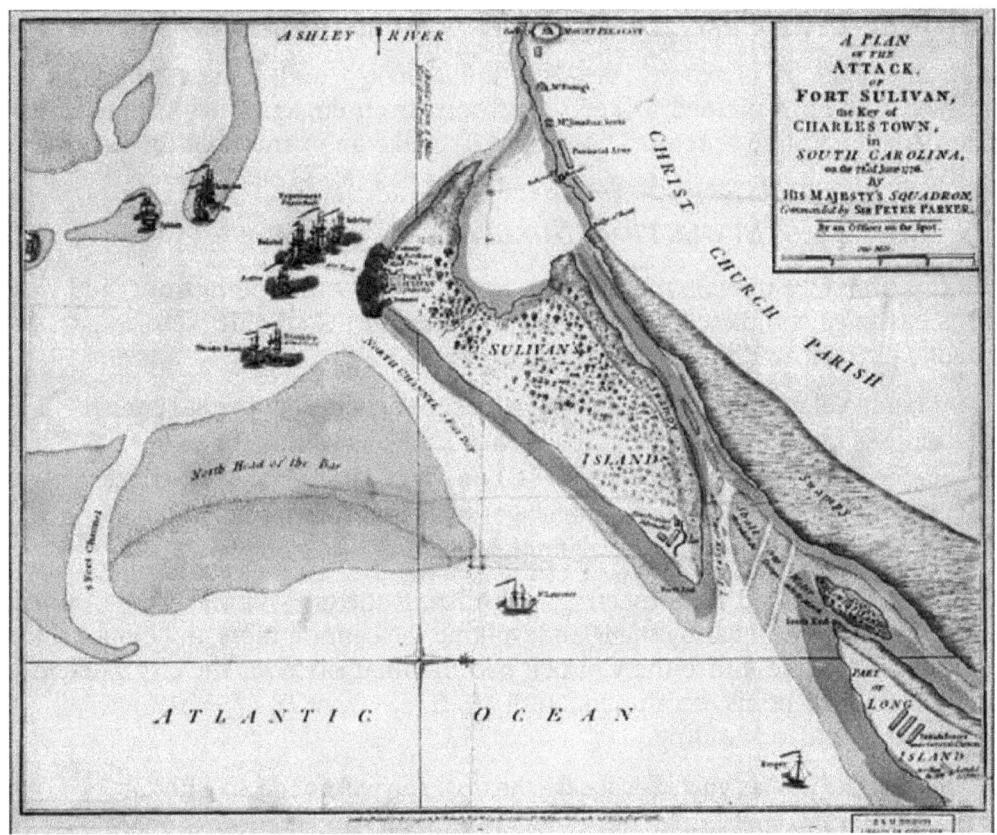

A map of the attack of Sullivan's Island, drawn by a British officer.
*Courtesy of the Library of Congress*

## 1776, June 16. *BATTLE OF SULLIVAN'S ISLAND*.

Clinton sent a brigade of 2,500 men under Maj. Gen. Charles Cornwallis to pitch camp on Long Island within sight of Breach Inlet. Cornwallis reported the Breach had a depth of two feet at low tide; in reality it was seven feet. Col. Moultrie had already stationed an Advance Guard of 400 men commanded by Col. William Thomson on the other side of the Breach to defend against the crossing, effectively stranding Cornwallis's force.

Sir Peter Parker informed Clinton that the Royal Navy could take Fort Sullivan alone. A survey of the fort bolstered Parker's confidence. The walls were sixteen feet wide, ten feet tall, constructed of palmetto logs and filled with sand. There were less than 400 men in the garrison, and the fort had thirty-one guns, most of them British 18-pounders and French 24-pounders. The British force consisted of eleven ships and 270 guns.

## 1776, June 18. *BATTLE OF SULLIVAN'S ISLAND*.

Gen. Clinton appealed to President Rutledge to cease hostilities. Rutledge rejected the plea.

## 1776, June 21. BATTLE OF SULLIVAN'S ISLAND. BREACH'S INLET.

Given the close proximity between the redcoats and Patriot militia, Col. Thompson was hard pressed to keep his troops from engaging with their British counterparts. Gen. Lee ordered Thompson to "make an example of the first man" who disregarded orders.

## 1776, June 22. REVOLUTION. SULLIVAN'S ISLAND.

By this time Ft. Sullivan was far from finished. Only the south (front) and west (right) sides were completed. The north (rear) and east (left) side were only a few feet high. Gen. Lee told the men at Sullivan:

> Courage alone with not suffice in war. True soldiers and magnanimous citizens must brandish the pick-axe and spade, as well as the sword, in defence of their country; one of two days labour, at this critical juncture, may not only save many worthy families from ruin, but many worthy individuals from loss of limbs and life.

Gen. Lee then called for a meeting with Pres. Rutledge and the Privy Council. Lee recommended evacuating the island, spiking the cannon there and demolishing the powder magazine. Since the Council had the final say over the city's defenses they refused to accept his recommendation.

Rutledge wrote to Moultrie:

> General Lee wishes you to evacuate the fort. You will not do so without an order from me. I would sooner cut off my right hand than write one.

## 1776, June 28. REV. COOPER PRAYS FOR BRITISH VICTORY.

Rev. Robert Cooper prayed from St. Michael's pulpit that "the King might be strengthened to defeat his enemies."

## 1776, June 28. BATTLE OF SULLIVAN'S ISLAND.

Early that morning, Col. Moultrie rode on horseback from Fort Sullivan to Breach Inlet to consult with Col. Thompson. As he and Thompson were talking, they observed the British men-of-war vessels loosening their topsails, a sure sign they were preparing to get under way. Moultrie galloped the three miles back to the fort and ordered the drummers to beat the long roll. The 435 troops in the fort sprang into action to man their posts.

The detachment inside the fort was comprised of infantrymen of the Second South Carolina Regiment and 33 artillerists from the Fourth South Carolina Regiment. Moultrie's staff included Lt. Colonel Issac Motte, Maj. Francis Marion, and Lt. Thomas Moultrie.

Marion was a severe taskmaster who did not tolerate nonsense. He kept the enlisted men busy upgrading the fortifications of the fort, alongside black slaves "whether they liked it or not." He ordered no beer or rum purchased without "specific permission."

## 1776, June 28. BATTLE OF SULLIVAN'S ISLAND.

The first major naval battle of the Revolution commenced at 11:30 A.M. when the *Thunder* lobbed a thirteen-inch explosive mortar shell over the fort, which landed on the roof of the powder magazine. It failed to explode and did little damage. Had the shell not been a dud, the battle could have come to an abrupt conclusion with that one shot.

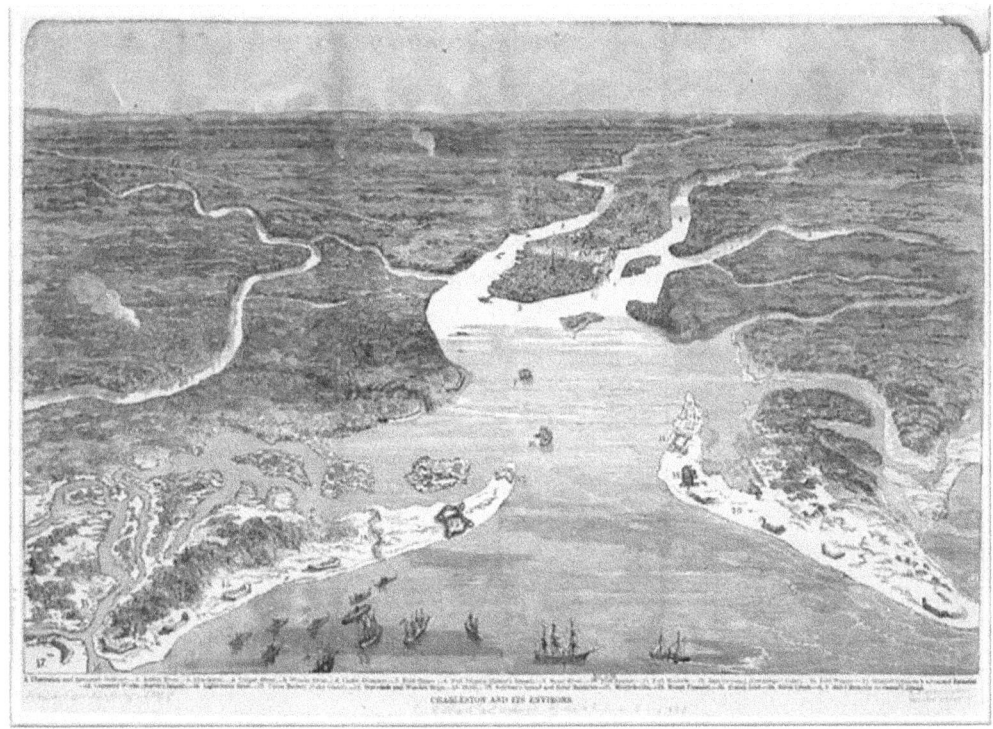

Charlestown harbor, 1776, with the British fleet approaching. Sullivan's Island to the right and Fort Johnson to the left, creating the narrow channel that ships must pass through to enter the harbor. *Courtesy of the New York Public Library*

As soon as the British ships came into range, Moultrie opened fire with the guns on the southeast bastion. Moultrie termed the situation "one continual blaze and roar, with clouds of smoke curling over ... for hours together."

Although greatly outnumbered, and with vastly inferior armaments, the South Carolina troops kept the British fleet from entering the harbor. The British cannonballs embedded themselves in the pulpy palmetto logs with no damage to fort. At the same time, Col. Thompson and his 400 men managed to hold The Breach, thwarting British efforts to cross and land troops on Sullivan's Island. British soldiers, weighted down with their equipment trying to cross the Breach, sank in water above their heads.

Two hours into the fight, Gen. Lee, observing the battle at Haddrell's Point, sent Maj. Francis Otway Byrd in a canoe to Fort Sullivan with a message to Moultrie, that "if the powder in the fort was expended" he should spike the guns and evacuate. To Moultrie, that was not an option. He was having good success and a retreat was unthinkable. Moultrie, however, *was* running short of powder, having expended 4,766 pounds of the available 5,400 pounds. The situation was so dire that Moultrie ordered cannons fired at intervals of ten minutes for each gun, only when there was a clear target sighted. Moultrie sent Francis Marion with a small party to the armed schooner *Defence* and returned with 300 pounds of powder.

Maj. Byrd returned to Haddrell's Point and informed Gen. Lee things were going "astonishingly well." Encouraged, Lee contacted Pres. Rutledge, who sent 500 pounds of powder to the fort with a note, "Honor and Victory, my good sir, to you and our worthy countrymen with you."

Seven miles away in the city, thousands of spectators watched the battle from waterfront vantage points or from rooftops and second-story piazzas.

Around 4 P.M. General Lee arrived at Fort Sullivan from Haddrell's Point. To allow Lee's entrance into the fort several of the Second South Carolina had to leave their guns and remove the timber that was barricading the back entrance. The British took that as a sign the fort was being abandoned. After inspecting the fort Lee told Moultrie, "Colonel, I see you are doing very well here, you have no occasion for me."

Three of the Royal ships, *Syren, Actaeon and Sphinx*, ran afoul of and grounded on a shoal called "Middle Ground" where Fort Sumter was eventually built.

In the midst of the battle, a British projectile broke the fort's flagstaff. Sgt. William Jasper called out to Moultrie, "Colonel, don't let us fight without our flag!" Moultrie, well aware of the audience watching in the city, asked Jasper what could be done. Jasper volunteered to retrieve.

Battle of Sullivan's Island, June 28, 1776. *Courtesy of the New York Public Library*

He "leapt over the ramparts" and, shouted, "Don't let us fight without a color!" Captain Horry described Jasper's action:

> He deliberately walked the whole length of the fort, until he came to the colors on the extremity of the left, when he cut off the same from the mast, and called to me for a sponge staff, and with a thick cord tied on the colors and stuck the staff on the rampart in the sand. The sergeant fortunately received no hurt, though exposed for a considerable time, to the enemy's fire.

Moultrie wrote, "Our flag once more waving in the air, revived the drooping spirits of our friends; they continued looking on, till night had closed the scene, and hid us from their view."

As American shot bombarded into the British men-of-war, one round landed on the *Bristol's* quarterdeck and rendered Sir Peter Parker's "Britches ... quite torn off, his backside laid bare, his thigh and knee wounded." The *Acteon* was grounded and severely damaged.

More than 2,500 British troops attempted to cross Breach Inlet from Long Island (Isle of Palms) to Sullivan's Island. They were stopped due to the depth of the water, and the fire from Thompson's troops on the Sullivan's Island side.

By 9:30 P.M. Parker withdrew and Francis Marion fired the last shot from Fort Sullivan at the retreating Royal navy. Moultrie sent word to Rutledge that the British ships had retired and that South Carolina was victorious. The reports came in from the ten-hour battle:

- BRITISH: 78 dead, 152 wounded. Lord William Campbell was wounded during the battle and later died of his wounds.
- AMERICAN: 12 dead, 25 wounded. 5 died of their wounds later.

The *Bristol* had been hit seventy times.

## 1776, June 28. *DECLARATION OF INDEPENDENCE.*

While the Battle of Sullivan's Island raged, in Philadelphia Thomas Jefferson, Benjamin Franklin, and John Adams presented a final draft of the Declaration of Independence to the Continental Congress. While South Carolinians were exchanging shot-for-shot with the British Navy, the Declaration was read to the Congress.

## 1776, June 29. *BATTLE OF SULLIVAN'S ISLAND.*

Early in the morning the British set fire to the grounded *Actaeon,* and abandoned it. The Americans, led by Lt. Jacob Milligan, rowed out to the burning ship on three small boats, boarded her while she was burning and fired several of its guns at the departing *Bristol.* They managed to take *Aceton's* bell and as much of her stores and sails as they could carry. While they were rowing away the ship's powder magazine blew up.

The South Carolina soldiers searched Sullivan's Island and "gathered up more shot, from 24-pounders down to the smallest size, than they had fired." The British shot had destroyed almost all of the island's huts and trees but Ft. Sullivan stood almost undamaged. Moultrie addressed his troops:

> My gallant companions, you see the advantage of courage and fortitude; you have fought and conquered, and the brave fellows who fell in the cannonade yesterday, are now in heaven, riding in their chariots like the devil.

Gen. Lee sent a "generous supply" of rum to the fort. Pres. Rutledge sent Moultrie a letter praising the "heroic behavior of yesterday."

Sgt. Jasper replacing the South Carolina flag during the battle of Sullivan's Island. *Courtesy of the New York Public Library*

## 1776, June 29. *RIDE OF DANIEL LATHAM.*

It was important to get the news to the Continental Congress as quickly as possible. Normal dispatches often took two or three weeks to travel to Philadelphia. Seventeen-year old Daniel Latham, "a very athletic young man," who was a distiller at 1 Hasell Street, set out early in the morning on horseback toward Philadelphia, spreading news of the victory everywhere he went. Within a week he arrived and announced to the news of the Sullivan's Island victory.

It is difficult to over-emphasize the importance of the June 28 victory at Sullivan's Island. When word reached the other American cities, it was seen as an early sign of the American capacity to oppose the British at arms. In hindsight, it ranks as one of the three most decisive American victories in the Revolution, with Saratoga and Kings Mountain. It also gave South Carolina a new patriotic symbol, the palmetto tree.

William Moultrie later wrote:

> This great nation we dare to oppose, without money, without arms, without ammunition, no generals, no armies, no admirals, and no fleets; that was our situation when the contest began.

## 1776, June 29. *CONTINENTAL CONGRESS. CHARLESTOWN HESITATES.*

Edward Rutledge, at the Continental Congress in Philadelphia, unaware of the events that had taken place in Charlestown, expressed his reluctance to declare independence from Britain. Contrary to the majority of his Congressional colleagues, Rutledge advocated patience with regards to declaring independence.

## 1776, June 30. *REVOLUTION. NAVAL.*

Two South Carolina sloops, *Vixen* and *General Washington,* commanded by Captain Hezekiah Anthony, encountered a Jamaican fleet of more than 100 vessels, escorted by four British men-of-war. They managed to capture the sloop *Salley,* loaded with rum and *Nancy*, bound for London with 250 hogshead of sugar, fifty of rum and eighty pipes of wine.

## 1776, July. *DEATH.*

Sabina Ellis Ramsay died at age nineteen, leaving Dr. David Ramsay widowed for the first time.

## 1776, July 2. *CONTINENTAL CONGRESS.*

Continental Congress adopted resolutions declaring independence from Great Britain. The South Carolina delegation, ignorant of the victory of Sullivan's Island, voted to preserve unity with England.

## 1776, July 4. *DECLARATION OF INDEPENDENCE.*

The Continental Congress approved the final wording of the Declaration of Independence. The ideals of individual liberty, first espoused by John Locke (partially in his *Fundamental Constitutions of Carolina)* were now clearly expressed by Thomas Jefferson.

John Hancock signed the document that day, and it was sent to John Dunlop's printing shop where 200 copies were printed. Copies were sent across the country to all major cities in America.

All four South Carolina delegates, still unaware of the events on Sullivan's Island, voted reluctantly for independence, unsure how their more conservative Carolinians would react.

- Arthur Middleton, thirty-four years old
- Thomas Heyward Jr., twenty-nine years old
- Thomas Lynch Jr., twenty-seven years old
- Edward Rutledge was the youngest signer of the Declaration, twenty-six years old

## 1776, July 4. *BATTLE OF SULLIVAN'S ISLAND AFTERMATH.*

President John Rutledge visited Ft. Sullivan to congratulate the garrison. His entourage included Maj, Gen. Charles Lee, Col. Christopher Gadsden, and Major Barnard Elliot. He presented his sword to Sergeant Jasper for heroic actions and gave the men a hogshead of rum from Charlestown merchant William Logan. Rutledge announced that Ft. Sullivan was to be renamed Fort Moultrie.

William Moultrie.
*Courtesy of the National Archive*

### 1776, July 8. *Revolution. British Leave Isle of Palms.*

British troops had spent ten miserable days on Long Island (Isle Of Palms) while Sir Peter Parker and the British fleet "licked their wounds." They were happy to board transports and leave the "mosquito-infested island."

### 1776, July 11. *Morris Island Lighthouse.*

A party of 320 Patriots attacked a detachment of Royal Marines at the Morris Island lighthouse, clearing the British out.

### 1776, July 14. *British Flagship Leaves Charlestown.*

The British flagship of Sir Peter Parker, HMS *Bristol*, left Charlestown for New York. By this time Parker and Clinton had already began to blame each other for their defeat.

### 1776, July 21. *Revolution. Naval.*

A British brigantine ran aground near Dewees Inlet and was captured by the provincial *Prosper*.

### 1776, July 31. *Revolution. First Jew Killed.*

Francis Salvador, part of the Ninety-Six militia, fell in battle against the Cherokee and an Indian took his scalp. He died "within three-quarters of an hour" at the age of twenty-nine. He was the first Jew killed in the Revolution.

### 1776, August. *Revolution. Privateering.*

The sloop *Swift* became the first vessel commissioned by South Carolina as a privateer. Initially commanded by Francis Morgan, in less than a month Captain Andrew Groundwater took command. *Swift* sailed out of Charlestown with the sloop *Vixen* looking for prizes.

### 1776, August. *Revolution. Lee's Plan to Attack Florida.*

General Lee, bolstered by the victory of Sullivan's Island, which he had opposed, devised a plan to lead troops on a mission to St. Augustine. He planned to attack the Loyalists of South Carolina and Georgia who had found safe haven on the Florida coast. Pres. Rutledge and the Privy Council were adamantly opposed using South Carolina troops, in fear that the British would return to Charlestown. Lee asked for volunteers from North Carolina and Virginia Continentals to accompany him.

### 1776, August 1. *Cooper Removed from St. Michael's.*

Rev. Robert Cooper, who supported the King, was removed as minister of St. Michael's Church and ordered out of the parsonage.

### 1776, August 2. *British Fleet Leaves Charlestown.*

The last of the British fleet, HMS *Active, Sphinx* and a troop transport left Charlestown.

**1776, August 2.** *DECLARATION ARRIVES IN CHARLESTOWN.*

A packet ship arrived from Philadelphia carrying a copy of the Declaration of Independence.

**1776, August 3.** *DECLARATION SIGNED.*

Most of the members of the Continental Congress officially signed the Declaration of Independence on this day. They then turned their attention to creating a union of the thirteen colonies.

**1776, August 5.** *REVOLUTION. DECLARATION READ PUBLICLY.*

The Declaration was read publicly in front of the Exchange on Broad Street. It was greeted "amidst loud acclamations of thousands." At noon the militia marched up Broad Street before President Rutledge and other officials. Later that night, Maj. Barnard Elliot read it to a large, enthusiastic crowd under the Liberty Tree.

Dr. David Ramsay wrote:

> The Declaration of Independence arrived in Charleston at a most favorable juncture. It found the people of South Carolina exasperated against Great Britain for her late hostile attack, and elevated with their successful defense of Fort Moultrie. It was welcomed by a great majority of the inhabitants ... with the firing of guns, ringing of bells ... and all the usual parade of a public rejoicing.

**1776, August 8.** *REVOLUTION. LEE'S EXPEDITION TO FLORIDA.*

Gen. Lee marched south with volunteers from the Virginia and North Carolina Continentals, about 1,300 men.

**1776, August 11.** *REVOLUTION. LEE'S EXPEDITION TO FLORIDA.*

Pres. Rutledge agreed to commit some troops to Lee's expedition. Col. Moultrie led a detachment of 240 South Carolinians to join Lee in Savannah. However, once united, Lee suggested that Moultrie take command of the regiment that would attack St. Augustine. Moultrie agreed, even though his brother, John Moultrie, was the royal governor of East Florida.

**1776, August 14.** *REVOLUTION. DECLARATION OF INDEPENDENCE.*

When Henry Laurens learned of the Declaration of Independence he exclaimed, "I am now by the will of God brought into a new world, and God only knows what sort of world it will be."

**1776, August 17.** *SLAVERY.*

As several colonies discussed the possibility of using black soldiers in the Continental Army, John Adams observed that South Carolinians "would run out of their wits at the least hint of a Negro battalion."

## 1776, August 19. *SLAVERY ISSUES. ARTICLES OF CONFEDERATION.*

Edward Rutledge wrote that the states would not approve the Articles of Confederation "as they stand now." The southern delegations opposed the provision that each state should contribute financially in proportion to their population, including slaves.

In an argument which was to continue for the next ninety years, Southern delegates argued that slaves were wealth-producing property, not people. Thomas Lynch, Jr. of South Carolina said that if the North wanted to debate whether slaves were property "there is an End of the Confederation.

Edward Rutledge argued it was "unfair to base taxes on one form of wealth-producing property and not others, such as land and livestock." He also wrote:

> I propose that the States should appoint a special Congress to be composed of new Members for this purpose – and that no Person should disclose any part of the present plan.

Signers of the Declaration of Independence from South Carolina.
Top: Arthur Middleton, Thomas Heyward, Jr. Bottom: Thomas Lynch, Jr.; Edward Rutledge. *Courtesy of the New York Public Library*

### 1776, September. *CULTURE.*

Charles Pinckney, son of Charles Pinckney, Junior, arrived in Philadelphia for a visit. He carried a letter of introduction from Dr. David Ramsay which he presented to Dr. Benjamin Rush. Ramsay described the young Pinckney as "a youth of merit and education."

### 1776, September. *REVOLUTION. POLITICS. NAVAL.*

President John Rutledge recommended the legislature pass an act to set up a board of commissioners to direct and administer the navy. It was also recommended that for incentive, prize money for each enemy ship captured would be split among the crew.

### 1776, September. *REVOLUTION. LEE RETURNS TO PHILADELPHIA.*

While waiting for supplies in Savannah, Gen. Lee received orders from Congress recalling him back to Philadelphia, leaving Moultrie in command. Lee also took with him most of the North Carolina and Virginia Continentals, which left the force undermanned for the attack on St. Augustine.

Summer in the Georgia swamps had also taken their toll on the force, with many soldiers and officers sick of fevers and other ailments. The group was recalled to Charlestown.

### 1776, September 1-6. *REVOLUTION. NAVAL.*

Joseph Vesey, who had lost his ship the *Hawke* to the British, signed on as master of the *USS Providence* under Captain John Paul Jones. During this week, the *Providence* captured three British ships, the *Solebay*, the *Sea Nymph* and the *Favourite*. The ships were carrying cargo such as sugar, rum, ginger and oil.

### 1776, September 17. *CONTINENTAL CONGRESS.*

Continental Congress promoted Col. Christopher Gadsden and Col. William Moultrie to the status of Brigadier Generals. Major Charles Cotesworth Pinckney was promoted to Colonel.

### 1776, September 17. *ASSEMBLY APPROVES THE DECLARATION.*

At a special session of the Assembly, presided by President John Rutledge, the Declaration of Independence was approved, writing:

> It is with unspeakable joy we embrace this opportunity of expressing our satisfaction in the Declaration of the Continental Congress constituting the United Colonies free and independent States absolved from their subjection to George III and totally dissolving all political union between them and Great Britain.

### 1776, September 20. *REVOLUTION. CONTINENTAL ARMY.*

All six South Carolina regular regiments became part of the Continental Army, with Brig. General Robert Howe the ranking officer in South Carolina. Despite his reputation in Charlestown as a notorious womanizer, Howe was well-respected for his military acumen. He sent Rutledge recommendations about the building of new fortifications which the Assembly approved, as well as the acquisition of land at Haddrell's Point for barracks.

### 1776, October. *COMMERCE.*

The South-Carolina Insurance Company was formed to sell fire policies.

### 1776, October 4. *COMMERCE. SLAVERY.*

A Charlestown grand jury recommended:

> that Jews and others may be restrained from allowing their negroes to sell good in shops, as such practice may induce other negroes to steal and barter with them ... a profanation of the Lord's Day.

### 1776, October 8. *REVOLUTION. NAVAL.*

A Board of Naval Commissioners was established, with Edward Blake as the first commissioner.

### 1776, October 14. *REVOLUTION. TEA TO BE SOLD.*

The General Assembly announced the sale of several hundred chests of tea, which had been stored in the Exchange basement for three years. The money was to be used in support of the Patriot cause in South Carolina.

Brig. General Robert Howe. Illustration from *A Brief History of the North Carolina Troops on the Continental Establishment: In the War of the Revolution.* Public Domain.

### 1776, October 18. *POLITICS. COMMERCE.*

An Act was passed, calling for ships drawing less than six feet of water, pay a piloting fee of £3, 15s; those drawing twenty feet paid £65, 15s.

### 1776, October 26. *SLAVERY.*

John Laurens wrote to his father, Henry:

> We have sunk the Africans and their descendants below the standard of humanity, and almost rendered them incapable of that blessing which equal Heaven bestowed upon us all.

### 1776, December. *REVOLUTION. FORTIFICATIONS.*

President John Rutledge approved Christopher Gadsden's proposal to construct a bridge connecting Sullivan's Island to Haddrell's Point, for better communication. The Rutledge family was, at this time, the most powerful in South Carolina. John served as President; brother Hugh was speaker of the Council; Thomas was in the General Assembly and youngest brother, Edward, was a member of the Continental Congress *and* the General Assembly.

# 1777

### 1777. *SLAVERY.*

A Frenchman noted the differences between the slaves in the French colonies versus Charlestown. The blacks on Charlestown streets did not "cringe or appear afraid of every white man as they do in our colonies; the Anglo-American Negro slaves have an air of self-respect about them that doesn't appear to be arrogance." He concluded it must be from the "training which the slaves receive while they are becoming civilized," or "kind treatment by white masters."

### 1777, January. *EDWARD RUTLEDGE RETURNS TO CHARLESTOWN.*

Edward Rutledge returned from Philadelphia and rented James Lauren's house at 117 Broad Street. His wife, Henrietta, was suffering recurring health problems, most likely bouts of malaria exacerbated by her weakened condition from the birth of her first child.

### 1777, January 10. *CONTINENTAL CONGRESS.*

Henry Laurens was elected a delegate to the Continental Congress.

### 1777, January 11. *CHURCH OF ENGLAND DISESTABLISHED.*

Christopher Gadsden introduced legislation to disestablish the Church of England in South Carolina. Rev. William Tennant of the Congregational Church argued that a State Church discouraged freedom, that goal of the Revolution. He commented:

> While you are contending for the rights of mankind with one of the greatest powers on earth, will you leave your own Constitution marked with injustice and oppression?

Many of the Charleston elite were divided by the issue. Gadsden, Charles Cotesworth Pinckney, Edward Rutledge and William Henry Drayton wished to disestablish the church, while Rawlins Lowndes, Richard Hutson, Charles Pinckney, Jr., and John Rutledge supported the Church.

### 1777, January 23. *AMERICAN REVOLUTION. RELIGION.*

Edward Rutledge wrote that "Religion is now become the subject of dispute and will I am afraid play the Devil with us."

### 1777, January 29. *CULTURE. EDUCATION.*

The Mount Zion Society was organized in Charlestown to "promote science and advance literature in the remote parts of this state." The officers of the Society were Daniel Cannon, Richard Hutson, and William Hasell Gibbes.

### 1776, February. *REVOLUTION. NAVAL.*

Hezekiah Anthony received a commission as a privateer for the sloop *General Washington*. Anthony became one of the most successful privateers during the Revolution.

### 1777, February 13. *REVOLUTION. OATH OF LOYALTY.*

An oath of abjuration (rejection) of loyalty to King George III and of allegiance to the new state was demanded of each white male citizen. Anyone who would not take the oath was banished.

### 1777, February 19. *REVOLUTION. PRIVATEERING.*

The South Carolina privateer *Notre Dame*, under Capt. Cochran, arrived with supplies from France, and towing a British prize captured with food provisions.

### 1777, March. *REVOLUTION. NAVAL. PRIVATEERING.*

The Continental frigate *Randolph* arrived in Charlestown with four prizes captured in the West Indies. The success of the *Notre Dame* and *Randolph* inspired to General Assembly to commission several more privateers, including the SCS *General Moultrie*, *SCS Polly* and *SCS Fair American*.

### 1777, March 10. *REVOLUTION. COMMERCE.*

Gabriel Manigault noted that, due to the British navy blockade of American ports, some merchants had opened "avenues of trade with the French, the Dutch, and their colonies in the West Indies.

## 1777, April 4. *REVOLUTION. COMMERCE.*

In a letter to Eli Kershaw, William Ancrum stated:

> We have had no arrivals lately, the miscarriage of our fleet and the many vessels that have been lately taken, will in all probability keep up the price of goods, rum is rising.

## 1777, April 6. *REVOLUTION. COMMERCE.*

John Adams commented that:

> South Carolina seems to display a spirit of enterprise in trade superior to any other state ... drive and flexibility, the tolerance for risk [and] roving quest for new markets.

## 1777, May 20. *INDIAN AFFAIRS. TREATY OF DEWITT'S CORNER.*

The Treaty of Dewitt's Corner was signed with the Cherokee at Due West in the backcountry. In the terms of the treaty South Carolina obtained most of present-day Greenville, Pickens, Oconee, and Anderson Counties.

Seal of the State of South Carolina

## 1777, May 22. *STATE SEAL USED FOR FIRST TIME.*

The state seal was used for the first time by President John Rutledge. The seal was made up of two elliptical areas, linked by branches of the palmetto tree. The image on the left is a tall palmetto tree and an oak tree, fallen and broken, which represents the battle fought on June 28, 1776, between defenders of the unfinished fort on Sullivan's Island, and the British Fleet. The standing palmetto represents the victorious defenders, and the fallen oak is the British Fleet. Banded together on the palmetto with the motto "Quis separabit?" (Who Will Separate [Us]?), are 12 spears that represent the first 12 states of the Union. At the bottom is the phrase "Animis Opibusque Parati," or "Prepared in Mind and Resources."

The other image on the seal depicts a woman walking along a shore littered with weapons. The woman, symbolizing Hope, grasps a branch of laurel as the sun rises behind her. Below her image is the word "Spes," (Hope) and over the image is the motto "Dum Spiro Spero," (While I Breathe I Hope.)

### 1777, June 8. *NAVAL. LIGHTNING STRIKE.*

The Philadelphia-built frigate *Randolph* had spent two months being refitted at Hobcaw shipyard. As the ship was being launched into Charlestown harbor a lightning bolt struck the mast and splintered it. The ship had to be pulled back into the shipyard for repairs.

Captain Nicholas Biddle spent the weeks in Charlestown courting Elizabeth Baker of Archdale Hall on the Ashley River. They became engaged by the end of the summer.

### 1777, June 9. *SLAVERY.*

Henry Laurens warned his friend Ralph Izard that "many of your negroes with vicious designs" were deserting Izard's plantation and running off to Charlestown, hoping to reach British vessels that would take them in. He urged Izard to "hire someone … to hunt down and retrieve" them.

### 1777, June 13. *REVOLUTION. LAFAYETTE ARRIVES.*

The Marquis de Lafayette (full name: Marie Joseph Paul Ives Roch Gilbert de Motier) and the Baron de Kalb arrived in America, on North Island in Winyah Bay. They proceeded to Benjamin Huger's house in Georgetown to join the American military cause. Huger brought Lafayette to Charlestown where he could catch a ship to Philadelphia and offer his services to the Continental Congress.

### 1777, June 15-25. *LAFAYETTE IN CHARLESTOWN.*

Lafayette spent an entertaining week in Charlestown. Christopher Gadsden and Gen. Moultrie gave the Frenchman a tour of the city's fortifications. He was so enthralled by the story of the defense of Sullivan's Island he presented Moultrie with "clothing, arms and accoutrements for one hundred men."

In a letter to his wife, Lafayette wrote:

> I have just passed five hours at a large dinner given in compliment to me by an individual of this town. Generals Howe and Moultrie, and several officers of my suite were present. We drank each other's health and endeavored to talk English, which I am beginning to speak a little.

### 1777, June 26. *LAFAYETTE DEPARTS.*

Lafayette departed for Philadelphia.

## 1777, June 28. PALMETTO SOCIETY. FIRST CELEBRATION.

The Palmetto Society was organized to celebrate Palmetto Day (later Carolina Day), June 28, 1776. The commemoration of the first anniversary of the Battle of Sullivan's Island was observed by the firing of artillery, the ringing of church bells and military parade. Glasses were raised to toast Gen. Moultrie, Sgt. Jasper and the men who died during the battle.

Francis Marion, a teetotaler, admonished the officers "to behave with sobriety and decency in the presence of ladies."

Marquis de Lafayette.
*Courtesy of the Library of Congress*

## 1777, July. REVOLUTION. LAURENS JOINS WASHINGTON'S STAFF.

John Laurens secured a place on George Washington's staff, with Alexander Hamilton and Marquis de Lafayette. Hamilton wrote that John had "stolen into my affections without my consent."

## 1777, July 4. CULTURE. SOUTH CAROLINA NAVY.

For the first anniversary of the Declaration of Independence:

An elegant Entertainment was given at the Council-Chamber by his Excellency the President [John Rutledge] to such Members of the Legislature as were in Town, to the Clergy, civil and military Officers, and a number of other Gentlemen. After Dinner, thirteen Toasts were given.

Captain Nicholas Biddle and *Randolph* had just been launched from Hobcaw shipyard and participated in the seventy-six-gun salute. Before *Randolph* could leave the harbor as a privateer, it was *again* struck by lightning, and a new mast had to be installed. In an attempt to keep lightning from striking a *third* time, Biddle installed a metal iron rod above the main masthead with a wire that led down to one of the backstays to the water. Biddle had read about this technique in Ben Franklin's *Poor Richard's Almanac*.

### 1777. August 8. REVOLUTION. SOUTH CAROLINA NAVY.

*Randolph* sailed toward St. Augustine searching for ships to capture. Less than 200 miles out of Charlestown Captain Biddle managed to capture three prizes.

### 1777, August 27. SOUTH CAROLINA NAVY.

*Randolph* returned to Charlestown barely a week after leaving, escorting his prizes, which totaled £90,000 sterling.

### 1777, September 7. SOUTH CAROLINA NAVY.

Captain Hezekiah Anthony, of the sloop *General Washington,* engaged with the British merchant 12-gun brig *Pensacola* bound for London. After a three-hour battle Anthony withdrew, his rigging badly damaged.

### 1777, September 25. SOUTH CAROLINA NAVY.

In the Bay of Honduras, *General Washington* captured the 300-ton *Spiers* filled with rum and mahogany. Upon his return to Charlestown with his prize, Captain Hezekiah Anthony was given command of a larger vessel, 14-gun brig *Polly*.

### 1777, September 25. PHILADELPHIA FALLS TO BRITISH.

The British occupied Philadelphia, the American capital.

### 1777, November. REVOLUTION. BRITISH BLOCKADE.

A Royal navy blockade was set off the Charlestown bar by four British ships, *Carysforts, Lizard, Perseus* and *Hinchinbrook*. The Tories living in Charlestown invited the officers to town nightly for entertainment.

This was a major problem for South Carolina. Many merchants ships were in the harbor, getting loaded with the summer's crop. With the blockade in place, most of the ships had no hope of leaving without running the risk of being captured, or destroyed.

### 1777, November 1. LAURENS ELECTED PRESIDENT OF CONGRESS.

Upon John Hancock's retirement, due to ill health, Henry Laurens was elected President of the Congress and served until December 9, 1778. During his term, Laurens dealt with the conspiracy to replace George Washington as commander-in-chief, perpetuated by several members of Congress and the military.

## 1777, November 17. *Articles of Confederation.*

The Continental Congress adopted the Articles of Confederation.

## 1777, December. *Revolution. Naval.*

Due to the success of American privateers, the British Ministry began to use armed naval vessels to escort merchant ships for the first time in its history.

## 1777, December 4. *Revolution. South Carolina Navy.*

President Rutledge proposed that Captain Nicholas Biddle command a force of four state warships to destroy the British navy blockade. He encouraged local merchants to offer enlistment bonuses so the ships could be manned quickly. The four ships were:

- *Randolph*, 36-gun frigate – Captain Biddle
- *General Moultrie,* 20-gun ship – Captain Sullivan
- *Notre Dame,* 16-gun brig – Captain Fryer Hall
- *Fair American,* 16-gun brig – Captain Charles Morgan
- *Polly*, 14-gun brig – Captain Hezekiah Anthony

## 1777, December 19. *Revolution. Valley Forge.*

George Washington's army, tattered and worn-out, settled into their winter quarters at Valley Forge, Pennsylvania, twenty-five miles northwest of Philadelphia.

## 1777, December 23. *Revolution. British Blockade.*

Concerned about the presence of British warships cruising outside the Charlestown harbor, Gen. Moultrie convened a meeting of the field officers of South Carolina's Continental regiments at his quarters to discuss Pres. Rutledge's request that the state's warships attack the British blockade vessels.

Even though the officers were against the attack, Rutledge and Gen. Howe convinced Moultrie to supply 150 soldiers for marine duty. Rutledge was concerned that South Carolina's commercial trade would suffer by the presence of the British.

## 1777, December 23. *Revolution. British Escape.*

Seven British prisoners in Charlestown escaped from jail, stole a boat and rowed out to the British blockade ships offshore. They informed the officers of the impending South Carolina naval attack.

## 1777, December 31. *Revolution. Naval.*

It was reported than American ships had captured 464 British ships.

George Washington and Lafayette at Valley Forge. *Courtesy of the Library of Congress*

# 1778

### 1778, January 14. *SLAVERY.*

John Laurens informed his father, Henry, that he had proposed arming and leading a regiment of black troops, with the promise of freedom after the war.

### 1778, January 15. *DISASTER. FIRE.*

A major fire started at the corner of Queen and Union (now State) Streets. It started in "either a bake-house or in a kitchen hired out to some negroes." Aided by a blustery wind, it burned across Charlestown for seventeen hours, destroying more than 250 buildings, including most of the holdings of the Charlestown Library Society (more than 6,000 volumes), Peter Timothy's printing shop, and Charles Pinckney, Junior's house on Queen Street. The city was "smoking ruins, and the constant falling walls and chimneys." The losses totaled more than $3 million.

William Ancrum noted that, due to the fire, "the distresses of many, before very great, now becomes almost insupportable." Elkanah Watson noted that "the flames reduced to indigence many who had retied to their beds in affluence."

Many suspected the fire had been started by British sailors disguised as civilians.

### 1778, January 23. *DISASTER.*

John Wells, Jr. commented that the fire had created "as complete a scene of woe and horror as the human imagination can picture."

### 1778, January 27. REVOLUTION. SOUTH CAROLINA NAVY.

The South Carolina naval ships sailed over the Charlestown bar. There were no British ships in sight. Biddle suspected that the Royal navy may have left when learning of the South Carolina squadron. In truth, the British ships were overloaded with prisoners from taking several prizes trying to enter Charlestown and had sailed north to their home base.

### 1778, February 16. REVOLUTION. COMMERCE.

Joseph Kershaw wrote to Henry Laurens, "Our port had been blocked up for a considerable length of time by two of three British cruisers, and some privateers out of Augustine."

### 1778, March 7. REVOLUTION. SOUTH CAROLINA NAVY.

The South Carolina naval squadron engaged the HMS *Yarmouth* east of Barbados. During the battle *Randolph* exploded, killing 311 of her crew, including Captain Biddle. The four survivors were picked up by *Yarmouth*. The other South Carolina ships fled.

### 1778, March 11. REVOLUTION. SOUTH CAROLINA NAVY.

Alexander Gillon, a Dutch merchant from Charlestown, was appointed Commodore of the South Carolina Navy. By this time, Gillon had amassed real estate holdings valued at £30,000, with his merchant business located next to the Exchange Building (present-day Gillon Street).

### 1778, March 19. NEW SOUTH CAROLINA CONSTITUTION.

The new Constitution of South Carolina was given a third reading and approved. It deprived the President of his veto. Only Protestants could be legislators or governor. The Anglican Church though disestablished, retained all its property.

President John Rutledge resigned his office because he felt this document surrendered all hope of reunion with Britain. Arthur Middleton was elected to succeed Rutledge but he declined. Rawlins Lowndes was then elected and served until Rutledge replaced him in January 1779. Christopher Gadsden was chosen as Vice-President and resigned from military service to serve the political office.

After his resignation Gadsden had some not-so-flattering words about General Robert Howe. The two men had passionately argued over the control that the Continental Army had over state officers and soldiers. Gadsden circulated a letter that questioned Howe's legal authority to issue orders to South Carolina Continentals and attacked the general's intelligence and ability as a commander.

### 1778, March 19. POLITICS. RELIGION.

President Rawlings Lowndes approved the changes to the state constitution that changed the title of South Carolina's chief executive's office from president to governor, although he was called "president" until the end of his term.

## 1778, March 24. *Religion.*

Reflecting on the disestablishment of the English church, Baptist minister Oliver Hart wrote that "religion is set free here."

## 1778, March 28. *Religion. Culture.*

Rev. Oliver Hart preached a sermon titled *Dancing Exploded: A Sermon Showing the Unlawfulness, Sinfulness, and Bad Consequences of Balls, Assemblies, and Dances In General.* Hart railed against "our merry gentry, who delight so much in frolicking and dancing." He also condemned their "filthiness, foolish talking, jesting and suchlike things."

## 1778, March 28. *Revolution. Test Act.*

The Assembly passed legislation ordering all males sixteen or older to swear allegiance to South Carolina and agree to defend the state against George III. All citizens had thirty days in which to comply or lose the right to hold office, vote, bring suit, bear arms, serve on juries, buy, sell or hold property, or pursue a trade. This precipitated the first mass exodus of Tories from Charlestown, making the city a predominant Patriot stronghold.

## 1778, March 28. *Religion. Culture.*

Due to the disestablishment of the State Church, St. Philip's Church Library donated all their books to the Charleston Library Society, and closed down its public library, open since 1700.

## 1778, March 29. *Revolution. South Carolina Navy.*

*General Moultrie* and *Fair American* returned to Charlestown with several prizes, and news of the loss of *Randolph* and Captain Biddle.

## 1778, April 1. *Legal. Circuit Court.*

Aedanus Burke was elected as one of several assistant judges for the common law court of South Carolina. It was a circuit court which served six backcountry districts. Twice a year, spring and fall, the judges would travel to Georgetown, Cheraw, Camden or to Beaufort, Orangeburg and Ninety-Six. Burke was also elected to Congress.

Timothy Ford described his impressions of Burke:

> I had formed an idea of his being a very great and dignified and Learned judge. I found him an arrant [sic] Irishman whose conversation though well enough aimed never contained a sentence of good English but on the contrary abounded with blunders, vulgarisms and Hibernianisms. The same was visible on the bench – his ideas seemed amazingly confused and he neither looked nor spoke nor acted like a judge. In short he carried with him less dignity than I have seen for a man of his learning and station ...

### 1778, April 3. *Politics. Election.*

Former President of South Carolina John Rutledge, was elected to the General Assembly.

### 1778, April 10. *Revolution. Backcountry Tory Uprising.*

Gen. Moultrie reported to Gen. Howe that two hundred South Carolina militia had killed and captured a group of Loyalists marching to Georgia. They had been pillaging and burning property on the march toward British-held East Florida.

### 1778, April 16. *Legal. Circuit Court.*

Aedanus Burke conducted his first court session in Orangeburg.

### 1778, April 20. *Politics. Test Act.*

John Lewis Gervais wrote to Henry Laurens that "two vessels full of Tories unwilling to take the oath were preparing to sail from Charlestown."

### 1778, May. *Revolution. South Carolina Navy.*

Alexander Gillon was commissioned as Commodore of the South Carolina State Navy and ordered to Europe to "purchase and equip three frigates." He was given a budget of £500,000 and authorized to sell rice and indigo in Europe to raise the funds.

### 1778, May 11. *William Pitt Dies in London.*

William Pitt, died in London. While rising in Parliament to defend the independence of the colonies, he suffered a heart attack and died.

### 1778, May 21. *Naval. Privateers.*

The Charlestown-based privateer, *Margery*, with Capt. Jacob Milligan, was captured off the Georgia coast.

### 1778, June 5. *Politics. Test Act.*

President Lowndes, pressured by the Continental Congress, issued a proclamation extending the deadline to take the oath set out by the Test Act.

### 1778, June 17. *Politics. Test Act.*

Lowndes wrote to president of the Continental Congress, Henry Laurens:

> Will you not be surprised Sir, to hear that before the Proclamation [extending the deadline for taking the oath] could pass through the formality of a publication the Bells of St. Michaels were set ringing, the people collected and my Conduct reprehended in the severest terms for Contravening an Express law, and superceding the Legislative Authority.

Christopher Gadsden wrote that the proclamation:

> was hardly got into the Sheriff's Hands before some Myrmidons Alarm'd the Town, Setting up a Proclamation against the Law; we were going to ruin their Liberties and what not!

South Carolina president, Rawlins Lowndes. *Author's Collection*

## 1778, June 17. *CONTINENTAL CONGRESS REJECTS CONCILIATION.*

Henry Laurens, president of the Continental Congress, presided over a unanimous vote by the Congress to reject the British offer of conciliation.

## 1778, June 18. *POLITICS.*

William Drayton was forced to resign as Chief Justice for the Province of East Florida, due to his sympathy with the Patriots during the Revolution.

## 1778, June 19. *REVOLUTION. SOUTH CAROLINA NAVY.*

Commodore Alexander Gillon led a South Carolina naval excursion and captured two British vessels.

## 1778, July 4. *REVOLUTION. INDEPENDENCE DAY ADDRESS.*

Dr. David Ramsay gave a public address in celebration of American independence. He stated that "our present form of government is everyway preferable to the royal one we have lately renounced."

## 1778, July 6. REVOLUTION. RIOTS.

A group of angry citizens smashed the windows of Christopher Fitzsimmons's shop for raising the price of candles.

## 1778, July 24. ARTICLES OF CONFEDERATION SIGNED.

The Articles of Confederation were signed by the South Carolina delegation to the Continental Congress, making it one of thirteen unified colonies. South Carolina signers were:

- 🌴 Henry Laurens
- 🌴 William Henry Drayton
- 🌴 John Mathews
- 🌴 Richard Hutson
- 🌴 Thomas Heyward, Jr.

## 1778, August 17. SATISFACTION DEMANDED BY GENERAL HOWE.

General Robert Howe demanded satisfaction from Christopher Gadsden, due to the unflattering letter that Gadsden had written about Howe's military ability.

## 1778, August 30. DUEL.

The duel between General Robert Howe and Vice-president Christopher Gadsden took place. Col. Charles Pinckney, Jr. served as Howe's second, while Col. Bernard Elliot served that role for Gadsden.

Howe missed his first shot at eight paces, grazing Gadsden's ear. Gadsden then intentionally fired into the air and demanded Howe fire a second time. Howe refused. The two men shook hands and parted.

## 1778, September. SOUTH CAROLINA NAVY. GILLON EXPEDITION.

Commodore Gillon, with Captains Joyner, Robertson and McQueen, sailed for France with $500,000 in stolen Spanish silver on *Notre Dame* and escorted by *Oliver Cromwell* of the Connecticut State Navy.

## 1778, September 5. REVOLUTION. COMMERCE.

William Ancrum wrote, "The embargo prevents the exportation of rice notwithstanding I believe some small parcels are shipped off clandestinely and with some risk."

## 1778, September 6. AMERICAN REVOLUTION. DRUNKEN SKIRMISH.

Several drunken French sailors made derisive remarks about Americans. Several drunken patriots take offense and chase the French back to their ship, from which they fired on the town with cannon and small arms. Local militia units returned fire for over an hour, with several casualties and wounded.

## 1778, September 6. POLITICS.

Robert Wells wrote to Henry Laurens that President Lowndes was "very unpopular" and that his "acceptance of the presidency when vacated by Mr.

Rutledge … have gained him the ill will of that powerful family." Lowndes was also unpopular due to "his dealing out the public money with a very sparing hand."

Major General Benjamin Lincoln.
*Courtesy of the New York Public Library*

## 1778, December 4. *GEN. LINCOLN TAKES COMMAND.*

Major General Benjamin Lincoln arrived in Charlestown and was confronted with a chaotic situation. The number of troops was far less than expected; provisions, money and munitions were severely lacking.

## 1778, December 9. *CONTINENTAL CONGRESS. LAURENS RESIGNS.*

Henry Laurens resigned as President of the Continental Congress.

## 1778, December 24. *PHILADELPHIA. DUEL. LAURENS VS. LEE.*

In Philadelphia, Col. John Laurens challenged Gen. Charles Lee to a duel over some insulting words Lee had uttered about George Washington. In an account of the duel, Laurens's second, Col. Alexander Hamilton, wrote:

> General Lee attended by Major Edwards and Col Laurens attended by Col Hamilton met agreeable to appointment on Wednesday afternoon half past three in a wood situate near the four mile stone on the Point no point road. Pistols having been the weapons previously fixed upon, and the combatants being provided with a brace each, it was asked in what manner they were to proceed. General Lee proposed, to advance upon one another and each fire at what time and distance he thought

proper. Col Laurens expressed his preference of this mode, and agreed to the proposal accordingly.

They approached each other within about five or six paces and exchanged a shot almost at the same moment. As Col Laurens was preparing for a second discharge, General Lee declared himself wounded. Col Laurens, as if apprehending the wound to be more serious than it proved advanced towards the general to offer his support. The same was done by Col Hamilton and Major Edwards under a similar apprehension. General Lee then said the wound was inconsiderable, less than he had imagined at the first stroke of the Ball, and proposed to fire a second time. This was warmly opposed both by Col Hamilton and Major Edwards, who declared it to be their opinion that the affair should terminate as it then stood.

## 1778, December 29. *REVOLUTION. SAVANNAH CAPTURED.*

The British captured Savannah, Georgia, giving them a strong base to build up a land force in the South. It placed South Carolina, and Charlestown, directly in the sights of British troops.

Gen. William Moultrie later called Howe's decision to defend Savannah with a too-small force:

> the most ill-advised, rash opinion ... It was absurd to suppose that 6 or 700 men, and some of them very raw troops, could stand up against 2 or 3,000 as good troops as any the British had ... we lost the aid of almost all the citizens of that state [Georgia] as the British immediately encamped the troops along the Savannah River up to Augusta... the loss of Savannah was the occasion of the fall of Charlestown.

# 1779

## 1779, January. *SLAVERY.*

John Laurens presented his plan to command a force of 3,000 armed slaves, with the promise of their freedom before the South Carolina Assembly. Even though Continental Congress had approved the plan, the proposal was rejected by the Assembly "with comtemptuous huzzahs."

Henry Laurens consoled his son that "rich men [do not] part willingly with the source of their wealth." Christopher Gadsden told Sam Adams that he was "disgusted" by such a "dangerous and impolitic step."

## 1779, January. *SOUTH CAROLINA NAVY. GILLON EXPEDITION.*

Commodore Gillon of the South Carolina State Navy arrived in Brest, France. Unfortunately, France was on a war footing and there were no acceptable ships available, most already have been conscripted by the French navy.

Gillon asked Benjamin Franklin to use his influence with the French, but Franklin refused, claiming that he represented the Continental Congress, not individual states. Gillon sarcastically called Franklin "Ye Superior American Naval Officer in Europe." This created a lifelong feud between Gillon and Franklin. John Paul Jones, a friend of Franklin, called Gillon "the red-ribboned commodore" due to his habit of overdressing in elaborate uniforms.

Lt. Colonel John Laurens
*Courtesy of the New York Public Library*

## 1779, January 27. *REVOLUTION. JOHN ASHE ARRIVES.*

Eleven hundred men of the North Carolina militia arrived in Charlestown, commanded by Maj. Gen. John Ashe.

## 1779, January 31. *REVOLUTION. BATTLE OF BEAUFORT.*

The British navy entered Port Royal Sound in Beaufort. At the same time, Gen. Moultrie arrived in Beaufort with 270 militiamen commanded by Brig. General Stephen Bull. A contingent of the Charlestown Artillery also arrived with two six-pound field pieces, led by Captains Edward Rutledge and Thomas Heyward, Jr., two signers of the Declaration of Independence.

The *South Carolina and American General Gazette* described Moultrie's arrival as, "an event that gave general joy, as it inspired us with a well-founded confidence that he would lead us to honor and victory."

## 1779, February. *SOUTH CAROLINA. PRIVATEERING.*

The 14-gun brigantine *Hornet*, built at Hobcaw shipyard, left Charlestown for her cruise. She almost immediately captured two British ships off the coast of Georgia, *Royal Charlotte* and *Prince of Wales*.

## 1779, February 3. *Revolution. Battle of Beaufort.*

The Americans established a position on the highest ground on Port Royal Island, called Gray's Hill. About 4 P.M. the British landed and emerged from the trees with fixed bayonets, and approached the American position. Gen. Moultrie ordered Capt. Heyward to open fire with the artillery, and then with musket volleys. The battle continued for about forty-five minutes until the Americans began running low on ammunition. Moultrie ordered a slow withdrawal. However, at the same time, the British retreated so Moultrie ordered a company of light horse militia led by John Barnwell to chase the British off the field, and almost cut them off from their boats.

The British suffered forty killed and wounded; the Americans suffered eight dead and twenty-two wounded, including Thomas Heyward, Jr. Even though the battle was a small skirmish, it was considered a positive tactical victory for the Americans.

In a letter to Charles Pinckney, Jr., Moultrie commented:

> I find my old bones yield much to fatigue; I hope, however, they will carry me through the war; then I will set me down in peace, and indulge myself the remainder of my days.

## 1779, February. *Election. Lowndes Resigns.*

Rawlins Lowndes stepped down as chief executive and John Rutledge was elected Governor of South Carolina less than one year after his resignation.

## 1779, February 16. *Revolution.*

Despite the victory at the Battle of Beaufort, British forces were steadily advancing from Savannah north toward Charlestown. Oliver Hart, minister of the First Baptist Church told his brother that "unless providence remarkably interposes on our behalf, we are an undone people."

## 1779, February 24. *Politics. Legal.*

The *State Gazette* reported that Aedanus Burke and Thomas Heyward had been elected assistant judges by the General Assembly.

## 1779, March. *South Carolina Navy.*

During a ten-day expedition, five ships of the South Carolina Navy – *General Moultrie, Sally, Family Trader, Hornet* and *Notre Dame* – captured four British merchant ships.

## 1779, March 2. *Birth.*

Joel Roberts Poinsett, future American statesman and botanist, was born in Charleston. The poinsettia was named after him.

## 1779, March 9. *REVOLUTION. EXECUTION.*

Andrew Groundwater and William Tweed were hanged for treason. Both men had refused to take the oath of fidelity and were arrested for carrying a message from a British prisoner of war to Colonel Archibald Campbell. According to Charles Pinckney:

> some interest was made for Groundwater ... he had been captain of a small vessel, and had been of service in the bringing in to us stores and many necessary articles which we were in want of ... [but also] strongly suspected of being concerned with Tweed in setting fire to the town on Trott's point ... the inhabitants were so incensed against him, that he suffered, to appease the people.

Aedanus Burke. *Courtesy of the New York Public Library*

## 1779, March 19. *SLAVERY. EXECUTION.*

A slave "was burnt on the Commons near this town for setting fire to his master's stable a few weeks since."

## 1779, April 19. *REVOLUTION. COUNCIL OF WAR.*

Gen. Lincoln called a council of war in Purrysburg (modern-day Hardeeville, S.C). to formulate a plan to cross the Savannah River with 5,000 troops and engage the British in Georgia. The plan would leave 1,200 troops in the Charlestown area for the defense of the lowcountry. The council included Lincoln, Gen. Moultrie, and Brig. Generals Issac Huger and Jethro Sumner of North Carolina.

Lincoln left Purrysburg and marched toward Augusta, Georgia with 2,000 light infantry and cavalry.

## 1779, April 28. COMMERCE.

William Ancrum noted: "Of late very few arrivals and no wagons as usual coming to town, little or no business is done in the shopkeeping way."

## 1779, May 3. JOHN LAURENS WOUNDED.

British troops are defeated in a skirmish at Coosawhatchie, but Col. John Laurens was wounded when his horse was shot out from underneath him.

## 1779, May 7. SLAVERY.

Thomas Pinckney complained that British raiders took nine slaves from his Ashepoo plantation and the rest "are now perfectly free and live upon the best provence of the plantation." He also complained that the negroes no longer paid any attention to the overseer.

## 1779, May 11. REVOLUTION. SIEGE OF CHARLESTOWN.

British general Augustine Prevost crossed the Ashley River onto the Charlestown peninsula with about 3,600 troops. He informed Governor John Rutledge that he would regard as prisoners of war those "inhabitants" who did not choose to accept his "generous offers of peace and protection" upon surrender of the city.

Rutledge offered to keep South Carolina out of the war for the safety of Charlestown and its garrison of 3,100 troops: He responded in writing:

> To propose a neutrality, during the war between Great-Britain and America, and the question, whether the state shall belong to Great Britain or remain one of the United States ... be determined by the treaty of peace between these two powers.

General William Moultrie and his officers were adamantly opposed to Rutledge's offer. When Moultrie asked Lt. Colonel John Laurens to deliver the message to Gen. Provost he replied, "I would do anything to serve my country, but I will not carry a message such as this."

Ultimately, Gen. Prevost rejected the proposal because it was a political decision, not a military one, He stated that his business was "with General Moultrie as military commander and has nothing to do with the governor."

Moultrie informed Rutledge and the privy council that he was "determined not to deliver up prisoners of war ... we will fight it out." He informed Gen. Prevost of his decision to defend the city.

## 1779, May 13. *REVOLUTION. FORTIFICATIONS.*

Gen. Prevost and the British army retreated back to Georgia. After that close call Gen. Lincoln determined that the city's fixed defenses needed to be improved along the neck - the narrow northern end of the peninsula. Back in the 1750s the "line" had been constructed under the direction of a French engineer William Gerard de Brahm – trenches and earthworks in a line that started along an Ashley River tidal creek (close to present-day Smith Street, north of present-day Calhoun Street) and ran eastward toward the Cooper River across King Street, (through present-day Marion Square) and Meeting Street along present-day Charlotte Street, turning northward to present-day Chapel Street.

## 1779, May 20. *REVOLUTION. SIEGE OF CHARLESTOWN.*

British troops, under the cover of darkness, attacked and routed a force of Patriot militia that had been guarding the Stono River plantation of Capt. John Raven Matthews. The British gave no quarter to the Patriots (a theme that was to be repeated often in South Carolina) and cut them to ribbons.

Lt. Col. Robert Barnwell was left for dead with seventeen bayonet wounds, but he survived and led his men at the Siege of Charleston the next year.

## 1779, June 20. *SIEGE OF CHARLESTOWN. BATTLE OF STONO FERRY.*

Gen. Lincoln attacked Gen. Prevost and the British at the Stono River Ferry. Due to Gen. Moultrie's delay in crossing onto James Island with a support unit of 750 men, the battle was a British victory.

## 1779, June 22. *SIEGE OF CHARLESTOWN. BATTLE OF STONO FERRY.*

A South Carolina naval squadron to moved down to the Stono River to support Moultrie's attack on Prevost's retreating troops. The galleys *Rutledge* and *Marquis de Bretagne,* and the schooner *Rattlesnake* anchored at Stono Ferry (present-day Limehouse Bridge) and fired at Prevot's retreating army.

*Rattlesnake* ran aground and was attacked by Hessian troops fighting for the British. Determining the situation hopeless, Captain Frisbie ordered *Rattlesnake* set on fire and abandoned. The crew managed to return to Charlestown on foot.

Alarmed by the British attack, Gov. Rutledge and General Lincoln wrote to French Admiral Comte D'Estaing in the West Indies pleading the French to come to South Carolina's aid. Seeing that a quick victory over the British was possible, D'Estaing decided to sail to Charlestown.

## 1779, July. *REVOLUTION. SIEGE OF CHARLESTOWN. SLAVERY.*

The South Carolina Assembly rejected "with horror" a Congressional recommenddation that South Carolina "raise three thousand black soldiers." Gadsden wrote that this "dangerous and impolitic Step ... much disgusted us."

## 1779, August 15. BIRTH.

Joseph Alston was born in Charleston. He was a future governor of South Carolina and inherited one of the state's largest fortunes.

## 1779, September. REVOLUTION. ECONOMY.

By this time paper money in South Carolina was practically worthless. Gen. Lincoln commented "that I apprehend that, unless something is done to increase its value, it will not long answer the purpose of carrying on the war."

Many wealthy lowcountry men, like Gen. Moultrie, loaned the government nine thousand pounds.

## 1779, September 4. REVOLUTION. FRENCH ARRIVE.

French Admiral Comte D'Estaing arrived in Charlestown with fifty-one ships and 4,000 troops, most likely the most powerful naval force ever off Charlestown.

## 1779, September 12. REVOLUTION. NAVAL.

Most of the French troops landed in the Tybee Island area. One of the troops was a young drummer boy, Henry Christophe, who later would become the future "King of Haiti" and lead the Haitian revolution against France.

## 1779, October 9. SIEGE OF SAVANNAH. JASPER KILLED.

A major assault on Savannah by 4,000 French and American forces failed to free the city from the British. Sgt. Jasper, hero of the Battle of Ft. Sullivan, died in the attack. Count Casimir Pulaski, a colorful Polish nobleman and considered the father of American calvalry, was also killed.

Gen. Moultrie wrote, "This disappointment depressed our spirits very much and we began to be apprehensive for the safety of these two southern states."

## 1779, October 15. MARRIAGE.

Gen. William Moultrie married the widow Hannah Motte Lynch, mother of Thomas Lynch Jr, a signer of the Declaration of Independence. The ceremony took place at St. Philips's Church.

## 1779, October 21. CONTINENTAL CONGRESS. POLITICS.

Henry Laurens was elected Minister to Holland by the Continental Congress. He was to procure a $10,000,000 loan to finance the war effort.

## 1779, November 4. REVOLUTION. NAVAL. DISASTER.

A hurricane hit the South Carolina-Georgia coast, damaging many of the South Carolina and French ships. The French returned to the West Indies, and South Carolina began to prepare for the coming British attack on Charlestown.

## 1779, November 5. *BIRTH.*

Washington Allston was born on a rice plantation, near Georgetown, on the Waccamaw River. He would grow up to pioneer America's Romantic movement of landscape painting.

## 1779, November 19. *REVOLUTION. ARRIVALS.*

Lt. Col. William Washington, second cousin to George Washington was transferred from New Jersey to the Southern theatre of war, to join the army of Major General Benjamin Lincoln in Charlestown.

## 1779, December. *REVOLUTION. FORTIFICATIONS.*

Gen. Lincoln wrote to the Continental Congress, reporting that Charlestown "is uncovered by works, and we have no expectation that it will soon be in a better state."

Washington Allston, self-portrait. Born in Georgetown, South Carolina.
*Courtesy of the Library of Congress*

## 1779, December 23. *SIEGE OF CHARLESTOWN.*

Commodore Abraham Whipple arrived in Charlestown with the 28-gun frigates *Providence, Queen of France* and *Boston* and the 18-gun sloop-of-war *Ranger*. Henry Laurens had convinced the Continental Congress to send what amounted to one-third of the Continental Navy's warships.

### 1779, December 26. *Siege of Charlestown. Naval.*

Sir Henry Clinton, British commander, left New York City with a fleet of over 100 ships to transport 8,700 men, horses and other supplies to attack Charlestown. Second in command of the force was Lt. General Charles Cornwallis.

Due to the military stalemate in the north, and despite the two previous efforts to take the city, Clinton still thought Charlestown was an attainable prize.

# 1780

### 1780. January. *Religion.*

Jacob Tobias purchased "a lot and brick building in Hasell Street for 310 guineas." From that time forward the Jewish congregation, Beth Elohim, "assembled in Hasell Street at the old synagogue lately occupied by Mr. Little, as a cotton gin manufactory."

### 1780. January. *Eutaw Flag Given to William Washington.*

William Washington and his troops camped at Charles Elliot's Sandy Hill Plantation. Elliott's daughter, Jane, inquired about Washington's flag and he responded "I do not have one."

Jane cut off the crimson silk end of a rich damask curtain and told him, "Let this be your flag, sir!" From that day forward, it was waved at the forefront of every battle in which he engaged. It picked up the name "Eutaw Flag," when Washington was injured and captured at the Battle of Eutaw Springs.

### 1780, January. *Revolution. Laurens Sails to Europe.*

Henry Laurens sailed to the Netherlands to negotiate Dutch support for the war.

### 1780, January 20. *Revolution. Clinton Sails South.*

Sir Henry Clinton arrived at Cape Fear, North Carolina. There he waited for the arrival of reinforcements from Britain.

### 1780, January 31. *Siege of Charlestown. Slavery.*

Continental Army General Benjamin Lincoln requested that Governor Rutledge "order 1,500 Negroes to assemble in the vicinity of this town with the necessary tools for throwing up lines immediately."

### 1780, February. *Politics. High Price of Salt.*

Aedanus Burke presented a petition to the Assembly in support of the backcountry men complaining about the "high price of salt" and that the per diem allowance to militiamen was "insufficient and not regularly paid."

### 1780, February 3. *Politics. "Dictator" Rutledge.*

With forethought rarely seen in modern politics, the General Assembly, in their last act before adjourning, gave Governor John Rutledge "extraordinary powers for a period to end ten days after the next meeting of the legislature." He thus became known as "Dictator" Rutledge.

### 1780, February 8. *Siege of Charlestown. Commerce.*

Peter Timothy closed his print shop, citing lack of material due to the British blocking supply lines by sea and by land.

### 1780, February 8. *Siege of Charlestown*

Colonel Charles Cotesworth Pinckney, commander of Ft. Moultrie, complained to Gen. Lincoln he was short both men and ammunition. He requested 1,215 troops to man the walls, artillery and defensive works. He only had 200. He wrote, "If half cannot be obtained, I shall make the best defense in my power with the number that may be allowed me."

### 1780, February 10. *Siege of Charlestown*

North Carolina militia, 1,250 strong, arrived in Charlestown. Meanwhile, the British fleet, commanded by Admiral Marriot Arbuthnot, sounded the North Edisto River and marked the channel.

### 1780, February 11. *Siege of Charlestown.*

British troops landed on Simond's Island (present-day Seabrook Island). Flat-bottomed boats carried troops and supplies up the Wadmalaw and Stono Rivers.

### 1780, February 15. *Siege of Charlestown.*

Peter Timothy took the post in the steeple of St. Michael's Church to report on British land and sea movements. He could see smoke from the British encampments on John's Island and numerous ships off the Charlestown bar.

The British army crossed the Stono River from John's Island to James Island, giving them a staging area and view of Charlestown across the Ashley River. They settled in to wait for the British navy to cross the Charleston bar to reinforce and resupply the army. Over the next five weeks Clinton's army seized corn, oxen, cattle, horses, pigs and other supplies from dozens of plantations in the area.

### 1780, February 16. *Siege of Charlestown. Harbor Blockaded.*

From his post in St. Michael's steeple, Peter Timothy reported that "3 of the British Men of War ... paraded before the Harbour" and an enemy frigate "in full view of the Town as if challenging our ships to go out." He also noted the ships "effectively blockaded the harbor.

### 1780, February 19. SIEGE OF CHARLESTOWN. BACON'S BRIDGE

Gen. Lincoln ordered Gen. Moultrie to take 600 men, cavalry and light infantry, to Bacon's Bridge on the Ashley River near Dorchester. Lincoln was convinced the British would cross the river there and approach Charlestown from the north. Two of Moultrie's officers were Lt. Col. William Washington, and Francis Marion.

### 1780, February 24. SIEGE OF CHARLESTOWN.

Lord Cornwallis's British force crossed onto James Island at Grimball's Cross Roads (near present-day James Island County Park).

### 1780, February 28. SIEGE OF CHARLESTOWN. FORT JOHNSON.

The British had advanced to the harbor side of James Island and the abandoned Fort Johnson.

### 1780, March. SIEGE OF CHARLESTOWN. EXECUTION.

Early in March Gen. Lincoln ordered that Hamilton Ballendine be hanged. Ballendine, who had attempted to leave the Continental garrison and provide information to the British, was "hanged at Charlestown today in Sight of our Lines," wrote Captain Russell.

### 1780, March 7. SIEGE OF CHARLESTOWN. BRIDGE CONSTRUCTED OVER WAPPOO.

British engineers constructed a bridge over the Wappoo Cut and Cornwallis's Light Infantry crossed onto the mainland.

### 1780, March 9. SIEGE OF CHARLESTOWN. SOUTH CAROLINA NAVY.

South Carolina decided to scuttle five ships – *Notre Dame, General Moultrie, Bricole, Truite* and *Queen of France* in the Cooper River near Shute's Folly. Chevaux de frize were placed on their decks and the five ships were bound together with a boom tied to their masts. This effectively blocked the upper Cooper River from British boats, which left that section of water available for Charlestown reinforcement and escape. This effectively ended operations of the South Carolina navy.

### 1780, March 9. SIEGE OF CHARLESTOWN. BACON'S BRIDGE.

Gen. Moultrie was forced to return to Charlestown for convalescence from the "nervous fever," a term used to describe typhoid. Gen. Issac Huger replaced Moultrie in command.

### 1780, March 10. SIEGE OF CHARLESTOWN. BACON'S BRIDGE.

Lt. Colonel William Washington's regiment joined forces with the remnants of the 1st Continental Light Dragoons at Bacon's Bridge (20 miles north of Charlestown) to reconnoiter, screen and disrupt the advancing British troop. They felled trees across roads, burned bridges and boats in an effort to slow the march toward Charlestown.

## 1780, March 14. *SIEGE OF CHARLESTOWN.*

The British mounted a battery of six 32-pounder guns at the north of Wappoo Creek at Fenwick's Point. These guns could shoot into the western side of the city, but were mainly used to keep South Carolina naval vessels off the Ashley River.

## 1780, March 17. *NEGROES CAPTURED BY BRITISH.*

By this time the British army had 317 captured Negroes in their service. Major John Andre requested "500 blankets and 500 hats for Negro clothing.

## 1780, March 19. *FRANCIS MARION BREAKS ANKLE.*

Captain Alexander McQueen held a dinner party at his home at 106 Tradd Street. After dinner, McQueen locked all doors and began to propose a series of toasts. One of his guests, Lt. Colonel Francis Marion, was not a heavy drinker. He removed himself from the house by dropping out of a second floor window, breaking his ankle.

106 Tradd Street, the John Stuart House, photo from the 1950s.

From one of these side windows, Francis Marion jumped onto Orange Street and broke his ankle.
*Courtesy of the Library of Congress*

## 1780, March 20. *BRITISH BATTERY AT ALBEMARLE POINT.*

Lt. General Cornwallis established a battery on the Ashley River at Albemarle Point, near the site of the first Charlestown settlement in 1670, less than 2,000 yards away, easily within reach of the three twenty-two pound and two twenty-pound cannons. That night, with the spring flood high tide, the British fleet finally crossed the Charlestown bar, blockading the harbor. Charlestown was now cut off by sea.

Col. Charles Cotesworth Pinckney was in command of the undermanned 1st South Carolina at Ft. Moultrie. It was the only defense between the British navy and the city. He knew, however, that the city expected the same performance from his troops as they had on June 28, 1776, when Col. Moultrie defeated Peter Parker.

## 1780, March 22. *SIEGE OF CHARLESTOWN. ANDREWS TAKEN.*

Gen. Clinton ordered "light troops" into St. Andrews Parish, west of the Ashley River, to facilitate the consolidation of British troops from Georgia.

## 1780, March 26. *SIEGE OF CHARLESTOWN. FORTIFICATIONS.*

Gen. Lincoln ordered Gen. Moultrie, now recovered from his "fever," to oversee the construction of batteries and works in Charlestown. Along the Charleston Neck seventy-nine guns were mounted in sixteen batteries. Along the waterfront, ninety-five guns were mounted in ten batteries.

## 1780, March 26. *WASHINGTON ENGAGES TARLETON.*

Lt. Colonel Washington had his first encounter with the British Legion, under command of Lt. Colonel Banastre Tarleton. It was a minor Patriot victory near Rantowle's Bridge on the Stono River. Later that same day, during the fight at Rutledge's Plantation on the Ashley River, Lt. Col. Washington again bested a detachment of Tarleton's dragoons and infantry.

Col. William Washington.
*Courtesy of the New York Public Library*

## 1780, March 27. SIEGE OF CHARLESTOWN.

From St. Michael' steeple, Peter Timothy reported over thirty British flatboats along the Wappoo Cut "skulking in the marsh."

## 1780, March 28. SIEGE OF CHARLESTOWN. DRAYTON HALL TAKEN.

Under the cover of darkness, the British rowed the flatboats up the Ashley River at Drayton Hall, thirteen miles north of Charlestown and then marched to Drayton Hall. Gen. William Moultrie noted in his diary, "The enemy crossed Ashley river, in force, above the ferry."

## 1780, March 29. BRITISH ARMY LANDS ON THE CHARLESTON NECK.

The British army advanced on the Neck, two miles north of the Continental lines, approximately near the present-day site of the Citadel. The army numbered 13,572 men, the largest operational force during the entire Revolutionary War.

Due to lack of men, the Continental army could not stop the British crossing. Gen. Lincoln gambled by keeping the bulk of the Southern Army within the city. However, he ordered a light infantry unit, led by Col. John Laurens, to take up a post outside the city's fortifications "to watch the motions of the Enemy and prevent too sudden an approach." He also wrote to the Continental Congress:

> We have to lament that, from the want of Men, we are denied the advantages of opposing them with any considerable force in crossing this river.

General Lincoln and General George Washington both preferred to let the British have Charlestown, and concentrate their forces in situations that were more advantageous to the Continental Army. However, Governor Rutledge, and other South Carolina authorities, refused to abandon the city, so Lincoln was forced to use his meager resources in an attempt to defend Charlestown.

In hindsight, had Lincoln decided to abandon Charlestown to the British, patriot support for the war may well have disappeared, and, different outcome of the Revolution may have happened.

## 1780, March 30. LAURENS ATTACKS BRITISH.

First action that morning was led by Col. John Laurens's unit against the advancing British light infantry. After several hours of scattered battle, Laurens's men retreated back behind the city's fortifications at dark. Laurens described it as "a frolicking skirmish for our young soldiers." It was the first engagement fought within sight of the city, or as one officer noted, "in view of ... many ladies."

The British set up camp at Gibbes Landing (present-day Lownde's Grove), which was a perfect staging area from which to lay siege to Charlestown.

## 1780, April 1. BRITISH SEIGEWORKS CONSTRUCTED.

Under cover of darkness, 3,000 men marched from the British camp at Gibb's Landing toward Charlestown. – including 1500 laborers. They stopped 1,000 yards from the city's fortifications and began construction of their own siege works. Due to the sandy soil "the work went quickly" and within one night Gen. Clinton was amazed they "completed 3 Redoubts and a communication without a singer shot."

The following morning, Samuel Baldwin of Charlestown wrote: "We were surprised ... at the sight of the works thrown up by our neighbors during the night."

### 1780, April 3. SIEGE OF CHARLESTOWN. FIRING ON THE BRITISH.

American artillery, which consisted of over 200 pieces, fired on the newly constructed British works all day with little effect – 300 shot and 30 shells. The British continued their construction of battlements without pause.

### 1780, April 4. DESCRIPTION OF BOMBARDMENT.

John Lewis Gervais in Charlestown wrote that the American batteries "fired a great deal all night & threw Several shells at the Ennemy's Works" - a total of 573 cannonballs. Since the British were unable to return fire, they continued the construction of their fortifications.

### 1780, April 5. SIEGE OF CHARLESTOWN. BRITISH RETURN FIRE.

After dark Gen. Clinton ordered the British battery at Fenwick's Point and the Wappoo Cut, across the Ashley River, to fire upon Charlestown. The cannonballs, whistling through the dark sky over the city, created a "terrible clamor" with "the loud wailing of female voices."

One of the British cannonballs struck Mr. Thomas Elfe's house at 54 Queen Street, and two damaged Governor John Rutledge's house on Broad Street. Rutledge wrote that he was appalled at "the insulting Manner in which the Enemy's Gallies have fired, with Impunity, on the Town."

Also, the British galley *Scourge* fired eighty-five times with "every shot ... into town." During the night three British soldiers deserted to the American side. One of the soldiers "paddled himself over on a plank from James Island

### 1780, April 7. AMERICAN REINFORCEMENTS ARRIVE.

A group of 700 battle-tested veteran Virginia Continentals sent by Gen. George Washington arrived in Charlestown. They crossed the Wando River and landed at Christopher Gadsden's wharf. They marched through town to the lines to the pealing of church bells. At the lines they were greeted with cheers and a firing of thirteen cannons, one for each of the independent states.

### 1780, April 8. SIEGE OF CHARLESTOWN. BRITISH NAVY ENTERS HARBOR.

During the afternoon, the British fleet weighed anchor and nine warships and three transports moved up the channel to Ft. Moultrie. At half past four Peter Timothy said that "the Admiral has received & returned the Fire of Ft. Moultrie and passed it without any apparent Damage." They landed at Ft. Johnson on James Island.

In less than ninety minutes eleven British ships had sailed past and were safely out of the range of Ft. Moultrie's forty guns. Peter Timothy commented:

> They really make a most noble appearance and I could not help admiring the regularity and intrepidity with which they approached, engaged, and passed Fort Moultrie. It will reflect great honor upon the admiral and all his captains, but 'tis pity they are not friends.

---

### SIEGE WARFARE

Three principal types of artillery were used during the Revolutionary War: field guns, howizters and mortars.

- **Field Guns:** Mounted on large-wheeled carriages and fixed to fire at low angles. Varied in size from three-pound (weight of solid shot fired) to forty-two pounds. Larger guns weighed appx. 5000 pounds (2½ tons).
- **Howizters:** Similar to field guns, but with shorter and stockier barrels. Could be fired at a low or high angle. Range: 1300-2000 yards.
- **Mortars:** A useful weapon because of its small size and ease of movement. It usually had a fixed trajectory (around 45 degrees), and the distance the shot traveled was adjusted by varying the powder charge. Just like the howitzer, the use of the exploding shell was popular to reach troops inside fortifications. Range: 2000 yards.

---

### 1780, April 8. SIEGE OF CHARLESTOWN. REFUSES TO SURRENDER.

General Henry Clinton issued a summons of surrender to be delivered to Gen. Lincoln who replied that "Duty and Inclination point to the propriety of supporting it [Charlestown] to the last extremity."

### 1780, April 12. SIEGE OF CHARLESTOWN. TARLETON'S QUARTER.

Col. Tarleton surprised General Issac Huger's mounted troops at Biggin's Bridge in Monck's Corner. The British captured forty-two wagons and 185 horses. Major Vernier was mortally wounded by Tarleton, *after* his surrender. This may be the first documented case of what become known as "Tarleton's Quarter."

### 1780, April 12. GOV. RUTLEDGE URGED TO LEAVE.

Lincoln called a meeting of his generals to sign a letter urging Gov. Rutledge to leave the city, in order to "Preserve the Executive Authority ... give confidence to the people and throw in the necessary succours and supplies to garrison."

Rutledge had resisted previous calls to leave out of fear that his reputation would suffer for having abandoned the city. This time, however, Rutledge agreed to leave, with three members of his Privy Council. Christopher Gadsden was appointed Lt. Governor, replacing Thomas Bee, who was attending the Continental Congress.

### 1780, April 14. *William Washington Captured & Escapes.*

Lt. Colonel Tarleton and his British dragoons took an American cavalry encamp-ment commanded by General Issac Huger, at Middleton's Plantation in Goose Creek. In a surprise attack, Tarleton's troops killed fifteen and captured eighteen. Tarleton noted that "Lt. Colonel Washington was Prisoner but afterward thro' the Darkness of the Morn escaped on foot."

This action effectively cut off Gen. Lincoln's escape route from Charlestown. The Continental Army was now stuck in the city.

### 1780, April 16. *Siege of Charlestown. Pitt Statue Damaged.*

A British cannon, fired from the James Island battery, shot off the arm of the statue of William Pitt in the intersection of Broad and Meeting Streets. After the war, the statue was later moved to the Grimke house at 321 East Bay Street. In 1808 it was moved to the Charleston Orphan House and in 1881 moved again to Washington Park. Presently it stands inside the entrance of the Charleston County Court House. *(See page 261)*

### 1780, April 18. *Siege of Charlestown. British Reinforced.*

More than 3,000 British reinforcements arrived from New York. Sir Clinton ordered 2,300 troops to Mt. Pleasant, in order to control the eastern side of the Cooper River. He named Lt. General Cornwallis commander of that force.

At this time, the Americans had 4,200 men in Charlestown fit for duty while the British counted 8,300.

### 1780, April 19. *Siege of Charlestown.*

Henry Laurens wrote to Gen. Lincoln, "I pray God to give you victory or open a door for an honorable retreat."

### 1780, April 20-21. *Lincoln Proposes Surrender Terms.*

Gen. Lincoln convened the council of war in the city. He informed his officers that the garrison had ten days of provisions left, and discussed offering terms of capitulation to Sir Henry Clinton,– surrendering the city. His terms were:

- The American army withdrawing from Charlestown within thirty-six hours, keeping their arms, artillery and all stores they were able to transport.
- Sir Clinton was to allow the Americans ten days "to march wherever Gen. Lincoln may think proper ... without any movement being made by the British troops."
- Security to the persons and property of the citizens

Clinton rejected the terms, considering the offer "insolence." At 10:30 P.M. the British resumed their bombardment, firing more than 800 rounds into the city.

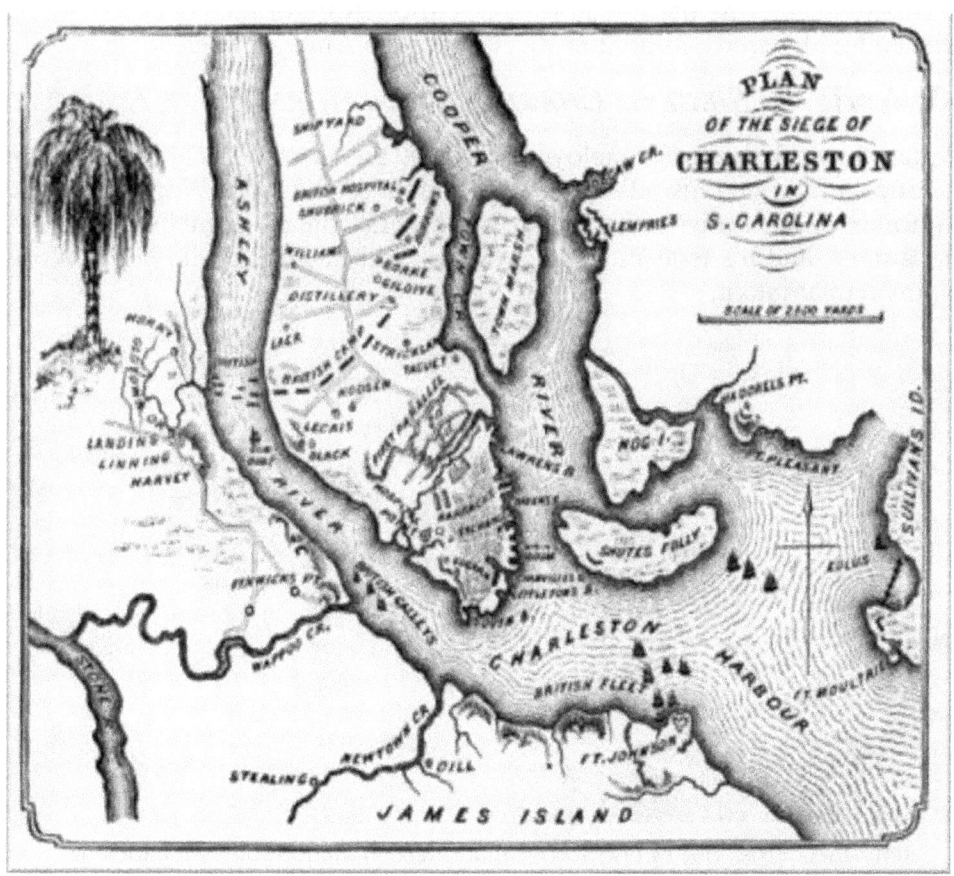
British plan for the siege of Charlestown, 1780. *Courtesy of the Library of Congress*

### 1780, April 23. *SIEGE OF CHARLESTOWN.*

The British were close enough to "easily throw a stone" into the American line trenches. Rifle fire was added to siege, in addition to the artillery barrage.

### 1780, April 24. *BRITISH LINES ATTACKED.*

At dawn, Lt. Colonel William Henderson attacked the British lines with 200 men – South Carolina and Virginia Continentals. They caught the British troops completely by surprise, killing several with bayonets before retreating. The attack "was done in a few Minutes without our partys firing a Single Gun & in the greatest order." Capt. Thomas Moultrie (brother of Gen. Moultrie) and two privates were killed.

### 1780, April 26. *SIEGE OF CHARLESTOWN.*

Gen. Lincoln and his war council vowed to continue the fight, although the city was effectively surrounded and the men worked "the whole day under the heaviest cannon and small arms fire." Due to the hellish nature of the conditions the line soldiers endured, desertions became an issue for the American defenders.

### 1780, April 29. SIEGE OF CHARLESTOWN. HORN WORK ENCLOSED.

American workers were "employed in closing the Horn Work" behind the lines. Gen. Lincoln informed his officers "that he intended the Horn Work as a place of retreat for the whole army" if the British drove them from the main line. Lt. Colonel John Laurens, and his light infantry, was assigned in front of the Horn Work to cover any retreat into it.

Remnants of the "Horn work" fortifications (left) in Marion Square, Charleston.
*Courtesy of the Library of Congress*

### 1780, May 1. SIEGE OF CHARLESTOWN. FOOD SUPPLIES SCARCE.

Provisions for the American army was reduced to seven weeks of rice. In order to taunt the Americans, the British began to fire shells armed, not with gunpowder and lead, but with rice & sugar.

Being cut off from supply lines, Lt. Governor Gadsden permitted Lincoln's officers to confiscate foodstuffs from citizen's houses. They discovered "scare a sufficiency for the supply of private families." So far, more than twenty civilians had been killed and thirty houses burned by British artillery.

### 1780, May 2. SIEGE OF CHARLESTOWN. HADDRELL'S POINT TAKEN.

Loyalist, Maj. Patrick Ferguson and sixty American Volunteers, marched to Haddrell's Point to attack the small fort that stood on a causeway that led to Fort Moultrie. The fort, about 150 yards from the mainland, was defended by Capt. John Williams and twenty soldiers of the South Carolina 1st Regiment. The British took the fort with the cannons from Fort Moultrie firing on them until dark. The British soon fortified the fort for a possible attack.

### 1780, May 3. *EDWARD RUTLEDGE CAPTURED.*

Edward Rutledge, brother of Gov. John Rutledge and signer of the Declaration of Independence, was captured by British cavalry with two other officers east of the Cooper. He was attempting to sneak out of the city with letters and communications to his brother and other officials.

### 1780, May 4. *SIEGE OF CHARLESTOWN. SULLIVAN'S ISLAND.*

The British landed 500 sailors and marines on Sullivan's Island.

### 1780, May 5. *SIEGE OF CHARLESTOWN.*

Col. Bantasre Tarleton defeated a large American cavalry, capturing sixty-seven officers and more than 100 horses.

### 1780, May 6. *SIEGE OF CHARLESTOWN.*

Knowing of the extreme conditions within the city, Sir Clinton was frustrated by the American resistance. He wrote, "I begin to think these people will be Blockheads enough to wait the assault."

### 1780, May 6. *SIEGE OF CHARLESTOWN. LANNEAU'S FERRY MASSACRE.*

The remnants of Gen. Issac Huger's dragoons, numbering about forty, werekilled and captured by Col. Tarleton.

### 1780, May 7. *SIEGE OF CHARLESTOWN. FORT MOULTRIE FALLS.*

Ft. Moultrie fell to the British. Not only was this militarily significant, but for most citizens it was psychologically devastating. Moultrie had successfully repulsed the British on June 28, 1776 – Carolina Day – but was now under the enemy's control, the British flag flying from its ramparts.

Several years later, Gen. Moultrie related his actions to secure the city's gunpowder from the British:

> The old magazine behind St. Philip's Church in consequence of that shelling so near, I had the powder (10,000 pounds) removed to the north east corner, under the exchange, and had the doors and windows bricked up. Not-withstanding, the British had possession of Charlestown so long, they never discovered the powder, although their provost was the next apartment to it, and after the evacuations, when we came into town, we found the powder as we left it.

### 1780, May 8. *SIEGE OF CHARLESTOWN. CEASE FIRE ORDERED. SURRENDER DISCUSSED.*

Colonel Grimke recorded, "no more Meat served out." The city was facing starvation conditions.

Gen. Lincoln convened the war council within the Horn Work to discuss Sir Clinton's new summons of surrender. A twenty-four-hour cease fire was ordered for the Americans to consider the offer. Most soldiers had survived on small rations of sugar, rice and coffee for several days. And now the rations had run out.

Gen. Moultrie welcomed the cease fire. He wrote that fatigue "was so great, for want of sleep, that many faces were so swelled they could scarcely see out of their eyes." Many of the militia "Looked upon all the business as settled, and without orders, took up their baggage and walked into town, leaving the lines quite defenceless."

Sixty-one officers composed the war council that met with Gen. Lincoln. A vote of 49-12 favored offering surrender terms to the British. The twelve dissenters included Col. Charles Cotesworth Pinckney and Lt. Col. John Laurens, natives of Charlestown. Lincoln ordered the officers to draw up articles for surrender, which was sent to Sir Clinton that night.

## 1780, May 9. *Siege of Charlestown. Clinton Refuses Surrender.*

Sir Clinton refused Lincoln's terms of surrender and order hostilities to commence at 8:00 P.M. Lt. Colonel Grimke wrote it was "a most furious cannonade & bombardment which continued throughout the night." Overnight the British launched 814 shots into the city, and the Americans responded with 380. Gen. Moultrie called it "a dreadful night."

## 1780, May 11. *Siege of Charlestown. Gadsden Encourages Surrender.*

Lt. Governor Gadsden wrote to Gen. Lincoln encouraging him that "no time should be lost in renewing the negotiation with Sir Henry Clinton on the Subject of Articles of Capitulation."

## 1780, May 12. *Surrender of Charlestown.*

At 2:00 P.M. Gen. Lincoln and Gen. Moultrie met the British commanders at the horn work and gate, and surrendered the city. It was the British army's greatest prize of the Revolutionary War, capturing the majority of the Southern Continental Army regulars, 5,500, and most of the South Carolina Navy. Sir Clinton wrote:

> Whatever severe Justice might dictate, we resolved not to press to unconditional Submission a reduced army whom we hoped Clemency might yet reconcile to us.

He ordered all regular army and militia to "bring all their arms with them, guns, swords and pistols." Henry Laurens complained about surrendering the troops, "Thousands of Muskets ... useless in Charlestown which might have been shouldered in our defence." The British also took possession of more than 200 cannon and 50,000 pounds of gunpowder.

The enlisted men of the Continental army were confined to barracks in the city, and the officers were sent to Haddrell's Point. Several senior officers were allowed to find quarters in private homes in the area. Gen. Moultrie and Charles Cotesworth Pinckney were confined at Snee Farm in Mt. Pleasant, owned by the Pinckney family.

Casualties during the Charlestown siege were:

- American: 150 dead; 138 wounded
- British: 99 dead; 217 wounded.

British soldiers were given the power to arrest people on any pretext; citizens could be jailed without a pre-trial hearing. They also cut down the Liberty Tree on Mazyck's Pasture and burned the stump. Thus began a two-and-a-half-year occupation.

## 1780, May 15. *BRITISH OCCUPATION. STOREHOUSE EXPLODES.*

The British transported all of the confiscated Continental weapons to a storehouse on Magazine Street, next to a powder magazine which contained 10,000 pounds of ammunition. Some of the citizens left the arms loaded, with some of them intentionally cocked.

As the British were transferring these arms to the storehouse, several discharged creating a powerful explosion and a blazing fire. The fire spread to several houses in the block, including a brothel and the poor house. Sixty British soldiers were killed, as well than 100 bystanders. Carcasses, torsos and other body parts were scattered several blocks away.

At the time of the blast, Gen. Moultrie was confined in a house next to St. Michael's Church. The building shook and windows rattled. Many in the city thought that they were suffering an earthquake. Moultrie left the shaking building, and learned the result of the shaking when he was stopped on the street by a Hessian officer, who accused the Continentals of causing the blast on purpose. Moultrie was placed under an armed guard for a few hours. Moultrie later wrote about the extreme destruction of the blast:

> One man was dashed with violence against the steeple of the new independent church [present-day Unitarian Church, one block away] and left the marks of his body there for several days.

## 1780, May 20. *BRITISH OCCUPATION.*

Most of the American militia were given parole and allowed to return to their homes. Many of the important men, stripped of their property, had little recourse than to pledge loyalty to the Crown.

John Wells, of the *South Carolina and American General Gazette,* quickly swore allegiance to the King to save his property. He was allowed to resume publication in July. Peter Timothy's paper, the *South Carolina Gazette*, was seized by the British and given to the Tory Robert Wells.

The Miles Brewton home at 27 King Street was turned into headquarters for Gen. Henry Clinton, and later for Lt. Colonel Nisbet Balfour, commandant of Charlestown, and Lord Rawdon, supreme commander of British troops in South Carolina.

Rebecca Brewton Motte, with an an invalid husband, refused to give up her brother's house to the occupying force, so they moved in with her. Although she was the mercy of her "guests," during meals, Rebecca always "sat at the head of her table in the drawing-room at each meal and commanded the respect, at least, of his lordship and followers." The officers "showed her the greatest courtesy and reffered to themselves as 'her guests'."

Rebecca's main concern was the care of her husband, and the safety of her three daughters. The Motte family was crowded into the small area of the house on the third floor, while the British lived in comfort in the large rooms on the lower floors.

### 1780, May 24. *Revolution. Backcountry.*

Governor John Rutledge arrived in Camden and learned the terms of Charlestown's surrender. Rutledge was disappointed by Lincoln's surrender and wrote "the Terms of Capitulation are truly mortifying." He demanded to know why Lincoln "did not evacuate the Town, & save his Troops." Things looked bleak for South Carolina militarily.

### 1780, May 25. *British Occupation.*

Sir Clinton noted that 200 citizens of Charlestown had congratulated them on their victory and that more than "1500 have already been here with their arms, desiring to join us." He was encouraged that all men of property "have most heartily joined us with their arms." Most organized resistance in South Carolina had been eliminated.

A Board of Police, made up primarily of former British Crown officials, was established to govern the city.

### 1780, May 29. *Waxhaws Massacre. Backcountry.*

Near the town of Buford, along the North and South Carolina border, Col. Tarleton surprised Col. Abraham Buford and 400 Virginia Continentals and demanded their surrender. Buford refused and resumed his march. Tarleton's line charged, and the British cavalry tore Buford's line to pieces. Many of the Americans laid down their arms and offered to surrender. According to Patriot accounts, Buford, who realized the cause was lost, dispatched a white flag toward Tarleton in an attempt to surrender. However, Tarleton was trapped beneath his dead horse and never responded to the surrender attempt and his troops, thinking their commander dead, continued to massacre the Continentals. This cemented the phrase "Tarleton's Quarter" and led to his nickname, "Bloody Tarleton.

American casualties were 113 men killed, 147 wounded. The British losses were 5 killed, 12 wounded. After the battle, the wounded were treated at nearby churches by the congregants, one of whom was a young Andrew Jackson.

### 1780, May 30. *Revolution. Naval. Gillon Expedition.*

Commodore Gillon signed a lease for 100,000 livres with Luxembourg for the frigate, *L'Indien*, which was rechristened *South Carolina*. The agreement stated that the Chevalier de Luxembourgh would receive one-fourth of its prizes. It had been a frustrating ten months for Gillon. He had trouble locating vessels for the South Carolina State Navy. He spent the next several months enlisting a crew.

## 1780, Summer. *British Occupation. The Balfour Baboon.*

Lt. Colonel Nisbet Balfour became the chief of staff on whom Cornwallis relied to keep supplies flowing to the troops in the backcountry. He also became one of the most despised of the British officers in Charlestown. General Moultrie said that Balfour had a "tyrannical, insolent disposition ... and treated the people as the most abject slaves." Dr. David Ramsay claimed that Balfour displayed:

> all the frivolous self-importance, and all the disgusting insolence, which are natural to little minds puffed up by sudden elevation, and employed in functions to which their abilities are not equal.

Tom Singleton, an elderly wealthy tobacco planter and merchant, gave much of his wealth in support of the Patriot cause. Singleton so hated Balfour that he dressed a pet baboon in an exact replica of Balfour's regimental uniform, and paraded him around town, addressing the baboon as "Lt. Col. Balfour." This enraged the prickly British officer, who had Singleton arrested and later exiled to St. Augustine.

## 1780, June. *British Occupation.*

Early in June, Gen. Benjamin Lincoln left for Philadelphia, under terms of his parole, leaving Gen. Moultrie as the highest-ranking Continental officer in the occupied city.

## 1780, June 1. *British Occupation. Oath.*

Sir Clinton revoked all paroles. He announced that all men were required to enroll in the service of the king. In the proclamation Clinton demanded no one in South Carolina remain neutral, "all persons should take an active part in Settling and Securing his Majesty's government and delivering the Country from that anarchy ..."

All prisoners who had not participated in the defense of Charleston were paroled as of June 20. If they did not pledge allegiance by that date they would be imprisoned. There was also a clause that, if so ordered, they would have to take up arms to defend Britain. He concluded by saying that all those:

> who shall afterwards neglect to return to their allegiance and to His Majesty's government will be considered as Enemies and Rebels to the same and treated accordingly.

Col. Issac Hayne signed the declaration of allegiance to avoid be separated from his dying wife and small children who were ill with small pox. He was told by General Patterson that he would not have to honor the clause about bearing arms against his fellow citizens. He then returned to his plantation in St. Paul's parish, forty miles south of Charlestown, present-day Colleton County.

Others who signed the Loyalty Oath included the elderly planters Charles Pinckney, Jr., Rawlins Lowndes, and Henry Middleton. The Oath of Allegiance that was forced upon South Carolinians read:

> I, _____, do hereby acknowledge and declare myself to be a true and faithful subject of his Majesty, the King of Great Britain, and that I will at all times hereafter be obedient to his government; and that whenever I shall be thereunto required, I will be ready to maintain and defend the same against all persons whatsoever.

Sir Henry Clinton, British commander during the Siege of Charlestown.
*Courtesy of the New York Public Library*

## 1780, June 4. *Clinton Reports on Charles Town's Surrender*

Gen. Henry Clinton wrote:

> With the greatest pleasure I further report ... that the inhabitants from every quarter repair to the detachments of the army, and to this garrison (Charles-town) to declare their allegiance to the King, and to offer their services in arms for the support of the Government. In many instances they have brought in as prisoners their former oppressors or

leaders; and I may venture to assert, that there are few men in South Carolina who not either our prisoners or in arms with us.

### 1780, June 5. *LOYALISTS CONGRATULATE CLINTON.*

The loyal citizens of Charlestown presented formal addresses of congratulations to General Clinton. Those who signed these addresses later had their property confiscated after the war.

### 1780, June 8. *BRITISH OCCUPATION. CLINTON LEAVES.*

Clinton left for New York, appointing Lord Cornwallis to take command of all British forces in the southern provinces.

### 1780, June 11. *AMERICAN REVOLUTION. CHURCH BURNED.*

Capt. Christian Houck (Huck), "Tarleton's chief butcher," burned a church in Chester, South Carolina

### 1780, June 14. *SLAVERY.*

Captain Thomas Hall informed Major Issac Harleston of Charlestown that "a one-eyed taylor negro fellow of yours went off to the English with his wife, children and enticed five more."

### 1780, July 1. *BRITISH OCCUPATION.*

James Simpson wrote to General Henry Clinton:

> Nothing but the evidence of my senses, would have convinced me that one half of the distress I am witness to could have been produced in so short a time in so rich a country. Numbers of family, who four years ago abounded in every convenience and luxury of life, are without food to live on, clothes to cover them or the mean to purchase them.

### 1780, July 3. *REVOLUTION. RUTLEDGE ARRIVES IN PHILADELPHIA.*

Gov. John Rutledge arrived in Philadelphia and immediately began to urge Congress to send troops to South Carolina.

### 1780, July 4. *BRITISH OCCUPATION. INDEPENDENCE CELEBRATED.*

The Continental officers at Haddrell's Popint celebrated "independence day," by singing, dancing, and drinking. Several officers discharged their weapons. The British termed that "an indecent abuse of lenity" and demanded that the officers turn over their pistols.

### 1780, July 25. *BRITISH OCCUPATION. ALLEGIANCE PROCLAMATION.*

A British military proclamation stated that mechanics and shopkeepers (who were overwhelming Patriots) must sweat allegiance to Britian in order to sell property, collect bebts, or leave the city. One hundred ssixty-three merchants swore allegiance in order to avoid financial ruin.

## 1780, August. *REVOLUTION. CORNWALLIS MARCHES NORTH.*

Cornwallis took the field and march north into the South Carolina backcountry. He left Lt. Colonel Nisbet Balfour as commandant of Charlestown.

## 1780, August 16. *REVOLUTION. BATTLE OF CAMDEN. PRISON SHIPS.*

Camden was another major defeat for the Americans. A new Southern Army, commanded by Major General Horatio Gates, was soundly defeated by Cornwallis at Camden. It was the worst American battlefield defeat of the Revolution, with more than 1,000 casualities. Thomas Pinckney, an aid-de-camp to Gen. Gates, was captured on the battlefield.

Most of the Americans captured were brought to Charlestown and placed on British prison ships in the harbor. The conditions on these ships were so horrific that Lt. Col. Nisbet Balfour triumphantly remarked that "the rebel Prisoners die faster even than they used to desert."

Gen. Moultrie described Balfour as "a proud and haughty Scot [who] carried his authority with a very high hand; his tyrannical disposition, treated the people as the most abject slaves."

## 1780, August 16. *BRITISH OCCUPATION.*

Francis Sheftall, a Jew who came to Charlestown after the fall of Savannah, wrote that after the occupation she:

> rented a house in St. Michael's Alley at the rate of 50 pounds sterling a year, and where the money is to come from god only knows for there is nothing but hard Money goes here and that I can assure you is hard enough to be got.

## 1780, August 16. *BRITISH OCCUPATION.*

Thirty-three people were arrested in Charlestown, and charged with encouraging residents to resist British authority. The prisoners, some of whom had been placed under house arrest, were dragged from their beds by British soldiers, and jailed in th Provost Dungeon of the Exchange Building. The arrested men included:

| | | |
|---|---|---|
| Dr. John S. Budd | William Johnson | Edward Rutledge |
| Dr Peter Payssoux | William Massey | Hugh Rutledge |
| Thomas Ferguson | Arthur Middleton | Thomas Savage |
| Christopher Gadsden | Alexander Moultrie | Tom Singleton |
| Thomas Grimball | Joseph Parker | Peter Timothy |
| Thomas Heyward, Jr. | Dr. John E. Poyas | Dr. Andrew Turnbill |
| Richard Hutson | Dr. David Ramsay | |

Within a few day the prisoners were transferred to the ship *Sandwich* in Charlestown harbor. Edward Rutledge learned of his two-year old son's death while inprisoned. Being unable to attend the funeral and comfort his wife only increased his bitterness toward Britain. Militiamen, like Charles Pinckney, were paroled to their homes. John Milner, a gunsmith:

> Was imprisoned in the basement of the old post offce [Exchange Building] at the head of Broad Street and East Bay and his Maiden Daughter [Martha] used to feed him through the iron bars ... with the boiled rice she carried in her pockets for him.

Peter Sinkler was betrayed to the British by his brother-in-law, James Boisseau. Sinkler died of typhus fever and his body was "secretly buried ... under the chancel of St. Philip's Church" while "his casket which was supposed to ghoue his body was filled with ammunition and carried to the army by his request."

Gen. Moultrie protested to Balfounr that sending Continenttal officers to prision ships violated the terms of capitulation agreed upon by Clinton and Cornwallis. Balfour responded the he "would do as he pleased with the prisoners ... not as General Moultrie pleases."

Other Charleston patriots who were latter arrested and imprisoned, or detained in the Provost included:

| | | |
|---|---|---|
| Col. Jonas Beard | Maj. John Habersham | Henry Peronneau |
| Edward Blake | William Harvey | Lt. Henry Ravenel |
| Maj. Peter Bocquet | Capt. Thomas Hall | Daniel Ravenel |
| Capt. George Sinclair Capers | Capt. William Hall | Mary Sarraszin |
| Capt. William Capers | Col. Issac Hayne | Peter Sinkler |
| Robert Cohran (Powder Receiver) | Issac Holmes | Col. John Stark |
| | Pvt. Solomon Legare | Daniel Stevens |
| Jacob Dedricks | Rev. John Lewis | Caspar Strobel |
| Henry Doyle (British deserter) | William Livingston | Sgt. John Sullivan |
| John Edwards | Robert Lushington | Jonathon Sarrazin |
| George Flagg | John Milner | Catherine Sarrazin |
| William Gibbes | Judge Henry Pendleton | Lt. Andrew Wells |
| Lt. Colonel John Grimke | | |

## 1780, September. *BRITISH OCCUPATION. PETER TIMOTHY'S DEATH.*

The Charlestown prsioners in the Provost Dungeon were transported to St. Augustine. During the voyage, the British reported that Peter Timothy was "lost overboard." Timothy, who published one of the most anit-British newspapers in the colonies, paid with his life for his political views.

## 1780, September. *BRITISH OCCUPATION. SEQUESTRATION.*

Cornwallis instituted the policy of sequestration. At first, it only affected the property of known, active rebels. Ultimately, however, it was expanded to all those with rebel sympathies.

## 1780, September 3. *Revolution. Henry Laurens Captured.*

During Henry Laurens's return voyage from the Netherlands, the British frigate *Vestal* intercepted his ship, the Continental packet *Mercury*, off the banks of Newfoundland. Laurens tossed his dispatches overboard, but they were retrieved by the British, who discovered the draft of a possible U.S.-Dutch treaty, prompting Britain to declare war on the Netherlands, The British charged Laurens with treason and transported him to England for trial.

## 1780, September 29. *Revolution. Backcountry.*

Francis Marion attacked the Royal militia at Black Mingo Creek Bridge, the first of dozens of quick strikes against the British, which slowly began to have effect.

## 1780, October 6. *Revolution. Sumter Commissioned.*

Gov. Rutledge commissioned Thomas Sumter as Brigadier-General in command of all state militia. His instructions to Sumter were to inspire the public, enroll as many men as possible, and "co-operate with the Continental forces."

Rutledge, in order to escape capture by the British, was living in the field, moving from Hillsborough, North Carolina to Salisbury, to Charlotte, to Cheraw.

Left: Tower of London. Right: Marker noting Henry Lauren's room in the Tower.
*Photos by author.*

## 1780, October 6. *Revolution. Laurens Sentenced to Tower.*

Henry Laurens was sentenced to the Tower of London for "suspicion of high treason." His imprisonment was protested by the Americans. In the field, most captives were regarded as prisoners of war, and while conditions were frequently appalling, prisoner exchanges and mail privileges were accepted practice.

During his imprisonment, Laurens was assisted by Richard Oswald, his former business partner and the principal owner of Bunce Island. Oswald argued on Laurens' behalf to the British government.

### 1780, October 7. REVOLUTION. KING'S MOUNTAIN.

The Patriot mountain men from North and South Carolina, Virginia and Tennessee, defeated a Tory militia at the battle of King's Mountain. British casualties were 290 killed, 163 wounded and 664 prisoners. Patriot forces lost twenty-eight killed and sixty-two wounded. This victory helped turn the tide of the war.

### 1780, October 14. REVOLUTION. GREEN APPOINTED COMMANDER.

Continental Congress appointed General Nathaniel Green as commander of the Southern armies.

### 1780, November 14. BRITISH OCCUPATION. PRISON SHIPS.

The British prison ship in Charleston harbor, *Concord*, was described as "infected with smallpox, putrid fever and influenza." Of the 2,100 prisoners on the ship, 800 died within a year.

### 1780, November 18. BRITISH OCCUPATION. SEIZURE OF PROPERTY.

Cornwallis issued a proclamation that he was seizing all the "real and personal property" of South Carolina's patriot leaders, including Henry Laurens and all the St. Augustine exiles.

### 1780, December 2. REVOLUTION. GREEN TAKES COMMAND.

Gen. Nathaniel Green arrived in Charlotte, North Carolina to take command of the Southern Continental Army.

# 1781

### 1781, January. BRITISH OCCUPATION.

The Knights Terrible Society was organized at Mr. Holliday's tavern, for the purpose of drinking once a week during the British occupation. They disbanded after the British left the city.

### 1781, January. BRITISH OCCUPATION. DEATH.

Jacob Motte died, leaving his widow, Rebecca Brewton Motte, to care for her daughters and deal with the occupying British force living in their home.

### 1781, January. BRITISH OCCUPATION. RECRUITING OF AMERICAN PRISONERS.

Gen. Moultrie complained to Lt. Colonel Balfour about his attempt to recruit American prisoners of war into British service.

Battle of Cowpens. Col. William Washington (center) and Banastre Tarleton (right).
*Courtesy of the New York Public Library*

## 1781, January 17. *REVOLUTION. BATTLE OF COWPENS.*

The term "cowpens" was a common nickname for pastureland for cattle. In the northeast corner of South Carolina, there was a large pastureland at the conjunction of two roads next to a ridge.

On a bitterly cold morning, a British force of 1,100 led by Banastre Tarleton, met an American force led by Continental Army Brig. General Daniel Morgan – 1,100 Continental riflemen and local militia, supported by Col. William Washington's eighty Continental dragoons and forty-five mounted Georgia infantry. In less than an hour the American forces routed the British, killing more than 800.

During Tarleton's hasty retreat, Col. Washington pursued and found himself isolated. He was attacked by Tarleton and two others. He managed to survive the assault and wounded Tarleton's right hand with a sabre blow, while Tarleton creased Washington's knee with a pistol shot that also wounded his horse. For his valor at Cowpens, Washington received a silver medal, awarded by the Continental Con-gress following the recommendation of Thomas Jefferson.

Congress also proclaimed "a complete and important victory." It was a major victory in turning the tide in the campaign to retake South Carolina from the British. Major General Lord Cornwallis wrote:

> I will not say much in praise of the militia of the Southern Colonies, but the list of British officers and soldiers killed and wounded by them ... proves but too fatally they are not wholly contemptible.

### 1781, January 24. *REVOLUTION. GEORGETOWN.*

Patriot commanders, Lieutenant Colonel "Light Horse" Harry Lee (father of Robert E. Lee) and Brigadier General Francis Marion, the "Swamp Fox" of the South Carolina militia, combined their forces and raided Georgetown, South Carolina, which was defended by 200 British soldiers.

### 1781, January 31. *REVOLUTION. NAVAL. GILLON EXPEDITION.*

Commodore Gillon was preparing to return to America, but the Dutch would not clear *South Carolina* until Gillon paid some outstanding bills due to the outfitting of the ship.

### 1781, February 9. *REVOLUTION. MONTAGUE RAISES A REGIMENT.*

Former Royal Governor, Lord Charles Montagu, returned to Charlestown in an effort to raise a regiment for military service in the West Indies. He managed to convince 400 Continental soldiers on prison ships to enlist by promising they would not have to serve against American forces.

### 1781, March. *BRITISH OCCUPATION. ARRESTS.*

Lt. Colonel John F. Grimke and Major John Habersham were arrested by the British on trumped-up parole violations. They were imprisoned in the dungeon beneath the Exchange Building in miserable conditions.

### 1781, March 3. *BRITISH OCCUPATION.*

*South Carolina Gazette* resumed publication as the *Royal Gazette*. The Tory publisher, John Wells, made sure the paper reflected the British perspective.

### 1781, March 3. *REVOLUTION. JOHN LAURENS ARRIVES IN FRANCE.*

Col. John Laurens arrived in France, as special minister, to secure immediate aid from France for the American cause. His undiplomatic, passionate arguments convinced the French to release their fleet immediately in support of the Americans.

### 1781, March 8. *REVOLUTION.*

Gen. Greene encouraged Gov. Rutledge to travel to Philadelphia to give Congress an accurate report of the military situation in the South, and to ask for additional aid. Rutledge wrote to Thomas Sumter and Francis Marion.

> My Journey will be tedious, for I must supply myself, with some Horses on the Road (my own being worn down) and I shall call on the Governors of No. Carolina, Virginia and Maryland on my way, to

represent the Situation ... which I believe very different from what People think.

Francis Marion chased by the British in the South Carolina backcountry.

Marion was one of the inspirations for Mel Gibson's Rambo-like character, Benjamin Martin, in the Hollywood blockbuster, *The Patriot*.

*Courtesy of the New York Public Library.*

## 1781, March 11. BRITISH OCCUPATION. MONTAGU TRIES TO RECRUIT MOULTRIE.

In a letter to Gen. Moultrie, Lord Montagu tried to convince the general to resign and join him in Jamaica "to fight the French and Spanish." Montagu argued that Moultrie's "honor and reputation would remain untarnished."

## 1781, March 11. *British Occupation. Moultrie Replies to Montagu.*

Gen. Moultrie was outraged by Montagu's proposal, looking at it as traitorous. From his confinement at Haddrell's Point, he wrote:

> When I entered into this contest, I did it with the most mature deliberation, and with a determined resolution to risqué [sic] my life and fortune in the cause. The hardships I have gone through I look back upon with the greatest pleasure ... You call upon me now, and tell me I have a fair open of quitting that service and reputation to myself by going with you to Jamaica.

> Good God! Is it possible that such an idea could arise in the breast of a man of honor. I am sorry you should imagine I have so little regard for my own reputation as to listen to such dishonorable proposals; would you wish to have that man whom you have honored with your friendship play the traitor? Surely not.

Henry William DeSaussure, imprisoned in a ship in Charlestown harbor, later wrote about Moultrie's refusal to join Montagu's regiment. He made the comparison with Benedict Arnold, who four months before Montagu's proposal, had yielded to British enticements. DeSaussure wrote, "But while in Arnold they found a traitor, in General Moultrie they met a true patriot who rejected with scorn the offers to abandon that struggle for liberty and independence."

## 1781, March 18. *Revolution. Sampit Bridge.*

Gen. Francis Marion routed the Tory and British army at the Sampit Bridge near Georgetown.

## 1781, March 21. *British Occupation. Slavery.*

William Bull observed that the city's slaves had:

> become ungovernable, absenting themselves often from the service of their masters. The code of laws calculated for the government of that class of people cannot be carried into execution.

## 1781, March 25. *British Occupation.*

When Cornwallis marched to Virginia, General Francis Edward Rawdon-Hastings, Lord Rawdon, was placed in command of South Carolina. Lord Rawdon decreed that all jobs in Charlestown were closed to any but Loyalists to the King. Many men who were sympathetic to the rebel cause were forced to pledge British allegiance out of the necessity of feeding their family.

## 1781, April. *British Occupation. Rebecca Motte Leaves.*

Rebecca Brewton Motte received permission from Lord Rawdon to move her family from the Miles Brewton house in Charlestown, to her Mt. Joseph plantation on the Congaree River (present-day Calhoun County). It was a strategic location on the British supply route between Charlestown and Camden.

Upon arrival, the family discovered Lt. McPherson and 165 British troops had commandeered the plantation house as quarters. They had erected fortifications around the property and renamed it Fort Motte.

## 1781, April. BRITISH OCCUPATION. GRIMKE ESCAPES.

John Grimke and John Habersham were released from the dungeon and returned to their barracks at Haddrell's Point. Grimke escaped and made his way through the British line and joined Gen. Greene's Continental Army.

## 1781, May. BRITISH OCCUPATION. FIRST APOTHECARY OPENED.

Dr. Andrew Turnbull arrived from St. Augustine, and opened Charleston's first apothecary (chemist/pharmacy) shop at the corner of King and Broad Streets, in Dr. John Lining's former home.

## 1781, May 3. BRITISH OCCUPATION. PRISONER EXCHANGE.

Cornwallis and Gen. Greene agreed on a prisoner exchange which included all the Charlestown prisoners in St. Augustine.

## 1781, May 7. BRITISH OCCUPATION.

Sir Henry Clinton issued a proclamation encouraging "Rebels or those serving in Rebel army or militia" to enlist in the British army. For a three-year enlistment, the British promised the "regiment of his choice, six guineas (a gold coin worth £1 sterling) and a grant of land."

## 1781, May 8. REVOLUTION. BATTLE OF FORT MOTTE.

Gen. Nathaniel Greene reinforced Gen. Marion's brigade which included Lt. Colonel "Light Horse" Harry Lee, and his Legion, with troops from the Continental Army. Their task was to capture and destroy the line of British forts that protected communications and supplies between Charleston and the backcountry, Rebecca Brewton Motte's house, Ft. Motte was one of those.

Fearing that British reinforcements were on their way, Marion and Lee decided to attack Ft. Motte at once. Rebecca and her family were ordered to move to a near overseer's cottage for safety.

## 1781, May 12. REVOLUTION. FT. MOTTE BURNED.

After four days, Ft. Motte was still in British hands. Gen. Marion decided the best thing to do was to set fire to the mansion and burn the enemy out. Rebecca was told of the plans and she "immediately and cheerfully consented, assuring him that the loss of her property was nothing compared to advancement of their cause."

To facilitate the effort, she handed General Lee three incendiary arrows given to her by her deceased brother, Miles Brewton. These East Indian, chemically-tipped arrows were supposed to be "ignited upon contact with any hard substance." The arrows had been kept at the plantation house, but Rebecca had managed to take them with her as she was forced to move to the cottage.

Marion's troops fired the combustible arrows from a musket. The first two sputtered out, but the third hit its mark and set fire to the roof of the house. The British began to sneak out of the second floor dormer windows attempting to douse the flames. They were easy targets for the Patriot riflemen, and were driven back inside. Lt. McPherson ran up the white flag, fearing that his troops would be blown up if the gunpowder stored in the house were set on fire. Together, the British and American soldiers put out the flames, saving the main body of the house.

Rebecca, as a true Southern hostess, then invited both the American and British officers to join her for dinner in the main house.

### 1781, May 17. *British Occupation. Pinckney Arrested.*

In violation of Gen. Lincoln's terms of surrender, Charles Pinckney and other militiamen on parole, were arrested and placed aboard two British prison ships in the Charlestown harbor – *Pack Horse* and *Torbay*. Conditions on the ships were horrendous. More than one third of the prisoners held in Charlestown died in captivity. Charles Pinckney wrote a letter to Colonel Balfour complaining about:

> a most injurious and disagreeable confinement ... the idea of detaining in close custody as hostages a number of men fairly taken in arms ... is so repugnant to the laws of war and the usage of civilized nations ...

### 1781, Summer. *England. Tower of London.*

Henry Laurens spent the summer in the Tower reading Gibbons' *Decline and Fall of the Roman Empire*. He also wrote letters that drew parallels with Great Britain, which included first-hand accounts of British troops' horrendous conduct in the America. These letters were circulated in Great Britain, and became a source of public embarrassment for the Parliament and King.

### 1781, Summer. *British Occupation. Allegiance Signers Ordered to Take Up Arms.*

Due to the battles in the backcountry going against the British, Lord Rawdon ordered all men who signed the allegiance to take up arms for Britain. Issac Hayne refused and, because he believed his parole to be broken, he became leader of a local militia unit and led several skirmishes against the British. The British quickly became irritated by the men who had sworn allegiance, but took up arms against the King.

### 1781, June 22. *Revolution. Prisoner Exchange.*

The American prisoners in the British ships in Charlestown, and many of the officers at Haddrell's Point, were exchanged and sent to Philadelphia.

### 1781, June 27. *British Occupation. Families Ordered Out of South Carolina.*

Col. Balfour ordered all wives and families of the St. Augustine exiles to leave South Carolina by August 1. Balfour had already learned of the prisoner exchange, and due to the difficulty the British were having in feeding the civilians, they were happy for an excuse to get rid of several hundred people.

He also ordered that the St. Augustine prisoners must go to either Philadelphia or Virginia, not Charlestown.

Etching which depicts Rebecca Brewton Motte, presenting a quiver of East Indian fire-arrows to Gen. Francis Marion and Colonel Lee.

From *Life of Francis Marion* by William Gilmore Simms, 1811. *Author's Collection*

## 1781, July 8. *Revolution. Prisoner Exchange.*

The Charlestown patriot exiles received word of the prisoner exchange, negotiated between Cornwallis and Gen. Greene, and learned they would be sent to Philadelphia.

## 1781, July 14. *Revolution. Fort Dorchester Taken.*

The British garrison abandoned Fort Dorchester when they were attacked by American cavalry led by Col. "Light Horse" Lee and Col. Henry Hampton.

## 1781, July 15. *Revolution. Quarter House Tavern.*

American forces capture a company of Tory dragoons at the Quarter House Tavern, five miles from Charlestown.

## 1781, July 27. *British Occupation. Execution Date Set.*

The British issued an official statement:

> The adjutant of the town will be so good as to go to Colonel Hayne in Provost Prison and inform him that in consequence of the court of enquiry held yesterday and the preceding evening Lord Rawdon and the commandant Lieutenant Colonel Nisbet Balfour have resolved upon his execution on Tuesday the thirty-first instant at six o'clock, for having been found under arms raising a regiment to oppose the British government, though he had become a subject and had accepted the protection of that government after the reduction of Charleston.

## 1781, July 30. *Revolution. Charleston Exiles in Philadelphia.*

The St. Augustine exiles arrived in Philadelphia. Edward Rutledge, Charles Cotesworth Pinckney, Thomas Pinckney, and their families rented a brick mansion in Germantown. The Pinckney brothers were met by their cousin, Charles, who had been sent from Charlestown a few weeks earlier, and had taken a room at Mrs. McFunn's boardinghouse on Second Street with Arthur Middleton.

Over the next few months Charles became friends with Pierce Butler, leader of his Charleston militia unit. Six years later, both men would later play major roles during the Constitutional Congress.

## 1781, August 3. *British Occupation. Plea for Hayne's Life.*

A group of citizens meet Lord Rawdon at the Miles Brewton House, to plead for Issac Hayne's life. Col Hayne's son, William Hayne, wrote:

> I recollect also going with my brother Issac & sister Sarah in Company of my Aunt Peronneau to Lieut. Col. Balfour ... and on our knees presenting a petition to him in favor of my father but without effect.

Col. Lawdon refused to stay the order.

## 1781, August 4. *Execution of Issac Hayne.*

At 5:00 P.M. Col. Issac Hayne "was escorted by a party of soldiers to a gallows erected within the lines of the town with his hands tied behind, and there hung up till he was dead."

Dr. David Ramsay reported:

> The military escort consisted of three hundred men. The place of execution was just without the city-lines, near Radcliffe's Garden, nearly in front, and within a stone's throw of the present Orphan House building. The troops formed a hollow square around the scaffold, the British troops occupying the front and rear, the Hessians on the right and left.

During the march through the city "the streets were crowded with thousands of anxious spectators." Someone in the crowd called to Hayne "Exhibit the example of how an American can die!" Hayne replied, "I will endeavor to do so." Upon arriving at the execution spot:

> He ascended the cart with a firm step and serene aspect. He enquired of the executioner, who making an attempt to get the cap over his eyes, what he wanted? ... He then affectionately shook hands with three gentlemen – recommended his children to their care – and gave the signal for the cart to move.

## 1781, August 4. *GILLON EXPEDITION*.

Commodore Gillon moved *South Carolina* a league off shore, beyond Dutch territorial waters, and prepared for the voyage back to America.

## 1781, August 6. *AMERICAN REVOLUTION. POLITICS*.

Gov. John Rutledge, in letter to the South Carolina delegation of the Continental Congress, wrote:

> I wish most anxiously to have an assembly elected, and sitting as soon as possible, but it would be ungenerous to exclude our worthy friends lately Prisoners in St. Augustine and Charles Town from a share in the Legislature ... and injurious to the public to deprive it of their Abilities and Services.

## 1781, August 8. *EXECUTION OF ISSAC HAYNE*.

The *Royal Gazette* wrote:

> Mr. Issac Hayne who since the capitulation of Charlestown, had taken protection, and acknowledged himself a subject of his Majesty's Government, having been taken in arms, and at the head of a Rebel Regiment of Militia, was therefore on Saturday morning last, executed as a Traitor.

## 1781, August 11. *BIRTH*.

Thomas Bennett, Jr. was born in Charlestown.

## 1781, August 12. *BIRTH*.

Robert Mills was born in Charlestown. His father was a tailor, respectable, successful, but solidly middle class. Mills is often erroneously referred to as America's first native-born architect, but Charles Bullfinch of Boston has a clearer claim to that honor.

## 1781, August 14. *REVOLUTION. GILLON EXPEDITION*.

Commodore Gillon was ready to sail for America when a large storm struck the area for more than a week. *South Carolina* was forced to ride out the storm at anchor. Gillon had taken on several passengers, bound for home:

- Lt. Colonel John Turnbull, a noted artist
- Charles Adams, youngest son of John and Abigail Adams

⚜ Lieutenant Joshua Barney of the Continental Navy, who had recently escaped from Mill Prison in Plymouth, England, by digging a tunnel beneath the wall.

## 1781, August 23. *REVOLUTION. GILLON EXPEDITION.*

Commodore Gillon ordered *South Carolina* to set sail through the North Sea toward America.

## 1781, August 25. *REVOLUTION. LAURENS RETURNS FROM FRANCE.*

Col. John Laurens arrived in Boston, with two shiploads of military supplies and half a million dollars in aid from the French.

## 1781, September. *REVOLUTION. PHILADELPHIA EXILES RETURN.*

Christopher Gadsden and a group of exiles left Philadelphia to join Gov. John Rutledge in the South Carolina backcountry. Sensing American victory was possible, they were anxious to avenge themselves against Cornwallis. Gadsden wrote:

> Revenge is below a brave man; vengence belongeth to the Almighty. He has claimed it expressly His right, wisely foreseeing the shocking havoc man would make with such a weapon left to his discretion. However, a just retaliation, upon an abandoned and cruel enemy, may be sometime absolutely necessary and unavoidable …

## 1781, September 8. *REVOLUTION. BATTLE OF EUTAW SPRINGS.*

This was the last major battle in the Carolinas, and Col. William Washington's final action. Midway through the battle, Gen. Greene ordered Washington to charge a portion of the British line positioned in a thicket along Eutaw Creek. During the last charge, Washington's mount was shot out from under him, and he was pinned beneath his horse. He was bayoneted, taken prisoner, and held under house arrest in the Charlestown area for the remainder of the war.

## 1781, September 16. *SLAVERY. DENMARK VESEY.*

Capt. Joseph Vesey purchased 390 slaves in St. Domingue. After Charlestown fell to the British, Vesey purchased a large ship, *Prospect*, which had a crew of sixty and twelve cannon. He began to transport slaves from Africa to the Caribbean Islands.

One of the slaves he purchased was a young boy "about 14 years old" named Telemaque. Vesey also noted the boy had "beauty, alertness and intelligence." Instead of keeping the boy chained below decks Vesey "adopted the boy as the ship's pet and plaything." He gave the boy a new set of clothes and used him as his cabin boy.

When the ship arrived at Cape Francois, Haiti, Vesey decided he "had no use of the boy" and turned him over to the slave agents Lory, Plomard and Compagnie.

## 1781, September 17. *Revolution. Loyalty Oath Extended.*

Gov. John Rutledge issued a proclamation offering amnesty to British supporters, specifically those who had voluntarily accepted British protection while under British control. They were given thirty days to take an oath of loyalty to South Carolina, and must agree to serve six months in the militia.

The exceptions to the amnesty were those:

> who held military or civil commissions under the British, those who had previously refused pardons and those guilty of conduct so 'infamous' as to be underserving of the privileges of American liberty.

Also, those Charlestonians who had welcomed the British in May 1780 were specifically excluded.

## 1781, October. *England. Tower of London.*

Henry Laurens' tower guard, Mr. Futerell, presented him with a bill for £97 as payment for his service for one year. Having depleted his funds, Laurens wrote:

> 'Tis enough to provoke me to change my lodging ... If I were possessed of as many guineas as would fill this room, I would not pay the warders, whom I never employed, and whose attendance I shall be glad to dispense with. Attempts, sir, to tax men without their consent, have involved this kingdom in a bloody seven years' war. I thought she had long since promised to abandon the project.

## 1781, October 14. *Revolution. Siege of Yorktown.*

A day-long assault by American infantry on British positions was led by Colonels Alexander Hamilton and John Laurens.

## 1781, October 15. *Revolution. Gillon Expedition.*

*South Carolina* left La Corunna, Spain for America.

## 1781, October 18. *Revolution. Yorktown.*

Cornwallis requested terms of surrender. John Laurens met with Cornwallis's emissaries to offer the American terms, which were essentially the same terms that Sir Clinton had imposed on Charlestown seventeen months before.

## 1781, October 19. *Revolution. Yorktown Surrender.*

Lord Cornwallis surrendered 8,000 British troops to George Washington at Yorktown, Virginia. Victory was assured by the arrival of the French fleet, secured by Col. John Laurens, which cut off Cornwallis' retreat by sea.

Aedanus Burke, serving with the Continental forces at Yorktown, witnessed the British surrender of arms. He wrote that he did "despise from my soul the mass of unfeeling men which compose its officers."

When word of the surrender reached Charlestown, Lord Rawdon was so concerned about an American attack he ordered forces from Wilmington, North Carolina relocated to Charlestown, constructed new fortifications across the Neck, and enlisted Negroes as soldiers.

### 1781, November 8. *REVOLUTION. CONTINENTAL ARMY MOVES CLOSER TO CHARLESTOWN.*

Gen. Nathaniel Green established the Continental Army at Round O, about forty-five miles west of Charleston.

### 1781, December 1. *ENGLAND. TOWER OF LONDON.*

Henry Laurens wrote a bitter note, which was smuggled from the Tower and sent to Congress:

> Almost fifteen months I have been closely confined and inhumanely treated. The treaty for exchange is abortive. There has been languor, and there is neglect somewhere. If I merit your attention, you will not longer delay speedy and efficacious means for my deliverance.

### 1781, December 13. *REVOLUTION. SKIRMISH ON JOHN'S ISLAND.*

Col. John Laurens, recently returned from Yorktown, led an American assault against 500 British infantry.

### 1781, December 17-18. *REVOLUTION. ELECTION.*

Elections were held for a General Assembly in South Carolina, which was to be convened at Jacksonborough on January 8, 1782. In parishes still held by the British, mainly around Charlestown, the election was lightly attended. A later study of the election revealed "that fifteen Charleston voters managed to elect thirty representatives and two senators from St. Philip and St. Michael."

### 1781, December 27. *REVOLUTION. GILLON EXPEDITION.*

Commodore Gillon and *South Carolina* approached Charlestown and discov-ered thirty-two British ships. For the next five days Gillon sailed up and down the coast looking for a place to land. Finally, Gillon sailed to Cuba to spend the winter.

# 1782

### 1782, January 8. *REVOLUTION. ASSEMBLY MEETS.*

Gov. John Rutledge and the Assembly convened in Jacksonboro, thirty miles from Charleston, near the site of the Stono Slave Rebellion on the Edisto River.

## 1782, January 13. *Revolution. Naval. Gillon Expedition.*

*South Carolina* arrived in Havana, Cuba. In tow were five Jamaican ships loaded with rum and sugar, which Gillon had captured while sailing past the Bahamas. The prizes netted £91,500, which Gillon used to refit *South Carolina*.

## 1782, January 17. *Rutledge's Charge to the Assembly.*

Gov. John Rutledge gave an address to the Assembly charging them with the duty to "determine whether the Forfeiture and Appropriation" of Tory properties was appropriate. He also stated that:

> the good People of this State have not only felt the common calamities of War, but, from the wanton and savage Manner in which it has been prosecuted, they have experienced such Severities as are unpracticed, and will scarcely be credited by civilized Nations ... They have tarnished the Glory of the British Arms, disgraced the Profession of a British soldier, and fixed indelible Stigmas of Rapine, Cruelty, Perfidy, and Profaneness, on the British name.

Christopher Gadsden was elected governor, but declined due to his health, which had suffered during his imprisonment in St. Augustine. John Mathews was chosen as the new governor, "a younger and more even-tempered individual."

Laws were quickly passed for raising Continental troops and for punishing "conspicuous Tories." Called the "Act for Disposing of Certain Estates and Banishing Certain Persons" it banished Loyalists, and provided for the confiscation and sale of their estates. The list of confiscation contained more than 700 individuals.

## 1782, January 21. *Slavery.*

Gen. Nathaniel Greene pleaded with John Rutledge to consider using armed slaves, by utilizing:

> this great resource that you have neglected to avail yourselves of, which if you had adopted before the reduction of Charlestown might have secured your country against all it has undergone.

## 1782, January 25. *Revolution. Jacksonborough Assembly. Slavery.*

Aedanus Burke, in a letter to Arthur Middleton, wrote that the Assembly was:

> Composed of very respectable good men and we are happily extricated from that Tory dead weight which used to embarrass our Councils in Charles Town ... Governor Rutledge conducted the business with good policy in excluding from voting all such persons who had not borne arms antecedent to 27th September ... I would think it madness to allow

men to influence our Election, who had borne arms against us without giving some Test of their attachment to us ...

He also had some prescient words concerning the Northern attitude toward slavery:

> the Northern people regard the condition in which we hold our slaves in a different light from us. I am much deceived indeed, if they do not secretly *wish* for a general emancipation.

## 1782, February. *REVOLUTION. THE PINCKNEYS RETURN.*

Charles Cotesworth and Thomas Pinckney left Philadelphia to return to Charlestown even though they were not officially paroled.

## 1782, February 4. *REVOLUTION. SLAVERY.*

John Laurens once again submitted his plan of arming blacks with the promise of freedom, with no success. He wrote to his friend Alexander Hamilton, "I was outvoted, having only reason on my side, and being opposed by a triple-headed monster of avarice, prejudice, and pusillanimity in our assemblies."

## 1782, February 23. *LAURENS RELEASED FROM THE TOWER.*

Henry Laurens was released from the Tower, in exchange for Lord Cornwallis, and the payment of £12,000. He wrote:

> On the 31st of December, being, as I had long been, in an extreme ill state of health, unable to rise from my bed, I was carried out of the Tower to the presence of the Lord Chief Justice of England, and admitted to bail "to appear at the court of king's bench on the first day of Easter term, and not to depart thence without leave of the court.

Laurens immediately sent for his daughters to join him from France in London. He then went for several weeks to recuperate with the waters of Bath.

Edward Rutledge argued forcefully against Cornwallis's release. Most South Carolina patriots blamed Cornwallis for the wholesale murder and plundering across the state. Rutledge wrote that Cornwallis should be "held a Prisoner for Life ... because he was a Monster and an Enemy to Humanity."

## 1782, February 26. *TORY PROPERTIES CONFISCATED.*

The estates of many Loyalists in South Carolina began to be confiscated, including Christopher Fitzsimmons, whose store had been vandalized in 1778 because he had raised the price of candles.

## 1782, February 27. *PARLIAMENT VOTES TO END WAR.*

Parliament voted to end the war.

## 1782, March 18. *BIRTH.*

John Caldwell Calhoun was born in Abbeville, in the South Carolina backcountry. His mother was described as being "full of intelligence and energy ... strong will and temper," attributes her son would inherit.

### BUILDINGS OF CHARLESTON
### David Ramsay House, 92 Broad Street

In 1782 Dr. David Ramsay purchased a home at 92 Broad Street at a cost of £3,500. It was in this home he began to research and write his *History of the Revolution in South Carolina,* which was published in 1785.

Dr. David Ramsay house, pictured in 1935. *Courtesy of the Library of Congress.*

## 1782, March 19. *REVOLUTION. NAVAL.*

Captain Michael Rudolph captured a British galley in the Ashley River.

## 1782, April. *REVOLUTION. TREATY OF PARIS.*

Negotiations between England and the American government began, involving Benjamin Franklin, John Jay, John Adams and Henry Laurens. Martha Laurens was living with her father, and often acted as a secretary for the American delegation.

### 1782, April. *REVOLUTION. PROTECTION TAX.*

The Assembly issued an order that anyone who had sought protection, and remained in Charlestown, should leave the city immediately or face confiscation or amercement (tax/fine) of their property. Colonel Charles Pinckney, Jr. refused to leave and his property was taxed at 12%. His cousin, Charles Cotesworth, urged him "to leave the British and come out of Charlestown."

### 1782, April. *REVOLUTION. GILLON EXPEDITION.*

Juan Manuel de Cagigal, Spanish Captain-General of Cuba, offered Commodore Gillon a command of a maritime force of sixty-two vessels, to attack the British-held Bahamas. Gillon accepted.

### 1782, April 21. *MARRIAGE.*

William Washington married Jane Elliott of Sandy Hill, South Carolina. Elliott and Washington met when she made his regiment a battle flag that he carried into combat from Cowpens to Eutaw Springs.

### 1782, April 22. *DEATH. PIRACY.*

Anne Cormac Bonny Burleigh, former pirate, died at the age of eighty-two.

### 1782, April 22. *REVOLUTION. GILLON EXPEDITION.*

*South Carolina* was the flagship of a Spanish invasion of the Bahamas that left Havana, Cuba. Included were fifteen American privateers carrying 3,000 troops.

### 1782, April 22. *REVOLUTION. MUTINY PLOT DISCOVERED.*

In Dorchester, a group of Pennsylvania and New Jersey troops were discovered plotting a mutiny against the Americans. Gen. Greene had them arrested and immediately hanged their ringleader, Gormel.

### 1782, April 23. *SLAVERY. DENMARK VESEY.*

Capt. Joseph Vesey returned to Haiti with another cargo of slaves. He was informed that his former "pet," Telemaque, was suffering from "epileptic fits" and a doctor had "certified that the lad was unwell." His sale was "thereupon cancelled," meaning that Vesey was forced to repurchase the boy. He was surprised to find that during the few months on the island, the boy had become proficient in French.

Vesey put Telemaque back to work again as his cabin boy and miraculously, the epileptic fits ceased as soon as they sailed from Haiti. Vesey must have seen this as more proof of the boy's intelligence and cleverness, and decided he would be more valuable as his personal servant.

### 1782, April 24. *BRITISH OCCUPATION.*

Charles Cotesworth Pinckney, camped with Gen. Greene's army on the Ashley River at Dorchester, wrote his brother-in-law, Arthur Middleton in Philadelphia, suggesting his younger cousin, Charles, should be in South Carolina.

### 1782, May 8. *Revolution. Gillon Expedition.*

The British governor of the Bahamas surrendered the island to the overwhelming Spanish force, led by Commodore Gillon. A few days later *South Carolina* sailed to Philadelphia.

### 1782, May 31. *Revolution. Gillon Expedition.*

Commodore Gillon and *South Carolina* arrived in Philadelphia. Gillon was soon prosecuted by the Chevalier de Luxembourg, for his share of the prize money captured by his ship *South Carolina.* Gillon resigned his commission and ordered his captain, John Joyner, to continuing cruising until June 1783, when the lease of the ship would be end.

### 1782, June 1. *Commerce. Culture.*

Hamilton Stevenson advertised his services as a "painter of miniatures or a hair sylist."

### 1782, July 11. *Revolution. British Evacuate Savannah.*

Gen. Anthony Wayne forced the British evacuation of Savannah, after restoring civil government.

### 1782, August 23. *Revolution. Gillon Expedition.*

*South Carolina* arrived in La Corunna, Spain to replenish stores. Gillon had taken two prizes during the voyage from the North Sea. These captured ships netted Gillon and the crew much needed £25,000 sterling.

### 1782, August 27. *British Occupation. Death of John Laurens.*

Col. John Laurens was killed at Tar Bluff on the Combahee River, about forty miles southwest of Charleston, in a completely useless skirmish. The British were trying to loot supplies of rice before leaving, and Laurens' company of fifty men were determined to stop them. John Laurens was the first Patriot killed in the battle.

Martha Laurens, living in Vigan, France, did not learn about her brother's death until three months later. However, during her morning prayers for her family, on this day, she stopped praying for her brother as she felt "there was no longer need."

Years later, while visiting Charleston, Lafayette stated, "Colonel Laurens was the most valiant officer and accomplished gentleman I ever knew. He was the beau ideal of gallantry."

### 1782, August 29. *Revolution. Marion's Last Action.*

In his last action of the war, General Francis Marion defeated British dragoons under the command of Loyalist Major Thomas Fraser.

### 1782, September 6. *Revolution. British Outposts Abandoned.*

Gen. Andrew Pickens and Gen. Nathaniel Greene discovered British posts on James Island had been abandoned.

## 1782, September 22. *British Occupation. Death.*

Colonel Charles Pinckney, Jr. died. Charles Cotesworth, his nephew, wrote to his sister Harriott saying, "Give vent to your tears for he was a man of worth."

Ignorant of his father's death, Charles Pinckney was in Philadelphia, making plans to travel to Europe and "sowing wild oats." When he received word of his father's death, he planned to return to Charlestown.

Gen. Francis Marion.
*Courtesy of the New York Public Library.*

## 1782, September 28. *British Occupation.*

The last issue of the *Royal Gazette* was published by John Wells. He left Charlestown after the British evacuation, fearing recrimination for not supporting the Patriots.

## 1782, November 6. *British Occupation.*

Upon receiving the news of John Laurens's death, John Adams wrote to Henry Laurens:

> I feel for you more than I can or ought to express. Our country has lost its most promising character, in a manner, however, that was worthy of the cause. I can say nothing more to you, but that you have much greater reasons to say, in this case, as a Duke of Ormond said of an Earl

of Ossory, "I would not exchange my dead son for any living son in the world."

Laurens replied, "Thank God, I had a son who dared to die in defence of his country."

## 1782, November 14. BRITISH OCCUPATION. LAST SOUTH CAROLINA MILITARY ACTION.

In the last action against the British in South Carolina, a Patriot group, commanded by Col. Thaddeus Kosciuszko, unsuccessfully tried to run off a British woodcutting party on James Island.

## 1782, November 29. REVOLUTION. TREATY OF PARIS.

Henry Laurens arrived in Paris from Vigan, France, to help negotiate a peace treaty between the United States and Great Britain. The next day he signed the preliminary articles with John Jay, Benjamin Franklin and John Adams.

## 1782, December 14. BRITISH EVACUATE CHARLESTOWN.

The British Army evacuated Charlestown. Wholesale looting by British troops had begun weeks before the withdrawal, private property stolen from houses. More than 5,000 slaves were taken by enterprising British officers, who transported them to the West Indies to be re-sold. Major Traile of the Royal Artillery, took down St. Michael's church bells and carried them away as British property.

As significant as the material losses were, perhaps in the long run, the loss of people was more devastating. Approximately 3,800 whites and 5,300 blacks joined the British exodus, resettling in Jamaica, Bermuda, England and St. Lucia. However, hundreds of British soldiers deserted, and remained in South Carolina.

The Continental Army entered the city that afternoon at 3:00 P.M. Gen. Nathaniel Greene escorted Gov. John Mathews and the Assemblymen into town. Gen. William Moultrie recalled:

> It was a grand and pleasing sight to see the enemy's fleet, upwards of three hundred sail, lying at anchor from Fort Johnson to Five Fathom Hole, in a curve line, as the current runs; and what made it more agreeable, they were ready to depart.
>
> I cannot forget that happy day when we marched into Charlestown with the American troops; it was a proud day to me, and I felt myself much elated ... both citizens and soldiers shed mutual tears of joy. The fourteenth day of December, 1782, ought to never be forgotten by the Carolinians; it ought to be a day of festivity with them, as it was the real day of their deliverance and independence.

At John Rutledge's invitation, Gen. Green made his headquarters at Rutledge's house on Broad Street. The thirty-month nightmare occupation was over, with bitterness lingering between both sides.

David Duncan Wallace, in *South Carolina: A Short History*, claims that Charlestown residents suffered losses valued at more than £300,000 sterling at the hands of the plundering British army.

Gen. Moultrie commented on the bitter partisanship between the Tories and Whigs that prevailed in South Carolina:

> Each party oppressed the other as much as they possibly could, which raised their inveteracy to so great a height, that they carried on the war with savage cruelty: although they had been friends, neighbors and brothers they had no feelings for each other, and no principles of humanity left. When the British party prevailed, after the surrender of Charleston, the Tories gave full scope to their interested and malicious passions ... and committed the most violent acts of cruelty and injustice, which was sanctioned by the British, provided they called themselves friends to the king.

### 1782, December 19. *REVOLUTION. SOUTH CAROLINA NAVY.*

*South Carolina* left Philadelphia with Captain John Joyner in charge. She was captured a few days later by British forces and taken to New York. Most of her crew were imprisoned on prison ships in New York harbor.

### 1782, December 20. *SLAVERY. COMMERCE. DENMARK VESEY.*

Capt. Joseph Vesey returned to Charlestown with his wife, Kezia, their son John and Vesey's personal servant - cabin boy, sixteen year-old Telemaque.

# 1783

### 1783. *ARRIVALS.*

Jonathon Lucas, a skilled English millwright, was shipwrecked off the coast of Charleston and settled in the city.

### 1783. *SLAVERY.*

Hector St. John de Crèvecoeur was on his way to a dinner party at a plantation near Charleston when he passed "a negro, suspended in a cage, and left there to expire." Crèvecoeur continued in his letter:

> I shudder when I recollect that the birds had already picked out his eyes, his cheek bones were bare; his arms had been attacked in several places, and his bodyseemed covered with a multitude of wounds. From the edges of the hollow sockets and from the lacerations with which he was disfigured, the blood slowly dropped, and tinged the ground beneath ... The living spectre, though deprived of his eyes, could still

distinctively hear, and begged me to give him some water to allay his thirst.

After Crèvecoeur reached the plantation, the owner explained to him that "the laws of self-preservation rendered such executions necessary."

## 1783, January. *GILLON RETURNS.*

Commodore Gillon retutned to Charlestown.

## 1783, January 6. *RESTORATION OF CIVILIAN GOVERNMENT.*

The General Assembly convened in Charlestown, four weeks after the British evacuation.

## 1783, January 14. *POLITICAL UNREST. AN ADDRESS TO THE FREEMEN OF SOUTH CAROLINA.*

Aedanus Burke published *An Address to the Freemen of South Carolina* in which he attacked the "excesses of confiscation and amercement." He argued that:

> the people of at large in whom the sovereignty of the State *should be vested,* ought to be informed whether public measures be right or wrong; and it therefore becomes the duty of every citizen to present the subject in as open and publick a light as opportunity or knowledge may enable him.

He also argued that John Rutledge was "not the first man to subvert liberty in the guise of preserving it" and that the "aggrandizement of family and perpetuation of power were often more important to the ambitious man than public freedom."

## 1783, January 24. *POLITICS.*

Gov. John Mathews addressed the Assembly.

## 1783, January 30. *COMMERCE. BRITISH OCCUPATION.*

A petition was submitted by "William Logan and others concerning the business practices of certain British Merchants in Charlestown" to Gov. John Mathews. They requested permission to "stay in the city long enough to sell their surplus goods and collect the debts owed them."

## 1783, February. *FREE BLACKS REQUIRED TO WEAR BADGES.*

An act was passed that required all free blacks in Charlestown wear a badge iden-tifying them as free, to purchase a license to practice trades, and pay an annual poll tax of four shillings, nine pence."

## 1783, February 4. *POLITICS. ELECTION. NEW GOVERNOR.*

Benjamin Guerard was elected governor of South Carolina. Guerard, a lawyer, helped defend Charlestown against the British siege in 1780, and was imprisoned on the schooner *Pack Horse* before being excelled to Philadelphia.

The Tax Act of 1783 placed a tax of one dollar on every one hundred acres of land, regardless of quality.

### 1783, February 17. COMMERCE. POLITICS.

The planter-dominated legislature extended the Loyalist merchants' stay an additional twelve months, until March 1, 1784. This benefited the planters, who had purchased slaves and other merchandise from these merchants. Charlestown quickly split into pro and anti-British merchant factions.

### 1783, March 1. SOUTH CAROLINA NAVY DISSOLVED.

The Assembly dissolved the South Carolina State Navy.

### 1783, March 18. MARRIAGE.

Dr. David Ramsay married Francis Witherspoon, daughter of the president of Princeton. They returned to Charlestown and took up residence at his house on Broad Street.

### 1783, April 2. CHARLES PINCKNEY RETURNS.

Charles Pinckney returned to Charlestown and lived at 2 Orange Street, helping his mother with his father's estate. The will reserved property valued at £53,000 and "sixty of the worst of my plantation slaves" to be sold to pay his debts. The mansion on Queen Street was left to his son, Charles. The remainder of his estate – three plantations, Fee Farm and Drainfield in St. Bartholomew's Parish and Snee Farm in Christ Church, were to be divided equally among his wife and children.

### 1783, May. SOUTH CAROLINA NAVY.

Captain John Joyner of *South Carolina* returned to Charleston. He faced a court-martial hearing and was honorably acquitted.

### 1783, May 12. CULTURE. THEATER.

The freemasons sponsored a production of *The Orphan* for the benefit of widows and orphans at the newly opened Mr. Strickland's Long Room. The actors were "a set of Young Gentlemen, who have studied this play for their amusement."

### 1783, May 18. COMMERCE.

Planter Pierce Butler commented that the war gave the city "a new spring for industry. Our wharfs present a scene of bustle and activity that I have not seen for many years."

### 1783, June. LEGAL. COURT OF GENERAL SESSIONS.

Aedanus Burke presided at the first Court of General Sessions in Charlestown after the war. He addressed the court:

It is going on four years since we enjoyed the privilege of meeting each other in the court of sessions, and now we offer you our warmest congratulations, that the bitter calamities through which you passed during that period, are by the blessings of heaven at an end; that happy peace is once more returned; our country in its independence, and hold dignity among nations. Our objective now must be to restore harmony under the protection of law.

Pierce Butler.
*Courtesy of the Library of Congress*

### 1783, June. *CONFISCATION ACT.*

Gen. Moultrie acquired the 700-acre Kent Plantation in Berkeley, confiscated from former governor James Colleton, for the crime of being an absentee British subject. Colleton's great-great-grandfather had been Sir John Colleton, one of original proprietors.

### 1783, June 8. *COMMERCE. RAMSAY TO RUSH.*

David Ramsay wrote to his friend Benjamin Rush: "This country is left destitute, and will not be like the former Carolina for years to come."

### 1783, June 11. *CULTURE. POLITICAL UNREST.*

David Ramsay wrote, "This revolution had introduced so much anarchy, that it will take half a century to eradicate the licentiousness of the people."

### 1783, June 11. *POLITICAL UNREST. RIOTS.*

The *South Carolina Gazette and General Advertiser* reported that "a considerable number" of artisans and mechanics marched the streets in protest against the Tory merchants. They dragged "four or five persons obnoxious to the state" to local water pumps for a "public dousing."

Gov. Guerard described these protests as "great riots and disturbances, or a most dangerous nature."

### 1783, June 21. *BIRTH.*

Theodosia Burr was born in Albany, New York, daughter of Aaron Burr. She would later marry South Carolina governor, Joseph Alston.

### 1783, July 2. *WEST INDIES CLOSED TO AMERICAN SHIPPING.*

The British closed their West Indian islands to American shipping. Only British ships could now carry Carolina cargo to the British Caribbean market. Rice planters, who needed to quickly replenish their plantations, became more deeply indebted to British merchants in Charlestown, who extended credit for slaves and other commodities.

### 1783, July 4. *COMMERCE.*

Alexander Gillon was optimistic about the Charleston economy. He anticpated the return of "a wide, general and extensive trade, hitherto unknown to many, and new channels of commerce hitherto unexplored and unthought of."

### 1783, July 12. *POLITICAL UNREST. RIOTS.*

Thomas Barron, a British subject, "imprudently and grossly insulted a citizen" on Broad Street. Within a few hours a Patriot mob, led by Commodore Alexander Gillon, started a riot against the Tory merchants still living in Charlestown, tarring and feathering several Loyalists.

### 1783, July 16. *SOUTH CAROLINA GAZETTE RESUMES PUBLICATION.*

Ann Timothy, widow of Peter Timothy, resumed publication of the *Gazette of the State of South Carolina,* continuing the tradition started by her mother-in-law, Elizabeth Timothy.

### 1783, July 16. *COMMERCE. SLAVERY.*

Capt. Joseph Vesey leased two town lots from John Christian Smith. Vesey and his wife lived at 281 King Street, and the other building on East Bay Street, became Vesey's business office.

He set himself up as a ship chandler – an importer and retailer of various commodities including naval stores, rum, sugar, and African slaves. To raise the capital for his business, Vesey sold his ship *Prospect* and liquidated his interest in two other Caribbean slave trading vessels, *Dove* and *Polly*.

Vesey's trusted manservant, Telemaque, enjoyed a quasi-freedom in the urban environment of Charlestown. He discovered a thriving black community living an illicit social life in the city's back alleys, hidden courtyards, street corners and church basements.

## 1783, August. *COMMERCE.*

Gadsden established a partnership with his sons, Thomas and Philip, called "Christopher Gadsden and Company." It was a factoring business located on Gadsden's Wharf, which became financial successful.

## 1783, August. *CULTURE. COMMERCE.*

A report was submitted to the Assembly on the discovery of 14,000 pounds of gunpowder inside the bricked-in walls of the Exchange Building. This was the powder that Gen. Moultrie had hidden in May 1780 before the British took the city. To their surprise most of the powder was still usable.

## 1783, August 6. *POLITICAL UNREST.*

The *Gazette of the State of South Carolina* reported many artisans and mechanics complained against the "mal-administration of men in power or public trust." In particular, they argued that "greedy planters and especially lawyers" were allowing their self-interest to trample the public good. As the prominent lawyers, they named:

| | |
|---|---|
| John Rutledge | Benjamin Guerard |
| Edward Rutledge | Charles Cotesworth Pinckney |
| William Drayton | Thomas Pinckney |
| Thomas Bee | Charles Pinckney |
| John Mathews | Jacob Read |

## 1783, August 13. *INCORPORATION BILL PROPOSED. NAME CHANGE.*

Edward Rutledge, Thomas Heyward, and Thomas Bee proposed a bill of incorporation for Charlestown. They claimed it was necessary "from the extent, growing trade and opulence of this metropolis." An elected intendant (mayor) and thirteen wardens would have the power to govern the city, whose name was changed to Charleston. All white males who paid a tax equal to three shillings could vote.

Some saw the incorporation as a move by the lowcountry elite to control the growing radical street demonstrations by groups of artisans and mechanics. Others realized it would also be a good administrative move, freeing the legislature from such issues as policing the slave population, maintaining the city markets, repairing streets, and regulating the harbor.

The Act to Incorporate Charleston also stated that the:

following public lands and buildings within said city, viz: the lands appropriated for the Exchange the beef market, the lower market, the fish market, the market at the Western end of Broad Street, with the buildings respectively thereon were to be vested in the City Council.

*Note: from this point forward in the manuscript, the city will be called "Charleston."*

## 1783, August 13. CULTURE. COMMERCE.

A seal of the city of Charleston was authorized, which was unveiled in 1790.

Seal of the City of Charleston.

## 1783, August 16. CHARLESTON INCORPORATED.

The *South Carolina Gazette and General Advertiser* noted that:

> The Assembly has now incorporated this town on principals very different from Royal Charters, and on a basis the most liberal for a free and independent people ... a new era in Charleston – may it be propitious to its rising glory, increasing commerce and growing opulence.

## 1783, August 16. ELECTION. FIRST INTENDANT.

Richard Hutson was elected the first Intendant of Charleston. He was educated at the College of New Jersey (Princeton), practiced law, and owned over 2,300 acres and seventeen slaves in St. Andrews parish. The first city council included:

| | |
|---|---|
| James Nelson | Thomas Heyward, Jr. |
| Thomas Bee | John Mathews |
| Alexander Alexander | George Flagg |
| Bernard Beekman | Thomas Radcliffe, Jr. |
| Joshua Ward | John Lewis Gervias |

## 1783, August 23. *Treaty of Paris. Laurens Leaves.*

Henry Laurens left the treaty negotiations in Paris to travel to Vigan, France in order visit his ailing brother, James.

## 1783, August 29. *Culture. Society of the Cincinnati Formed.*

The Society of the Cincinnati formed a chapter in Charleston. Membership was limited to Continental Army staff officers and their oldest sons. General William Moultrie was voted president. Their bylaws stated that "no person who has joined the Enemy or taken protection from them since the Declaration of Independence" would be eligible for membership.

## 1783, September. *Revolution. Statistics.*

During the Revolution, South Carolina was the site of more than 130 battles and skirmishes. In proportion to population, South Carolina exceeded all the other states in her contributions to the cause. With 100,000 white residents, the state had spent $11,523,299.29. Massachusetts, with three times the population, contributed the same amount to the cause. Eighteen per cent of the battlefield deaths during the war took place in South Carolina.

## 1783, September 3. *Treaty of Paris Signed.*

Treaty of Paris was signed by Benjamin Franklin, John Jay and John Adams. In a letter to his wife Abagail, John Adams stated:

> I have the Satisfaction to inform you that the definitive Treaties were all Signed yesterday, and the Preliminaries with Holland were Signed the day before. Dr. Franklin has fallen down again with the Gout and Gravel ... Mr. Laurens, has a Brother declining, so that he will go to the south of France, untill he knows his Brother's Fates.

## 1783, September 9. *Commerce.*

David Ramsay reported to Benjamin Rush that "the genius of our people is entirely turned from war to commerce. Schemes of business and partnerships for extending commerce are daily forming."

## 1783, September 26. *Politics. Culture.*

The city of Charleston ratified an ordinance "to restrain the exhibition of theatrical entertainments within the city" without permission of the city council. Failure would incur a fine of 10 sterling for each offense. Any tavern keeper who permitted performances would lose his license for seven years. The ordinance claimed theatrical enterprises corrupt "the morals of youth ... and encourage idleness, riot and disorder."

## 1783, September 28. *COMMERCE. SLAVERY.*

Capt. Joseph Vesey placed an advertisement in the *South CarolinaGazette* as "J. Vesey & Co." which offered more than "100 Prime slaves from Tortola for sale every fair day except Sunday."

Richard Hutson, first Intendant (mayor) of Charleston. *Courtesy of the National Archives*

## 1783, October. *SOCIETY OF THE CINCINNATI ATTACKED.*

Aedanus Burke published *Considerations on the Society or Order of the Cincinnati*, denouncing the order as a way to establish "an impregnable hereditary peerage, reducing the mass of people to subservience before the experiment [of liberty] was fairly begun."

His pamphlet sparked a national debate, and was reprinted in Philadelphia, Hartford, New York and Newport. John Jay, John Adams and Elbridge Gerry were some of the most prominent men who sided with Burke and were critical of the Society.

Other writers defended the Society, often deriding Burke as "one of those men who are born to disappoint every expectation of their friends," a "radical Irish immigrant," and that man who "appeared on the bench in a lady's black petticoat."

### 1783, October 7. POLITICS.

The new city council appointed constables, passed laws "governing mariners and seamen within the city" and established a nightly guard and town watch.

### 1783, October 27. SLAVERY.

In a letter to the *South Carolina Gazette and General Advertiser,* a writer who called himself "Another Patriot," expressed outrage over the sight of the American flag flying "in every yard where the unfortunate Africans are penned for sale … War veterans must burn with indignation at such an affront offered to it."

### 1783, December. COMMERCE. ANTI-BRITANNIC SOCIETY FOUNDED.

Alexander Gillon, Henry Peronneau, Benjamin Waller, Benjamin Cudsworth and James Fallon founded the Marine Anti-Britannic Society and the Whig Club of 600. They were opposed to all trade with Britain and British merchants. Gillon advocated confiscation of Loyalist property and "the removal of the state capital to the Congaree River in the interior" of the state.

### 1783, December 20. CULTURE. THEATER.

The first theatrical performance in Charleston after the war, approved by the city after the British evacuation, was held in the Exchange Building.

### 1783, December 27. COMMERCE.

Business was so good that Dr. Robert Pringle set aside his medical practice and formed a mercantile partnership with his brother-in-law, William Freeman, Jr., of Bristol, England. Pringle owned 235 acres and fifty-eight slaves near Jacksonborough, south of Charleston. He claimed his customers were "gentlemen of fortune and means [who] attach themselves wholly to our store for everything they want."

# 1784

### 1784. DEATH. MARTHA LAURENS PREDICTION.

James Laurens died in Vigan, France. That morning, Martha Laurens, in London, started out of her bed. She declared, "Uncle James is dead," to her father. She requested that her friend, Miss Catherine Futerell, record the day and hour. Several weeks later a letter arrived informing them of James Laurens' death, precisely at the day and hour Martha had stated.

### 1784, January 14. TREAT OF PARIS RATIFIED.

Congress ratified the Treaty of Paris, officially ending the Revolutionary War.

### 1783, January 30. POLITICS.

John Rutledge was sworn into his seat in the Assembly by Judge Aedanus Burke, who had written the infamous *An Address to the Freemen of South Carolina* the year before, which was very critical of Rutledge.

## 1784, February 4. *CHAMBER OF COMMERCE RE-ESTABLISHED.*

In an effort to promote new non-British avenues of trades, a group of thirteen Charleston merchants met at the City Tavern to reestablish the Chamber of Commerce. Their number soon grew to seventy. Founding members included Edward Darrell, Alexander Gillon, and John Lewis Gervais. Membership was denied to all foreign merchants.

They opened correspondence with Thomas Jefferson, who whose the American minister to Paris, seeking to increase South Carolina trade with France.

## 1784, February 16. *ELECTION.*

Benjamin Guerard was elected governor and William Moultrie Lt. Governor.

## 1784, March 2. *POLITICS.*

Charles Pinckney took his seat in the South Carolina General Assembly.

## 1784, March 5. *POLITICAL UNREST. WHIG CLUB OF 600.*

James Fallon, a well-known rebel-rouser, began holding nightly meetings at the City Tavern of what he called "a committee of 600." Fallon was a man involved in "perpetual broils" and claimed that liberty was "smothered ... by the aristocrats and tories." Fallon printed handbills naming certain British merchants who should leave the state within the month.

## 1784, March 8. *POLITICAL UNREST.*

Late in the evening, after a spirited meeting of the "committee of 600":

> a multitude of men ... burst forth from the City Tavern, formed an array in the street and marched with colours flying, towards the square of St. Michael ... the peaceable part of the citizens flew to their arms and met in the square, some on foot, some on horseback.

The mob was dispersed by Thomas Pinckney, William Washington, and John Blake. Aedanus Burke wrote that the ringleader of the mob, James Fallon "kept behind the curtain, as if he had no hand in it."

## 1784, March 17. *THOMPSON TAVERN SCANDAL. DUEL.*

William Thompson was a tavern owner and former Continental Army officer. He was also a member of the Marine Anti-Britannic Society. His business catered to the radical democratic crowd, who had a history of agitation against the aristocrats of the city. He had recently claimed that dancing was frivolous and inconsistent with the principals of democracy. He requested that the dances hosted in the State House by the legislature cease.

On St. Patrick's Day, John Rutledge sent a slave woman to Thompson's business to watch an artillery display from the second floor of his tavern. Thompson refused to allow the woman into the tavern. Rutledge considered this a personal insult and demanded an explanation. Thompson challenged Rutledge to a duel, which was illegal. Rutledge informed the legislature, and Thompson was arrested for a week.

Upon Thompson's release, the Marine Anti-Britannic Society adopted a resolution thanking Thompson for:

> his *spirited, manly,* and patriotic conduct ... when Aristocratical principles endeavored to subvert and destroy every *genuine idea of real republicanism.*

Many in Charleston were outraged by Thompson's treatment by the aristocrats, fueling months of attacks on "aristocrats, lawyers, Tories." The anti-British sentiment was strong. Riots became commonplace on the street. Tories were burned in effigy and others were threatened to leave town, or else.

## 1784, March 23. *POLITICS.*

The Assembly elected the following delegates to the Confederation Congress in Trenton, New Jersey:

Henry Laurens (did not serve)    Alexander Gillon (did not serve)
Jacob Read                       David Ramsay
John Bull                        Charles Pinckney

## 1784, March 26. *LEGAL.*

The manner in which an alien could become a citizen of South Carolina was described by law.

## 1784, April 8. *COMMERCE.*

David Ramsay informed Benjamin Rush that "our next business will be to improve our country, cutting canals and building bridges."

## 1784, April 8. *SOCIETY OF CINCINNATI. POLITICAL UNREST.*

The Society of the Cincinnati was still defending itself against the attack started by Aedanus Burke. George Washington wrote to Thomas Jefferson, asking for his opinion. Washington wrote that "the Pamphlet ascribed to Mr. Burke ... had its effect. People are alarmed, especially in the Eastern States."

Jefferson's suggested that Washington should distance himself from the Society.

## 1784, April 26. *BIRTH.*

Jean Jacques Audubon (later Anglicized to John James) was born on the island of Santo Domingo.

## 1784, April 29. *POLITICS.*

William Thompson published an account of his arrest by the Assembly, attacking the elites as "the NABOBS of this State, their servile *Toad-eaters,* the BOBS, and their serviley-servile tools and lick-sprittles of Power to *both,* the BOBBETTES." He also claimed that the objective had been:

> To humiliate a *Publican*, a *stranger* a wretch of no higher rank in the Commonwealth than that of a *Common-Citizen*: for having dared to dispute with a *John Rutledge* or any other of the NABOB tribe.

Thompson ultimately lost his tavern lease and left town the next year.

## 1784, Spring. *JOSEPH BROWN LADD ARRIVES.*

Nineteen-year old Dr. Joseph Brown Ladd arrived in Charleston from Rhode Island to establish a medical practice. He was fleeing vicious rumors about his character spread by the relatives of a woman, Amanda, he wished to marry. Amanda, an orphan, was adopted by a wealthy family, but her fortune was held in a trust controlled by her uncle, who would lose access to the fortune if she married.

However, none of that scandal was known to the residents of Charleston, and Ladd quickly became a popular man about town. Over the next two years he published over seventy poems in the *American Museum,* one of the most influential magazines in America, with a subscription list that included Benjamin Franklin, John Jay, Thomas Jefferson, James Madison and George Washington.

## 1784, July 28. *COMMERCE.*

Thomas Jefferson wrote from Paris to Goose Creek planter, Ralph Izard, inquiring about importing South Carolina produce.

## 1784, July 29. *POLITICAL UNREST.*

William Hornby wrote in the *Gazette of the State of South Carolina:*

> In these days we are equal citizens of a DEMOCRATIC REPUBLIC, in which *jealousy* and *opposition* must naturally exist, while there exists a difference in the minds, interests and sentiments of mankind.

## 1784, August 14. *POLITICAL UNREST.*

Christopher Gadsden wrote to Sam Adams in Boston "'tis our common interest too support government and not let a few designing men set us by the ears for their own purposes."

## 1784, Fall. *POLITICS. ELECTION.*

Alexander Gillon, head of the Whig Club of 600, challenged incumbent Intendant, Richard Hutson, in the election. The democrats insisted a vote for Hutson was a vote for the aristocracy. The Hutson faction claimed a vote for Gillon was a vote for disorder. Huston won 387-260. A letter to the *Gazette* stated: "Do not send wealthy men to the legislature, or elect anyone … who did not reside in the district he represented."

Christopher Gadsden accused Gillon of being able to "govern and influence a few weak and deluded men." Hutson's election was referred to as "law and liberty trampling on anarchy and tyranny."

## 1784, August 27. CULTURE.

Ralph Izard wrote to Thomas Jefferson about the psychological damage the British left behind, noting that "the hatred planted in the breasts of our Citizens against each other is the most serious injury they have done us."

## 1784, September 16. POLITICS. WHIG CLUB OF 600.

The "Secret Committee" for the Whig Club of 600 argued that a "few wealthy families" were using "*family influence* into the government" in order to establish an "odious *aristocracy* over their betters." They warned that:

> enormous wealth is seldom the associate of pure and disinterested virtue. Elect no wealthy candidate ... above all never place confidence in or take your political creed from lawyers – that double-tongued race of men who are bred up to chicanery and deceit.

This was a direct attack on the Rutledge and Pinckney families, who were the most powerful in South Carolina.

## 1784, September 23. COMMERCE. ECONOMY IMPROVES.

Henry Laurens was delighted by the economic activity in Charleston.

> The merchant, the farmer, the mechanic are all busy in their respective vocations, each one anxious in the pursuit of his own, at the same time without seeming to know or mean it, contributing to the public weal. In a word, everybody appears to be busy in some way or other.

## 1784, September 27. POLITICAL UNREST. A FEW SALUTARY HINTS.

Aedanus Burke published his third political pamphlet, *A Few Salutary Hints, Pointing Out the Policy and Consequences of admitting British Subjects to Engross our trade and become our Citizens*. Burke argued that allowing British merchants to remain would be ruinous.

> I was one, whose opinion it was, that they would soon incorporate with us, make good citizens, and that after the war was over, our enmities should be forgotten; but I am sorry that I fell into such an error; for the conduct of Great Britain since the peace ... now convince me, that I did not know them.

## 1784, October 9. COMMERCE. DENMARK VESEY.

Capt. Joseph Vesey imported "3000 Gallons of rum and 1 Negroe Woman from Guadaloupe on the brig *Le Vigilant.*"

By this time his manservant, Telemaque, as he was known in the African population, had been taught to read by his master, and was an important part of Vesey's business. Telemaque realized city slaves had larger freedom of movement than those living on plantations. More than half of Telemaque days were spent apart from his Master's house and business, a freedom of movement enjoyed by a majority of the slaves in Charleston. As Frederick Douglass wrote, "A city slave is almost a freeman, compared with a slave on the plantation."

Through the years Telemaque became fluent in French, English, and Gullah, the common language among the slaves, born out of a diverse linguistic pool. His formal name was difficult for most Africans to pronounce, so it had been simply shortened to a nickname, "Telmak."

### 1784, November 1. *POLITICS. CONGRESS.*

Charles Pinckney arrived in Trenton, New Jersey for Congress, and lived at the French Arms Tavern.

### 1784, November 20. *POLITICAL UNREST.*

After the verbal attacks from the Whig Club of 600, the *Gazette and General Advertiser* responded by calling them "an assemblage of drunken tavern-keepers, Mountebank [dishonest] doctors, pettifogging attorneys and necessitous speculators."

### 1784, December 11. *RELIGION. INDEPENDENT CHURCH.*

The repaired Independent Church on Meeting Street was consecrated by the new pastor, Rev. William Hollinshead. During the British occupation the church had fallen into disuse. The British ripped out the pulpit and pews, and used the building as a hospital, and later a storehouse for provisions for the Royal army. When the British evacuated Charlestown "they left only the shell of the church building."

### 1784, December 14. *BIRTH. DEATH.*

Fifteen months after her marriage to Dr. David Ramsay, Francis Witherspoon Ramsay died while giving birth to a son.

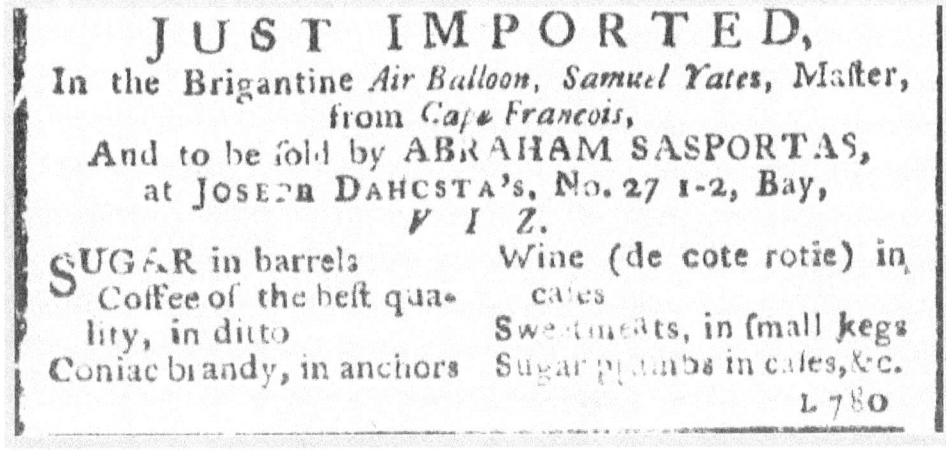

*South Carolina Gazette*, November 11, 1784.

# 1785

## 1785, January. *COMMERCE. CONGRESS.*

Congress appointed James Madison to head a committee to lobby the states for greater power to regulate commerce. Monroe argued for a general navigation act in an attempt to deal with the British ban on American trade to the West Indies.

## 1785, January 14. *ARRIVALS. LAURENS FAMILY RETURNS.*

The Laurens family returned from France. Henry, his daughters Martha and Mary Eleanor (Polly), their Aunt Mary, and cousin Francis moved into his deceased brother James's house at 117 Broad Street. The house was in disrepair due to neglect and use of British troops during the occupation.

After being in Europe for more than four years, Henry wrote that he had "become a stranger in my native land." He estimated that damage to his property exceeded £40,000.

## 1784, January 27. *POLITICS. STATE CAPITAL.*

More than 220 citizens of the District between the Broad and Catawba Rivers, petitioned the legislature for "removal of the seat of government, county courts, a college, a revision of the state constitution and tobacco inspection warehouses." They asked that the new capital "be fixed as centrical as possible for the ease and convenience of the community at large."

John Lewis Gervais presented a plan to move the capital to Friday's Ferry on the Congaree River. His plan called for the division of 640 acres near Friday's Ferry into half-acre lots. The legislature passed "an act to appoint Commissioners to purchase lands for the purpose of building a town and for removing the seat of government thereto." The new town would be named Columbia.

## 1785, February. *EDUCATION.*

The Mount Zion Society of Charleston petitioned the legislature for a college to be erected in Winnsborough in the Camden District.

## 1785, February. *SLAVERY.*

Henry Laurens wrote that he hoped "slavery in the United States, so far as Virginia southward is either totally abolished or dwindling. I think I see the rising gradations to unlimited freedom." He predicted a "direful struggle" if the South did not abolish slavery.

## 1785, February 11. *POLITICS. ELECTION.*

William Moultrie became the thirty-fifth governor of South Carolina. In his first address to the Assembly, Moultrie emphasized the need for military preparedness. "However distant or improbable a War may seem to be, a policy requisite to be served in Peace, is to prepare for the event."

## 1785, February 15. COMMERCE.

A petition was submitted by "fifty free-holders living on the Edisto River for a road "whereof the intercourse between your petitioners' settlements both with the town of Orangeburgh and Charleston would be more convenient and direct."

## 1785, February 27. RELIGION. FIRST METHODIST SERVICE.

Methodist Bishop Francis Asbury, and Rev. Jesse Lee, held the first service of Methodists in Charleston at a deserted Baptist Meeting House. Asbury called Charleston "the seat of Satan, dissipation and folly."

Due to their rigid morality and their passionate evangelism, Methodists infuriated many people. Methodists were quick to point out the fiery fate sinners unless they repented. The services continued every evening for fourteen days. This would become the Cumberland Street Methodist Episcopal Church, with forty white and thirty-five black members the next year.

## 1785, March 16. ARRIVALS. CULTURE. THEATER.

The American Company of Comedians, led by Mr. Ryan, arrived in Charleston and obtained permission from the Magistrate to perform.

## 1785, March 19. COLLEGE OF CHARLESTON CHARTERED.

The Assembly granted a charter for College of Charleston to "encourage and institute youth in the several branches of liberal education." Many things had stalled the school's progress ,including the Revolution. The founders of the College included three signers of the Declaration of Independence (Edward Rutledge, Arthur Middleton, and Thomas Heyward, Jr.) and three future signers of the United States Constitution (John Rutledge, Charles Cotesworth Pinckney, and Charles Pinckney).

## 1785, March 22. CULTURE. THEATER.

The American Company of Comedians performed *The Roman Father,* dedicated to "His Excellency, George Washington. The performance took place in the "large room over the City Exchange."

## 1785. March 24. LEGAL. COUNTY COURT ACT.

The County Court Act divided South Carolina into counties and established a system of county courts.

## 1785, March 28. CULTURE. THEATER.

The American Company of Comedians of Dennis Ryan gave the second of nineteen performances at the Exchange Building. Evidently, Ryan was quite an ambassador of entertainment. An editorial in the *Columbian Herald* praised Ryan for lessening the prejudice against the theater.

### 1785, April 19. *SLAVERY*.

Henry Laurens, in a letter to his deceased son's best friend, Alexander Hamilton, noted that:

> some of my negroes to whom I have offered freedom have declined the bounty, they will live with me, to some of them I already allow wages, to all of them every proper indulgence.

### 1785, May 18. *LEGAL. DEBTOR CHARGES*.

A Charleston attorney noted that so many planters were facing debtor charges, many "were torn to pieces by the legal process."

### 1785, June. *RELIGION. METHODIST*.

Rev. John Tunnel was appointed by Methodist Bishop Francis Asbury to the Charleston Circuit. He continued to lead services in the Baptist Meeting House until one Sunday they found the church boarded up and the benches tossed into the street.

Noah Webster.
*Courtesy of the Library of Congress*

### 1785, June. *CULTURE. NOAH WEBSTER.*

Noah Webster arrived in Charleston for a lecture. He was traveling across the country trying to gain support for his idea of simplifying English spelling and to explain his phonetic alphabet.

### 1785, July 4. *CULTURE. DR. LADD LECTURES.*

At the invitation of Gov. William Moultrie, Dr. Joseph Brown Ladd delivered a patriotic address before the Sons of Cincinnati of South Carolina.

### 1785, August 5. *CULTURE. COMMERCE.*

Henry Laurens moved away from Charleston to Mepkin Plantation, and retired from public life. He was struggling to rebuild his shattered post-war life. He wrote:

> I live in a house of my son, a garden of my own affords many good things, and a Plantation of my own for supplying that house with Necessaries and comforts of Life, and I owe no Man any thing and so We live ... tolerably well ... enabled to help some who ... have not been quite so fortunate.

### 1785, August 11. *CHAMBER OF COMMERCE.*

The Charleston Chamber of Commerce decided that, as long as Britain had to negotiate with thirteen different governments to regulate trade and commerce, American merchants would remain at a disadvantage. The Chamber urged the Assembly to grant Congress the power to negotiate American commerce.

### 1785, August 24. *AGRICULTURAL SOCIETY FOUNDED.*

The Agricultural Society of South Carolina was founded. Thomas Heyward, Jr. invited a select group of planters to the Exchange Building for "the purpose of forming a Society in this state to encourage Agriculture and other Rural Concerns." They called for crop diversification, and experimentation to find additional staple crops that would open new markets for South Carolina planters. The officers were:

- Thomas Heyward, Jr. - president
- Thomas Pinckney – vice president
- Peter Smith – treasurer

Members at large included:

| | |
|---|---|
| Ralph Izard | John Rutledge |
| Charles C. Pinckney | Thomas Bee |
| William Drayton | Issac Harleston |
| John Mathews | Aaron Loocock |

In addition to his two plantations, Loocock was also a partner in the Rumney Distillery in Charleston with Nathaniel Russell.

## 1785, September 10. CULTURE. TREE PRESERVATION.

Henry Laurens wrote about the wasteful use of live oak trees across South Carolina. The words come across as eerily prophetic in more ways that just environmental responsibility:

> The day is not distant in the long tract of Time, when we shall be stripped of that essential article [live Oaks]. The Europeans will laugh at us, our Children will rue the folly of their Fathers. For every live Oak you cut down you ought to Plant ten young trees ... but few of us Southern Americans have patience to look forty years forward, we are for grasping all the golden Eggs at once.

## 1785, Fall. CULTURE. DR. LADD LECTURES.

Dr. Joseph Brown Ladd delivered a series of popular public lectures on chemistry.

## 1785, October 1. COMMERCE. INDIAN AFFAIRS.

The Assembly voted 51-47 against West Indian slave trade ban. Charles Cotesworth Pinckney argued that South Carolina was not suited for supporting small white farmers because the land "was not capable of being cultivated by white men" – a reference to the unhealthy swamp lands of the lowcountry.

Alexander Gillon, Edward Rutledge and David Ramsay voted for the trade ban. Ramsay stated "that every man [who] went to church last Sunday, and said his prayers, was bound by a spiritual obligation to refuse the importation of slaves."

## 1785, October 1. POLITICS. SLAVERY.

As a bill to prohibit the slave trade was being discussed in the Assembly, Charles Cotesworth Pinckney wrote that "this country was not capable of being cultivated by white men ... was it not well understood that no planter could cultivate his land without slaves?"

Many planters were in deep debt in post-war Charleston, due to the record number of slaves imported. The planters realized that shutting down foreign slave importation would increase the value of domestic slaves. The bill lost by four votes.

## 1785, November 14. DUEL. CRIME.

A duel was fought between Major William Clay Snipes and Col. Maurice Simons. Snipes complained of testimony given by Simons in a civil suit between Snipes and Rawlins Lowndes. During the duel, Simon was killed by Snipes, who was arrested and charged with murder. Dueling was as a capital offense at the time.

## 1785, December. CONGRESS. CULTURE.

While in New York City, serving in Congress, Dr. David Ramsay met Noah Webster, and fully supported his work in purifying the language. Ramsay wrote, "The principals of their mother tongue were first unfolded to the Americans since the Revolution by their countryman Webster."

### 1785, December 7. *CULTURE. PUBLISHING.*

Dr. David Ramsay published his two-volume *History of the Revolution of South Carolina*. In an attempt to gain maximum profits, he paid for the printing himself – 3,200 copies printed by Issac Collins of Trenton, New Jersey.

### 1785, December 17. *POLITICS. CONGRESS.*

In Congress, Charles Pinckney was appointed to a committee to determine whether a minister of Spain should be appointed. Other committee members included, John Jay (New York), Elbridge Gerry (Massachusetts) and James Monroe (Virginia). Pinckney and Monroe became good friends.

# 1786

### 1786, January. *POLITICS. STATE CAPITAL.*

The Assembly voted 62-50 that they should "meet near the Center of the State as conveniency will admit." Edward Rutledge led the opposition of moving the State House from Charleston.

They drew a thirty-mile diameter circle in the state's center and decided to build the new capital at Friday's Ferry, on the west bank of Congaree River, to be called Columbia.

### 1786, January. *CULTURE. HARMONY HALL.*

Mr. James Verling Godwin, with the assistance of a "principal merchant" of Charleston, invested £300 for the construction of a building "beyond the city limits, near Mr. Partridge's Amphitheatre." Godwin said the building would be named Harmony Hall, after a hall of the same name in Kingston, Jamaica, where he had performed.

### 1786, January 13. *RELIGION. ASBURY RETURNS.*

Francis Asbury, first Methodist bishop in America, returned to Charleston.

### 1786, January 15. *RELIGION. ASBURY IN CHARLESTON.*

Asbury preached two sermons, one on Sunday morning and another in the evening. He wrote in his diary:

> Our congregations here are large, and our people are encouraged to undertake the building of a meeting house this year. Charleston has suffered much – a fire about 1700, another in November, 1740, and lastly the damage sustained by the late war. The city is now in a flourishing condition.

## 1786, January 19. CRIME.

Four sailors allegedly "attacked a gentleman on the Bay, supposed with the intent to rob him." The victim retreated to his store, "where he not only ... defended himself, but ... at length beat them off."

## 1786, February. COMMERCE. SANTEE CANAL COMPANY.

The Assembly incorporated the Company for Inland Navigation from Santee to Cooper Rivers. Original members of the company were John and Edward Rutledge, William Moultrie and Ralph Izard. The goal was to connect several rivers so that trade from North Carolina could more easily flow to Charleston. It became known as the Santee Canal Company, and later the Santee-Cooper Company.

## 1786, February 13. EDUCATION.

Henry Laurens approved of all the new schools being opened throughout South Carolina, writing:

> Our people are not inattentive to the rising generation, schools and seminaries are growing in different parts of the country even to the remotest, hence I have great hopes the children will be wiser and better than their fathers.

## 1786, February 14. COMMERCE.

Fifty-three residents of Ninety-Six and Orangeburg petitioned the Assembly that the Edisto River be cleared for the "easy carriage of tobacco, flour, lumber and naval stores to Charleston."

## 1786, February 17. COMMERCE. CULTURE.

Lewis Hallam and John Henry petitioned the Assembly for permission to build a new theater in Charleston. The petition was denied.

## 1786, February 18. LEGAL. TRIAL. DUEL.

Major William Clay Snipes appeared before Judge Aedanus Burke for the murder of Col. Maurice Simons in a duel. Charging the jury, Burke said:

> Although dueling was in point of law a capital offense, yet such was the prevalence of custom ... that dueling might be considered as the law of some countries; schoolmen might employ themselves in writing books against it – divines execrate this practice from their pulpits – and lawyers harangue against it with all the powers of eloquence, yet so long as mankind continued to consider the fighting of duels as the only manner in which points of honor could be adjusted it was improbable that dueling would fall into disuse.

Snipes was convicted of manslaughter, but was given a full pardon by the court and released.

## 1786, March 3. *Politics. State Capital.*

The argument over moving the state capital from Charleston, to some point in the center of the state, was opposed by the lowcountry elites. The *Charleston Morning Post and Daily Advertiser* published the views of several lowcountry gentlemen. Ralph Izard claimed removal of the capital would:

> strengthen the country interest in a proportion of four to one. It would be neither grateful nor just to compel those gentlemen to travel 140 miles.

Charles Cotesworth Pinckney argued that "men from good families with virtue, wealth and political talents" should not give up power to "proprietors of barren acres." Thomas Bee stated that the economic capital of the state should be the political capital. Edward Rutledge claimed that "country gentlemen were more in the habit of traveling than town gentlemen."

## 1786, March 11. *Politics. Commerce.*

South Carolina ratified an amendment to the Articles of Confederation which gave the Continental Congress the power to regulate trade with foreign nations.

## 1786, March 22. *Commerce. Santee Canal Company.*

The General Assembly chartered the "Company for Inland Navigation from Santee to Cooper River," commonly called the Santee Canal Company.

## 1786, March 25. *Culture. Amphitheater Riding School.*

Mr. Partridge announced the re-opening of his Amphitheater Riding School at the northern end of Meeting Street to "display his feats of Horsemanship on one, two and three horses." This theater was located out of the city limits and thus, not regulated by the Council.

## 1786, April. *Legal. Debtor Relief Laws.*

The Assembly passed debtor relief laws, fully supported by the planters and farmers. John Lloyd, president of the state senate wrote that:

> The interference of the legislature in the private contracts of individuals cannot in my opinion be justified upon any plea whatsoever [and will] forever blast out national character with foreigners.

## 1786, June. *Commerce. Culture.*

Mr. Godwin, formerly of the David Douglass Company of Comedians, built Harmony Hall north of Boundary Street. Since it was outside the city limits, Godwin did not have to pay the £100 license fee the city charged theater owners. However, his theater drew a rougher crowd than the usual aristocratic patrons in town, bringing condemnation from most city officials.

## 1786, June 15. *Disaster. Fire.*

Fire swept down Broad Street, destroying fourteen buildings.

## 1786, June 17. COMMERCE. LEGAL.

A Charleston attorney commented on the legal situation of planters, "we are, it is true, independent. But we are not yet a happy people. The want of money is the great cry, the want of economy is the great want."

## 1786, June 22. CULTURE. THEATER.

The *Columbian Herald and Independent Courier* announced:

> We hear Harmony Hall will be opened some time next week with a Grand Concert of music, interspersed with an exhibition of ancient and modern heads and dancing by Mr. Godwin ... The Hall is elegantly fitted up, having twenty-two boxes a large pit, an excellent orchestra.

## 1786, July. *RAMSAY MEETS MARTHA LAURENS.*

Dr. Ramsay returned to Charleston from New York (after serving a term in Congress) and took over the treatment of the ailing Henry Laurens. It was during this time he first met Martha Laurens.

## 1786, September. BIRTH. SLAVERY.

Jehu Jones, Jr., a mulatto, was born in Charleston as a slave. He would gain his freedom in 1798, and later became a successful tailor.

---

# CHARLESTON FIRST

### GOLF TIMELINE IN CHARLESTON

**1743:** David Deas of Charlestown received the first documented shipment of golf equipment in the American colonies – 432 balls and 96 clubs.

**1759:** Andrew Johnston returned from a trip to Scotland with golfing equipment in order to play on his plantation. When he died the inventory of his estate listed "twelve goof [golf] sticks and balls."

**1786, SEPTEMBER 29:** The South Carolina Golf Club was organized.

**1788, MAY 28:** An advertisement in the *Charleston City Gazette* requested that members of the South Carolina golf Club meet on "Harleston's Green, this day, the 28th."

### 1786, September 29. *CULTURE. CHARLESTON FIRST.*

Several Scottish merchants organized the South Carolina Golf Club on Harleston's Green - a rough rectangle used as a public pleasure ground, wedged between present-day Calhoun & Beaufain Streets and Rutledge & Barre Streets. Slaves apparently served as the earliest "finders" (caddies). They cleared the Green for the golfers, yelling "be forewarned!" to alert children and families.

### 1786, October 12. *CULTURE. LADD – ISSACS FEUD.*

Dr. Joseph Brown Ladd responded to a public smear campaign by Ralph Issacs in the *Charleston Morning Post*. Issacs was jealous of Ladd's success in Charleston society, and publicly called Ladd a "social climber that cared only for money ... a quack."

Ladd responded in the paper by writing, "I account it one of the misfortunes of my life that I ever became friends with such a man."

### 1786, October 16. *CULTURE. LADD – ISSACS FEUD.*

Ralph Issacs responded to Dr. Ladd:

> I dare affirm that the event of a little time will convince the world that the self-created doctor is as blasted a scoundrel as ever disgraced humanity.

Issacs then challenged to settle the affair "with honor" – a duel.

### 1786, October 28. *DUEL. LADD – ISSACS FEUD.*

Dr. Joseph Brown Ladd met Ralph Issacs in a duel on Philadelphia Alley at dawn, approximately 6:30 A.M. There was a fog hanging on the narrow alley next to St. Philip's Church graveyard. Dr. Ladd had the honor of the first shot and fired into the air. Issacs, not able to clearly see Ladd, due to the fog, hollered out, "hah! You missed!" Then he fired at the vague outline of Dr. Ladd standing in the mist. Ladd was stuck in the right knee, shattering bone. Ladd fell in to the ground screaming in agony.

### 1786, November 2. *DEATH. LADD – ISSACS FEUD.*

Dr. Joseph Brown Ladd "lapsed into a delirium fever as it turned gangrenous." Five days after the duel, he died from his injuries. Ralph Issacs "escaped unhurt, and for three or four days lay hid in the thatched roof of Milligan's Tavern, to escpae the vengeance of the friends of Dr. Ladd."

### 1786, November 3. *MICHAUX ARRIVES.*

Andre Michaux arrived from France to establish aa 111-acre garden and nursery north of the city. In this botanic garden he propagated and cultivated the plants he collected for the French government.

### 1786, November 8. *THEATER. RIOT.*

Because of a sore foot, Mr. Godwin of the Harmony Hall theater, could not perform his popular comic dance "The Drunken Peasant." The audience hurled bottles on stage, which Godwin tossed back and charged the audience with a drawn sword. The theater was cleared of all in attendance and closed by the authorities for the evening, upon further investigation.

### 1786, November 24. *CULTURE. THEATER.*

The next performance at Harmony Hall had been delayed for sixteen days, due to the riot at the Hall on November 8. There were no disturbances on the night when performances renewed.

### 1786, December 5. *POLITICS. ELECTION.*

Winners of the seats in the Assembly from the Charleston area were:

| | |
|---|---|
| David Ramsay (426 votes) | Rawlins Lowndes (207) |
| Edward Rutledge (426) | Alexander Gillon (203) |
| William Johnson (424) | William Somersall (202) |
| Charles C. Pinckney (422) | Michael Kalteisen (201) |

# 1787

### 1787. *COMMERCE. RICE MILL.*

Jonathon Lucas invented a system that combined rice-grinding and mortar-and-pestle technology, and built the world's first water-powered mill. This replaced the laborious task of hand-pounding and threshing rice. His tidal-powered mill revolutionized the industry and he became the foremost builder of rice mills along the Georgia and Carolina coasts.

The first rice water mill was constructed at Peach Island Plantation on the Santee River.

### 1787. *ARRIVALS. RELIGION. BAPTIST.*

Rev. Richard Furman moved to Charleston after being called to the pulpit at the First Baptist Church.

### 1787, January. *CONSTITUTIONAL CONVENTION.*

Gov. William Moultrie announced that "the appointment of a Convention of the States appears to be indispensable."

### 1787, January 1. *DEATH.*

Arthur Middleton died and was buried at Middleton Plantation. The death notice from the *State Gazette of South-Carolina* described him as a "tender husband

and parent, humane master, steady unshaken patriot, the gentleman, and the scholar.

### 1787, January 22. CRIME.

The *Columbian Herald* called for drastic measures to prevent burglaries and robberies:

> The danger which threatens the inhabitants from a gang of villains who now actually invest this city [Charleston], calls loudly for an extraordinary exertion of the police, but also of the inhabitants themselves. It were to be wished that voluntary associations might be entered into to patrol the streets, guard the property of citizens, detect the villains, and bring them to condign punishment.

### 1787, January 28. MARRIAGE.

Dr. David Ramsay married Martha Laurens, his third wife.

### 1787, January 30. CULTURE. THEATER.

*She Stoops To Conquer* was performed at Harmony Hall.

### 1787, February. RELIGION. METHODIST.

The Methodist Meeting House was completed on Cumberland Street, across from the Powder Magazine. The Charleston Methodists raised so much money that the church was debt free when Rev. John Tunnel held his first service. The congregation consisted of forty whites and fifty-three blacks.

### 1787, February 17. CULTURE. THEATER SCANDAL.

The performance of *The Merchant of Venice* at Harmony Hall created a furor because the actresses playing Portia and Nerissa appeared in breeches in the fourth act.

### 1787, February 20. ELECTION.

Thomas Pinckney became the thirty-sixth governor of South Carolina, replacing William Moultrie.

### 1787, February 20. CONSTITUTIONAL CONVENTION.

The Assembly chose five men to attend the Constitutional Convention:

- John Rutledge
- Charles Cotesworth Pinckney (older brother of the governor)
- Henry Laurens, who declined to serve, citing health concerns
- Charles Pinckney (the governor's 2<sup>nd</sup> cousin)
- Pierce Butler

Tomb of Arthur Middleton at Middleton Place, Charleston, SC.
*Photo by Brian Stansberry.*

### 1787, March 1. *INCORPORATION OF CHARLESTON.*

Over 170 artisans and mechanics asked that the incorporation of the city be abolished, and a new government be established that would not "be dissonant to Revolution principals, derogatory to the rights of American freemen, subversive to our constitution." The City Council was called:

> an engine of oppression in the hands of a *potent* few to Lord it over the equal rights of other oppressed fellow citizens of Charleston ... leaven of that garbage of monarchy, those tinseled trapping of royalty which republican Freemen of this state have but lately shaken off.

No action was taken. Charleston's merchant-planter-lawyer elite class continued to serve in most elected positions, but they now received more vocal opposition.

### 1787, March 28. *POLITICS. ACTORS CLASSIFIED AS BEGGARS.*

The Assembly passed a vagrancy act that classified actors the same as unlicensed peddlers, beggars and fortune tellers. Plays could not be performed legally in South Carolina until the law was amended in 1791. It was not good news for Mr. Godwin and his Harmony Hall.

### 1787, April. *SLAVERY. POLITICS.*

The Assembly voted to end slave trade for two years.

## 1787, April 4. COMMERCE. JEFFERSON SENDS RICE SAMPLES.

In an attempt to find rice more palatable to Southern Europeans, Thomas Jefferson sent samples of Mediterranean and Asian rice to Ralph Izard and Edward Rutledge, members of the Agricultural Society. Apparently, none of the rice grew well enough in the lowcountry to make it economical feasible.

Thomas Pinckney, 36th governor of South Carolina.
*Courtesy of the Library of Congress*

## 1787, May 11. CONSTITUTIONAL CONVENTION.

John Rutledge arrived in Philadelphia for the Constitutional Convention and found lodgings at the Indian Queen Tavern on Third Street, which he described as having "sixteen rooms for lodgers, plus four garret rooms ... greeted by a liveried servant in coat, waistcoat, and ruffled shirt."

Other delegates who stayed at the Tavern included George Mason and Alexander Hamilton. Charles Pinckney stayed at the home of Mrs. Mary House, at the corner of Fifth and Market Street with his good friend, James Madison.

## 1787, May 19. COMMERCE. ECONOMIC RECESSION.

Crop failure for three consecutive years, 1784-86, compounded an already bleak and precarious economic situation in the lowcountry. Many planters were suffering, such as Jacob Read of Christ Church. His law practice was able to provide for his family and slaves, but his plantation was in poor condition. He asked for a loan from John Tunno of £1,500 pounds, and promised to "mortgage houses in Charleston, land & slaves to four times the value and pledge my Honour to you for an exact and punctual compliance. He assured Tunno he could "700 barrels of ice in 1787 and repay the loan by 1789."

It was estimated that at this time, South Carolinians carried a debt of about £2,000,000 sterling.

## 1787, May 25. CONSTITUTIONAL CONVENTION.

The Convention opened and George Washington was chosen as president. Charles Pinckney was appointed to the Committee of the Rules with Alexander Hamilton, to set up the rules of the convention.

## 1787, May 29. CONSTITUTIONAL CONVENTION. PINCKNEY'S DRAUGHT.

Charles Pinckney presented a complete outline of a constitution. James Madison wrote in his diary:

> Mr. Charles Pinkney [sic] laid before the house the draught of federal Government which he had prepared to be agreed upon between the free and independent States of America.

Pinckney's Draught (as it came to be known) compromised thirty-one of the provisions of the Constitution as finally adopted. They included:

- A strong central government consisting of three separate and distinct branches
- Legislative branch divided into a Senate and a House of Delegates, elected proportionate to the white population; blacks would be counted as three-fifths.
- The President has control over the military
- Federal power to order militia into any State
- House with powers of Impeachment.
- "No religious test shall ever be required as a qualification to any office or public trust under the authority of the United States."
- The president should annually report on the "condition of the United States" – a state of the union address.

Pinckney reminded the delegates that the citizens were watching the Convention. He said:

> From your deliberations much is expected. The eyes, as well as hopes of your constituents are turned upon the convention; let their expectations be gratified. Be assured, that, however unfashionable for the moment your sentiments may be, yet, if your system is accommodated to the situation of the Union, and founded in wise and liberal principals, it will, in time, be consented.

## 1787, June 8. CULTURE. VAGRANCY ACT.

Due to the limitations set out by the Vagrancy Act, which included actors, Mr. Godwin of Harmony Hall began a series of patriotic lectures based on popular

American figures of the day, John Hancock, John Adams, John Rutledge, Benjamin Lincoln, Henry Laurens and George Washington.

Harmony Hall became available only for "concert and lectures." The Act was so effective that no acting troupes appeared in Charleston for the next five years.

### 1787, June 25. CONSTITUTIONAL CONVENTION.

Charles Pinckney gave a speech, refuting Alexander Hamilton's claim that solutions to certain issues at the Convention could be found using the British system of government. Pinckney passionately disagreed:

> The people of the United States are perhaps the most singular of any we are acquainted with. Among them are fewer distinctions of fortune and less of rank than among the inhabitants of any other nation. Every freeman has a right to the same protection and security ... None will be excluded by birth and few by fortune from voting for proper persons to fill the offices of government.

### 1787, July 13. CONSTITUTIONAL CONVENTION. FUGITIVE SLAVE LAW INTRODUCED.

Menassah Cutler, noted in his journal that he saw James Madison, George Mason, Alexander Hamilton, John Rutledge, and Charles Pinckney having dinner at the Indian Queen. Most historians interpret this meeting as a backroom deal on the slavery question.

Pierce Butler of South Carolina introduced the Fugitive Slave law.

### 1787, April 14. SLAVE TRADE BAN MISINTERPRETED BY JEFFERSON.

The April vote by the South Carolina Assembly to ban the slave trade for two years was misinterpreted by Thomas Jefferson as abolishing the trade altogether. Jefferson wrote to Edward Rutledge, "The abomination must have an end, and there is a superior bench reserved in heaven for those who hasten it."

Every northern state was in the process of prohibiting slavery, starting with Vermont in 1777 and ending with New Jersey in 1804. A similar bill in the Continental Congress, authored by Jefferson, to ban slavery in the southwest territory (Kentucky, Tennessee, Alabama and Mississippi) failed by one vote in 1787. South Carolina was uncomfortable with the thought of a federal government tampering with slavery where it was already established.

### 1787, August 22. CONSTITUTIONAL CONVENTION.

Charles Pinckney addressed the Convention on the slavery issue. "If slavery is wrong, it is justified by the example of the whole world ... in all ages one half of mankind have been slaves," he stated, citing the history of Greece and Rome. He warned that halting the slave trade would meet with firm resistance by the southern delegations.

Constitution of the United States, South Carolina signatures in the box.

## 1787, September. *DISASTER. HURRICANE.*

A hurricane hit Charleston, killing twenty-three people.

## 1787, September 17. *CONSTITUTION SIGNED.*

South Carolina delegates John Rutledge, Charles Cotesworth Pinckney, Charles Pinckney, and Pierce Butler signed the new Constitution of the United States.

## 1787, September 18. *POLITICS*

George Washington wrote a letter of introduction for Charles Pinckney for the Marquis de Lafayette. Pinckney planned on finally fulfilling his dream to travel to Europe, delayed first by the Revolution, and then his father's death. However, he delayed the trip again, in order to return to South Carolina to campaign for the ratification of the Constitution.

## 1787, October 1. *CULTURE.*

Mr. Juhan gave a vocal performance at the City Tavern, accompanied by flute, violin and piano.

### 1787, October 2. *CONSTITUTION PUBLISHED.*

In an "Extraordinary Issue," the *State Gazette of South Carolina* published the new United States Constitution.

### 1787, October 23. *COMMERCE.*

Edward Rutledge wrote Thomas Jefferson in Paris regarding trade between Charleston and France.

> I have endeavored, and not without success, to convince several of our mercantile people, as well as some of our planters, how highly beneficial it will be to change the consignment of their rice from Great Britain to France.

### 1787, October 31. *COMMERCE.*

Thomas Morris and William Brailsford, mercantile partners and members of the Charleston Chamber of Commerce, wrote to Thomas Jefferson, "France is indisputably a much better market for our rice and tobacco than England." They also boasted of "considerable exports to the German, Holland and Spanish markets."

### 1787, December. *CULTURE. EDUCATION.*

Samuel Chandler opened an academy in Charleston. Classes ran from 6:00 am until 6:00 pm. Subjects taught were English and French, geography, writing, arithmetic and philosophy. He also offered an evening school specializing in trigonometry, accounting, navigation, surveying and methods of architecture.

# 1788

### 1788. *BUILDINGS OF CHARLESTON.*

Edward Rutledge purchased John Laurens' house at 117 Broad Street and added the Greek Revival piazzas.

### 1788. *RELIGION. METHODIST.*

Bishop Francis Asbury preached a sermon at the Cumberland Street Church. A mob of Methodist haters gathered on the street and hurled bricks and stones through the window. Some female members were so frightened that they escaped through the side windows. Bishop Asbury continued the sermon during the attack.

### 1788. *BUILDINGS OF CHARLESTON. SECOND INDEPENDENT CHURCH.*

Rev. Issac Keith became co-pastor of the Independent Church. Due to the increase in size of membership, the Second Independent Church was finished on Archdale Street. For the next thirty years the two pastors, Revs. Hollinshead and

Keith, preached one sermon in both churches each Sunday, alternating morning and afternoon services.

## 1788. *ARRIVALS. CATHOLIC.*

Rev. Matthew Ryan, an Irish priest, arrived in Charleston to organize a Roman Catholic parish.

## 1788, January. *RATIFICATION OF THE CONSTITUTION.*

The "Broadside on the Ratification of the Constitution by South Carolina" was published, and claimed that ratification of the Constitution would ensure that:

> One of the greatest human revolutions will be accomplished – a free government erected by a free people, capable of reviving our trade, protecting out manufactures, and rendering us happy at home and respected abroad.

## 1788, January 1. *CRIME.*

The *City Gazette* reported that a man "was paraded through the streets, covered with feathers, stuck in a coat of tar, as a spectacle for the execration of others more honest than himself." The man had apparently gone "on board of a vessel, where he saw some goods so bewitching as to induce him to break at least one of the commandments, which says 'Thou shalt not steal.'"

## 1788, January 18. *POLITICS. RATIFICATION CONVENTION.*

The Assembly, at the urging of John Rutledge, Cotesworth Pinckney and Charles Pinckney, agreed on a ratifying convention for the Constitution.

## 1788, February 5. *DISASTER. FIRE. STATE HOUSE BURNED.*

The State House building burned. Sparks in the senate chamber fireplace accidenttally became lodged behind the wall paneling and started a fire, which was discovered about nine o'clock in the evening. "But before proper assistance could be obtained, it had got to such a height as to prevent any possibility of saving that elegant building." Although the structure was a total loss, most of the provincial documents lodged on the ground-floor rooms were saved.

Backcounty advocates wasted little time in using the disaster to their advantage, pushing for the removal of the capital to Columbia.

## 1788, February 14. *CULTURE. ENTERTAINMENT.*

Mr. Poole announced an exhibition to "perform a variety of feats with his trained horses." There was also to be "a clown to entertain the Ladies and Gentlemen between the Feats."

## 1788, February 22. COMMERCE. SEAMTRESSES.

Sixty-six seamtresses in Charleston petitioned the legislature to raise imports duties on "ready-made clothes" that could be made in Charleston.

## 1788, March. CITY MARKET.

Plans for a "City Market" began to take shape when six prominent citizens donated land to the city to build the new street. Much of the property was a canal created by building up the banks of a tidal creek that ran from the Cooper River to Meeting Street. The donors gave the city four years to fill the canal property from Meeting to Church Street and six additional years to fill it from Church to East Bay. The donors were:

- Charles Cotesworth Pinckney
- John Deas
- Thomas Jones
- Sims White
- John Wyatt
- Mary Lingard

The canal to be filled to make the street was thirty-three feet wide and divided what is now North and South Market Streets, with spaces along each side of the canal about thirty-three feet wide as well.

## 1787, April. JAMES HOBAN ARRIVES.

Irish architect James Hoban arrived in Charleston from Philadelphia. He was contracted to build the court house on the site of the ruins of the old State House.

## 1788, April 24. CULTURE.

Mr. Willman hired the "Great room on Tradd Street" for his exhibitions of trained birds and little dogs "dressed in uniform." The instructions listed it "at seven o' Clock, the corner of Tradd-street, late Williams's coffee house ... Mondays, Wednesday, Fridays ..."

## 1788, April 27. MARRIAGE. "ENTERED HYMEN'S SHACKLES."

At Mepkin Plantation, Charles Pinckney married eighteen-year old Mary Eleanor (Polly) Laurens, with the blessing of her father, Henry. Pinckney's friend, John Sanford Dart, sarcastically wrote that he had "entered Hymen's shackles with Miss Laurens."

## 1788, May 12. RATIFICATION CONVENTION.

The delegates for the Constitutional Ratifying Convention gathered in Charleston at the Exchange Building. Charles Pinckney gave a long opening statement in strong defense of the Constitution. Thomas Bee was chosen chairmen of the delegates. The convention then began a discussion of the document paragraph by paragraph.

## 1788, May 15. *RATIFICATION CONVENTION. SLAVERY.*

Rawlins Lowndes objected to a Federal government having the power to ban the slave trade after 1808. He claimed that, without slaves, South Carolina:

> would degenerate into one of the most contemptible [states] in the Union ... Negroes were our wealth, our only natural resource, yet behold how out kind friends in the north were determine soon to tie up our hands, and drain us of what we had!

## 1788, May 20. *RATIFICATION CONVENTION. OPPOSITION.*

Aedanus Burke emerged as one of the leaders *against* the Constitution. He wrote that "anarchy was not so dangerous as despotism, for a war must be succeeded by a peace, but despotism was a monster very difficult to get rid of."

## 1788, May 23. *RATIFICATION CONVENTION.*

Presided by Gov.Thomas Pinckney, the Assembly ratified the U.S. Constitution by a vote of 149-73, the eighth state to do so. Voting was divided among the lowcounty planters and merchants for ratification, and the backcountry farmers against. Edward Rutledge wrote to his good friend John Jay:

> We had a tedious but trifling opposition to contend with ... well administered, the people will cherish and bless those who have offered them a Constitution which will secure to them all the Advantages that flow from government.

Christopher Gadsden was "struck with amazement" by the document. He claimed that the "essentials to a republican government, are, in my opinion, well secured." Aedanus Burke complained that outcome was a natural result of being held in Charleston where:

> not fifty inhabitants [were] unfriendly to the new government ... the merchants, the mechanics, the populace, and the mob ... 4/5 of the people do, from their souls detest it. The minority are chiefly from the backcountry where the strength and numbers of our republic lie – and although the vote of the Convention has carried it.

## 1788, June 11. *CRIME. EXECUTION.*

Five men and one woman – Robert Stacy, Josiah Jordan, John George, Edward Hatcher, Thomas Smith and Ann Connely – were hanged for the robbery and murder of Nicholas John Wightman.

## 1788, June 16. *CRIME. EXECUTION. PIRACY.*

Richard Cain, Richard Williams, William Rogers, John Masters, and William Pendergrass, from the schooner *Two Friends,* were executed for piracy and murder at Hangman's Point opposite the city of Charleston.

The bodies of William Rogers and Richard Williams, being the principal aggressors, were cut down and conveyed to Morris's island, there to be hung in chains.

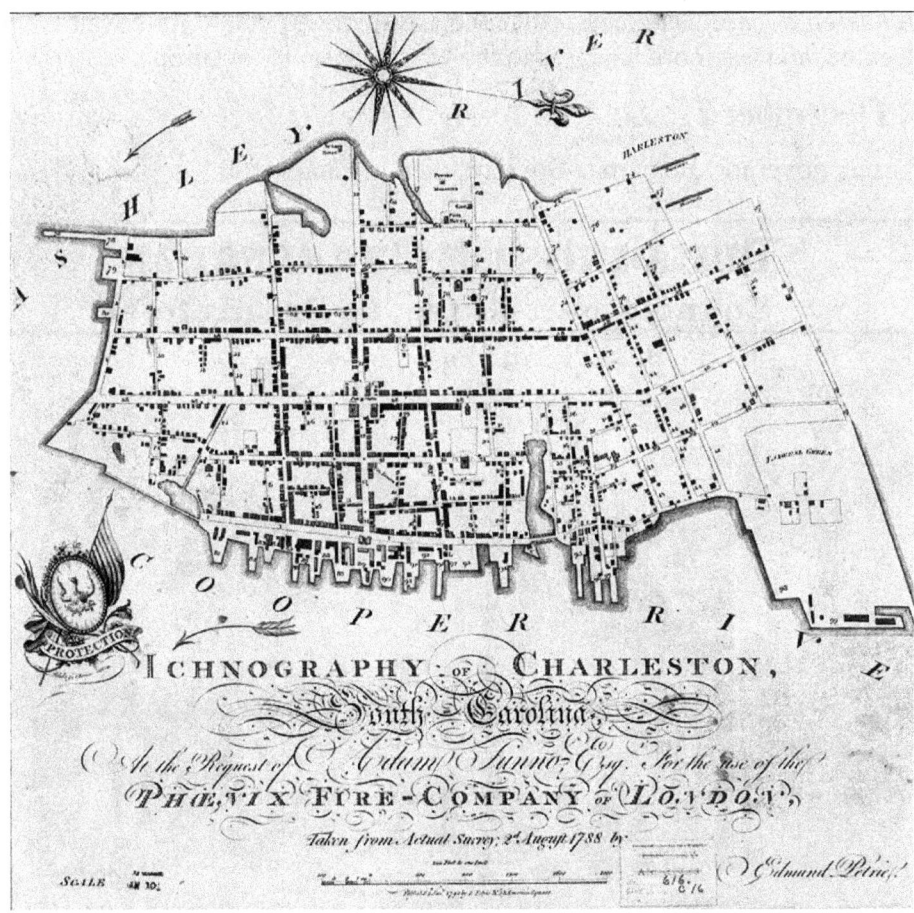

Iconography of Charleston, Phoenix Fire Company map, London, 1788.
*Courtesy of the Library of Congress*

## 1788, September. *BUILDINGS OF CHARLESTON. COURT HOUSE.*

Tons of sandstone arrived from Virginia aboard the schooner *Betsey*, for the construction of the new Court House on the site of the burned State House. A local stonecutter, Robert Given, was hired "to fabricate the window lintels, sills, east and west frontpieces, and the door surrounds, cornice, and Ionic capitals of the south facade."

## 1788, November 24. *POLITICS. SLAVERY.*

David Ramsay, who as a native Philadelphian was known to have anti-slavery views, was running for Congress against William Loughton Smith, who had been living in England for thirteen years. When Ramsay questioned Smith's residency requirement, Smith responded with rage in the *State Gazette of South Carolina:*

> It is well known that *he is principled against slavery ...* and must be taught that *without slavery, this district must be abandoned and rendered a mere wilderness;* that the slaves of this country are well treated, and live more happy than the white peasantry in Europe.

## 1788, December 21. *DEATH.*

Former governor, Benjamin Guerard, died in Charleston.

### BUILDINGS OF CHARLESTON
**County Court House, 84 Broad Street**

Judge William Drayton, an amateur architect, supervised the construction of the new County Court House in 1788-92. James Hoban assisted in its design. By the time of its completion in 1792, Columbia had replaced Charleston as the state capital, so the building became a center for various legal activity, housing the circuit, state and federal courts as well as the sheriff's offices. *Courtesy of the Library of Congress*

# 1789

**1789, January 16.** *POLITICS. STATE CAPITAL.*

Arthur Simkins, of the Ninety-Six District in the backcountry, introduced a bill to move the capital to Columbia.

**1789, January 16.** *POLITICS. STATE CAPITAL.*

Rawlins Lowndes wanted assurance that if the capital was moved to Columbia, the Assemblymen would not have to "sleep in the open air." He wondered if they would be making laws of "hewing down logs and building houses?" Edward Rutledge claimed that he had been to Columbia and "found nothing there."

**1789, January 21.** *PINCKNEY ELECTED GOVERNOR.*

Charles Pinckney was elected governor.

**1789, January 26.** *POLITICS. STATE CAPITAL.*

Not all wealthy planters were against the move of the capital. Pierce Butler, who owned 8,200 acres in the backcountry, argued that the capital "like the sun, ought to be in the center, visible to all."

**1789, January 30.** *POLITICS. STATE CAPITAL.*

The Assembly voted to move the capital from Charleston to Columbia by a vote of 89-71. December 1, 1789 was the date set for transferring public records to Columbia.

**1789, February.** *WASHINGTON ELECTED FIRST PRESIDENT.*

George Washington was elected the first president of the United States. All seven of South Carolina's electoral votes were cast for Washington. Gen. William Moultrie wrote a letter congratulating Washington:

> Possessed of every feeling that can act on grateful hearts, the Society of Cincinnati in the State of South Carolina beg leave to congratulate you on the happy occasion which has once again placed you in a situation of rendering general good to their country.

**1789, March 4.** *POLITICS. NEW STATE CONSTITUTION.*

The Assembly agreed on a convention the following year to revise the state constitution.

**1789, March 4.** *FIRST CONGRESS CONVENES.*

The First Congress convened in New York, with only eleven of the thirteen states represented – North Carolina and Rhode Island had yet to ratify theUnited States

Constitution. Only the South Carolina delegation had a majority of represent-tatives who had opposed the Constitution. The South Carolina's representatives were:

- Aedanus Burke (Antifederalist)
- Daniel Huger (Federalist)
- Thomas Tudor Tucker (Antifederalist)
- William Loughton Smith (Federalist) During the sessions Smith became a confident of Alexander Hamilton.
- Thomas Sumter – (Antifederalist)

Burke, Tucker and Huger, took lodgings at Michael Huck's Boarding House, corner of Wall and Smith Streets.

Charleston 1788. St. Michael's Church to the left. Exchange Building in the center. St. Philip's church to the right. *Courtesy of the New York Public Library*

## 1789, March 15. *CULTURE. FRENCH REVOLUTION.*

As the French Revolution was underway, Pierce Butler warned them not to be careful, and heed the lessons learned when the Loyalists and the Patriots fought a bitter civil war within South Carolina. He stated that if the French could feel:

> as much of the miseries of the Civil War, they would enter on the business with caution. Once the dogs of civil war are let loose it is no easy matter to call them back.

## 1789, April. *SLAVERY IMPORT BAN EXTENDED.*

The Assembly voted to extend 1787 slave importation ban for three more years.

## 1789, April 1. COMMERCE.

Edward Rutledge wrote to Thomas Jefferson, explaining his planting strategy.

> We must change in part the articles that we raise; we must import as little as possible; and we must find new markets for our produce. As I can afford to make experiments, I am doing it in the articles of hemp and cotton to a pretty considerable degree.

## 1789, May 10. BIRTH.

James Louis Pettigrew was born near Abbeville, South Carolina. (*The spelling to "Petigru" was changed later in his life.*)

## 1789, May 21. POLITICS.

Edward Rutledge wrote to John Jay, commenting that so many of the rank and file had been "democratized by the Revolution" they "found it very difficult to fall back in the ranks."

## 1789, August 24. RELIGION. CATHOLIC.

The grounds on the south side of Hasell Street, between King and Meeting Streets, were conveyed to the trustees of the Roman Catholic Community.

## 1789, August 25. FRENCH REVOLUTION.

In France, the National Assembly published the Declaration of the Rights of Man, declaring all men free and equal. In Saint-Domingue, the Declaration was widely welcomed on the island. Wealthy whites saw an opportunity to gain independence from France, which would allow elite plantation-owners to take control of the island, and create trade regulations that would further their own wealth and power. They underestimated the effect the Declaration would have on the enslaved black population, more than 450,000 souls.

## 1789, September. POLITICS.

George Washington asked Sen. Ralph Izard "if he thought either John or Edward Rutledge, or Charles Cotesworth Pinckney, would accept appointment to the Supreme Court."

## 1789, September 29. RUTLEDGE APPOINTED TO SUPREME COURT.

George Washington formally asked John Rutledge to serve as the senior associate justice on the U.S. Supreme Court. Rutledge accepted, even though he was in poor health. Privately, Rutledge and his friends were disappointed he was not chosen as chief justice. Rutledge claimed his legal knowledge was "at least equal to Mr. Jay's, with the Additional Weight, or much longer Experience, and much greater Practice."

### 1789, November 18. *POLITICS.*

William Drayton received a recess appointment from Pres. George Washington to become the first judge of the United States District Court for the District of South Carolina.

### 1789, December 1. *POLITICS. STATE CAPITAL.*

All records of state government were moved to the new capital, Columbia.

# 1790

### 1790. *POPULATION.*

The first Federal census listed Charleston with a population of 8,089 whites and 8,831 blacks. It also listed that eighty per cent of South Carolina's white population lived in the backcountry.

### 1790. *CULTURE. LIBRARY SOCIETY MOVES.*

The Charleston Library Society moved its "sizable collection" into the third floor of the County Courthouse. It was soon followed by the collection of the Charleston Museum.

### 1790, January. *POLITICS. STATE DEBT. ASSUMPTION.*

The Assembly passed a resolution to press Congress to consider assumption – that is, the assumption of the state's debt accumulated during the war. They thought the new federal government should assume the debt "having been incurred in Consequence of the War between the United States and the Kingdom of Great Britain."

### 1790, January 9. *CULTURE. ENTERTAINMENT.*

Miss Wall and Mrs. Robinson announced a concert.

> This evening, at the lecture room, late Harmony Hall, will be a concert, between the parts will be rehearsed the musical piece of THOMAS AND SALLY OR HARLEQUIN SHIPWRECKED.
>
> To begin at 7 o' clock. Tickets to be had at M'Crady's tavern, Singleton's bar and at the printing press.

### 1790, January 23. *CULTURE. ENTERTAINMENT.*

An equilibrist who called himself the "famous Saxon," hired Harmony Hall for regular performances to "dance upon the wire" and "catching an orange on a fork behind his back."

### 1790, February. *CULTURE. THEATER. CONTORTIONIST.*

William Powers Knight gave nightly programs of acrobatic stunts in McCrady's Long Room. His most famous stunt was described in which he "lay down a snuffbox in front of his feet, throw his head backward between his legs, put his finger, his nose and his toes all in the box together."

### 1790, February 9. CONGRESS. DRAYTON NOMINATED.

William Drayton was formally nominated to the U.S. District Court and confirmed by the Senate.

### 1790, February 11. CONGRESS. QUAKER SLAVERY PETITIONS.

Three Quaker petitions were filed in Congress to abolish the slave trade. The petitions complained of "the licentious wickedness of the African slave and the inhuman tyranny and blood guiltiness inseparable from it." The South Carolina delegation wasted no time in protesting their outrage.

Aedanus Burke of South Carolina immediately stood up and claimed the Quakers were "inciting a bloody insurrection" and demanded the petitions be thrown out. He argued that "the rights of Southerners ought not be threatened and their property endangered to please people who would be unaffected by the consequences."

For South Carolinians, the slavery question was closed after the Constitutional Convention of 1787.

### 1790, February 12. CONGRESS. QUAKER SLAVERY PETITIONS.

The argument over the slavery petitions continued. South Carolina representtatives, Aedanus Burke, William Loughton Smith and Thomas Tudor Tucker argued that the petitions were unconstitutional and should be dismissed. Burke claimed that, if adopted, it:

> would sound an alarm, and blow the trumpet of sedition in the Southern states. The Northern States adopted us with our slaves, we adopted them with their Quakers ... I don't think my constituents want to learn morals from the Quakers.

Smith denounced the Quaker slave petitions as an:

> attack upon the palladium of the property of our country ... there is no point on which we [Southerners] are more jealous and suspicious than on a business with which we think the government has nothing to do.

Thomas Tudor Tucker was incredulous that the Quakers expected them to free their slaves. "This would never be submitted to by the Southern states, without a civil war," he warned ominously. The measure was defeated 43-14.

### 1790, February 15. CONGRESS. QUAKER SLAVERY PETITIONS.

William Loughton Smith assured Edward Rutledge in a letter that they had defended slavery and were "trimming the Quakers in the gallery pretty soundly."

### 1790, February 16. SLAVERY.

Citizens complained about the "licentiousness of the negroes of this town" and that they "patronized the city's abundant dram shops, congregated unlawfully, sold merchant-dise illegally and gambled on the city streets and wharves."

## 1790, February 17. CONGRESS. ASSUMPTION ISSUE.

Aedanus Burke argued in favor of Federal assumption of state's debts. South Carolina's "large debt was contracted for the common cause." He stated that:

> South Carolina was no more able to grapple with her enormous debt, that a boy of twelve years age is to grapple with a giant ... and if she in now suffered to fall, every thinking man must lay the blame on the United States.

## 1790, February 28. CONGRESS. QUAKER SLAVERY PETITIONS.

Not all the Quakers took the defeat of the slavery bill calmly. A Mr. Mifflin, "a great fellow near seven-foot high" cornered William Laughton Smith at his lodgings in Philadelphia and berated him for two hours "in his own parlor," with no success of changing Smith's mind.

Smith then suggested that Mifflin try his luck convincing his father-in-law, Senator Ralph Izard, who owned 550 slaves. For over an hour, Mifflin and Izard argued "in close debate attacking each other with texts of scripture." Senator Pierce Butler of South Carolina joined the argument and, realizing he was outnumbered, Mifflin invited the Carolina men to have dinner with his entire "Society." The Southern gentlemen politely declined.

Aedanus Burke complained that "placing the government in a settlement of Quakers (Philadelphia), was equivalent of South Carolina pitching its tent under a tree with a hornet's nest."

Senator William McCray of Pennsylvania criticized the South Carolina delegation, saying, "Pride makes fools of them, or rather completes what nature began."

## 1790, March 23. CONGRESS. ASSUMPTION ISSUE.

Debate on the assumption issue commenced, whether or not the Federal government would assume the debts of each state. South Carolina carried one of the heaviest debts after the war. Many in Congress attacked South Carolina particularly that the state had outfitted its own navy.

James Jackson (Georgia) argued that South Carolina, had "no legal authority to outfit a ship of war ... she aimed at a high sounding fame, of possessing vessels of war in her own employ." Now that they were in debt "they have only themselves to blame."

## 1790, March 31. CONGRESS. BURKE-HAMILTON FEUD.

Aedanus Burke took the floor to defend his state's debt, and to praise the South Carolina militia, which had been maligned by Sec. of the Treasury Alexander Hamilton, during a eulogy to Gen. Nathaniel Greene. Burke stated:

> A gentleman now high in office in a public assembly called this militia, these brave men, the very mimickry of Soldiery ... Sir in behalf of these brave men I give the lie to Colonel Hamilton, yes in the face of this

Assembly and in the presence of this gallery ... I say I give the lie to Colonel Hamilton.

Burke was called to order, but he refused to back down. Hamilton was promptly informed of Burke's outburst. The animosity between Burke and Hamilton stemmed from several sources. Hamilton was a leading figure in the Society of the Cincinnati, which Burke opposed, and was the leader of the Federalist faction. Burke was also courting the daughter of New York governor George Clinton and Clinton "hated Hamilton mortally."

## 1790, March 31. *SLAVERY.*

Charles Cotesworth Pinckney wrote to Revolutionary War hero, Gen. Thomas Sumter, serving in Congress. Pinckney claimed, that, although he had supported the Constitution and the new government:

> I have no idea of them intermeddling with our negroes. This is altogether a matter of domestic regulation. The great art of government is not to govern too much.

## 1790, April 1. *CONGRESS. BURKE-HAMILTON FEUD.*

Alexander Hamilton wrote to Aedanus Burke, responding to being called a liar. Hamilton suggested that Burke had misunderstood Hamilton's remarks about the militia. He wrote, "It remains to you to judge what conduct, in consequence of the explanation, will be proper on your part."

Burke immediately wrote Hamilton back that day.

> The attack which I conceived you made on the southern Militia, was, in my opinion a most unprovoked and cruel one ... you proclaimed aloud in the face of, I may say, thousands that the Militia were the mere Mimicry of Soldiery ... you may have forgot it, but some of your Friends and all of your acquaintances have not forgot it.

## 1790, April 4. *CONGRESS. BURKE-HAMILTON FEUD.*

Senator William Maclay (Pennsylvania) wrote in his journal, "The town is much agitated about a duel between Burke and Hamilton. So many people concerned in the business may really make the fools fight."

The quarrel was smoothed over by the intervention of several members of Congress. Hamilton wrote another letter to Burke, explaining he meant no insult to the militia. Burke responded with an apology and the matter was forgotten.

## 1790, May 10. *NEW STATE CONSTITUTION.*

The Constitutional Convention of South Carolina convened in Columbia. John Rutledge was elected to serve, but declined due to his duties on the U.S. Supreme Court.

## 1790, May 18. *DEATH*.

William Drayton, first U.S. District judge of South Carolina, died. He was succeeded by Thomas Bee.

## 1790, June 3. *NEW STATE CONSTITUTION RATIFIED*.

The new state constitution was ratified which contained several major democratic changes. It included full religious freedom for the first time, and abolished the aristocratic privy council. It required a quorum of fifty per cent of the members to conduct business, which prevented any area (including Charleston) from passing beneficial legislation.

The loss of the state capital, and the new provisions in the constitution, shifted the balance of political power away from Charleston. In 1778 Charleston held 48% of the legislatives seats and the backcountry held 37%. By 1790 those numbers hand flipped: Charleston 35 %; Backcountry 46%.

## 1790, June 11. *BEE NOMINATED AS FEDERAL JUDGE*.

Pres. George Washington nominated Thomas Bee to the seat vacated by the death of William Drayton. He was later confirmed by the Senate.

## 1791, July 29. *U.S. SUPREME COURT*.

While in New York for the Supreme Court session, John Rutledge came down with a severe case of gout. He was unable to attend the court's session that summer.

## 1790, October 28. *ORPHAN HOUSE. CHARLESTON FIRST*.

Charleston City Council passed an ordinance that established the Charleston Orphan House. Until a structure could be built, Mrs. Elizabeth Pinckney provided a building on Market Street, close to the Sailors' Homes, for children too young to be bound out.

## 1790, November 1. *CULTURE. BROWN FELLOWSHIP SOCIETY*.

The Brown Fellowship Society was chartered in Charleston by "five brown men." James Mitchell, George Bampfield, William Cattel, George Bedon, and Samuel Saltus, were all mulatto members of St. Philip's Episcopal Church. The church was interracial, but the attached cemetery was restricted to whites. The Fellowship Society aimed to establish their own cemetery for "brown," believing it would foster a sense of social unity among them.

Encouraged by Rev. Thomas Frost, the white minister of St. Philip's Church, the Brown Society was for light-skinned (Browns) freepersons of color, most whom had been given their freedom by their white fathers, after their sexual indiscretions with slave women. The Society was the Browns' attempt to create their own exclusive club that mirrored the several dozen clubs in the white society.

The Brown Fellowship Society's charter defined that it was open to fifty men, who had to pay an initiation fee of fifty dollars as well as monthly dues. The money was used to support older members who were too ill to work, and guaranteed a funeral and burial in the Society's private cemetery.

Despite these goals, the Society ultimately created a schism between the browns and the (mostly enslaved) blacks of the lowcountry, who resented the Browns' attempt to ingratiate themselves more to the whites, and not the blacks.

Brown Fellowship Society Cemetery. *Photo by author*

# 1791

### 1791, February. *COMMISSION OF PUBLIC ACCOUNTS.*

The Assembly elected three commissioners to settle the public treasury accounts prior to 1791. The three commissioners were William Moultrie, Arnoldus Vanderhorst (Charleston intendent), and Sen. John Lewis Gervais.

### 1792, February. *MARRIAGE.*

Two years after his first wife died in 1789, William Alston married Mary Brewton Motte, youngest daughter of Rebecca and Jacob Motte. His son, Joseph, was twelve years old at this time.

### 1791, February 19. *RELIGION. ST. MARY'S CATHOLIC FORMED.*

The congregation of St. Mary's was incorporated as the Roman Catholic Church of Charleston.

## 1791, March. RUTLEDGE RESIGNS FROM SUPREME COURT.

John Rutledge resigned from the U.S. Supreme Court and accepted the position of Chief Justice of South Carolina's Court of Common Pleas and General Sessions. George Washington asked Edward Rutledge and Charles Cotesworth Pinckney if either man would accept the vacancy. They both declined, citing personal financial reasons.

## 1791, March 1. ILLNESS.

Edward Rutledge's wife, Henrietta Middleton, "fell into a Fit .. and has had repeated Attacks since. She has almost lost her memory."

## 1791, March 21. GEORGE WASHINGTON'S TOUR OF THE SOUTH.

George Washington left Philadelphia to begin his southern tour. In a letter to Thomas Jefferson he wrote:

> I shall halt one day at Fredericksburg and two at Richmond; thence I shall proceed to Charlestown by the way of Petersburg, Halifax, Tarborough, Newbern, Wilmington and George Town.

## 1791, March 24. EXECUTION.

Thomas Walsh "was assisted in his devotions by the Rev. Dr. Keating, pastor of the Roman Catholic church" before he was hanged for counterfeiting in Charleston. He "politely waved his hand to the crowd and said, 'Good day, gentlemen'" before he "pulled the cap over his face" and was "immediately launched into eternity."

## 1791, March 24. CRIME.

Charleston's sheriff was reimbursed for the "hire of a Pilot boat to convey Pirates to place of Execution" – Hangman's Point in the city's harbor.

## 1791, April 19. GEORGE WASHINGTON'S VISIT.

The *South Carolina Gazette* reported:

> The members of the Society of Cincinnati established in this State intend to pay every respect and honor due the president of the United States on his arrival in this city; it is therefore to be hoped that those members who may be in the country, will make it a point to be in town at or before the 10th instant, the time when the president may be expected.

## 1791, April 28. CULTURE. ST. CECILIA SOCIETY.

The St. Cecilia Society sponsored a concert of music at McCrady's.

## 1791, April 29. GEORGE WASHINGTON'S VISIT.

William Alston entertained Pres. George Washington at his plantation, Clifton, on the Waccamaw River, "in a style which the president pronounced to be truly Virginian."

Gen. William Moultrie, Col. William Washington, the president's second cousin, and John Rutledge, Jr., son of the former South Carolina governor, were present at Clifton to escort and accompany the president to Charleston. Moultrie took on the role of Washington personal chaperone during his entire visit in the Charleston area.

## 1791, May 1. *GEORGE WASHINGTON'S VISIT.* *HAMPTON PLANTATION.*

The president's party had breakfast at Hampton Plantation, the home of the widowed Harriet Pinckney Horry. Her mother, Eliza Lucas Pinckney had been living with her daughter for several years. During the visit, Eliza asked Washington whether a certain oak tree should be cut down to create a better view from the portico. Washington replied that he liked the tree and the view. The tree was saved, and from that day it was known as the Washington Oak.

The Washington Oak at Hampton Plantation. *Photo by the author.*

## 1791, May 2. *GEORGE WASHINGTON'S VISIT.* *1ST DAY IN CHARLESTON. (Monday)*

Washington had breakfast at Snee Farm, the home of Gov. Charles Pinckney. Pinckney apologized for the house, calling the home "a place so indifferently furnished and where your fare will be entirely that of a farm." This was the same house in which Moultrie and Charles Cotesworth Pinckney had lived as captives after Charlestown was taken by the British.

After breakfast Washington crossed into Charleston from Haddrell's Point, which was the eastern terminus of the ferry. Waiting to greet the group was Brig. General Charles Cotesworth Pinckney, Maj. Edward Rutledge and Col. John Dart.

Washington was rowed across the river on a large barge by "12 American Captains of Ships, most elegantly dressed." It was noted:

> There were a great number of boats and barges on the river filled with Gentlemen and Ladies, as well as two boats of musicians, all of whom attended Washington across the river.

A month after the meeting Washington once again offered both Pinckney and Rutledge the vacant seat on the Supreme Court. Both men declined.

Once in the city, Washington was greeted by Gov. Charles Pinckney, Lt. Gov. Isaac Holmes, Charleston intendant (mayor) Arnoldus Vanderhorst, and South Carolina's two U.S. Senators, Pierce Butler and Ralph Izard. The president was greeted at the Exchange Building, where he stood on the balcony facing East Bay Street and watched a "procession in his honor to whom he politely and gracefully bowed as they passed in review before him."

Washington was then taken to his lodgings on Church Street (Heyward-Washington House) where he was attended by several of Mr. Heyward's servants.

## 1791, May 3. GEORGE WASHINGTON'S VISIT. 2ND DAY IN CHARLESTON. (Tuesday)

The president had breakfast with Elizabeth Grimke Rutledge at her home on 116 Broad Street (John Rutledge House). Mr. Rutledge (Chief Justice of the S.C. Supreme Court) was on the Circuits and not in the city.

Later in the day, at his lodgings, Washington:

> was visited about 2o'clock, by a great number of the most respectable ladies of Charleston – the first honor of the kind I had ever experienced and it was flattering as it was singular.

## 1791, May 4. GEORGE WASHINGTON'S VISIT. 3RD DAY IN CHARLESTON. (Wednesday)

Before breakfast Washington visited and examined the lines of Attack and Defense of the city on horseback and proclaimed them adequate.

For the evening meal Washington dined with the Members of Cincinnati in the long room of McCrady's Tavern on East Bay Street. A choir of singers entertained the diners throughout the meal.

After the meal Washington attended "an elegant dancing Assembly at the Exchange – At which were 256 elegantly dressed & handsome ladies." According to newspaper reports the ladies were "all superbly dressed and most of them wore ribbons with different inscriptions ... such as "long live the President."

## 1791, May 5. GEORGE WASHINGTON'S VISIT. 4TH DAY IN CHARLESTON. (Thursday)

Washington visited Fort Johnson and Fort Moultrie, during which Gen. Moultrie recounted the victorious battle against the British fleet. For the evening, Washington was once again entertained at the Exchange at a dinner hosted by Gov. Pinckney and other principal gentlemen of the city.

The dinner must have been as spectacular as the previous evening for Washington wrote in his diary "there were at least 400 ladies – the Number & appearance of which exceeded anything of the kind I had ever seen."

## 1791, May 6. GEORGE WASHINGTON'S VISIT. 5ᵀᴴ DAY IN CHARLESTON. (Friday)

He viewed the town on horseback for most of the day, riding up and down the principal streets. Sometime during the day Washington stopped to ob-serve the work on the courthouse and talk with the supervising architect, James Hoban. Washington had recently been given the duty by Congress to build "the President's House" in D.C.

The evening meal was at Sen. Pierce Butler's home, and then a party at Gov. Pinckney's home.

## 1791, May 7. GEORGE WASHINGTON'S VISIT. 6ᵀᴴ DAY IN CHARLESTON. (Saturday)

Before breakfast, Washington visited the Orphan House at which there were 107 boys and girls, and he was impressed with the management of the house. After touring the house and gardens, the President had breakfast with the children.

Washington wrote:

> I also viewed the City from the balcony of [St. Michael's Church from whence the whole is seen in one view and to advantage, the Gardens & green trees which are interspersed adding much to the beauty of the prospect. Charleston stands on a Pininsula [sic] between the Ashley & Cooper Rivers and contains about 1600 dwelling houses and nearly 16.000 Souls of which about 8000 are white—It lies low with unpaved streets (except the footways) of sand. —There are a number of very good houses of Brick & wood but most of the latter—The Inhabitants are wealthy, —Gay—& hospitable; appear happy and satisfied w'ith the Genl. Government.

## 1791, May 8. GEORGE WASHINGTON'S VISIT. 7ᵀᴴ DAY IN CHARLESTON. (Sunday)

The president attended "crowded churches" in the morning (St. Michael's) and evening (St. Philip's); the evening meal was with Gen. Moultrie at his home at 60 Meeting Street.

## 1791, May 9. GEORGE WASHINGTON'S VISIT. 8ᵀᴴ DAY IN CHARLESTON. (Monday)

Early in the morning Washington left for Savannah in the company of Moultrie, Gov. Pinckney, Charles Cotesworth Pinckney and Sen. Pierce Butler. They escorted Washington twenty-eight miles to his cousin's (Col. William Washington) plantation Sandy Hill for the evening meal and lodgings. Moultrie and Butler remained with Washington for the entire journey to Savannah, where Butler owned several plantations.

## 1791, August. *CULTURE*.

Twenty Charleston men purchased a portion of the Orange Grove Plantation from Robert Gibbes to establish the Washington Race Course – a one-mile oval track. Members of the group included:

- William Alston
- William Washington
- Andrew Johnson
- Wade Hampton

## 1791, August 22. *SLAVERY. HAITIAN REVOLUTION*.

Hundreds of slaves revolted in the French colony Saint Domingue. The signal for revolt was given by Dutty Boukman, a high priest of vodou.

Within the next ten days, slaves had taken control of the entire Northern Province, in an unprecedented slave revolt of "pillage, rape, torture, mutilation, and death." Led by a forty-eight year old house servant, Toussiant, the number of slaves who joined the revolt reached some 100,000, who killed 4,000 whites, and burned or destroyed 180 sugar plantations and hundreds of coffee and indigo plantations.

When word of the rebellion reached Charleston, the white population immediately became concerned. Peter Freneau, editor of the *City Gazette*, printed hundreds of additional copies of his daily paper to meet the demand from the locals, including Capt. Vesey's house servant, Telemaque, or "Telemak." One of Telemak's friends, Jack Purcell, later recalled that he:

> was in the habit of reading to me all the passages in the newspapers that related to Saint Domingue ... [and] every pamphlet he could lay his hands on, that had any connection with slavery.

The whites were horrified as they learned day-by-day the events unfolding on the Caribbean island, and saw the undisguised delight of their slaves in Charleston This revolution set the template which defined the way whites viewed every facet of black life in Charleston from this day forward.

The city outlawed all large gatherings of blacks. West Indian slaves were banned. Any abolitionist literature was forbidden. All free blacks were viewed with suspicion. One writer in the newspaper even proposed a ban of any news of the Santo Domingo insurrection so more intelligent slaves could not "explain to the more ignorant of their class the full force of this dangerous doctrine."

## 1791, October. *JOHN RUTLEDGE'S WEALTH AND DEBT*.

At this time, John Rutledge's holdings in Charleston included three houses, fifteen slaves and twenty-nine town lots. In addition, he also 148,000 acres across South Carolina, and 300 additional slaves. Despite that, Rutledge was coming to realize that he did not have enough property to cover his debts, which had accumulated during the Revolution.

### 1791, October 21. *Commerce. Culture.*

Mr. Lafar, a French refugee from Santo Domingo, opened a dancing academy in order to "alleviate the distresses of his family."

### 1791, October 21. *Vagrancy Act Revoked.*

The State Assembly revoked the Vagrancy Act of 1787, thereby legalizing the acting profession in South Carolina.

### 1791, November 19. *Commerce.*

Ralph Izard, U.S. Senator for South Carolina, supported the new branch of the Bank of the United States because it would "facilitate our inland navigation business, and establish the credit and importance of our state, and promote the happiness of our citizens."

# 1792

### 1792. *Commerce. Buildings of Charleston.*

For £7,000 sterling, William Alston bought out the interests of his new wife's family and moved into the Miles Brewton house on King Street. Mary Motte Brewton was able to move back into her childhood home.

### 1792. *Buildings of Charleston. Orphan House.*

Anthony Toomer was given a contract to construct the brick walls of the three-story Orphan House.

### 1792, February 15. *Culture.*

The first Race Week was held at the new Washington Race Course, won by Fox Hunter, owned by Mr. Lynch.

### 1792, March 8. *Commerce.*

The Bank of South Carolina opened with a capital stock of $200,000. Thomas Jones was the president.

### 1792, April 10. *Commerce.*

Due to the lobbying efforts of the Charleston Chamber of Commerce, a branch of the Bank of the United States opened in Charleston.

## 1792, April 22. DEATHS.

Henrietta Middleton Rutledge, wife of Edward Rutledge, finally succumbed to her long illness and died. That same day, her mother-in-law, Sarah Hext Rutledge, John and Edward's mother, also died.

## 1792, May 28. SLAVERY. HAITIAN REVOLUTION.

In response to the disturbing news of the slave rebellion in Santo Domingo, Gov. Charles Pinckney instructed Col. Vanderhorst that the state should institute "strict and unceasing" militia drills and slave patrols.

## 1792, May 30. COMMERCE. CULTURE.

Thomas West and John Bignall, successful theater owners in Richmond, Virginia, obtained permission from Charleston City Council to construct a new theater. They planned to model the proscenium of their Charleston theater on the new London opera house. To raise money for the construction, they were selling shares at fifty pounds each.

## 1792, June 6. DEATH.

Six weeks after the death of his mother, John Rutledge lost his wife, Elizabeth "after an illness so slight and short ... that her death might be called sudden." Rutledge "was taken to long periods of brooding." With the burden of his crushing debt, Rutledge slowly descended into a deep depression.

Ralph Izard wrote that "After the death of his Wife, his mind was frequently so much deranged, as to be in a great measure desprived of his senses."

## 1792, June 26. CRIME.

The *City Gazette* reported:

> John Fuller, condemned for forgery in 1792, received support from Rev. Mr. Hamett when he "threw himself upon his knees, and prayed aloud with great fervency and apparent devotion."29 "solemnly swore that he was not guilty of the crime for which he was about to suffer," although he admitted that he "had lived a vicious life."

## 1792, July 31. COMMERCE. CULTURE.

West and Bignall reported that they had raised 2,500 pounds for the construction of a new theater.

## 1792, August 9. COMMERCE. CULTURE. THEATER.

The contract to construct the new theater for West and Bignall was given to Captain Anthony Toomer, with the understanding that the building be finished in January 1793. The lot for the theater was a triangle parcel at Broad and Middleton streets, and the high ground of Savage's Green (present-day New Street), purchased from Henry Middleton for £500 sterling.

There is some evidence that the theater was designed by James Hoban, who had lived in Charleston for a couple of years, while helping design and build the Charleston County Courthouse.

### 1792, August 25. *SLAVERY. HAITIAN REVOLUTION.*

Charles Cotesworth Pinckney wrote to his brother, Thomas, who had replaced John Adams as Minister to Great Britain, about his sympathy for the "very genteel but unfortunate" white refugees who were pouring into Charleston, seeking refuge from the slave insurrection. Over the next four years more than 600 white Santo Domingans arrived in Charleston.

Many of the refugees brought their slaves with them. A Charlestonian wrote, "From the moment we admitted the St. Domingo negroes into our country, security from that source became daily precarious."

### 1792, September 3. *ARRIVALS. FRENCH CONSUL.*

The French consul to the Carolinas and Georgia, Michel-Ange-Bernard Mangourit, arrived in Charleston. He and Gov. Moultrie became close friends.

### 1792, September 28. *SLAVERY.*

Ralph Izard claimed the agitation of Northerners against slavery would produce a "convulsion which will be severely felt by the Southern states."

### 1792, October. *POLITICS. FEDERAL COURT CONVENED.*

South Carolina District judge Thomas Bee convened the federal circuit court for the first time in the new County Court House.

### 1792, October 28. *MARRIAGE.*

Six months after his wife Henrietta had died, Edward Rutledge married Mary Shulbrick Eveleigh, widow of Nicholas Eveleigh.

### 1792, November 20. *CULTURE. CHARLESTON THEATER.*

In a letter to her husband, Gabriel, who was conducting business in the new state capital, Columbia, Mrs. Manigault wrote that she "drove up to the new Playhouse this morning, and was surprised by the odd turn of the new street there."

### 1792, November 26. *BIRTH.*

Sarah Grimke was born in Charleston, daughter of Judge John Grimke, planter, slaveholder, lawyer and politician.

### 1792, December 16. *POLITICS. ELECTION.*

Aedanus Burke wrote to James Monroe concerning the fight for the vice-presidency in the upcoming national election. He argued against Aaron Burr and John Adams, and supported his friend, New York governor, George Clinton.

# 1793

### 1793. *POLITICS. SLAVERY.*

Secretary of State Thomas Jefferson warned Gov. William Moultrie that "Chastaing, a small dark mulatto" and a quadroon named La Chaise, had left Philadelphia en route to Charleston "with a design to excite an insurrection among the negroes."

### 1793. *COMMERCE. CITY MARKET.*

Capt. Joseph Vesey was one of the men contracted to oversee the construction of the new City Market on Daniel's Creek.

### 1793, January 11. *CULTURE. PARADE.*

The French consul, Michel-Ange-Bernard Mangourit, hosted a grand party to celebrate the "auspicious events" in France. Gov. Moultrie called out all of Charleston's military units to parade down Broad Street to the strains of "La Marseillase" to Church Street and then to William's Coffee House on Tradd Street.

While passing the French Huguenot Church Mangourit stopped the procession and "as an expiation for the persecutions of Louis XIVth against the church, he took off his hat, and saluted it."

### 1793, February 11. *CULTURE. CHARLESTON THEATER.*

West and Bignall's Charleston Theater opened for its first performance, *The Highland Reel* by O'Keefe. John Love, who had leased the refreshment concessions, hired "two reliable white men and three Negro men, for which wages will be given." They were to supply the patrons with fruit and liquor between the acts.

The opening was a rousing success, coming two days before the opening of the Jockey Club races, the climax of the Charleston social season. Crowds arrived early for the races and bought tickets for the Charleston Theater. West and Bignall took advantage of their captive audience and presented plays for six consecutive nights. After Race Week, they settled into a regular schedule of Monday, Wednesday and Friday performances.

During that first season, a good proportion of the troupe consisted of the Sully family from Philadelphia - Matthew and Sarah Sully, their three daughters, Misses Charlotte, Elizabeth and Julia, and their sons, Matthew, Jr, Chester and Thomas. All three Sully daughters married while they were in Charleston.

Charles Fraser in *Reminiscences of Charleston*, wrote:

> The opening of the theater ... was quite an event ... Theatricals had been so long discontinued here, that the rising generation were strangers to the fascinations of the stage; and I can never forget the delight which this new amusement produced in all classes of our community.

### 1793, April 8. POLITICS. FRENCH MINISTER ARRIVES.

Edmond Charles Genet, Minister of the French Republic to the United States, arrived in Charleston. He announced that he was going to encourage privateering against all the "national enemies of France." Genet became friends with Aedanus Burke during the Frenchman's visit.

### 1793, April 13. CULTURE. CHARLESTON THEATER.

Business at the Charleston Theater was so good, that West and Bignall began to open for Saturday night performances, the first which was *The Beggar's Opera.*

### 1793, April 18. PRIVATEERING.

Before leaving for Philadelphia, French Minister Genet commissioned five local Charleston privateers, with permission of Gov. Moultrie, who wrote Genet a letter of introduction to George Washington.

### 1793, April 29. POLITICS. PRIVATEERING.

Gov. Moultrie's political opponents, outraged that he had allowed the French privateers to be commissioned, called a meeting of all "pro-British citizens" at the Exchange Building.

### 1793, May 3. PRIVATEERING.

The Charleston-commissioned privateer *le Citoyen Genet* captured the British brig *Betsey.* This created an international incident with the British crying foul.

### 1793, May 26. ELIZA LUCAS PINCKNEY DIES.

Eliza Pinckney died of cancer in Philadelphia. For several years she had been living with her daughter Harriot. George Washington, who had first met Eliza two years before during his tour of the South, served as one of her pallbearers. She was buried at St. Peter's Churchyard in Philadelphia.

### 1793, May 31. CULTURE. THEATER.

The theater season closed with a performance of *Romeo and Juliet.* The Charleston Theater had presented fifty performances in four months, and was an unqualified success. Shareholders who had invested the initial £50, were now selling their shares upwards to £70.

West and Bignall pledged to continue a "well-regulated theatre."

### 1793, June 5. PRIVATEERING.

The Federal government was outraged by French Minister Genet's encouragement of privateering in Charleston. They resolved to place restraints on France's ability to commission privateers.

### 1793, June 24. FRENCH REVOLUTION. HAITIAN REVOLUTION.

The 1793 French Constitution abolished slavery throughout their empire.

Edmond Charles Genet, Minister of the French Republic in the United States. From *Harper's Encyclopædia of United States History, Vol. IV*, Harper & Brothers. Public Domain.

### 1793, July 9. *Slavery. Crime. Murder. Execution.*

The murder of Stephen Saint Johns by his slave, Titus, sent shockwaves through the slave owners' community. Titus was executed in Charleston.

### 1793, July 15. *Privateering.*

President George Washington issued an injunction against privateers using American ports.

### 1793, July 18. *Privateering.*

French privateer, Jean Bouteille, sailed his vessel *la Sans Pareille* into Charleston harbor with three captured prizes.

### 1793, July 28. *Privateering.*

The Charleston-based privateer *le Citoyen Genet* sailed into Philadelphia harbor. The first officer, Gideon Henfield was arrested for violating the neutrality proclamation. The U.S. Circuit Court refused to hand down an indictment.

### 1793, August. *Commerce. City Market.*

The city advertised for "carpenters and bricklayers" to refit the "City Market." Capt. Joseph Vesey was one of the men contracted.

### 1793, August. *Slavery. Rumored Revolt.*

Gov. Moultrie received a disturbing package of letters from Lt. Gov. James Wood of Virginia, detailing plans for a slave uprising in Charleston. One letter, discovered by pure accident, was addressed to the "Secret Keeper" in Norfolk from the "Secret Keeper" in Richmond, which claimed that six thousand blacks in Charleston with access to arms and powder was organizing an uprising.

Another letter in the package was addressed to Charleston Intendent Arnoldus Vanderhorst, from a gentleman in Virginia. He claimed that six thousand blacks in South Carolina were "determined on the 15th of October, next in concert with others of the Different States, to massacre the Inhabitants without discrimination." The plan also included, for a diversion, the setting fire to houses throughout the city.

Moultrie ordered the militia to increase their patrols and informed the residents of the backcountry to be on alert. With the horror of the St. Domingue revolt fresh in their minds, these precautions did little to allay the apprehensions of the whites in Charleston.

### 1793, August 12. *French Revolution. Haitian Revolution.*

The abolition of slavery by the French government, and the Haitian slaves' response to the Declaration of the Rights of Man, frightened many of the Charleston leaders. Senator Ralph Izard claimed "South Carolina would be one of the first victims to the principals to the principles contained in the Rights of Man, without distinction, to persons of colors."

### 1793, September 20. *Culture. Theater.*

Mr. West, manager of the Charleston Theatre, returned to "superintend the necessary alterations in the theatre" in preparations for the next season. He also announced his intention to produce an original play titled THE AMERICAN AND FRENCH AT THE SEIGE OF YORKTOWN, OR THE SURRENDER OF CORNWALLIS, but there is no record it was ever staged.

### 1793, October 3. *Slavery. Haitian Revolution.*

The ship *Maria*, bearing refugees from Haiti, docked in the city's harbor. Rumors of an insurrection by armed slaves had panicked the locals. Whites called for a meeting to demand that Governor Moultrie ban any further Haitian blacks, free or slave.

### 1793, October 10. *Slavery. Rumored Revolt.*

Gov. Moultrie received a letter from "A Black" warning of a revolt in Charleston. The free black, who claimed he was being watched and was in fear for his life if he spoke to the governor in person, wrote:

> Altho I am one of those too unpopular characters here, a free black ... tis my love to a people among whom I have been all my life, would urge me to tell you personally what I do in this way [by letter] ... be on your guard against certain strangers, don't let your attention be directed to

Frenchmen alone... we also have enemies to the northward ... don't be lulled by the seeming humility of those about you.

### 1793, October 10. *AMERICAN HISTORY. COTTON GIN.*

Eli Whitney sent a drawing of his new invention, the cotton gin, to Secretary of State Thomas Jefferson in application for a patent. Jefferson replied on November 16 that:

> the only requisite of the law now uncomplied with is the forwarding a model, which being received, your patent may be made out & delivered to your order immediately.

### 1793, October 15. *SLAVERY. RUMORED REVOLT.*

Governor Moultrie, bowing to the pressure due to fears of blacks from St. Domingue, issued a proclamation, ordering:

> all free foreign blacks who had arrived in the state less than a year before to leave the state within ten days' time, [as there are] many characters amongst them, which are dangerous to welfare and peace of the state.

### 1793, October 28. *SLAVERY. HAITIAN REVOLUTION.*

Sen. Pierce Butler asked the Assembly to ban all West Indian blacks before a revolt happened in South Carolina. He claimed that "our Eastern [Northern] and French friends will do no good to our blacks." He also chided about "the folly of some idle people in America will sooner or later give us some trouble with our negroes."

### 1793, December. *CRIME. SLAVERY.*

Intendent, John Huger, arrested Joukain, "a very dangerous negro" because he had formerly "headed a parcel of colored people in Santo Domingo and engaged in a pitched Battle with the Whites."

### 1793, December 13. *CULTURE.*

Pastor Laval, recently from Santo Domingo "compelled ... to abandon his property," opened a fencing hall.

### 1793, December 17. *CULTURE. CONCERT.*

Four French minister, Messers. Petit, LeRoy, Foucard, and Villars, gave a concert at Mr. Williams' Coffee House.

### 1793, December 17. *CULTURE. ENTERTAINMENT.*

Mr. Ricketts opened a circus on Tradd Street for equestrian performances.

## 1793, December 23. *SLAVERY. RUMORED REVOLT.*

Thomas Jefferson wrote to Gov. Moultrie about a report he had received about a slave revolt planned in Charleston, as part of a larger plan, the first branch of which has been carried into execution at St. Domingo." Although Jefferson doubted the credibility of the report, he thought it risky to ignore.

> PASTER LAVAL, an inhabitant of St. Domingo being compelled on account of the misfortunes of the colony to abandon his property, and finding himself here divested of any other means of acquiring a decent livelihood, than those which his education have procured him; with pleasure announces to the public, that he has taken a house behind the Old Market, near the state-house, and that on Monday next, he will open a fencing hall. The young gentlemen of South-Carolina, who are desirous of learning to fence, may be assured that all the pains of the teacher will be employed to perfect them in an art so useful for the graces and safety of the body. Enquire for further particulars of Mr. Paille, next door to Mr. Theric's, on the Bay.

Newspaper announcement by "Pastor Laval."

# 1794

## 1794. *DEATH. NEW YORK.*

Theodosia Prevost Burr, wife of Aaron Burr died, leaving him with an eleven-year old daughter to raise, Theodosia. For Aaron Burr, raising his daughter and directing her education became a lifelong obsession. He was determined to raise a female version of himself. James Parton wrote:

> The little Theodosia was now beginning her education, every step of which was thoughtfully superintended by her father. From her earliest years, she began to manifest a singular, almost morbid fondness for her

father, who, on his part, was resolved that she should be peerless among the ladies of her time.

## 1794. *COMMERCE.*

The following businesses were operating in Charleston:
- Young's Book-store, Broad St.
- Muirhead's Book-store, Elliott St.
- Mr. Love's fruit shop, Tradd St.

## 1794. *LOWCOUNTRY NATIVE AIDS LAFAYETTE ESCAPE.*

Lafayette, imprisoned by the Jacobins in Austria, escaped with the assistance of Francis Kincloch Huger, the son of Benjamin Huger, who had welcomed Lafayette to America at Georgetown.

## 1794, January 1. *ARRIVALS. CULTURE.*

The players for the Charleston Theatre returned to Charleston from Richmond, Virginia, on the sloop *Eliza.*

## 1794, January 22. *CULTURE. CHARLESTON THEATER.*

The Charleston Theatre opened for its second season with two performances, Henry Jones' *The Earl of Essex* and O Keefe's comic opera *The Farmer.* The orchestra consisted of thirteen players. For this season "coffee and tea were available in the bar room, adjoining the upper boxes."

## 1794, February 8. *CULTURE. BENEFIT FOR FRENCH REFUGEES.*

A benefit was held for Santo Domingo refugees at the Charleston Theatre. The performance included "some French play actors lately from Santo Domingo, after being plundered by privateers ... have at length arrived at Charleston." The performers were listed as Mr. and Mrs. Vall, Mr. Francisqui and Mr. Danville.

## 1794, February 16. *POLITICS. PRIVATEERING.*

In a letter to French Minister Edmond Genet, Aedanus Burke wrote discussing Pres. Washington's injunction against privateers:

> We have in Charleston one thing in common with her sister cities of Philadelphia and New York, that is a ministerial party, tuned to perfect unison with a strong British party, both together celebrating at this moment, a sort of jubilee or triumph, for the victory supposed to be obtained over you, while the few Republican in town, and the mass of Inhabitants of the Country, are seriously afflicted for it.
>
> You have in South Carolina the veneration and affections of that great body of men who, in our late conflict for overturning Royalty, have on

many honorable and hard trials, given good proof how warm was their love for Republican Liberty.

## 1794, February 24. *Disaster. Theater.*

The French actors, who were in the process of building their own theater on Lot #40 on Church Street, opposite the location on which David Douglass had built his 1774 theater, suffered a disaster. According to the *State Gazette*:

> Early yesterday morning, in consequence of a remarkably high wind, the frame of the new French Theatre ... was entirely blown down and part of the brick work demolished.

Many Charlestonians who were not supportive of "theatre entertainments," expressed their satisfaction of the destruction of the theater. A writer in the *State Gazette* opined:

> Wherever God erects a House of Pray'r
> The Devil's sure to build a Chapel near!
> The proximity of the New French Theatre to the New Church must strike every antiquated gentleman as a circumstance highly shocking and indecent. To this alone may be attributed the downfall of that profane temple, and for the promotion and encouragement of the Devil and all his Works!

## 1794, Spring. *Slavery.*

Charleston held another mass meeting and demanded that all ships entering the harbor be screened for blacks having French connections, particularly Santo Domingo.

## 1794 March 6. *Culture. St. Cecilia Society Benefit.*

The St. Cecilia Society held a "grand concert" benefit for the "distressed inhabitants of St. Domingo." It included the French actors and the cast from the Charleston Theatre.

## 1794, March 14. *American History. Cotton Gin Patented.*

Eli Whitney was issued a U.S. patent for his cotton gin, which changed the South in a multitude of ways. In South Carolina, it put the backcountry farmers on an equal footing with the lowcountry rice planters. Tens of thousands of slaves were relocated from the coast to inland cotton plantations.

## 1794, March 17. *Culture. Charleston Theater. Riot.*

During a performance at the Charleston Theatre, "two or three French pirates were evicted after "disturbing several ladies in the boxes. The "pirates Captain Branzon and Lieutenant Langlois of the privateer *le Lascazas*, returned to their ship and reported that one of their crew had been murdered. They convinced "a considerable number of sailors" to retaliate against the theatre.

As the audience emerged from the building at the end of the evening, the sailors rushed forward with cutlasses, wounding several people, demolished several waiting carriages on Broad Street, and cut horses' traces. As the alarm bell was sounded, many Charlestonians leapt from their beds and rushed to the scene. The volunteer militia, Captain T. Morris' Light Dragons, quelled the riot and arrested fourteen sailors, who were jailed and fined.

Eli Whitney's cotton gin. Illustration from *Harper's Weekly*. Courtesy of the Library of Congress

## 1794. March 26. *CULTURE. FRENCH THEATER.*

It was announced that the French Theatre would soon present programs three times a week.

## 1794, April. *PRIVATEERING.*

The French privateer, *la Montagne,* arrived in Charleston harbor towing a Spanish prize with seventy-five Santo Domingo slaves.

## 1794, April 8. *CULTURE. FRENCH THEATER.*

Three housewrights inspected the new French Theatre and certified that it was "soundly constructed." The property was owned by John Sollee, a Huguenot who arrived in Charleston in 1791 with "$300,000 of portable wealth." He purchased a plantation, Charliewood, and married Harriet Neyle.

## 1794, April 8. *CULTURE. FRENCH THEATER.*

The opening night program at the French Theatre included *Pygmalion, The Three Philosophers* and "dancing on the tightrope by Signor Spinacuta and Mr. Placide. Charles Fraser reported:

> The great increase of French population in Charleston ... led to the establishment of a French theatre ... with a good company of

comedians, pantomimists, rope dancers, etc ... My liveliest recollection of it is the frantic enthusiasm with which ... used to accompany the orchestra when playing the "Marseillois.

This was the beginning of a fierce competition between the French Theatre and the Charleston Theatre for patrons. Several of the French members of West and Bignall's troupe left to join their fellow countrymen.

### 1794, June. *CULTURE. ENTERTAINMENT.*

Signior Falconi performed acrobatics and tricks on the slack rope at Mr. Turner's Long Room.

### 1794, June 20. *SLAVERY.*

A writer named "Rusticus" (most likely Alexander Garden) wrote a letter to the editor about white anxiety over the presence Haitian slaves:

> The circumstances which occasion'd their introduction gave new ideas to our slaves which the opportunities of conversation with the new comers could not fail to ripen into mischief. It may be perhaps true that the generality of those admitted were not immediately concerned in the revolt - their hands were free from blood but they witnessed [sic] all the horrors of the scene – they saw the dawning hope of their countrymen to be free – the rapidity with which the flame of liberty spread among them ...

### 1794, June 28. *CULTURE. FRENCH THEATER.*

Mr. Placide, manager of the French Theatre, introduced a new pantomime that evening, *The Attack on Fort Moultrie,* based on the battle against the British on June 28, 1776. It was an ingenious bit of marketing. That date had already become the most patriotic holiday for most Charlestonians, and the performance was wildly successful, repeated for three consecutive nights before sold-out audiences.

### 1794, July 4. *POLITICS.*

David Ramsay complained about the political stranglehold a few families held over the state. He argued that "Among us no one can exercise any authority by virtue of birth. All start equal in life. No man is born an Assembly."

### 1794, July 12. *FRENCH THEATER. THOMAS SULLY.*

The three Sully brothers, Matthew, Chester and Thomas (age 10), joined the French troupe for the summer season.

Thomas, who was an expert tumbler, would later become a famous portrait artist in Philadelphia, painting portraits of Andrew Jackson, John Quincy Adams, Thomas Jefferson, Lafayette, and famous actress Fanny Kemble. One of his most famous works was his 1819's *The Passage of the Deleware*, illustrating the famous 1776 Christmas night crossing river by George Washington.

Thomas Sully, in his later years. *Public Domain*

### 1794, August 11. *CULTURE. DEATH.*

John Bignall, co-owner of the Charleston Theatre, died. The *State Gazette* lament-ed that "as an actor his loss is irreparable."

### 1794, August 13. *FUNERAL.*

Bignall's funeral was attended by "all the Orphans whom he had helped" and by the Fraternity of Ancient York Masons, of which he was a Brother.

### 1794, September 9. *CULTURE. FIREWORKS DISPLAY.*

Mr. Spinacuta and Mr. Bulet, conducted a fireworks display in the Charleston College yard, charging 5 shillings for admission. It was reported that "several hearts are said to have caught a flame that evening, which is not yet extinguished."

### 1794, September 24. *SLAVERY. PUNISHMENT.*

Noel, a "french negro" was convicted of theft and sentenced "to Receive thirty & nine Lashes on the Bare back at the Lower Market." The same day a slave named Silvan was also whipped for theft.

### 1794, October 6. *CULTURE. CHARLESTON THEATER.*

The third season for the Charleston Theatre opened.

### 1794, October 6. *DEATH.*

Commodore Alexander Gillon died.

## 1794, October 18. *Charleston First. Orphan House Opens.*

The Charleston Orphan House opened to 115 children at 160 Boundary Street (present-day Calhoun Street) on the outskirts of the city.

### CHARLESTON FIRST

**OCTOBER 18, 1794**
**THE FIRST PUBLIC ORPHAN HOUSE**

The Charleston Orphan House opened to 115 children at 160 Boundary Street (present-day Calhoun Street) on the outskirts of the city. Designed by Thomas Bennett, the structure consisted of a main building 40x40 feet, with two wings 65x30 feet each. Brickwork was done by Anthony Toomer. It cost $11,000 to construct and was the first public orphanage house in America.

The original Board of Commissioners were:

| | |
|---|---|
| John Mitchell | William Marshall |
| John Robertson | Thomas Jones |
| Richard Cole | Samuel Beckman |
| Thomas Corbett | Arnoldus Vanderhorst |
| Charles Lining | *(Intendent / Mayor)* |

Charleston Orphan House. *Author's collection.*

## 1794, November 19. *Politics. Jay's Treaty.*

Jay's Treaty was negotiated by and signed in London by John Jay. In the Treaty, the United States gave up her definition of neutral shipping for twelve years. Britain would not be required to stop their practice of impressment – stoppimg American vessels and seizing alleged British subjects for forced service in the navy. The British also did not have to compensate Americans for slaves kidnapped or freed during the Revolution.

South Carolinians were outraged by the treaty. Christopher Gadsden, in a speech at the Exchange complained that he would "as soon send a favorite virgin to a Brothel, as a man to England, to make a treaty."

Charles Fraser commented on the outpouring of hatred for England:

> The excitement was tremendous ... among other manifestations of it, was a gallows erected in front of the Exchange in Broad Street, on which were suspended six effigies, designed to represent the prominent advocates of [George] Washington's policy, who had maintained the treaty ... John Jay, John Adams, Timothy Pickering, Jacob Read, and William Loughton Smith ... who had warmly advocated in the House of Representative, the appropriation necessary for carrying the treaty into effect. Tie sixth effigy was his satanic majesty ... in the evening they were carried off to the Federal green, where they were burnt.

## 1794, November 20. *Slavery.*

Ralph Izard expressed fear about the Frenchmen arriving in Charleston, that they would:

> fraternize with our Democratical clubs and introduce the same horrid tragedies among our Negroes which have been fatally exhibited in the French islands.

## 1794, November 30. *Fortifications. Fort Mechanic.*

Gov. William Moultrie reported that the construction of fortifications at the tip of the Charleston peninsula "had sufficiently advanced." He praised:

> the Patriotic Exertions of the Mechanics .... Who undertook the Erection and Completion of the Work ... on respectable Battery mounting ten heavy Pieces of Cannon.

The battery was named Fort Mechanic. Also, Fort Johnson now boasted fourteen heavy cannon and Fort Moultrie was described as being in a state of "forwardness."

## 1794, December 17. *Politics. Election.*

Arnoldus Vanderhorst replaced William Moultrie as governor, who retired to the life of a gentleman farmer.

## 1794, December 20. CULTURE. THEATER.

The second season for the French Theatre opened. It was now under the management of Mr. Edgar, formerly of the Charleston Theatre. Its players again included most of the Sully family.

The Theater also reduced the price of admission, undercutting the prices of the Charleston Theatre.

# 1795

## 1795, January. METHODISTS CALL FOR EMANCIPATION.

A group of twenty-three Methodist ministers met in Charleston, and called for the immediate emancipation of slaves.

## 1795, January 18. COMMERCE. SANTEE CANAL COMPANY.

Ralph Izard argued that improved inland navigation would overcome the mistake of having an inland capital. He wrote:

> When men of property and education are distributed through all parts of the state, an exact apportionment in the representation will be much less important that it is at present.

## 1795, February 27. FRANCIS MARION DIES.

Francis Marion died at Pine Bluff, South Carolina.

## 1795, March 3. PINCKNEY'S TREATY.

Congress approved, and George Washington later signed, the Treaty of San Lorenzo, also known as Pinckney's Treaty. This opened the Mississippi River to American navigation and set the boundary between the United States and Spanish colonies. The treaty was negotiated by Thomas Pinckney for the United States, and Manuel de Godoy for Spain.

## 1795, March 13. CULTURE. THEATER FEUD.

The feud between the Charleston Theatre and the French Theatre spilled out into public. Both theatres had lost money during the 1794 season. The French Theatre was short-staffed with "indifferent actors." Yet owner John Sollee applied to renew his license.

The subscribers to the Charleston Theatre "to the number of 50 and upwards" attempted to block Sollee's license with tactics that the *Columbian Herald* called "diolutely illegal." They printed numerous copies of a petition and carried them house-to-house in the city for signatures, urging the city council to only grant a license to one theatre.

### 1795, March 26. *CULTURE. CHARLESTON THEATER.*

Despite the efforts of the subscribers of the Charleston Theatre, John Sollee's application for the French Theatre was reissued for the next season.

### 1795, April.

John Rutledge's battle with chronic gout gave him considerable trouble in his duties on the court circuit as Chief Justice of South Carolina. After convening court an hour late, a grand jury accused him of constant tardiness. Rutledge replied, "Gentlemen, I would have you know that it is *never* 10 o'clock till I am in Court."

### 1795, June 30. *JAY RESIGNS FROM SUPREME COURT.*

John Jay resigned as Chief Justice of the U.S. Supreme Court.

### 1795, July 1. *WASHINGTON APPOINTS RUTLEDGE CHIEF JUSTICE.*

Pres. Washington offered the position of Chief Justice of the U.S. Supreme Court to John Rutledge. Washington reminded Rutledge that he must be in Philadelphia for the Court's term on August 1. The Senate would consider and vote on Rutledge's nomination in December.

### 1795, July 12. *JAY'S TREATY. RUTLEDGE SPEECH.*

Public reaction to the Jay Treaty in Charleston included marching in the streets, with effigies of John Jay and King George III burned. The house of Sen. Jacob Read, who had supported the treaty, was damaged. The British flag was ripped down from the British consul's house and dragged through the streets. John Rutledge, in a speech at St. Michael's, called the Treaty:

> an humble acknowledgement of our dependence upon his majesty; a surrender of our rights and privileges, for so much of his gracious favour as he should be pleased to grant.

Many historians have pointed to Rutledge's opposition to the Treaty as why his nomination as Chief Justice of the U.S. Supreme Court was not approved. His "political indiscretion," was viewed as not being loyal to the party.

### 1795, July 17. *POLITICS. JAY'S TREATY.*

A committee of citizens was elected to study Jay's Treaty. Those elected were:

| | |
|---|---|
| Christopher Gadsden | Edward Rutledge |
| John Rutledge | Charles CotesworthPinckney |
| Aedanus Burke | Thomas Tudor Tucker |
| David Ramsay | |

### 1795, July 23. *POLITICS. JAY'S TREATY.*

The committee that studied Jay's Treaty presented their findings at a meeting at St. Michael's Church. Charles Pinckney opened the meeting by asserting that "the treaty deserves the censure of every friend to this country, and of every man who wishes to see its commerce extensive and flourishing."

Christopher Gadsden then reported the committee's findings. He concluded by saying that "great evils would result to these states from this treaty, if ratified."

### 1795, July 29. RUTLEDGE RESIGNS FROM STATE OFFICE.

John Rutledge resigned as South Carolina Chief Justice, and set out for Philadelphia for the session of the U.S. Supreme Court.

### 1795, August. POLITICS. U.S. MINT DIRECTOR.

Henry William de Saussure was appointed the second director of the U.S. Mint by President George Washington.

### 1795, August 12. U.S. SUPREME COURT.

John Rutledge took his seat as Chief Justice of the U.S. Supreme Court. He was met with opposition over his position against Jay's Treaty. Many senators publicly claimed that Rutledge's nomination "should be withheld if possible." During the session, the court only heard four cases.

John Rutledge, by John Trumbull.
*National Archives.*

### 1795, August 18. POLITICS. JAY'S TREATY.

Pres. George Washington signed Jay's Treaty against fierce opposition.

### 1795, September. EDUCATION.

Twenty-one-year old Joseph Alston enrolled in the College of New Jersey (Princeton) as a junior. Alston was the favored son of one of South Carolina's richest families. His property, valued at £200,000 sterling, included 100 slaves and The Oaks, a rice plantation on the Waccamaw River.

### 1795, September 21. POLITICS. SLAVERY.

Mechanics and artisans petitioned the Assembly against "jobbing Negro Tradesmen" and other "dangerous and illegal" slave activity that could "destroy that subordination which the situation of this state requires from the slave towards his master and all other citizens."

### 1795, October. POLITICS.

John Rutledge, as Chief Justice, took his place on the bench in the U.S. Circuit Courtroom at the Charleston County Courthouse, along with district Judge Bee.

### 1795, October 6. CULTURE. FRENCH THEATER.

John Sollee, of the French Theatre, engaged the entire troupe of actors from the Federal Street Theatre in Boston. They had suffered from such bad management that the entire troupe resigned. Sollee also began to call his business the "City Theare."

### 1795, October 27. PINCKNEY'S TREATY.

Pinckney's Treaty was officially signed and enacted.

### 1795, November 17. CITY THEATER. SLAVERY.

The City Theatre printed the following notice:"Agreeably to the regulation of the city council, no people of colour to be admitted to any part of the house."

### 1795, November 21. RUTLEDGE FALLS ILL.

On the court circuit in Raleigh, North Carolina, John Rutledge "was taken so unwell that he was obliged to return to Mr. Evans's." After several days rest he was able to return home to Charleston.

### 1795, December 15. RUTLEDGE REJECTED BY SENATE.

The U.S. Senate rejected John Rutledge's nomination as Chief Justice of the U.S. Supreme Court by a vote of 14-10. His opposition to Jay's Treaty had tarnished Rutledge's reputation.

### 1795, December 26. RUTLEDGE ATTEMPTS SUICIDE.

John Rutledge, in poor health, and severely depressed over debt and the controversy over his appointment as Chief Justice (as yet, he did not know the Senate had rejected his nomination eleven days before.) The family became so concerned about his mental health they had him "constantly guarded" for his safety.

In the early morning, Rutledge snuck out of his house on Broad Street and walked two blocks to William Gibbe's Wharf on the Ashley River. "At dawn he walked deliberately into the water fully clothed until the water was over his head. He sunk but struggling sometimes rose."

Several "negro Fellows had the presence of mind to run with a Boat hook and catch hold of his arm – he made violent opposition to them but they dragged him out and detained him by force." John Blake, who lived nearby, took Rutledge to his house. According to Blake, Rutledge:

> was prodigiously agitated and shook with cold and perhaps shame – He persisted in his intention ... said he had a right to dispose of his own life as he pleased – he had long been a Judge and he knew of no Law that forbid a man to take away his own Life ... that if he had not been prevented he would by this time have been happy.

### 1795, December 26. *RUTLEDGE RESIGNS.*

Later that day, John Rutledge had recovered enough to write an eloquent letter to George Washington, resigning as chief justice, not knowing the Senate had rejected his nomination. He claimed he was "totally unequal to the discharge of the duties of the Office."

# 1796

### 1796. *CULTURE.*

William Moultrie, aged sixty-six, and living in retirement, began to write his *Memoirs of the American Revolution.*

### 1796. January 4. *ARRIVALS. CULTURE.*

James Chalmers arrived from Philadelphia. It was said that "He had talents and powers as an actor in comedy, but ... consummate vanity with utter carelessness of anything but self-gratification." He was to become the first major star of the theater world in Charleston.

### 1796, February 13. *CULTURE. CITY THEATER.*

John Sollee announced the opening of a Long Room at the City Theatre for use of private parties during Race Week.

### 1796, February 13. *CULTURE. CHARLESTON THEATER.*

The Charleston Theatre opened their season.

### 1796, June 13. *FIRE. SLAVERY. LEGEND OF "OLD BONEY."*

A fire broke out in Lodge Alley. Winds blew it westward, toward the center of the city where it burned "a vast Number of Houses and ... left many Citizens without the Means of being otherwise accommodated."

Many citizens believed the fires were started by "French Negroes ... intended to make a St. Domingo business of it."

St. Philip's was also in the path of the fire, but was saved by the heroic actions of a slave. The fire:

> would have destroyed that venerable building but for the heroic intrepidity of a negro, who, at the risk of his life, climbed to the very summit of the belfry, and tore off the burning shingles.

St. Philip's vestry gave the slave's name only as Will, belonging to Charles Lining, a church vestryman.

This was the roots of the legend of "Old Boney." Generations of Charlestonians have been taught that there is a friendly guardian spirit that haunts St. Philip's graveyard, a lanky figure of an African man, who is seen walking in the shadows beneath the magnolia tree.

## 1796, June 22. *Culture. Disaster.*

James Godwin performed a benefit for "the sufferers of the late fire."

## 1796, July. *Epidemic.*

An epidemic swept through the city, resulting in several dozen deaths through the summer.

## 1796, August. *Michaux Leaves Charleston.*

Andre Michaux left Charleston after establishing his botanical garden.

## 1796, August 14. *Slavery. "Old Boney" Given His Freedom.*

Two months after the fire, St. Philip's vestry voted to reward Will by making him a free man. The next month, they paid $707.14 to Charles Lining for "his fellow, Will," and freed Will legally with a deed of manumission.

## 1796, September 5. *Epidemic.*

The Medical Society announced that "the number of cases of the present prevailing epidemic fever have very CONSIDERABLY diminished within the last seven days."

## 1796, September 7. *Slavery. Execution.*

A young slave named Molly was executed for arson, after being convicted of "robbing her master, and setting fire to Capt. Vesey's house at the Grove." In her confession, Molly apparently not only admitted to "being guilty of these crimes, and also that she was the person who set fire to her master's house at Belvedere."

Molly added to the terror by declaring that:

> she was persuaded to the commission of these atrocious acts by a Frenchman, named Renaud, her master's gardener, formerly a servant to Mr. Michaud...belonging to the French Republic.

### 1796, September 9. *POLITICS. XYZ AFFAIR.*

Charles Cotesworth Pinckney was named Minister to France by Pres. George Washington at a time when American relations with the French was poor. The Jay Treaty between the U.S. and Great Britain had angered France. They ordered the French Navy to seize American merchant vessels trading with Britain.

### 1796, OCTOBER. *RUTLEDGE ASKED TO RETURN TO S.C COURT.*

Members of the South Carolina bench paid "a formal visit" to John Rutledge, and asked if he would return as Chief Justice of South Carolina. He delined, and continued to live a quiet life, almost a recluse.

### 1796, November. *POLITICS. XYZ AFFAIR.*

Charles Cotesworth Pinckney arrived in France. When he presented his diplomatic credentials to the government they were refused. He was told that no ambassador could be accepted until the outstanding crisis was resolved. Pinckney was outraged by the offense.

Charles Cotesworth Pinckney.
*Courtesy of the Library of Congress*

### 1796, December 8. *CRIME. CONDITION OF JAILS.*

Judge Aedanus Burke complained to the General Assembly of the poor conditions of the jails throughout the state. He claimed they were "so flimsy that sheriffs were obliged to take extreme measures to prevent escapes." In fact, many prisoners were chained to each other or to walls. He also recommended that "some bedding" be provided.

# 1797

### 1797. *ARRIVALS.*

Joseph Alston returned to Charleston and began to study law in the office of Edward Rutledge.

### 1797. *COMMERCE. INSURANCE COMPANIES.*

The Mutual Insurance Company Against Fire and the Charleston Insurance Company for Marine Insurance were incorporated during the year.

### 1797. *CASTLE PINCKNEY CONSTRUCTION.*

Construction began on a small fort located on Shute's Folly, a small island in the Charleston harbor. Named after Gen. Charles Cotesworth Pinckney, the new Castle Pinckney was built on the ruins of the old "Fort Pinckney."

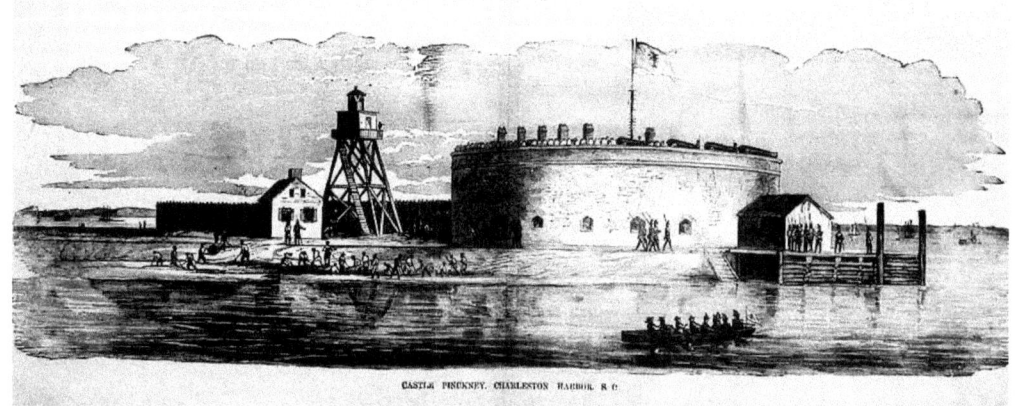

Castle Pinckney during the Civil War. From *Frank Leslie's Illustrated Newspaper*.

### 1797, January 9. *CULTURE. THEATER.*

The City Theatre opened their season with *The Grecian Daughter*.

### 1797, February 27. *POLITICS. XYZ AFFAIR.*

United States Secretary of State, Timothy Pickering, informed Congress that during the previous eleven months, France had seized 316 American merchant vessels. Since the American navy had been disbanded after the Revolution, the United States government was almost powerless to respond. French ships cruised the length of the Atlantic seaboard unopposed.

### 1797, March. POLITICS. XYZ AFFAIR.

France's foreign minister, Charles de Talleyrand, demanded that the American diplomats, Charles Cotesworth Pinckney, John Marshall and Elbridge Gerry, pay a substantial bribe to meet with him. Pinckney's response was "No! No! Not a sixepence! Millions for defense, but not one cent for tribute!"

### 1797, March 27. CULTURE. THEATER.

*Richard III* was performed at the City Theatre, and according to the *City Gazette*, the production was "miserably represented."

### 1797, April 26. CULTURE. THEATER.

Penina Moïse was born in Charleston. Her parents, Abraham and Sarah Moïse, had arrived in Charleston five years earlier, refugees from the Haitian slave insurrection. Penina became known as the first Jewish American women to achieve success in literature as a poet.

### 1797, April 26. CULTURE. THEATER.

It was revealed that both the City Theatre and Charleston Theatre were $2,400 in debt. The reasons cited were "poor management, lazy actors and a permissive audience."

### 1797, May 20. CULTURE. THEATER.

The City Theatre's season closed. It had produced fifty-two performances, including five Shakespearean pieces.

### 1797, November 14. SLAVERY.

Several "French Negroes" were charged with plotting to murder whites, and "fire … the town." Due to the testimony of several slave witnesses, two slaves were banished from the city, and three others were sentenced to hanging "for treason against the state."

### 1797, November 18. THEATER. ELIZA ARNOLD PERFORMS.

A "Miss Arnold" age 10, performed in Charleston for the first time with her family, singing "Market Lass." This is notable mainly due to the fact that in 1806, the nineteen-year old "Miss Arnold" (real name Eliza, married a fellow actor, David Poe, Jr. Their son, Edgar, would be born three years later.

### 1797, December 2. CULTURE. THEATER.

For the second consecutive season, the Charleston Theatre was unable to open, due to financial considerations.

### 1797, December 2. *SLAVERY. EXECUTION.*

Two slaves, Jean Louis and Figaro, and a free black were hanged, accused of planning "to set fire to the city as they had formerly done in St. Domingo." They were:

> led to the place of execution at the bottom of Tradd Street facing the Lower Market between "the Hours of Twelve and One o'Clock and hanged by the Neck.

### 1797, December 18. *SLAVERY.*

Several prominent citizens petitioned the Assembly to establish a permanent "Guard ... composed of infantry and cavalry" due to "conspiracies of Negroes."

One white man was found guilty of "having talked wildly in the moment of intoxication about conspiracy and house buring." Unable to pay the $10,000, he was imprisoned for two years.

### 1797, December 31. *CULTURE. THEATER.*

The City Theatre announced that their troupe was transferring to the Charleston Theatre on Broad Street, where:

> the largeness and elegance of that house will give ample scope for the merits of the performers, which with a few exceptions can vie with any on the Continent.

# 1798

### 1798. *SLAVERY. DENMARK VESEY.*

By this time, Joseph Vesey's manservant, Telemaque (Telmak), preferred to be called Denmark. His wife, a slave named Beck owned by John Paul a grocer, gave birth to their child, Sandy Vesey, "a fat black fellow who looked very much like Denmark."

Due to the fact they both were slaves owned by different white masters, the marriage was ultimately doomed to failure.

### 1798, January 12. *DISASTERS. FIRE.*

On a Friday night, a fire broke out at Broad and Union (now State) Streets. Several blocks away at the Charleston Theatre, the fire alarm brought the audience to its feet and out into the street. The performance was discontinued.

### 1798, February 8. *CULTURE. THEATER.*

A performance of an allegorical drama, *Americana and Eleutheria*, was performed at the Charleston Theatre. Written by an "unknown Charlestonian" it was never performed again. It was described as, "The scenery did not appear to be well calculated to give all the effect ... the allegorical design ... was understood by few."

### 1798, March 3. THEATER. STREET ALTERCATION.

John Sollee was in severe financial difficulty. During the morning rehearsal his actors demanded their salaries, which Sollee could not pay. Mr. Edgar and a companion began to pass out handbills on the street, announcing that there would be no performance tonight "since the best performers don't play anymore."

In front of Mr. Ryan's apothecary shop Mr. Edgar was accosted by Alexander Placide, owner of the Vauxhill Gardens on Broad Street. Placide spit on the handbill and stuck it under Edgar's nose. Edgar raised his cane and his companion stuck his fist in Placide's face. Placide responded that "it was ungenerous for two to attack one."

### 1798, March 3. CULTURE. THEATER.

In debt over $11,000, Sollee put the City Theatre on Church Street up for rent. Messrs. Williamson, Jones and Placide assumed management on the condition that Sollee have nothing to do with the theatre for the next four years.

### 1798, April. XYZ AFFAIR.

Charles Cotesworth Pinckney left France to return to Charleston.

### 1798, April 6. CULTURE. THEATER.

Many of the theatrical cast who had lost their salaries to Sollee, formed a troupe called the Charleston Comedians, and began to offer weekly performances at the Charleston Theatre in order to generate an income.

### 1798, May. POLITICS. FEAR OF FRENCH INVASION.

The fear of an invasion by France was so great, that a mass meeting was held at St. Michael's Church to help calm the citizens' anxiety.

### 1798, May. RUTLEDGE'S DEBTS.

John Rutledge had mentally and physically recovered enough that he was "exclusively engaged by his pecuniary embarrassments." He began to sell off property to settle as much of his debts as possible. Over the next three years there were more than forty judgements for debt filed against him, totaling more than £13,000.

### 1798, June 2. CULTURE. EDUCATION.

After the theatrical season closed, the Charleston Theatre was rented out for six months to the Charleston Seminary to pay debts.

### 1798, July 4. POLITICS.

Henry DeSaussure complained that:

we have no privileged casts or orders of citizens to monopolize the public employments. Talents combined with virtues are the passports to public favor and to public appointments – all enjoy equal rights and protection under the laws.

### 1798, August 14. *CULTURE. THEATER.*

Sollee's Long Room, behind the City Theatre on Church Street, acquired a reputation as being a "Sink of dissipation with gaming."

### 1798, December 18. *EDWARD RUTLEDGE ELECTED GOVERNOR.*

Edward Rutledge was elected governor of South Carolina.

# 1799

### 1799. *RELIGION.*

The predominately-black Bethel Methodist Church was organized.

### 1799, February 9. *CULTURE. THEATER.*

The City Theatre opened the new season with a new production, *The Charleston Celebration, or The Happy Return,* in honor of Charles Cotesworth Pinckney's return from Europe, and his role in the XYZ Affair.

### 1799, March 10. *CULTURE. THEATER.*

The stairs over the lobby of the City Theatre collapsed, injuring several members of the audience. The troupe moved their productions to the Charleston Theatre on Broad Street until repairs were made.

### 1799, May 8. *CULTURE. ENTERTAINMENT.*

Alexander Placide re-opened his Vauxhall for the season.

### 1799, June. *CULTURE.*

When Theodosia Burr was almost sixteen-years old, Edward Livingstone, mayor of New York, escorted her to visit a French warship visiting the city. He remarked, "You must bring none of your sparks on board, Theodosia. We have a magazine here, and we shall all be blown up."

### 1799, June 5. *NAVAL. QUASI-WAR WITH FRANCE.*

The frigate, USS *John Adams* built by contributions by Charleston citizens, was launched in New York. This was an effort to combat to marauding French ships along the Atlantic seaboard.

### 1799, September. *DUEL. BURR VS. CHURCH.*

While visiting New York, Aedanus Burke acted as second to Aaron Burr in a duel with John B. Church, Alexander Hamilton's brother-in-law.

The duel was precipitated by Hamilton when he supplied Church with some inflammatory gossip about a land dead in which Burr (supposedly) offered a bribe. Burr invoked the *code duello*.

The flintlock dueling pistols, owned by Church, were made by Wogdon & Barton, of England, and would later be used in the famous Burr-Hamilton duel in 1804. Burr survived a near miss by Church when the bullet passed through Burr's coat at the first shot. While the second shot was being prepared, Church suddenly apologized and the duel ended.

### 1799, September 20. *SLAVERY.*

William Read wrote to his brother, Senator Jacob Read that "there is some disturbance among the blacks. Ten are now weekly punished and rigidly confined … from fever and plotting slaves good Lord deliver us."

### 1799, September 30. *SLAVERY. COMMERCE. LOTTERY.*

Capt. Joseph Vesey's manservant Telemaque (Telmak, or "Denmark" as he now preferred to be called) purchased an East Bay Lottery ticket #1884.

### 1799, October 24. *KING COTTON. SLAVERY.*

Charlestonian, Charles Caleb wrote that, "The culture of cotton is now the great staple. Never was so much of this planted before." Indeed, cotton production in South Carolina rose from 131 pounds in 1788 to 6.4 million pounds in 1800, fifty per cent of all cotton exported from the United States.

The over reliance on cotton and rice for economic stability also shackled South Carolina to slave labor dependency.

### 1799, November 9. *SLAVERY. COMMERCE.*

The Charleston *City Gazette* announced that the "Thirteenth Day's Drawing" of the East Bay Lottery was ticket #1884, and that the top prize was $1,500. The ticket was owned by the slave, Denmark Vesey. Capt. Vesey agreed to allow Denmark to purchase his freedom for $600.

### 1799, December 14. *GOV. RUTLEDGE RETURNS HOME.*

Citing poor health, Gov. Edward Rutledge left Columbia to return to Charleston. In his impatience, Rutledge rode for several days through a cold rain and reached Charleston with "a severe cold."

### 1799, December 14. *GEORGE WASHINGTON DIES.*

Washington died at Mt. Vernon of pneumonia.

## 1799, December 21. *CHARLESTON WATER WORKS.*

The Charleston Water Works, the city's first public utility, was established to bring water from Goose Creek.

## 1799, December 31. *SLAVERY.*

On the last day of the 18th century, Denmark Vesey handed over one-third of his earnings from the lottery. In return, he was handed his manumission papers, signed by Capt. Joseph Vesey. To Denmark, the future looked bright. As Archibald Grimke, a Charleston mulatto and Denmark's first biographer, wrote, Vesey was:

> In possession of a fairly good education – was able to read and write, and to speak with fluency the French and English languages ... [and had] obtained a wealth of valuable experience.

At that time, the total free black population in South Carolina was 3,185, the majority of them being of mixed race ancestry – Browns. After being a dark-skinned slave for seventeen years in Charleston, Denmark, at thirty-three years of age, entered the 19th century as a free black man.

<br>

The End of

**CHARLESTON ALMANAC**

*From Founding Through The Revolution*

<br>

# Coming Soon

**CHARLESTON ALMANAC**

*From Patriots to Rebels – the 19th Century*

# BIBLIOGRAPHY

**ARTICLES & PAPERS**

Bargar, B.D. "Charles Town Loyalism in 1775: The Secret Reports of Alexander Innes." *South Carolina Historical Magazine*, 1962.

Calhoon, Robert M. and Weir, Robert M. "The Scandalous History of Sir Egerton Leigh *William and Mary Quarterly,* XXXII, 1958.

Crouse, Maurice A. "Gabriel Manigault Charleston Merchant." *South Carolina Historical Magazine*, 1967.

Gottilieb, Gabriele. *Theater of Death Capital Punishment in Early America, 1750-1800.* (PhD. Diss. University of Pittsburg, 2005).

Hart, Oliver. "Dancing Exploded: A Sermon Showing the Unlawfulness, Sinfulness, and Bad Consequences of Balls, Assemblies, and Dances In General, Delivered in Charlestown, South Carolina March 22, 1778.

Klein, Rachel N. "Order in the Backcountry: The South Carolina Regulation." *The William and Mary Quarterly.* October 1981.

Litterfield, Daniel C. "Charleston and Internal Slave Redistribution." *South Carolina Historical Magazine*, 1986.

Nichols, Elaine. "Sullivan's Island Pest Houses: Beginning an Archaeological Investigation," Digging the Afro American Past: Archaeology and the Black Experience, A Conference held at the Univ. of Mississippi, Oxford, Mississippi, May 17-20 1989.

Rogers, George C., Jr. "The Charleston Tea Party: The Significance of December 3, 1773." *South Carolina Historical Magazine*, 1974.

_____. "Aedanus Burke, Nathanael Greene, Anthony Wayne, and the British Merchants of Charleston." *South Carolina Historical Magazine*, April 1966.

Smith, D.E. Huger. "Commodore Alexander Gillon and the Frigate *South Carolina. South Carolina Historical and Genealogical Magazine,* Vol. 9, No. 4 (Oct. 1908).

Williams, G.W. "Early Organists at St Philip's, Charleston." *South Carolina Historical Magazine*, 1953.

**ON-LINE RESOURCES**

http://civilwaref.blogspot.com/2014/10/john-laurens-born-october-28-1754.html

## Newspapers

*Charleston Morning Post and Daily Advertising*
*Charleston Courier*
*City Gazette*
*Columbian Herald and Daily Advertising*
*Gazette of the State of South Carolina*
*South Carolina Gazette*
*South Carolina Gazette and Country Journal*
*South Carolina Royal Gazette*
*State Gazette of South Carolina*

## Books

Anderson, Dorothy Middleton and Eastman, Margaret Middleton Rivers. *St. Philip's Church of Charleston: An Early History of the Oldest Parish in South Carolina.* Charleston: History Press, 2014.

Aston, Anthony. *The Fool's Opera or the Tests of the Age.* London, 1731

Bates, Susan Baldwin and Leland, Harriott Cheves, Ed. *Proprietary Records of South Carolina, Volume One.* Charleston: The History Press, 2005.

_____. *Proprietary Records of South Carolina, Volume Two.* Charleston: The History Press, 2006.

_____. *Proprietary Records of South Carolina, Volume Three.* Charleston: The History Press, 2007.

Bellows, Barbara L. *Benevolence Among Slaveholders: Assisting the Poor in Charleston, 1670-1860.* Baton Rouge: Louisiana State University Press, 1993.

Berkeley, Edmund and Smith, Dorothy. *Dr. Alexander Garden of Charles Town.* Chapel Hill: University of North Carolina Press, 1966.

Borick, Carl P. *A Gallant Defense, The Siege of Charleston, 1780.* Columbia: University of South Carolina Press, 2003.

Bowden, David K. *The Execution of Issac Hayne* Lexington, S.C.: Sandlapper Press, 1977.

Bowes, Frederick P. *The Culture of Early Charlestown.* Chapel Hill: University of North Carolina Press, 1942.

Bragg, C.L. *Crescent Moon over Carolina William Moultrie & American Liberty.* Columbia: University of South Carolina Press. 2013.

Breibart, Solomon. *Explorations in Charleston's Jewish History.* Charleston: The History Press, 2005.

Brown, Alphonso. *A Gullah Guide to Charleston.* Charleston: The History Press, 2008.

Calhoun, Joanne. *The Circular Church: Three Centuries of Charleston History.* Charleston: The History Press, 2008.

Carmichael, Sherman. *Forgotten Tales of South Carolina.* Charleston: The History Press, 2011.

Carney, Judith A. *Black Rice: The African Origins of Rice Cultivation in the Americas.* Cambridge, MA: Harvard University Press, 2002.

Caskey, James. *Charleston's Ghosts: Hauntings In The Holy City.* Savannah: Manta Ray Books, 2014.

Cheves, Langdon, Esq. *The Shaftesbury Papers and Other Records Relating to Carolina.* Published by the South Carolina Historical Society, 1897. Charleston: Tempus Publishing, Inc., 2000.

Clark, William Bell. *Captain Dauntless: The Story of Nicholas Biddle of the Continental Navy.* Whitefish, Mt.: Literary Licensing, LLC, 2012.

Coker, P.C. III. *Charleston's Maritime Heritage, 1670-1865.* Charleston: Coker Craft Press, 1987.

Cohen, Henning. *The South Carolina Gazette, 1732-1775.* Columbia: University of South Carolina Press. 1953

Cote, Richard N., ed. *Dictionary of South Carolina.* Easley, S.C., 1985.

_____. *Theodosia: Theodosia Burr Alston: Portrait of A Prodigy.* Mt. Pleasant: Corinthian Books, 2003.

Chittenden, W.B. *The Literary Remains of Joseph Brown Ladd, M.D.* New York: H.C. Sleight, 1832.

Curtis, Mary Julia. *The Early Charleston Stage, 1703-1798.* Ann Arbor: UMI, A Bell & Howell Company, 1968.

Deaton, Stanley Kenneth. *Revolutionary Charleston, 1765-1800.* Ann Arbor: UMI Dissertation Services, a Bell & Howell Company, 1998.

Doar, David. *Rice and Rice Planting in the South Carolina Low Country.* Charleston: The Charleston Museum, 1936.

Downey, Christopher Byrd. *Stede Bonnet: Charleston's Gentleman Pirate.* Charleston: The History Press, 2012.

_____. *Charleston and the Golden Age of Piracy.* Charleston: The History Press, 2013.

Edgar, Walter. *South Carolina: A History.* Columbia: University of South Carolina Press, 1998.

_____ *South Carolina in the Modern Age.* Columbia: University of South Carolina Press, 1992.

_____, ed. *The South Carolina Encyclopedia.* Columbia: University of South Carolina Press, 2006.

Egerton, Douglas R. *He Shall Go Out Free: The Lives of Denmark Vesey.* Madison: Madison House Publishers, 1999.

Fant, Jennie Holton, ed. *The Travelers' Charleston: Accounts of Charleston and Lowcountry, South Carolina.* Columbia: University of South Carolina Press, 2016.

Fraser, Walter J. *Charleston! Charleston! The History of a Southern City.* Columbia: University of South Carolina Press, 1989.

_____. *Patriots Pistols and Petticoats: Poor Sinful Charles Town during the American Revolution.* Columbia: University of South Carolina Press, 1993.

Godbold, E. Stanly, Jr. and Woody, Robert H. *Christopher Gadsden and the American Revolution.* Knoxville, TN.: University of Tennessee Press, 1982.

Gordon, John W. *South Carolina and the American Revolution: A Battlefield History.* Columbia: University of South Carolina Press, 2003.

Hagy, James William. *This Happy Land: The Jews of Colonial and Antebellum Charleston.* Tuscaloosa: University of Alabama Press, 1993.

Harris, J. William. *The Hanging of Thomas Jeremiah: A Free Black Man's Encounter with Liberty.* New Haven, Ct.: Yale University Press, 2009.

Hart, Emma. *Building Charleston: Ton and Society in the Eighteenth-Century British Atlantic World.* Charlottesville: University of Virginia Press, 2010.

Haw, James. *John and Edward Rutledge of South Carolina.* Athens: University of Georgia Press, 1997.

Heitzler, Michael J. *Goose Creek: A Definitive History, Volume I.* Charleston: The History Press, 2005.

_____. *Goose Creek: A Definitive History, Volume II.* Charleston: The History Press, 2006.

Heyward, Duncan Clinch. *Seed From Madagascar.* Chapel Hill: University of North Carolina Press, 1937.

Hoffer, Peter Charles. *Cry Liberty: The Great Stono River Slave Rebellion of 1739.* New York: Oxford University Press, 2010.

Hoole, William Stanley. *The Ante-Bellum Charleston Theatre.* Tuscaloosa: University of Alabama Press, 1946.

Isenberg, Nancy. *Fallen Founder: The Life of Aaron Burr.* New York: Viking Penguin, 2007.

Jacoby, Mary Moore, ed. *The Churches of Charleston and the Lowcountry.* Columbia: University of South Carolina Press, 1994.

Johnson Elmer D. and Sloan, Kathleen Lewis, ed. *South Carolina: A Documentary Profile of the Palmetto State.* Columbia: University of South Carolina Press, 1971.

Jones, Mark R. *Wicked Charleston: The Dark Side of the Holy City.* Charleston: The History Press, 2005.

Kelly, Joseph. *America's Longest Siege: Charleston, Slavery and the Slow March Toward Civil War.* New York: Overlook Press, 2013.

Kidd, Thomas S. *The Great Awakening: The Roots of Evangelical Christianity in Colonial America.* New Haven: Yale University Press, 2007.

Koger, Larry. *Black Slave Owners, Free Black Masters in South Carolina, 1790-1860.* Columbia: University of South Carolina Press, 1995.

Lambert, Robert Stansbury. *South Carolina Loyalists in the American Revolution.* Columbia: University of South Carolina Press, 1987.

Lander, Ernest M., Jr. and Ackerman, Robert K., ed. *Perspectives In South Carolina History: The First 300 Years.* Columbia: University of South Carolina Press, 1973.

Leland, Jack. *62 Famous Houses of Charleston,* South Carolina, Charleston: Post & Courier, 1997.

Lerner, Gerda. *The Grimke Sisters From South Carolina: Pioneers for Women's Rights and Abolition.* New York: Oxford Press, 1998.

Littlefield, Daniel C. *Riceand Slaves: Ethnicity and the Slave Trade in Colonial South Carolina.* Champaign: University of Illinois Press, 1991.

Lilly, Samuel Alvin. *The Culture of Revolutionary Charleston.* Ann Arbor: UMI Dissertation Services, A Bell & Howell Company, 1972.

Lounsbury, Carl R. *From Statehouse to Courthouse: An Architectural History of South Carolina's Colonial Capital and Charleston County Courthouse.* Columbia: University of South CarolinaPress, 2001.

Massey, Gregory D. *John Laurens and the American Revolution.*Columbia: University of South Carolina Press, 2000.

McCowen, George Smith. *The British Occupation of Charleston, 1780-82.* Columbia: University of South Carolina Press, 1972.

McCrady, Edward. *The History of South Carolina under the Proprietary Government, 1670-1719.* New York, 1897; New York: Russell & Russell, 1969.

_____. *The History of South Carolina under the Royal Government, 1719-1776.* New York, 1897; New York: Russell & Russell, 1969.

_____. *South Carolina in the Revolution, 1775-1780.* New York: MacMillian, 1901.

_____. *South Carolina in the Revolution, 1780-1783.* New York: MacMillian, 1902.

McDonough, Daniel Joseph. *Christopher Gadsden and Henry Laurens: The Parallel Lives of Two American Patriots.* Ann Arbor: UMI Dissertation Services, Bell & Howe Company, 1990.

Matthews, Marty D. *Forgotten Founder: The Life and Times of Charles Pinckney.* Columbia: University of South Carolina Press, 2004.

Meister, Charles W. *The Founding Fathers.* Jefferson, North Carolina: McFarland & Company, Inc., Publishers, 1987.

Middleton, Margaret Simmons. *David and Martha Laurens Ramsay.* New York: Carlton Press, Inc., 1971.

Miles, Suzannah Smith. *Scoundrels, Heroes and the Lowcountry Outdoors: A Masculine Side to Lowcountry History.* Mt. Pleasant: King's Highway Publications, 1999.

Miller, Ruth M. and Andrus, Ann Taylor. *Charleston's Old Exchange Building: A Witness to American History.* Charleston: The History Press, 2005.

Menendez, Al and Shirley. *South Carolina Trivia.* Nashville: Rutledge Hill Press, 1996/

Moore, Margaret H. *Complete Charleston: A Guide To The Architecture, History, and Gardens of Charleston and the Low Country.* Charleston: TM Photography, Inc. 2000.

Moore, Warner Oland. *Henry Laurens: A Charleston Merchant in the Eighteenth Century, 1747-1771.* Ann Arbor: UMI Dissertation Services, Bell & Howe Company, 1994.

Mould, David R. and Loewe, Missy. *Historic Gravestone Art of Charleston, South Carolina, 1695-1802.* Jefferson, North Carolina: McFarland & Company, Inc., Publishers, 2006.

Moultrie, William. *Memoirs of the American Revolution.* New York: Arno Press, Inc., 1968.

Murray, John E. *The Charleston Orphan House: Children's Lives in the First Pubic Orphanage in America.* Chicago: University of Chicago Press, 2013.

Nevens, Allan. *Slave Trading in the Old South.* New York: Frederick Ungag Publishing, 1959.

Nicholson, Watson. *Anthony Aston: Stroller and Adventurer.* South Haven, Michigan, 1920.

Oliphant, Mary C. Simms *The History of South Carolina.* Atlanta: Laidlaw Brothers, 1958.

Pease, William H. and Jane H. *A Family of Women: The Carolina Petigrus in Peace and War.* Chapel Hill: University of North Carolina Press, 1999.

_____. *James Louis Petigru: Southern Conservative, Southern Dissenter.* Columbia: University of South Carolina Press, 2002.

Petit, James Percival. *South Carolina and the Sea: Day by Day toward Five Centuries, 1492 – 1976 A.D.* Charleston: Walker, Evans & Cogswell, 1976.

Phipps, William E. *Amazing Grace in John Newton: Slave Ship Captain, Hymn Writer, and Abolitionist.* Macon: Mercer University Press, 2004.

Pinckney, Charles. *Observations on the Plan of Government Submitted to the Federal Convention.* New York, 1787.

Pinckney, Elise, ed. *The Letterbook of Eliza Lucas Pinckney, 1739-1762.* Chapel Hill: University of North Carolina Press, 1972.

Poston, Jonathon H. *The Buildings of Charleston: A Guide to the City's Architecture*, Columbia: University of South Carolina Press, 1997.

Ramsay, David. *The History of the American Revolution, 2 vols.* New York: Russell and Russell, 1968.

Raven, James. *London Booksellers and American Customers: Transatlantic Literary Community and the Charleston Library Society, 1748-1811.* Columbia: University of South Carolina Press, 2002.

Ravenel, Mrs. St. Julien. *Charleston, the Place and the People.* New York: McMillian, 1912.

Ravenel, Harriott Horry. *Eliza Pinckney.* New York: Charles Scribner's Sons, 1896.

Ripley, Warren. *Charles Towne: Birth of a City.* Charleston: Post & Courier, 1970.

_____. *The Battery: Charleston, South Carolina.* Charleston: Post & Courier, 1975.

Robertson, David. *Denmark Vesey:The Buried History of America's Largest Slave Rebellion.* New York, New York: Alfred A. Knopf, Inc., 1999.

Robinson, W. Stitt. *James Glen: From Scottish Provost to Royal Governor of South Carolina.* Westport, CN.: Greenwood Press, 1996.

Rogers, George C. *Charleston in the Age of the Pinckneys.* Norman: University of Oklahoma Press, 1969; Columbia: University of South Carolina Press, 1980.

_____, ed. *A South Carolina Chronology, 1497-1970.* Columbia: University of South Carolina Press, 1973.

_____, Chesnutt, David R., and Clark, Peggy J., ed. *The Papers of Henry Laurens, Volume 1-16.* Columbia: University of South Carolina Press, 1968-2003.

Rosen, Robert. *A Short History of Charleston.* Columbia: University of South Carolina, 1997

Rubin, Hyman, III. *South Carolina Scalawags.* Columbia: University of South Carolina Press, 2006.

Ryan, William R. *The World of Thomas Jeremiah: Charles Town on the Eve of the American Revolution.* New York: Oxford University Press, Inc., 2010.

Shaffer, Arthur H. *To Be An American: David Ramsay and the Making of the American Consciousness.* Columbia: University of South Carolina Press, 1991.

Shatzman, Aaron Mark. *Servant Into Planters: The Origin of an American Image: Land Acquisition and Status Mobility in Seventeenth Century South Carolina.* Ann Arbor: UMI Dissertation Services, A Bell & Howell Company, 1993.

Sirmans, M. Eugene. *Colonial South Carolina: A Political History: 1663-1763.* Chapel Hill: University of North Carolina Press, 1966

Smith, Mark M, ed. *Stono: Documenting and Interpreting a Southern Slave Revolt.* Columbia: University of South Carolina, 2005.

South Carolina Historical Society. *The Shaftesbury Papers.* Columbia: University of South Carolina Press, 2010.

Stedmen, E.C. and Hutchinson, E.M. *A Library of American Literature: An Anthology in Eleven Volumes.* New York: Charles L. Webster & Company, 1891.

Stello, R. Alan. *Arsenal of History: The Powder Magazine of South Carolina.* Charleston: The History Press, 2013.

Thomkins, Stephen. *John Wesley: A Biography.* Grand Rapids: William B. Eerdmans Publishing Company, 2003.

Timothy, Peter. *Letters of Peter Timothy, Printer of Charleston, South Carolina to Benjamin Franklin.* Chicago: Black Cat Press, 1935.

Uhlendorf, Bernhard A. *The Siege of Charleston.* Ann Arbor: University of Michigan Press, 1938.

Unger, Harlow Giles. *The Last Founding Father: James Monroe and a Nation's Call To Greatness.* New York: Da Capo Press, 2009.

Van Ruymbeke, Bertrand. *From New Babylon to Eden: The Huguenots and Their Migration to Colonial South Carolina.* Columbia: University of South Carolina Press, 2006.

Vipperman, Carl J. *The Rise of Rawlins Lowndes, 1721-1800.* Columbia: University of South CarolinaPress, 1978.

Wallace, David Duncan. *South Carolina: A Short History.* Columbia: University of South CarolinaPress, 1951.

_____. *The Life of Henry Laurens.*Columbia: University of South CarolinaPress, 1915.

Weir, Robert M. *Colonial South Carolina: A History.* Columbia: University of South CarolinaPress, 1983.

Williams, Arthur V., Jr. *Tales of Charleston 1930s.* Charleston: College of Charleston Library in association with the Jewish Historical Society of South Carolina, 1999.

Williams, Francis Leigh. *A Founding Family: The Pinckneys of South Carolina.* New York: Harcourt Brace Jovanovich, 1978.

Williams, George W. *St. Michael's Charleston, 1751-1951.* Columbia: University of South Carolina Press, 1951.

Willis, Eola. *The Charleston Stage in the SVIII Century.* Columbia: The State Company, 1924.

Wood, Peter H. *Black Majority: Negroes in Colonial South Carolina from 1670 through the Stono Rebellion.* New York: Alfred A. Knopf, 1974.

Zahniser, Marvin R. *Charles Cotesworth Pinckney, Founding Father.* Chapel Hill: University of North Carolina Press, 196

# INDEX

## A

*A Few Salutary Hints, Pointing Out the Policy and Consequences of admitting British Subjects to Engross our trade and become our Citizens*, 410
Act for Repairing and Expeditious Finishing the Fortifications, 88
Act for Disposing of Certain Estates and Banishing Certain Persons, 390
Act for Rebuilding, 178
Act for Settling a Pilot, 55
Act for suppressing idleness, drunkenness, and profanity, 51
Act for the Encouragement of the Importation of White Servants, 71
Act for the Good Government of Charles Town: repealed, 133
Act for the Good Government of Charles Town, An, 131
Act of 1721: licenses for taverns, 128
Act of Union, 88
Act Preventing the Spreading of Contagious Distempers, 95
Act to Incorporate Charleston (1783), 402
*Acteon*: grounded, 325
Adams, Charles, 386
Adams, John, 276, 325, 405; about John Laurens' death, 395; comments on Charlestown politics, 317; comments on Laurens, 404; comments on Negro soldiers, 330; comments on South Carolina commerce, 336; description of Edward Rutledge, 292; observations about Charlestown delegates, 292; Treaty of Paris, 392
Adams, Samuel, 289, 348, 409; assured of Charlestown support, 289; called names, 291; letter from Gadsden, 289
*Address to the Freemen of South Carolina, An*, 398
Admiralty Court: established by South Carolina, 316
Adron, William: erects Pitt statue, 263
*Adventures of Harlequin and Scaramouch, with the Burgomaster Trick'd, The*, 154
Advocate General of Admiralty: Joseph Morton appointed, 72
Agent in London: office created, 96; office established, 96
Agricultural Society of South Carolina: founded, 415; officers, 415; receives rice samples from Jefferson, 425
Agriculture: description of crops, 50
*Albemarle*, 25; destroyed, 27
Albemarle Point, 359; construction of wooden buildings, 33; fort completed, 40; named and settled, 32; renamed Charles Town, 34; *Three Brothers* arrives, 32
Allein, Richard: replaces Trott as Chief Justice, 122
Allston, Washington: birth, 355; image, 355
Alston, Joseph: birth, 354; enrolls in Princeton, 467; returns to Charleston, 472; studies law under Edward Rutledge, 472
Alston, William: entertains George Washington, 444; marries Mary Brewton Motte, 443
Amazing Grace: hymn, 197
American Company of Comedians, 227, 233, 413; given permission to perform, 413; perform at Exchange, 413; present *The Distressed Mother*, 237
American Revolution: "Don't Tread On Me" flag designed, 309; 200 Carolina militia killed, 344; American ships deemed lawful prizes, 310; Article of Confederation adopted, 340; Battle of Beaufort, 349, 350; Battle of Cowpens, 378; Battle of Eutaw Springs, 387; Battle of Fort Motte, 382; Battle of Hog Island Channel, 308; British blockade, 340, 346; British blockade of American ports, 302; British evacuate Charlestown, 396; British flagship leaves, 329; British fleet appears in Charlestown, 317; British fleet approaches Charlestown, 317; British fleet leaves Charlestown, 329; British fleet sails to Cape Fear, 311; British naval reinforcements

reach Cape Fear, 316; British officers entertained in town, 339; British troops approach Charlestown, 350, 351; call for disestablishement of English Church, 316; Carolina exiles leave Philadelphia, 387; Charleston exiles learn of prisoner exchange, 384; Charlestown delegation attacked by British ship, 313; colonies declared in open rebellion, 306; death for aiding British, 315; drunken brawl, 346; duel between Laurens and Lee, 347; effects on Charlestown economy, 312; English church disestablished, 335; foreshadowing of, 55; French fleet arrives, 354; gunpowder seized off Georgia, 302; harbor blockaded, 305; John Ashe arrives, 349; John Laurens arrives in France, 379; John Laurens joins Washington's staff, 338; John Laurens proposes to lead Negro troops, 341; John Laurens returns with French supplies, 387; King's Mountain, 377; Lafayette arrives, 337; last SC action, 396; Laurens imprisoned in Tower, 377; Laurens released from Tower, 391; Lee marches to Florida, 331; Lee plans to attack Florida, 329; Morris Island lighthouse taken by Patriots, 329; new signals for harbor, 312; Parliament votes to end war, 392; paroled officers ordered to take up arms, 383; Patriot troops seize supplies from British ship, 305; prisoner exchange, 382; prisoners enlisted to fight, 379; Salvadore killed, 329; Savannah captured, 348; Siege of Charlestown, 352; South Carolina delegation votes against Decla-ration, 327; South Carolina naval fleet, 340; South Carolina navy formed, 307; South Carolina regiments join Continental Army, 333; state loyalty oath demanded, 335; Test Act passed, 343; trade opens with French, 335; Treaty of Paris negotiations, 392; troops in Charlestown, 317; Valley Forge, 340; Virginia announces freedom for fighting against rebelious colonists, 307; Waxhaws Massacre, 370; Yorktown, 388; Yorktown surrender, 388

*Americana and Eleutheria*: performed once at Charleston Theater, 474

Amicable Society, 162

Anabaptist Church, 72

Anglicans: population, 75

Anne, Queen: ascends to throne, 80

Anson, George, 186; arrival, 135; attacks Capt. Gordon, 147; attacks Spanish, 177; captains *Squirrel*, 147; description of, 135; leaves Charlestown, 154; orders Bowling Green to be laid into streets, 186; plunders Spanish gold, 183; purchases Ansonborough, 137

Ansonborough: deed recorded, 155; description of, 186; established, 186; laid out in streets, 186; purchased by George Anson, 137

Anthony, Hezekiah: captain of *George Washington*, 339; commander in South Carolina Navy, 327; commissioned as privateer, 335; given new command, 339

Archdale Street: named for John Archdale, 49

Archdale, John, 52, 66; accomplishments as governor, 66; becomes governor, 66; biography, 49; campaign to attract new colonists, 54; description of commerce, 89; leaves, 69; purchases Propreietor's share, 49

Armstrong, John: arrival, 315

Arnold, Benedict, 381

Arnold, Eliza (Poe): performs in Charleston, 473

Arrivals: *Carolina* returns from Barbados, 35; colonists from New York, 38; Dutch from New York, 43; Irish immmgrants for backcountry, 247; Scottish prisoners, 105; settlers from Barbados with Yeamans, 36; settlers from New York, 34

Articles of Confederation, 419; adopted, 340; adopted by 1st Provincial Congress, 299; arguments over slavery, 331; signed, 346; South Carolina signers, 346

Asbury, Francis, 414; attacked by mob, 429; description of Charleston, 413; first Methodist service, 413; preaches sermons, 417; returns to Charleston, 417

Ash, John: introduces bill to regulate elections, 81

Ashe, John: arrival with North Carolina militia, 349

Ashe, Thomas: about crops, 50

Ashley Ferry: billard table, 151; executions, 281; Gordon's fair, 194; hosts Assembly, 219; hosts fair, 162; treaty with Cherokee, 219

Ashley Hall Plantation, 93

Ashley River: named, 23

Assembly, 332; 1782 meeting, 389; act for importing white servants, 71; act to build Battery, 68; act to repair fortifications, 100; announces sale of tea, 333; appoints committee to investigate election, 223; approved construction of statehouse, 199; approved rice to pay taxes, 62; approves statue of Pitt, 238; arms slaves, 101; asks to void Proprietor's charter, 101; banishes Colleton, 61; Barbadian control of, 37; bill introduced to regulate elections, 81; calls for Montagu's removal, 274; Catholics right to vote, 80; challenged by governor, 222; chooses delegates to Constitutional Convention, 423; claims taxes should only by enacted by local authorities, 235; commissions more privateers, 335; convenes in Charlestown, 398; convens for first time, 315; convens in Shepheard's Tavern, 152; convention of the people, 121; created to replace the Assembly, 314; delegates to Confederation Congress, 408; denied authority to pay Wilkes' debt, 261; description of 1782, 390; discovers gunpowder in Exchange, 402; dissolves SC Navy, 399; doubled tax on exported skins, 78; encourages white servant immigrants, 108; endorses Townsend protest letter, 250; establish courts and sheriffs, 247; establish courts in backcountry, 245; establish library, 74; establish new provisional government, 121; establish watch on Sullivan's Island, 62; establishes free school, 92; Establishment Act passed, 84; first meets, 37; forces out Montagu, 279; gains power during French and Indian War, 220; gives Congress power to regulate trade, 419; gives Rutledge unlimited power, 357; lifts ban on slave importation, 251; Mace purchased, 207; meets in Beaufort, 272; passes an act against privateers, 55; passes Commodity Act, 59; passes debtor relief, 419; passes Negro Act, 130; passes new Negro Act, 175; passes Vagrancy Act, 424; pays debts from piracy excursions, 119; pays for military service with rice, 104; petitions King George to purchase Carolina, 121; petitions King to become a Royal colony, 108; prevents men and women cohabitating, 83; reformed to usurp Proprietors, 120; refuses to pay officers' rents, 211; rejects Laurens' plan for armed Negro troops, 348; rejects Negro troops, 353; requires ministers to support Patriot cause, 315; restricts clandestine trade, 222; revises election law, 119; Security act passed, 128; selects Legislative Council, 314; stand against govenor, 224; suspends business until governor apologizes, 224; suspends business with governor, 272; taken by Dissenters, 88; urges Congress to assume state debt, 438; votes against Indian slave trade ban, 416; votes to move capital, 417, 435; votes to pay Wilkes' debts, 258; warned to ignore Townsend letter, 250

Association: abandoned by other colonies, 261; attacked by Drayton, 255; attacked by locals over Smythe Horse Affair, 297; broken by Rhode Island, 262; castigates Georgia, 262; effect on economy, 260; effect on imports, 264; formed, 255; Manigault refuses to join, 257; meets at Liberty Tree, 288; non-importation agreement takes effect, 293; orders Gillon not to sell wine, 259; organized, 253; position on Smythe Horse Affair, 297; prostests against Rhode Island, 262; publishes names of non-members, 256; resurrected, 286; thirty-one refuse, 256; violaters publicly identified, 262; votes to remain in support of non-importation, 261

Assumption Issue, 440

Aston, Anthony: performs first play, 81

*Attack on Fort Moultrie, The*: performed at French theater, 461

Audubon, John James: birth, 408

Austin and Laurens, 200; number of slavey imported, 190

Autopsy: first performed in Carolina, 63

## B

Backcountry: Battle of Cowpens, 378; Campbell floods with pamphlets, 301; Cherokee massacre, 215; commerce, 262; complaints about new state constitution, 315; courts established, 245; courts open, 273; dangerous conditions, 244; description of residents, 240; district courts established, 254; exploration of, 78; formation of Regulators, 241; lack of courts, 241; mounted rangers approved, 300; protest Charlestown politicians, 250; Regulators ordered to disband, 245; stampede of immigration, 226; trade with Charlestown, 271

Backhouse's Tavern, 229

Balfour Baboon, 371

Balfour, Nisbet, 378, 383; brags about prisoners' deaths, 374; orders patriot's families to leave, 383; ridiculed with baboon, 371; sets execution date, 385

Ball, Eleanor: marries Henry Laurens, 198

Ballendine, Hamilton: hanged for desertion, 358

Bank of South Carolina: opens, 449

Baptists: arrival, 54; population, 75

INDEX / 491

Barbadian Adventurers, 20; encouraged by Proprietors, 21; established, 20; organized under Yeamans, 21; plan to settle Carolina, 21; proposal for grants, 21
Barbadians: against Navagation Act, 55; all West Indies colonists called, 39; attitude toward *Fundamental Constitutions*, 37; attitude toward the English settlers, 36; control Council, 37; description of their attitude, 36; ignore English law, 55
Barbados: asylum for Royalists, 16; baronages extended, 17; Carolina expedition arrives, 27; seen as a place to find colonists, 20; settled, 13; settlers arrive, 35; settlers wanted from, 25; sugar production, 15; title of, 14; trade with England prohibited, 16
Barker, Thomas: massacred by Catawba, 102
Barnwell, John, 130; Battle of Beaufort, 350; captures *Phillipa*, 302; commissioned commander of southern forces, 130; goes to England, 125; goes to London to present Carolina's case to the King, 121
Bassett, Nathan: baptizes negro, 156, 161
Battle of Bacon's Bridge, 358
Battle of Beaufort: description of, 350
Battle of Cowpens: description, 378; image, 378
Battle of Fort Motte: house burned, 382
Battle of Hog Island Channel, 308
Battle of Lexington and Concord, 298
Battle of Stono Ferry, 353
Battle of Sullivan's Island: Breach's Inlet crossing, 325; British evacuate Isle of Palms, 329; British fleet cross the bar, 319; casualties, 325; Charlestown preperations, 320; Clinton appeals for surrender, 321; Clinton's plan for Breach Inlet, 320; Clinton's plan to take fort, 319; description of, 323, 325; first anniversary, 338; first major naval battle of the Revolution, 323; Ft. Sullivan state of readiness, 322; image, 324; importance of, 327; Lee recommends evacuating Ft. Sullivan, 322; Lee reviews fort, 319; map, 321, 323; news of victory spread, 327; Patriots guard Breach Inlet, 321; Patriots plunder *Aceton*, 325; preparations in Charlestown, 318; Rev. Cooper prays for British victory, thousands watch, 322
Battle of Sullivan's Island: Battle of the Ponds. *See* Yemassee War
Bayly's Medley of Entertainments and Uncommon Performances, 247
Beale, Othniel: commissioned to build, 182; designs palisade, 182

Beaufort, 101; Assembly meets, 272; attacked by Yemassee, 101; chartered, 93
Bedon, George, 64; claims land from Yeamans, 43; death from hurricane, 201
Bee, Thomas, 278, 402; appointed as Federal judge, 442; birth, 167; chairmen of ratification convention, 431; complaints about moving capital, 419; convenes in new courthouse, 451; proposes city incorporation, 402
Bellinger, Edmund, 74
Bennett, Thomas , Jr.: birth, 386
Berkeley, John: death, 44; Proprietor, 18
Berkeley, Sir William: Proprietor, 18
Biddle, Nicholas, 339; death, 342; to destroy British blockade, 340
Bignall, John: death, 462; plans to build new theater, 450
Blackbeard, 110; blockades Charles Town, 111; demands ransom, 111; meets Bonnet, 110; profile, 111
Blake, Joseph, 72, 74; accused of piracy, 72; appointed governor, 69; chosen as acting governor, 65; comment on rice, 75; Deputy Governor, 66; gives Independent Church money, 66; land grant conveyed to, 71; signed religious act, 70
Bloodless Revolution, 114; airing of grievances, 120; Assembly asks to void Proprietor's charter, 101; Barnwell goes to England, 125; citizens association formed to repeal Proprietor's charter, 120; Craven pleads case in London, 105; Declaration of Causes, 121; Johnson establishes, 125; Lords of Admiralty agree to send ship, 119; new provisional government established, 121; Royal Privy Council recommends, 126; tensions increase between Assembly and Proprietors, 112
Blythe's Court-Room, Mrs., 195
Board of Police: established by Clinton, 370
Board of Trade: created, 68
Boatswain: convicted of arson, 179
Bohun, Edmund: appointed Chief Justice, 71; death from yellow fever, 74
Bolton, Thomas, 85; sells shipyard, 202
Bolzius, Rev. John Martin: conducts first Lutheran communion, 151
Bonnet, Stede, 112; appeal to Johnson, 118; arraigned by Trott, 115; blockades Charles Town, 111; captured, 113; escapes disguised as woman, 114; execution, 117; execution image, 117; grounds vessel, 112; image, 116; imprisoned at Patridge's house, 113; lays off Charles Town, 108; meets Blackbeard, 110;

profile, 109; recaptured, 115; sentenced to death, 115; writes appeal to Johnson, 115
Bonny, Anne Cormac: 2nd marriage, 130; arrival, 81; born, 80; captured, 128; death, 393; description of as a child, 81; freed, 128; image, 126; marriage, 119; profile, 129; sails to Bahamas, 119
Bonny, James, 119
Boon, John: purchased ship with sugar, 44
Boone, Joseph: argues to revoke Proprietor's charter, 114
Boone, Thomas, 221; arrives as Royal Governor, 220; leaves Charlestown, 227; refuses to administer oath, 222; treaty signed with Cherokee, 226
Border Survey, 271
Boston: founded, 14
Boston Massacre, 260; reported in *Gazette*, 260
Boston Tea Party: image, 287
Boundary Commission: border between North and South Carolina, 143; completes survery of North and South Carolina, 161
Boundary Street, 419, 463; northern border, 256
Bouquet, Henry: commander of British troops, 210; orders citizens to pay rent, 211
Bowling Green: opens, 192
Bowling Green Plantation. *See* Ansonborough
Boyd, Jean: arrival, 56; description of Charles Town, 56
Braine, Henry: captain of *Carolina*, 33
Breach's Inlet: Cornwallis' troops unable to cross, 325
Brewton, Francis: marries Charles Pinckney, Jr., 202
Brewton, Miles, 280
Brewton, Miles, Sr.: arrival, 53
Brewton, Robert: house, 125
*Britannia*: tea dumped, 293
British Occupation, 369, 370, 373, 395; all jobs closed to Patriots, 381; arrests for parole violations, 379; Balfour baboon, 371; citizens plea for Hayne's life, 385; death of John Laurens, 394; description of prison ship, 377; effect of, 397; families ordered out, 384; Greene camps at Dorchester, 393; Hayne execution, 385; Hayne execution date set, 384; Johns Island skirmish, 389; last SC action, 396; Loyalty oath, 371; magazine explodes, 369; Pinckney arrested, 383; Rebecca Motte leaves, 382; seizure of property, 377; slaves ungovernable, 381
*Briton*: launched at Hobcaw, 282

Broad Street Tavern, 163
Brookes, Robert, 46
Broughton Island Packet: seized, 243
Broughton, Thomas: assumes governorship, 155; portrait painted by Henrietta Johnston, 92; received Mulberry Plantation, 90
Broughton's Battery, 173
Brown Fellowship Society: charter, 442; chartered, 442; image, 443
Brown, Morris: birth, 260
*Brownlow*, slave vessel, 194
Bruce, Peter Henry: arrival, 187; His Majesty's Engineer, 187
Bryan, Hugh: blames fire on Anglican Church, 179; imprisoned, 180; letter to Bull, 180; preaches to slaves, 180
Buildings of Charleston: County Court House, 434; David Ramsay House; image, 392; Exchange Building, 246; Governor's House Inn; image, 216; John Lining House; image, 104; John Rutledge House; image, 223; Miles Brewton House, 279; Pink House, 67; Powder Magazine; image, 98; Robert Brewton house, 127; St Michael's Church, 221; St. Andrews Hall; image, 142; St. John's Lutheran Church, 228; statehouse approved, 199; Unitarian Church, 273; William Bull house, image, 127; William Rhett House; Image, 95
Bull, Stephen, 26; appointed Surveyor General, 54
Bull, William: account of Stono Rebellion, 170; becomes governor, 164; constructs house, 125; death, 206
Bull, William, Jr., 125, 235, 258; appointed acting governor, 227; attacks the *Gazette*, 234; birth, 93; blames Gadsden for protests, 235; complains about backcountry, 257; confers with Cherokee, 219; congratulated on his handling of tea situation, 285; denounces Stamp Act protests, 233; moves Assembly to Ashley Ferry, 219; orders militia to guard city, 236; refuses to recognize Provincial Congress, 296
Bullman, John: critical of Committee, 291; dismissed from St. Michael's, 292; preaches sermon critical of Boston Tea Party, 291
Bunce Castle, 190
Burke, Aedanus, 356, 408, 418, 432, 435, 439, 441; acts as Burr's second in duel, 477; against Constitution ratification, 432; argues for assumption of debt, 440; arrival, 309; attacks Cincinnati Society, 405; attacks confiscation, 398; attacks Hamilton, 441;

attacks slavery ban petition, 439; befriends Genet, 453; birth, 183; complains about jails, 471; complaints about Quakers slave ban, 440; concerns about national election, 451; conducts first court session, 344; defends SC militia, 440; describes 1782 Assembly, 390; description of, 309; discusses injunction against privateers, 458; elected circuit judge, 343; elected judge, 350; elected to Congress, 343; image, 351; impressions of, 343; presides at first court, 399; publishes 3rd pamphlet, 410; Yorktown, 388

Burleigh, Joseph: marries Anne Bonny, 130

Burning of Sodom, The, 178

Burr, Aaron, 401, 451, 457; wife dies, 457

Burr, Theodosia: birth, 401

Butler, Pierce, 399, 440, 446, 447; arrives in Philadelphia, 385; asks to ban all West Indian blacks, 456; birth, 185; hosts George Washington, 447; image, 400; introduces Fugitive Slave law, 427; marries Mary Middleton, 268; remarks on French Revolution, 436; supports moving capital, 435

# C

Calhoun, John Caldwell: birth, 392

Campbell, William: advice to Clinton about taking Charlestown, 315; arrives as Royal Governor, 301; asked to return to city, 306; condemnation of Charlestown, 309; despair over Jeremy hanging, 304; marries Sarah Izard, 226; moves into Miles Brewton House, 301; moves to Meeting Street, 301; on board *Cherokee*, 308; response to General Committee, 306; stirs up backcountry against lowcountry, 301; supports Jeremy's innocence, 303; urges attack on South Carolina, 317; warned to ignore Jeremy trial, 303; wounded, 325

Cape Fear, 23; abandoned in Cooper's plans, 25; misfortunes, 22; settlement, 22; settlement abandoned, 24

Cardy, Samuel: designs lighthouse, 240

*Carolina*, 25; arrives in Bermuda, 28; arrives in Charleston harbor, 32; cargo, 32; crew, 27; damaged by storm, 28; repaired in Bahamas, 28; returns with settlers, 35; returns with supplies, 33; sails to Barbados for supplies, 33; sails to Virginia, 33; slips past Spanish blockade, 33

Carolina Coffee House, 52, 211

Carolina Colony, 2, 38, 61, 122; 2nd charter, 18; Barbadian interest in settlement, 20; Barbadian slave code adopted, 36; building of roads, forts, 35; campaign to recruit settlers, 35; colonists recruited, 25; company of adventurers organized, 21; *Concessions and Agreements*, 21; description of, 23, 34; divided into four counties, 51; expedition arrives in Barbados, 28; exploration by Hilton, 20; first litigation, 37; first Spanish settlement abandoned, 10; food shortage, 33; formal possession taken, 23; *Fundamental Constitutions of Carolina*, 25; Locke's observations, 34; lure of the colony, 36; plans for settlement, 20; promotional pamphlet, 52; Proprietors establish a fund, 19; Proprietors renew commitment, 43; Sandford recommends settlement, 23; second charter drafted, 21; security concerns, 33; Spanish blockade, 33; stock company established, 20; weekly food allotment, 36

Carolina Day: first celebration, 338

Carolina Expedition: arrives at Bull's Island, 31; arrives at Port Royal, 31; arrives in Barbados, 27; arrives in Charleston harbor, 32; expedition leaves Ireland, 27; first election, 32; greeted by Cassique, 31; leaves Barbados, 28; leaves Bermuda, 31; *Port Royal* stranded in Bahamas, 28; takes on new passengers in Bermuda, 31; voted to settle on the Ashley River, 32; West commissioned commander, 27; Woodward joins, 28; Yeamans joins on board *Port Royal*, 28; Yeamans returns to Barbados, 31

*Carolina Packet*, 232, 258; boarded by angry citizens, 233; delivers Pitt statue, 261

Carteret, George: death, 46; Proprietor, 19

Carteret, Nicholas: description of Indians, 31

Cary, Thomas, 49

Cassique: argues for settlement on Ashley River, 31; friend of the English, 31; greets expedition, 31; greets the Carolina expedition, 31; lives with English, 23

Castle Pinckney: built, 472; image, 472

Catawba tribe: allies with English, 103; during the Yemassee War, 102; slaughtered, 103

Catesby, Mark: arrival, 131

Catholics: land for church, 437; not allowed rights of Englishmen, 70; parish organized, 430; right to vote, 80; St. Mary's formed, 443

*Cato*: performed at Dock Street, 161

Chalmers, James: arrival, 469

Chamber of Commerce, 429; correspondence with Jefferson, 407; established, 284; reaction to, 284; reestablished, 407; urges Assembly to give Congress power to negotiate commerce, 415

Chamberlain, Sarah: execution, 165

Chandler, Samuel: opens academy, 429

Charles I: arrested for treason, 16; charter for Maryland, 14; crowned, 12; Eleven Year Tyranny, 13; execution, 16; first Carolina land grant, 14; guilty of treason, 16; raises standard of war, 15; trial, 16

Charles II: arrives in London, 17; bestows title to Cooper, 40; birth, 14; crowned, 17; death, 54; encourages privateers, 53; exhumes Cromwell, 18; goes into exile, 17; grants charter for Carolana, 18; nullifies Heath Charter, 21

Charles II, 43

Charles Town: officially named, 34; ships trading with England, 92

Charlesfort: abandoned, 10; destroyed by fire, 10; settlement established, 10

Charleston; 1774 image, 266; 1708 description of, 91; 1725 description of, 137; 1762 description, 222; 1765 description of, 229; 1769 population, 258; 1770 description of, 264; 1773 churches, 286; 1773 description of, 280; 1773 description of, 276; 1774 image, 295; 1778 map, 433; 1783 incorporation, 402; 1788 image, 436; association formed to repeal Proprietor's charter, 120; attacked by French, 87; blockaded by Blackbeard, 111; blueprint established for the "old South", 37; British evacuate, 396; description by George Washington, 447; description of, 51, 224, 285; description of by Jean Boyd, 56; description of Grand Modell, 40; description of houses, 244; divided into two parishes, 199; early image, 44; first city council, 403; first English walled city, map, 57; first French church, 59; French attack, 86; harbored explored, 12; hurricane, 97; in terror of pirates, 113; incorporated first time, 131; learns about Battle of Lexington, 299; name change from Charlestown, 402; original town plan, 41; petitions to become a Royal colony, 108; piracy encouraged, 107; prepares for 1776 British attack, 320; ships in port, 48; slaves whipped and emasculated, 69; surrenders to British, 368; tea dumped, 293; votes to move to Oyster Point, 44

Charleston Comedians: formed by French troupe, 475

Charleston First: Anglican hymnbook published, 163; Chamber of Commerce, 284; English walled city, 57; fire insurance company, 158; first female painter, 92; golf club, 420; Insurance fire company; image, 157; museum, 275; newspaper edited by woman, 167, 169; opera performed, 154, 155; public orphan house, 463; published Anglican hymnbook, 162; rice cultivated, 54; theater opens, 158; weather observations, 164

Charleston harbor: explored by Sandford, 23

Charleston Insurance Company for Marine Insurance: incorporated, 472

Charleston Library Society, 194; founded, 193; holdings destroyed by fire, 341; locations, 193; moves to county courthouse, 438; provides collection of artifacts, 274; recieves collection from St. Philip's, 343

Charleston Museum: established, 274; moves to county courthouse, 438

Charleston Orphan House: image, 463; opens, 463

Charleston Theater: Charleston Theater, 459, 462, 466, 475; 1st season closes, 453; 3rd season opens, 462; 4th season opens, 469; *Americana and Eleutheria* performed once, 474; announces original play, 455; benefit for refugees, 458; description, 451; description of opening night, 452; feud with French Theater, 465; fire disrupts performance, 474; French troupe moves in, 474; in competition with French theater, 461; in debt, 473; opens, 452; opens for Saturday performances, 453; players return for 2nd season, 458; rented by seminary, 475; season opens, 458; unable to open, 473

Charleston Water Works: opens, 477

Chassereau, Peter: architect, 153

Cherokee tribe: allies with English, 105; chiefs return from London, 144; during the Yamassee War, 102; during Yemassee War, 103; fort built for, 209; French and Indian War uprising, 214; signs treaty of Dewitt's Corner, 336; signs treaty with King George II, 144

Chicken, George: slaughters Catawbas, 103

Christophe, Henry: serves as drummer boy, 354

Church of England: dencounced by Presbyterians, 92; disestablished, 335; established as state religion, 84
Church of the Tides. *See* Huguenot Church
Circuit Court Act, 248, 254
Circular Church, 83
City Council: appoints constables, 406; establishes orphan house, 442
City Market: land donated, 431
City Tavern, 407, 428
City Theatre: opens Long Room, 469; 3rd season closes, 473; blacks banned from attending, 468; in debt, 473; opens 3rd season, 472; put up for rent, 475; *Richard III* performed, 473; Sollee's Long Room acquire reputation, 476; troupe moves to Charleston Theater, 474
Clark, Richard: religious extremism, 212
Clarke, William: first surgeon, 45
Clinton, Henry, 362, 368, 373; appeals to Rutledge to surrender, 321; blames Parker for defeat, 329; commander of British forces in South, 317; congratulated on victory, 370; demands loyalty oath, 371; describes surrender, 372; frustrated by resistance, 367; image, 372; issues summons to surrender, 363; lands on Isle of Palms, 319; leaves for New York, 373; leaves New York for Charlestown, 356; new surrender summons, 368; orders batteries to fire upon city, 362; orders troops into St. Andrews, 360; orders troops to Mt. Pleasant, 364; plan for Breach Inlet, 320; pleas for return, 319; refuses terms of surrender, 368; rejects Lincoln's surrender, 364; revokes all paroles, 371; sends Cornwallis to Isle of Palms, 321
Club Forty-Five, 261, 262; meets, 260; tea protests at Liberty Tree, 282
Cock, John: builds house, 125
Cohen, Moses, 195
Cole, Richard, 38
Collection of Psalms and Hymns: published, 162
College of Charleston, 71; barracks constructed on site, 211; bill to establish passed, 260; founders, 413; plans made, 226
Colleton, James: arrival, 58; banished by Sothell, 61; commissioned governor, 58; disbands Grand Council, 59; imposes martial law, 59; orders exepdition disbanded, 58; reputation for tyranny, 59
Colleton, Peter, 20
Colleton, Sir John, 27; conveys Mulberry Plantation, 90; extended baronage, 17; interest in moving to Carolina, 20; Proprietor, 19

Colleton, Thomas, 35
Colonial Dames of America in the State of South Carolina, The, 96
Colonial Lake: commissioners, 247; established, 247
Columbia: new state capital location, 417
Columbus, Christopher, 10
Coming Street Cemetery: established, 204
Coming, John, 38; comments on Barbadians, 37; marries Affra Harleston, 39; returns land, 40; surrenders land on Oyster Point, 39
Commerce: 1678, 45; 1720 ships, 125; 1731 ship traffic, 145; 1735, 152; 1748 ship total, 191; 1763, 224; 1765 ships, 229; 200 acres sold, 46; 3000 gallons of rum imported, 410; 330 tons of rice exported, 76; ad to rent theater, 292; Bank of South Carolina opens, 449; Bank of the United States opens, 449; businesses open, 458; Charleston Insurance Company for Marine Insurance, 472; cotton becomes king, 477; effects of Revolution, 312; exports, 1713, 96; first barrel of rice shipped, 39; first paper currency printed, 159; first service established, 140; harbor clogged with ships, 235; hemp prices set, 160; Indian traders licensed, 45; indigo, 2nd most profitable crop, 194; inspection system fo tobacco, 268; land grant conveyed to Blake, 71; livestock imported, 49; Miles Brewton house sold, 449; Mutual Insurance Company Against Fire incorporated, 472; naval stores exported, 50; new city market land donated, 431; new wharves, 182; number of wharves, 167; outfitting a ship, 55; partnership for a saw mill, 56; real estate, 253; real estate, 166; real estate sale, 152; rice enumerated, 85; Rice exports, 73; rice used as currency, 68; salt manufacturing, 137; Santee Canal Company, 465; semi-annual fairs established, 132; seventeen ships anchor, 88; shipbuilding, 110; ships trading, 92; Stamp Act shuts down, 235; tax on exported animal skins, 62; ten vessels registered in Charles town, 68; trade between SC and France, 429; trade with backcountry, 271; water-powered rice mill, 422
Commissioners of the Indian Trade of South Carolina: established, 93
Committee of Grievances: members, 272
Committee of Ninety-nine, 290
Commodity Act, 59
*Common Sense*: presented to Provincial Congress, 313; published, 312

Company for Inland Navigation from Santee to Cooper Rivers. *See* Santee Canal Company
Compilation of the Provincial Statues, 96
Concessions and Agreements, 21
Confederation Congress: delegates, 408
Congregationalists: arrival, 48
Considerations on the Society or Order of the Cincinnati, 405
Constitution Ratification Convention: called, 430; constitution ratified, 432; opposition, 432; slavery arguments, 432
Constitutional Convention, 422, 426; Butler introduces Fugitive Slave law, 427; Pinckney's Draught, 426; SC delegates, 423
Continental Congress, First: delegates return, 293
Continental Congress, First, 292; Charleston delegates, 290; opens, 292; suspends trade with Britain, 292
Continental Congress, Second, 298; Carolina delegation attacked by British ship, 313; Charlestown be defended, 307; Charlestown delegates, 299; creates War Department, 313; *Declaration of the Causes and Necessity of taking up Arms*, 302; establishes American Navy, 309
Continental Congress, Third: adopts Articles of Confederation, 340; Laurens elected president, 339; rejects British offer of conciliation, 345
Cooke, Mary, 220; sued William Lennox over non-marriage, 217
Cooper, Anthony Ashley: appointed Chancellor of the Exchequer, 18; appointed Lord Chancellor, 41; arrested for treason, 49; attitude toward Yeamans, 41; Barbados property, 18; biography, 41; death, 52; encourages recruitment of French settlers, 46; flees to Holland, 52; *Fundamental Constitutions* written, 25; granted amnesty, 17; instructions to Yeamans, 38; introduces *Habeas Corpus Act*, 46; meets Locke, 24; named Earl of Shaftesbury, 40; orders colony move to Oyster Point, 40; plan for Carolina settlement, 25; praise of Coming, 38; proprietor, 19; purchases three ships, 25; removed from Privy Council, 42; river named for, 23; takes control of the Proprietors, 25; treason charges dropped, 49; trial for treason, 49; warns against Catholics, 42
Cooper, Robert: prays for British victory, 322; removed as minister, 329

Corbet, Thomas: becomes high baliff of Westminster, 195
Cormac, William, 80; arrival, 81; bribes governor, 128
Cornwallis, Charles, 139, 321, 356, 358, 364, 371, 377; appointed SC commander, 373; arrival in Carolina, 316; comments on militia, 379; described by Edward Rutledge, 391; erects battery at Albemarle Point, 359; exchanged for Henry Laurens, 391; lands on James Island, 358; requests surrender terms, 388; surrenders Yorktown, 388
Cotesworth, Mary: marriage to Pinckney, 70
Cotton Gin: image, 460
Cotton, John, Jr.: arrival, 70
Council of Foreign Plantations, 18
Council of Safety, 302, 306; charged with running colonial business, 301; orders fortification of Sullivan's Island, 311; proposed, 295; requests palmetto logs for Fort Sullivan, 312; to enforce non-importation, 296
Council of Trade and Plantations,, 46
*Country Journal*, 247, 252, 255
County Court Act, 413
Court of Chancery: established, 130
Court of Guard: at Half Moon Battery, 84
Courten, Sir William: given title of Barbados, 13
Craven, Charles, 52; appeals for help from Proprietors, 102; arrives as governor, 95; declares martial law, 101; engages Yemassee, 101; pleads Carolina's case for Royal Colony, 105; worries about Trott's power, 100
Craven, William: Proprietor, 19
Crescent Insignia: first design, 217
Crime, 182, 423; building a jail, 244; burglary ring, 287; condition of jails, 471; counterfeiting, 444; description of workhouse, 248; Dutartre family, 133; forgery, 450; inciting a slave to robbery, 282; Kate convicted of setting fire, 179; pillory and lashes, 287; slave convicted of poisoning, 198; stealing a Negro, 283; stealing clothes, 162; street magic, 269; tarred and feathered, 430; theater vandalized, 226; witchcraft, 86
Cripps, Mary Splatt: arrival, 239; marries to Alexander Gillon, 240
Crisp Map of Charles Town, 57, 99
Cromwell, Oliver, 15, 16; death, 17; signs Navagation Acts, 17
Crops, 249; killed by first winter, 35

Crowfield. *See* Oaks Plantation, The
Culinary: description of meal, 277, 278; largest Plum pudding, 159; *pastry-cook*, 190
Culpepper, John: surveys Oyster Point, 40
Curfew Act, 79; for slaves, 161

# D

D'Estaing, Comte: arrival, 354; asked to help defend South Carolina, 353
DaCosta, Abraham, 195
DaCosta, Issac: establishes Coming Street Cemetery, 203; first Jew to join Masonic lodge, 200; first minister of Beth Elohim, 195
Dalton, Joseph, 32, 34; secretary of the colony, 34
Dancing Exploded: A Sermon Showing the Unlawfulness, Sinfulness, and Bad Consequences of Balls, Assemblies, and Dances In General, 343
Daniel, Robert: appointed deputy governor, 101
Dart, Benjamin: appointed joint Treasurer, 262; sons of Liberty, 250; supports Wilkes Fund, 262
Dart, John: greets Washington, 445
de Ayllón, Lucas Vasquez: settlement on Carolina coast, 10
De Brahm, William, 206, 209, 353; finishes batter sea wall, 208; hired, 206; hired to rebuild fortifications, 201; presents plan, 202
de Grammont, Sieur: pirate, 52
de Leon, Ponce, 10
de Saussure, Henry William: appointed director of U.S. Mint, 467
de St. Julien, Benjamin, 195
de, St. Julien, Damaris Elizabeth: marries William Moultrie, 195
Dealy, James: tarred and feathered, 299
Dearsley, George: opens shipyard, 85
Death: from yellow fever, 75
DeBordeaux, James: builds house, 75
Declaration of Causes: against the Propreitors, 121
Declaration of Independence: anniversary celebration, 338; approved by Assembly, 332; final wording approved, 327; presented to Congress, 325; signed by Hancock, 328; signed by most members, 330; South Carolina signers, 328; image, 331
Declaration of the Causes and Necessity of taking up Arms, 302

Declaration of the Rights of Man: frightens Charleston whites, 455
Declaratory Act: passed, 238; viewed as threat to American liberty, 238
DeCosta, Solomon, 192
*Defence*: schooner of the SC navy, 308
Defoe, Daniel: criticism of Proprietors, 30
Delancey, Peter: killed in duel, 270
DeSaussure, Henry William: praise of Moultrie, 381
Description of the American Yellow Fever, A: image, 191; published, 191
Dickenson, Sarah: execution, 86
Did You Know: Charleston older than, 58; rum consumption, 209; servants, 50
Dillon's Tavern, 249, 254, 260, 262, 268, 282; Association organized, 254; Stamp Act celebration, 234; Stamp Act protest, 232; Stamp Act repeal celebration, 238
Disasters: 1728 hurricane, 140; 1740 fire, 177; 1752 hurricane, 201; 1778 fire, 341; 1796 fire, 469; 1798 fire, 474; description of 1778 fire, 341; earthquake, 71; fire, 71; fire destroys new French theater, 459; great fire of London, 24; hurricane, 97, 183, 211; State House destroyed by fire, 430
Dissenters, 51; allowed to hold office, 85; becomes majority of population, 56; bill to regulate elections, 81; complaints about election, 80; hatred of Trott, 81; majority of new colonists, 50; protest the Establishment Act, 84; send Boone to England, 83; take control of Assembly, 88
Dock Street Theater, 154, 156, 159, 162, 164, 174, 205, 206; destroyed by fire, 177; image 158; opens, 157; put up for auction, 159; second season opens, 161; vandalized, 226
Dodson, Sam: protest of boarding his ship, 57
Dorchester: founding of, 66
Doughty's Long-Room: wax display, 203
Douglass Troupe, 283
Douglass, David, 233, 281; abandons Charlestown investments, 292; builds new theater, 227; signs lease for theater, 281
Douglass, Frederick: difference between city and plantation slave, 411
*Dove of London*: purchased interest with sugar, 44
Drayton Hall: land purchased, 165
Drayton, Charles: arrival, 46
Drayton, John: purchases Drayton Hall, 165
Drayton, William, 439; appointed Florida Chief Justice, 232; appointed to U.S. District Court,

437; birth, 147; death, 442; supervises construction of court house, 434
Drayton, William Henry, 308; accompanies the Pinckneys to England, 202; birth, 182; chosen Chairman of Assembly, 315; designs state seal, 316; elected Chief Justice of South Carolina, 314; image, 316; name published, 256; orders blocking Hog Island Channel, 307; refuses to join Association, 255; Secret Committee of Five, 298; voted president of 2nd Provincial Congress, 307
Dueling: attitude toward, 291; Burr vs. Church, 476; Grant and Middleton, 220; Haley vs. Delancy, 270; Howe vs. Gadsden, 346; Laurens vs. Lee, 347; Simon vs. Snipes, 417; Snipes trial, 418; Thompson vs. Rutledge, 407; trial of Haley, 270
Dutartre, Judith: arrested, 134; pregnant, 134
Dutartre family, 132, 133, 134; attack on, 134; conviction, 136; execution, 136; falls under spell, 132; scandal, 132
Dutartre, Peter: arrested, 134
Dyssli, Samuel: description of Charlestown, 164

## E

East India Company, 281
Ecija, Francisco: exploration of Charleston harbor, 12
Economy: 1727 recession, 138; 1765, 229; financing of slaves, 249
Economy Currency values: chart, 143
Eden, Charles: arrangement with Blackbeard, 111; sends reinforcments, 103
Edict of Nantes: issued, 12; revoked, 55
Edisto River, 418; Baptist settlement, 54
Edisto tribe, 20, 23
Education: College of Charleston chartered, 413; dancing school, 293; free school, 252; free school established, 92, 96; French school, 186; French School opens, 196; Miller advertises teaching services, 150; music school, 293; new schools, 418; Pike's Dancing School, 270; teaching of geography, 170; writing instruction, 295
Egan, Edmund, 222
Election Act: scandal, 222
Elections: 1768, 250; 1782, 389; first Jew elected, 293; parishes created, 130; reapportionment of Assembly, 119
Elections Act of 1716, 105
Electricity demonstration, 192, 241
Eleven Year Tyranny, 13

Elfe, Thomas: house hit by shell, 362; makes table for Council chamber, 212
Elliott, Jane: marries William Washington, 393; presents Washington a flag, 356
Elliott, William: donates land for church, 72
Ellis, John, 203
English Civil War: begins, 15; Commonwealth collapses, 17
Entertainments, 156; 1774 theater season closes, 289; 1774 theater season opens, 285; a ball, 218; acrobatic stunts, 438; ad to rent the New Theater, 292; advertisement for subscriptions, 155; American Company of Comedians perform, 413; American Company of Comedians season, 227; Apple-eating, 184; at Mrs. Blythe's Court-Room, 195; Bayly's Medley of Entertainments, 247; benefit concert, 147; benefit for refugees, 458; billiard table, 151, 192; bonfires and fireworks, 189; Bowling Green opens, 192; chemistry lectures, 416; cock fight, 149, 208; complaints about, 227; concert at Harmony Hall, 438; dancing and cards, 146; decency observed, 247; electrical fishes, 289; English and Scottish songs, 149; fair at Ashley Ferry, 162, 194, 200; firework displays, 462; first advertised concert, 147; first show performed, 153; foot race and sack race, 183; given by troops, 218; Harmony Hall, 417; hermaphrodite sheep, 222; high wire act, 438; horsemanship, 275; lecture on gardening, 170; Lewis Hallam Company of Players, 205; magic show, 273; must have permission for performances, 404; New Vauxhall opens, 243; Orange Gardens, 218; patriotic lecture by Ladd, 415; *Richard III* performed, 287; shuffle board, 183; slack rope, 204; St. Celilia's Day concert, 164; street magic, 269; *The Distressed Mother*, 237; *The Fair Penitent*, 205; the white Negro, 183; vocal concert, 428; wax display, 203; wax exhibition, 268
Epidemics, 470; cure for small pox, 165; measles, 271; small pox, 70, 71, 72, 165, 215, 225; small pox hospital opens, 226; small pox inoculation, 215; yellow fever, 74, 75, 87, 141, 147, 172, 219
Establishment Act: passed, 84; repealed, 88
Eutaw Flag: given to Washington, 356
Exchange Building, 242, 453; Act passed, 242; Declaration read, 330; delegates chosen for 1st Continental Congress, 290; description of, 276; First Provincial Congress convenes, 296;

gunpowder found in walls, 402; hosts ball for Washington, 446; hosts Constitution ratification convention., 431; image, 246; land purchased, 245; meeting to protest Tea Act, 283; more tea stored, 290; new state constitution read, 315; plans for construction, 241; stone arrives, 251; tea stored in, 285; theatrical performance, 406; Washington watches procession, 446

Exclusion Act: passed to exclude Dissenters, 83; voided, 83

Execution, 86; ax-wielding slave, 150; Boatswain burned at the stake, 179; Bonnet's crew, 115; burned at stake, 255; Charles I, 16; description of, 204; Dutartre family, 136; for arson, 470; French Negroes executed, 474; hanged for aiding runaway slave, 268; hanged for stealing a Negro, 273, 283; hanged for treason, 351; Issac Hayne, 385; Jacob Weber, 217; pirates, 74, 444; Sarah Chamberlain, 165; slave burnt, 351; slave hanged, 214; slaves, 198; slaves burned, 204; slaves burnt and hanged, 126; slaves hanged, 281; Stede Bonnet image, 117; Thomas Jeremy hanged, burned, 304

Exports, 48; 12 planks of cedar, 34; 1678, 45; 1681, 49; 1713, 96; 1718, 110; 1731, 145; 1750, 196; 1759, 213; 1763, 224; 1769, 258; 330 tons of rice, 76; affected by British blockade, 302; description of, 90; first, 34; indigo, 184, 190; rice, 138, 221, 224, 264; rice exceeds 2000 barrels, 72

# F

Factors: definition, 199; most successful, 199
Faculty of Physic, 206
Fallon, James: Whig Club of 600, 407
Fellowship Society, 247; founded, 222
Fenwick, Robert: arrival, 64
Ferguson, Thomas: letter to Gadsden, 306
First Baptist Church, 72; Furman takes pulpit, 422
First Scots Presbyterian: first service at Meeting House, 152; founded, 145
*Flamborough*: first Royal navy ship, 120
*Flora, or Hob In The Well*: history of, 155; performed at Shepheard's Tavern., 154
Flud, William, 165
Ford, Timothy: impressions of Burke, 343
Fort Dorchester: taken by Lee, 384

Fort Johnson: British soldiers stationed, 189; holds British stamps, 232; new name for Windmill Pont, 89; refortified, 306
Fort King George: constructed, 130; established, 130
Fort Mechanic: contructed, 464
Fort San Marcos: on the site of Charlesfort, 11
Fort Sullivan: completed, 314; description of, 314; during the battle, 323; floating bridge constructed, 320; renamed Fort Moultrie, 328; state of readiness, 322
Fortifications, 68, 100, 182, 206; along Boundary Street, 353; Assembly repairs, 119; Battery wall at White Point, 464; bids requested, 248; brick wall built along Bay Street, 65; bridge between Sullivan's and Haddrell's Point approved, 334; built on northern edge, 187; completed, 84; completed at Albemarle Point., 40; construction along Water Street., 206; De Brahm presents plan, 202; deemed ruinous, 244; description of, 89; description of, 1776, 320; fall into disrepair, 194; finished along Oyster Point, 208; first fortifications built, 33; first Royal navy ship arrives, 120; Fort King George, 130; Fort Sullivan construction begins, 312; Haddrell's Point, 310; Half Moon Battery, 79; Half Moon Battery., 79; Lincoln's accessment of, 355; money appropriated for brick wall, 68; Moultrie in charge of, 360; new signals, 312; palisade constructed, 182; patrol vessels, 97; powder magazine approved, 95; repaired, 120; repairs urged, 81; watch established, 62; William De Brahm hired, 201; Windmill Point constructed, 83, 89
Franklin, Benjamin, 210, 325, 349, 396, 404, 409; hires Timothy as printer, 146; nominates Garden to Royal Society, 281; praise for Elizabeth Timothy, 168; sends printer, 145; Treaty of Paris, 392
Fraser, Charles: comments about Jay's Treaty, 464; describes French theater, 460
Frediche, George: organizes St. John's Church, 210
Free School, 206
Freemasonry, 205, 241, 399; first Jew, 200; first lodge in Charlestown established, 160; Lodge of St. John, 165; private performance, 162
French and Indian War, 206; beginning, 204; burning Cherokee villages, 219; Cherokee negotiate for peace, 219; conclusion and results, 225; court-martial trial, 219;

Crescent insignia, 217; general muster called, 214; list of prominent officers, 217; Lyttelton returns, 215; Montgomerie arrives, 216; officially delcared, 209; privateering, 224; Quartering Act scandal, 211

French Huguenot Church, 452; Lutherans worship at, 210

French Revolution, 436

French Theatre, 459, 460, 461, 466; 2nd season opens, 465; feud with Charleston Theater, 465; renamed City Theater, 468

Freneau, Peter: editor of *City Gazette*, 448

Friday's Ferry. *See* Columbia

Friendly Brothers of St. Patrick, 280, 285

Friendly Society for the Mutual Insurance of Houses Against Fire: established, 156; goes bankrupt, 178

Frost, Thomas, 442

*Fundamental Constitutions of Carolina*: 2nd version, 31; 3rd version, 51; 4th version, 52; adopted, 25; impracticality of, 42; influence on Charleston, 25; system of government, 26

Furman, Richard: calls for disestablishment of English Church, 316; moves to Charleston, 422

## G

Gadsden flag, 309; presented to Provincial Congress, 313

Gadsden, Christopher, 235, 313, 390, 409, 467, 482; 1st Continental Congress, 290; advertises for Negroes, 252; amazed by Constitution, 432; anxious to avenge, 387; appointed lt. governor, 364; appointed to investigate his own election, 223; assures Adams of support, 289; attends Stamp Act Congress, 232; birth, 135; blamed for Stamp Act protests, 235; chosen colonel of First Provincial Regiment, 300; concerns over black population, 238; departs for 1st Congress, 291; description by John Adams, 292; description by Silas Dean, 292; description of, 264; designs, 309; elected Vice-President, 342; finishes Philadelphia apprenticeship, 187; French and Indian War, 214; friendship with Laurens, 135; gives Lafayette a tour, 337; image, 256; insults Drayton, 257; introduces legislation to disestablish English church, 334; leads tea protest, 283; letter to Sam Adams, 289; makes Fort Johnson headquarters, 313; marries Jenny Godfrey, 189; named member of Congressional Marine committee, 309; on English oppression, 253; opens store, 192; opens wharf, 241; opinion of Gillon, 409; opposed to Jay Treaty, 464; organizes Sons of Liberty, 236; promoted to Brigadier General, 332; purchases Gadsdenboro, 212; Smythe Horse Affair, 297; speech at Mazyck's pasture, 238; speech at Stamp Act Congress, 232; to Sam Adams, 289

Gadsden, Thomas, 142; appointed Collector of Customs, 131; death, 178; sells land to Anson, 137; settles in Charles Town, 110

Gadsden's Wharf: description of, 241, 279; opened, 241

Gage, Thomas, 236

*Gambia,* slave ship, 207

Gambrell, Joseph, 302

Garden, Dr. Alexander: administers small pox inoculations, 215; arrival, 200; categorizes local plants, 200; elected to Royal Society, 281; studies in fauna, 203

Garden, Rev. Alexander, 141, 160; arrival, 119; calls on Whitefield to explain offense, 175; first convention of clergy, 144; opens free school for Negroes, 183

Gardenia: named for Dr. Alexander Garden, 281

Garth, Charles, 232; informs Carolina about Stamp Act, 229

Gazette of the State of South Carolina: location of, 75

General Committee: asks Campbell to return, 306; position on Smythe Horse Affair, 297

General History of the Robberies and Murders, 126

*General Washington*, 335, 339; SC Navy, 327

Genet, Edmond Charles, 458; arrives, 453; image, 454

Gentleman Pirate. *See* Stede Bonnet

George I, King, 100; issues piracy pardon, 110

George II, King, 202; grants charter for Georgia, 147

George III: proclamation ceremony, 217

George, Christian: arrested, 134; arrival, 131; befriends Dutartre family, 132; execution, 136

Georgetown, 337, 379; designated port of entry, 145; founding, 141

Georgia colony, 173; chartered, 147; importance of, 149

German Friendly Society, 259; organized, 237

Gervais, John Lewis: describes American batteries, 362; presents plan to move capital, 412
Gibbes, Robert: bribes Council member, 92; death, 103; elected governor, 92; replaced as governor, 95
Gibbes, William: Secret Committee of Five, 298
Gibbes' Wharf: built, 258
Gibbon, William: elected first mayor, 131
Gillon Expedition, 348, 355, 371, 379, 386, 388; leaves for France, 346; passengers to America, 386; Spanish invasion of Bahamas, 393
Gillon, Alexander: appointed Commodore of SC Navy, 342; birth, 179; captures British ships, 345; challenges Hutson for Intendant, 409; confident about economy, 401; death, 462; forms Anti-Britannic Society, 406; forms Whig Club of 600, 406; instigates a riot, 401; marriage, 240; meets Mary Splatt Cripps, 239; ordered to not sell the wine, 259; ordered to purchase ships, 344; returns to Charlestown, 398; sails to France, 346; violates Association, 259; votes for slave ban, 416
Gilman, Samuel, 273
Girad, Peter: comment on Huguenot population, 72
Gist, Mordecai, 221
Glebe Lands, 71, 73
Glen, James, 196, 202; arrival, 184; discusses trade, 196; grants privateer commission, 173; hired De Brahm William, 201; requests British regulars, 187
Godwin, James Verling, 417, 419; attacks audience with sword, 422
Golf: equipment shipped, 420; first equipement, 420; first golf club, 421; first shipment, 182
Goose Creek: bastion for Barbadians, 36; in control of government, 83; M'Arion arrives, 61; oppose Sothell, 63; vulnerable during Yamassee War, 102
Gordon, John: conducts a fair, 194
Gordon's Tavern, 202, 203, 204, 205, 206, 208, 218
Governor's Bridge: finished, 256
Governor's House Inn, 216
Governor's Bridge, 242
Governors of Carolina, Proprietary: list, 123
Grand Council: approved fortifications, 45; approves the move to White Point, 44; Barbadian control, 37; declares war on the Kussoes, 38; describes defenses, 89; disbanded by Colleton, 59; established, 37; hears first litigation case, 37; order to prohibit taverns open during divine worship, 63; orders French church to worship at 9 a.m., 63; orders survey, 38; Oyster Point officially named Charles Town, 47; passes new Church Act, 88; shipmasters ordered to post bond, 39; survey of Oyster Point, 38; using *Fundamental Constitutions* as blueprint, 36
Grand Modell: approved by Proprietors, 26; description of, 40
Grant, James, 217, 242; burns Cherokee villages, 219
Grant, Oswald & Company, 214; controls slavey trade, 190
Granville Bastion, 87, 208; named, 69
Gray's Tavern, 262
Great Awakening, 166
Great Fire of London, 24
Green, Nathaniel, 377; appointed commander of South, 377; at Round O, 389
Greene, Nathaniel: army camps at Dorchester, 393; enters Charlestown, 396; pleads to arm slaves, 390
Griffin, Dempsey: execution, 273
Griffith, Thomas: riding school, 269
Grimball, Paul: leader of Dissenters, 63
Grimke, Elizabeth: marriage to John Rutledge, 226
Grimke, John, 451
Grimke, John F.: arrested, 379
Grimke, Sarah: birth, 451
Groundwater, Andrew: hanged for treason, 351
Guerard, Benjamin: death, 434; elected governor, 398; governor, 407
Guerard, Peter: patent on rice-husker, 62
Guttery, Gilbert: first health commissioner, 95

# H

Habeas Corpus Act, 46
Habersham, John: arrested, 379
Haddrell's Point: barracks approved, 333; floating bridge contructed, 320; image, 311; Lee observes battle from, 323; Moultrie imprisoned at, 381; Patriot battery erected, 310; taken by British, 366
Haitian Revolution, 448; Charleston institutes slave patrols, 450; sparks fear of slave revolt, 455; white refugees arrive, 451
Haley, John: duel, 270; trial for murder, 270
Half-Moon Battery, 79, 84

Hallam, Lewis: petition to build theater, 418
Hamilton, Alexander, 391, 414, 425, 427, 436; about John Laurens, 338; attacked by Burke, 441; attacks SC milita, 440; desciption of duel between Laurens and Lee, 347; responds to Burke, 441; Yorktown, 388
Hampton Hill, 213
Hampton Plantation: image, 445
Hancock, John: retires as president of Congress, 339; signs Declaration, 328
Hangman's Point, 150, 432, 444
Harleston, Affra, 28, 29, 39, 73; comment on small pox, 72; gives land to church, 71; marries John Coming, 39; on epidemic, 71
Harleston's Green: first golf club, 421
Harmony Hall, 423, 426, 438; built, 417; closed due to riot, 422; description of shows, 420; *Merchant of Venice* controversy, 423; opens, 419; opens for lectures and concerts, 427; riot, 422
Hart, Oliver: about British advancement, 350; calls for disestablishment of English Church, 316; comments on English church, 343; sermon against dancing, 343; travels backcountry to rally Patriot support, 302
Harvey, Alexander, 271
Harvey, John: chained to tree, 241
Hayne, Issac, 319; birth, 188; execution, 385; execution announcement, 386; execution date set, 384; refuses to fight for British, 383; signs loyalty oath, 371
*Heart of Oak*: largest ship built in Carolina, 224
Heath Charter: nullified, 21
Heath, Sir Robert: given first Carolina grant, 14
Henderson, William: elected librian of Library Society, 206
Henfield, Gideon: arrested for violating neutrality, 454
Henry, John: petition to build theater, 418
Henry, Patrick: description of John Rutledge, 292
Herriot, David, 112; escapes, 114; imprisoned with Bonnet, 113; joins Blackbeard and Bonnet, 110; killed, 115
Hext, Mary: advertises boarding, 178
Hext, Sarah, 153; marries Dr. John Rutledge, 166
Heyward,Thomas, Jr., 415; 2nd Continental Congress, 299; Battle of Beaufort, 349; defends Haley on murder charges, 270; elected judge, 350; proposes city incorporation, 402; wounded, 350

Hildesley, John: commander of *Flamborough*, 120
Hilton Head, 25; named, 20
Hilton, William: description of Carolina wildlife, 20; engaged to explore Carolina, 20; explores Carolina, 20
History of South Carolina, 201
History of the Revolution of South Carolina, 417
HMS Flamborough, 187
HMS *Rose*, 187
Hoban, James, 434, 451; arrives in Charleston, 431; meets George Washington, 447
Hobcaw, 85, 180, 202, 251, 339, 349; *Briton* launched, 282; during Queen Anne's War, 87; *Heart of Oak* launched, 224; lightning strikes *Randolph*, 337
Holliday, Giles: death, 166; purchases Dock Street Theater, 159
Holmes, Samuel: advertised architectural services, 149
Holt, Henry, 154; advertises dancing lesson, 152; conducts final ball, 162
Hopkins, Esek: recieves flag from Gadsden, 309
Horlbeck, Adam: constructs Exchange, 245
Horlbeck, Peter: constructs Exchange, 245
Horn work: image, 366
Hornigold, Captain Benjamin, 111
Horry, Daniel: arrival, 64
Horry, Harriot Pinckney: goes to England, 202; returns from England, 212
Horse racing, 151, 157, 183, 186, 188, 194, 218, 247, 448, 449; description of, 279; first race season, 154
Hospital / Workhouse: constructed, 167
How, Millicent: indentured servant to West, 27
Howe, Robert, 318, 346; becomes highest ranking Continental officer, 332; complaints about by Gadsden, 342; demands satisfaction from Gadsden, 346; image, 333
Huger, Francis Kincloch: helps Lafayette escape, 458
Huger, Issac, 305; Biggin's Bridge, 363
Huguenot Church, 63; lot donated, 59; organized, 49
Huguenots, 26; arrival, 48; arrive on *Margaret*, 55; complaints about threats, 64; establish Charlesfort, 10; flee France, 55; more than 1500 arrive, 55; population, 75; skills, 48; win five of six seats, 63
Hunter, George: surveys path from Charleston to Columbia, 144
Hutchinson, Thomas, 212

Hutson, Richard, 234; comments on Fort Sullivan, 319; elected first Intendant, 403; friends with Ramsay, 286; image, 405; reelected Intendant, 409
Hyde, Edward: death, 44; Proprietor, 19
Hyrne, Edward: requests money for plantation purchase, 78

# I

Imports: 1729, 141; 1735, 153; 1773 slaves, 274
Indenture Service: terms, 71
Independent Church, 66; 2nd church opens, 430; new building, 148; reopened, 411; Whitefield preaches, 174
Indian Affairs, 89, 416; attack on Yamessee, 140; chiefs entertained, 147; Stuart arrested, 299; Treaty of Augusta, 227; treaty signed with Cherokee, 144; treaty with Cherokee, 336
Indian Trade, 54, 93; act repealed by Proprietors, 112
Indians, 171; description of, 31; population, 32; trade with, 36
Indigo: 1759 exports, 213; becomes 2nd most profitable crop, 194; experiments by Eliza, 173; first successful crop, 184; Pinckney's indigo deemed excellent, 186; seeds sent to Charlestown, 173
Intendant: mayor, 403
Intolerable Acts: description of, 288; passed in response to Boston Tea Party, 288
i'on, Richard, 184, 185
Isle of Palms: Clinton plans to land troops, 320; Cornwallis lands, 321; evacuated by British, 329
Issacs, Ralph: challenges Ladd to duel, 421; duel, 421; insults Ladd publicly, 421
Izard, Ralph, 270, 290, 337, 409, 410, 415, 418, 419, 425, 440, 446, 449, 465; concerns about Northern agitation, 451; conveys lot for French Church, 59; fear about French refugess, 464; response to "Delcaration of the Rights of Man, 455; supports Bank of the Unites States, 449
Izard, Sarah: marries William Campbell, 226

# J

Jackson, Andrew, 370
Jackson, Originall, 37; observations of Rev. Williamson, 47
Jacksonboro: Assembly convenes, 389
James I, King, 43
James II, 21, 41, 52; becomes King, 54; deposed, 60; goes into exile, 17
James Island: British marines land and are driven back, 312
Jamestown, Va.: established, 12
Jasper, William: killed at Savannah, 354; raises flag during battle, 324; raises flag over Ft. Sullivan; image, 326
Jay, John, 319, 396, 404, 405, 409, 417, 432, 437, 464; burned in effigy, 466; resigns from Supreme Court, 466; Treaty of Paris, 392
Jay's Treaty, 464; committee rejects, 466; creates poor realtions with France, 471; protests against, 464; signed by Washington, 467; violent protests against, 466
Jeffereys, William, 39
Jefferson, Thomas, 325, 328, 379, 407, 408, 409, 410, 427, 429, 436, 444, 461; sends rice, 425; warns Moultrie of slave insurrection, 452
Jemmy: leader of Stono Rebellion, 171
Jeremy, Thomas: arrested, 303; execution, 304; found guilty, 303
Jews: establish cemetery, 204; first congregation, 193; first meeting, 195; first mention of a Jew, 66; Meeting house established, 228; substantial immigration, 173
Jockey Club, 24
Johnson, Nathaniel: appointed governor, 81; arrival, 60; creates reservation for Yemassee, 89; description of trade, 90; leads opposition against Sothell, 63; orders construction of Windmill Point, 83; portrait painted by Henrietta Johnston, 92; refuses to support William & Mary, 60; refuses to surrender, 87; ruse against the French, 87; urges fortifications repair, 81
Johnson, Robert, 105; appointed 2nd Royal Governor, 144; appointed governor, 105; battles pirates, 115; commissions Rhett to end piracy, 113; complains about piracy, 112; death, 155; establishes government in exile, 125; establishes townships, 144; first address to Assembly, 109; hunts pirates, 114; pays ransom to Blackbeard, 112; places bounty on Bonnet, 114; supports Proprietors, 121; writes account of piracy, 114
Johnson, Samuel: dictionary arrives, 206
Johnson, William: electricity demonstration, 229, 242
Johnson, William Jr.: birth, 271

Johnston, Gideon: arrival, 90; death, 105; description of Charles Town, 91; financial struggles, 92; journey to Charles Town, 90; love of Madeira, 90; stranded on island, 90

Johnston, Gideon,: appointed Bishop's Commissary, 90

Johnston, Henrietta: arrival, 90; first female painter, 92; portrait painting, 92

Jones, Edmund: execution, 268

Jones, Jehu, Jr.: birth, 420

Jones, John Paul, 332; comments about Gillon, 349

Jones, Samuel: slave baptised, 156

Jordan, Joseph: execution, 268

Jovial Club, 269

## K

Kahal Kadosh Beth Elohim: early member list, 195; established on Hasell Street, 356; first Jewish meeting, 195; founded, 193

Keith, Issac: minister of 2nd Independent Church, 429

Kennett, Margaret: description of Charlestown, 137; opens shop, 136

*Keppel,* slave ship, 213

Kettleby, Abel: named first Agent in London, 96

Kiawah Island, 23

Kiawah tribe, 31, 32; population, 32

King George's War. *See* War of Jenkin's Ear

King William's War, 60

Kingdom, Richard: shipped first barrel of rice, 39

Knight, William Powers: acrobatic stunts, 438

Kussoes Tribe, 38

Kyrle, Richard: governor, 53

## L

Ladd, Joseph Brown, 415; arrives in Charleston, 409; chemistry lecture, 416; death, 421; duel, 421; responds to insults, 421

Lafayette, Marquis de, 338, 428; arrives in Carolina, 337; escapes prison, 458; image, 338; remarks on John Laurens, 394; time in Charlestown, 337

Lamboll, Thomas: description of hurricane, 97

Landgraves: definition of, 26

Latham, Daniel: rides to Philadelphia, 327

Laughing Club. *See* Loyal Society

Laurens, Eleanor: death, 261

Laurens, Henry, 418, 420; 1766 net worth, 236; accepts position in London, 184; advertises in *Gazette*, 199; attacks Gadsden, 250; birth, 135; bitterness about Tower treatment, 389; captured by British, 376; care of Negroes, 230; changing attitude toward slavery, 414; comments about John's death, 395; comments on Declaration, 330; comments on Declaratory Act, 239; complains about surrender, 368; complains to British about harboring Negroes, 310; confronts Moore, 244; death of wife, Eleanor, 261; description of new Assembly, 315; description of slave cargo, 207; description of slave suicide, 257; effects of British blockade, 305; elected Minister to Holland, 354; elected to Congress, 334; elected vice-president of South Carolina, 314; extension of Meeting Street, 242; fears about tea protests, 289; financing of slaves, 249; French and Indian War, 217; hopes for slavery, 412; house searched, 233; income; 1769 income, 259; leaves Paris, 404; letter to Martha, 270; marries Eleanor Ball, 198; moves to Mepkin, 415; number of Negroes sold yearly, 206; opens business, 190; opinion on No.45, 271; placed in Tower, 376; prays for honorable retreat, 364; presented bill for time in Tower, 388; profile, 139; purchased Mepkin Plantation, 222; purchases *Wambaw* back, 244; rationalization of slave trading, 257; rejects British offer of conciliation, 345; released from Tower, 391; remarks to son about armed Negroes, 348; replaces Hancock, 339; resigns as President of Congress, 347; retains John Rutledge as lawyer, 220; returns from London, 293; returns to Charleston, 412; sails to London, 270; sails to Netherlands, 356; signs preliminary articles in Paris, 396; spends summer in Tower, 383; Stamp Act comments, 236; tensions between lowcountry and backcountry, 296; treaty of Paris, 392; unhappy with Oxford and Cambridge, 281; warns of deserting slaves, 337

Laurens, James: death, 406

Laurens, John, 135, 361, 366, 368, 379, 388, 429; challenges Lee to duel, 347; comments on slavery, 334; discusses surrender terms, 388; image, 349; joins Washington's staff, 338; killed, 394; presents plan of Negro troops, 348; proposes to lead black troops,

341; refuses to carry capitulation message to Prevost, 352; returns from France, 387; returns to Charlestown, 389; sails to London, 270; skirmish against British in the Neck, 361; submits plans again to arm Negroes, 391; thoughts on the Revolution, 297; wounded, 352; Yorktown, 388
Laurens, Mary Eleanor: left in care of uncle James, 270; marries Charles Pinckney, 431
Lawson, John, 79; discovers wreckage, 79; leaves Charles Town, 78
Le Jau, Francis: arrival, 85; commits on witch trial, 86; dismayed by church attendance, 88
Lee, Charles, 315; address to Sullivan troops, 322; arrival, 317; challenged by John Laurens, 347; commander of the South, 313; criticism of Fort Sullivan, 319; description of, 317; image, 318; observes battle from Haddrell's Point, 323; plans to attack Florida, 329; recalled to Philadelphia by Congress, 332; recommends evacuating Ft. Sullivan, 322; sends rum to Ft. Sullivan, 326; visits Ft. Sullivan during battle, 324
Lee, Jesse: first Methodist service, 413
Lee, Light Horse Harry, 384; Battle of Ft. Motte, 382; joins Marion, 379
Legal: circuit courts, 343; courts open in backcountry, 273; first case, 37
Legare, Solomon: filled cisterns remark, 77; purchases island, 141
Legislative Council: created, 314; replaces Privy Council, 314
Leigh, Egerton: marriage, 243; orders *Wambaw* seized, 243; scandal, 252
Lempriere, Clement, 302; seizes British gunpowder, 303
Lennox, William: sued by Mary Cooke over non-marriage, 217
Letter Concerning Toleration, A, 25
Lewis Hallam Company of Players: arrival, 205; performs *The Orphan*, 205
Liberty Bell, 228
Liberty Boys. See Sons of Liberty
Liberty Tree, 254; Association discussed, 264; Association formed, 255; Association meets, 261; burned by British, 369; celebrates John Wilkes, 249; Declaration read, 330; first meeting, 238; image, 239; radicals meet, 249; tea protests, 282; tea tax protest, 269
Library: first established, 74
Lighthouse: Morris Island, 240
Lightning rod: installed, 207; installed on *Randolph*, 339

Lincoln, Benjamin: arrival, 347; asks for Negro laborers, 356; calls for fortifications along Boundary Street, 353; declines offer to surrender, 363; image, 347; leaves, 371; prefers to let British have Charlestown, 361; proposes surrender, 364
Lindo, Moses, 222
Lining, John, 190; arrival, 143; conducts first weather observations, 164; publishes yellow fever paper, 191; summer heat, 188
Linnaeus, Carolus, 203
Livingston, Rev. William: description of hurricane, 97
Lloyd, Caleb, 233; promises not to perform duties, 234
Locke, John: *Fundamental Constitutions* written, 25; image, 24; meets Cooper, 24; observations about Carolina, 34; secretary to the Council for Trade, 24; travels through France, 46
*London*: arrives with tea, 283
*London Magazine*: *1762* description of Charleston, 222
*London Merchant*: opens at Dock Street, 159
Long Island. See Isle of Palms, See Isle of Palms
Loocock, Aaron, 415
Loocock, William, 226
Lord Rawdon, 381, 383; orders forces to reinforce Charlestown, 389; sets execution date, 385
Lost Colony, 11
Low, Edward, pirate: captures ships, 133
Lowndes, Charles: arrival, 143; commits suicide, 159
Lowndes, Rawlins, 432; birth, 128; concerns about moving capital, 435; elected President, 342; image, 345; letter to Laurens, 344; resigns as President, 350; signs loyalty oath, 372; speaker of Assembly, 274
Lowther, George, pirate: off Charlestown, 131
Loyal Society, 190
Loyalty oath, 299
Lucas, George, 131; arrival, 164; death, 190; leaves Eliza in charge, 167; named Lt. governor of Antigua, 184
Lucas, Jonathon: arrival, 397; invents water-powered rice mill, 422
Ludwell, Philip, 63; commissioned governor, 63; Jacobite ban, 64; problems facing, 63; removed, 65
Lutherans: petition to build a church, 203; St. Johns organized, 210
Lynch, John: purchases slaves, 47

Lynch, Thomas: 1st Continental Congress, 290; 2nd Continental Congress, 299; argument over slavery in Articles, 331; attends Stamps Act Congress, 232; birth, 194; commitment to Association, 264; departs for 1st Congress, 291; description of, 278; governor of Jamaica, 53; informs Geroge Washington about Fort Sullivan, 312

Lyttelton, William Henry, 210; arrival, 209; marches with troops, 214; replaced by Boone, 220

# M

M'Arion, Benjamin: arrival, 61; death, 153
Mace of the House: purchased, 207
Madagascar Rice: first time, 101
Madeira, 90
Madison, James, 425; comments on Picnkey's Draught, 426
Magnolia Plantation: established, 46
Mahone, Dennis: punished as a runaway servant, 38
Mangourit, Michel-Ange-Bernard: arrival, 451; parade, 452
Manigault, Gabriel: 1769 income, 259; birth, 83, 211; financing of slaves, 249; houses Library Society collection, 193; on trade with French, 335
Manigault, Peter, 249; description of Charles Pinckney, 204; elected as Speaker, 250; refuses to cede power to governor, 271; returns to Charleston, 205; visits Pinckneys in London, 203
Marine Anti-Britannic Society: founded, 406; takes side against Rutledge, 408
Marion, Francis, 61, 338, 359; at Bacon's Bridge, 358; at Sampit Bridge, 381; Battle of Ft. Motte, 383; Battle of Sullivan's Island, 322; birth, 146; breaks ankle, 360; captain in Second Provincial Regiment, 300; chosen for 1st Provincial Congress, 296; commissioned lieutenant, 219; death, 465; death of father, 153; defends Dorchester, 307; distaste for vengance, 219; fires last shot of battle, 325; first military service, 207; first quick strike, 376; French and Indian War, 214; image, 380, 395; joins with Lee, 379; last military action, 394; purchases Pond Bluff, 274; receives Hampton Hill, 213; retrieves gunpowder during battle, 324
Market Street, 442

Marshall, Samuel, 71; appointed Register of Births, 70; arrives,Anglican minister, 68; death, 74; salary set, 70
Martin, Laughlin: tarred and feathered, 299
Maryland: chartered, 14
Massachusetts Bay Colony: Plymouth Colony established, 12
Massey, Joseph: first paper currency printed, 159
Mather, Cotton, 70
Mathews, Benjamin and Ann: violaters of the Association, 262
Mathews, John: elected governor, 390
Matthews, Maurice: dismissed as Surveyor General, 54
Mazyck's pasture, 238; celebrate repeal of Stamp Act, 251
McCray, William: description of SC delegation, 440
McQueen, Alexander: dinner party, 359
Mechanics, 255, 464; asks for city incorporation be abolished, 424; complain about greedy lawyers, 402; definition, 248; learn about Battle of Lexington, 299; nominate radical candidates, 249; petition against Negro tradesmen, 468; protest against Tory merchants, 401; response to Bull's sermon, 291
Medical Society, 470
Medicine: cure of all sorts, 148; dissection room opened, 235; first apothecary, 382; first autopsy, 63; first health commissioner, 95; first surgeon, 45; midwife advertised, 251; surgery performed, 146
Medlin, Richard, 46
Mellichamp, William: given rights to manufacture salt, 137
Mepkin Plantation, 415, 431; purchased by Henry Laurens, 222
Mercier,Peter: death, 204
Methodists: attacked by mob, 429; building attacked, 414; call for slave emancipation, 465; Cumberland Street Meeting house, 423; first service, 413
Michaux, Andre: arrives in Charleston, 421; birth, 189
Middle Wharf: largest wharf, 167
Middleton Place: founded, 178
Middleton Plantation, 422
Middleton, Arthur: arrival, 45; calls out militia, 138; complains about runaway slaves, 140; death, 160; denounces anti-tax protests,

138; elected speaker of new Assembly, 120; governor, 137; receives grant, 53
Middleton, Arthur (Declaration signer), 390; 2nd Continental Congress, 299; arrives in Philadelphia: attends school in London, 203; birth, 182; death, 422; designs state seal, 316; image, 424; Secret Committee of Five, 298
Middleton, Edward: arrival, 45
Middleton, Henrietta: marries Edward Rutledge, 287
Middleton, Henry, 287, 450; 1st Continental Congress, 290; elected president of 1st Continental Congress, 293; signs loyalty oath, 372
Middleton, Mary: marries Pierce Butler, 268
Middleton, Thomas: French and Indian War, 216
Miles Brewton House: Campbell moves in, 301; image, 279
Millegen-Johnston, George, 224
Monck, George, 17; Proprietor, 19
Monroe, James, 451
Montagu, Charles Grenville, 381; arrival, 239; battles with Assembly, 274; demands Aeembly give up rights, 271; establishes Colonial Lake, 247; fines levied against dead Negroes in river, 252; lives at Fort Johnson, 270; moves Assembly to Beaufort, 272; orders Regulartors to disband, 245; outsmarted by Assembly, 272; pardons Regulators, 270; resigns, 279; returns for third term as governor, 270; returns to raise a regiment, 379; tries to recruit Moultrie, 380; warned Assembly to ignore Townsend letter, 250
Montgomerie, Archibald: arrival, 215; burns Cherokee villages, 216
Moody, Christopher, 114; off Carolina coast, 115
Moore, Daniel: appointed customs collector, 242; attacked by Laurens, 244; charged with extortion, 244; description of, 244; most hated man, 244; scandal, 242
Moore, James: attacks Florida, 81; comments on yellow fever, 75; destroys Spanish ships, 83; encourages attack on Florida, 80; orders seawall, 81
Morgan, Henry: knighted, 53
Morris Island lighthouse, 240, 312, 314; attacked by Patriots, 329
Morton, Joseph: accused of piracy, 72; appointed Advocate General, 72; appointed governor, 51; house raided, 58; reappointed governor, 55; replaced, 53
Morton, Robert, 58
Motte, Issac: Battle of Sullivan's Island, 322
Motte, Jacob: death, 262; marries Rebecca Brewton, 212; ordered to pay Wilkes' debts, 258
Motte, Mary Brewton: marries William Alston, 443
Motte, Rebecca Brewton, 382; birth, 162; burns house down, 382; leaves Charlestown, 381
Moultrie, John, 190; arrival, 139; describes troops, 218; French and Indian War, 216; president of Faculty of Physic, 206; pronounces Martha Laurens alive, 215
Moultrie, William, 415, 418, 443, 452, 464; acquires plantation thru confiscation, 400; appointed to survey, 271; arrives at Fort Sullivan, 313; attends court-martial, 219; Battle of Beaufort, 349; becomes comander of Florida force, 332; birth, 144; colonel of Second Provincial Regiment, 300; commissioned a captain, 217; confidence in Fort Sullivan, 320; congratulates Washington on election, 435; criticism of, 306; criticism of Howe, 348; describes militia organization, 296; describes powder explosion, 369; description of British evacuation, 396; description of British fleet, 317; description of partisanship, 397; developed new signals for lighthouse, 312; elected governor, 412; escorts Washington to Charleston, 445; first wife's death, 308; French and Indian War, 214, 216; given command of Fort Sullivan, 313; gives Lafayette a tour, 337; image, 328; in charge of city's defense, 315; in charge of fortifications in the Neck, 360; inspects defenses on Sullivan's Island, 322; loans government money, 354; lt. governor, 407; marries Damaris Elizabeth de St. Julien, 195; marries Hannah Lynch, 354; opposes to Rutledge's offer, 352; orders foreign blacks out of state, 456; paroled to Snee Farm, 369; president of Cincinnati Society, 404; promoted to Brigadier General, 332; refuses Grenville's offer, 381; reports on enlistments, 302; retires to plantation, 464; secures gun powder in Exchange, 367; sick with typhoid, 358; takes troops to Florida, 330; tells Prevost he will defend the city, 352
Mount Zion Society, 335, 412
Mr. Pike's Long Room: next door to New Theater, 285
Muhlenberg, Henry Melchior: arrival, 180

description of whites and blacks, 149
Mulberry Plantation, 90
Muschamp, George: arrives as Customs Collector, 54; Collector of the King's Revenue, 55; seizes vessel, 59
Mutual Insurance Company Against Fire: incorporated, 472

## N

Narborough, John: commands fleet to suppress piracy, 60
Naval stores: becomes major export, 50
Navigation Acts: 1696 Act, 68; arguments against, 55; enforcement of, 55; signed by Cromwell, 17; strengthened, 68
Naylor, William Rigby, 241
Negro Act, 130;1740 Act, 194; passed in response to Stono Rebellion, 175
Nevis: Henry Woodward stranded in Nevis, 25; *Port Royal* arrives, 28
New Amsterdam: founded, 13; renamed New York, 21
New Church Act, 88; creates ten parishes, 88
New Theater: location, 281, 285; opens, 285
New Vauxhall, 243; opened, 243
New York: named, 21
Newton, John: arrival, 194; hires Laurens to sale slaves, 194; profile, 197
Nicholson, Francis: arrival, 130; asks to be released as governor, 135; cracks down on opposition, 131; departs, 137; description of, 128; description of Rhett, 130; first Royal Governor, 127
Non-importation Agreement. See Association
North Briton #45. See John Wilkes Affair

## O

O'Sullivan, Florence, 38; claims two lots, 46; description of Carolina, 34; request for clergy, 33
Oaks Plantation., 45
Ocracoke Island, 112, 113
Officer's Punch, 170
Oglethorpe, James: arrival, 149; explores Savannah River, 149; invasion of Florida approved, 176; lands at Savannah, 149; seeks assistance to invade Florida, 174
Orange Gardens: opened, 218
Orangeburg: settlement of, 155
Otranto. See Oaks Plantation, The

Owen Roberts: constructs temporary fort, 311
Owen, William: contests first election, 32
Oyster Point, 40, 244; houses erected on, 47; hurricane, 97; John Coming surrenders land, 39; land set aside for settlement, 35; named, 32; officially named Charles Town, 47; sea wall constructed, 248; sea wall finished, 208; survey, 38; survey ordered, 40; trenches built, 89

## P

Pachelbel, Charles Theodore, 194; arrival, 159; becomes organist at St. Philip's, 175; marriage, 161; organizes St. Celcilia's Day concert, 164
Paine, Thomas, 312
Palmer, John: attacks Yamassee, 140
Palmetto Day. See Carolina Day
Palmetto Society: organized, 338
Panting, Thomas: appointed headmaster, 252
Parker, Peter: blames Clinton for defeat, 329; britches blown off, 325; commander of British navy, 316-17; confident of taking Ft. Sullivan, 321
Partridge, Nathaniel: Provost Marshall, 113
Partridge, William: complaints about club membership, 269
Passenger List of Carolina, 29
Penn, William, 49, 80
Percivall, Andrew, 51; governor of Proprietor's plantation, 43
Peronneau, Henry: appointed joint Treasurer, 262; granted citizenship, 68
Pest House, 231
Peter Minuit, 13
Petigru, James Louis, 221; birth, 437
Peyne, James, 191, 192
Philadelphia: falls to British, 339; founded, 52
Philadelphia Alley: duel, 421
Phillips, Eleazar: arrival, 143; death, 147; first printer to his Majesty, 143
Pickens, Andrew, 394
Pike's Dancing School, 270
Pinckney, Charles: appointed Agent for South Carolina, 202; appointed Chief Justice, 200; death, 212; death of first wife, 185; description of, 204; engagement to Eliza Lucas, 185; gives Eliza access to library, 174; marries Eliza Lucas, 185; returns from England, 212
Pinckney, Charles (1732-82), 178, 211, 393; admitted to bar, 200; calls on Campbell, 301;

comments on execution for treason, 351; death, 395; given votes, 250; house destroyed by fire, 341; marries Francis Brewton, 202; President of 1st Provincial Congress, 296; purchases Snee Farm, 204; signs loyalty oath, 372

Pinckney, Charles (1757-1824), 332, 407, 426, 466; addresses slavery issue, 427; arrested and imprisoned, 383; becomes friends with James Monroe, 417; birth, 211; challenges Hamilton, 427; give speech at ratification convention, 431; learns of father's death), 395; marries Polly Laurens, 431; returns to Charlestown, 399

Pinckney, Charles Cotesworth, 360, 368, 393, 395, 416, 447; appointed to Colonel, 332; arrives in Philadelphia, 385; birth, 189; complains of shortages, 357; complaints about moving captial, 419; concerns about Haitian Revolution, 451; description of Charlestown fortifications, 320; dines with Quincy, 278; donates land for market, 431; educated in England, 202; erected battery at Haddrell's, 310; greets Washington, 445; image, 471; leaves France, 475; named Minister to France, 471; paroled to Snee Farm, 369; refused by French government, 471; returns to Charlestown, 391; Secret Committee of Five, 298; upset that Congress attacked slavery, 441; urges Middleton to return to SC, 393

Pinckney, Eliza Lucas: 1740 description of Charleston, 176; arrival, 164; birth, 131; describes her family responsibilities, 185; description of Charleston people, 179; description of soil and crops, 181; dismisses suggestions for a husband, 173; engagement, 185; experiments with indigo, 173; goes to England, 202; grief stricken, 212; in society, 174; marries Charles Pinckney, 185; news about indigo quality, 186; prepares to leave Charleston, 184; receives indigo seeds, 173; returns from England, 212; sends indigo to England, 190; serves breakfast to George Washington, 445; small pox observations, 215; successful indgo crop, 184; takes control of plantations, 167

Pinckney, Grace Bedon: death, 69

Pinckney, Thomas, 407; arrives in Philadelphia, 385; birth, 198; complains about slaves taken, 352; educated in England, 202; image, 425; Minister to Great Britain, 451; negotiates treaty, 465; presides over ratification convention, 432; report from Ft. Johnson, 318; returns from England, 286; returns to Charlestown, 391

Pinckney, Thomas (1666-1705): arrival, 64; death, 85; first wife dies, 69; marriage to Mary Cotesworth, 70; marries to Grace Bedon, 64

Pinckney, William: gives up son to brother, 178; impoverished by fire, 178

Pinckney's Draught, 426

Pinckney's Treaty, 465, 468

Pink House: image, 67

Piracy, 52, 53, 56, 60, 63, 64, 73, 74, 96, 108, 113, 114, 115, 131, 133, 444; battle between Rhett and Bonnet, 113; blockade of Charles Town, 112; Bonnet escapes, 114; Bonnet executed, 117; captures Seth Sothell, 47; complains to Proprietors, 112; complaints about, 53; execution, 74, 108, 115, 432; first serious attempt to restrain, 60; first trial, 105; in Charles Town, 107; infamous party, 113; Sothel released, 60; the King's Pardon, 110; William III offers pardon, 80

Pitt, William, 210; death, 344; supports colonies against Stamp Act, 237

Placide, Alexander: attacks Sollee, 475; manager of French theater, 461; re-opens Vauxhall, 476

Plantation and Stores of the Proprietors, 40

*Planter's Adventure*: carries British stamps, 232

Plymouth Rock: image, 13

Poe, David, Jr: performs in Charleston, 473

Poetry: humorous, 151

Poher, Henry: opened New Vauxhall, 243

Poinsett, Elisha, 208; opens tavern, 198

Poinsett, Joel Roberts: birth, 350

Poinsett's Tavern, 163, 242

Politics, 49; attacked over anti-slavery views, 433; clamor for West to be reinstated, 42; Dissenters complain about election, 80; Dissenters take control of Assembly, 88; English law enforced in Carolina, 94; first election in Charles Town, 37; Grand Council established, 37; new bicameral system, 63; petition to move state capital, 412; piracy scandal, 53; plan to expel non-Anglicans, 83; power sturggle between Colleton and Sothell, 61; tax rate doubled on exported skins, 78; tension between Barbadians and English, 42; tougher slave law, 68; voting act passed, 64

*Polly*: carries seized gunpowder to Continental Congress, 302; sized by British, 305

Pon Pon Plantation, 188

Pond Bluff, 274

Popple, William, 73
Population: 1672, 39; 1677, 45; 1680, 47; 1682, 50; 1686, 56; 1690, 61; 1699, 72; 1700, 75; 1720, 125; 1722, 131; 1724, 134; 1730, 143; 1733 slave, 149; 1739 slaves, 167; 1740, 174; 1760, 215; 1763, 224; 1769, 258; 1770, 260; 1773, 286; 1780, 90; 1790 census, 438; black majority for first time, 90; during Proprietary years, 123; majority, white servants, 35; origin of early colonists, 39; slave, 1720, 125; Yamassee, 90
*Port Royal*: blown off course to Nevis, 28; expedition arrives, 31; site abandoned by English, 32
Port Royal (town), 25
Port San Marco: abandoned, 11
Powder Magazine, 423; approved, 95; constructed, 96; lightning rod installed, 207
Powell, Henry: settles Barbados, 13
Powell, Thomas: publishes Council proceedings, 282
Presbyterians, 54; arrival, 48; founded Stuart's Town, 53; population, 75
Prevost, Augustine: lands on peninsula, 352; rejects Rutledge's offer, 352
Price, Hopkin: Sons of Liberty, 250
Prileau, Elias: first French minister, 59
*Princess Carolina*: built in Charles Town, 101
Pringle, Robert, 406; arrival, 137
Prioleau, Phillip: description of waterfront fortifications, 208
Privateers, 25, 53, 55, 64, 83, 86, 173, 184, 185, 210, 224, 302, 335, 339, 344, 458, 460; Assembly commissions more, 335; Bouteille sails into Charleston, 454; Charleston-based ship sails into Philadelphia, 454; during Queen Anne's War, 80; incite riot at theater, 459; injunction against, 454; international incident created, 453; James II enforcement against, 54; Joseph Vesey, 311; Pres. Washington outlaws, 456; South Carolina Navy, 329; success, 175
Proprietors: 1705 list of, 85; 2nd Charter drafted, 21; 2nd version of *Fundamental Constitutions*, 31; advertise Carolina, 20; amount of investment, 46; approve Grand Modell, 26; campaign to recruit settlers, 35; charter purchased by George II, 141; colony as a business venture, 35; close Land Grant office, 120; convinced by Cooper to finance colony, 25; disappointed in governors, 58; dismiss Carolina grievances, 120; dismiss Matthews as surveyor, 54; encourage Barbadian settlement of Carolina, 21; established, 18; establish Proprietor's plantation, 43; forbid Indian enslavement, 38; *Fundamental Constitutions* adopted, 25; hear grievances, 120; Indian traders licensed, 45; instructions to Joseph West, 27; instructions to the New Reciever General, 93; issue fourth version of *Fundamental Constitutions*, 52; list of, 18; Locke becomes secretary, 24; meet with Trott, 100; move to attract Dissenters, 51; orders Assembly to disolve, 112; overthrown, 121; Oyster Point appointed as port, 48; pressured to surrender charter, 103; proclaim Yeamans as governor, 39; promise 150 acres, 26; renew commitment to Carolina, 43; refuse to send livestock, 43; repeal several acts by the Assembly, 112; warn against Goose Creek men, 64; Yeamans issued a commission, 26
Prospect of Charlestown, A, 170
Provincial Assembly: appoints Council of Safety, 296
Provincial Congress, First: adopts a bill of rights, 299; approves infantry regiments, 300; calls for new election, 293; convenes, 296; declares independence from British authority, 296; issues paper currency, 299; not recognized by Bull, 296; passes loyalty oath, 299; tensions between lowcountry and backcountry, 296
Provincial Congress, Second: adjourns to become General Assembly, 315; called into emergency session, 307; discusses type of government to establish, 314; drafts state constitution, 314; establishes General Assembly and Council, 314; gives delegates permission, 314
Provincial Regiments: recruitment, 302
Pulaski, Casimar: killed, 354
Purry, Jean Pierre: 1731 description of South Carolina, 145; arrival, 148

## Q

Quarantine Act: list of physicians, 190; revived, 190
Quarry, Robert: appointed governor, 53; dismissed for piracy, 56; involved in piracy trade, 53; named Naval Officer, 55; replaced by West, 53
Quartering Act: Assembly refuses to obey, 249; new barracks constructed, 211; part of the

Intolerable Acts, 289; passed, 229; report presented to Assembly, 212
Queen Anne's War: attack on Florida, 81; begins, 80; French & Spanish repulsed, 87; French attack Charles Town, 87; French attack Charles Town, 86; French demand Charles Town surrender, 87; Rhett attacks, 87; Spanish land in Mt. Pleasant, 87; St. Augustine attack debt, 82
Quincy, Josiah, 267, 278, 280; 1773 description of Charlestown, 276; attends Assembly, 280; attends St. Cecilia, 276; describes white Charleston, 276; description of, 276; description of Charlestown from harbor, 276; description of meal, 277, 278; dines at Miles Brewton house, 277; last day in lowcountry, 280; leaves, 280; purchases Madeira, 280; race week, 279; religious impression, 277
Quitrent Act: passed, 145

## R

Race Week, 469; first, 449; theater open during, 452
Rackham, Calico Jack: becomes pirate captain, 117; captured, 128; execution, 128; granted pardon, 120; with Vane, 113
Ramadge's Tavern: Council of Safety proposed, 295
Ramos, Jacob: sentenced to pillory, 282
Ramsay, David, 401, 404, 408; 2nd wife's death, 411; arrival, 286; attacked over anti-slavery views, 433; attitude on dueling, 291; comments on Laurens and Gadsden, 135; comments on morality of slave trade, 416; complains about powerful families, 461; Declaration description, 330; description of 1728 hurricane, 140; description of Aedanus Burke, 309; description of Balfour, 371; description of convention, 290; description of Hayne execution, 385; description of hurricane, 201; description of John Rutledge's success, 220; economy destitute, 400; first marriage, 297; first wife dies, 327; in defense of American government, 345; marries Francis Witherspoon, 399; marries Martha Laurens, 423; medical degree, 281; meets Martha Laurens, 420; publishes *History of the Revolution of South Carolina*, 417; *Sermon on Tea*, 291; supports Webster's dictionary, 416

Ramsay, Martha Laurens, 270; birth, 214; left in care of uncle James, 270; marries David Ramsay, 423; reaction of uncle's death, 406; reacts to brother's death, 394; returns to Charleston, 412; Treaty of Paris, 392
Ramsay, Sabina Ellis: death, 327
*Randolph*: struck by lightning, 337, 339
Randolph, Edward: accuses Blake of piracy, 72; arrival, 72; description of Stuart's Town destruction, 58; rice production, 76
Rawdon, Lord, 385; in command of SC, 381
Read, Mary: captured, 128; death, 128
*Recruiting Officer, The*, 156; closes the second season, 162; performed at Dock Street, 157; performed at New Theater, 288
Regulators, 245; force Assembly to pass Court Act, 254; formation of, 241; ordered to disband, 245; pardoned by Gov. Grenville, 270
Religion: Anabaptists; arrival, 69; appeal for clergy, 33; arrivals, 54; city divided into St. Philip's and St. Micheal's, 199; Establishment Act passed, 84; Establishment Act repealed, 88; first convention of clergy, 144; first Dissenters arrive, 48; first Lutheran communion, 151; first mention of a Jew, 66; first Methodist service, 413; First Scots founded, 145; Huguenot Church organized, 49; Huguenots arrival, 48; Jews register for citizenship, 70; New Church Act passed, 88; Proprietors allow French to worship "with the tide", 64; request for clergy, 34; Society for the Propagation of the Gospel; charter issued, 80; struggle to establish Anglican Church, 92; Williamson dismissed, 53
Republic of South Carolina: created, 314
Revenue Act of 1764: enforced by Moore, 242
Rhett, William, 108; arrives, 65; attacks French & Spanish in harbor, 87; birth, 24; builds house, 94; commissioned to end piracy, 113; death, 132; description of, 130, 132; engages Bonnet, 113; executes Bonnet, 117; image, 116; likeness placed on ship, 202; pirate expedition leaves Charles Towh, 113; portrait painted by Henrietta Johnston, 92; recaptures Bonnet, 115; returns with Bonnet, 113; secret correspondence with Proprietors, 112
Rhettsbury, 187
Rhode Island: founded, 15
Ribault, Jean, 10
Rice: 1730s exported, 196; enumeratered, 85, 86; export chart, 264; exports exceed 2000 barrels, 72; first barrel of rice shipped, 39;

more rice than ships, 75; patent on rice-husker, 62, 68; praised, 73; production doubles, 167; smuggling, 91; used as currency, 68; used to pay for military services, 104; used to pay taxes, 62; water-powered mill, 422

*Richmond*: arrival, 48

Right Worthy and Amicable Order of UBIQUARIANS: organized, 179

Riots: against Tories, 401; during performance at theater, 460; Thompson Tavern Scandal, 408; windows smashed, 346

*Rising Sun*: destroyed by storm, 76; wreckage discovered, 79

Rombert, Peter, 134; arrested, 134; arrival, 131; befriends Dutartre family, 132; claims ressurection, 136; declares God trumps Man, 132; execution, 136; marriage, 132; sleeps with members of Dutartre family, 134; vision from God, 133

Rose, William, 200

Roupell, George: collusion with Moore, 242

Royal Colony: established, 141

*Royal Jamaica*, 64; arrival, 64

Royal Privy Council: recommends Carolina become Royal colony, 126

Ruck, Andrew: petitions for relief from slave labor competition, 185

Rush, Benjamin, 291, 332, 400, 404, 408

Russell, Nathaniel, 415; raises money for Irish immigrants, 243

Rutledge, Andrew: announces cancellation due to small pox, 225; arrival, 143; counsel for George Whitefield, 176; death, 207; marries Sarah Hext, 153

Rutledge, Dr. John: arrival, 153; death, 198; marries Sarah Hext, 166

Rutledge, Edward, 306, 331, 418, 427, 429, 439; 1st Continental Congress, 290; 2nd Continental Congress, 299; argues against Cornwallis exchange, 391; argument over slavery in Articles, 331; arrives in Philadelphia, 385; Battle of Beaufort, 349; birth, 195; called to English bar, 272; captured, 367; comments on constitution ratification, 432; committee to draft Washington's commission, 300; complaints about, 437; complaints about moving capital, 419; description by John Adams, 292; elected governor, 476; falls ill, 477; greets Washington, 445; image, 288; marries Henrietta Middleton, 287; mother dies, 450; opposes moving capital, 417; opposition to Declaration of Indepedence, 319; proposes city incorporation, 402; proposes War Office, 312; reluctance to sign Declaration, 327; remarks about moving capital, 435; rents James Laurens' house, 334; returns from England, 274; supports trade embargo, 289; thoughts on English church, 335; votes for slave ban, 416; wife dies, 450

Rutledge, Elizabeth Grimke: entertains George Washington, 446; dies, 450

Rutledge, Henrietta Middleton: dies, 450

Rutledge, Hugh, 228

Rutledge, John, 390; 1st Continental Congress, 290; anxious to call Assembly, 386; assumes role of father, 228; attempts suicide, 468; attends Stamp Act Congress, 232; birth, 172; Burke attacks, 398; chronic gout, 466; confronts debt, 475; description by John Adams, 292; description by Patrick Henry, 292; elected as governor, 350; elected President of South Carolina, 314; elected to Assembly, 344; first legal case, 217; has Thompson arrested, 408; house damange by shells, 362; image, 467; learns of city's surrender, 370; marriage to Elizabeth Grimke, 226; mother dies, 450; moves to avoid capture, 376; nicknamed, 357; offered Chief Justice of Supreme Court, 466; offers to keep South Carolina out of war, 352; opposes Stamp Act, 232; orders Moultrie to defend Ft. Sullivan, 322; power of his family, 334; promises amnesty to Loyalists, 388; refuses to surrender city, 361; rejected by Senate, 468; rejects Clinton's plea, 319; rejects Clinton's second plea to surrender, 321; report on election, 223; resigns due to new Constitution, 342; resigns from S.C. Supreme Court, 467; resigns from U.S. Supreme Court, 469; returns to Charlestown, 215; serves as Chief Justice of U.S. Supreme Court, 467; sits on Federal circuit, 468; speed against Jay's Treaty, 466; stays at Indian Queen Tavern, 425; studies law in England, 211; takes seat in Assembly, 406; urged to leave city, 363; visits Ft. Sullivan, 328; warns of British attack, 313; wealth of, 295; wife dies, 450; wins first legal case, 220

Ryan, Dennis: American Company of Comedians, 413

Ryan, Matthew: arrival, 430

## S

*Sally George*: slave ship, 261
Salt manufacturing, 137
Salvador, Francis: arrival, 274; elected to office, first Jew, 293; first Jew killed in Revolution, 329; killed by Cherokee, 329
Sandford, Robert: explores Carolina coast, 23; explores Charleston harbor, 23; lands on Kiawah, 23; recommends settlement in Carolina, 23
Sandy Hill: George Washington stays, 447
Sandy Hill Plantation, 356
Sanford, Robert, 23; comments about marriage, 431
Santee Canal Company, 418, 465; chartered, 419
Savage, John: first president of Chamber, 284; sells Snee Farm, 204
Savage, Thomas: Sons of Liberty, 250
Savage's Green, 450
Savannah: captured by British, 348
Saxby, George, 233; hanged in effigy, 233; house searched, 233; promises not to perform duties, 234
Sayle, Nathaniel: death, 93
Sayle, William: appeals for clergy, 33; becomes governor of Bermuda, 15; death, 35; dependency on West, 35; land set aside for settlement, 35; learns of the Westoes, 31; letter from the Proprietors, 93; named governor by Yeamans, 31; organizes council, 32
Scandal: 1768 election, 250; bribing Council member, 93; Gadsden election, 222, 223, 224, 225; Gov. Quarry accused of piracy, 53; Mary Simmons publicly shamed, 161; Mary Simmons runs away with Henry Holt, 162; *Merchant of Venice* actresses, 423; Rev. Wintley dismissed, 141
Schermmerhorn, John, 140
Screven, Elisha, 141
Scriven, William: arrival, 69
Scrivener, William: request for clergy, 34
Seal of the City of Charleston: designed, 403; image, 403
Searle, Robert: attacks St. Augustine, 25
Second South Carolina Regiment: arrives at Fort Sullivan, 313; prepares for battle in Ft. Sullivan, 322
Secret Committee of Five: formed, 298; members, 298; orders tar and feathering, 299; seizes British mail, 298; seizes gunpowder, 298
Security Act: requires white men to carry firearms to church, 170
Segoon-Pop Club, 194
Sermon on Tea, A, 291
Servant: definition of, 27, 50
Seven Years War. *See* French and Indian War
Sewee tribe, 79
Shagnuffey, John: guilty of street magic, 269
Shem Creek: Queen Anne's War, French troops cross, 87
Shepheard, Charles: tavern opened, 151
Shepheard's Tavern, 170; first masonic lodge, 160; first public presentation of an opera, 154; hosts first show performance, 153; houses Assembly, 152
Shinner, Charles: adjourns court due to Stamp Act, 235
Shipbuilding, 101, 110, 178, 181, 223, 239, 258; *Heart of Oak* launched, 224; Hobcaw sold, 202; *Mary Anne* launched, 192
Short Description of the Province of South Carolina, A, 224
Shot heard 'round the world, 298
Shute's Folly. *See* Castle Pinckney
Shute's Wharf, 189
Siege of Charlestown, 353, 356, 357, 361; Americans fire on British, 362; battery at Albemarle Point, 360; Battle of Bacon's Bridge, 358, 359; Battle of Stono Ferry, 353; bridge contructed over Wappoo, 358; British construct seigeworks, 361; British enter harbor, 363; British fire upon the city, 362; British land on James Island, 357; casualties, 369; British land on Seabrook, 357; British land on the Neck, 361; British mount guns at Fenwick Point, 359; British take Drayton Hall, 361; cease fire, 367; city surrendered, 368; Clinton asks for sur-render, 363; Clinton frustrated by Charles-town resistance, 367; Clinton refuses surrender, 368; Cornwallis lands on James Island, 358; effects on economy, 357; first skirmish, 361; Ft. Johnson seized, 358; Haddrell's Point taken, 366; harbor block-aded, 357; horn work, 366; Lanneay's Ferry massacre, 367; Lincoln proposes sur-render, 364; map, 365; Negro laborers, 356; Pitt statue damaged, 364; Prevost lands on peninsula, 352; SC Navy scuttles ships, 358; St. Andrews taken, 360; supplies scarce, 366
Siege of Savannah: Jasper killed, 354; Pulaski killed, 354

Sign of Bacchus, 247
Sign of the Harp and Crown., 165
Simmons, Ebenezar: land sold for Exchange, 245; purchases lot on East Bay, 166
Simmons, Issac: warns about his wife, 161
Simmons, Mary: publicly shamed by husband, 161; runs away to New York, 162
Simonds, Francis: donates plot for White Meeting House, 83
Simons, Maurice: killed in duel, 416
Single house: description, 133
Singleton, Tom: Balfour baboon, 371
Slave badges: free blacks required to wear, 398
Slave Codes: defined, 176
Slavery, 111, 442, 462, 474; 1720 population, 125; 1724 population, 134; 1733 population, 149; 1769 imports, 254; 1769 population, 258; 1773 imports, 274; ad for runaway, 308; Adams comments on Negro soldiers, 330; African importation ban, 255; Barbadian slave code adopted, 36; bill to prohibit trade defeated, 416; blacks outnumber whites for the first time, 90; British take 5000 slaves, 396; care of Negroes, 230; comments by John Laurens, 334; complaints about, 310; complaints about behavior, 272; concerns about Negro population, 165; dangers of slave majority, 162; defined by *Fundamental Constitutions*, 26; Denmark Vesey left in Haiti, 387; description of tensions, 182; deserting to the British, 337; differences between French and English noted, 334; execution, 150; execution, 204; execution, 204; execution, 213; execution, 281; execution by burning, 351; execution, burned at stake, 179, 255; financing options, 249; first African slaves in Carolina, 10; first Carolina slave law passed, 62; first petition to ban slavery, 439; first slaves brought, 33; foreign ban lifted, 251; foreign blacks ordered out of state, 456; free school opens, 183; French Negroes charged with plot, 473; Haitian Revolution, 448; hanged for robbery, 282; hanged for runaway, 268; heavy duties imposed, 100; heavy tax levied, 237; horrors of, 397; image, 208, 265; import chart, 290; import duty set higher on West Indian slaves, 81; importance to for rice cultivation, 153; in Barbados, 15; Indian slavement forbidden, 39; insurrection plot, 126; insurrection rumors, 144; Jeremy hanged for inciting insurrection, 303; John Laurens proposes to lead black troops, 341; Laurens' rationalization, 257; loss of income due to Association, 260; militia in control of security, 128; Molly executed for arson, 470; Negro Act passed, 130; Negro gang killed, 310; Negro meeting camp, 181; new duty imposed by Assembly, 110; new slave code, 62; number imported by Laurens, 190; number sold by Laurens, 206; patrols increased, 236; permanent guard discussed, 474; pest house, 231; profile, 265; promised freedom for fighting for British, 307; ratio of black slaves vs. white servants, 71; rice trade, 54; rumored uprising, 455; runaway, 189, 261; runaway ad, 271; runaways whipped and emasculated, 69; *Sally George* not allowed to unload, 261; Security Act passed, 170; slave sale, 47; Spain promises freedom for desertion, 150; Stono Rebellion, 170; Sullivan's Island slave quarantine, 215; Titus arrested for murder, 454; tougher new law, 68; trade ban extended, 436; trade banned for 2 years, 424; trade monopoly removed by Parliament, 70; Vesey slave sale, 405; white anxiety over Haitian slaves, 461; white complaints about, 272; whites demand French slave be refused, 460
Small pox: cure for, 165
Smith, Benjamin, 260
Smith, Josiah: complaints about economy, 312; meets with Newton, 195; preaches against balls and theater, 174; publishes *The Burning of Sodom*, 178
Smith, Robert; complains about poor, 240
Smith, Thomas, 278; arrested, 138, 139; commissioned governor, 65; declares himself president, 138; organizes anti-tax protest, 138; resigns, 65; Sons of Liberty, 250
Smith, William Loughton: assures that slavery was defended, 439; attacks Ramsay over anti-slavery views, 433
Smoking Club, 196
Smythe Horse Affair, 297; conclusion, 297
Snee Farm, 369, 399, 445; established, 204
Snipes, William Clay: arrested for murder after duel, 416
Society for the Propagation of the Gospel, 85; charter issued, 80; Wesley brothers, 156
Society of Brooms, 203
Society of the Cincinnati: defends against Burke's attacks, 408; formed in Charleston, 404

Society Street: named, 213
Sollee, John, 460, 465, 466, 468; attacked on street, 475; in deep debt, 475; opens Long Room at City Theater, 469
Sollee's Long Room: acquires reputation, 476
Sons of Liberty: Association resurrected, 286; called hypocrites, 252; hangs effigy, 262; officers chosen, 249; organized, 236
Sothell, Seth: arrives at Albemarle, 60; arrives in Charles Town, 61; banished from Albemarle, 61; becomes Proprietor, 47; calls a Parliament, 61; captured by pirates, 47; claimed governorship, 61; entering Charles Town, image, 61; forced to step down, 63; reforms passed, 62
South Carolina: asks to become a Royal Colony, 101; becomes Royal Colony, 141; name used for the first time, 65; overthrows Proprietary government, 121
*South Carolina & American General Gazette,* 227, 281
*South Carolina Gazette*: attacked by William Bull, Jr., 234; established, 145; first edition under Timothy, 151; first issue by woman, 167; image, 169; publishes Council proceedings, 282; publishes first edition, 146; resumes publication, 228, 401; resumes publication as *Royal Gazette,* 379; seized by British, 369; suspended due to Stamp Act, 234; suspends publication, 227; Timothy becomes publisher, 150; warns about tea, 283
South Carolina Golf Club, 421
South Carolina Navy, 338, 342, 343; Battle of Stono Ferry, 353; Board of Commissioners, 333; board of commissioners recommended, 332; captures, 339; captures four British ships, 350; captures *Polly,* 320; captures rum, 327; ends operations, 358; formed, 307; Gillon appointed Commodore, 342; Gillon sails to France, 346; *Hornet* launched, 349, 350; plans to attack British blockade, 340; privateers, 329; *Randolph* captures three ships, 339; scuttles ships near Shute's Ferry, 358; ships in the fleet, 340
South Carolina Society, 176; charter confirmed by George II, 202; established, 163; incorporated, 198; purchases land in Ansonborough, 213
*South Carolina Weekly Gazette*: renamed, 227
South-Carolina Insurance Company, 333
Spotswood, Alexander: military supplies, 103
St. Andrew's Club, 219
St. Andrew's Hunting Club: stipulations, 210

St. Andrew's Society, 148; founded, 142
St. Augustine: attacked by Charles Town, 81; expedition against disbanded, 58; founded, 11; Woodward taken to, 25
St. Cecilia Society, 164, 276, 277; benefit for French refugees, 459; concert, 444
St. Celilia Society: established, 220
St. George's Society: rents Shepheard, 151; founded, 150
St. John's Lutheran Church: completed, 228; organized, 210
St. Mary's Catholic: formed, 443
St. Michael's Church: bells arrive, 228; bells taken by British, 396; bells toll for first time, 228; benefit concert, 238; cornerstone laid, 200; description of, 286; houses troops, 210; image, 221; meeting against Jay's Treaty, 466; used as military lookout, 357
St. Philip's Church, 442; description of, 132; donates books to Library Society, 343; established, 47; first service in new church, 132; image, 136; John Wesley preaches, 160; Quincy attends, 277; relief of poor, 152; Richard Clark resigns, 212; Whitefield preaches, 166
Stamp Act, 232, 235, 237; clogs Charlestown harbor, 236; courts shut down, 237; *Gazette* suspends publication, 234; goes into effect, 235; image, 234, 237; merchants pledge not to use stamped paper, 235; passed, 229; protests, 232, 233; repealed, 238, 251; viewed as threat, 229
Stamp Act Congress, 232, 235; convenes, 232
State Capital, 412, 417, 419; petition to move, 412; records moved to Columbia, 438
State Constitution: 1778 version approved, 342; 1790 version ratified, 442; changes President to Governor, 342
State House: arms taken, 298; construction begins, 202; cornerstone laid, 202; description, 206; destroyed by fire, 430; image, 300; opened, 206
State Seal: authorized, 316; description of, 336; image, 336; used for first time, 336
Stono Rebellion: description of, 170
Stono, Archibald, 92
Streets of Charleston, 213, 242, 256; Ansonborough laid out, 186; Meeting and Church streets named, 148
Stuart, John, 227; arrested, 299; flees to St. Augustine, 298
Stuart's Town: attacked by Spanish, 58; destruction of, 57; founded, 53
Sugar: production begins in Barbados, 15

Sugar Act, 227; passed, 229
Sullivan's Island: 500 runaway slaves, 307; Bonnet hides out, 114; Bonnet recaptured, 115; British fortify, 367; Fort Sullivan construction begins, 312; guard placed, 89; pest houses, 95, 265; Queen Anne's War, 86; recommended be fortified, 311; slaves recieved, 215; watch established, 62
Sully, Thomas: image, 462; performs at French theater, 461
Sumter, Thomas: named Brigadier General, 376
Swallow's Tavern, 284, 288
*Swift*: first ship commissioned as privateer for South Carolina, 329

# T

Tarleton, Banastre, 363, 367; Battle of Cowpens, 378; Biggin's Bridge, 363; captures Washington, 364; Lanneau's Ferry, 367; nicknamed, 370; Waxhaws Massacre, 370
Tarleton's Quarter: Waxhaws Massacre, 370
Tarring and Feathering, 299, 303
*Tartar*, 270; arrival, 184
Taverns: 1763 licenses, 224; 1768 licenses, 245; act to regulate sailors, 198
Tax Act of 1783, 399
Taylor, Anthony: offical protest against the sea and wind, 63
Tea Act: enacted, 281; news reaches Charlestown, 282; protest meeting at Exchange, 283; public outcry, 283; repeals tea taxes, 282; tea arrives in Charlestown, 283; tea stored in Exchange, 285; threats to burn Exchange, 283
Tea Protests, 292; at Liberty Tree, 269; cargo of salt and coal dumped, 296; tea dumped, 293
Teach, Edward. *See* Blackbeard
Teach's Hole, 112
Telemaque. *See* Denmark Vesey
Tennant, William: fears about new state constitution, 315; friends with Ramsay, 286; travels backcountry to rally Patriot support, 302
Tennant, William III: urges restaint of tea drinking, 291
Test Act, 343; deadline extended, 344
Test Oath: Tories leave city, 344
*The Orphan, or the Unhappy Marriage*, 153; performed at Dock Street, 158; performed at Shepheard's Tavern, 154
Theater, 158, 159, 174, 288; 2nd season at Charleston Theater, 458; 1754-55 season, 205; 1774 season closes, 289; 1774 season opens, 285; 1785 season begins, 414; 2nd season opens, 161; 3rd season opens for Charleston Theater, 462; 4th season at Charleston Theater opens, 469; Charleston limits performances, 404; Charleston Theater opens, 452; City theater in deep debt, 475; City Theater troupe moves to Charleston Theater, 474; construction of Dock Street Theater, 154; description of Harmony Hall, 420; first opera presentation, 154; first season closes, 154; first theatrical season, 153; French theater destroyed by fire, 459; petition to build new, 418; plans for new theater, 450; s2nd season closes, 162; season opens at French theater, 460; street altercation, 475; *The Merchant of Venice* scandal, 423; unable to open, 473
Thomas, John: performs first autopsy, 63
Thompson Tavern Scandal, 407
Thompson, William: challenges John Rutledge to duel, 407; publishes account of arrest, 408
Thornburgh, William: recommendation of Carolina rice, 73
*Three Brothers*: arrives in Carolina, 32; arrives in Virginia, 28; attacked by Spanish, 32; returns with slaves, 33; sails to Bermuda, 33; sloop, 28
Thurber, John, 101; gifted rice seed, 54
Timothy, Ann, 75; resumes publicaton of *South Carolina Gazette*, 401
Timothy, Elizabeth: birth, 80; career, 168; description of 1740 fire, 177; first newspaper edited, 167; official printer of colony, 168; opens book store, 189; takes over the Gazette, 166
Timothy, Lewis, 80, 147, 157; arrives in Philadelphia, 145; becomes publisher of the *Gazette*, 150; death, 166; publishes *Collection of Psalms and Hymns*, 162
Timothy, Peter, 166; 1768 description of Charlestown, 249; addresses power struggle between Assembly and Montagu, 275; announces tea arrival, 282; appointed colonial postmaster, 210; attacks Gillon for breaking Association, 259; blacks out royal insignia, 260; closes print shop, 357; describes British movements, 363; describes lack of celebration for king's birthday, 262; name on masthead, 167; opinions on Revolution, 304; print shop destroyed by fire, 341; reports 30 British boats, 361;

reports on British ships, 357; requests debts be paid, 228; Secretary of 1st Provincial Congress, 296; suspends *Gazette*, 227; suspends *Gazette* to protest Stamp Act, 234; takes lookout post, 357; takes over *Gazette* from mother, 189

Tobias, Jacob, 356

Toomer, Anthony: builds bridge, 242; builds walls for orphan house, 449; contracted to build theater, 450

Tories: definition of, 308

Tower of London, 384, 388, 389; Cooper imprisoned, 49; image, 376; Laurens imprisoned, 376

Townsend Acts, 245; Carolina joins other colonies in prostest, 249; Charlestown and Boston allied against, 250 letter sent urging colonies to oppose, 247; opposed by Assembly, 250; passed, 243; repealed, 260

Traile, Major: takes St. Michael's bells, 396

Treaty of Augusta: signed with Cherokee, 227

Treaty of Dewitt's Corner, 336

Treaty of Paris: preliminary articles signed, 396; ratified, 406; signed, 404

Treaty of San Lorenzo,. *See* Pinckney's Treaty

Treaty of Utrecht, 96

Trott, Nicholas, 65, 96, 108; appointed Attorney General, 70; appointed Chief Justice, 81; becomes Judge of Admiralty, 105; called unfit, 88; defends Church Act, 88; given unlimited power, 100; granted leave, 96; holds piracy trial, 105; meets with Proprietors, 100; pirates found guilty, 115; removed from office, 122; returns as Attorney General, 80; returns to Charles Town, 100; secret correspondence with Proprietors, 112; sentences Bonnet to death, 115; trial for witchcraft, 86

Tucker, Thomas Tudor, 436, 439; argues against slavery ban, 439; birth, 187; image, 188; profile, 187

Tunnel, John: appointed Methodist bishop, 414; first servince in new meeting house, 423

Turnbull, Andrew: first apothecary, 382

Turnbull, John, 386

Turner's Long Room, 461

Tweed, William: hanged for treason, 351

Two-Bit Club. *See* South Carolina Society

Two-Bit Society. *See* South Carolina Society

Tynte, Edward: death, 92

## U

Unitarian Church, 369; image, 273

## V

Vagrancy Act: changes theatrical performances, 426; defines actors as beggars, 424; revoked, 449

Valentine, George: performs surgery, 146

Vanderhorst, Arnoldus: elected governor, 464

Vane, Charles, 113, 117; off the Carolina coast, 113

Vauxhill Gardens, 475

Vesey, Denmark: life in Charleston, 402, 410; marriage, 474; pays for his freedom, 478; purchases lottery ticket, 477; reacquired by Joseph Vesey, 393; reads new reports of Haitian Revolution, 448; wins lottery, 477

Vesey, Joseph, 410; beaches ship on coast, 313; house set on fire, 470; invests in property, 242; opens business as ship chandler, 401; oversees Market construction, 452; picks up Congessional delegation, 311; purchases Telemaque, 387; re-acquires Telemaque, 393; returns to Charlestown, 397; serves under John Paul Jones, 332; slave sale, 405; takes prize, 311

*Vixen*, 320, 329; SC Navy, 327

## W

Walker, George: tarred and feathered, 303

Walsh, Thomas: launched into eternity, 444

*Wambaw*: ordered to be sold, 243; seized, 243

Wappoo Plantation, 167

War of Jenkin's Ear, 180; Anson plunders Spanish gold, 183; declared, 173; declared in Charlestown, 176; ends, 192; Florida invasion disaster, 176; renamed King George's War, 185

Washington Oak, 445; image, 445

Washington Race Course, 449; established, 448; first Race Week, 449

Washington, George: advice on oak tree, 445; appoints de Saussure to Mint, 467; breakfast at Rutledge house, 223; breakfast at Snee Farm, 445; crosses into Charleston, 445; description of Charleston, 447; descrition of Charleston ladies, 447; dies, 477; elected President, 435; Heyward house, 446; informed about Fort Sullivan, 312; leaves

Charleston, 447; talks with Hoban, 447; Valley Forge image, 341; visits orphans, 447
Washington, Sarah Izard, 301
Washington's Visit To Charleston: Clifton Plantation, 445; Day 1 in Charleston, 445; Day 2 in Charleston, 446; Day 3 in Charleston, 446; Day 4 in Charleston, 446; Day 5 in Charleston, 447; Day 6 in Charleston, 447; Day 7 in Charleston, 447; Day 8 in Charleston, 448
Washington, William, 407; arrives in Charlestown, 355; at Bacon's Bridge, 358; Battle of Cowpens, 378; Battle of Eutaws Springs, 387; birth, 200; captured and escapes, 364; escorts Washington to Charleston, 445; given a flag, 356; hosts George Washington, 447; image, 360; injured and captured, 387; marries Jane Elliott, 393
Weather: coldest day, 192; drought, 140; first observations, 164; first recorded snowfall, 137; first winter, 35; summer heat, 188
Weber, Jacob: execution, 217
Weberites, 217
Webster, Noah: arrives for lecture, 415; image, 414
Webster, Pelatiah, 230, 231; describes militia, 230; description of Charlestown, 229; leaves Charlestown, 231; trip to Sullivan's Island, 231
Wells, John: assumes control of South Carolina and American General Gazette, 298
Wells, Robert, 292; description of Lowndes, 346; given the *Gazette*, 369; imports *Samuel Johnson's Dictionary*, 206; largest book store in America, 286; leaves Charlestown, 298; notice of magazines available, 210; opens book shop, 203
Wesley, Charles: arrival, 156; arrives in Charlestown, 160; returns to England, 160
Wesley, John, 160; arrival, 156; arrives in Charlestown, 160; encourages John Newton, 197; leaves Charlestown, 164; preaches at St. Philip's, 160; publishes *Collection of Psalms and Hymns*, 162
West and Bignall, 452, 453; contract to build theater, 450; lose French members, 461; open the new Charleston Theater, 452; raise money for theater, 450
West, Joseph, 37; accused of Indian slave trading, 51; appointed governor by Sayle, 35; appointed Superintendent of the Plantation and Stores, 40; commissioned commander of Carolina expedition, 27; commissioned governor, 53; commissioned governor, 43; complaints about heat and low morals, 33; complaints about rum drinking, 33; concerns about Sayle, 34; declares war on the Kussoes, 38; instructed to obtain seeds, 27; made Landgrave, 43; praised by Proprietors, 39; provisions shortage, 33; resigned as govenor, 55
West, Thomas: announces original play, 455; plans to build new theater, 450
Westo tribe, 31 skirmish with, 44
Weyman, Edward: Secret Committee of Five, 298
Whig Club of 600, 406, 407; attacked in print, 411; attacks Rutledge and Pinckney families, 410; mob dispersed, 407
Whigs: definition of, 308
White Meeting House, 70
White Point. *See* Oyster Point
White servants, 35
White, Ezra: architect, 255
Whitechapel Bell Foundry, 228
Whitefield, George: 2nd arrival, 174; accuses locals of sinful behaviour, 174; attacks slavery, 175; comments on Charlestown, 166; conducts service without Book of Common Prayer, 175; defends against Anglican violations, 176; description of, 166; description of Charlestown, 174; first arrival, 166; image, 177; preaches at St. Philip's, 166; reception of sermon, 175; suspended from Anglican church, 176
Whitmarsh, Thomas, 146; arrival, 145; death, 150
Whitney, Eli: applies for patent, 456; cotton gin patented, 459
Wilkes Affair, 226, 258, 260, 268
Wilkes Fund, 258, 260, 261, 268; battle between governor and Assembly, 272
Wilkes, John, 226; arrested, 226; elected mayor of London, 286; released, 260
William and Mary: ascend to throne, 60; take power, 60
William III, King: death, 80
William of Orange: deposes James II, 60
William Pitt statue, 263; approved, 238; arrival, 261; damaged, 364; dedicated, 262; image, 263
Williams Roger, 15
Williamson, Atkin: baptises a bear, 53; dismissed from pulpit, 53; land granted, 47

Wilson, Samuel, 52; description of exports, 48; secretary to the Proprietors, 48
Windmill Point, 83; renamed Fort Johnson, 89
Winteley, John: dismissed from pulpit, 141
Witherspoon, Francis: marries David Ramsay, 399
Woodes Rogers, 120
Woodmason, Charles: 2nd returns, 200; arrives in Charlestown, 220; description of backcountry, 240; outrage over election, 252; presents petition from backcountry residents, 245; returns from England, 240; returns to England, 228
Woodward, Henry: captured by Spanish, 25; freed, 25; joins the Carolina expedition, 28; sold cows, 51; solicits help from Indians, 33; stays with Edisto Indians, 23; stranded in Nevis, 25; treaty with Westos, 44
Woolford, Jacob: owns Broad Street Tavern, 163
Woory, Joseph: description of Carolina, 23; description of Carolina, 23
Worley, Richard: killed, 115
Wragg, Samuel: builds *Princess Carolina*, 101; captured by Blackbeard, 111; persuades Parliament to relax rice restrictons, 144; slave ship plundered and destroyed, 182

## X

XYZ Affair: intensifies, 472

## Y

Yeamans, John, 21, 23, 27; accepts commission as governor, 28; arrives in Charles Town, 36; attitude toward English colonists, 34; chosen as speaker, 37; comments on West, 37; commissioned at governor for a second time, 26; commissioned governor, 38; Cooper's description of, 41; creates power struggle, 36; death, 43; description of, 37; devotion to profit, 42; expects to be governor, 36; expedition battered by storm, 22; extended baronage, 18; fights over governorship, 36; image:, 42; imported cattle, 37; joins the Carolina expedition, 28; named governor of Carolina, 21; names Sayle as new governor, 31; proclaimed governor by Proprietors, 39; removed as governor, 43; returns to Barbados, 31; sailed to Carolina, 22; sends exports to Cooper, 34
Yeamans, William, 21
Yemassee tribe, 93, 101, 140; kills Charles Town delegation, 101; lands opened for settlement, 105; reservation set aside, 89
Yemassee War, 101, 104; Battle of the Ponds, 103; Catawbas ally with English, 103; Cherokee ally with English, 105; conclusion, 105; Craven appeals for help, 102; England sends supplies, 103; image, 102, 106; negotiations, 101; North Carolina sends reinforcements, 103; reasons for, 101; Yemassee ask for peace, 105
Yonge, Francis: arrives to meet with Proprietors, 120; bitterness toward Trott and Proprietors, 120; returns to Charles Town, 120

## ABOUT THE AUTHOR

Mark R. Jones is an eighth generation native of the South Carolina lowcountry. He is an author, historian, licensed guide and tour operator in Charleston, S.C. With his wife, novelist and tour guide Rebel Sinclair, Jones operates Black Cat Tours, conducting tours that cover the darker history of the Holy City. He has conducted more than 20,000 tours.

He is the author of seven other books. His first book kicked off the wildly popular *Wicked* series for The History Press. *Wicked Charleston: The Dark Side of the Holy City* (2005), was followed by *Wicked Charleston, Vol. II: Prostitutes, Politics & Prohibition* (2006).

In 2007, Jones published two true crime anthologies, *Palmetto Predators: Monsters Among Us* and *South Carolina Killers: Crimes of Passion*. Jones, and one of the *Predator* stories, was featured in the Investigation Discovery program "A Crime To Remember" in 2016.

In 2013, Jones published *Doin' the Charleston: Black Roots of American Popular Music & the Jenkins Orphanage Legacy* and *Kingdom By The Sea: Edgar Allan Poe's Charleston Tales*. In 2015, Jones published *Charleston Firsts*.

Jones is also an active speaker, creating historical presentations for a wide variety of organizations - schools, libraries, corporate and civic organizations.

For more information about Mark, his books and tours, or to inquire about booking Mark for a speech or presentation, go to:

MarkJonesBooks.com
BlackCatTours.com
Contact: markjonesbooks@outlook.com